BODY

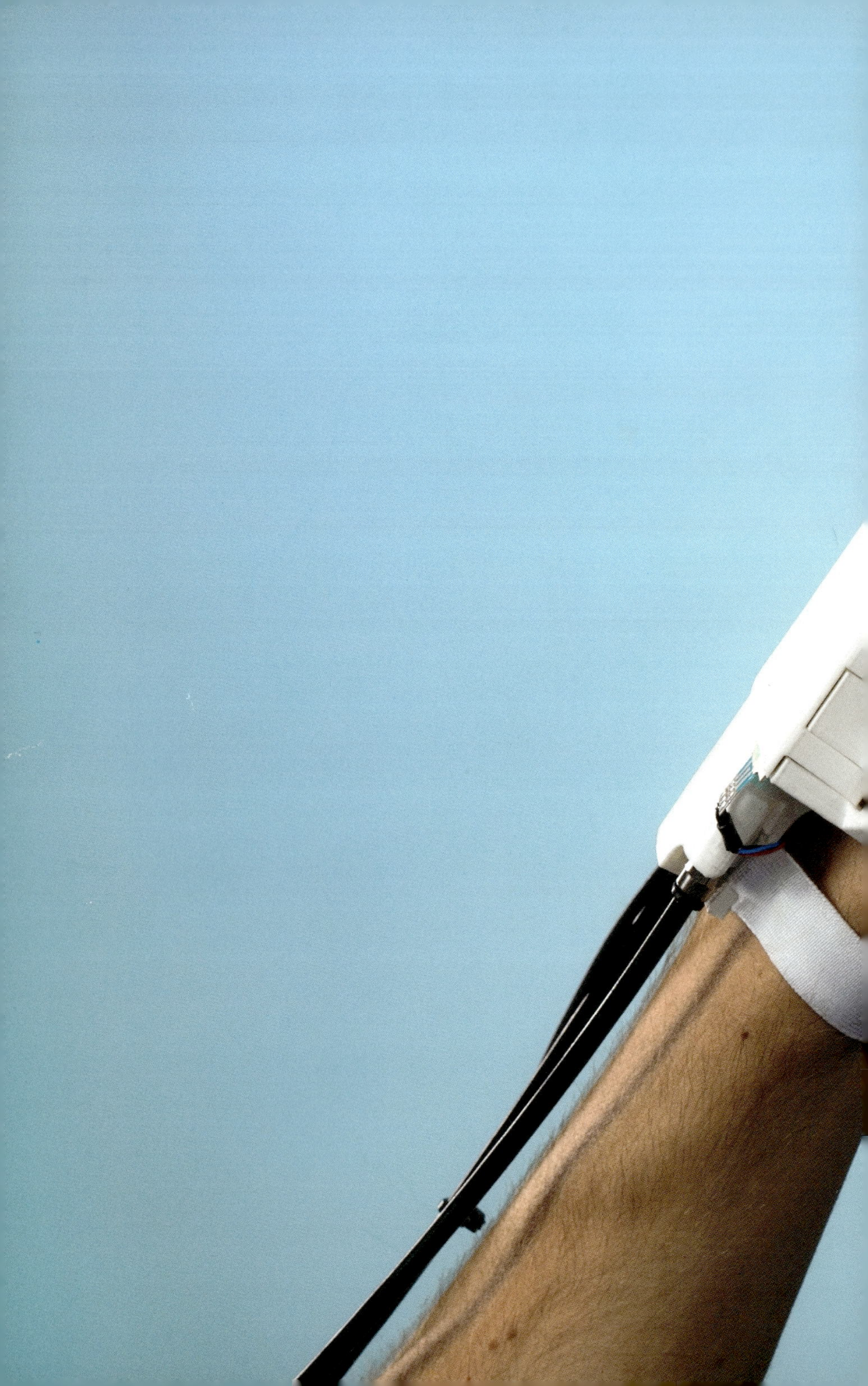

BODY

THE PHOTOGRAPHY BOOK

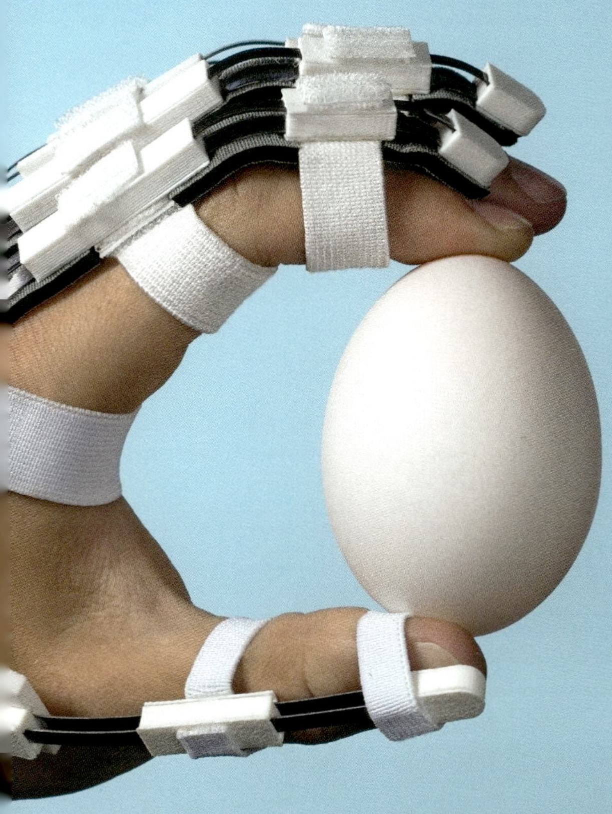

NATHALIE HERSCHDORFER

369 ILLUSTRATIONS

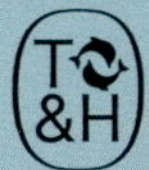

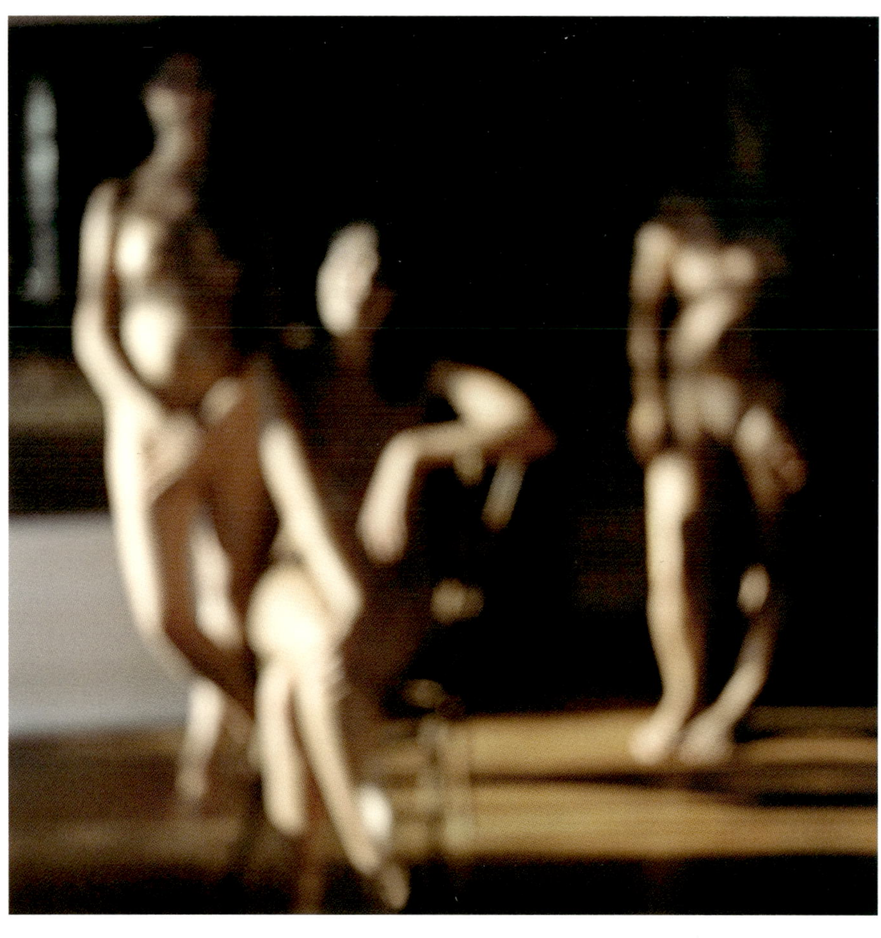

CONTENTS

PREFACE

Nathalie Herschdorfer

The diversity of the body is more visible today than perhaps at any other time in photography's 180-year history. Whatever its skin colour or age, whether it's angular or curvy, healthy or sick, the body has become a globalized object, a fact reflected in changing societal standards of beauty. With renewed thought around notions of identity, and gender identity in particular, catalyzing shifts within society, the body — and the self within — can now advertise its own ambiguity more openly. Contemporary photography reflects this, showing us the body from every angle and opening up new pathways for bodily representations and perspectives beyond the traditional nude. Such is already the case for the female nude, which has always been dominant in photography and subject to the artistic reification of the female. In *Ways of Seeing* (1972), John Berger recognized how few works of art — and, by extension, photographs — depicted a woman for herself, rather than as a desirable ideal, noting that 'To be naked is to be oneself. To be nude is to be seen naked by others.' With this, Berger innovatively repositioned the artistic nude through a feminist prism, reminding us that it was, above all, a matter of the male gaze. Forty years later, the nude is no longer the sole preserve of men: the sexualized and stereotyped body is now being tackled by the female gaze.

From the physical signs of identity to the cultural, such as body-building and make-up, photography bears witness to the metamorphoses, both real and imaginary, to which the contemporary body may be subjected throughout its life — interventions that allow us to know each other, to recognize each other and to be recognized in turn. However, in a world of images, the body-as-object has gained the upper hand over the body-as-subject, which constantly evades our grasp: the rise of the selfie is both symptom and proof of this. As we increasingly recognize our own bodies via images, we suffer a kind of double vision: on one hand there is the gaze of the other, which allows us to perceive ourselves as subjects; on the other is our perception of our own bodies, from which 'the self' is constructed and which we control. Between the two lie visual representations: those of other bodies — real and fictionalized — which we often admire, and those of ourselves, which frequently disappoint us.

Beginning at a very young age, this tyranny of appearance is reinforced by images that obey the hegemonic norms and ideals of the society in which we live, by those perfectly photographed bodies reproduced in magazines and online that make us insecure about our own. Defining the identity of one's own body is now a common preoccupation, and although images of perfect bodies continue to proliferate, there is an increasing desire to show something other than the ideal that we are supposed to live up to. One of the defining features of 20th-century art and culture was the exposition, through two world wars, of the human capability for dehumanization of the body; not only in our capacity for harm, but in our taste for modification and 'improvement'. As focus returns to the tensions between the public and private body, artists remind us that what makes the body unique is its vulnerability. Despite science's promise that the limits of the body can be pushed back, the sick and suffering body — which is no less a part of human life — reminds us of its finite nature. Although the 'de-physicalization' of bodies in the 21st century is one possible response to our obsession with death, death cannot be eradicated.

Ultimately, while the body is of course an object — in a physical sense, at least — it is also subjective: the mind allows us to escape bodily constraints, to create doubles, to alter the body or to present it in a particular way — in other words, to leave our bodies behind. Faced with a ubiquity of visual imagery, we feed our imaginations primarily on images: when we go online, we discover other possible lives and make them for ourselves through the images we each create and share. Images can reveal the mortal body, but they can also come to its aid, offering another form of life that could potentially be eternal.

ALL THE STATES OF THE BODY

Nathalie Herschdorfer

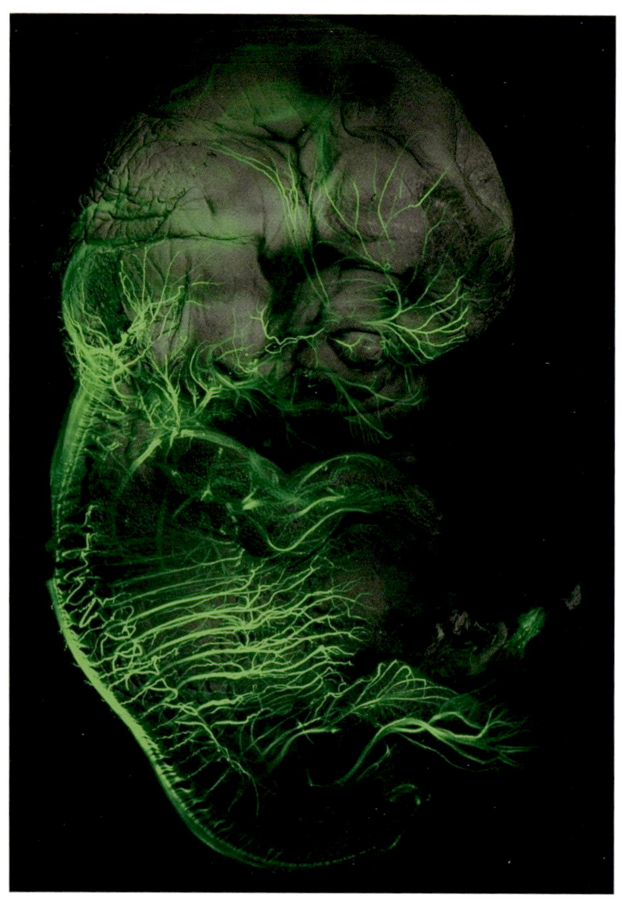

↑ **Alain Chédotal and Morgane Belle,** An eight-week foetus, with peripheral
nerves marked in green; the head is about 9 mm, 2017

In 2017, the scientific journal *Cell* published fascinating images of human embryos aged between 6 and 14 weeks and measuring between 8 mm and 9 cm long. They revealed anatomy in its tiniest details: blood vessels, nascent muscles, central and peripheral nervous system, embryonic organs, and so on. These extremely precise images, produced by a team of French researchers from the Institut de la Vision and the Institut National de la Santé et de la Recherche Médicale in Paris, were compiled to form an interactive atlas of the human embryo and foetus. Combining techniques ranging from tissue marking to the latest 3D imaging, and including optical microscopy, the images — which form part of the international project to map human cells, the Human Cell Atlas — have opened up new lines of medical research. Quite apart from their aesthetic appeal, they offer new prospects in paediatrics and also in the study of cancer. They have been produced using 21st-century technology and science, yet they form part of a long tradition. Since the Renaissance, the representation of the human body has been based on morphology (the study of the forms of things), which is itself based on anatomy and dissection. The new scientific investigation is accompanied by images that make it easier to understand the complexity of the body, its organs, and its many organic, biological and physical interactions. Much still remains to be discovered, and the photographic image plays a fundamental role in our understanding of the human body.

For centuries, painters and sculptors in the West have tried to represent the body in an anatomically correct way. From the 1840s on, photography overturned that approach to the body. The new medium became a vital tool for scientists, who, before its invention, had been forced to resort to drawings to transcribe their observations. Photography now allowed them to see the exterior and the interior, and to show isolated details. It documents, explores, deconstructs and allows medical science to learn and understand more about the way the body functions and its anomalies. Scientists were obviously not alone in embracing photography. Artists posed their subjects, staged them, created compositions that gradually moved away from the grand tradition of painting. Photographers glorified the silhouette, retouching where necessary, while endeavouring to capture the body in its natural and intimate state. Photography reveals what was invisible, secret, hidden. It lays the body bare, in both the real and figurative sense.

In his 1994 book, *The Body*, William A. Ewing looked back at the history of representation of the human form through photography. He showed how the subject aroused great interest among photographers from the moment the medium was invented in the 19th century. Scientists, doctors, ethnologists, police investigators and others began to base their observations on the photographic image. Ewing also noted the popularity of the nude among Pictorialist, Modernist and Surrealist artists, as well as in magazines and advertising throughout the 20th century. In fact, war photography and photography used for political ends have always given a prominent place to the human body. This book follows in the footsteps of the wide-ranging research Ewing carried out twenty-five years ago, providing a vast survey of the way the body has been represented in the course of the history of photography. We will take up the story where Ewing stopped, i.e. shortly before 2000. The passion for this subject has not abated in the 21st century; on the contrary it seems more evident than ever. In an era of virtual reality and cyborgs, the subject seems to have become even more complex. New mutations have appeared, both at human level and in photography. Digital evolution has opened up new horizons not dreamed of thirty years ago. The augmented body has become a reality, while the virtual image can now take us on a geographical journey without any need for physical movement. Today, we seem to be confusing our physical body more and more with our body-image — we need only think of the impact of the many screens in our daily lives, of the internet and social networks. Never before in human history has it been so easy to manipulate our flesh, to create new identities for ourselves and to disseminate images so widely. And never before in human history have we been exposed to so many photographs depicting magnified, scrutinized, restructured, modified or enhanced bodies.

This book looks at the works of more than 175 photographers from different backgrounds, countries and generations. Each of them depicts, composes, distorts, reconstructs or questions the contemporary body. Their images are challenging because they raise a number of questions that are pertinent to 21st-century humanity. For nearly 180 years photography has had a profound impact on our understanding of the body. From medical images to advertising images to images used for artistic, scientific, documentary, political or pornographic purposes, photography touches on every area relating to the body and has a profound influence on our way of experiencing it. Whether they show the body as an alter ego, a finished model, a work in progress or a high-performance machine that still needs constant fine-tuning, photographers are taking part in the debate. The images in this book are organized by subject matter rather than chronologically or by photographer. We humans are constantly rethinking the body. That is why it seemed important to indicate some of the ways it can be looked at, in an attempt to show the dialogue we engage in with our own bodies.

The first chapter, PHYSIQUE, shows that life is first and foremost corporeal. We are our body. We are creatures of flesh and bone, governed by the laws of anatomy and physiology. We cannot escape this fate even if, in the virtual era, we feel increasingly disconnected from our flesh. The body is the site of our presence in the world. Photography divides the body into elements, examines its complex technology, explores its organs and functions in depth, analyzes its performance, its failings and its sufferings. The images produced in order to document and understand the body allow researchers to construct an atlas of the 21st-century human being, thanks in particular to new 3D imaging methods. Images are still very much needed. In the bio-medical field, much still remains to be researched, especially in the fight against cancer, a disease that remained for a long time invisible.

The second chapter, entitled ALTER EGO, concerns the theatrical aspects of the body. The body carries us, but we carry it too. It is like a stage on which our dreams and our achievements, our games, joys, impulses, emotions, problems and sadnesses all play their part. It is no more possible to escape the reflection of its mirror than that of the smartphone screen. Digital photography encourages us to play and experiment with different poses and identities based around our own image. Our phones have turned us into potential photographers and, above all, into great consumers and disseminators of images. In our narcissistic society, the selfie — shared primarily through social networks — is taken everywhere and by people of all ages. In earlier times, self-portraits were the preserve of artists. Today, both ordinary people and celebrities go through this ritual in which the body is shown as a staged version of the self.

The chapter entitled CONSTRUCTIONS situates the body within the consumer culture. The ways people care for their bodies on a daily basis — eating, washing, applying cream, doing their hair, shaving, putting on make-up, dabbing on perfume, dressing, resting, exercising, massaging — show that looking after the body is an endless task. It involves on one hand the demands relating to beauty and health — which, for some, means the search for perfection and eternal youth — and on the other the concept of the body as a source of identity, a sort of body politic. Our Western society is a society based on looks, in which we exist only in the eye of others. In that sense, the body is like a boxing ring. The manner in which it is represented resonates with the questions that pervade society. It is the object on which the invention of collective or individual mythologies is based. More than ever before, photography plays a prime part in the construction of our bodies. We scrutinize ourselves, sometimes in astonishment, and above all we look at how others represent themselves or are represented. The body fashions the image and the image fashions the body.

The obsession with a beautiful and flawless body is leading us to aspire to a stronger and more intelligent body so that we will live longer. The chapter on MUTATIONS describes this ideal of the high-performance body — which could even be described as superhuman. From the time our distant ancestors first used tools to the more daring inventions of science fiction, human beings have always dreamed of unleashing the body's forces, making up for the defects of its organism and discovering the secret of youth. Today, transhumanism is promising to provide the material techniques of physical, cognitive and emotional improvement. It seems to become more and more difficult to establish the limits between what can or cannot be changed. The advent of an enhanced, not to say incorporeal, body seems more real in the 21st century than it has ever been. Artists are also seeking this utopia. Aside from the prosthetic body, they have always fantasized, transfigured the body, playing with metamorphoses and opening up new fields of representation.

CELEBRATION looks at the magnified, admired, dream body. From the very beginning, photography has celebrated beauty, often perceived through the bodies of women. This tradition dates back to antiquity, which already deified the forms of the body. The body the photographers glorify is often shown naked, in the tradition of works of painting and sculpture. The female nude is a silhouette with perfect curves, sometimes exaggerated, often retouched, always idolized. Male beauty is more heroic and muscular. After being restricted for a long time to displays of virility and bravery, the male body has recently become more sexualized, sometimes even feminized. Some photographers are trying to rediscover a joyful and untamed energy in this highly sought-after male body that is often pushed to its limits. Celebrating the beauty of the body also means glorifying a body that is liberated and at one with nature.

Existence is primarily corporeal. The chapter on FLESH is concerned with that reality. What makes the body singular is precisely its vulnerability. It is exposed to weariness, suffering and disease. We have still not found a way to kill death or abolish ageing. Life-spans have become longer in the 21st century and, despite all our efforts to hide or embellish, we are faced at times with disfigured bodies. The natural body, the one that bears the marks of life, is sometimes hard to look at. We are offended by images of diseased or suffering bodies. We feel out of sync with flesh and its imperfections because we are so accustomed to retouched images. In reaction to the enhanced images we are constantly exposed to, contemporary photographers are helping us towards an acceptance of our fragility, that is to say our humanity.

The survey concludes with a chapter on LOVE, which looks at the body in terms of reactions, emotions, sensations and pleasure. Sex is one of the subjects most exploited by photographers, who treat it either with veneration or as a provocation. 'Obscene' images were already circulating in the 19th century. Now, in the internet era, images of physical 'love' are more widespread than ever and, notably, accessible to all. These images of bodies — generally shown naked, offered up to the viewer — often seem seductive and exciting. Photography becomes the vector of desire. Yet such photographs do not only express sexuality; they can also celebrate real love through the language of bodies that touch and cherish one another. The intimacy shared with their fellow beings also offers photographers many opportunities to depict the body in terms of emotions. But, focused inevitably on the physicality of the body, can photography really illuminate the mind? Though the debate continues, modern science is increasingly revealing that our thoughts, emotions and behaviours may in fact be as much physical as mental or rational processes. Professor of Psychology David Sander sets out some of the latest scientific ideas on the mind–body relationship in his essay 'Mind and Body'.

Both intimate and universal, the human body is one of the prime subjects of Western art history. It expresses both the divinity and the wounds of humanity. This book is an attempt to highlight the great richness of the subject in photography. The concept of the body is such a vast topic that it could be explored ad infinitum. The way the body is represented photographically, now that photography has become the main contemporary medium, takes us back to the big questions of our society. Mingling different worlds, genres, aesthetics and techniques, this book shows that the body pervades contemporary photography just as it pervaded art history until the late 20th century. The journey shown here reveals that photography is never neutral and always raises questions about what it means to be human today. The body has been seen in terms of self-heroification, stereotypes, aspirations, transgressions, research, games and experiments, yet today, in the 21st century, it still remains open to a whole range of fascinating interpretations.

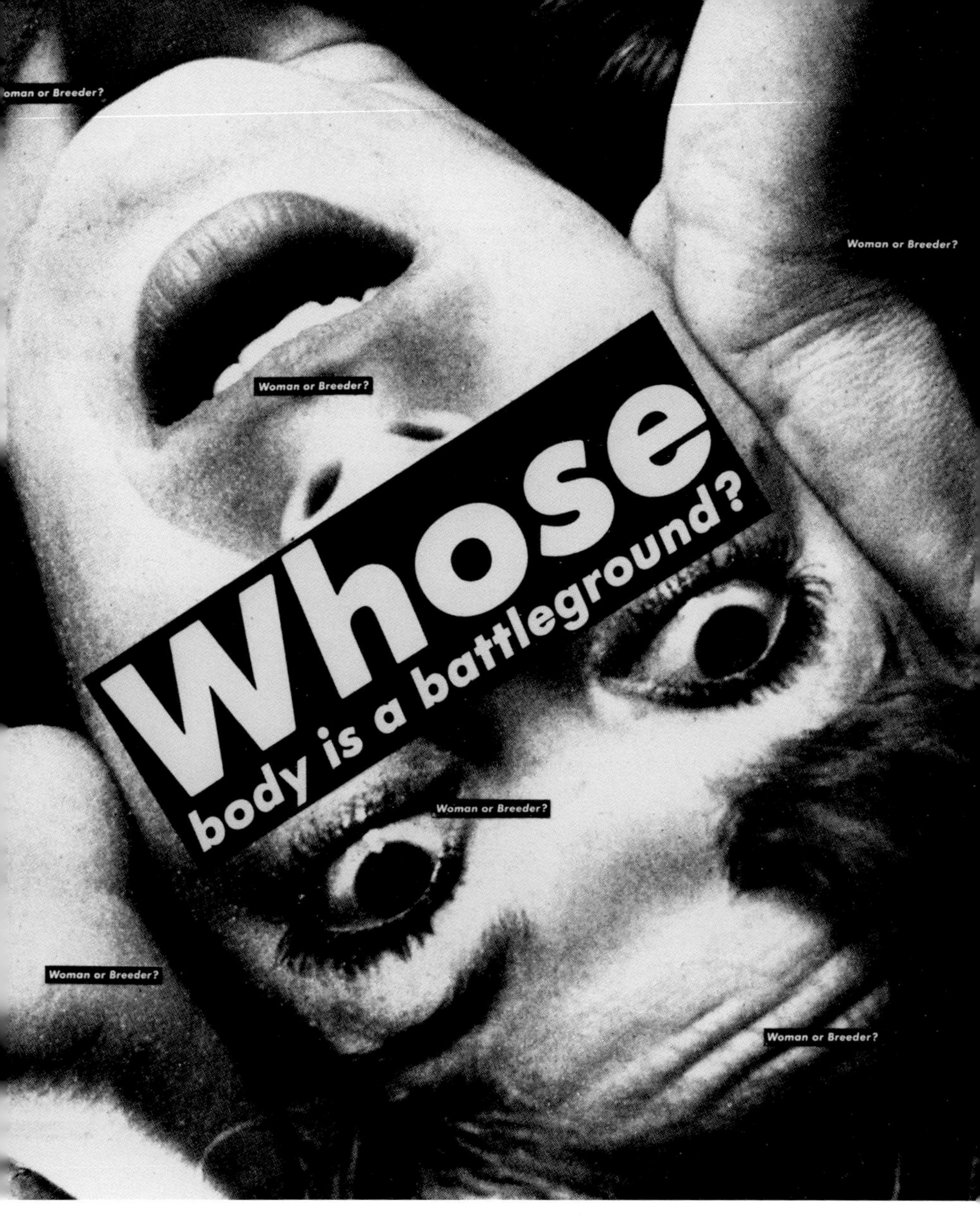

↑ Barbara Kruger, *Untitled (Whose Body is a Battleground?)*, 1982—89

PHYSIQUE

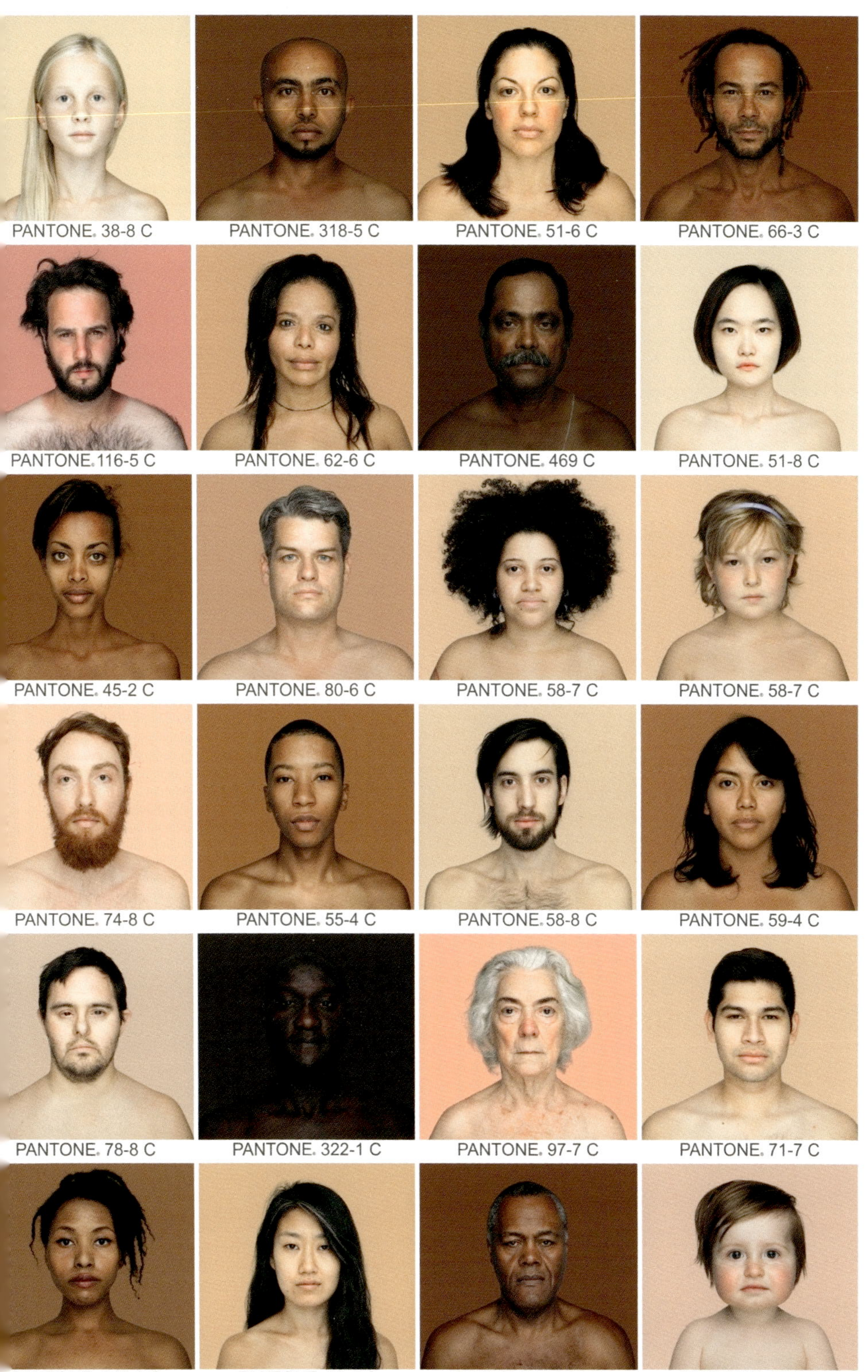

PANTONE 38-8 C
PANTONE 318-5 C
PANTONE 51-6 C
PANTONE 66-3 C
PANTONE 116-5 C
PANTONE 62-6 C
PANTONE 469 C
PANTONE 51-8 C
PANTONE 45-2 C
PANTONE 80-6 C
PANTONE 58-7 C
PANTONE 58-7 C
PANTONE 74-8 C
PANTONE 55-4 C
PANTONE 58-8 C
PANTONE 59-4 C
PANTONE 78-8 C
PANTONE 322-1 C
PANTONE 97-7 C
PANTONE 71-7 C
PANTONE 316-6 C
PANTONE 53-7 C
PANTONE 317-5 C
PANTONE 92-9 C

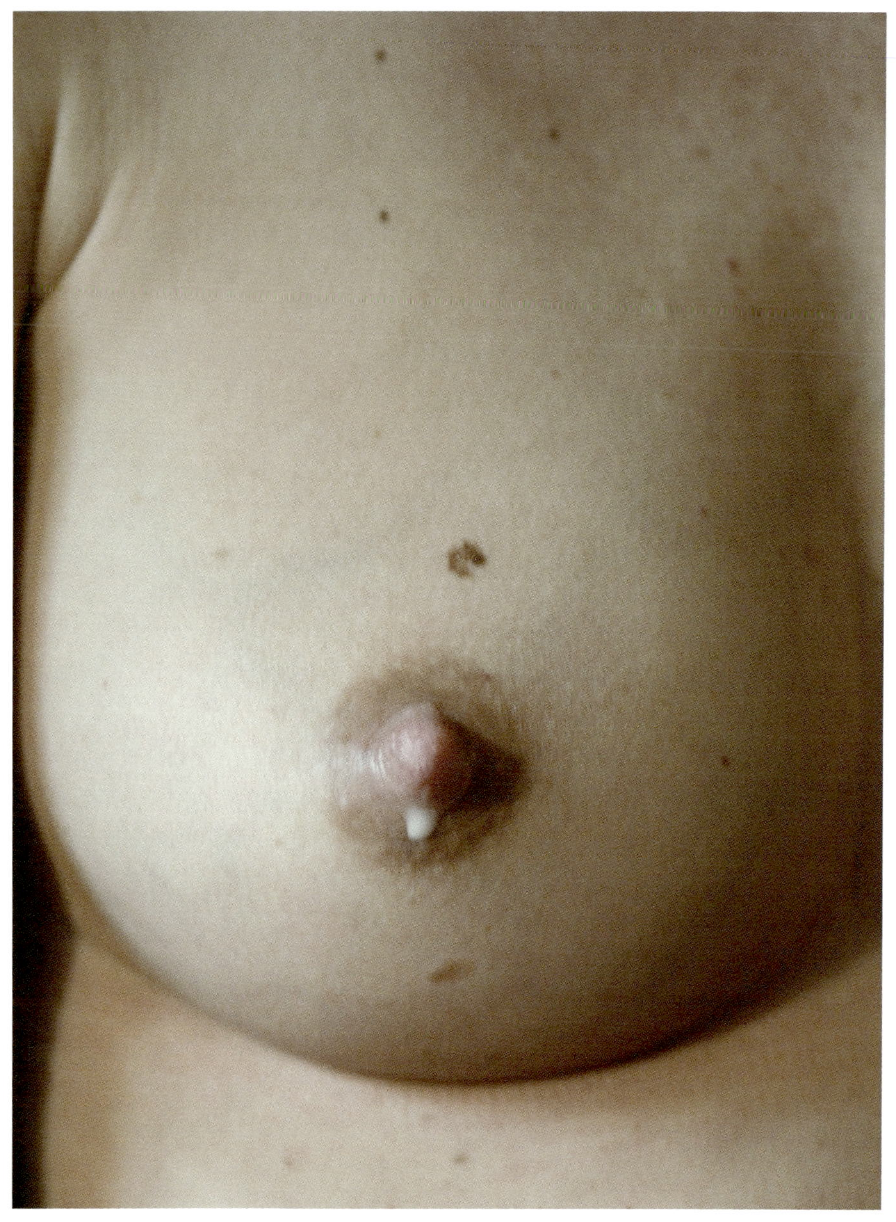

↑ **Nolwenn Brod,** *The Breast,* from the series 'La Ritournelle', 2015
←(Previous) **Angélica Dass,** *Humanae (Work in Progress),* 2012–ongoing

While photography accompanies the most anodyne moments of our daily life in the 21st century, the very first image of our photographic existence is now taken before we are born: this is the ultrasound image (pp. 28–29) that parents are given after one of their medical visits during pregnancy. Today the photo album of a life begins with the image of the foetus. Two-dimensional foetal ultrasound scans first appeared in 1974; twenty years later 3D ultrasounds could show the foetus in terms of volume, a technique that was further developed during the 2000s. While the ultrasound has now become an imaging technique known to everyone, we must remember that in 1965 people were greatly shocked to discover the series of spectacular images produced by the Swede Lennart Nilsson, a pioneer of *in utero* photography. His images of human embryos and foetuses floating in their amniotic sac became famous around the world.

It was, in fact, soon after the birth of photography itself that scientists became eager to use the new medium to study the human body. In the 19th century, they still preferred illustrations — the tradition of representing the body and its parts precisely dates back to the Renaissance — but they recognized the potential of photography. The functions of medical photography are to measure and classify the body, to explore it in depth and produce images of its tiniest details, down to the individual cell. These photographic images make it easier to understand the structure and functioning of organs and tissues, including parts that cannot be seen with the naked eye, but also to document diseases and observe the course of treatments. Today, medical imaging still enables researchers to construct a modern atlas of the human body, observed from every angle and at every level. It reveals the anatomy in all its detail, and the tools are constantly being perfected.

Laboratories are today engaged in a technology war and producing ever more sophisticated means of understanding the functioning and anomalies of the body and its organs. The selection of images reproduced here (pp. 8, 30–37, 40, 41) shows how astounding they can be. At the same time we must remember that over and above the beauty of these images, the

Human Cell Atlas that is being compiled at international level is opening up new medical prospects. Today, observation by microscope is accompanied by new methods of 3D imaging and the data is compiled with the help of increasingly fine-tuned software, in order to help us understand the laws of anatomy and physiology.

Medical images are taken in order to document and understand the body – a body that is, in turn, proving to be ever more complex. For centuries now our Western society has held the scientific study of human anatomy in high regard, and it is true to say that we are still as transfixed as ever by images of microscopic details of the insides of our body. We are fascinated, but also astonished at the sight of these abstract landscapes, which have been coloured using computer software to make them easier to understand.

On the other hand, we see nothing aesthetic in the image of an open body, bleeding, diseased, disabled or simply distorted by old age. Eamonn Doyle (pp. 42, 43) has produced a powerful series showing the elderly with their bent bodies. When we are faced with a photograph that shows an afflicted body too directly we tend to avert our eyes. We do not like images of bodies that bear the scars of their personal history. We find the worn-out, suffering body too much to take in and spend our lives fighting against its inadequacy. Lauren Greenfield (pp. 44–45) shows how constant the fight against this weak body actually is, specifically in our youth- and fashion-oriented world. Throughout life we have to watch over our mortal body, to battle it. We turn away from images that remind us of the fragility of the human condition and the precarious nature of all life. Even natural processes such as women's menstruation are rarely photographed. Yet what makes the body so singular is precisely its vulnerability.

Although we are fascinated by images reflecting a bio-medical knowledge of the body – the 'official' knowledge that underpins the practices of medical and research institutes – humans, governed by the laws of anatomy and physiology, remain creatures of flesh and bone. Howard Schatz, in collaboration with his wife Beverly Ornstein (pp. 46–47), has made collages of athletes who practise many different disciplines of sport to

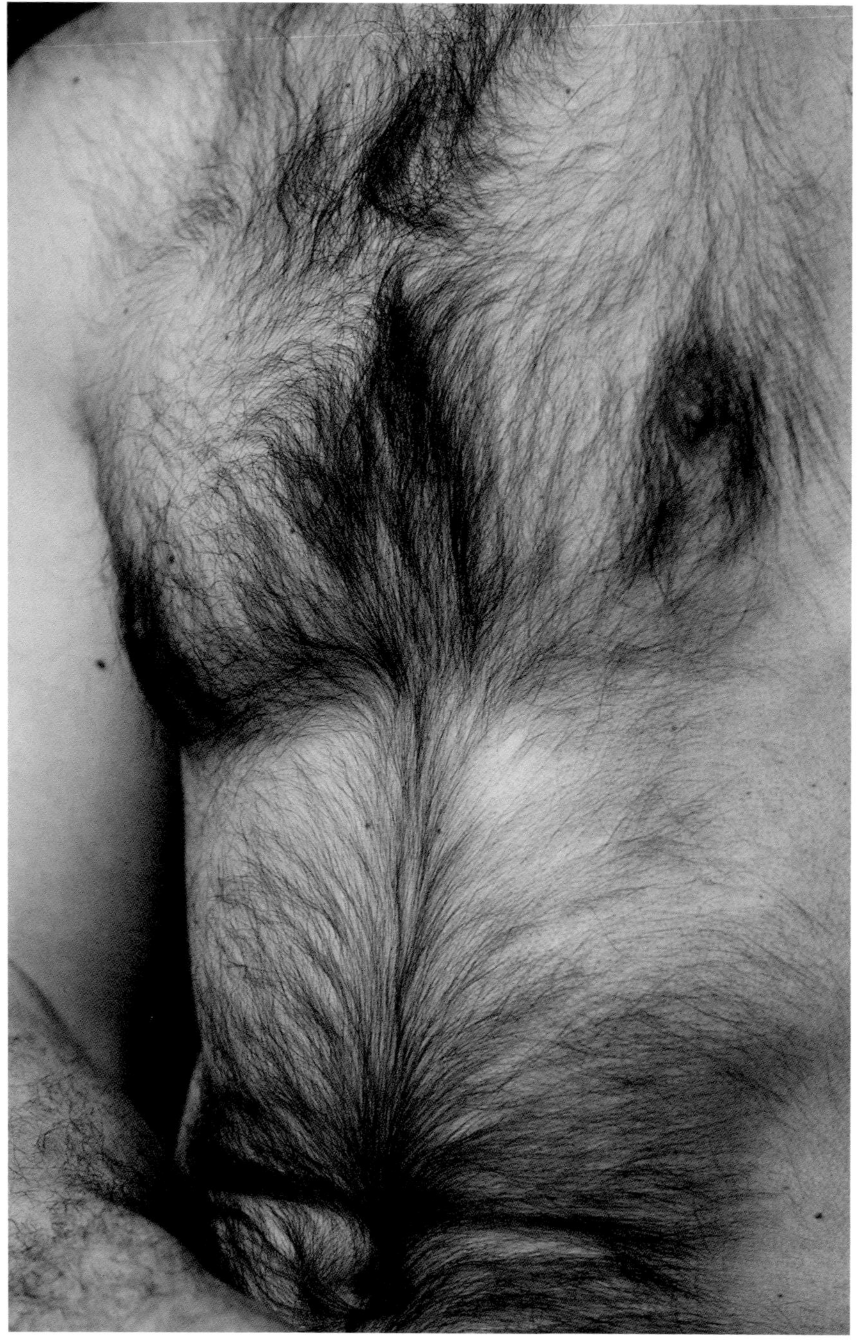

↑ **Nolwenn Brod**, *The Torso*, from the series 'La Ritournelle', 2015

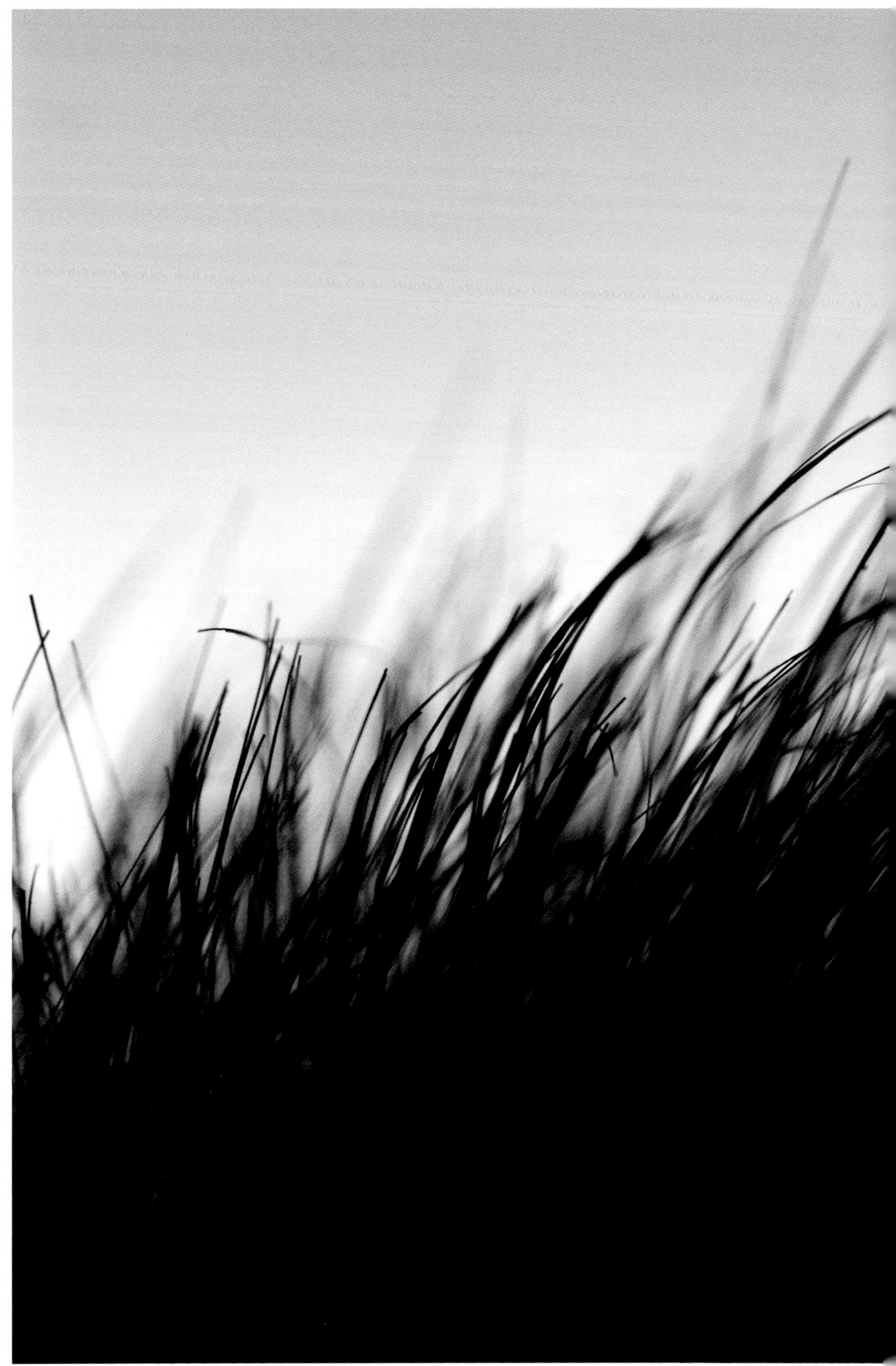

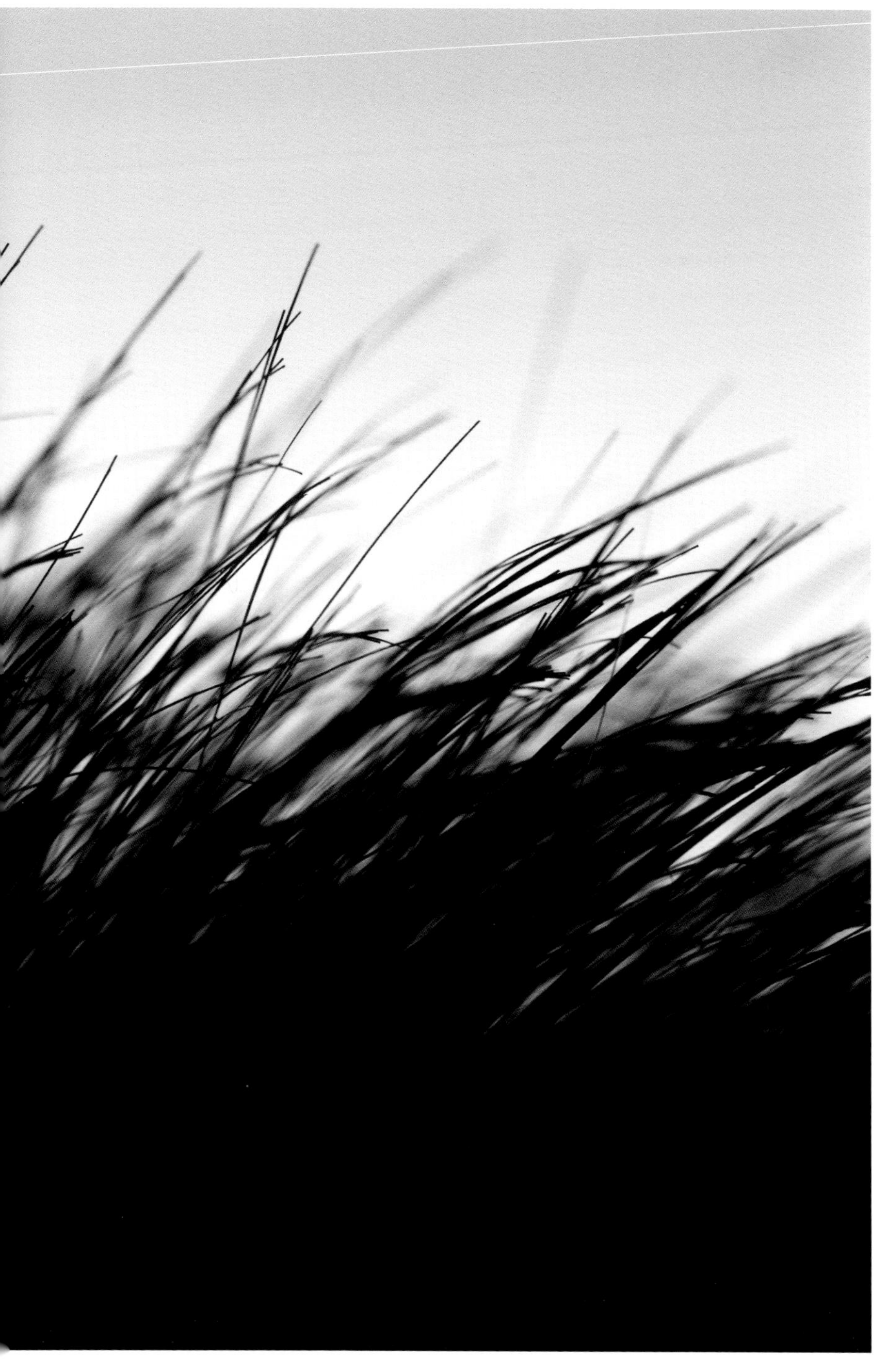

↑ **Sean Lee,** *Plain,* 2013

demonstrate how the body fits the sport, or how the body is trained in order to perform. The series of photos by Angélica Dass (p. 17) highlights skin tones, which she compiles into to a kind of colour chart, pointing out that her work 'challenges the concept of race, attempting to document humanity's true colours rather than the untrue labels "white", "red", "black" and "yellow"'. The works of Pieter Hugo (pp. 50, 51), by contrast, are disturbing: his black-and-white portraits have been manipulated in such a way that the skin tones reflect their pigmentation and are accentuated as much as possible. He shows faces on which the imperfections of the skin rise to the surface: tiny veins, fine lines, beauty spots, liver spots, the marks of age. Neither black nor white, Pieter Hugo's models (who all come from South Africa, a country where skin colour is still a deep source of tension) suddenly acquire an unreal look, with piercing gazes that make the blood run cold.

This gives rise to a question: whether to submit to the body or act with it? The human condition is a corporeal condition. Laia Abril's work (pp. 75, 76) focuses on the fragility of women's rights and women's liberation. In 'A History of Misogyny' — a long-term project — she uses various materials and objects to explore the suffering and damage inflicted on female bodies. Meanwhile, Elinor Carucci (pp. 52–55), in her various self-portraits, shows that we are our flesh and that it remains possible to attend to our most intimate sensations despite the fact that the society in which we live is telling us to separate ourselves, to disconnect from our physical body. The world of medicine fragments the body into its various components and encourages us to dissociate ourselves from it. Yet again and again we are reminded that our existence is primarily corporeal and that we make contact with the outside world through our skin. Nicholas Nixon (pp. 60, 61) is just one of the photographers who celebrates this physical relationship that we have with the world and with others.

→(Above and below) **Jeff Mermelstein**, *New York City*, 2016

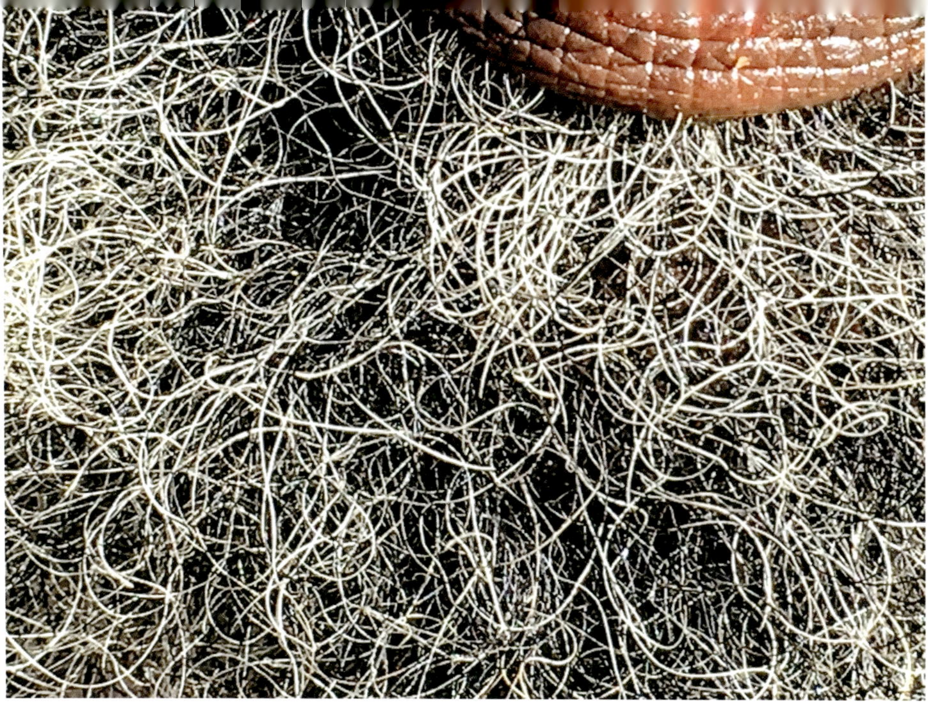

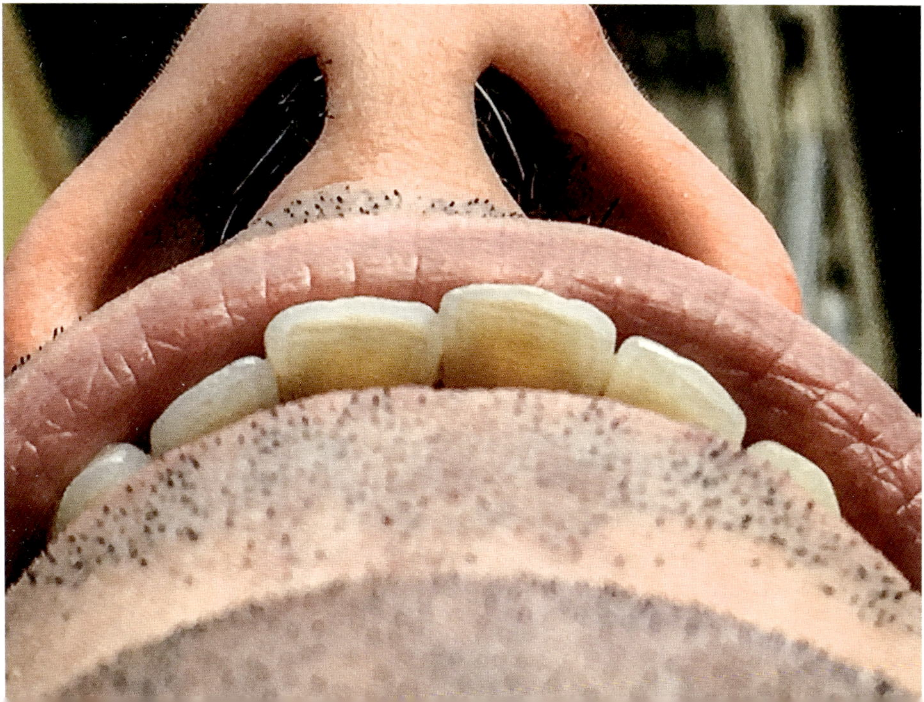

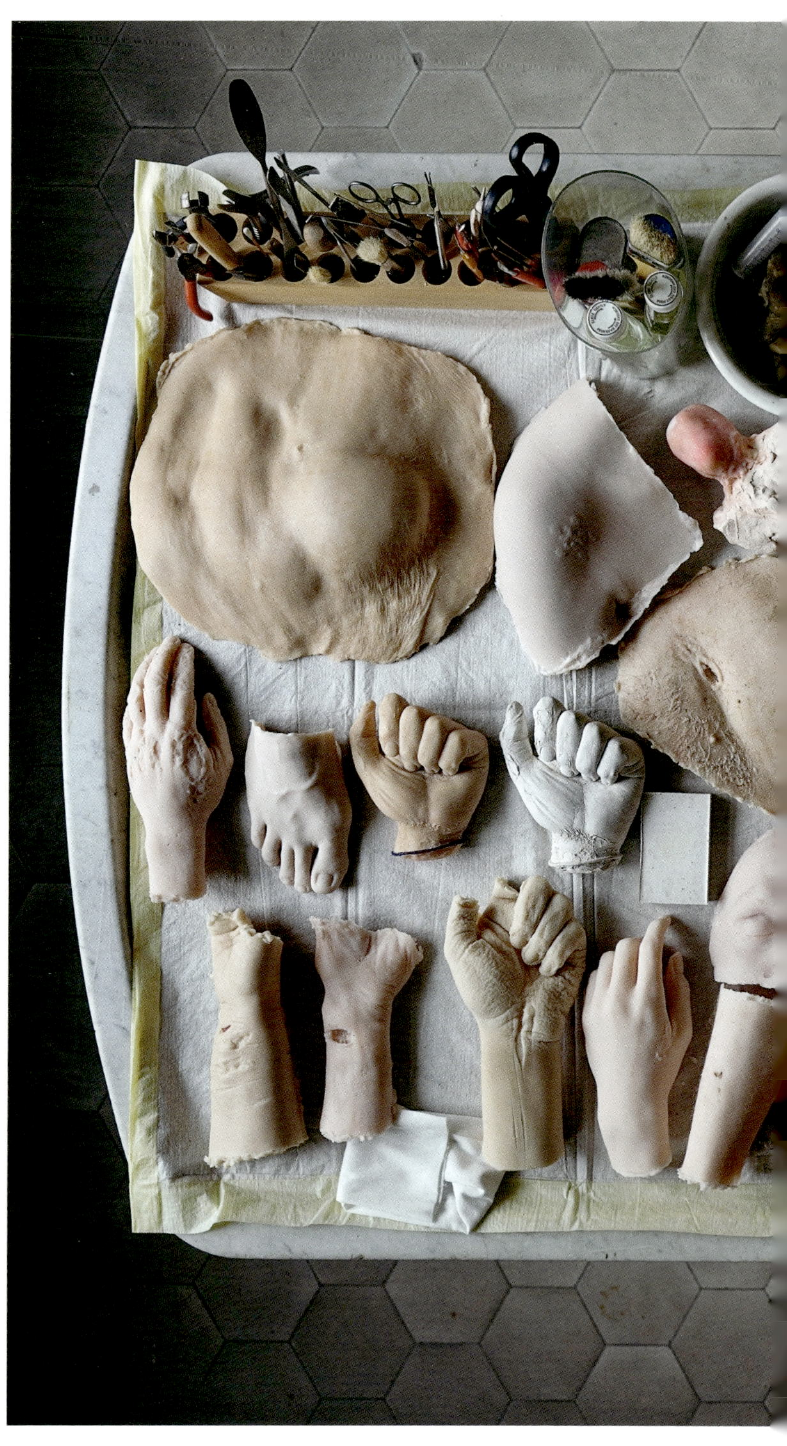

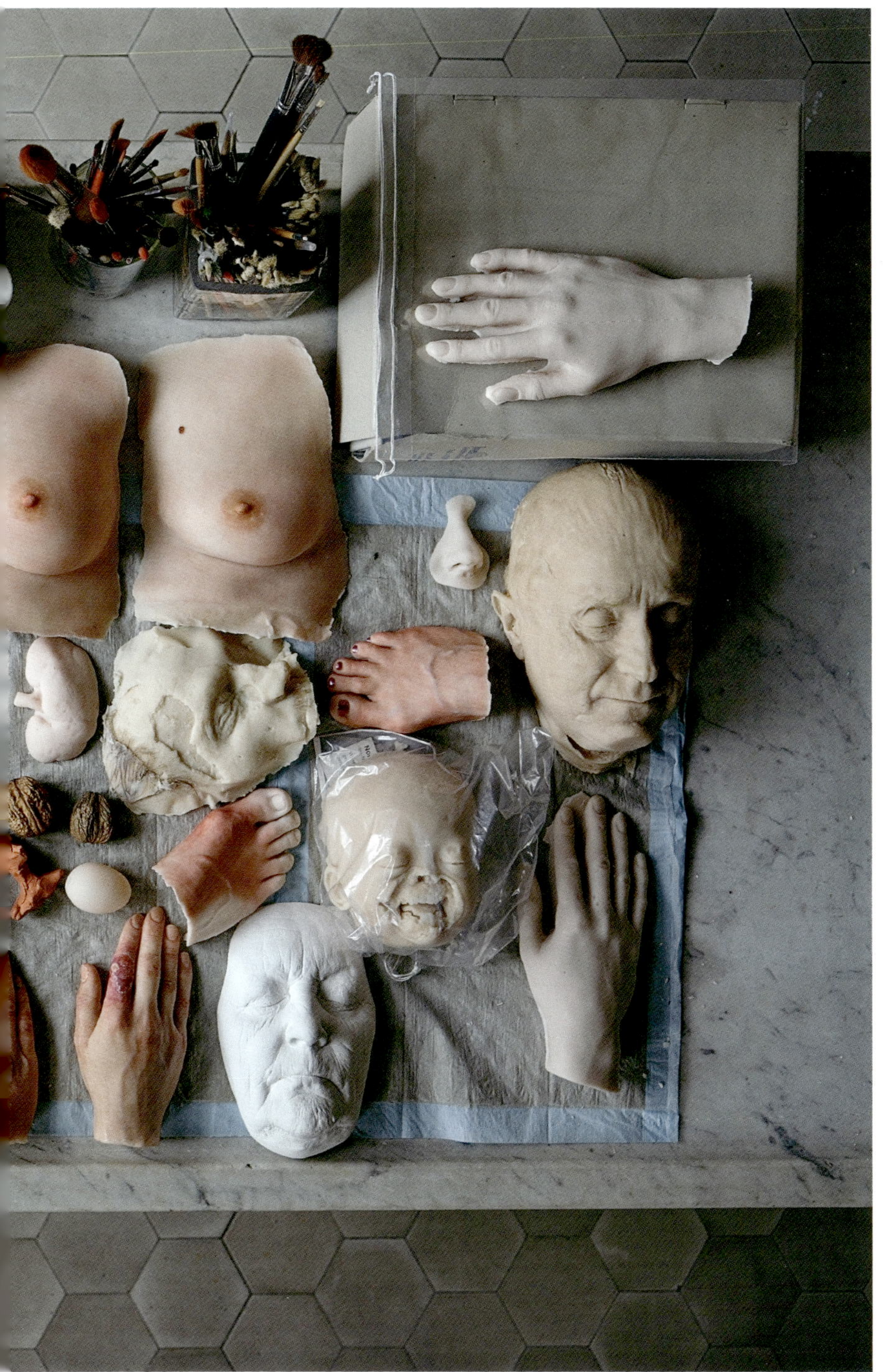

↑ **Thomas Struth,** *Study, Charité, Berlin,* 2015

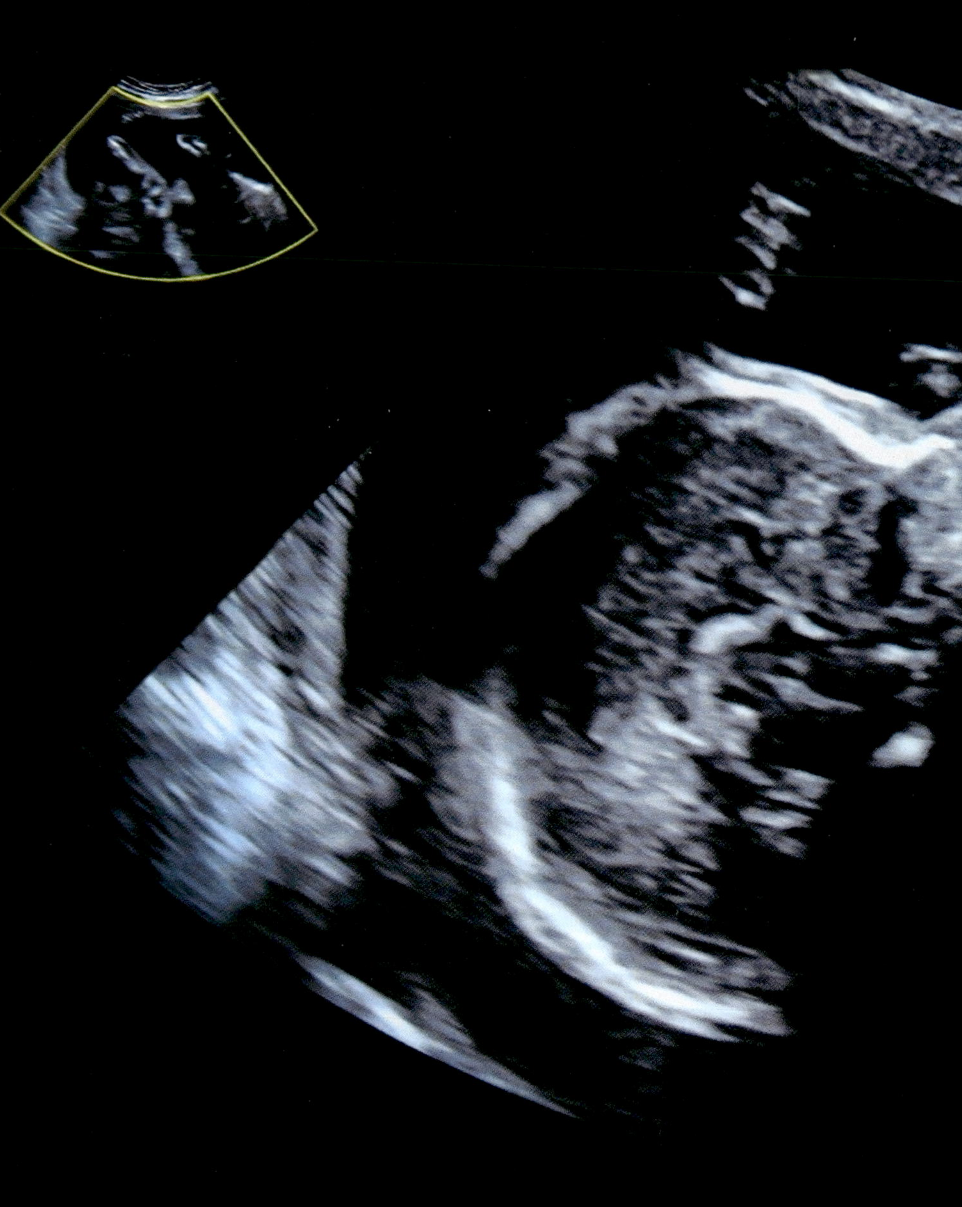

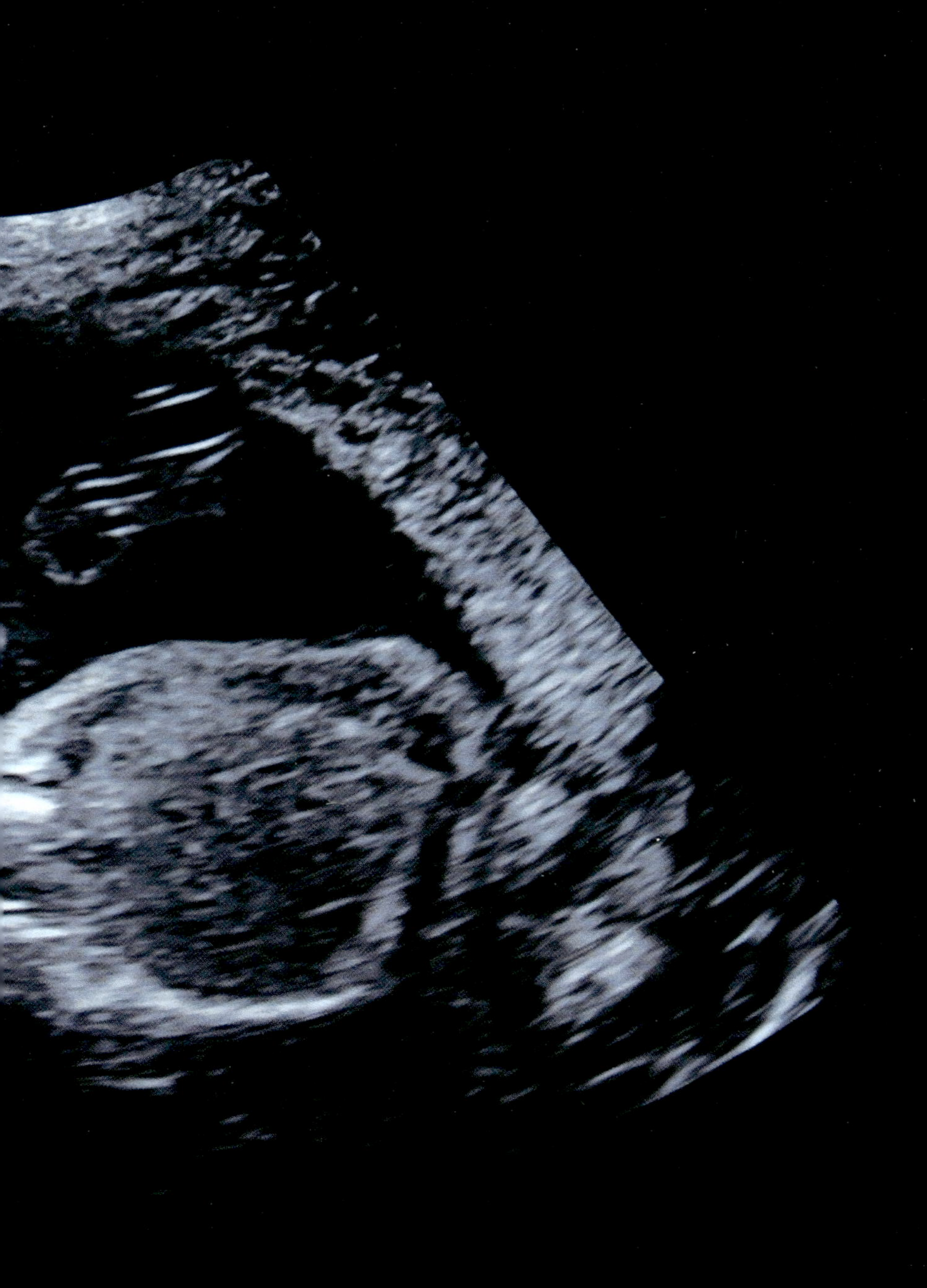

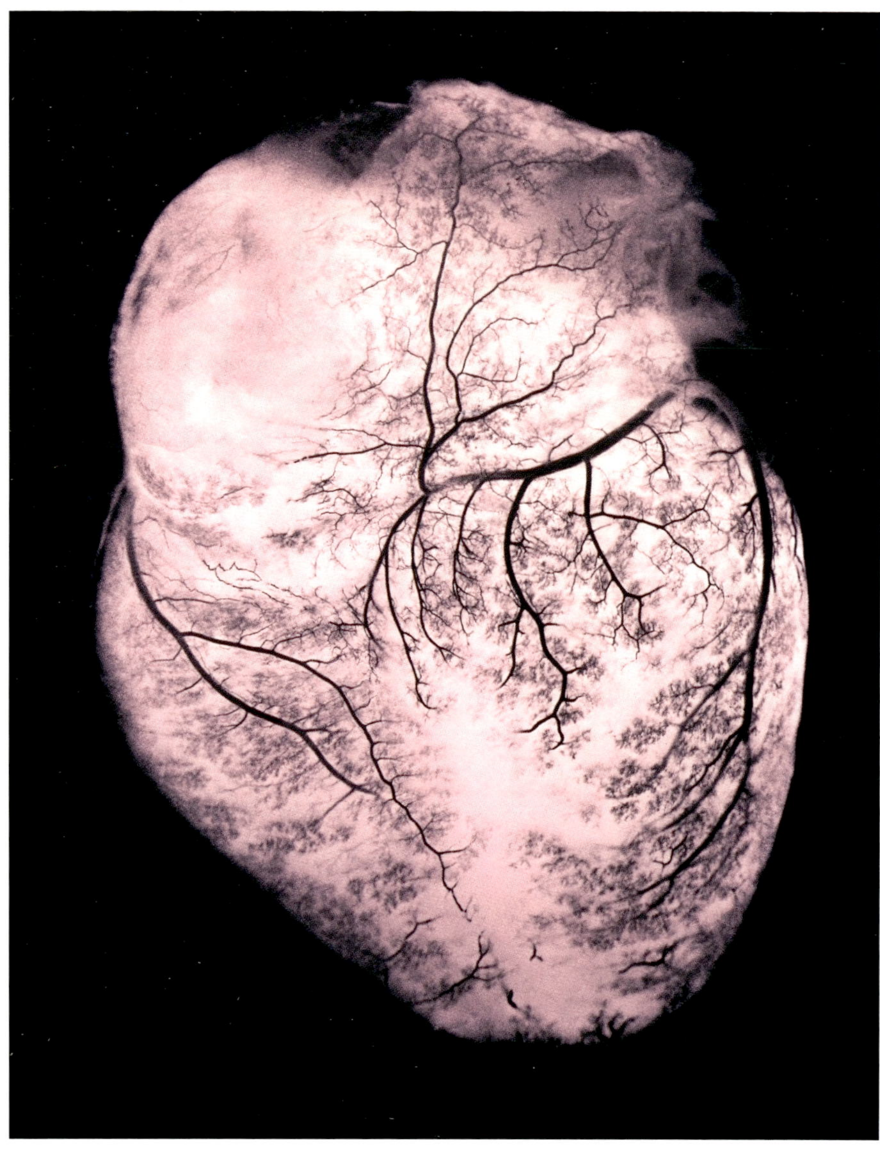

↑ **Science Photo Library,** Human heart, showing the arteries
and veins that supply blood to the cardiac muscles
←(Previous) **Imagerie du Flon,** *Iris,* 2017

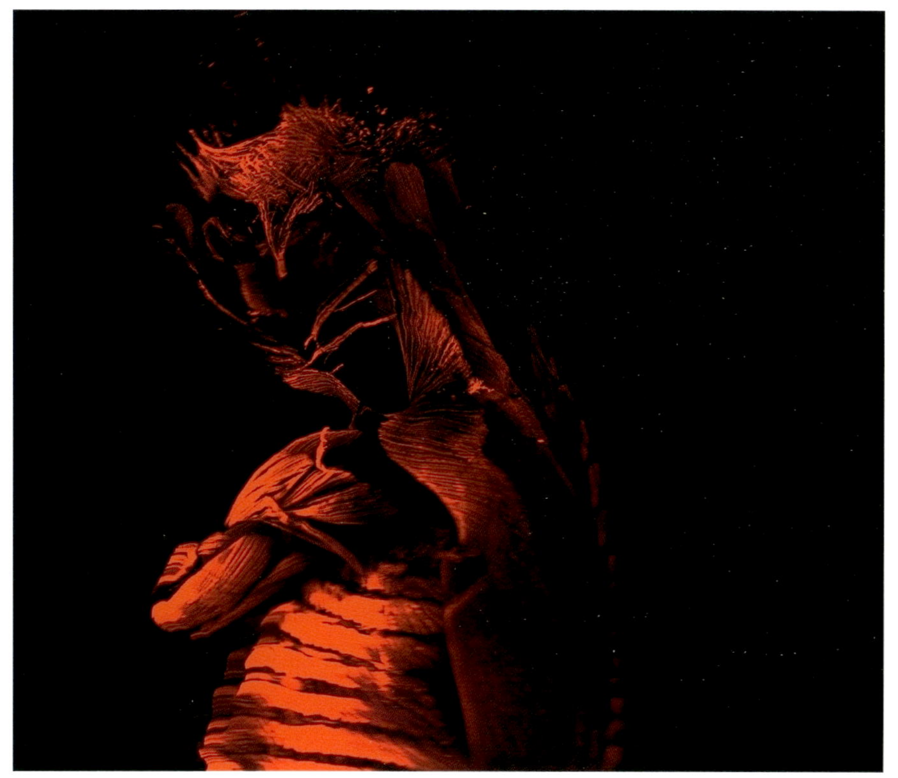

↑ **Alain Chédotal and Morgane Belle,** Motor system of the
shoulder and neck in an eight-week-old embryo, 2017

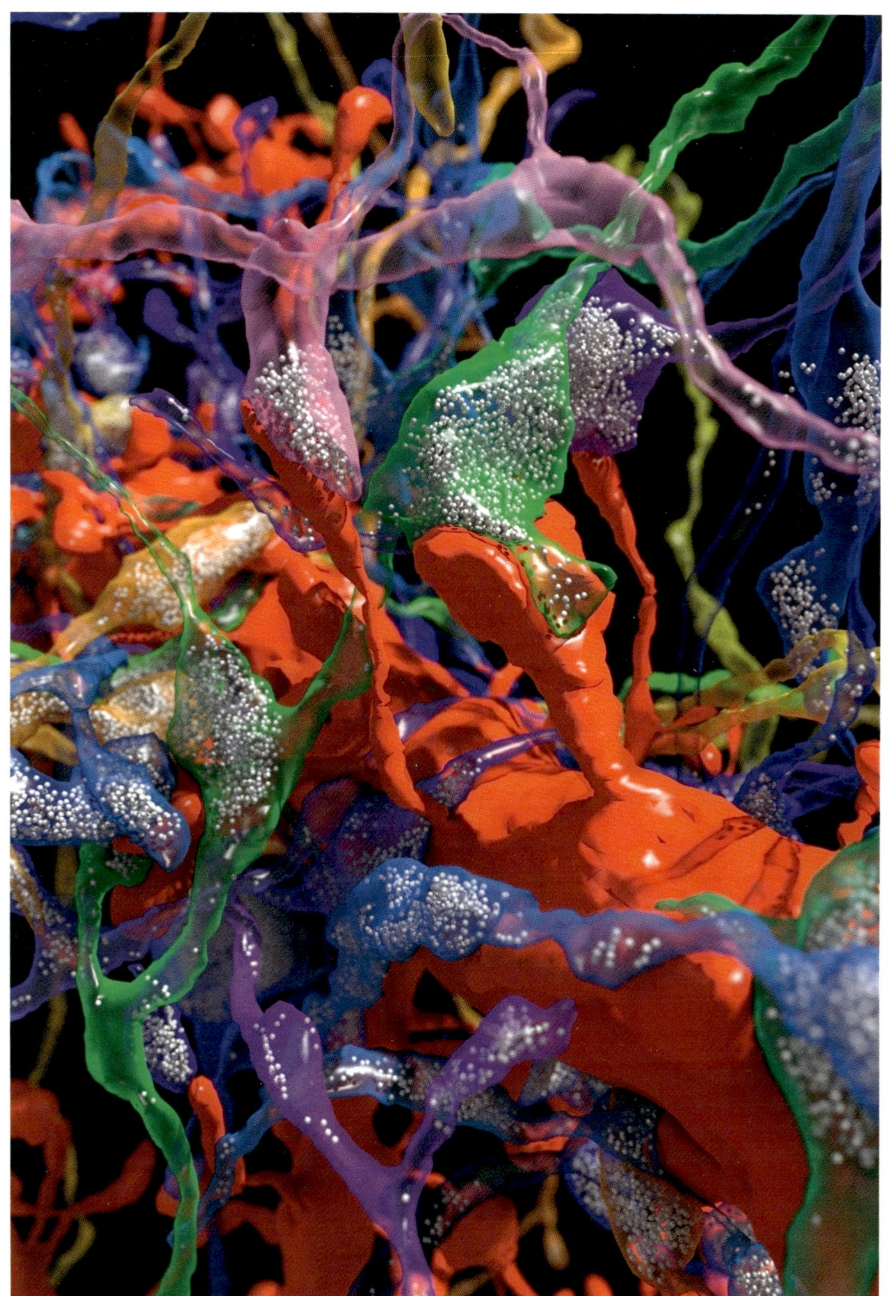

↑ **Daniel Berger, Narayanan Kasthuri and Jeff Lichtman,**
Highly magnified view of the connections between nerve cells, 2015

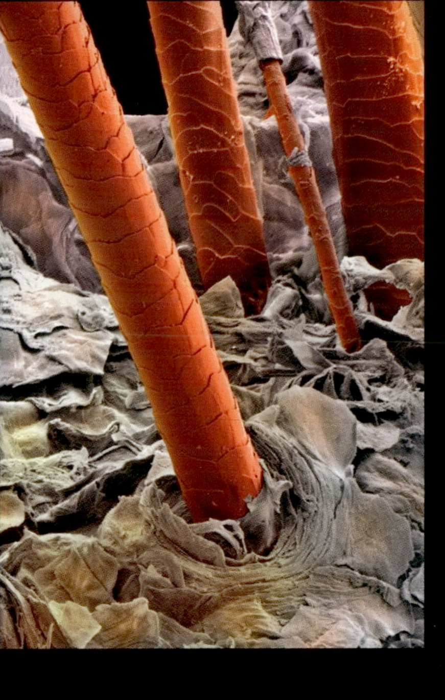
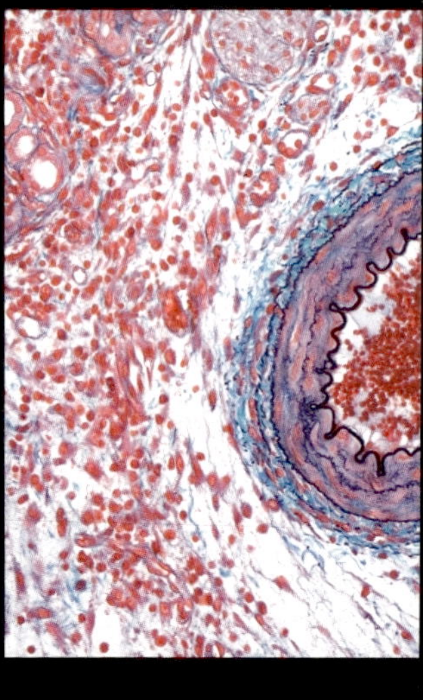
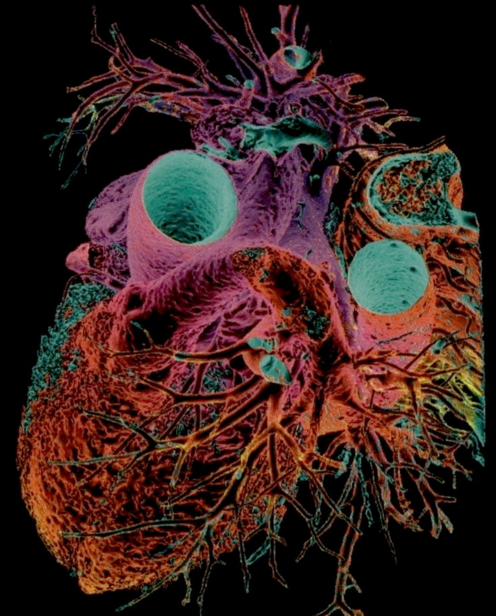
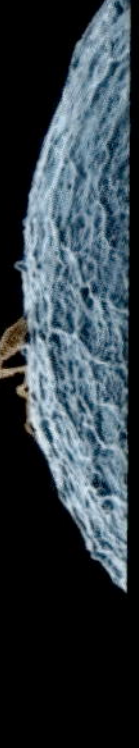

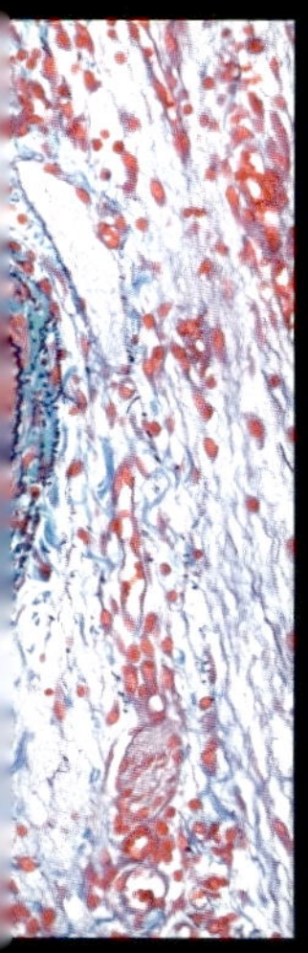
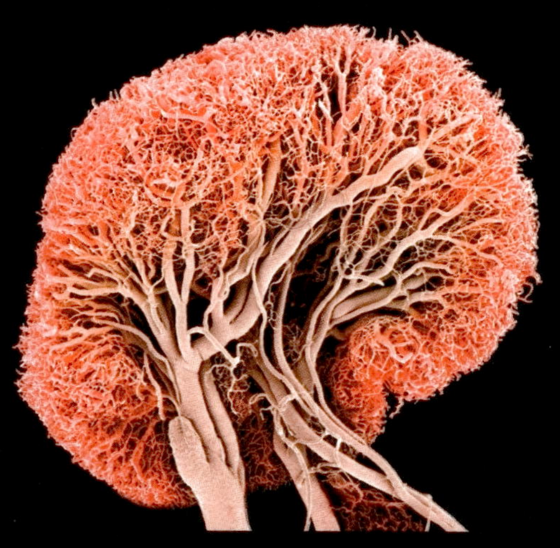
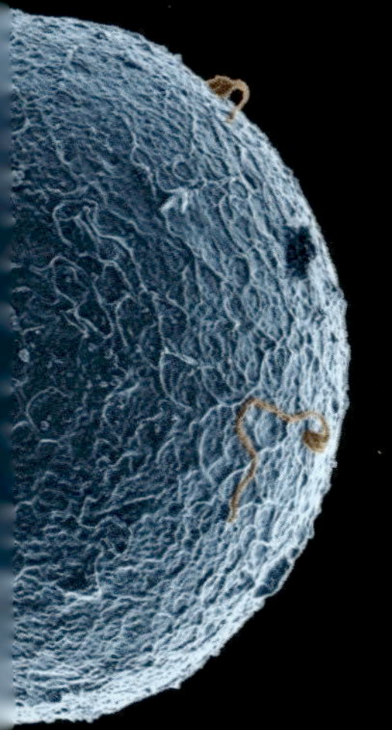
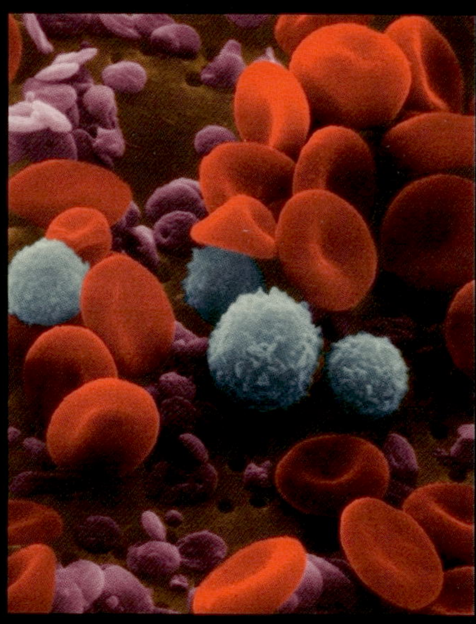

↑ (Clockwise from top left) A coloured Scanning Electron Micrograph (SEM) of hair shafts growing from the surface of human skin; a light micrograph of a cross-section through a small muscular artery and surrounding tissue; an SEM of blood vessels in a lymph node; an SEM of blood cells; an Environmental Scanning Electron Microscopy (ESEM) image of a human egg cell and sperm cells; a coloured 3D Computed Tomography (CT) scan of a section through a healthy adult human heart, showing the pulmonary artery and its branches (Y-shaped, centre), ascending and descending aorta (blue, rounded) and ventricles (bottom left), with spine seen at right

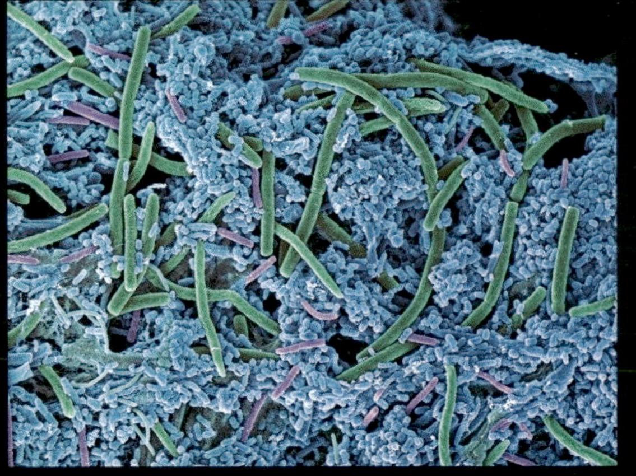

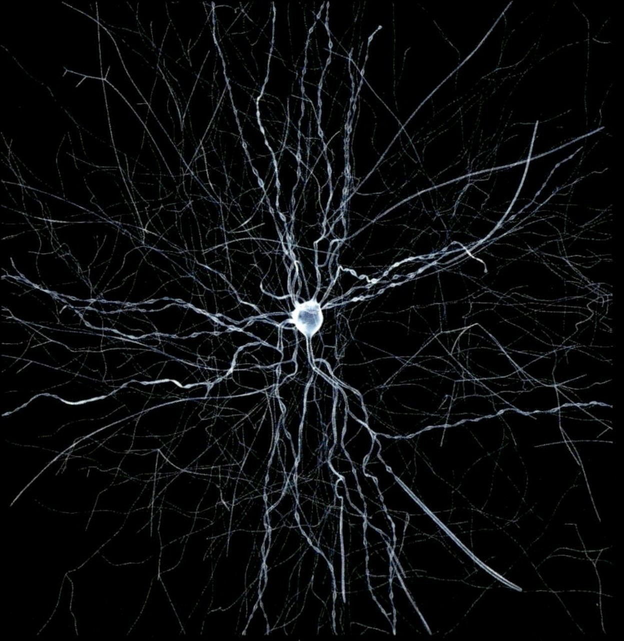

(Clockwise from top left) A Scanning Electron Micrograph (SEM) of dental plaque-forming bacteria; an SEM of a human embryo at the eight-cell stage; an SEM of a sweat pore; Steven Daniel, *Aechorea #06*, 2016 (separation of nucleic acids DNA and RNA through an agarose gel matrix); an SEM of lamellae from compact bone; a large, layer 2/3 basket cell in a digital reconstruction of neocortical microcircuitry

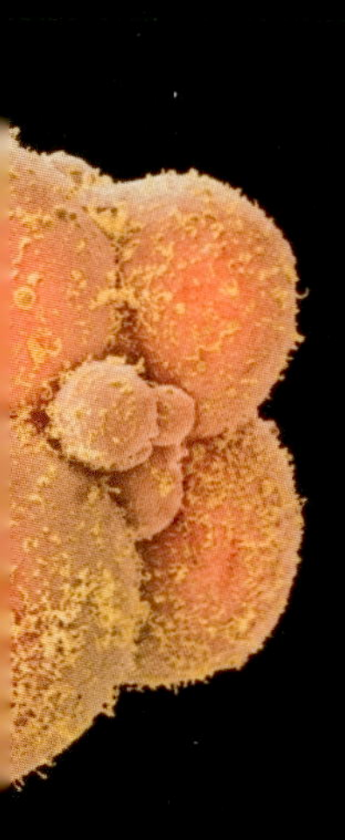
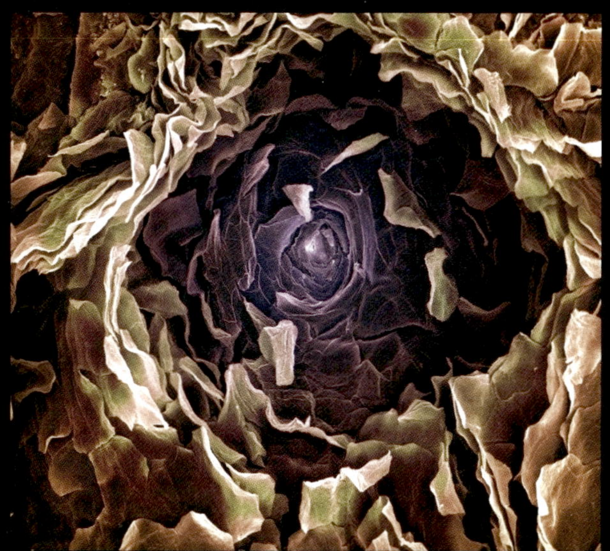
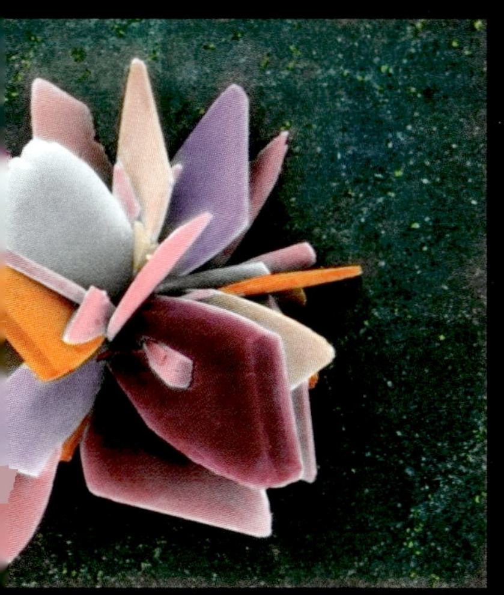
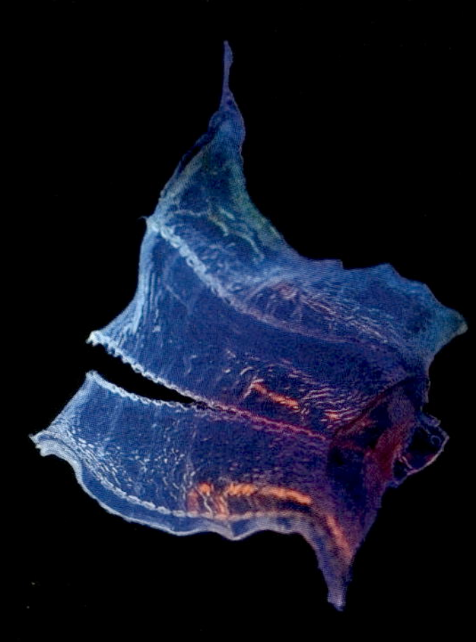

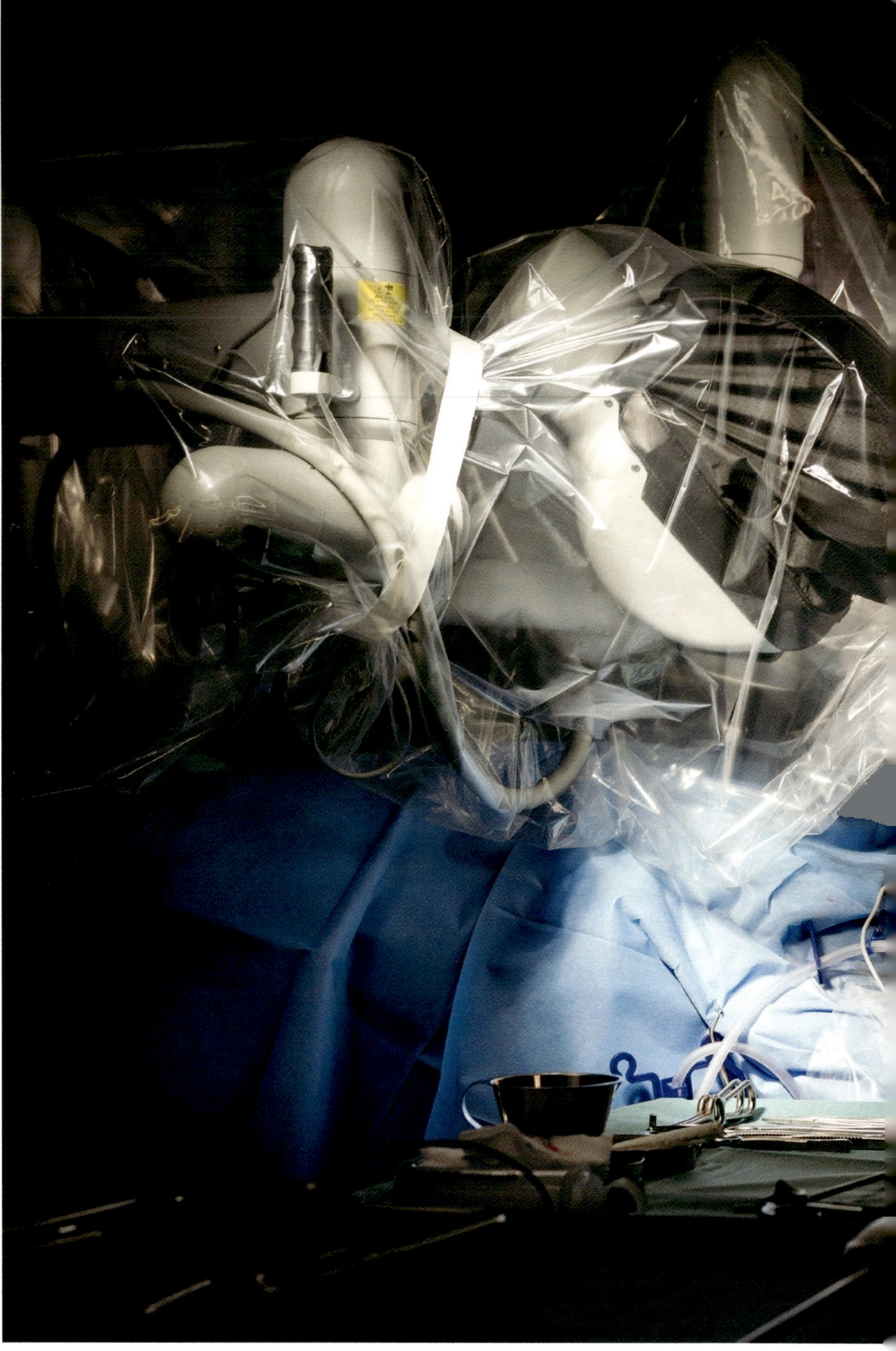

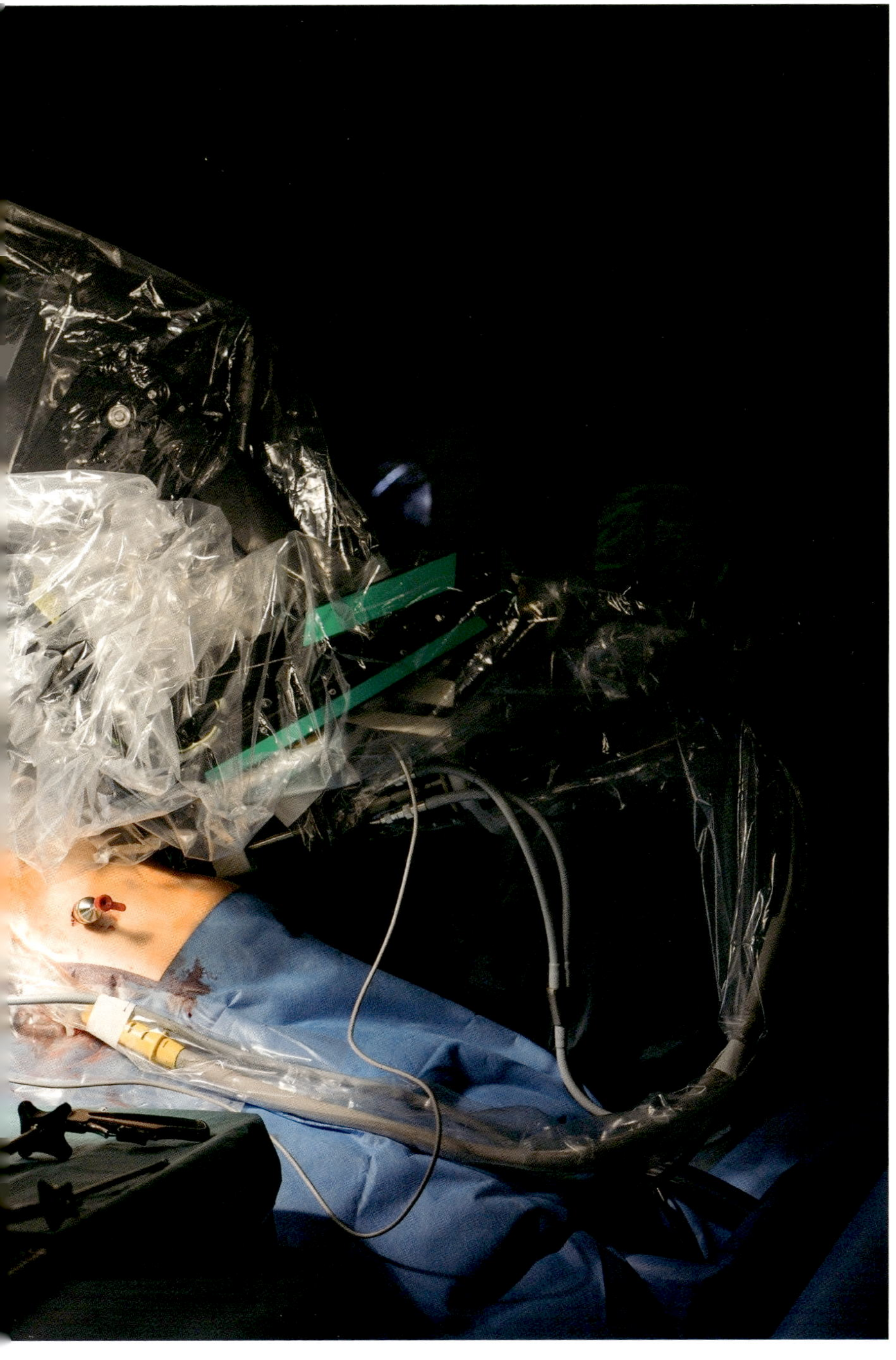

↑ **Thomas Struth**, *Figure, Charité, Berlin, 2012*

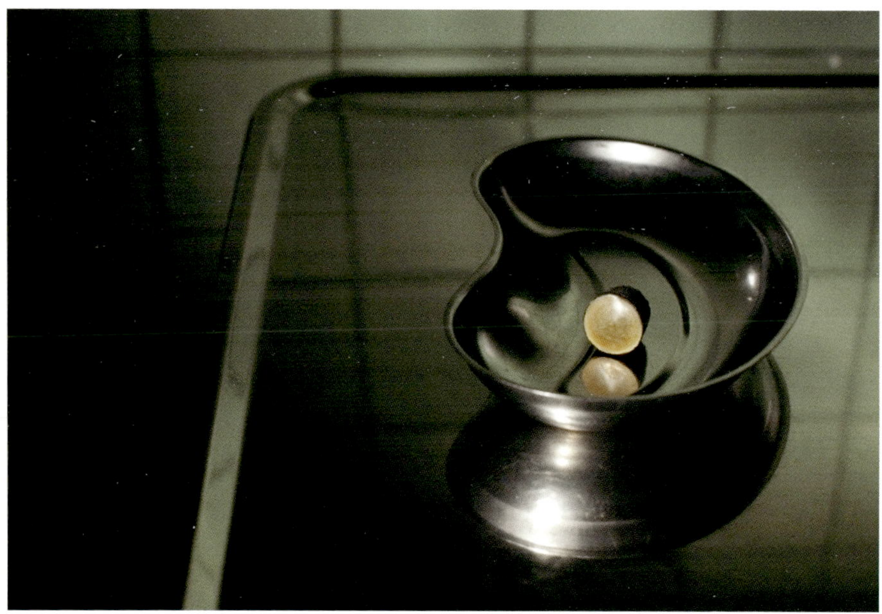

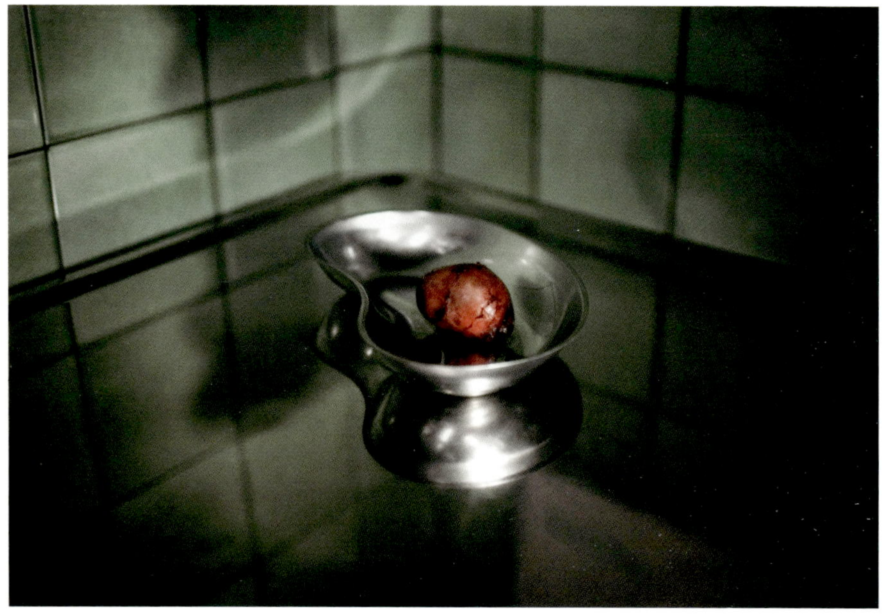

↑ (Top) **Maija Tammi,** *Gallstone #2*, from the series 'Removals', 2011–13
↑ (Above) **Maija Tammi,** *Goiter #1*, from the series 'Removals', 2011–13

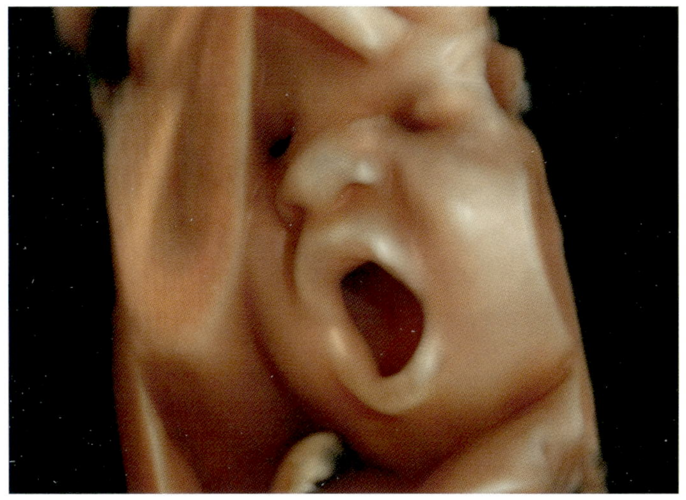

↑ **Bernard Benoit,** 3D ultrasound scan of a foetus, yawning,
at the start of the eighth month of pregnancy, 2018

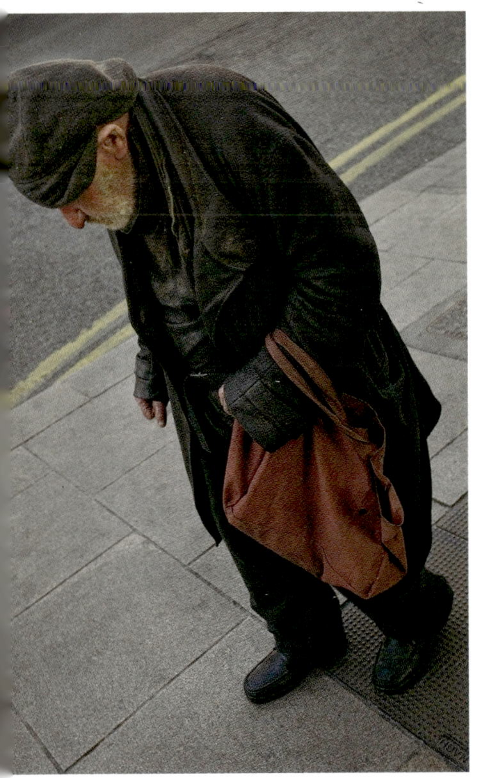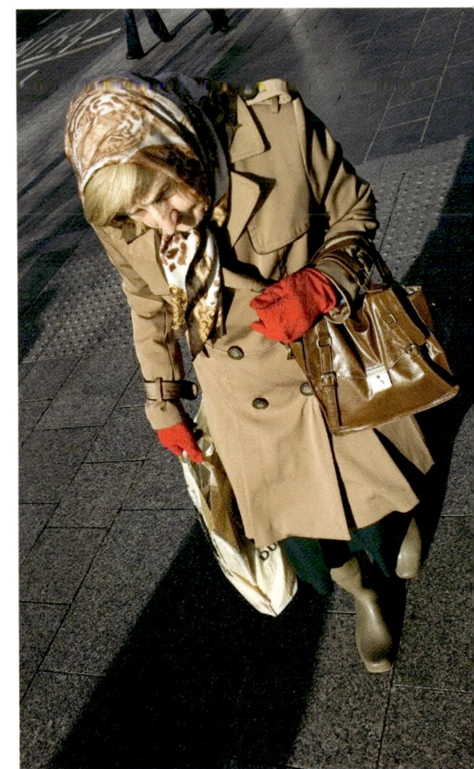

↑ (Left) **Eamonn Doyle,** *Untitled 3*, from the series 'i', 2013
↑ (Right) **Eamonn Doyle,** *Untitled 14*, from the series 'i', 2013

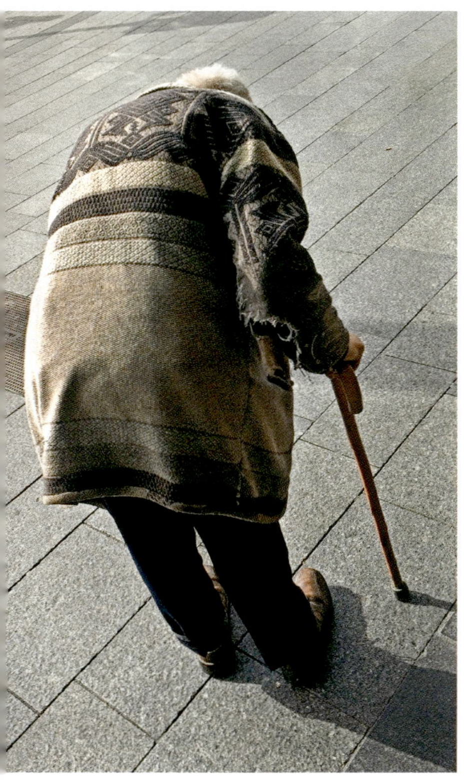 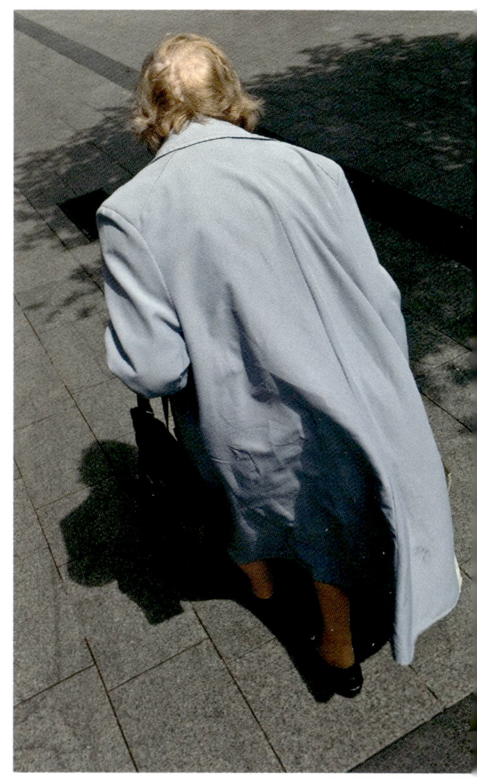

↑ (Left) **Eamonn Doyle,** *Untitled 15*, from the series 'i', 2013
↑ (Right) **Eamonn Doyle,** *Untitled 19*, from the series 'i', 2013

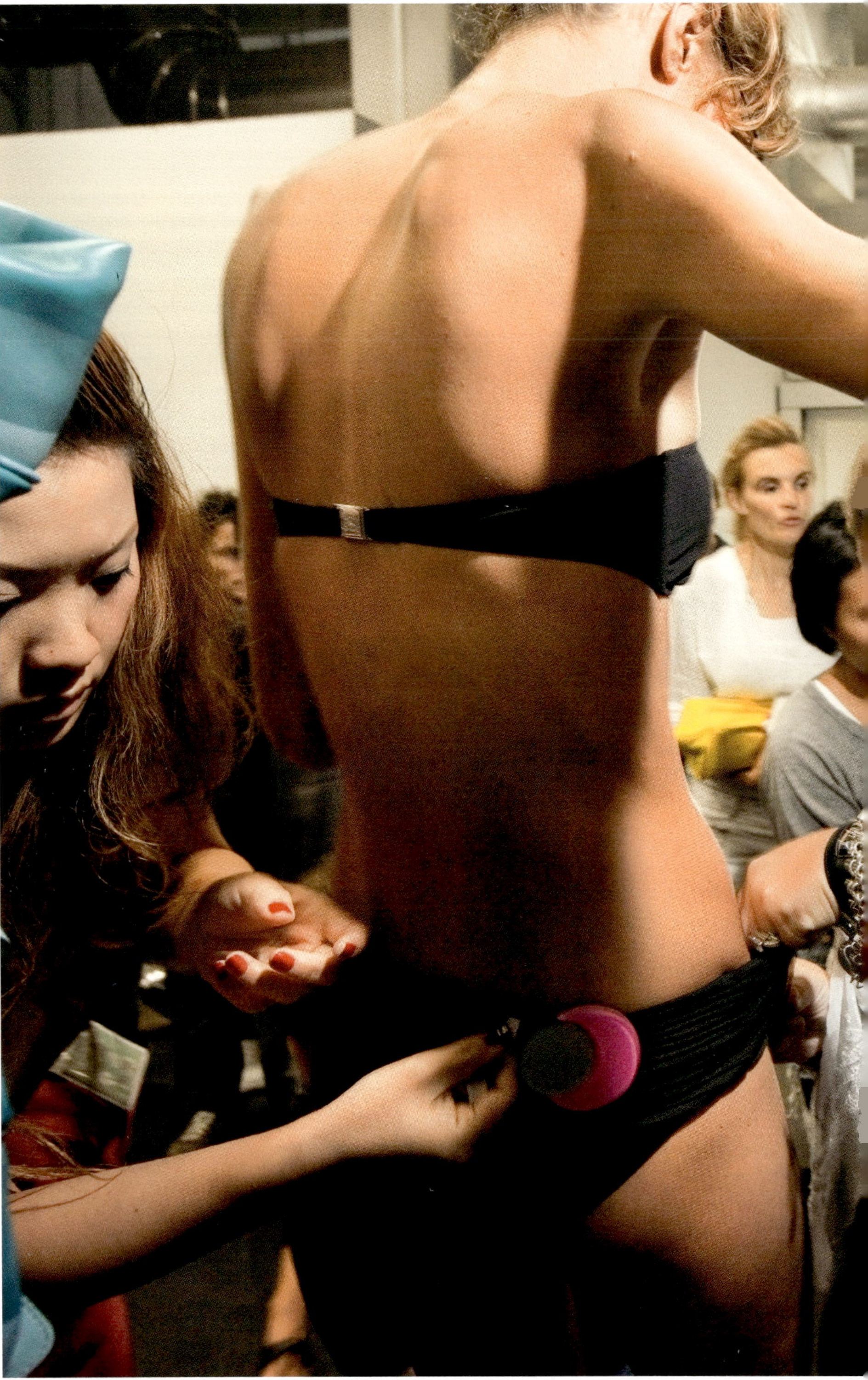

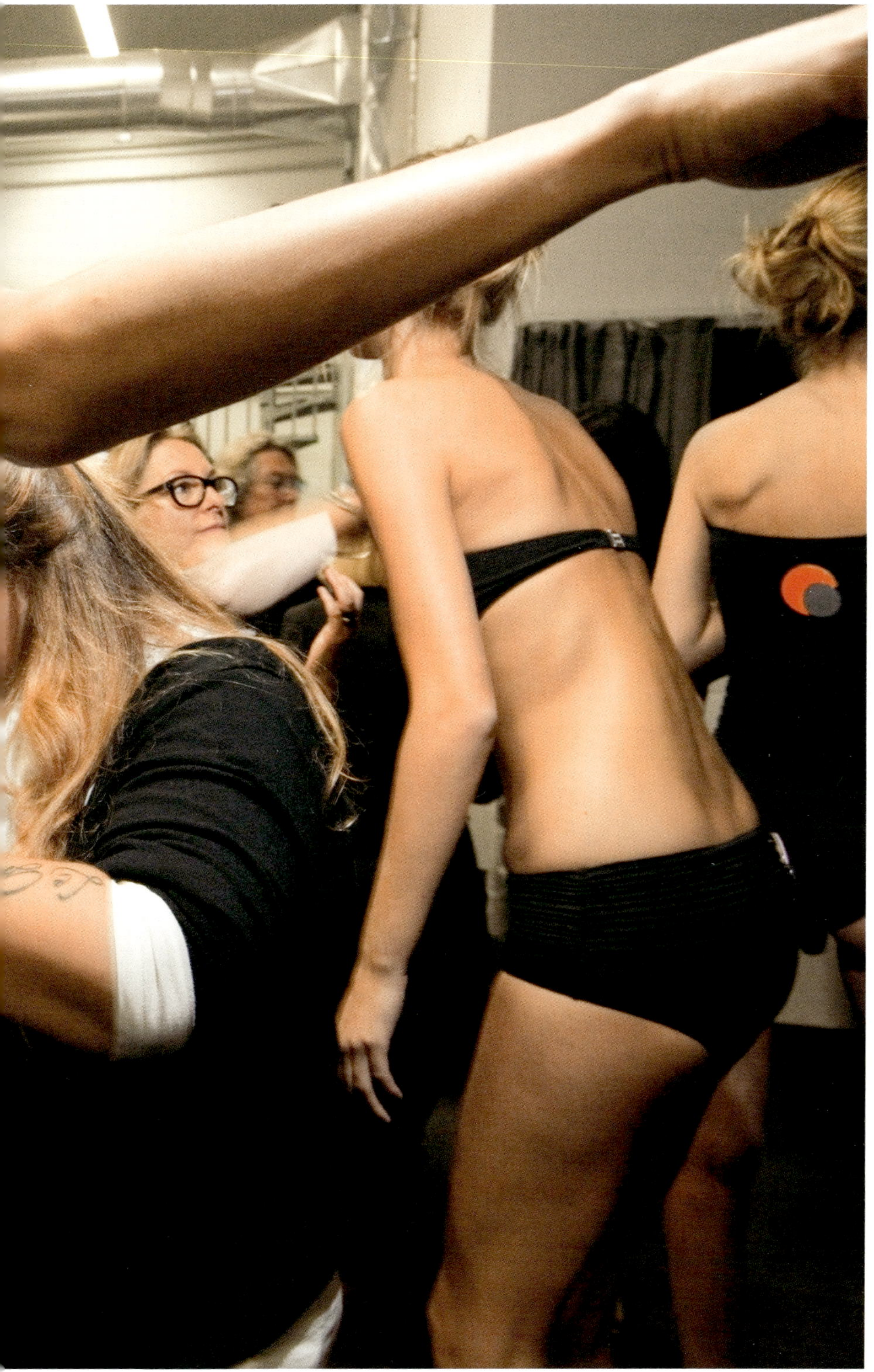

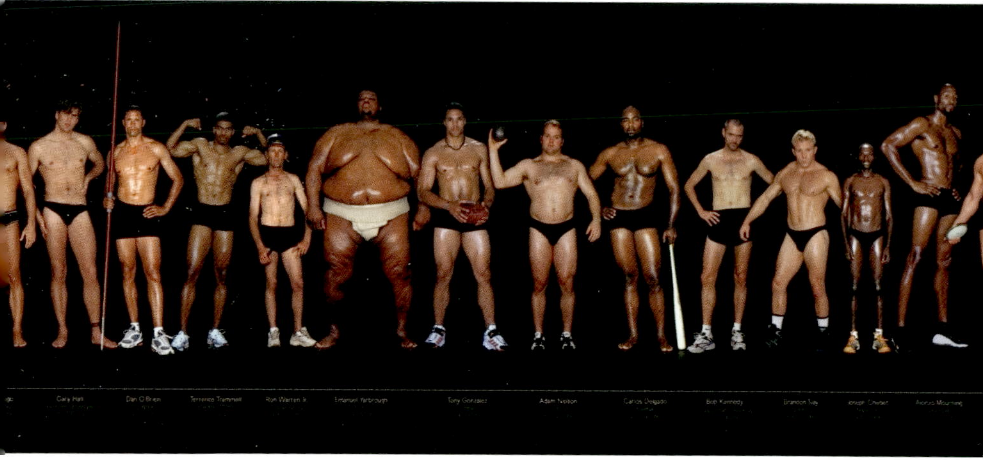

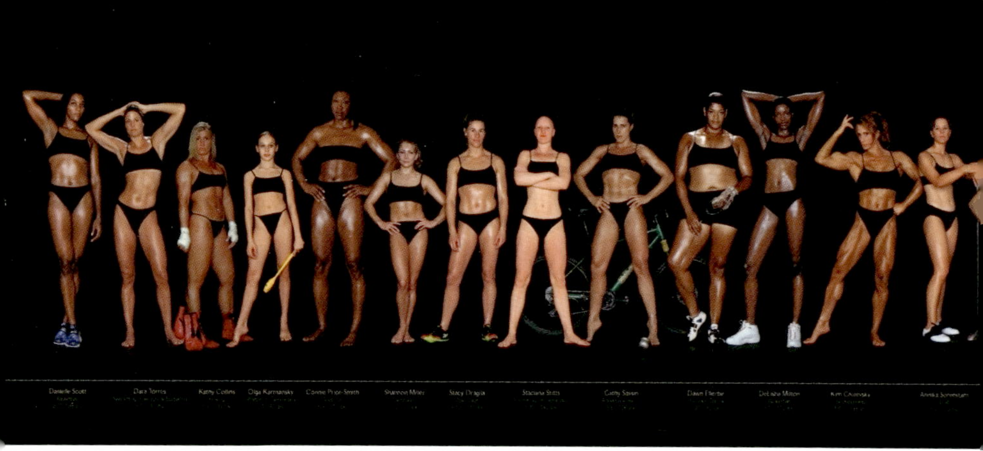

← (Previous) **Lauren Greenfield,** *Fashion Week,* 2009

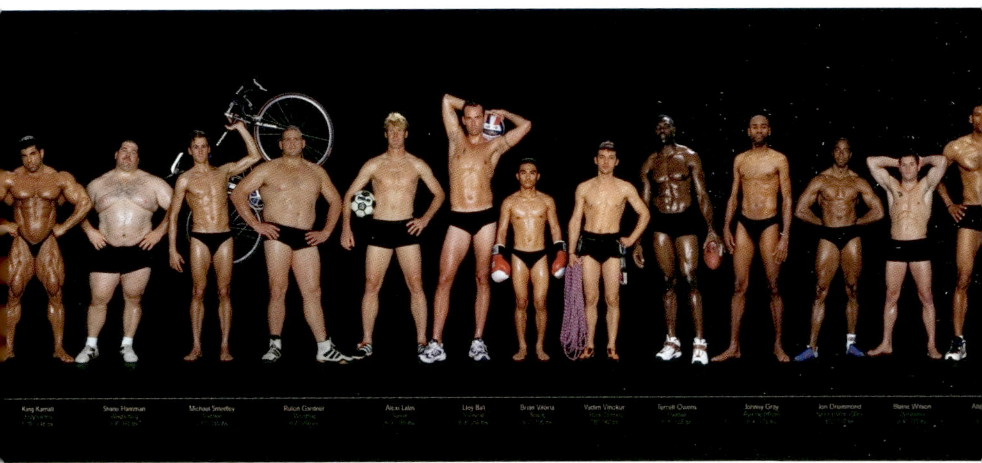

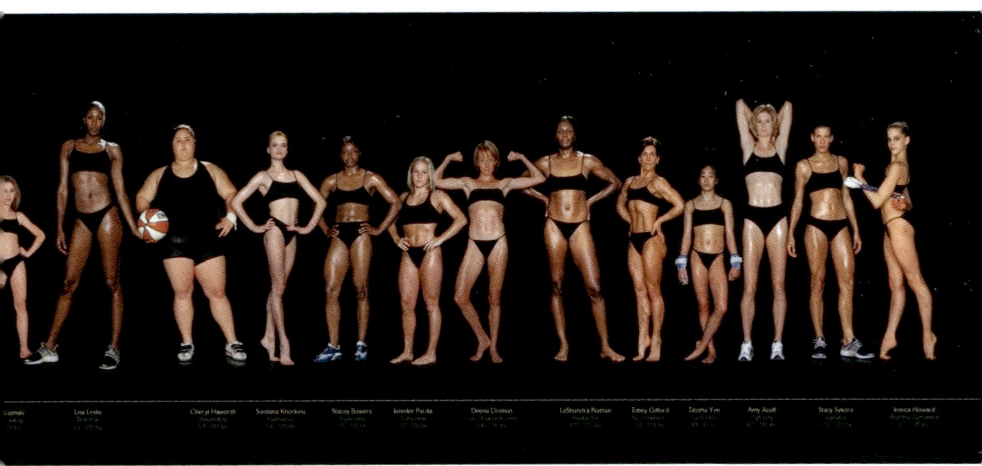

↑ (Top and above) **Howard Schatz**, *Athletes*, 2000—02

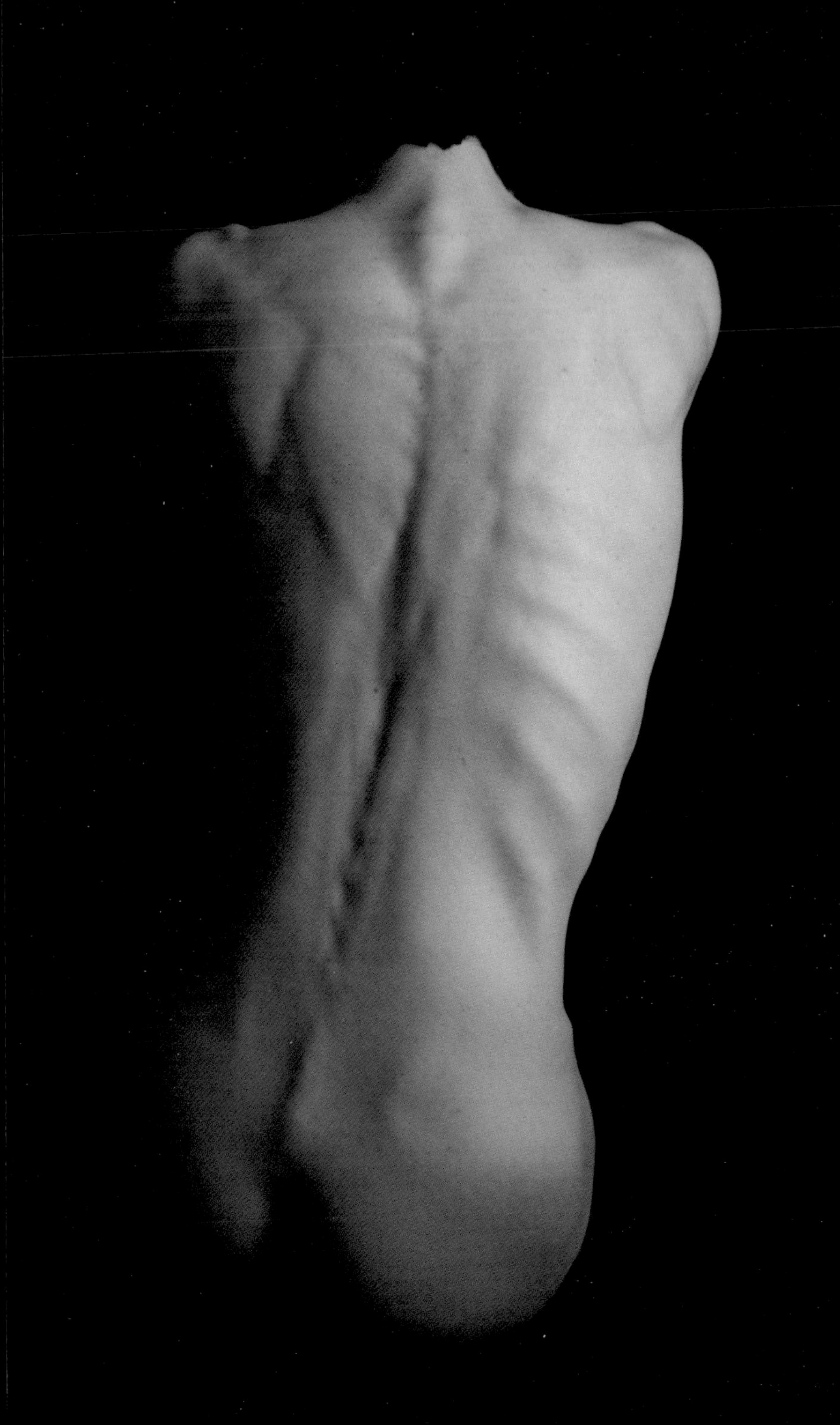

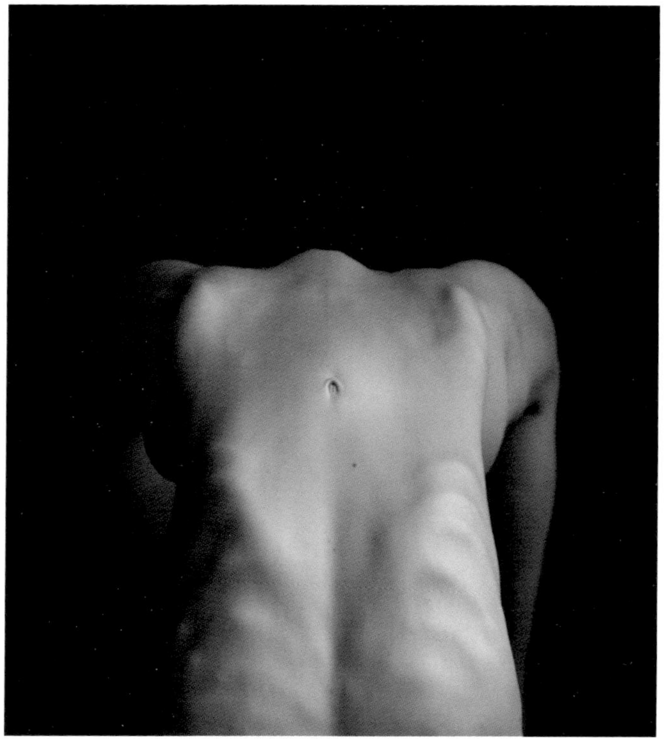

↑ **Juul Kraijer,** *Untitled (C.M. #10),* 2015
←**Juul Kraijer,** *Untitled (C.M. #3),* 2015

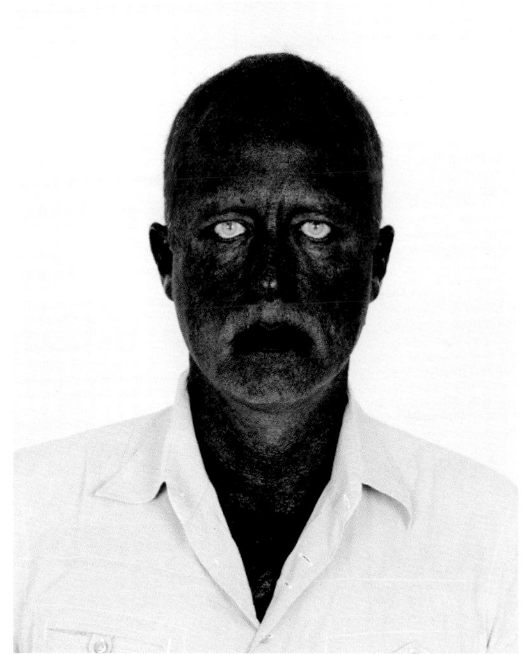

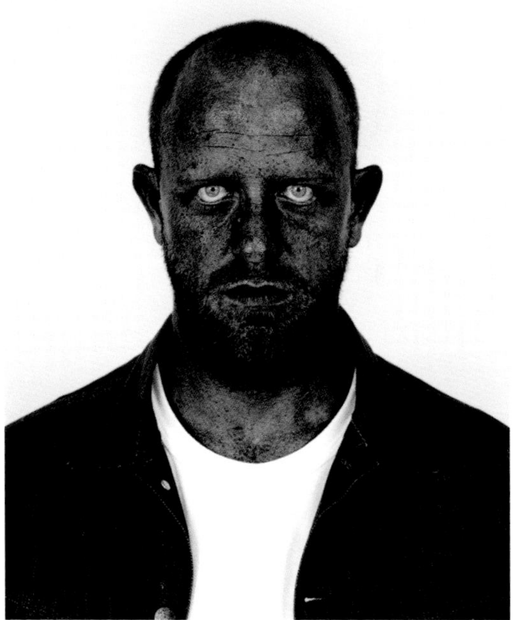

↑ (Top) **Pieter Hugo,** *Michael Stevenson,* from the series 'There's a place in hell for me & my friends', 2012
↑ (Above) **Pieter Hugo,** *Pieter Hugo,* from the series 'There's a place in hell for me & my friends', 2011

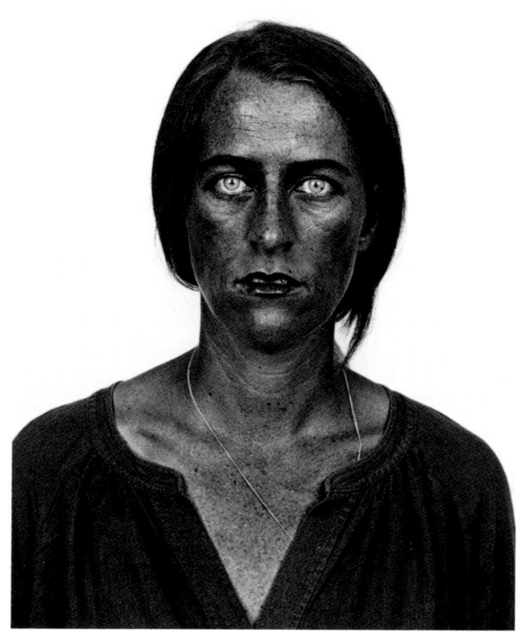

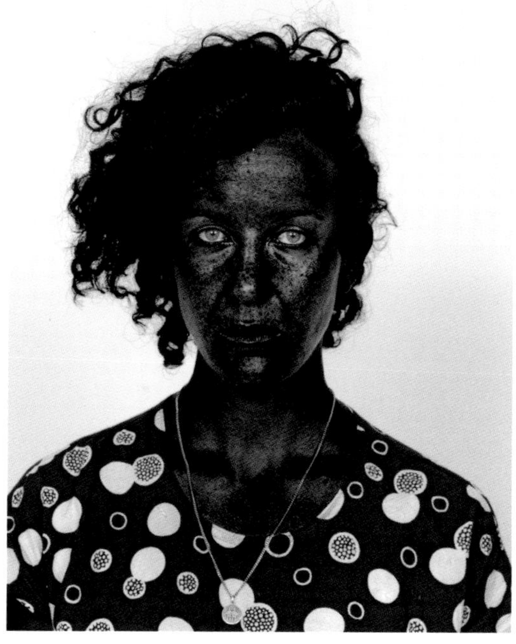

↑ (Top) **Pieter Hugo,** *Annebelle Schreuders*, from the series 'There's a place in hell for me & my friends', 2012
↑ (Above) **Pieter Hugo,** *Trasi Henen*, from the series 'There's a place in hell for me & my friends', 2011

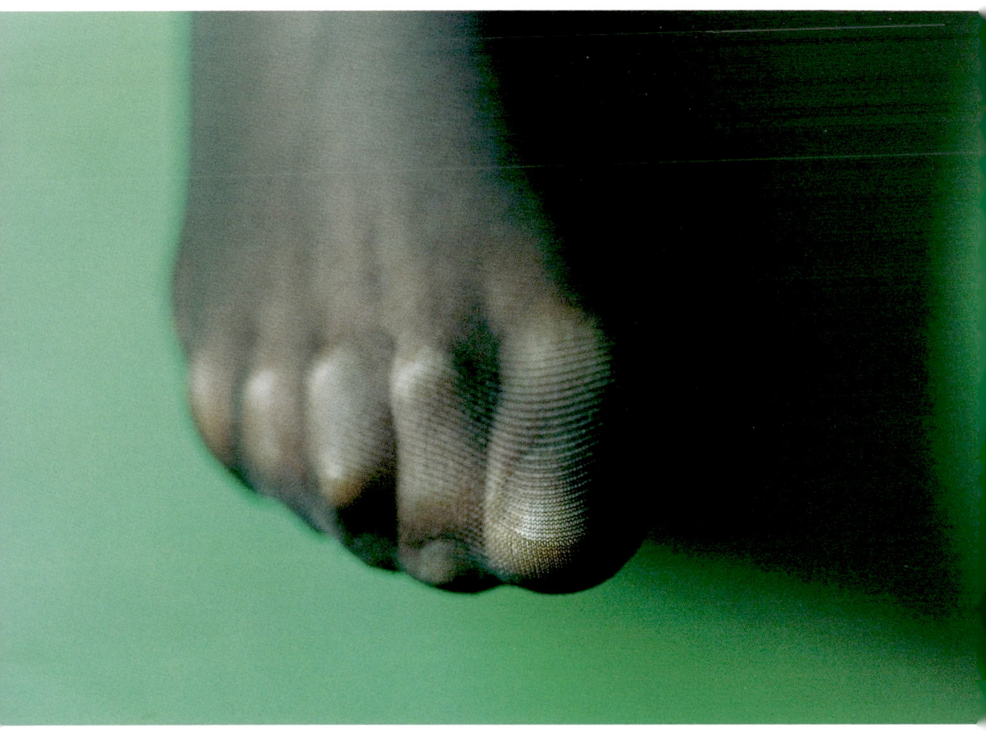

↑ **Elinor Carucci,** *Foot in stocking,* 1997

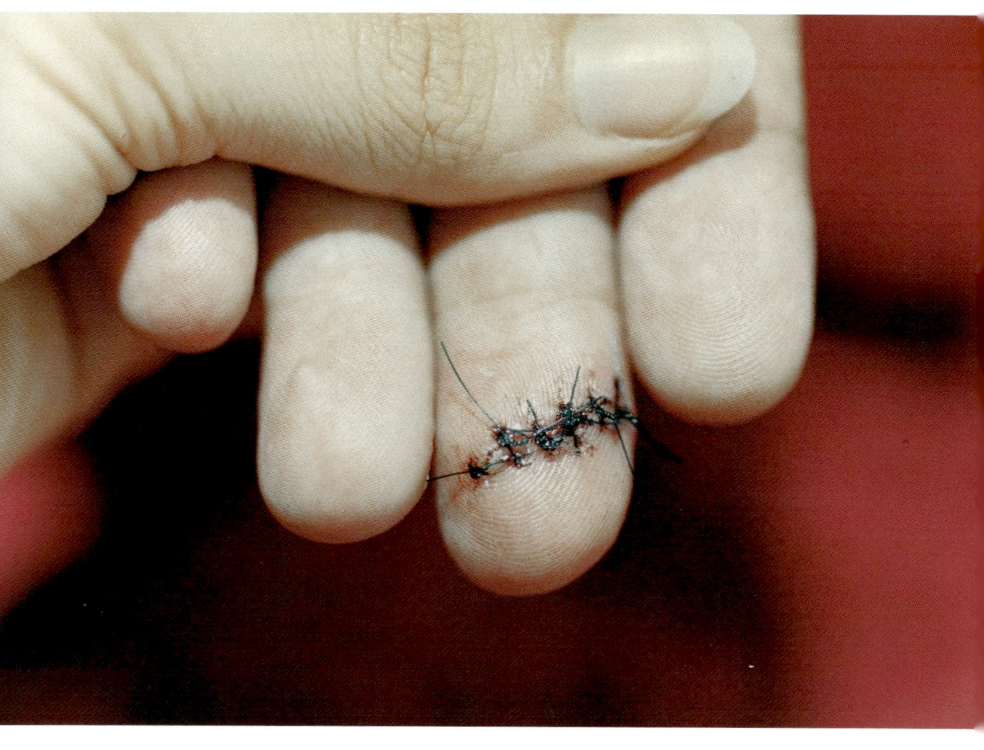

↑ **Elinor Carucci,** *I hold Eran's wounded hand,* 1998
→(Overleaf) **Elinor Carucci,** *Feeling me,* 2004

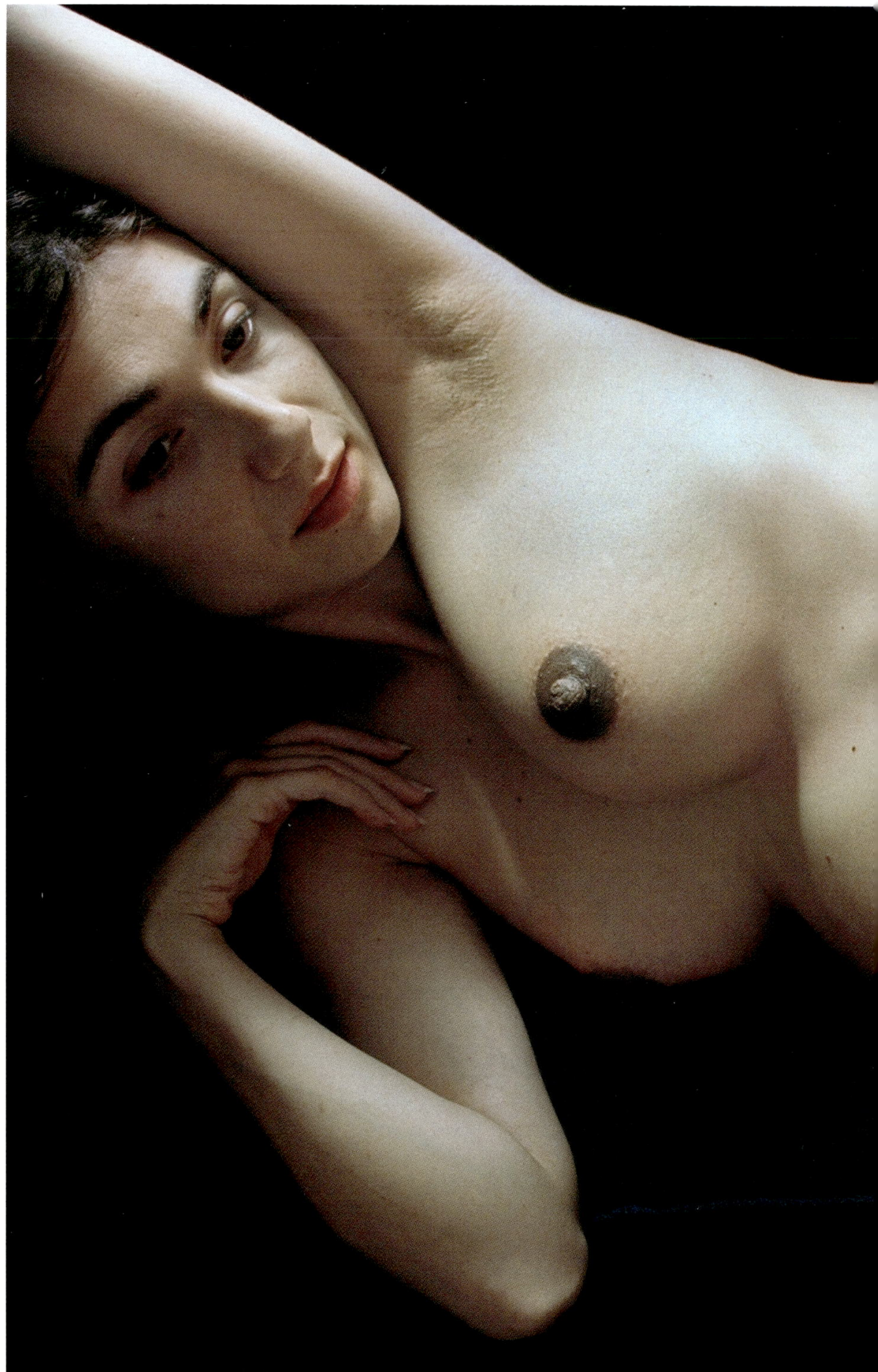

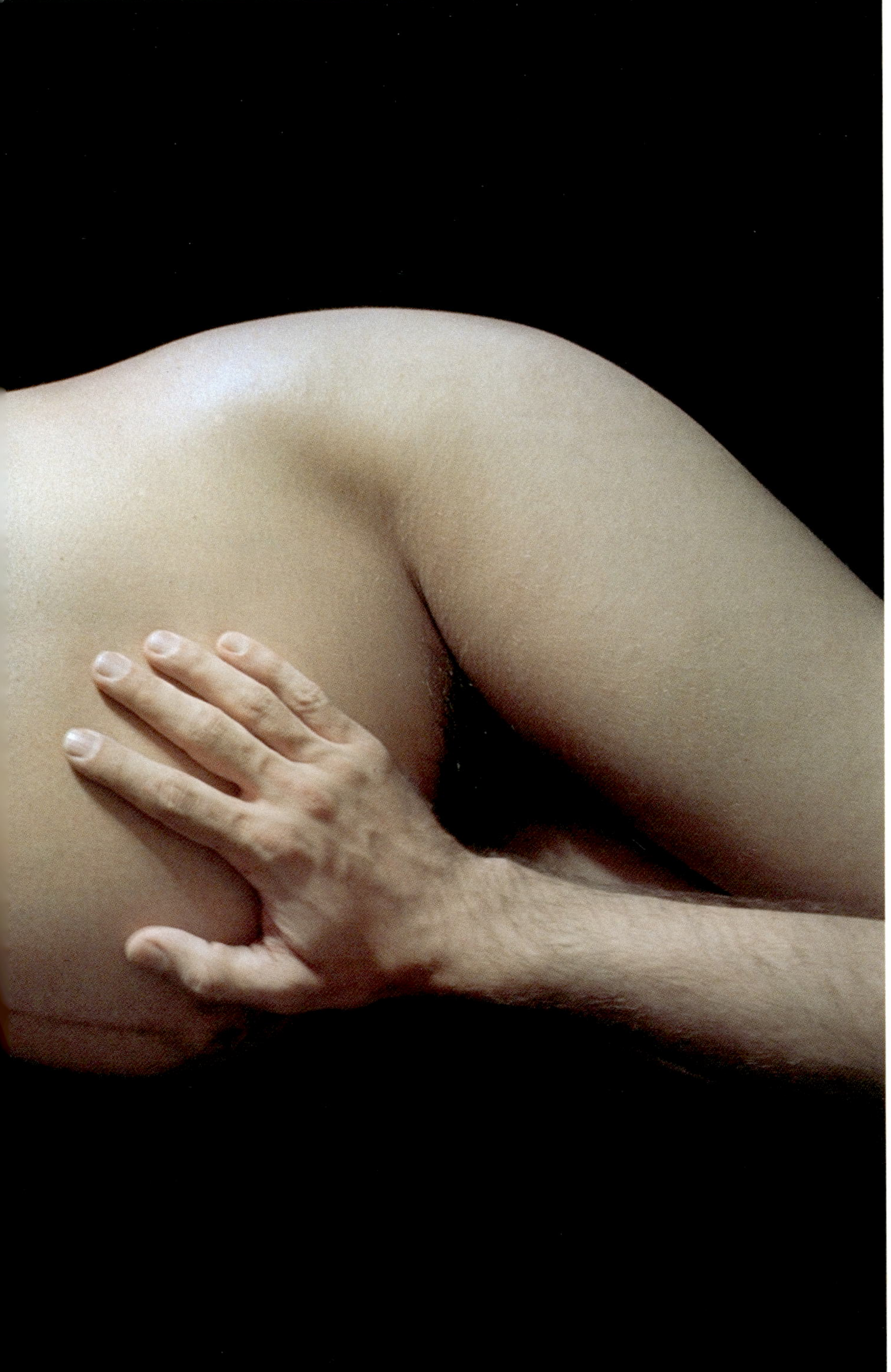

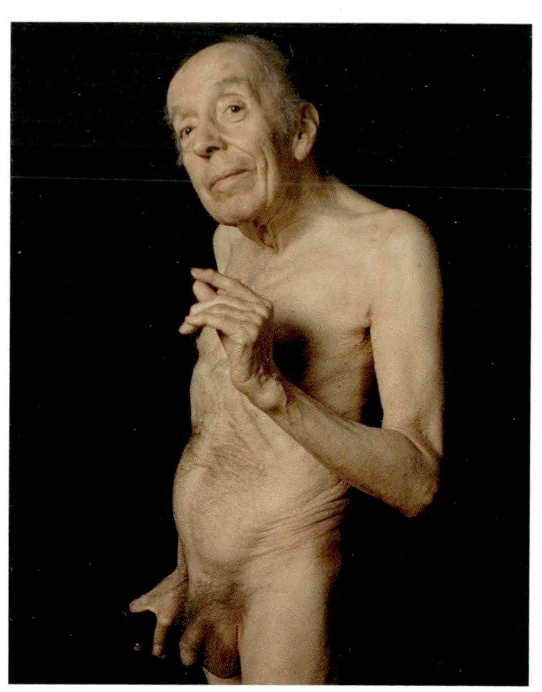

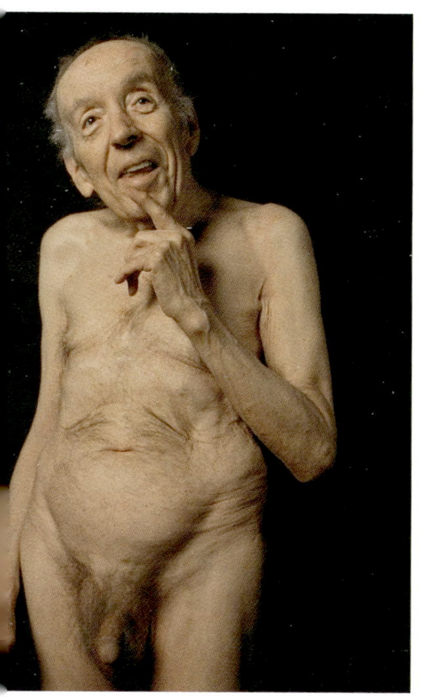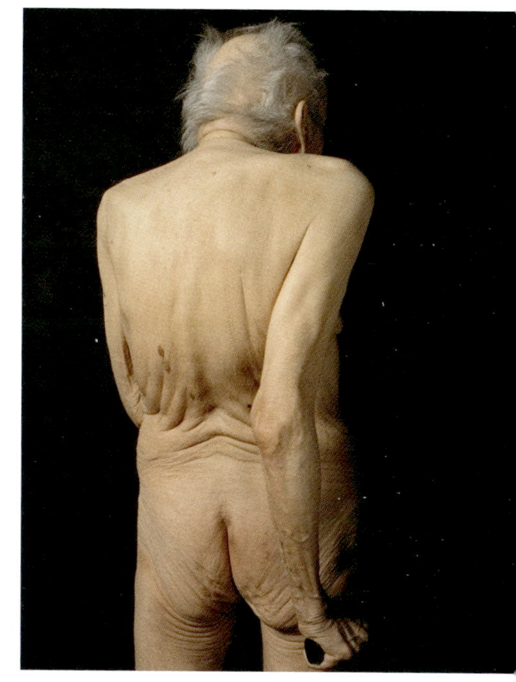

↑ **Andres Serrano,** *Taylor Mead Triptych (Nudes)*, 2009

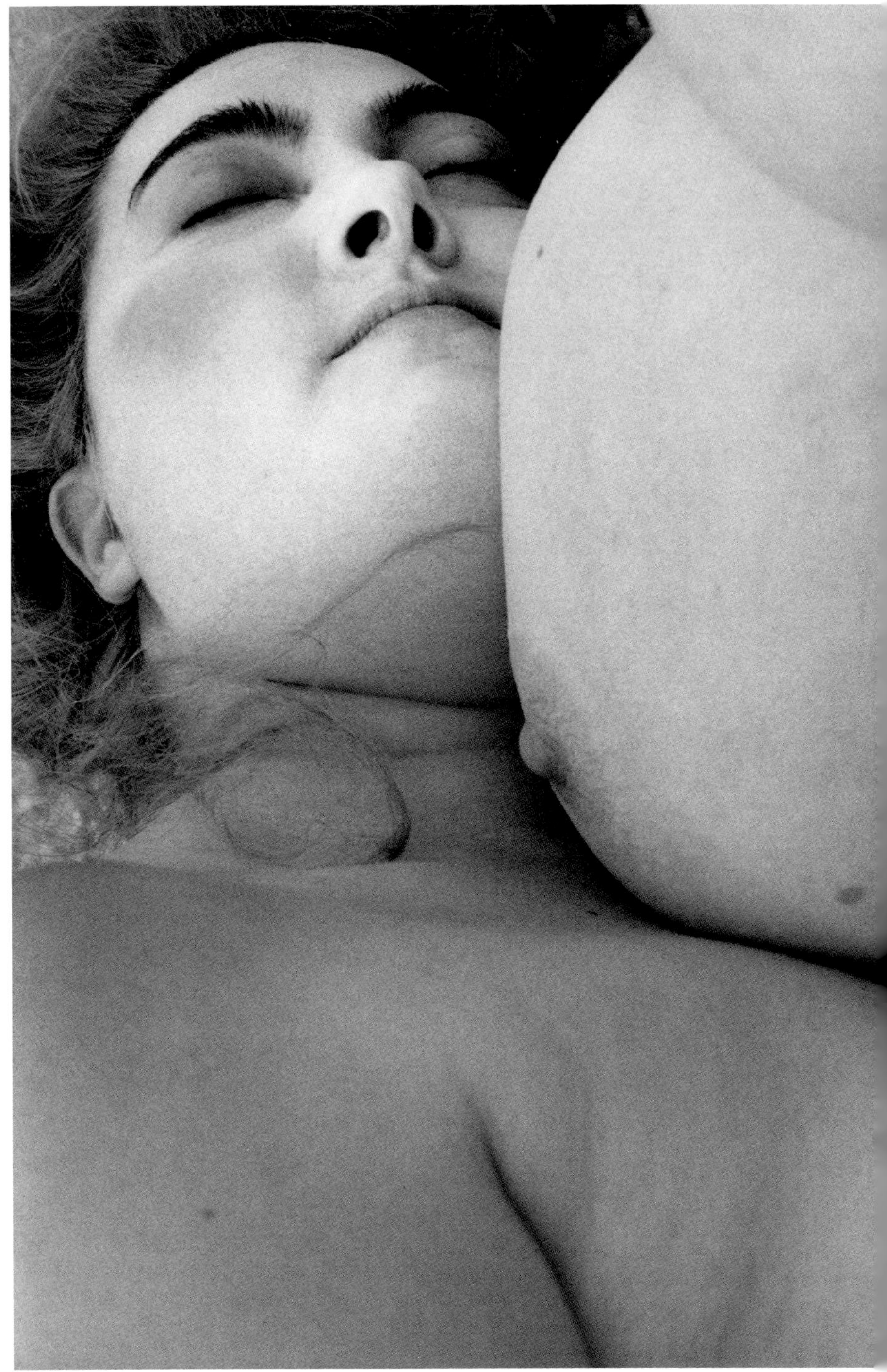

↑ Jamie Hawkesworth, *Nudes*, 2017

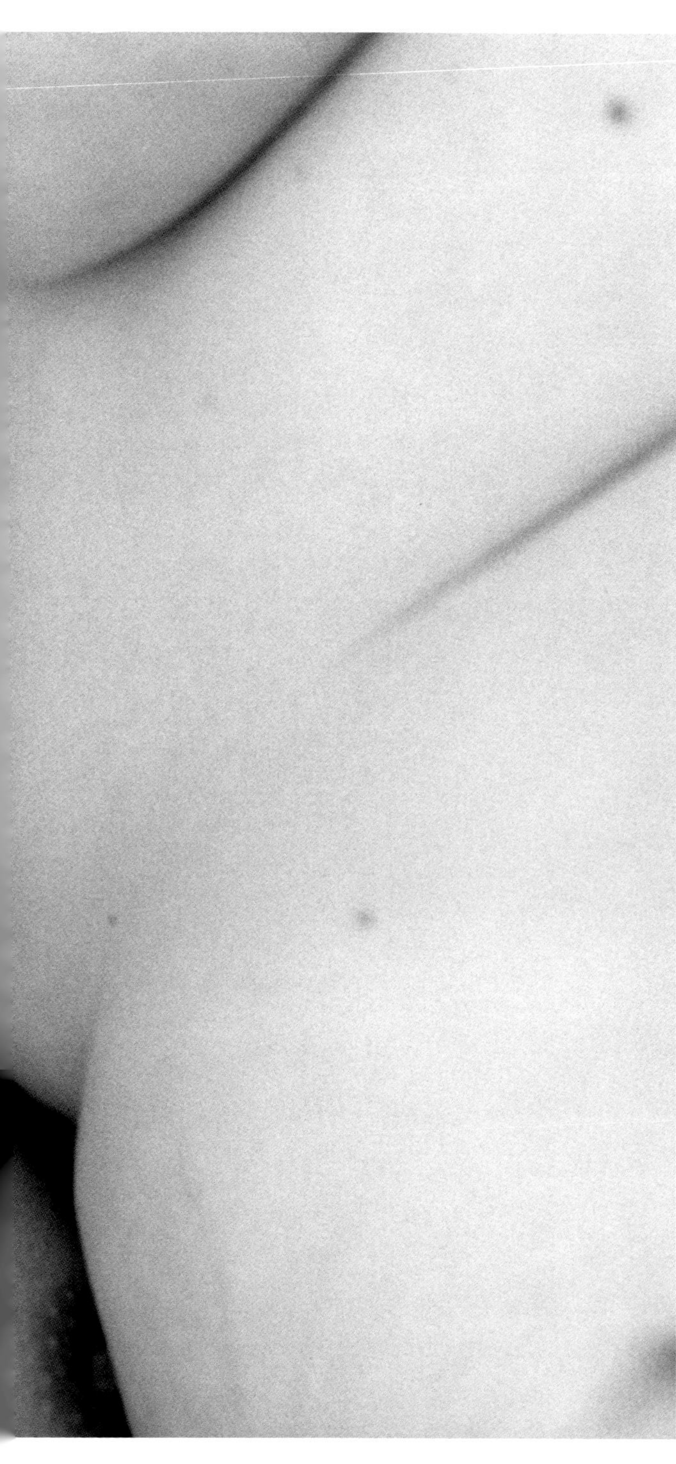

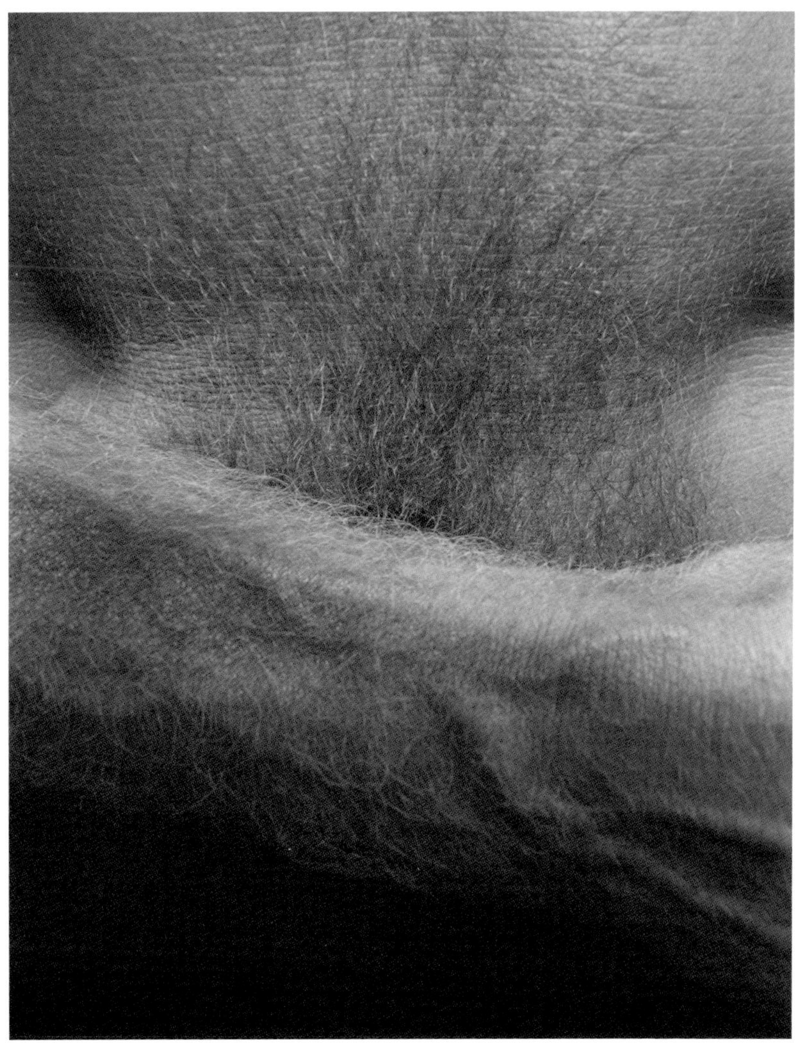

↑ **Nicholas Nixon,** *Self, Lexington,* 1998

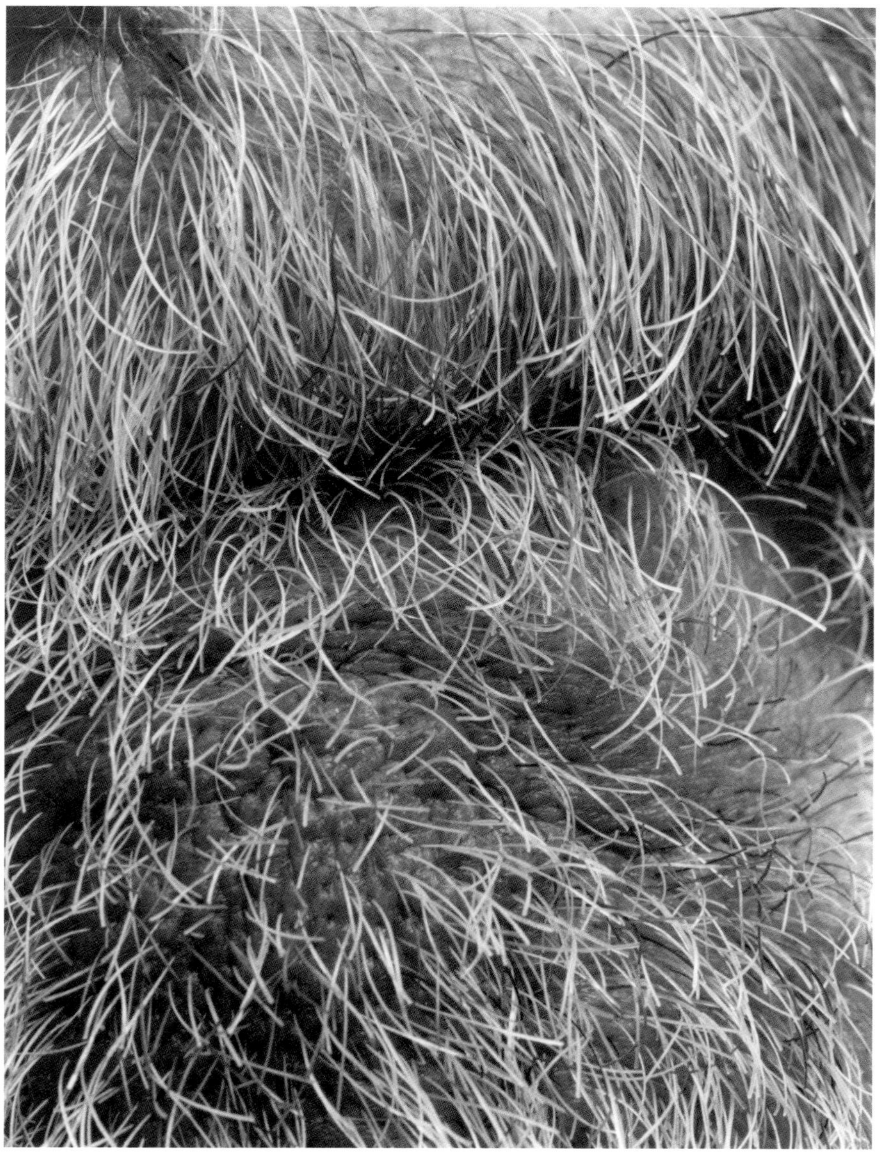

↑ **Nicholas Nixon,** *Self, Brookline,* 2008

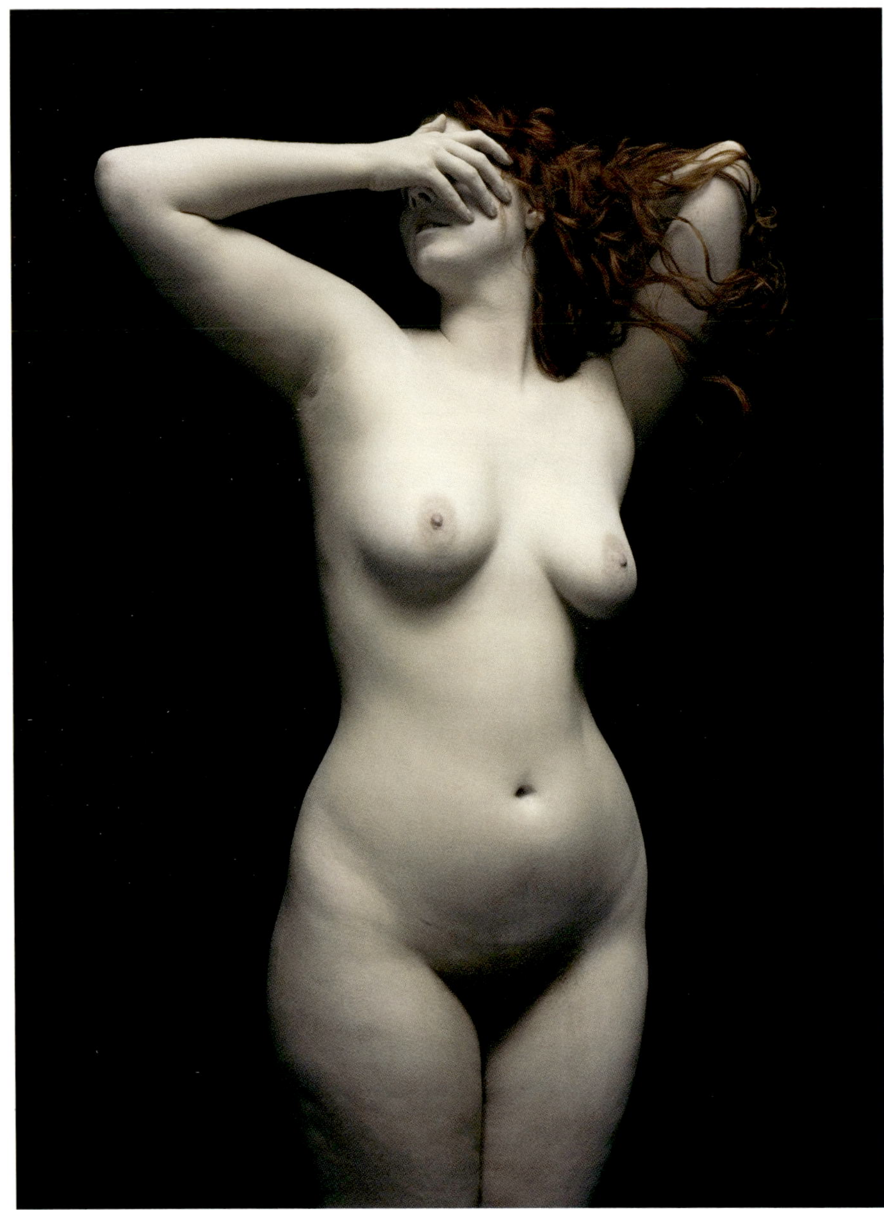

↑ **Nadav Kander,** *Isley standing,* 2010

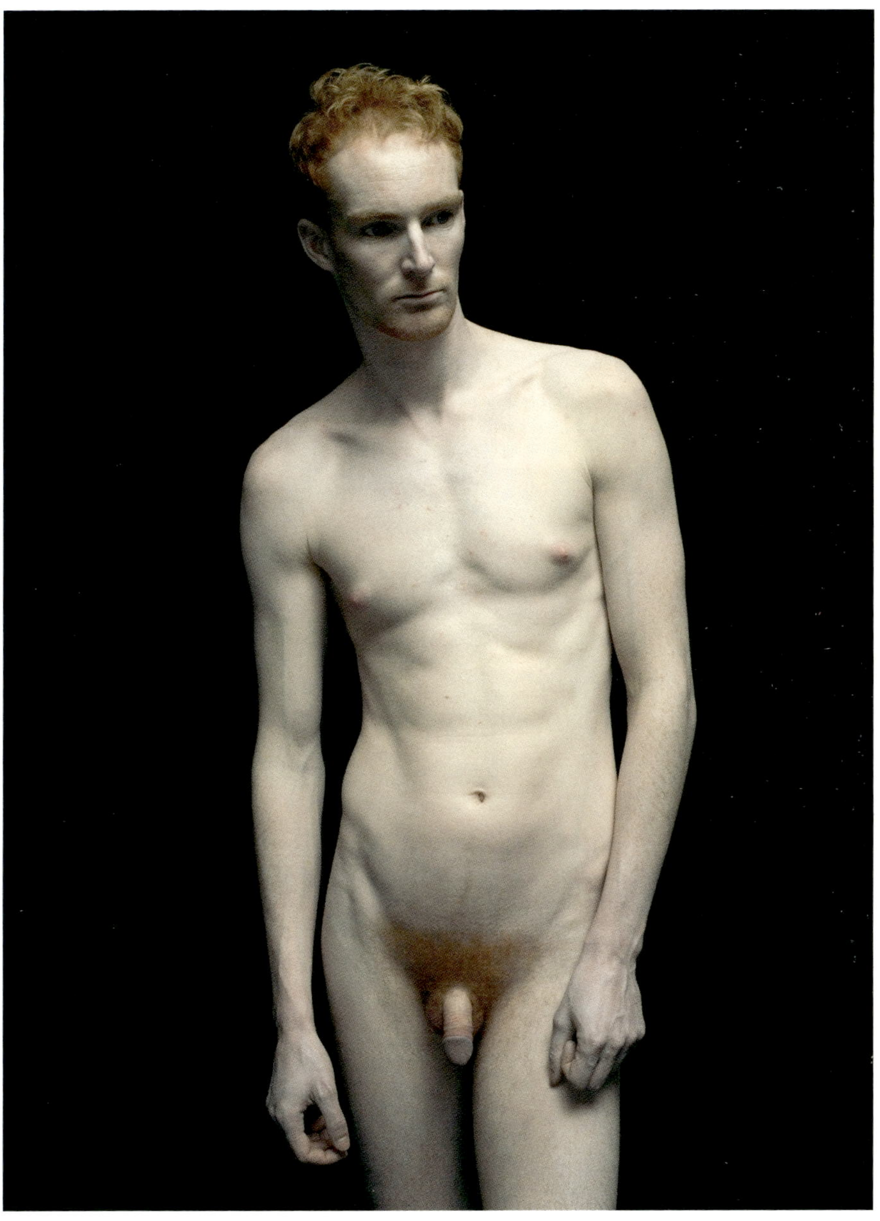

↑ **Nadav Kander,** *Michael standing*, 2010

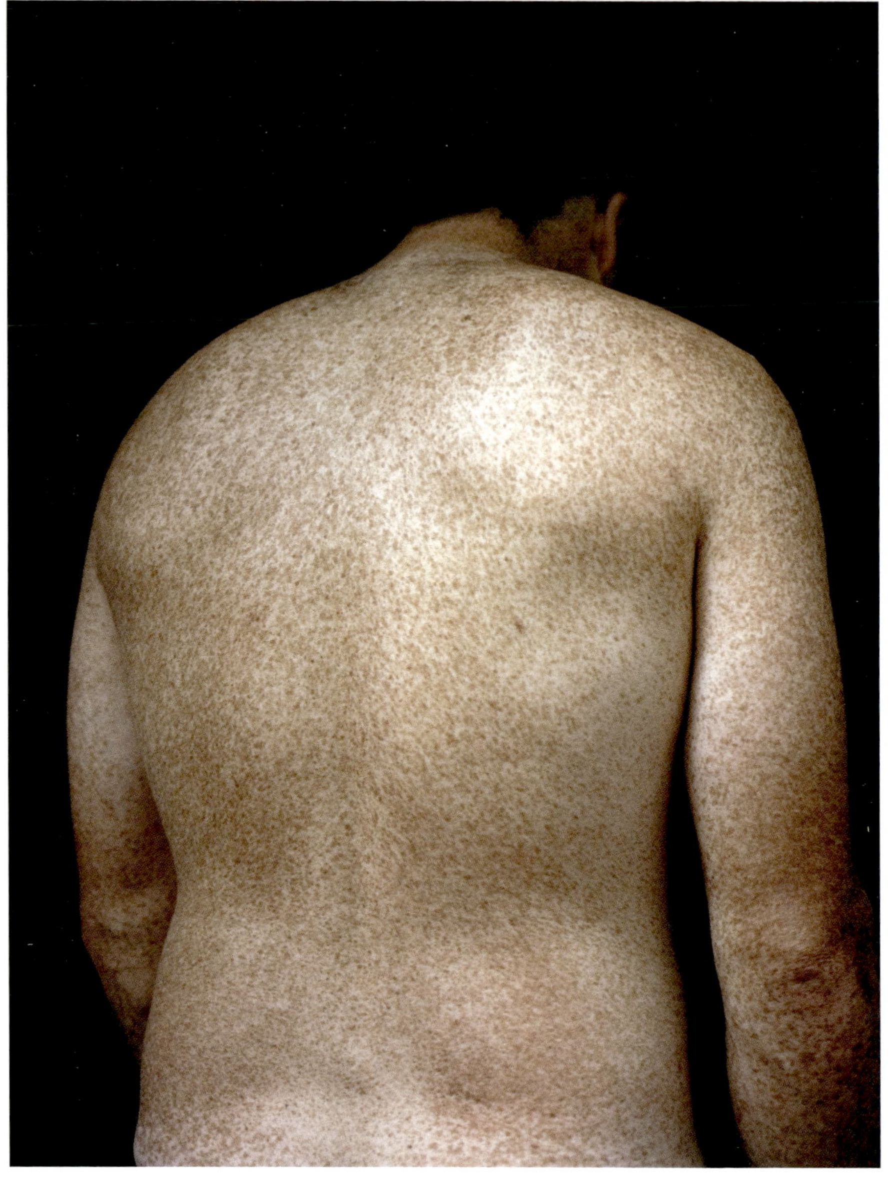

↑ **Anne Golaz,** *The Back,* from the series 'La Grande Scène', 2015

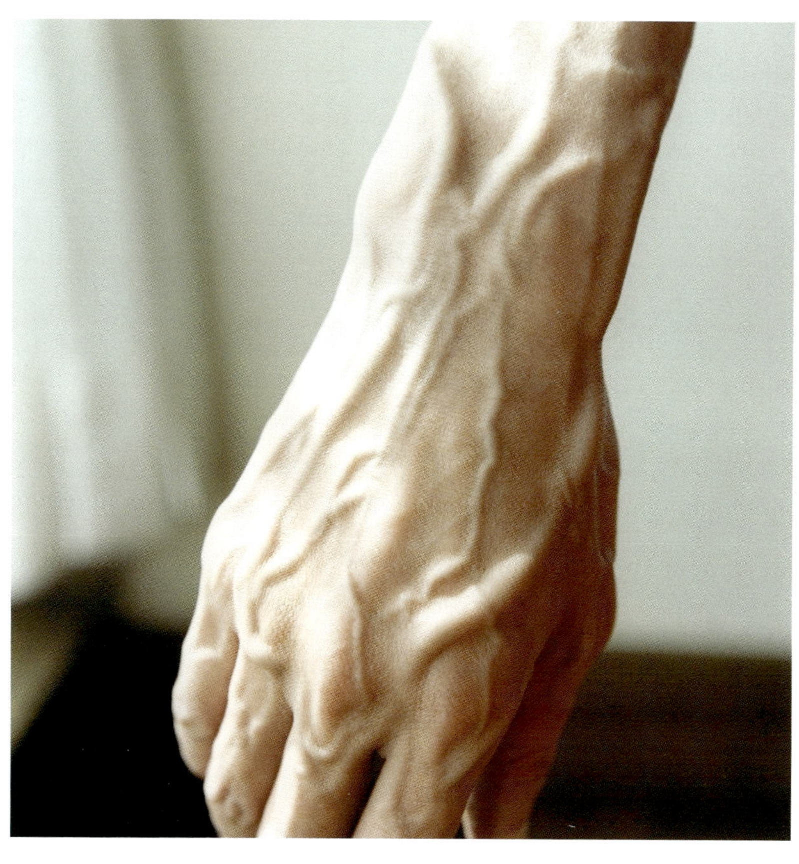

↑ **Rinko Kawauchi,** Untitled, from the series 'Utatane', 2001

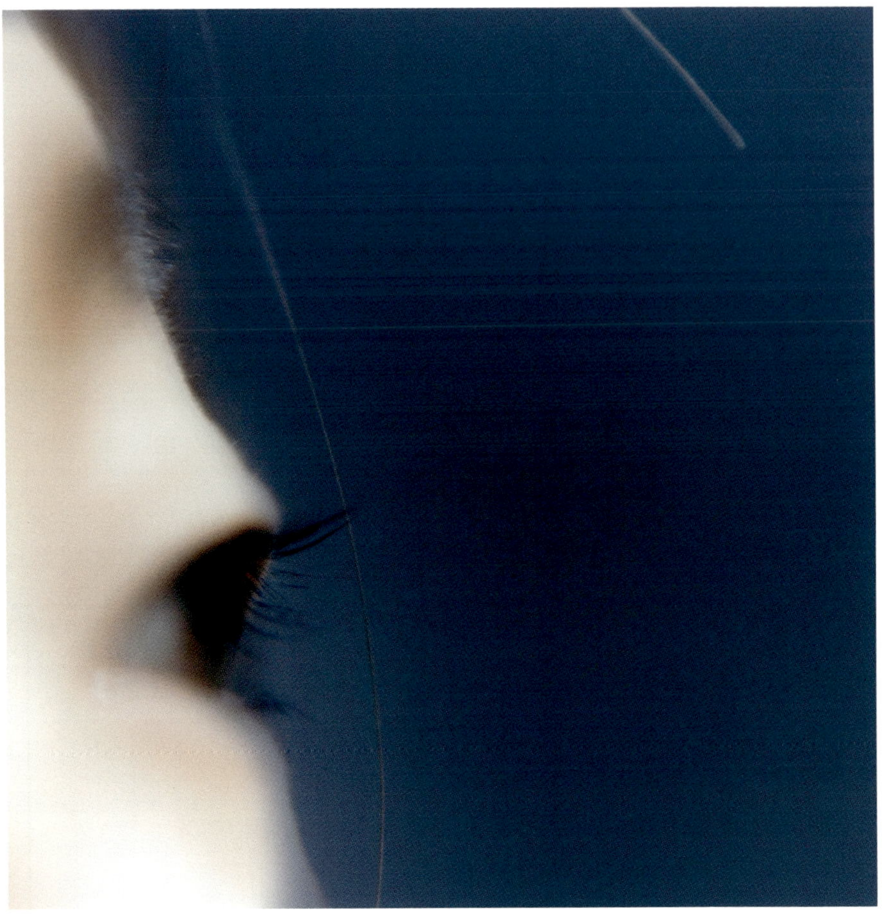

↑ **Rinko Kawauchi,** Untitled, from the series 'the eyes, the ears', 2005

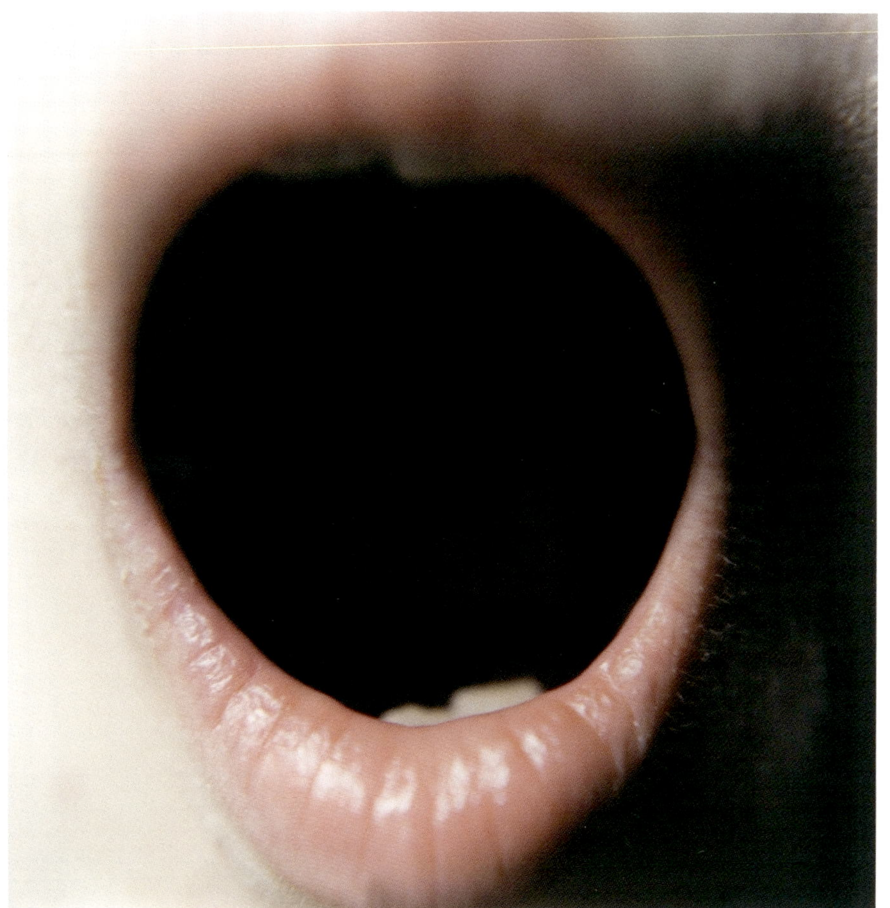

↑ **Rinko Kawauchi,** Untitled, from the series 'AILA', 2004

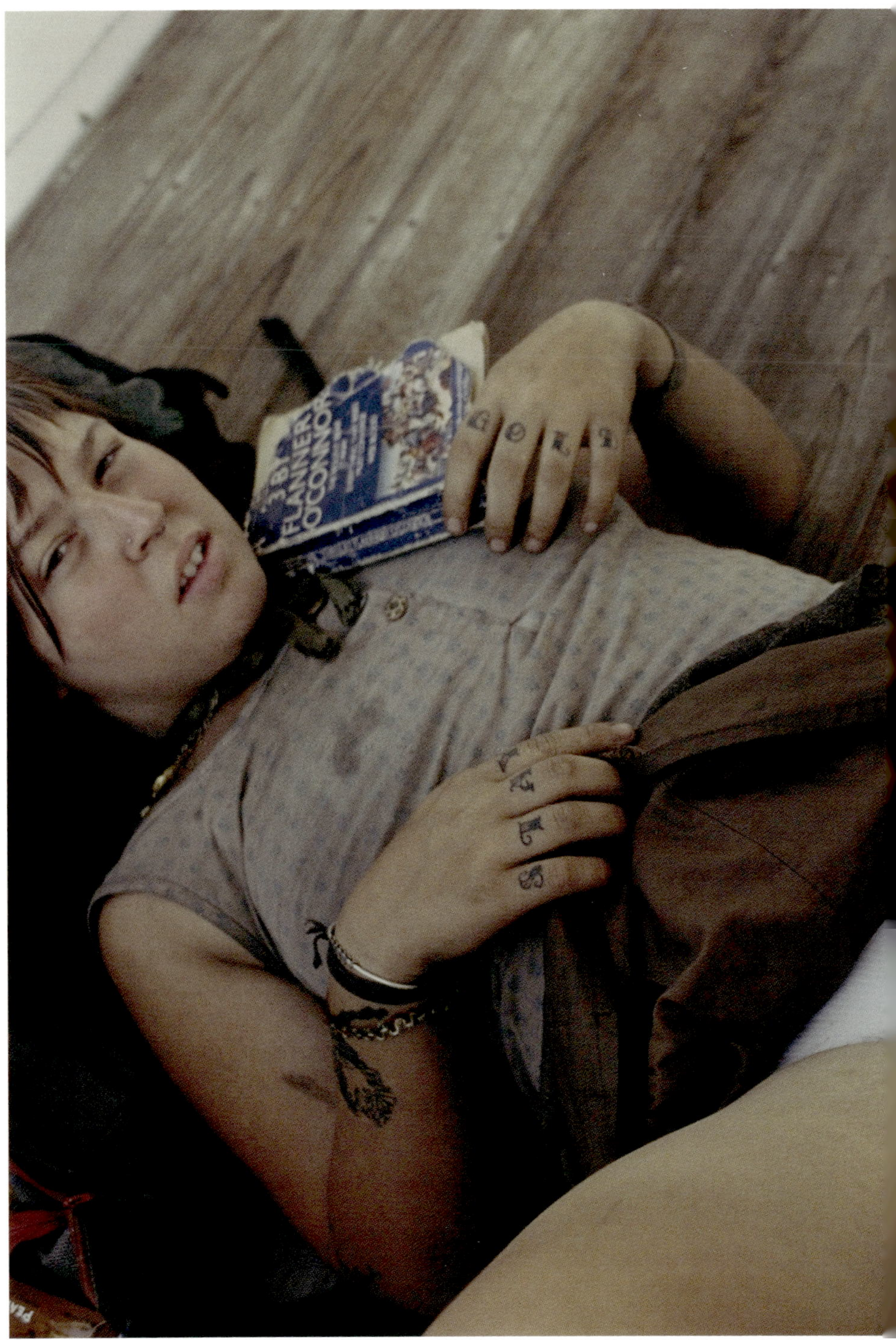

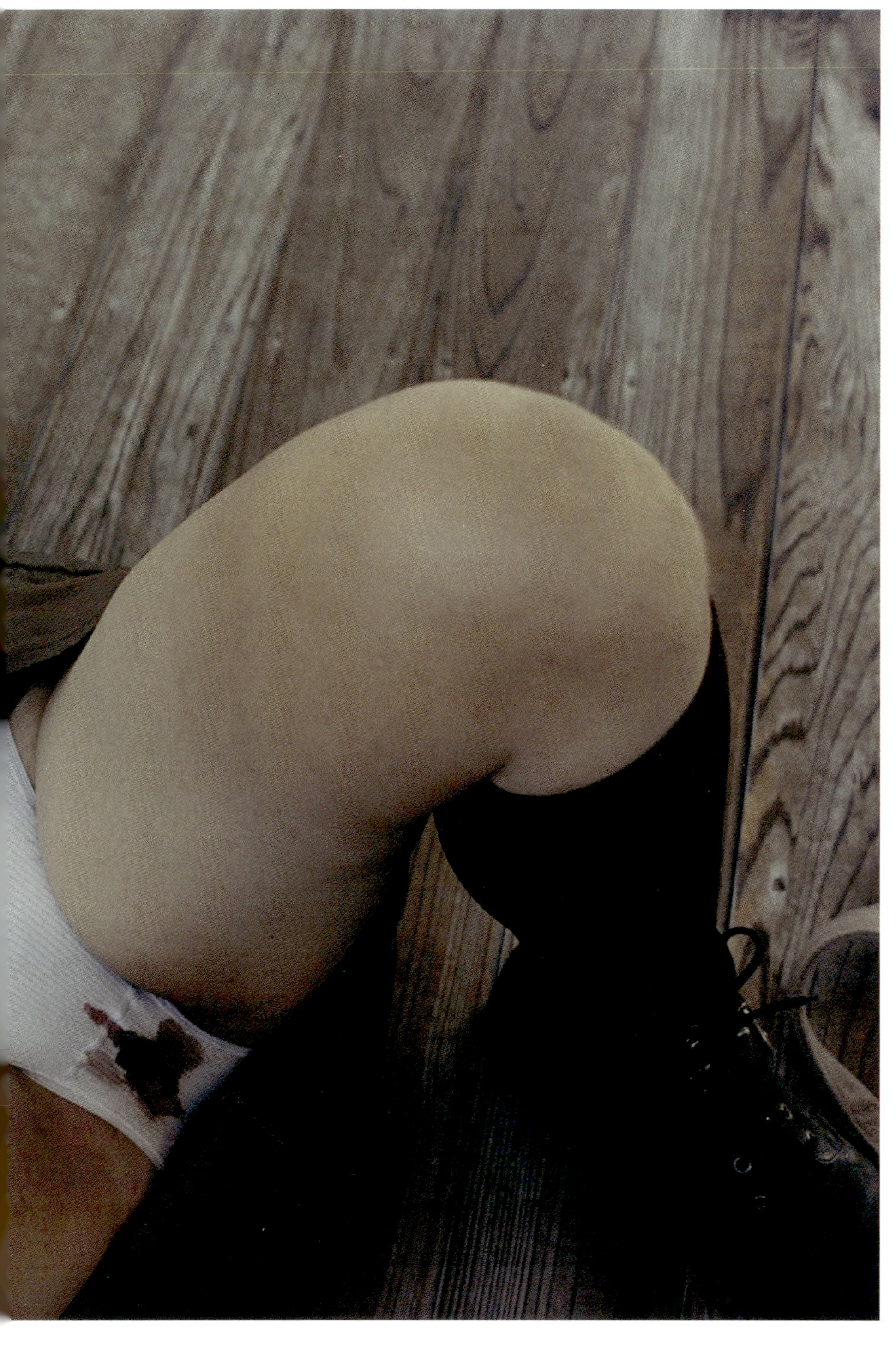

↑ **Mike Brodie**, *#1064*, from the series 'A Period of Juvenile Prosperity', 2006–9

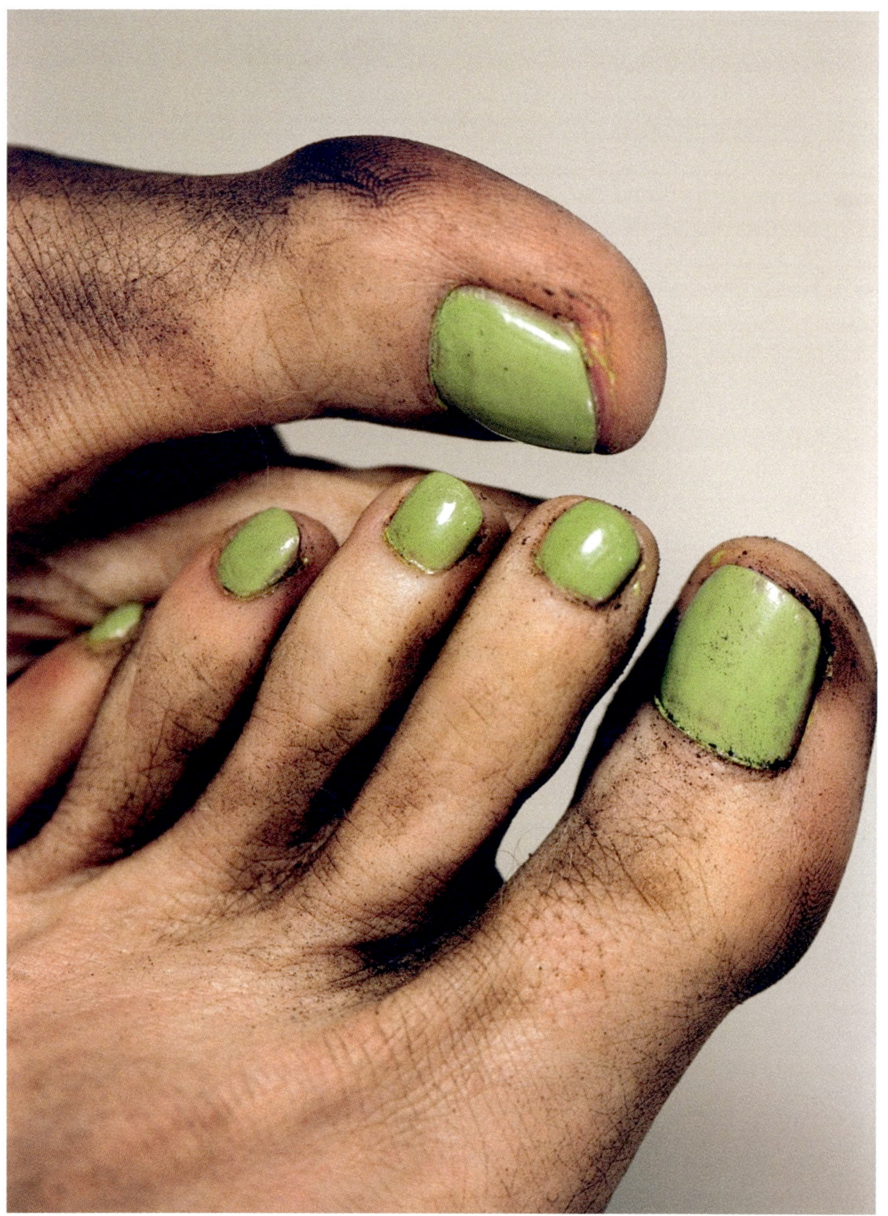

↑ **Marilyn Minter,** *Soiled,* 2000

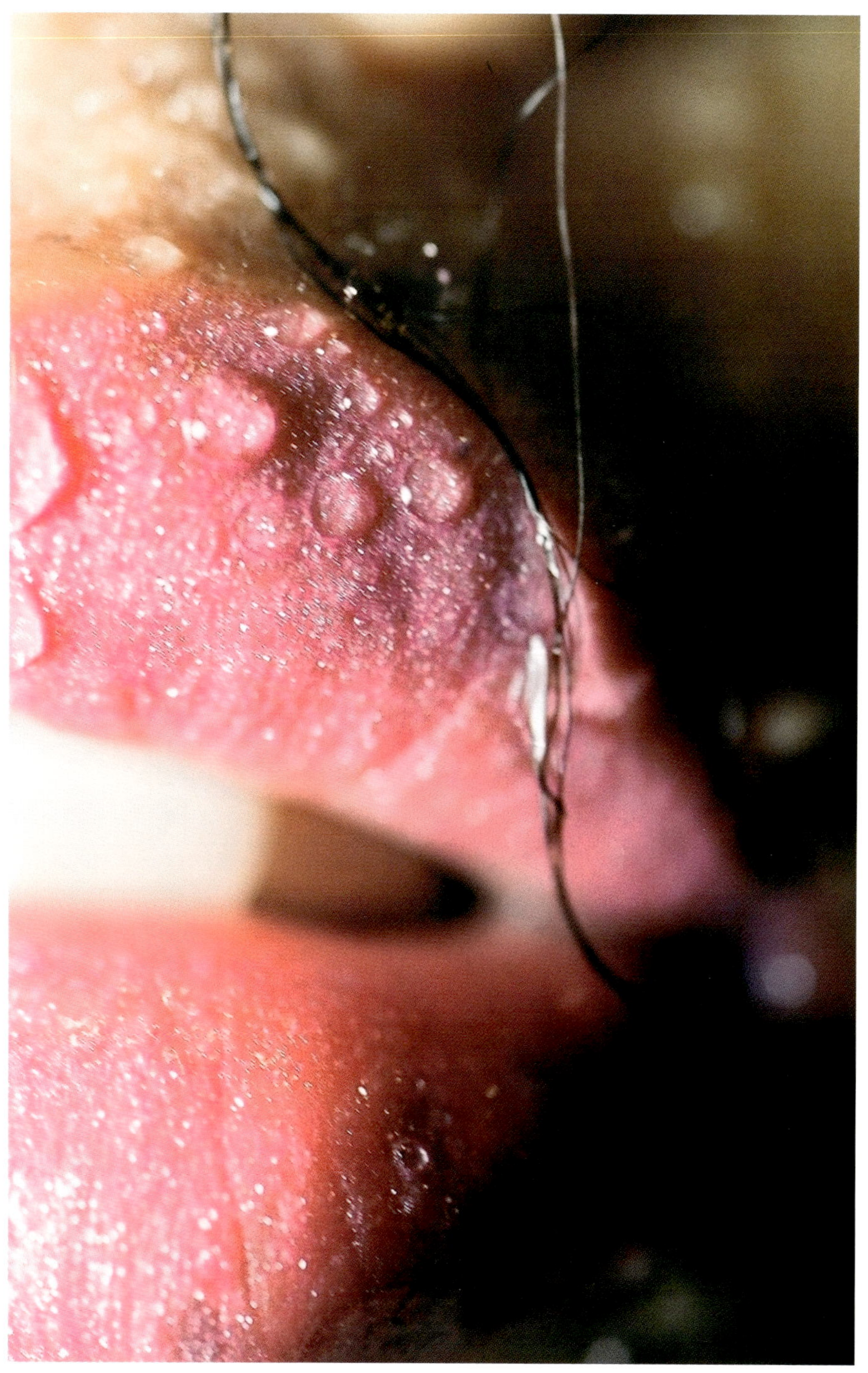

↑ **Marilyn Minter,** *Bubble Gum,* 2005

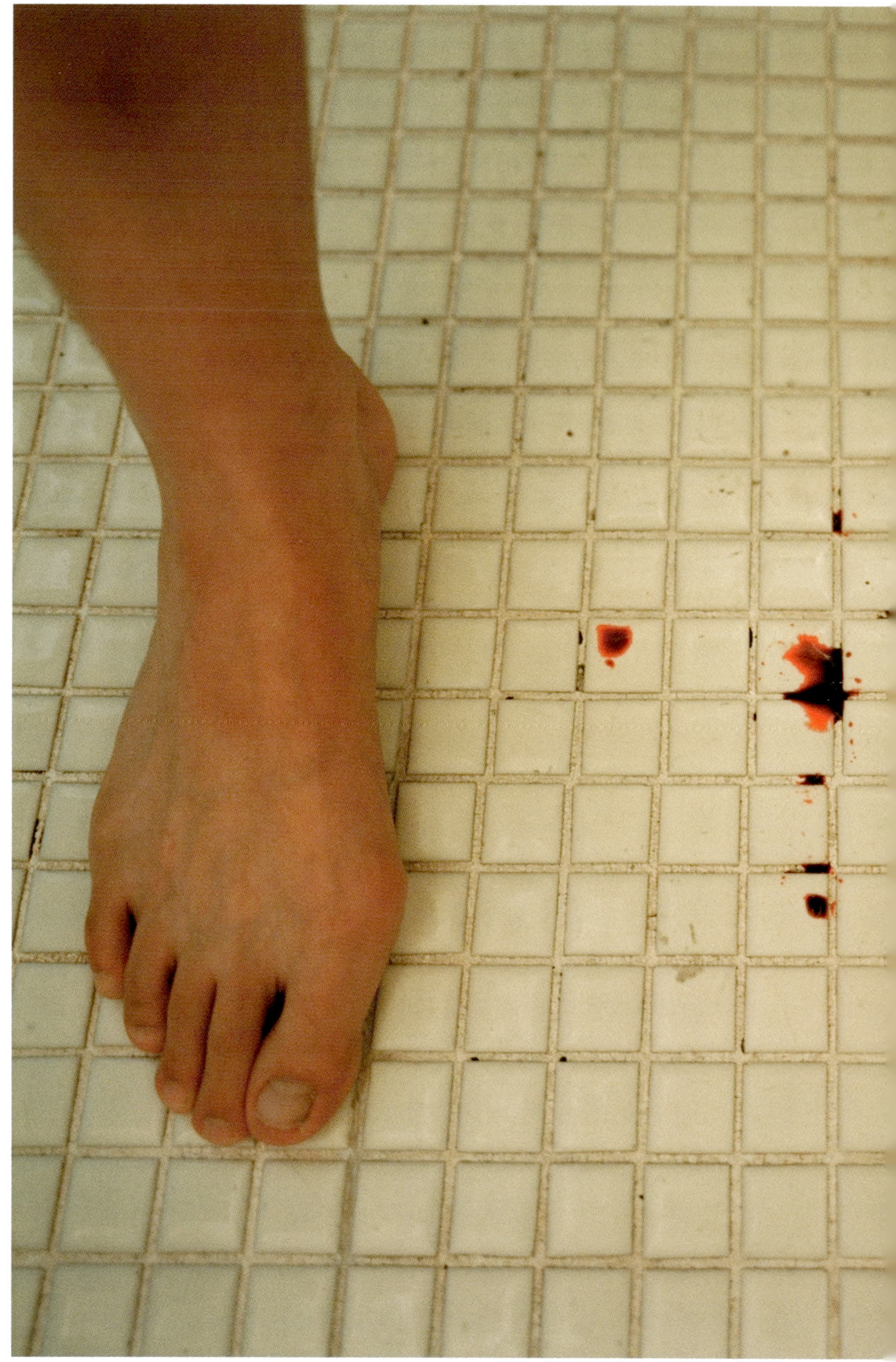

↑ **Yurie Nagashima,** *Self-Portrait,* 2001

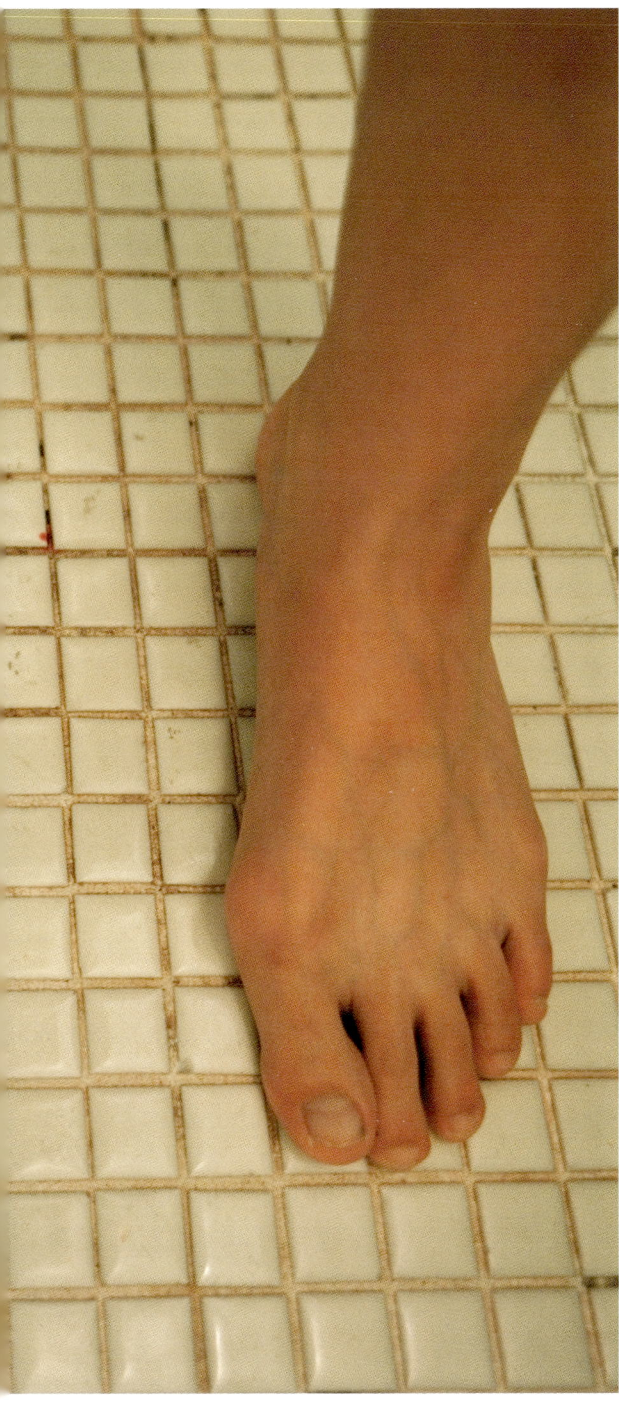

→ **Laia Abril,** *Illegal Instrument Kit*, from the series 'On Abortion', 2016. 'Throughout the 20th century, tools such as the assortment pictured here were used in illegal abortions: forceps and specula opened the cervix (and continue to be used for routine gynaecological examination and operations). During late-stage abortions, sharp, pointed instruments like the urinary catheter were used to sweep the uterus, as were repurposed household tools such as coat hangers. These instruments are extremely dangerous, due to the high risk of puncturing other organs such as the uterus, bladder or intestine.'

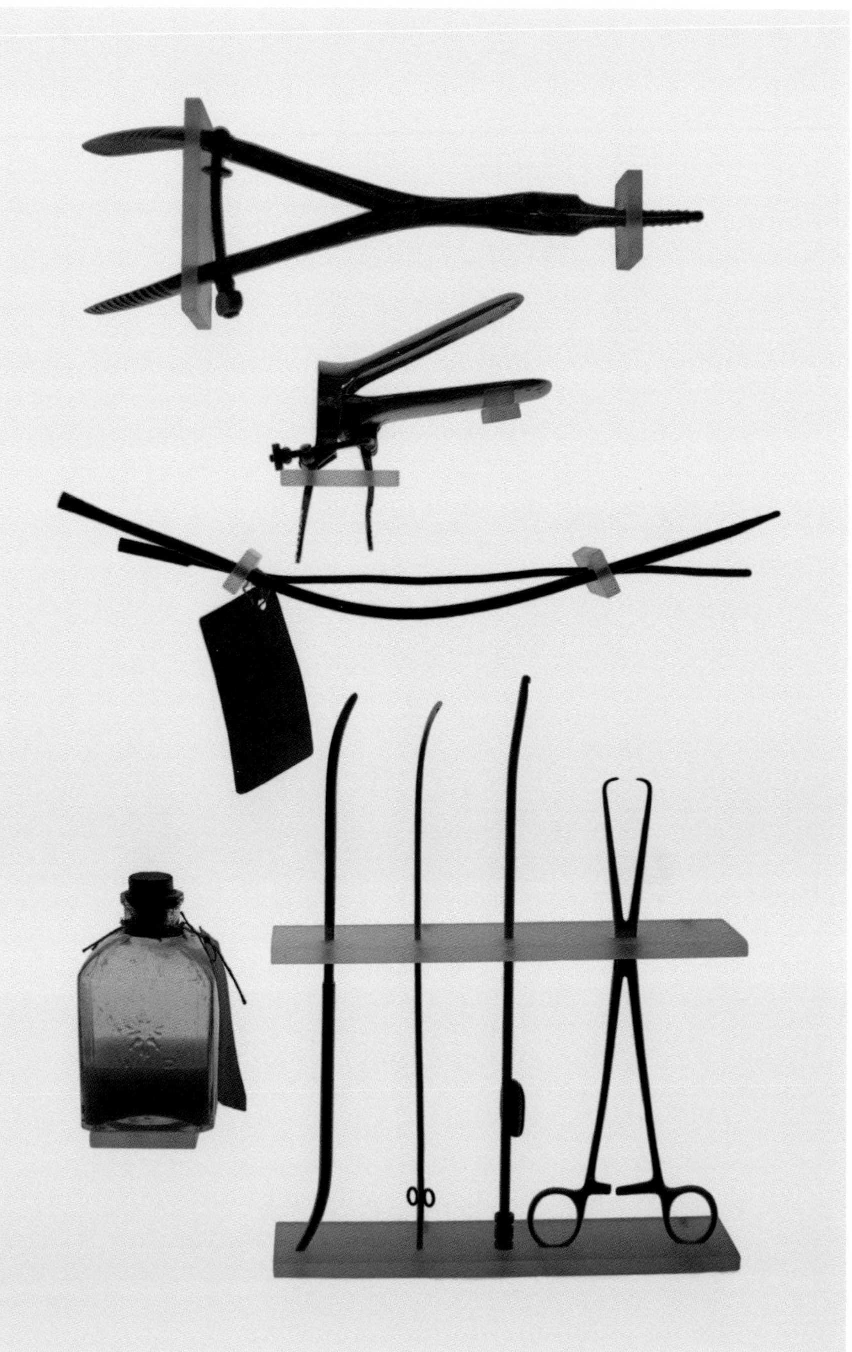

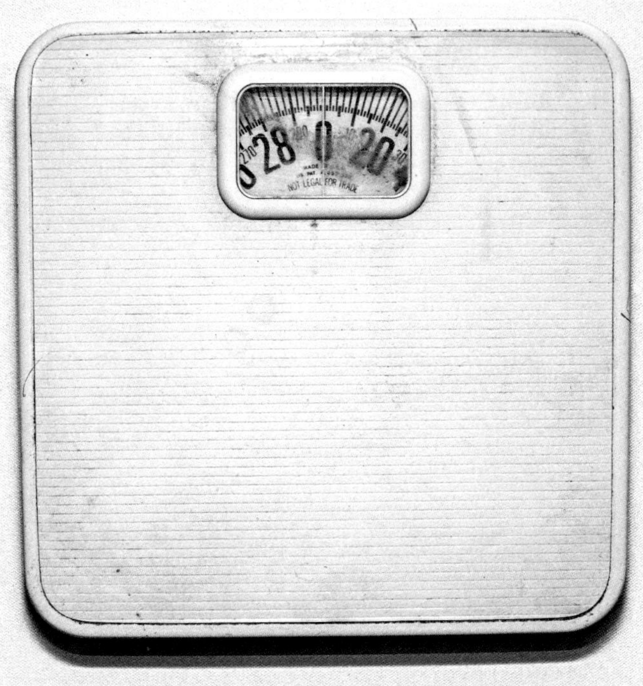

↑ **Laia Abril,** from the series 'The Epilogue', 2014. 'I finally allowed myself to understand that everything I did, I did it with love, and I would never have hurt her in any way, knowingly. People said: "You would not have done any different." But yes, I would have. — Jan, Cammy's mother. In the picture, Cammy's scale at her parents' house.'

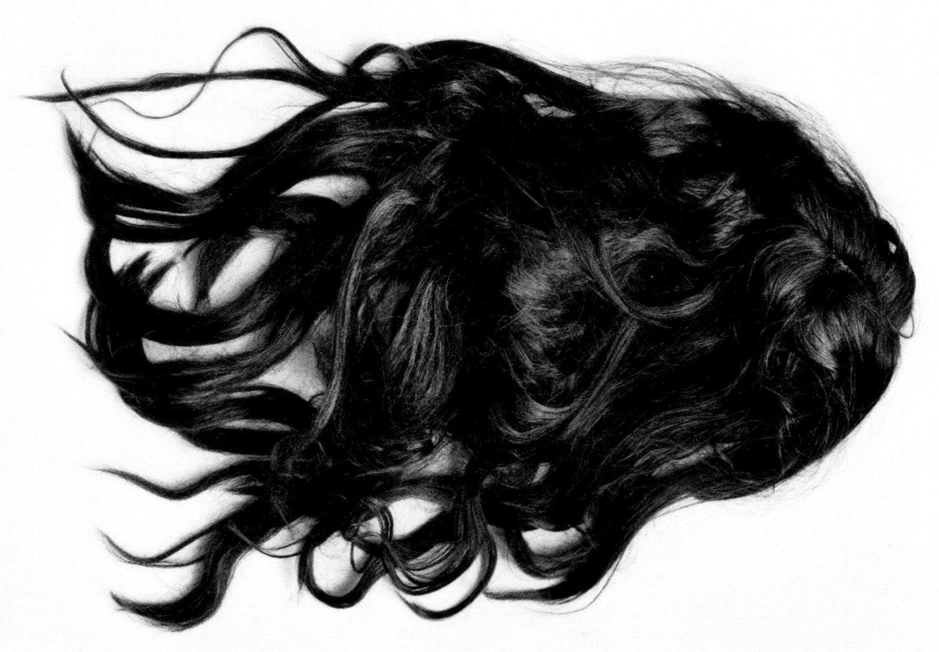

↑ **Neige Sanchez,** *Untitled,* 2015

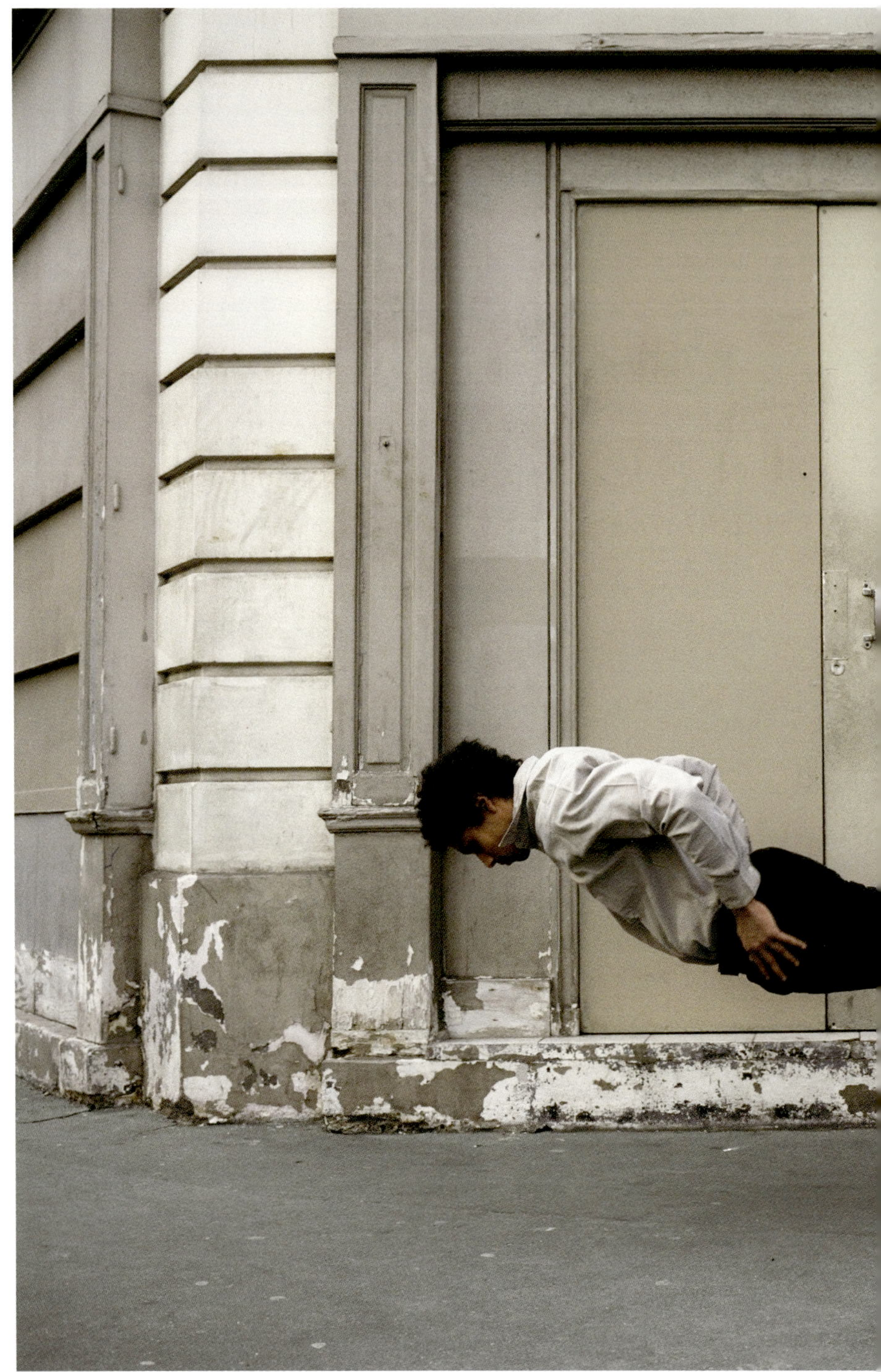

↑ Denis Darzacq, *The Fall No. 09,* 2006

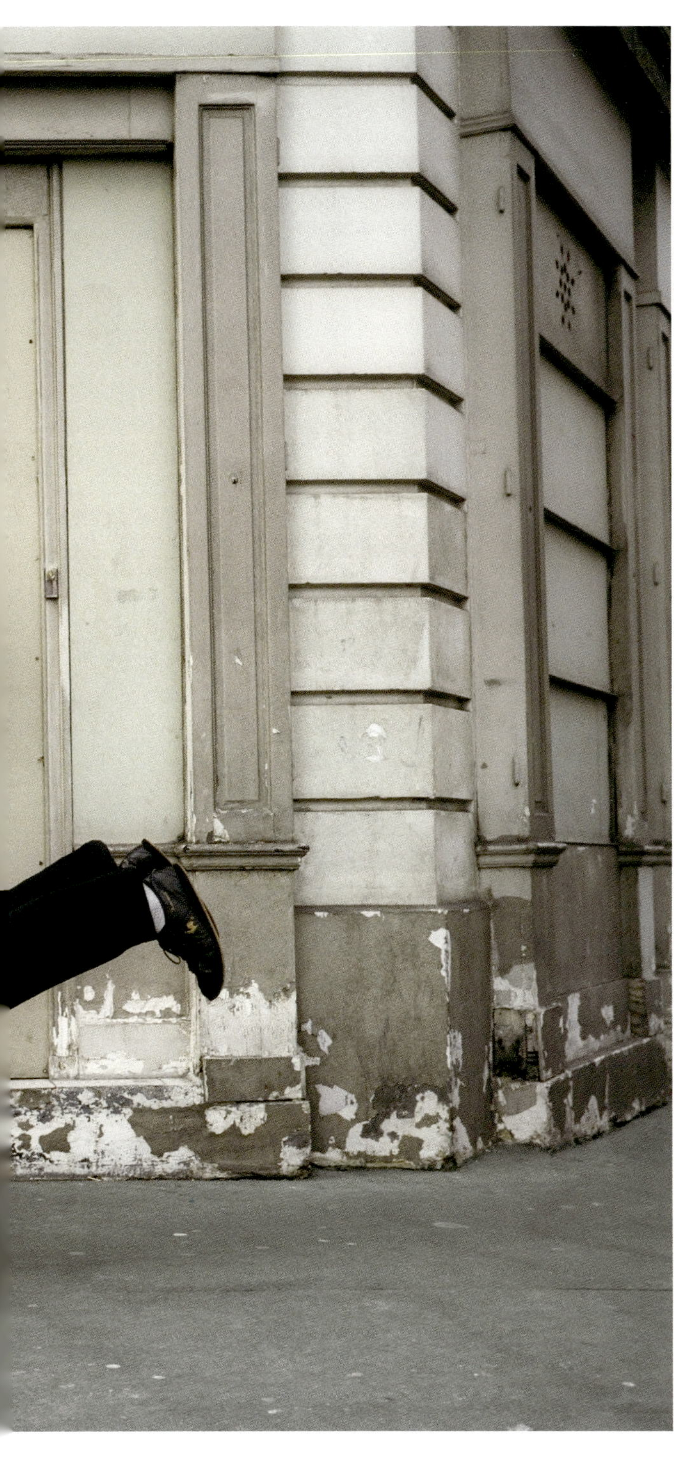

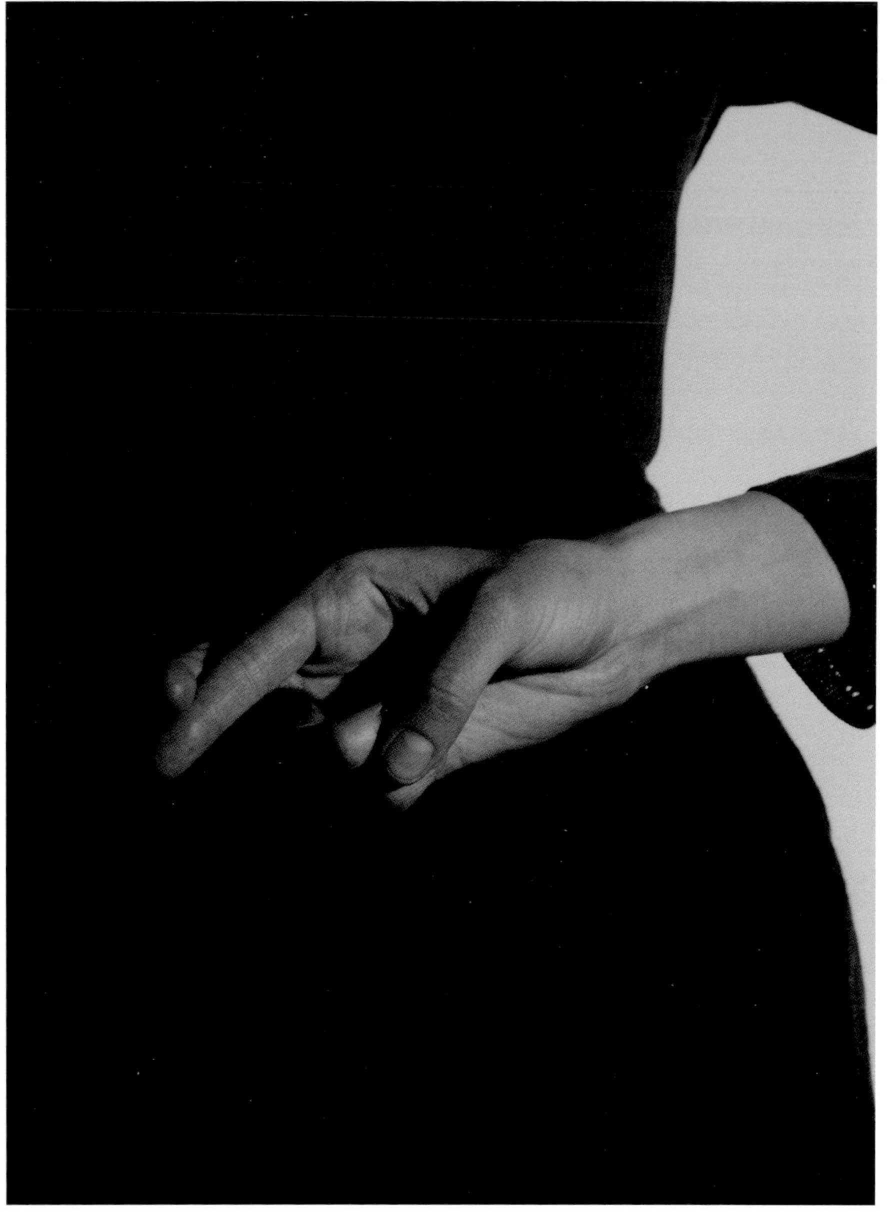

↑ Yuliya Khan, *For Those Who Listen*, 2017

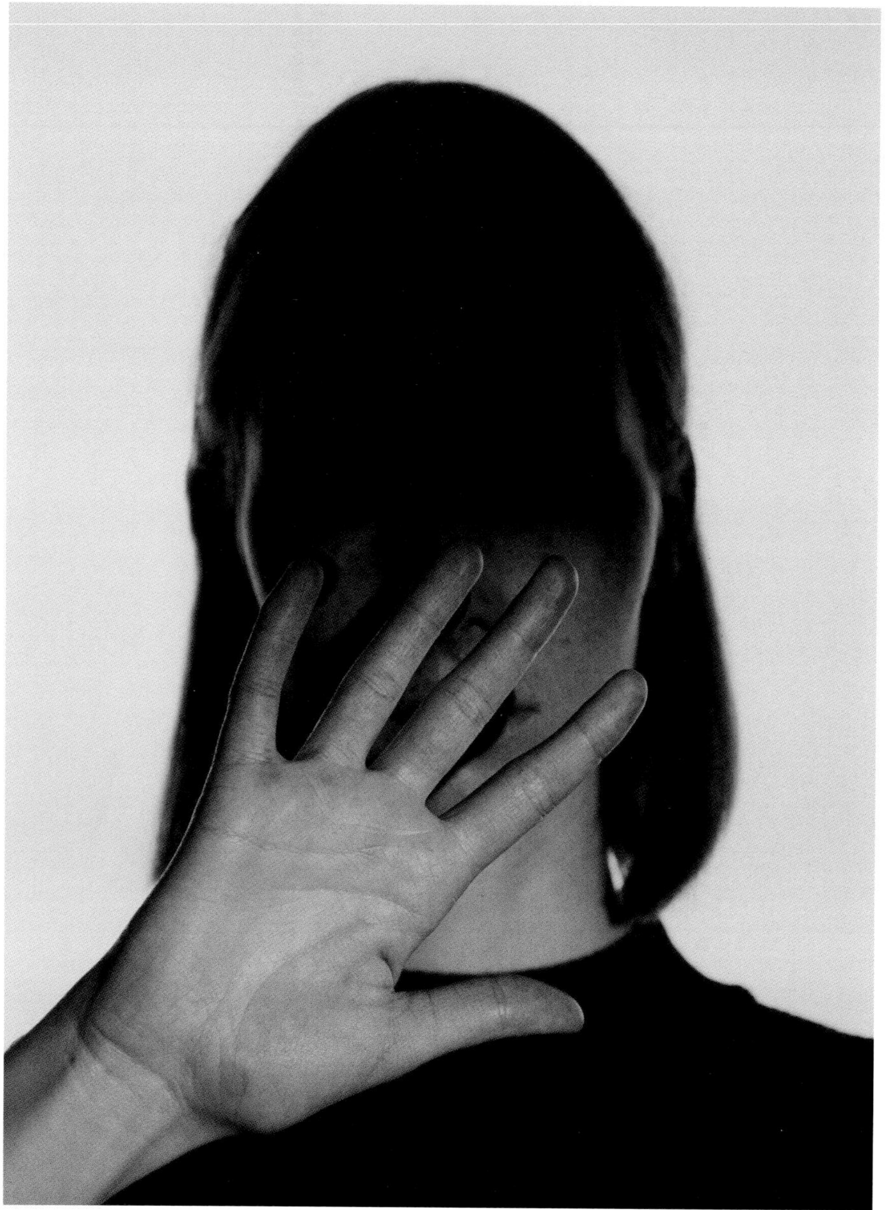

↑ **Yuliya Khan,** *For Those Who Listen,* 2017

ALTER EGO

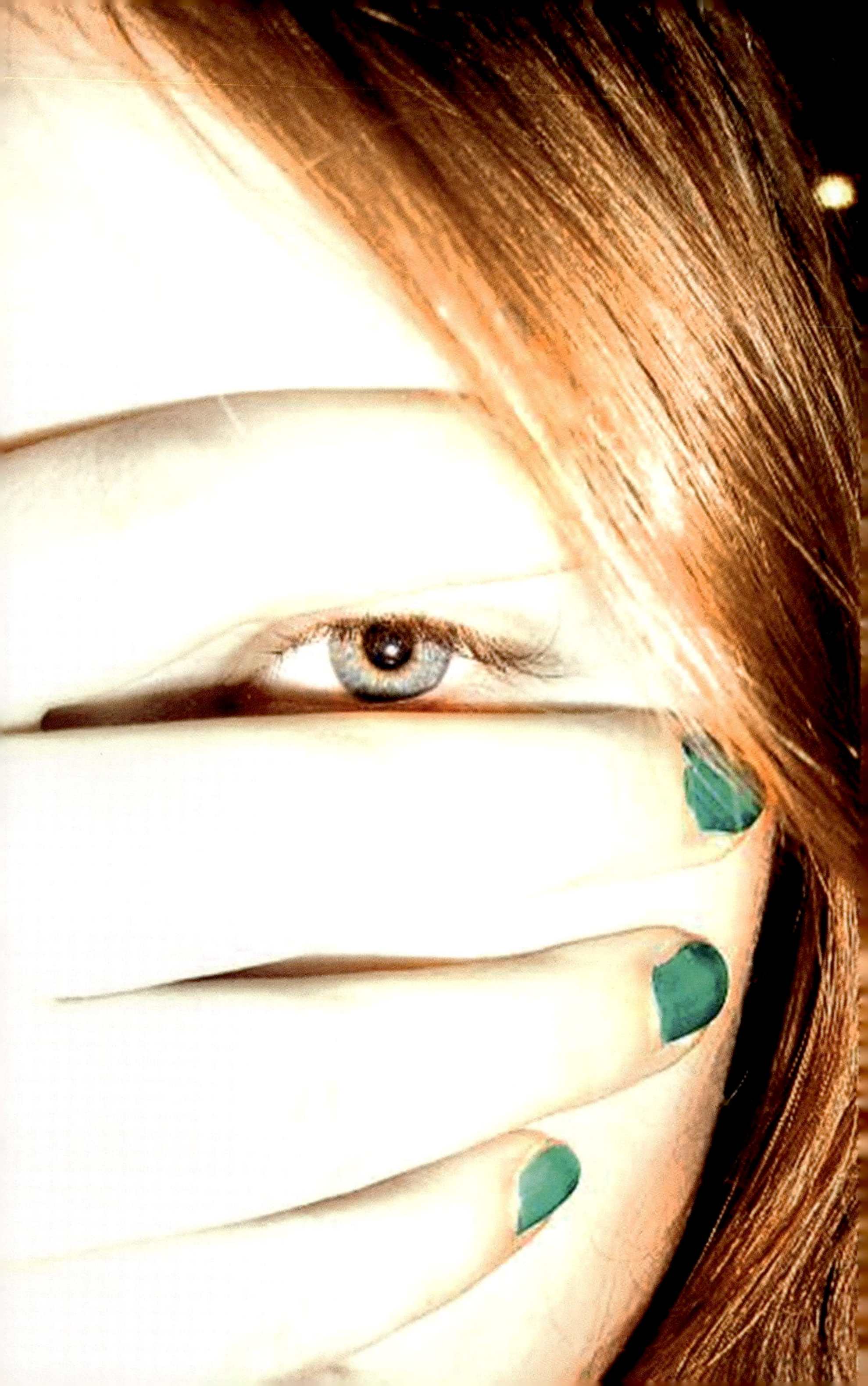

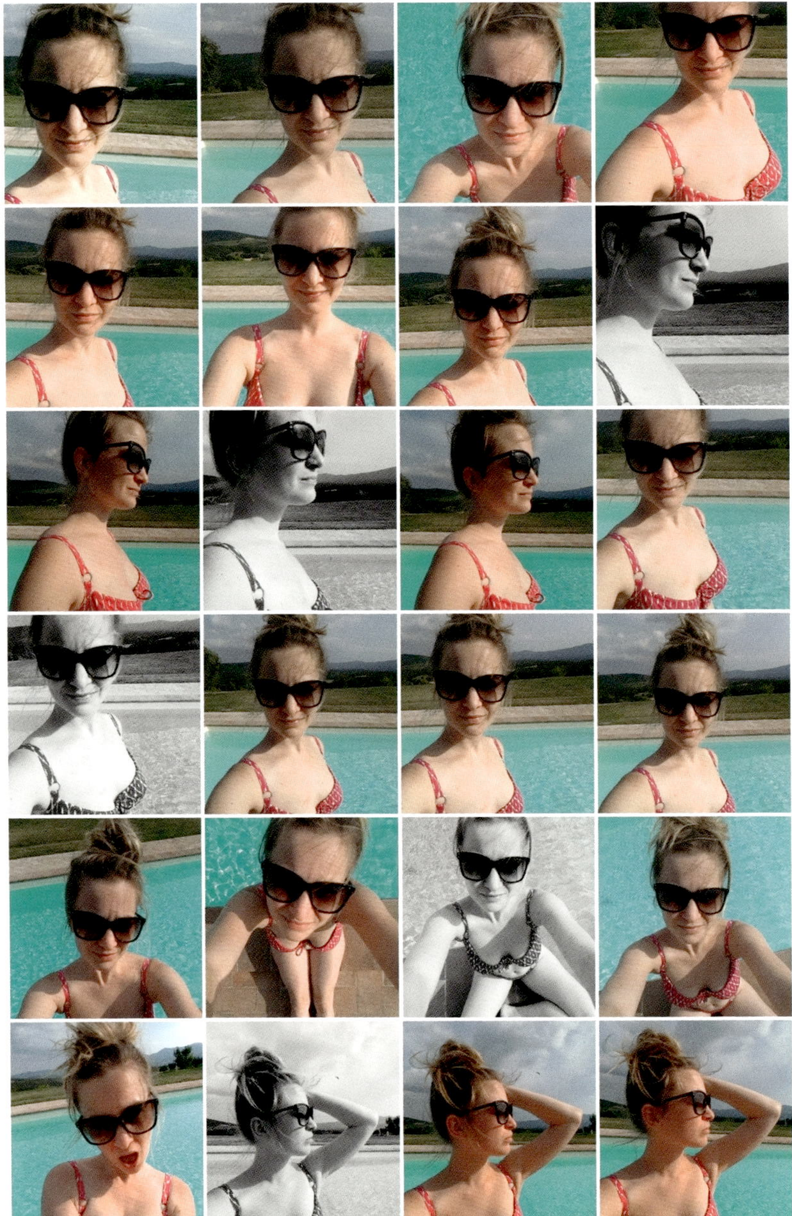

↑ **Anonymous,** *Selfie,* 2017
← (Previous) **Ole John Aandal,** *Juvenilia no 33 (Eye),* 2009

The thousands of selfies shared on social networks every minute show how common the self-portrait has become in the digital era. Most people have posed in front of their cell-phone screen to immortalize an event or simply an everyday moment. The continuous flow of selfies on social networks is growing apace. Photographing oneself and then sharing this image with friends or strangers is now a practice found all over the world. Note that the actual term 'selfie' entered the *Oxford English Dictionary* in 2013.

These images that have become so familiar are evidence of the important role photography plays in our everyday life. Today, photography is not primarily a tool that allows us to discover the planet, but rather a means of promoting an image of our own body. Since its invention, in fact, the medium — this 'mirror of memory', as daguerreotypes were once known — has been used for portraits. The photographer Nadar said that his clients actually found it difficult to recognize themselves when they were handed their portrait. But since the 19th century photography has profoundly changed our view of our own bodies in many ways. Gone is the sense of disappointment when faced with our own image. It has become common practice to ask photographers to retouch, improve, embellish our portraits. In the 21st century we no longer have to sit still and face the photographer's lens. The camera follows our every gesture and tempts us to look at ourselves on its little screen that has become more ubiquitous than the mirror on the bathroom wall.

We have become our own photographers. It is up to us to pose and compose, to immortalize (sometimes just for a few seconds), and then to share. The younger generation are creating sophisticated images. They are fully aware that this is primarily a way of shaping our appearance, constructing the way we present ourselves to the world. Photography helps us to take our body in hand, to scrutinize it in order to understand it better. Ole John Aandal (pp. 83, 88, 89), who has compiled images taken by teenagers, shows how for them the body is constantly experienced as a kind of self-performance.

The body is the site of our presence in the world, yet we experience it as an alter ego, as another self, a spokesman of our being. It is a testimony to our identity and to our singularity, and a fiction that we offer the world and ourselves. The image we convey to others gives us a status, and the body appears as a tangible form of our self-image. Through this image, we demonstrate that we are the inventors of our own existence. The body — treated as an alter ego — is constructed as though it were a character in a play. This is also a means of concealing anything that is too intimate. Kim Kardashian (pp. 96, 97) certainly shows herself undressed in her selfies, but in fact she is not revealing anything intimate about herself. Through her self-portraits she builds herself a double in order to escape her own body and disguise it, play on its appearance. Her external body becomes a promotional object for what her fictional being would be: the body becomes posture.

The body we allow others to see is central to our society of images. We perceive our body through the image we fashion. That is how we show ourselves to ourselves and to others. In her self-portraits taken over a period of several years, Yurie Nagashima (pp. 72–73, 114–17, 166) questions her own identity, whether in relation to her family or to her transformed body during pregnancy. This sense of identity is constructed, worked on, throughout life. We start out with a face that needs to be shaped, beautified. Then we build up our body-image not only from our mirror-image but also and above all from the way others view us and the way we want others to look at us. Interactions result from the way our image is viewed, which explains the importance attached to the body and to the appearance. The way we are viewed predominates in modern times. The people photographed by Deana Lawson (pp. 102, 103, 384–85) are keenly aware of how others see them.

But there is not only the question of how subjects are viewed; there is also the impact of the physical contact between bodies. When Tabitha Soren photographs baseball players (see p. 113), she reveals the curious relationship that brings two people together, and that is reflected in the way one body touches the other — its alter ego. The relationship with the other is created by the way their bodies come together. This form of complicity also struck Alec Soth (see p. 121) when he observed

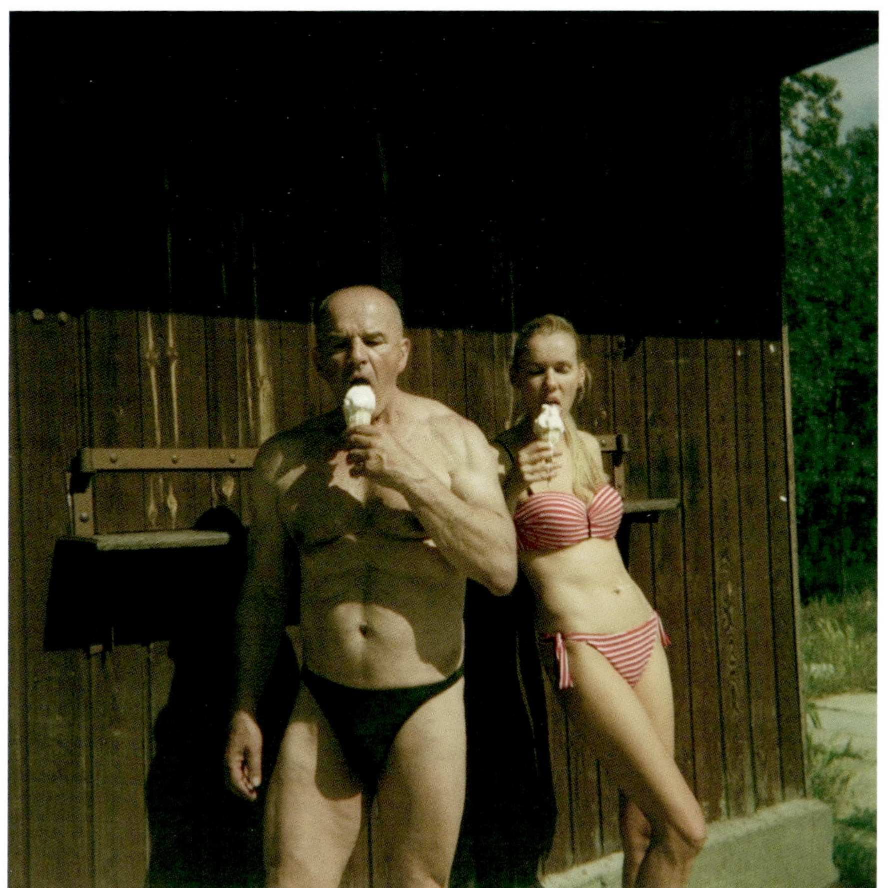

↑ **Aneta Bartos,** *Lody,* 2017

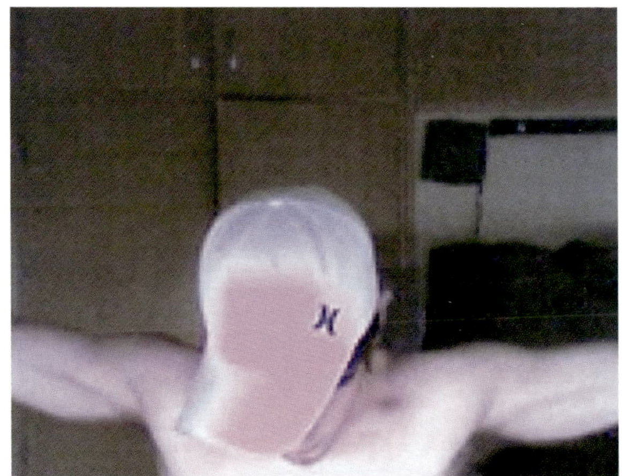

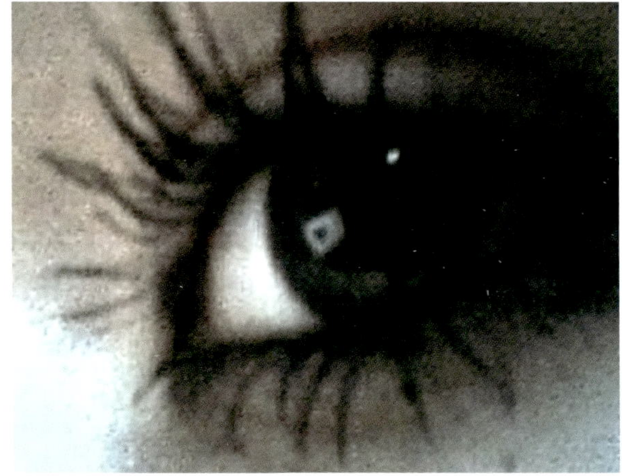

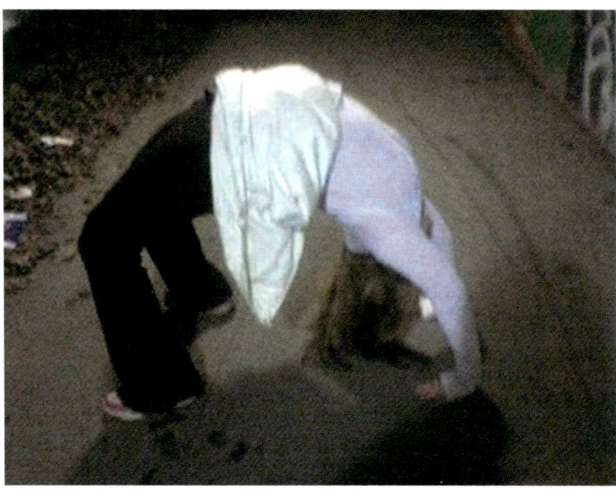

↑ (Top) **Ole John Aandal,** *Juvenilia no 25 (Pink Boy)*, 2009
↑ (Centre) **Ole John Aandal,** *Juvenilia no 6 (Eye II)*, 2009
↑ (Below) **Ole John Aandal,** *Juvenilia no 3 (Bridge)*, 2009

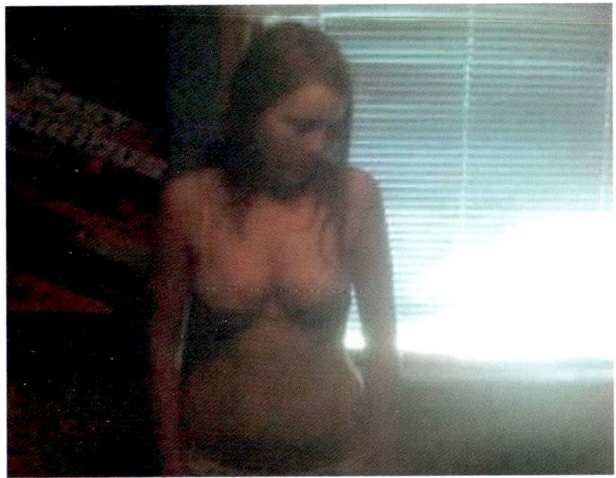

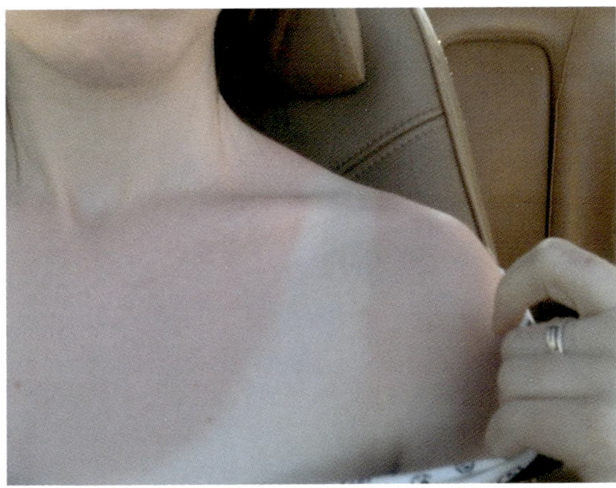

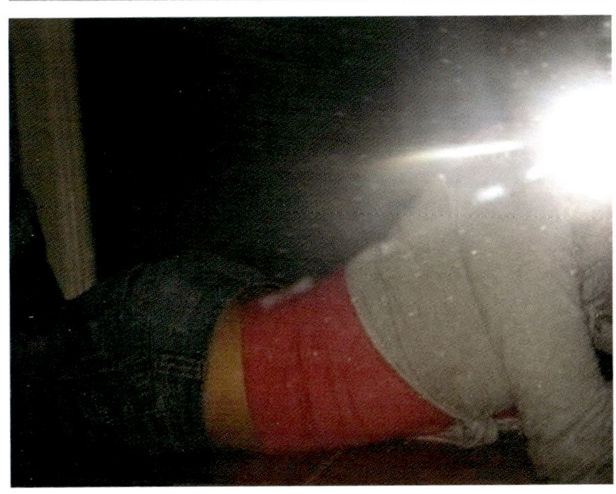

↑ (Top) **Ole John Aandal,** *Juvenilia no 28 (Girl by Window),* 2009
↑ (Centre) **Ole John Aandal,** *Juvenilia no 37 (Burnt),* 2009
↑ (Below) **Ole John Aandal,** *Juvenilia no 1 (Flash),* 2009

the interaction between some of the couples posing in the nude in front of his camera. The body forms the social link with the other; the body touches and is touched. At intimate moments it allows itself to be seen in its smallest details.

In the works of Mona Kuhn (pp. 4, 122–23, 288, 289), the body is exposed and it feels; it is something that is both external and internal. Kuhn's photographs, which oscillate between bodies that are hazy and distinct, close or distant, reflect her models' sense of ease with their own bodies and the bodies of those close to them. Kuhn shows us liberated bodies; bodies apparently without ego. For her, there is no dichotomy between the body that we are and the body that we own.

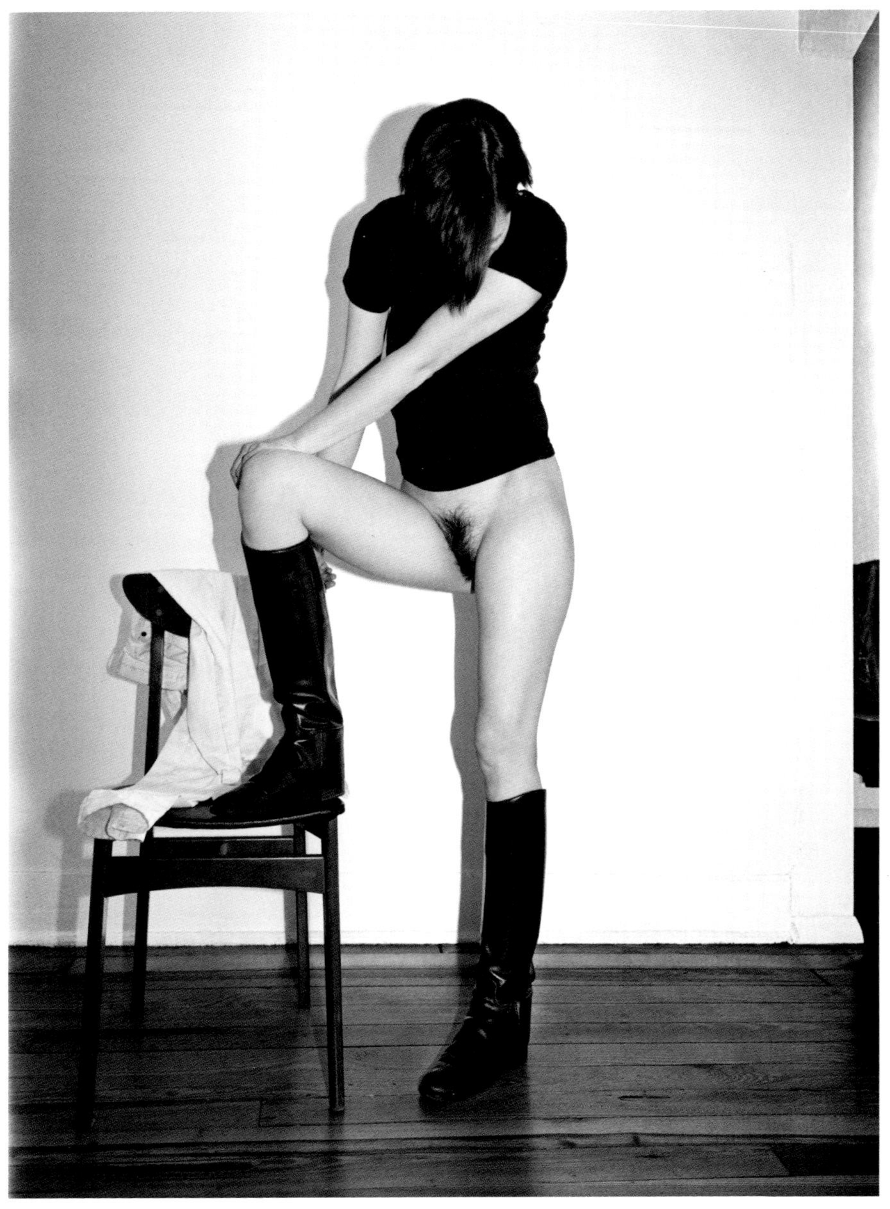

↑ **Collier Schorr,** *Boots, Chair, Hair,* 1998—2014

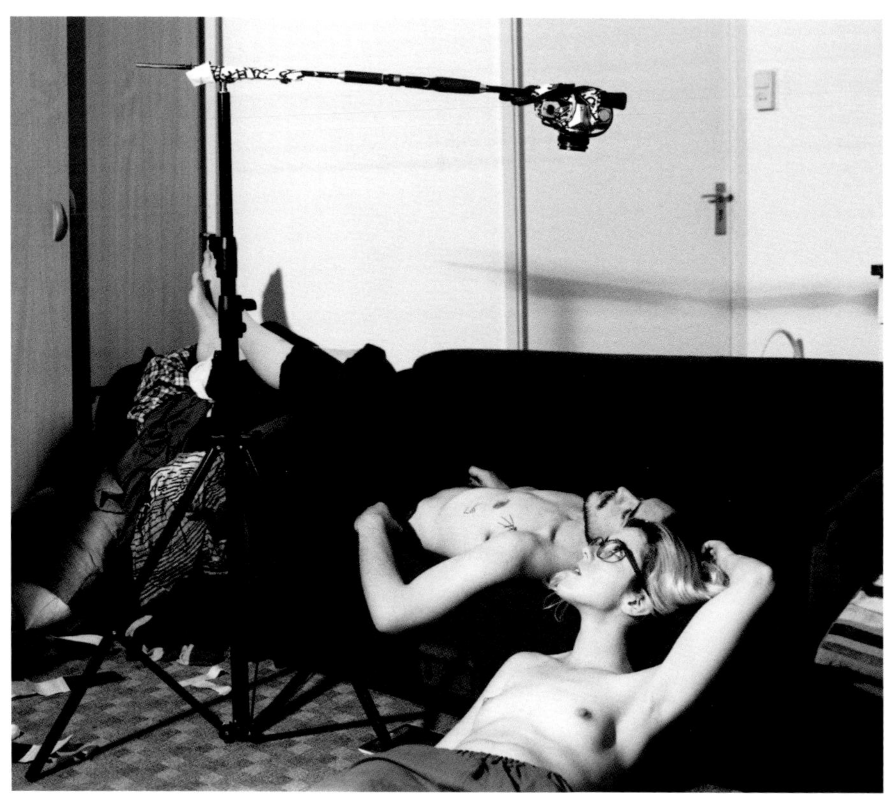

↑ **Jeanne Tullen,** *Self-Portrait with Device,* from the series 'Womb', 2014

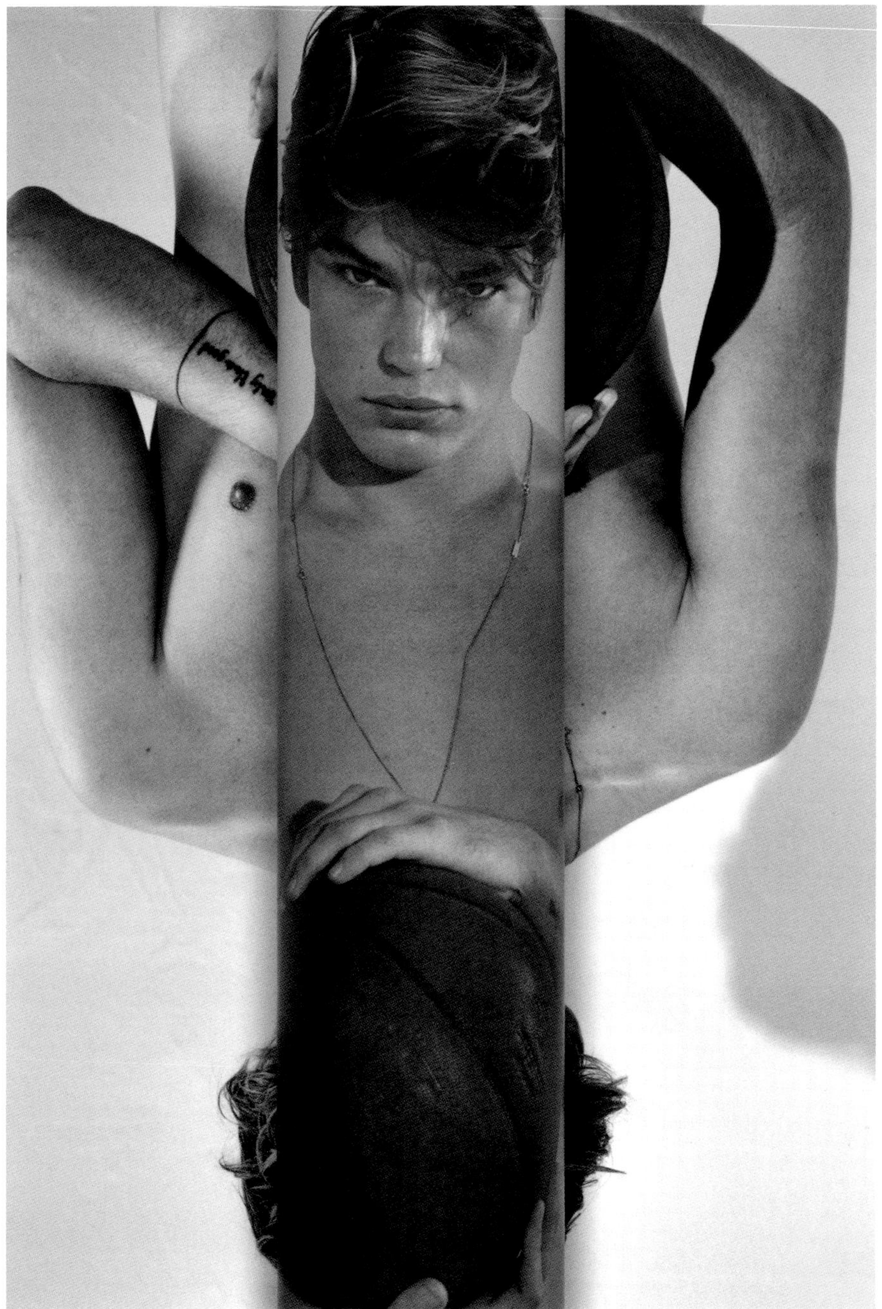

↑ **Collier Schorr**, *A Hand With Illusion*, 2015

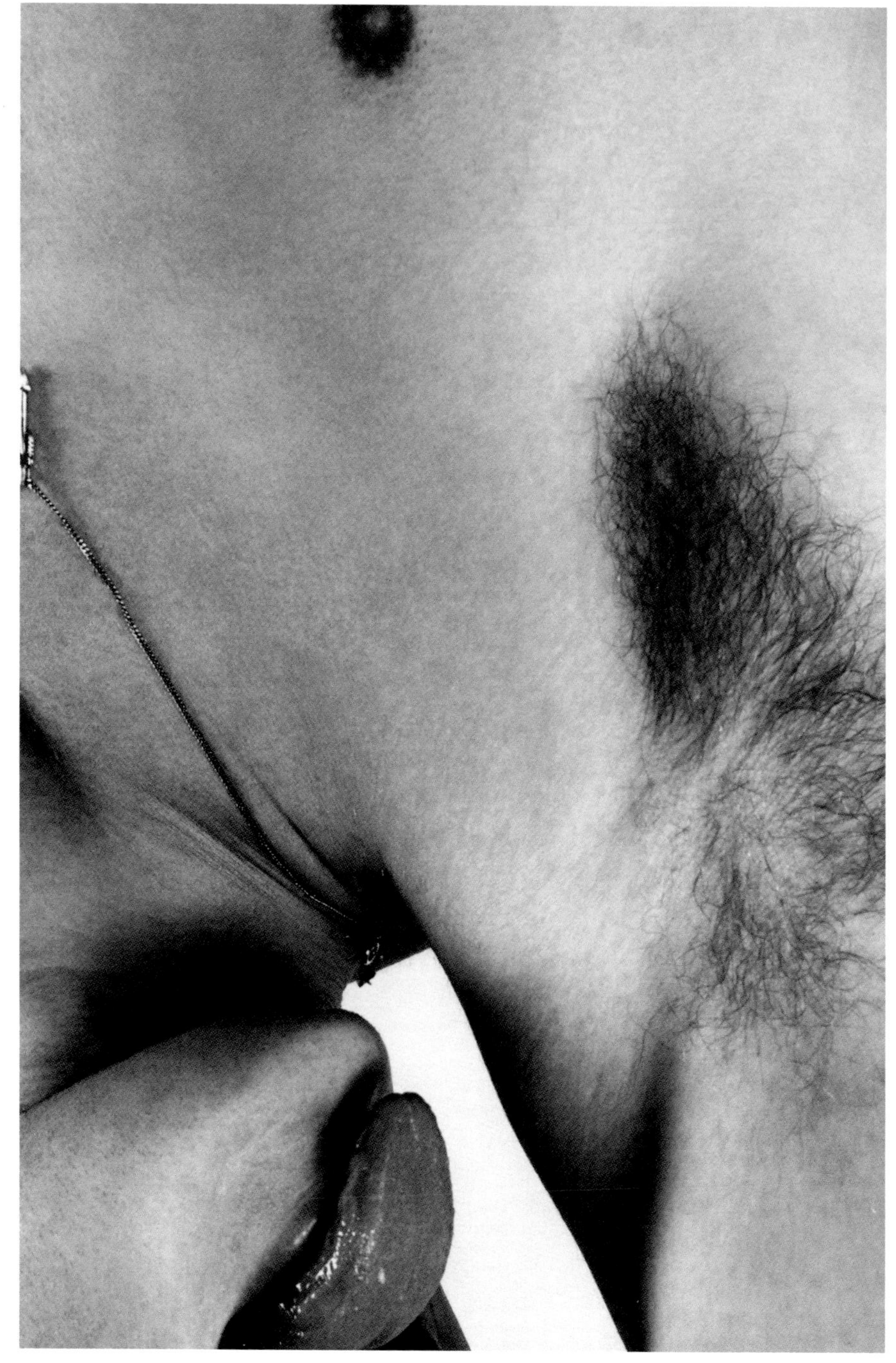

↑ **Collier Schorr,** *Another Spiritual,* 2015

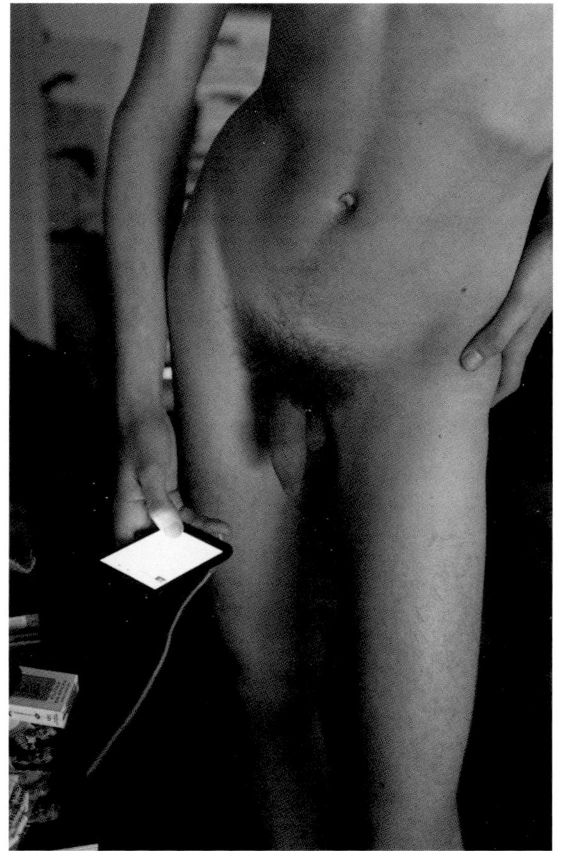

↑ **Collier Schorr,** *Paul and Text,* 2016

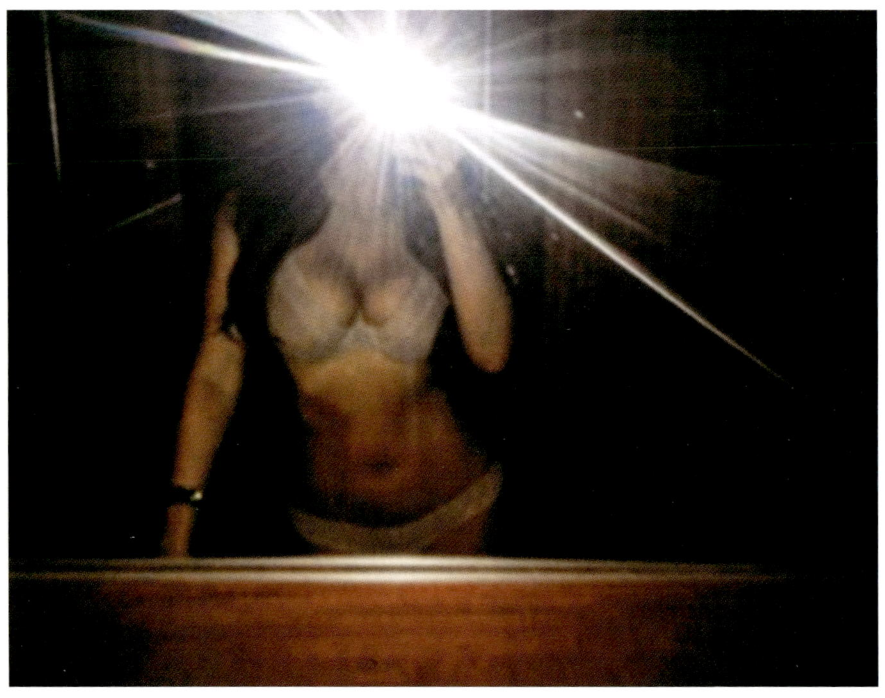

↑ **Kim Kardashian,** Untitled, from the series *Selfish*, 2015–16

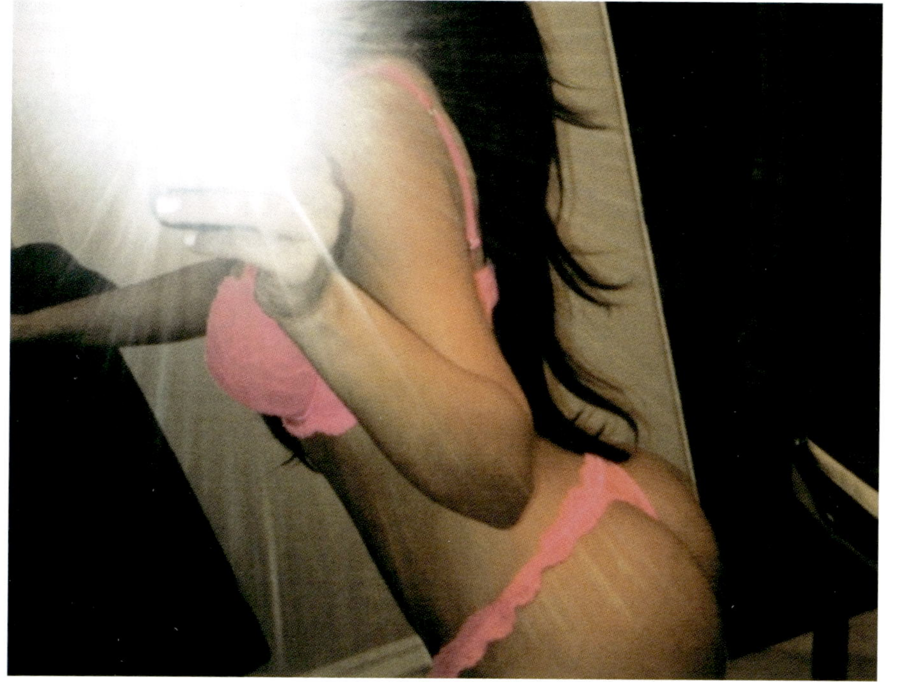

↑ **Kim Kardashian,** Untitled, from the series *Selfish*, 2015—16

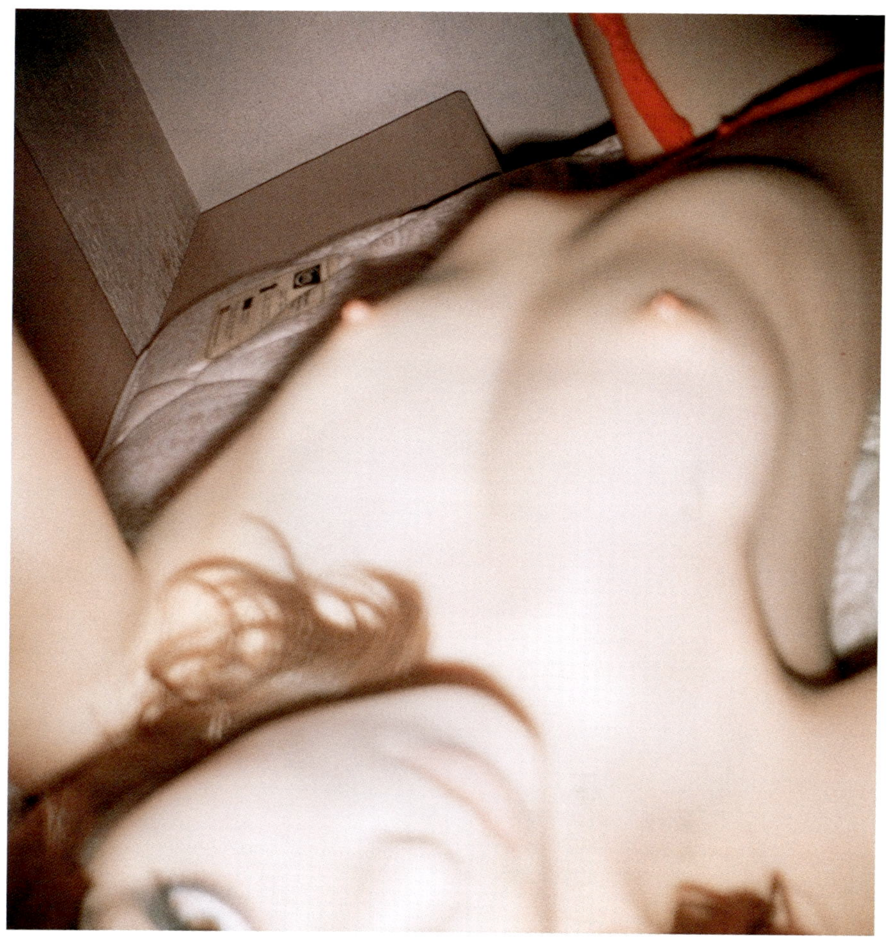

↑ **Todd Hido,** *Untitled, #8338-c,* 2009
→(Overleaf) **Pierre et Gilles,** *Narcisse,* 2012

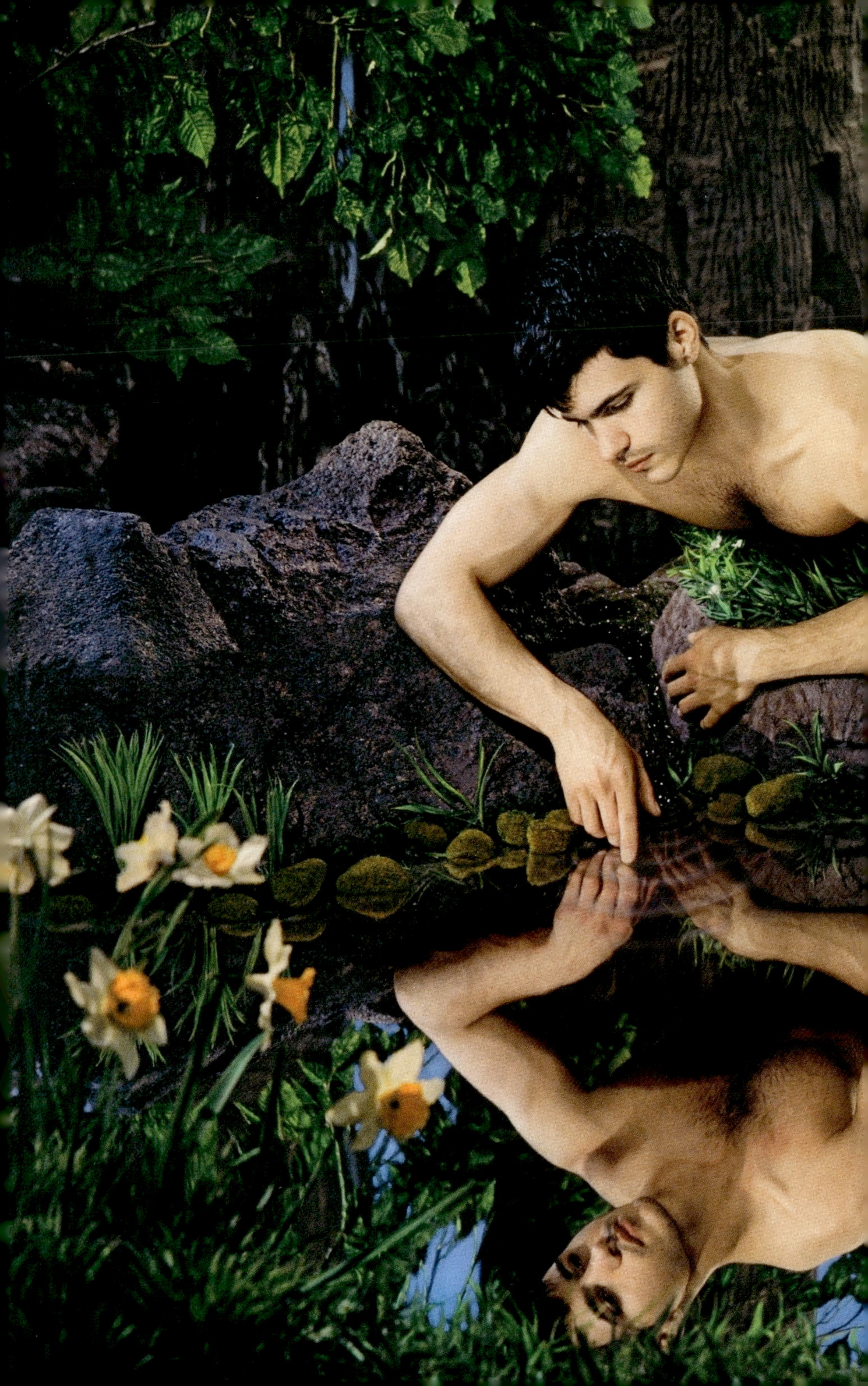

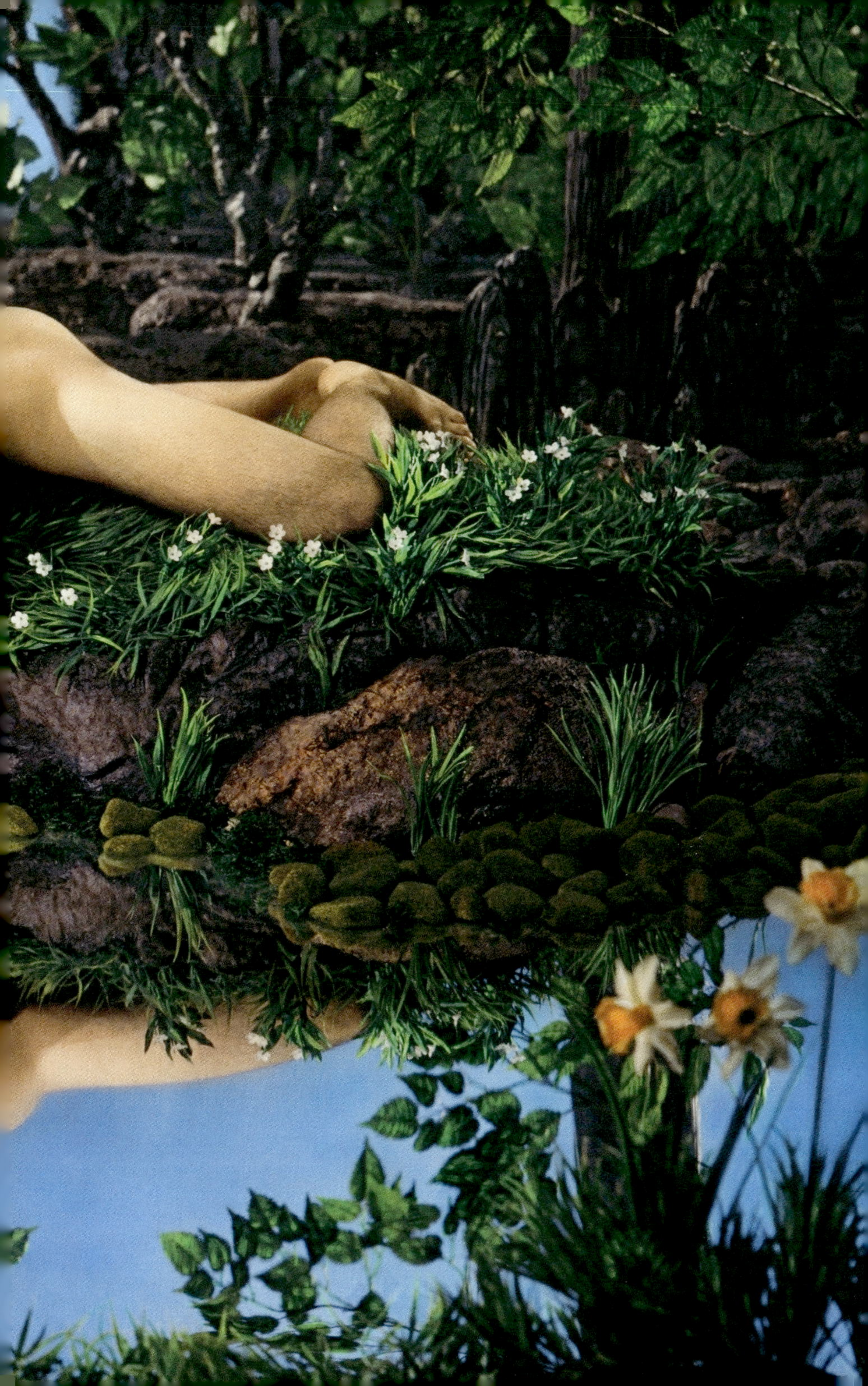

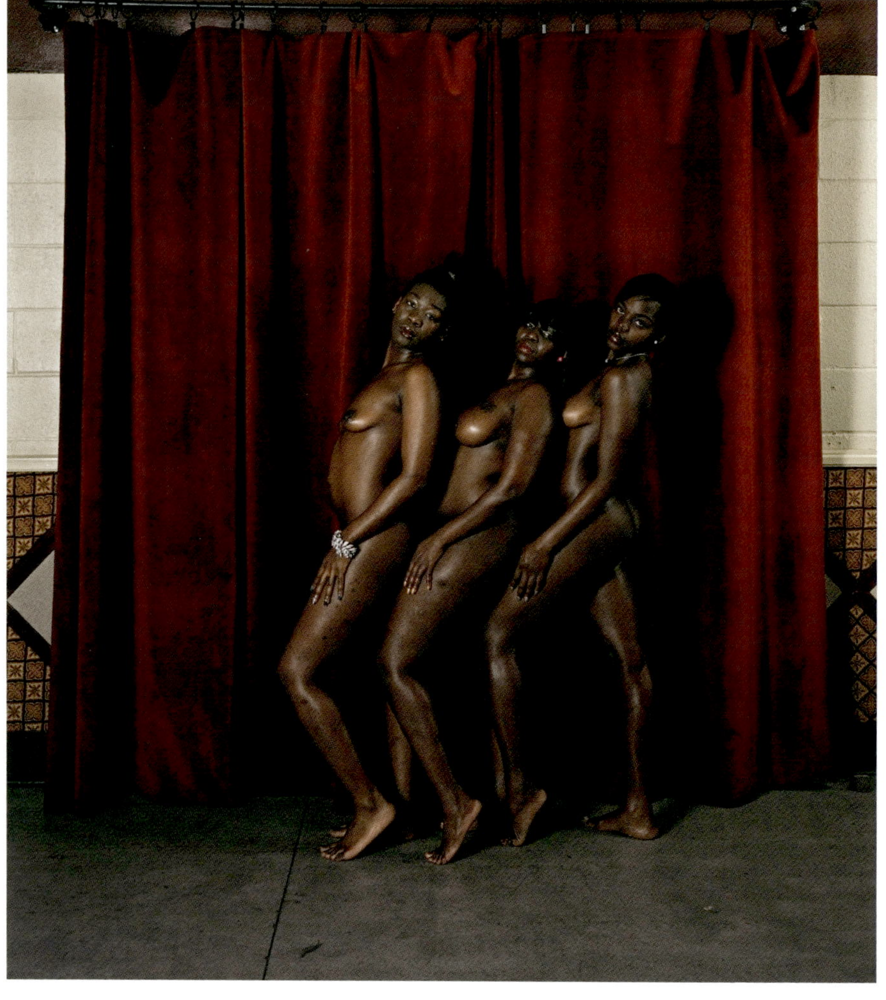

↑ **Deana Lawson,** *Three Women*, 2013

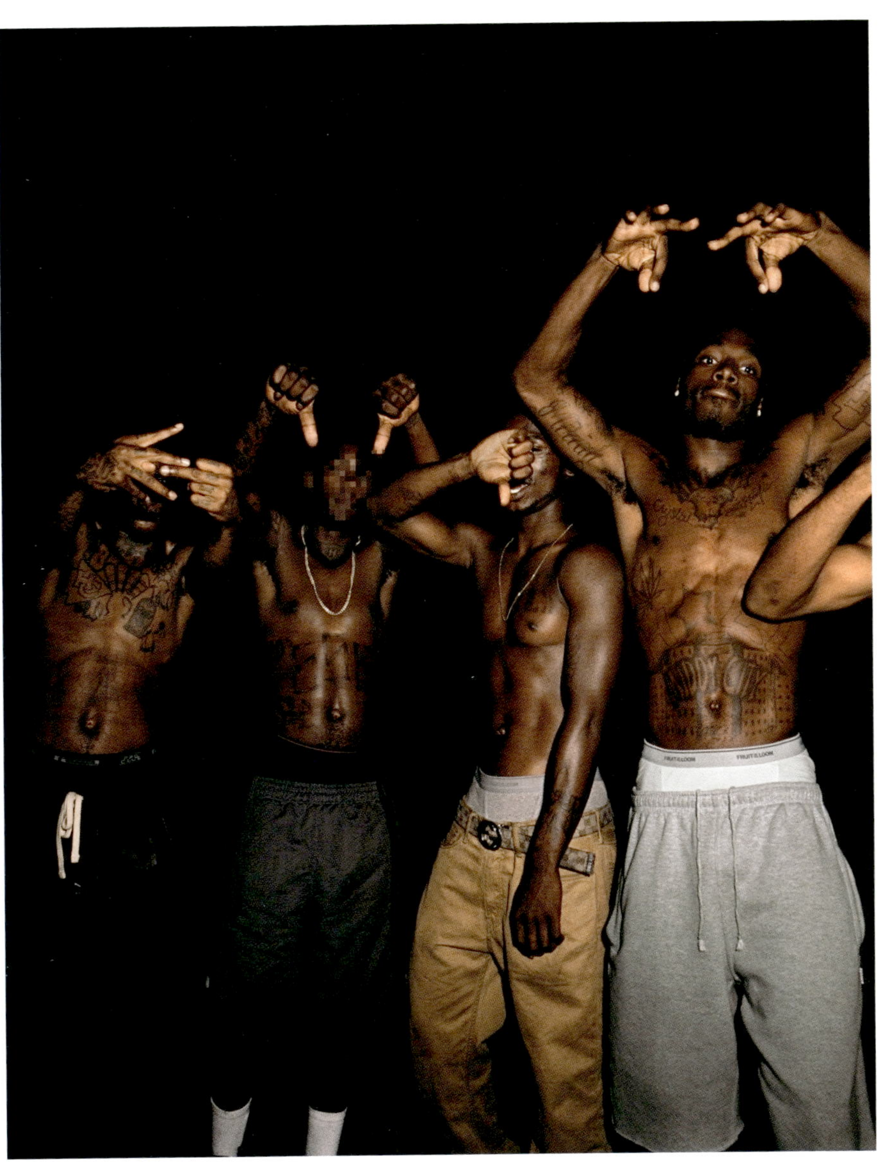

↑ **Deana Lawson**, *Signs*, 2016

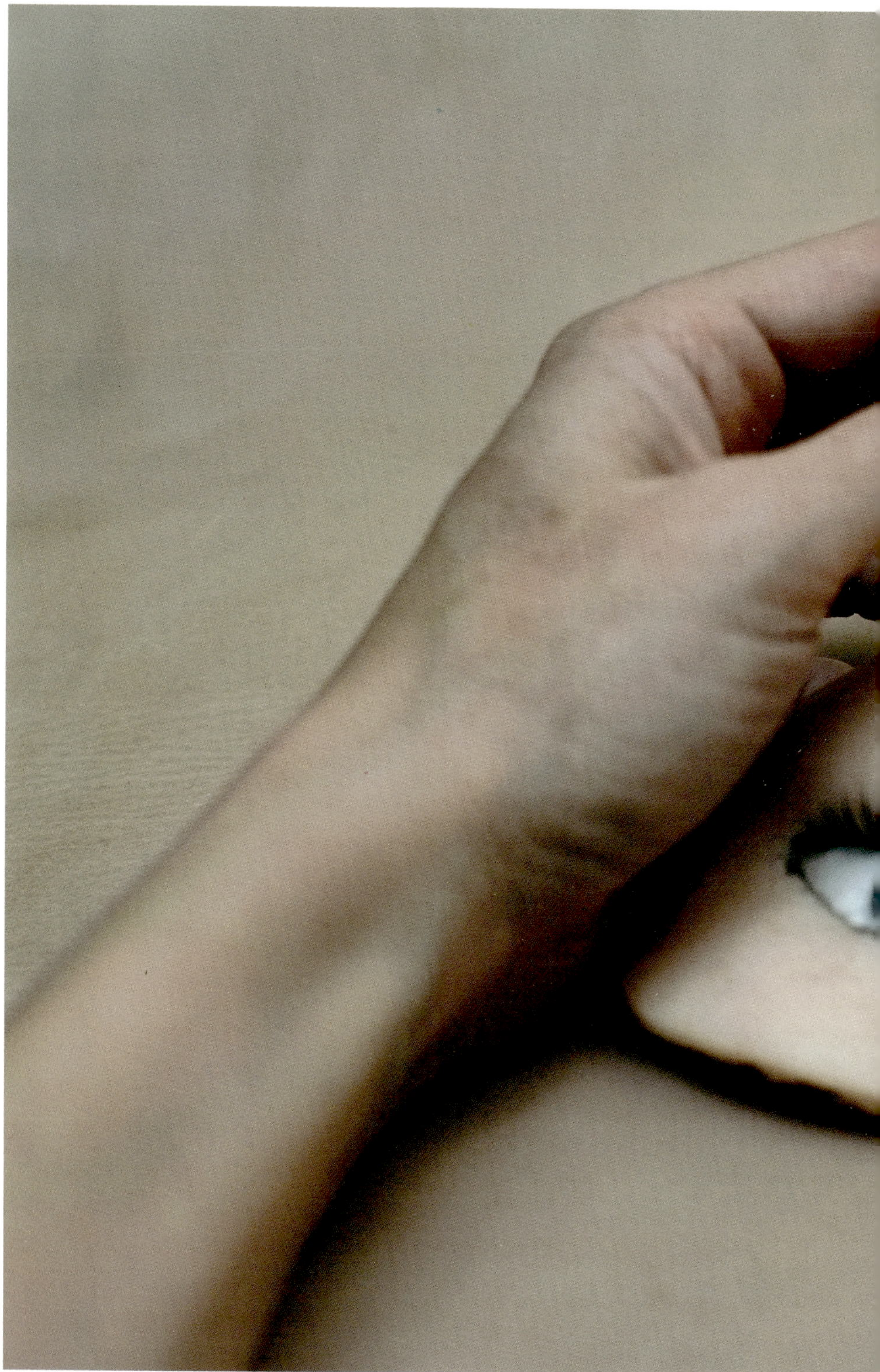

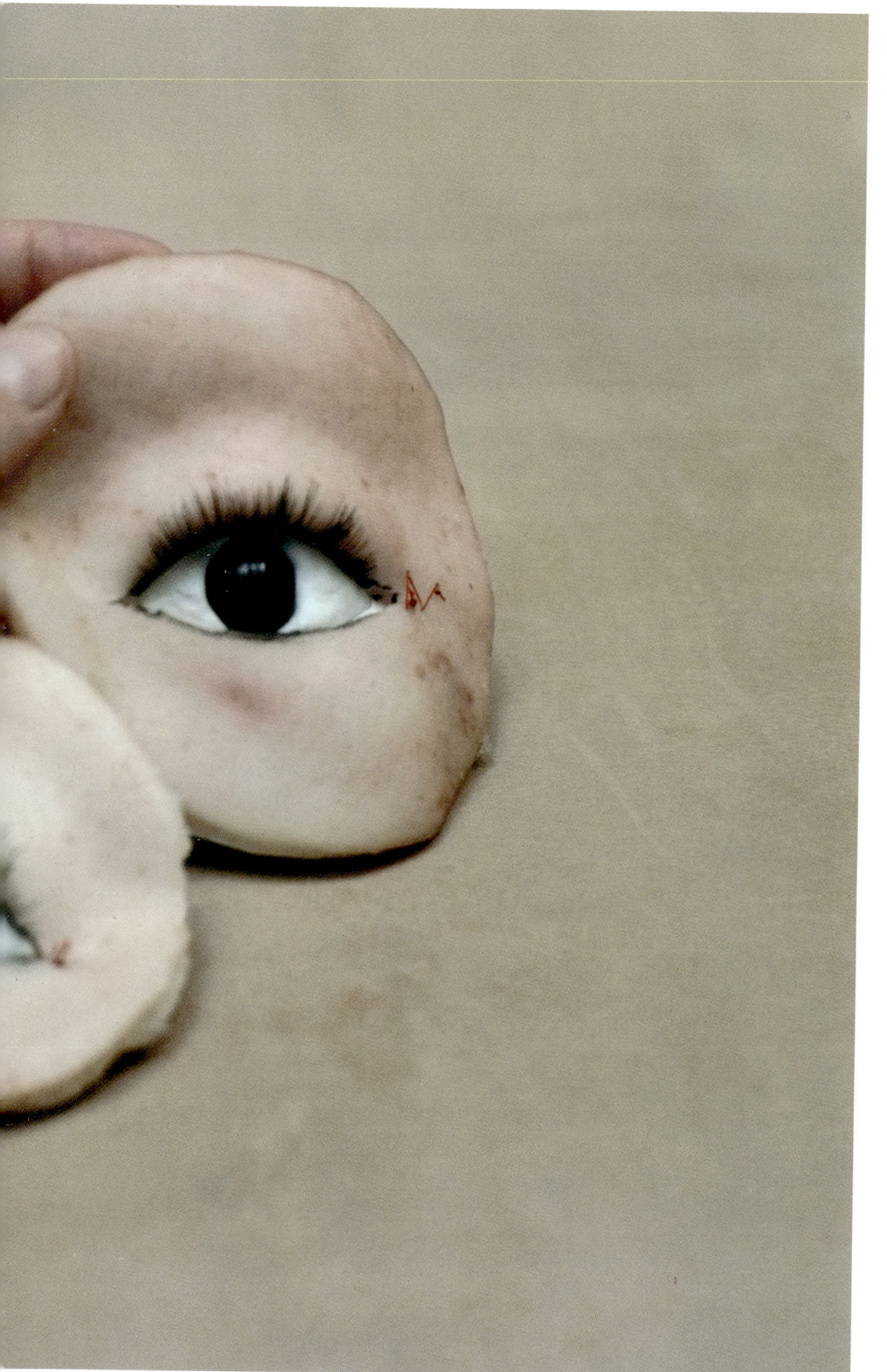

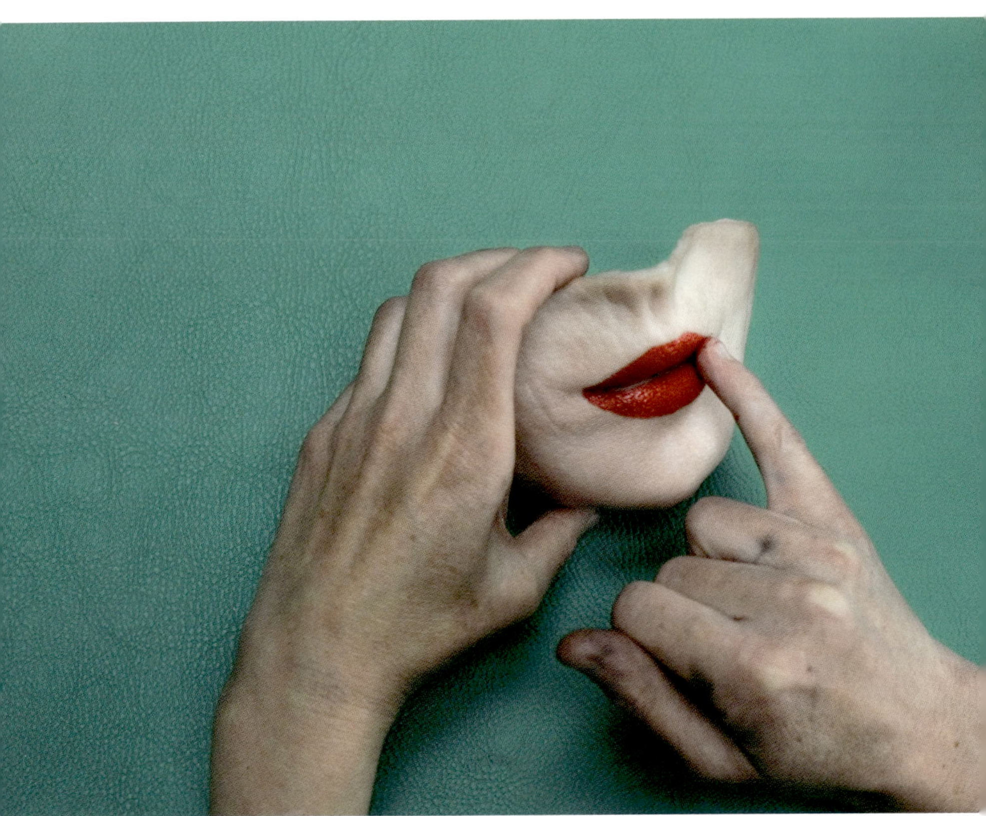

↑ **Aneta Grzeszykowska**, *Selfie #18*, 2014
← (Previous) **Aneta Grzeszykowska**, *Selfie #10*, 2014

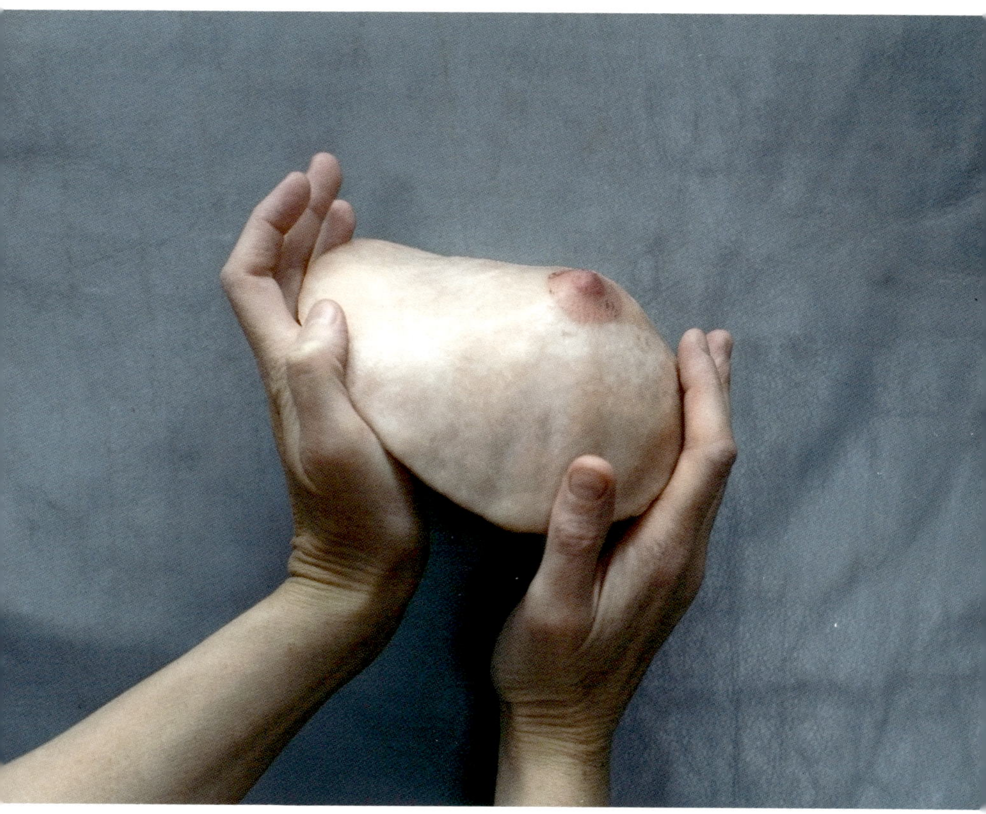

↑ **Aneta Grzeszykowska,** *Selfie #12,* 2014

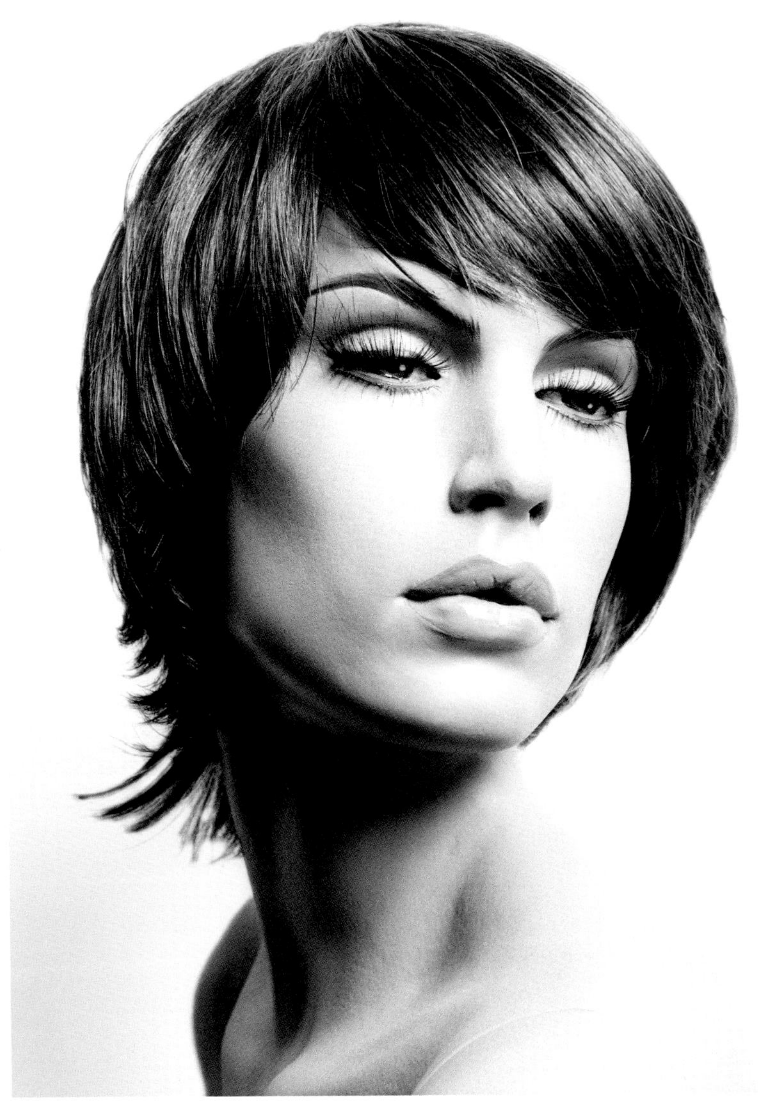

↑ **Valérie Belin,** *Untitled,* from the series 'Mannequins', 2003

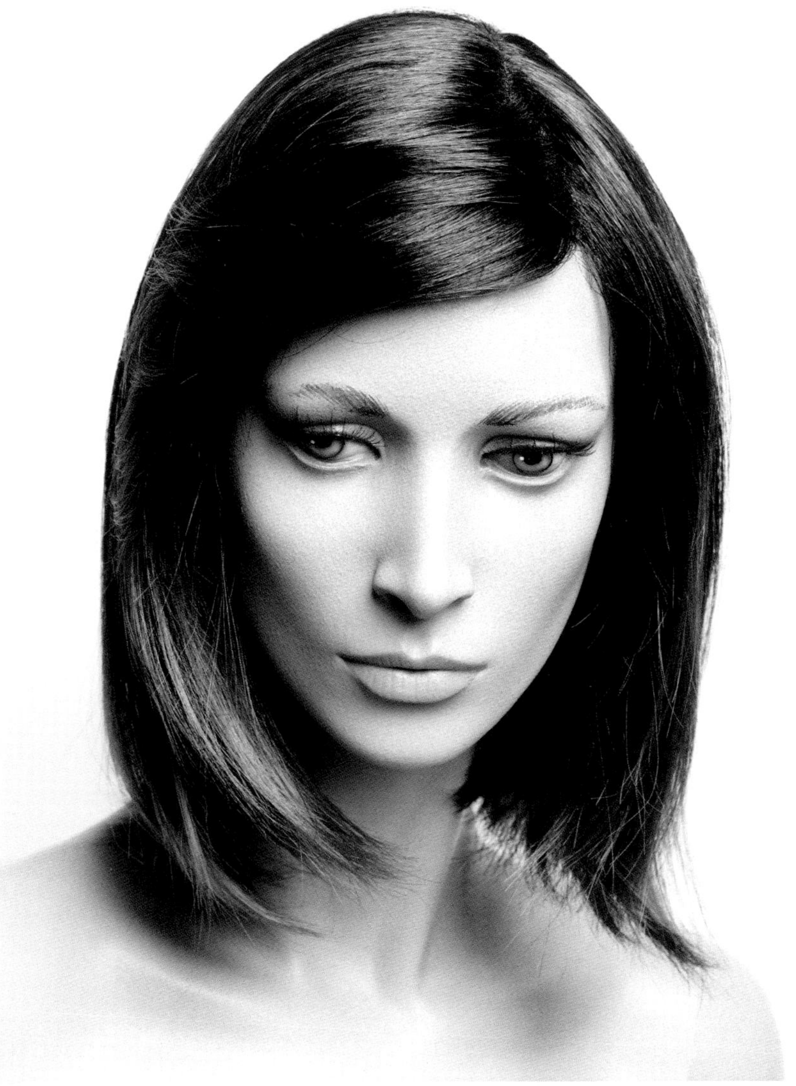

↑ **Valérie Belin,** *Untitled,* from the series 'Mannequins', 2003

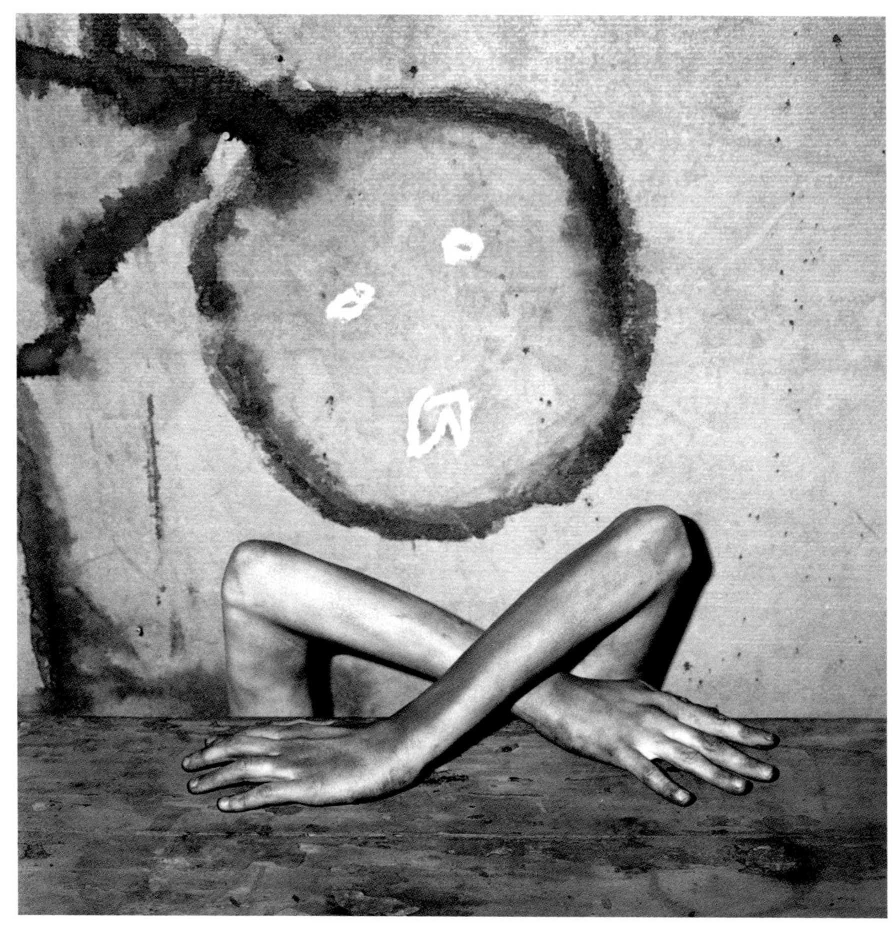

↑ **Roger Ballen**, *Mimicry*, 2005

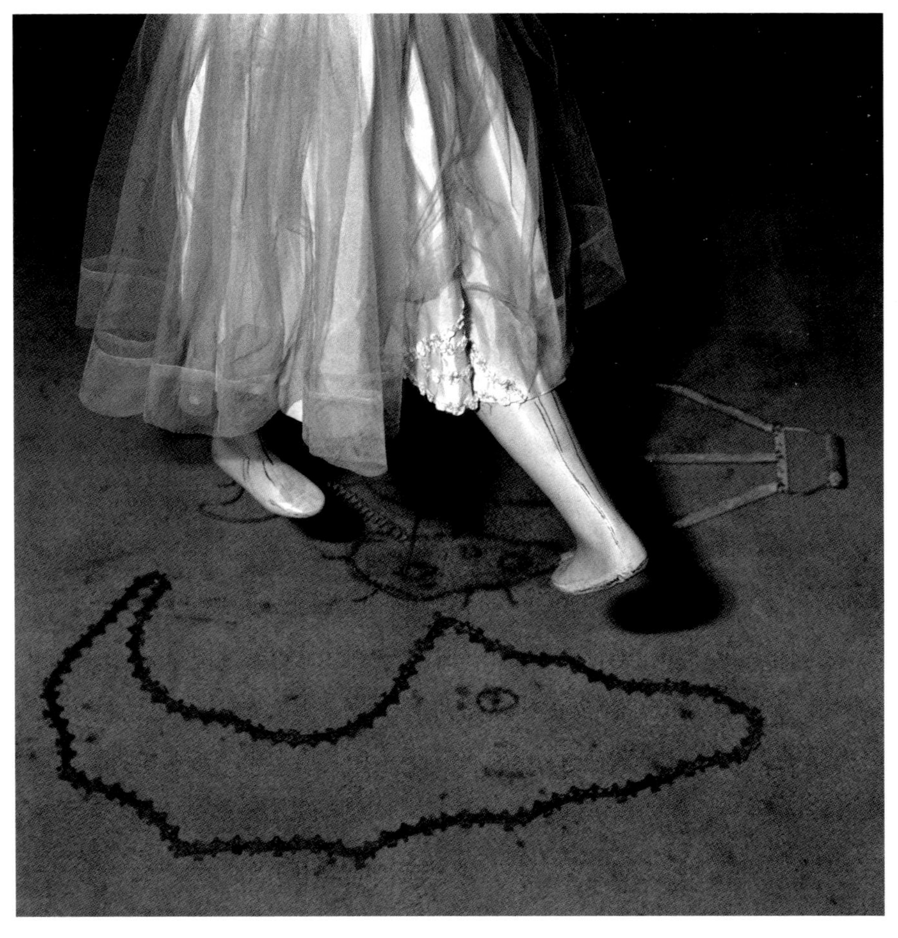

↑ Roger Ballen, *Closet*, 2004

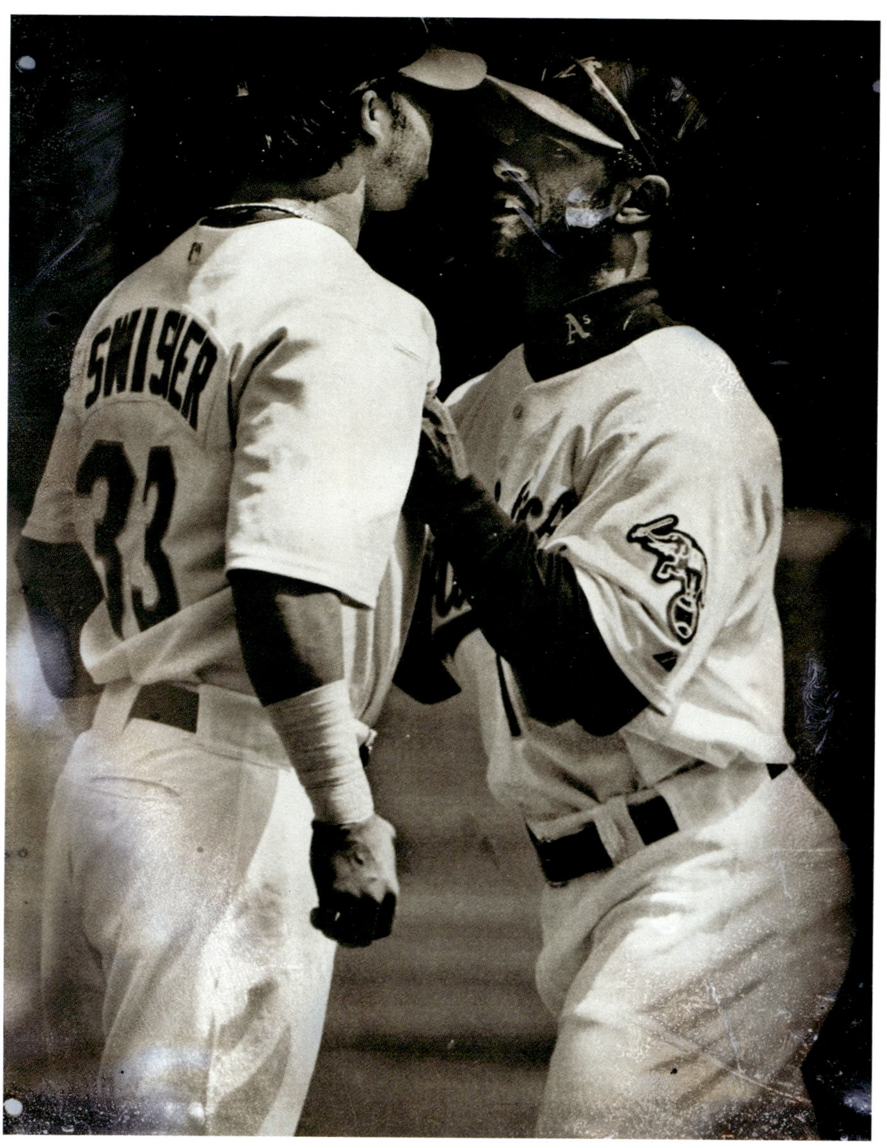

↑ **Tabitha Soren,** *Nick Swisher and Jay Payton, Oakland A's play-fight, Oakland, CA,* from the series 'Fantasy Life: Baseball and the American Dream', 2005

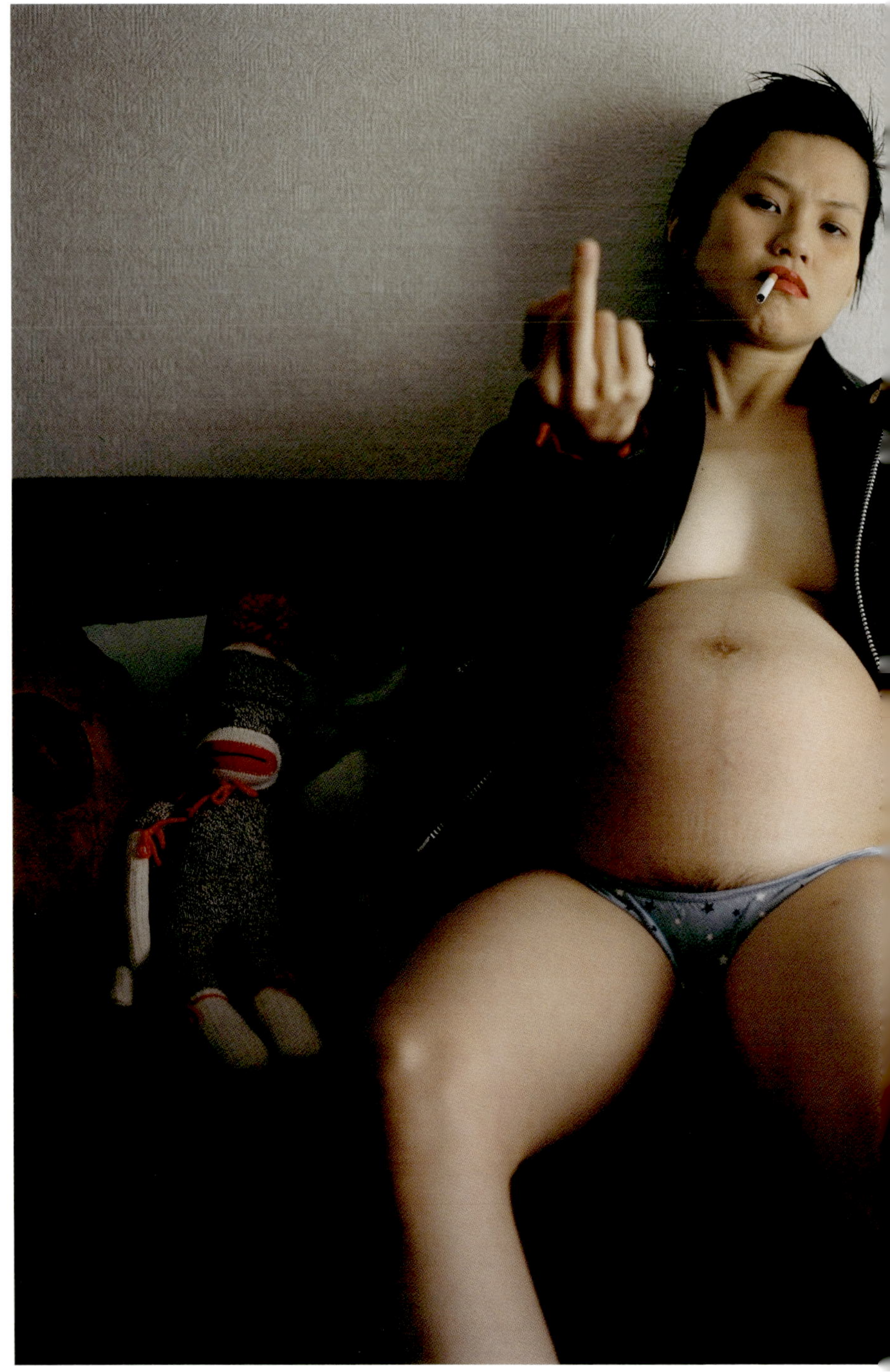

↑ **Yurie Nagashima,** *Self-Portrait,* 2002

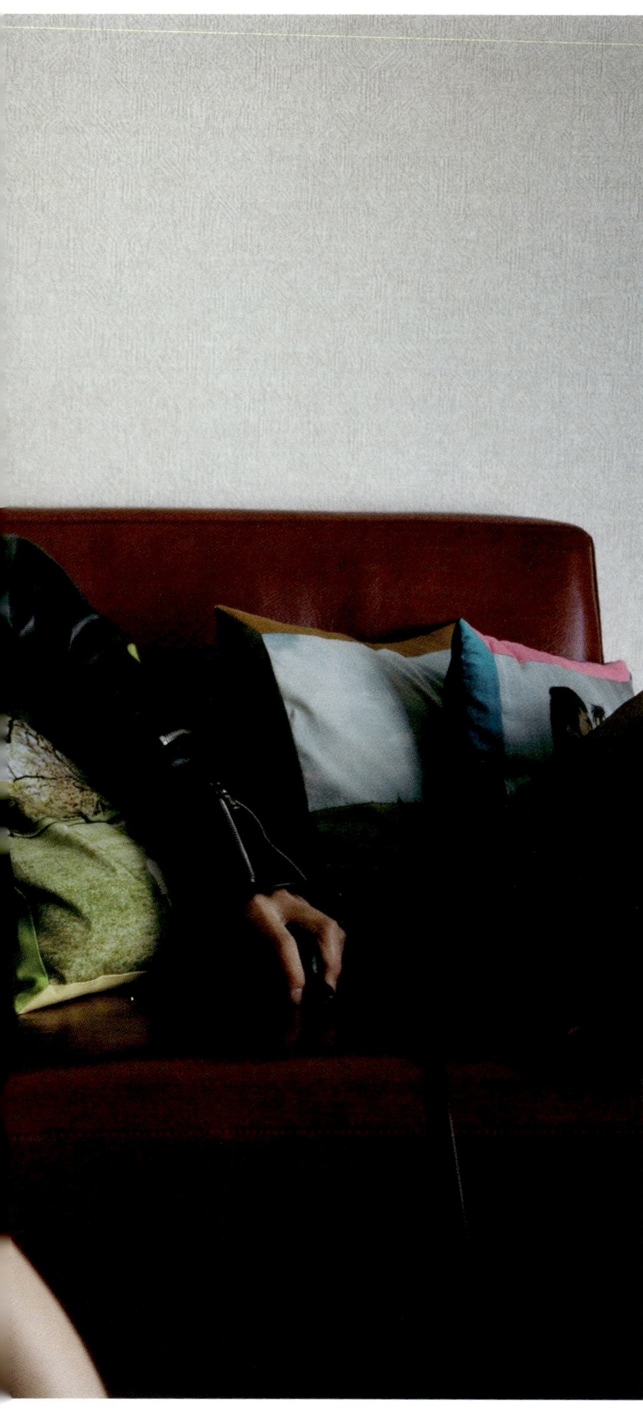

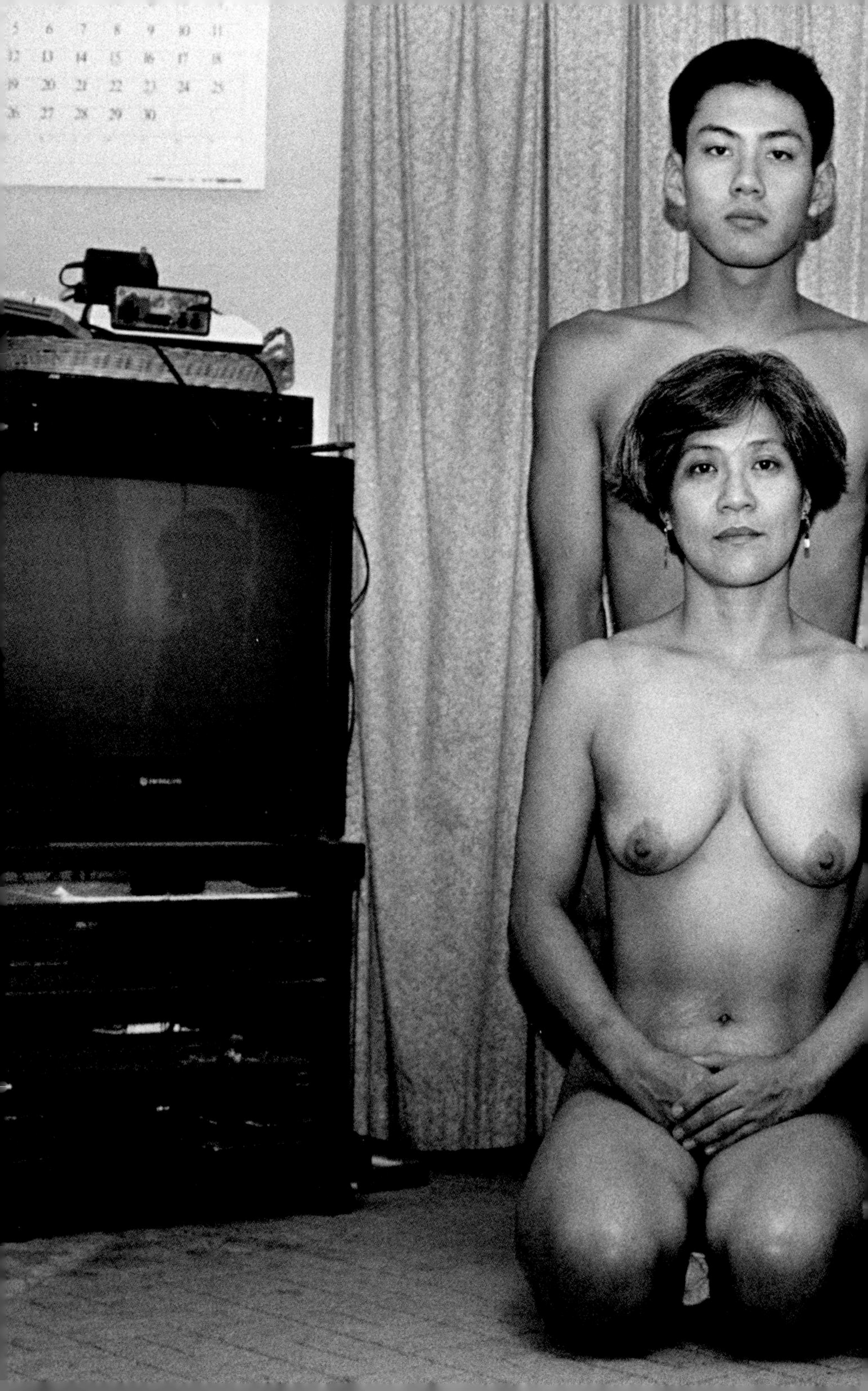

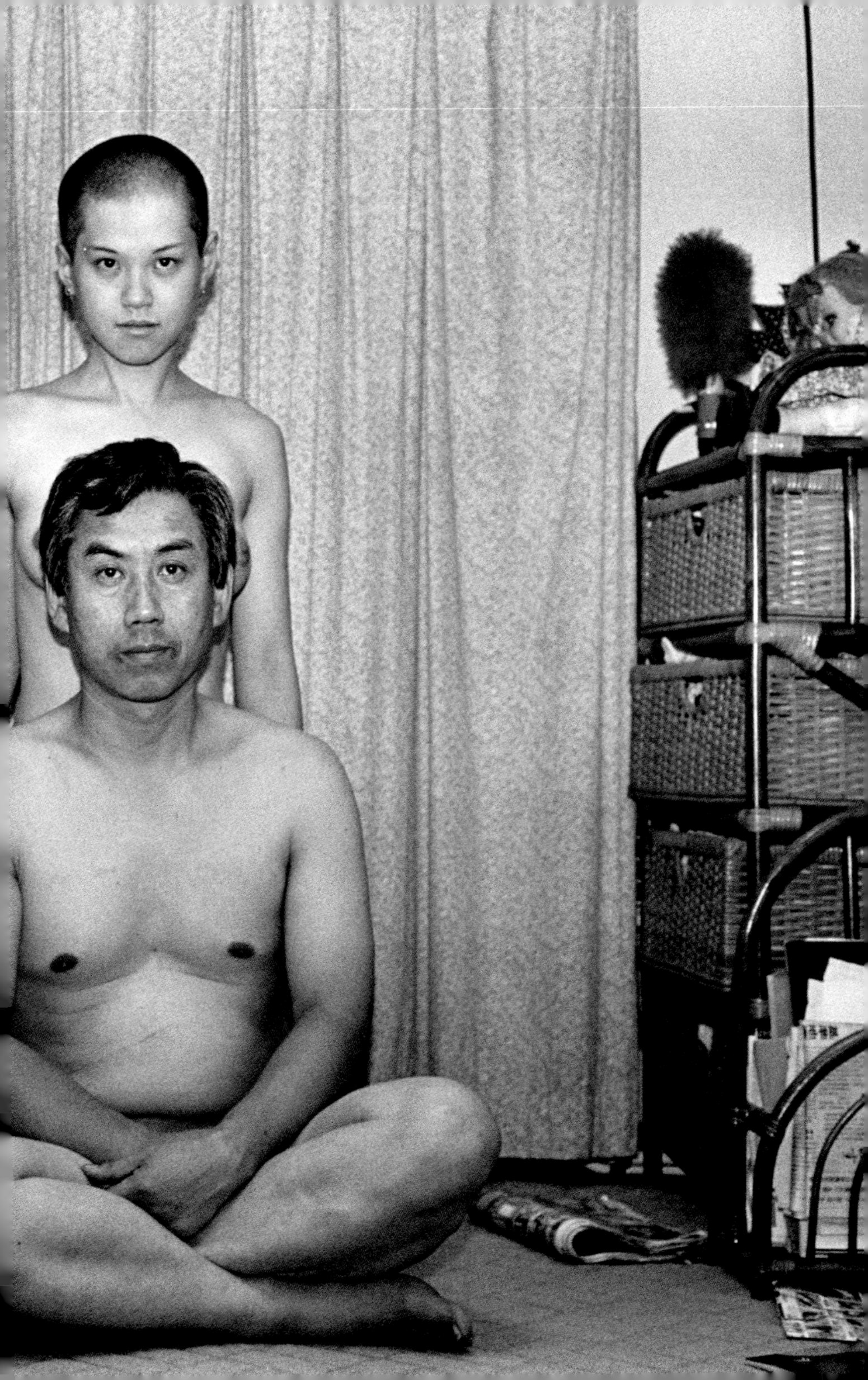

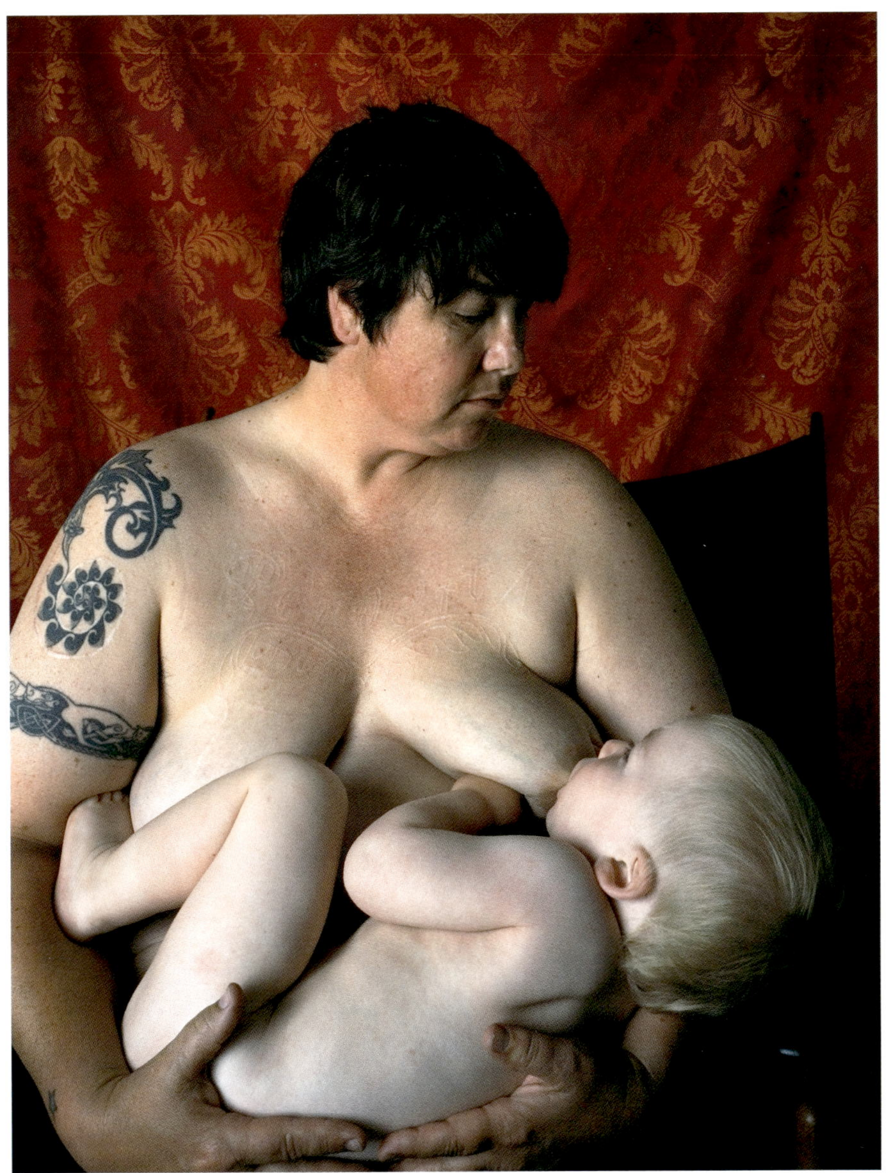

↑ **Catherine Opie**, *Self-Portrait / Nursing*, 2004

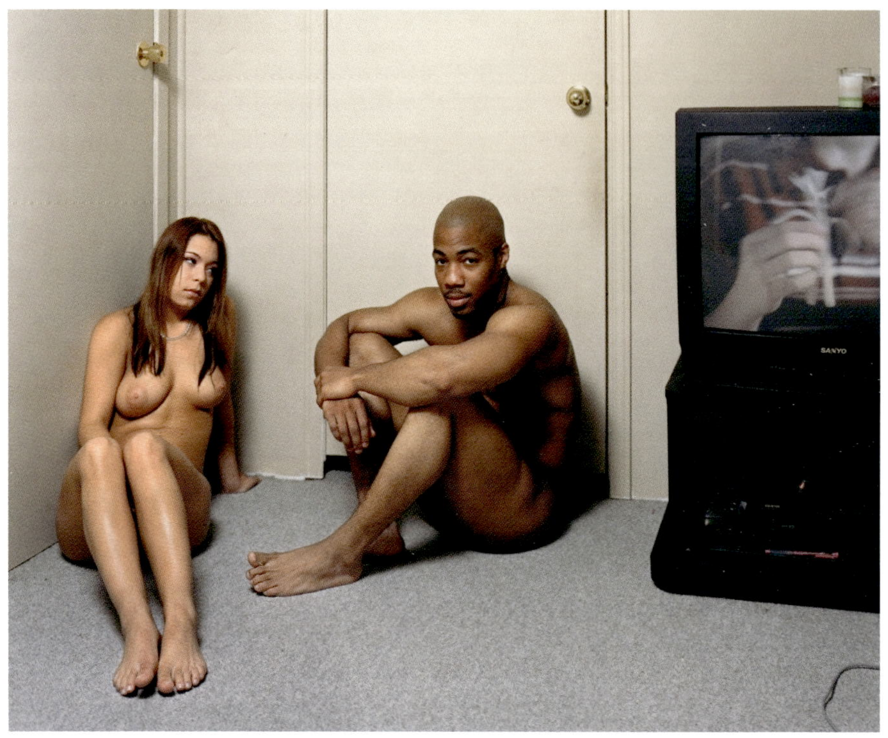

↑ **Alec Soth,** *Jennifer and Terrell, Canada,* 2005

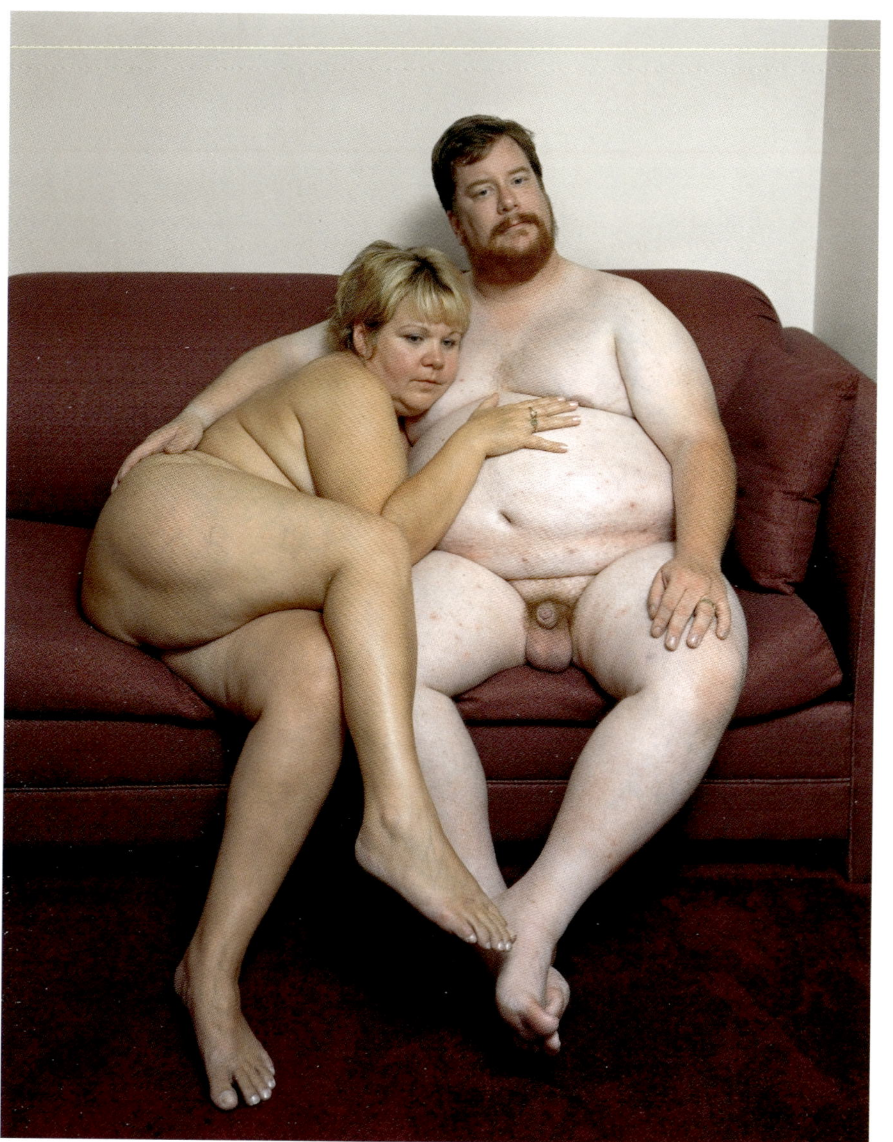

↑ **Alec Soth,** *Michele and James, Canada,* 2004

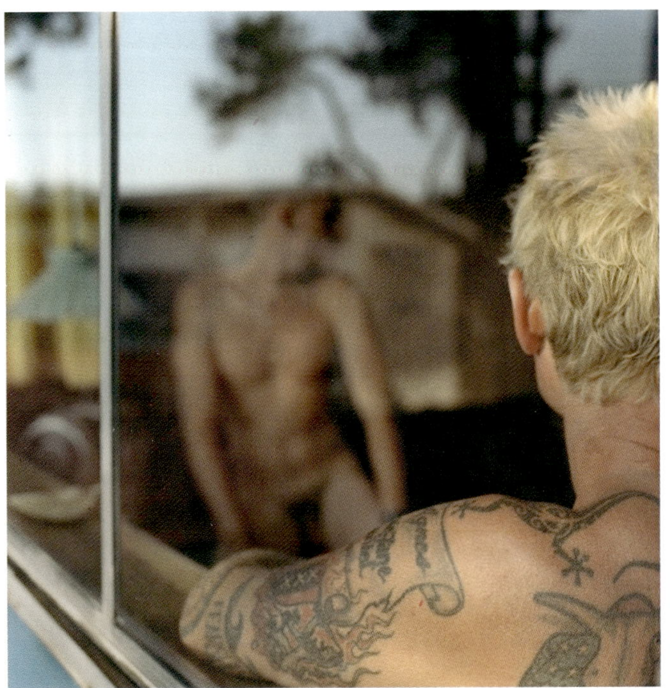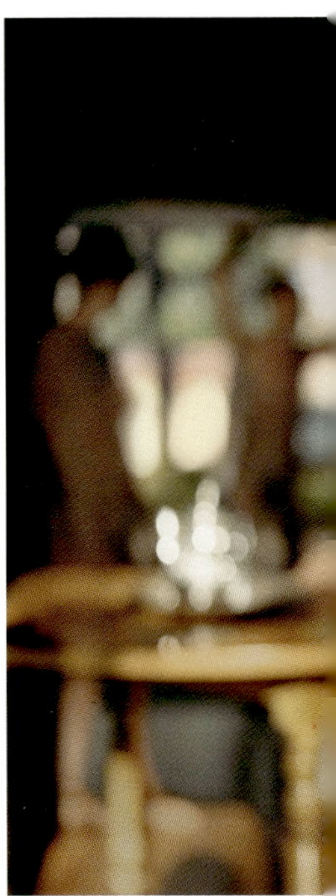

↑ (Left) **Mona Kuhn,** *Johnny,* 2006
↑ (Centre) **Mona Kuhn,** *Refractions,* 2006

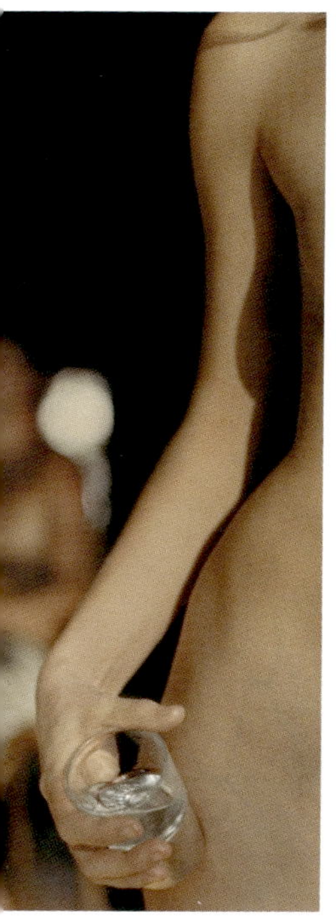
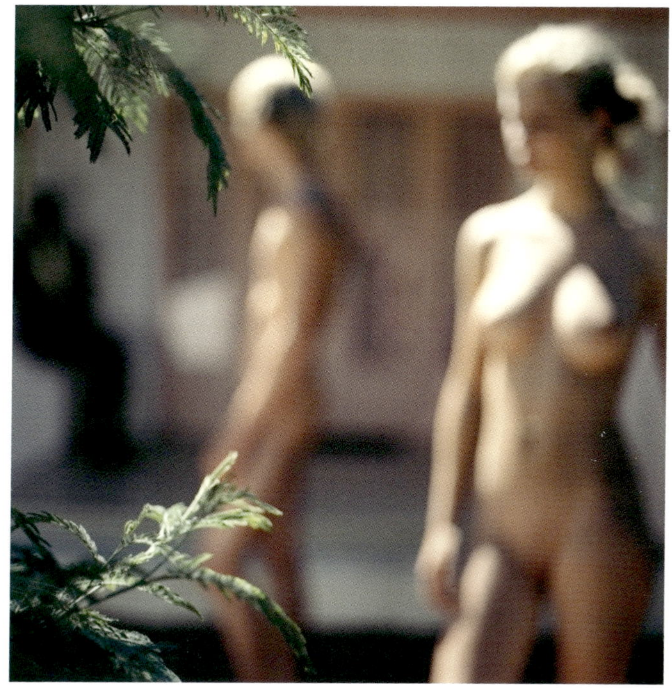

↑ (Right) **Mona Kuhn,** *All About Eve,* 2006
→(Overleaf) **Zhang Huan,** *To Add One Meter To an Anonymous Mountain,* 1995

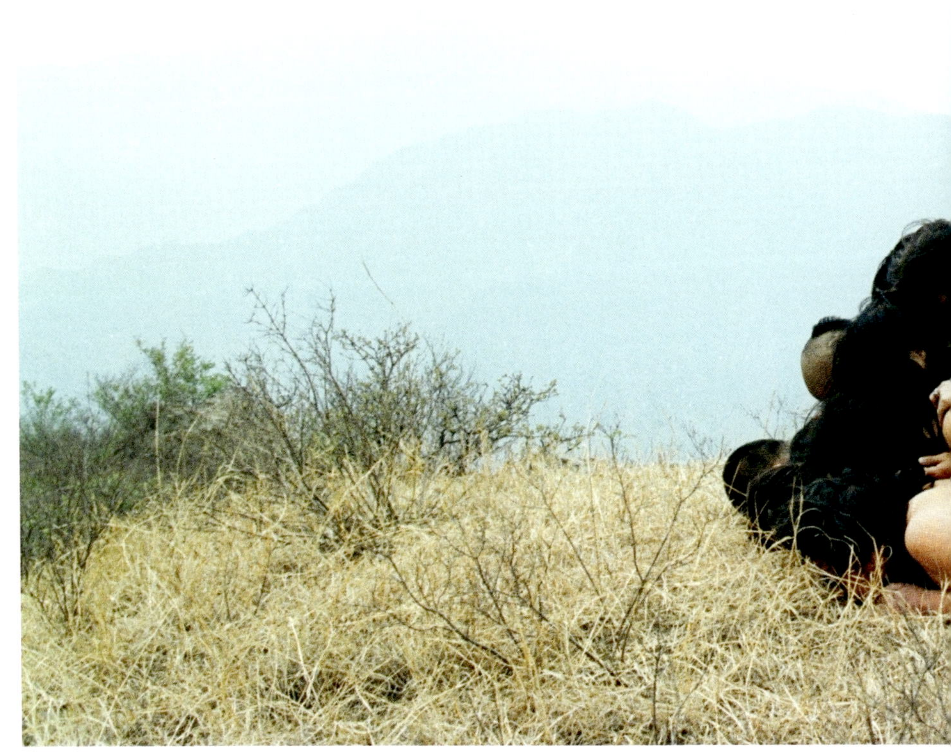

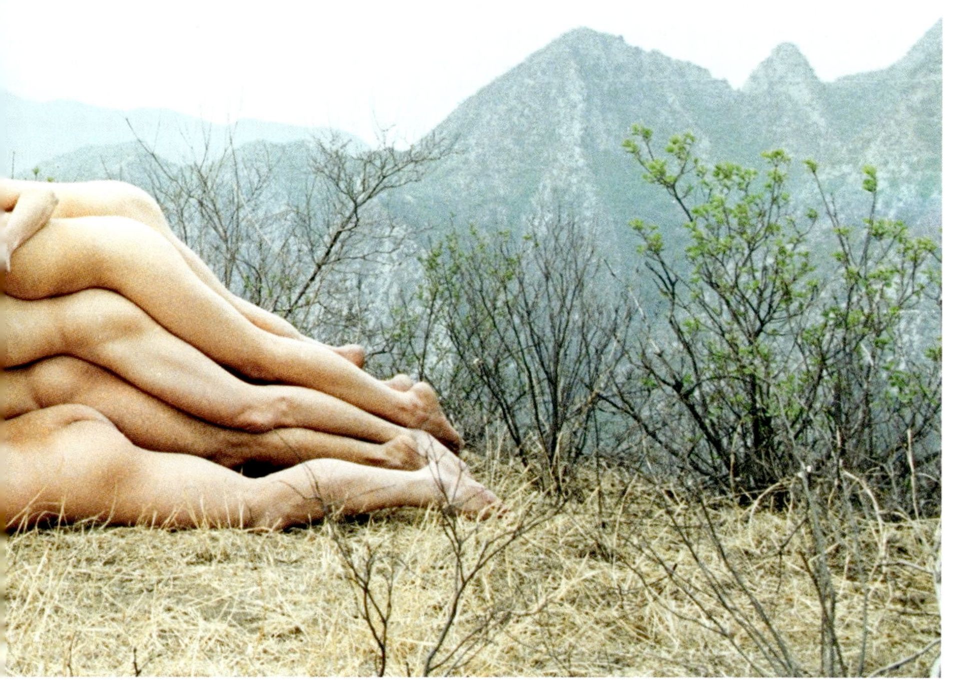

CONSTRUCTIONS

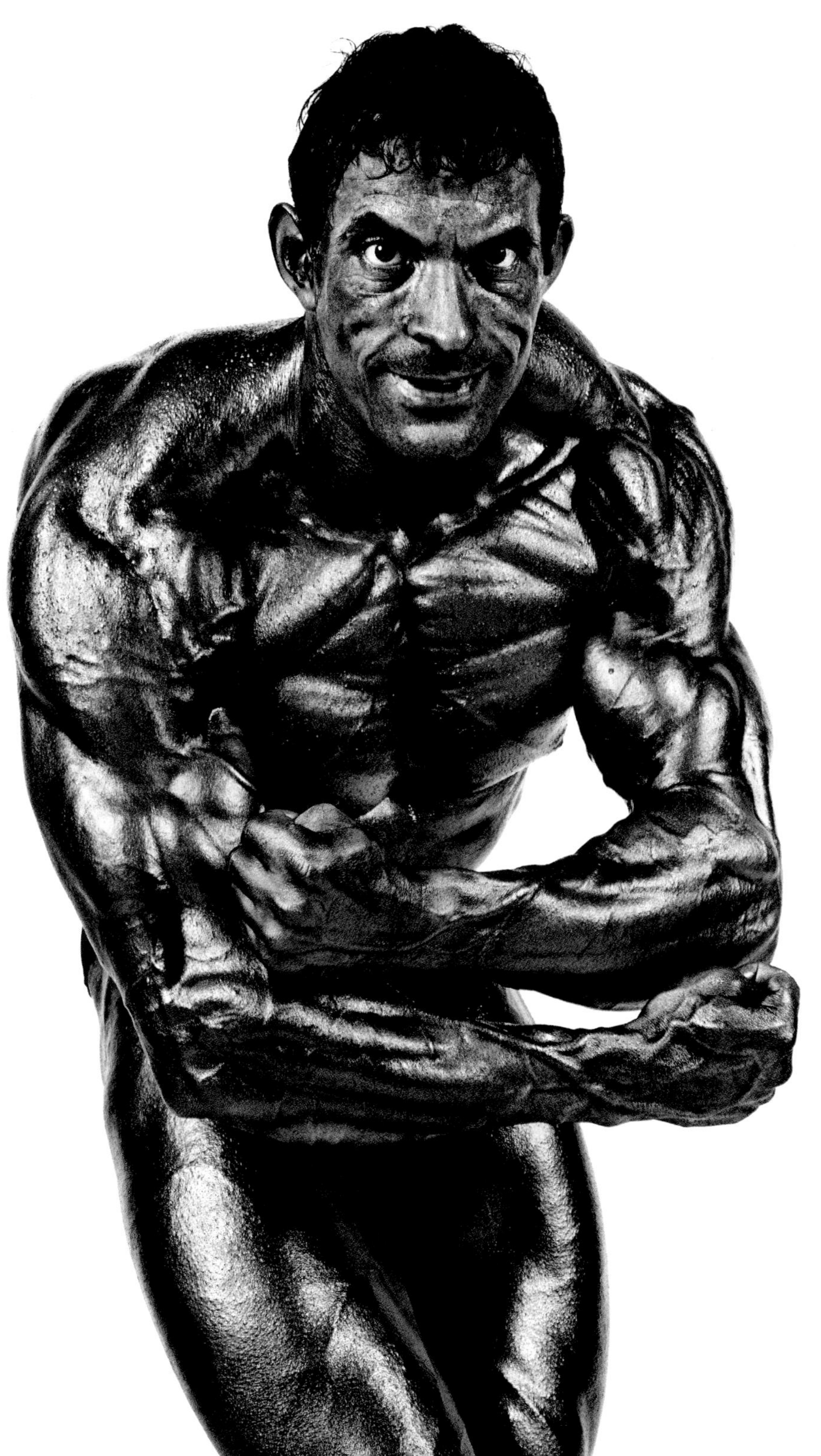

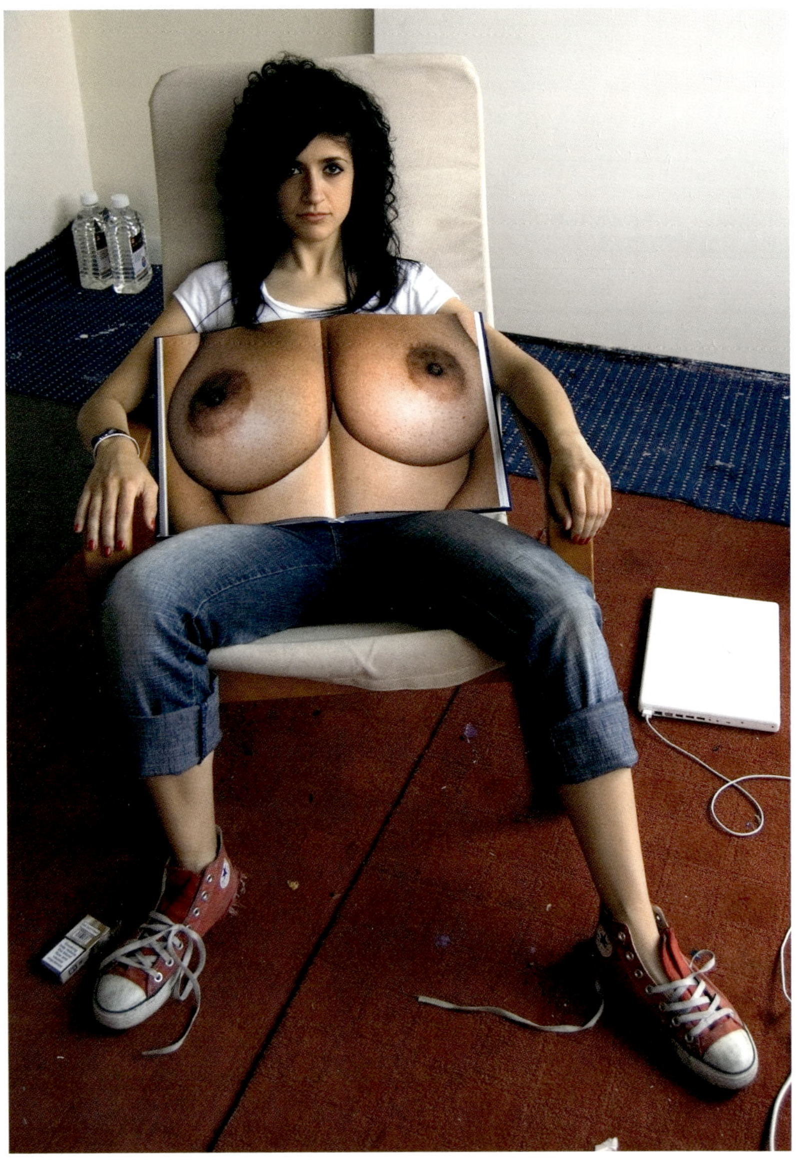

↑ **Sarah Maple,** *Self-Portrait With Fried Eggs*, 2008
← (Previous) **Valérie Belin,** *Bodybuilders I*, 1999

We are living in an era when self-acceptance is the mantra of the day, yet paradoxically we have never been so exposed to ideas we are supposed to conform to, especially through social networks. Although canons of beauty have always existed, today they seem more demanding — if not easier to attain, thanks to the countless beauty tips available on the internet. Diets, physical exercise, make-up, creams, pills, vitamins: injunctions to stay beautiful and healthy (i.e. young, slim and radiant) are now reaching more and more people. In the 19th century, bodybuilding was the preserve of a small group of men who performed at fun fairs. Gradually, physical exercise became more popular at various levels of society. Photography played a prime part here because the first 'before and after' images, which we still find on social media today, appeared in the 1880s. At that time the 'after' images depicted athletes with strong physiques, but from the end of the 19th century an awareness of health began to encourage *everyone* to exercise outdoors, walk, swim and take up various sports. During the 1930s, the American illustrated press devoted pages to beauty creams and to the so-called natural beauty acquired by sun-bathing. In Europe, Hitler promoted the Greek ideal — a slender, muscular body — and the Soviets extolled the body as one of the perfectly oiled cogs of a mechanized society. Henceforth, sport, health and appearance went hand in hand.

Today the body has become an object that is entirely malleable and can be altered in an infinite number of ways. Flesh can be controlled, muscled, sculpted. Aside from working out and the cult of healthy eating, we are now offered products to be applied or swallowed, accompanied by surgical interventions of varying degrees of severity. In some countries, cosmetic surgery seems to have become an everyday, if not essential, procedure. Wrinkles and traces of age are less marked, breasts are inflated, the fat in the stomach and thighs melts away, the eyes open wider, the teeth are whitened, the hair is dyed, the eye colour changes, hair is shaved or otherwise removed, skin is artificially tanned, and so on. It is not only athletes who subject their body to the dictates of performance and force it to boost its output and efficiency. We are all being encouraged to tame and mould our bodies by mechanical, chemical, biological, pharmaceutical and other means. Perhaps we are in the process of creating mutant bodies, a new race. The French anthropologist David Le Breton calls this as a 'farewell to the body', and describes the body as a rough draft that needs to be corrected. Mastery of the body is achieved by a fierce battle that takes place throughout life, and sometimes begins even before birth. Test tubes, medically assisted reproduction, surrogate motherhood and incubators are some of the options offered to parents who want to create a child and bring it to term.

Once childhood is over, we must detach ourselves from the body we were born with and impose physical discipline on it in an attempt to achieve an ideal that has been disseminated in images fashioned by Western culture for more than a century. We are living in a society that has learned the art of mastering the body. Valérie Belin (pp. 108, 109, 127, 146, 147, 181) looks at this tyranny over the envelope of the body in several series. The body has become a fiction in the 21st century, a self-construction. We no longer work with it but on it, since it has become an aesthetic implement designed to be looked at and assessed. Lauren Greenfield (pp. 44–45, 148–49) is an attentive observer of the dictates imposed on it. But we must not be too quick to mock her subjects. Studies have shown that the body also reflects social inequalities: people who are regarded as unattractive get paid less and tend not to go on to further education. So the body is also a marker of our social position. That means it is vital to turn it into a beautiful sculpture. We control and standardize our bodies on the basis of certain measures and ideals, but we also pierce or tattoo them in order to create a personal identity, assume a certain attitude, and, above all, exist in the eyes of others.

In the 21st century the body and the face are no longer down to fate but down to a decision. Annette Messager (pp. 154–55) entitles her work, consisting of dozens of images of parts of the body, 'Mes Voeux' (My Vows) — offering a fragmented identity that composes itself like a kaleidoscope. The transsexuals depicted by Luis Arturo Aguirre (pp. 150, 151) and Bettina Rheims (pp. 152, 153) show the strenuous work involved. We need no longer be subjected to our body but can act with (or against) it in order to fashion the desired identity. Cindy Sherman (p. 142)

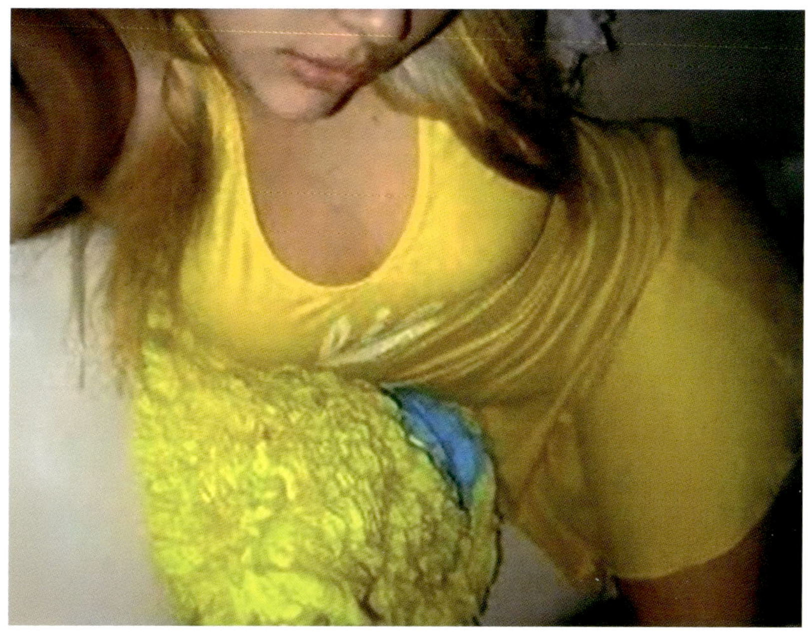

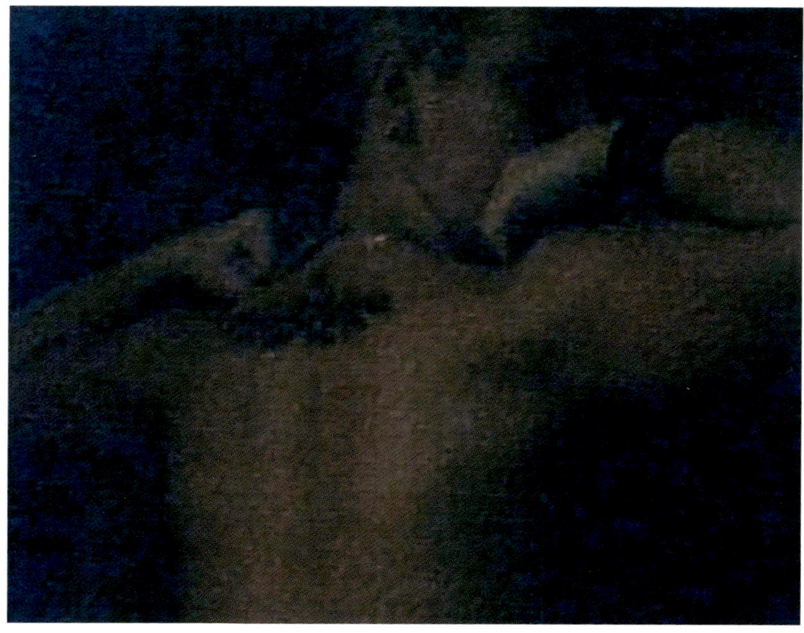

↑ (Top) **Ole John Aandal,** *Juvenilia no 31 (Girl in Yellow),* 2009
↑ (Above) **Ole John Aandal,** *Juvenilia no 16 (Dark Thorax),* 2009

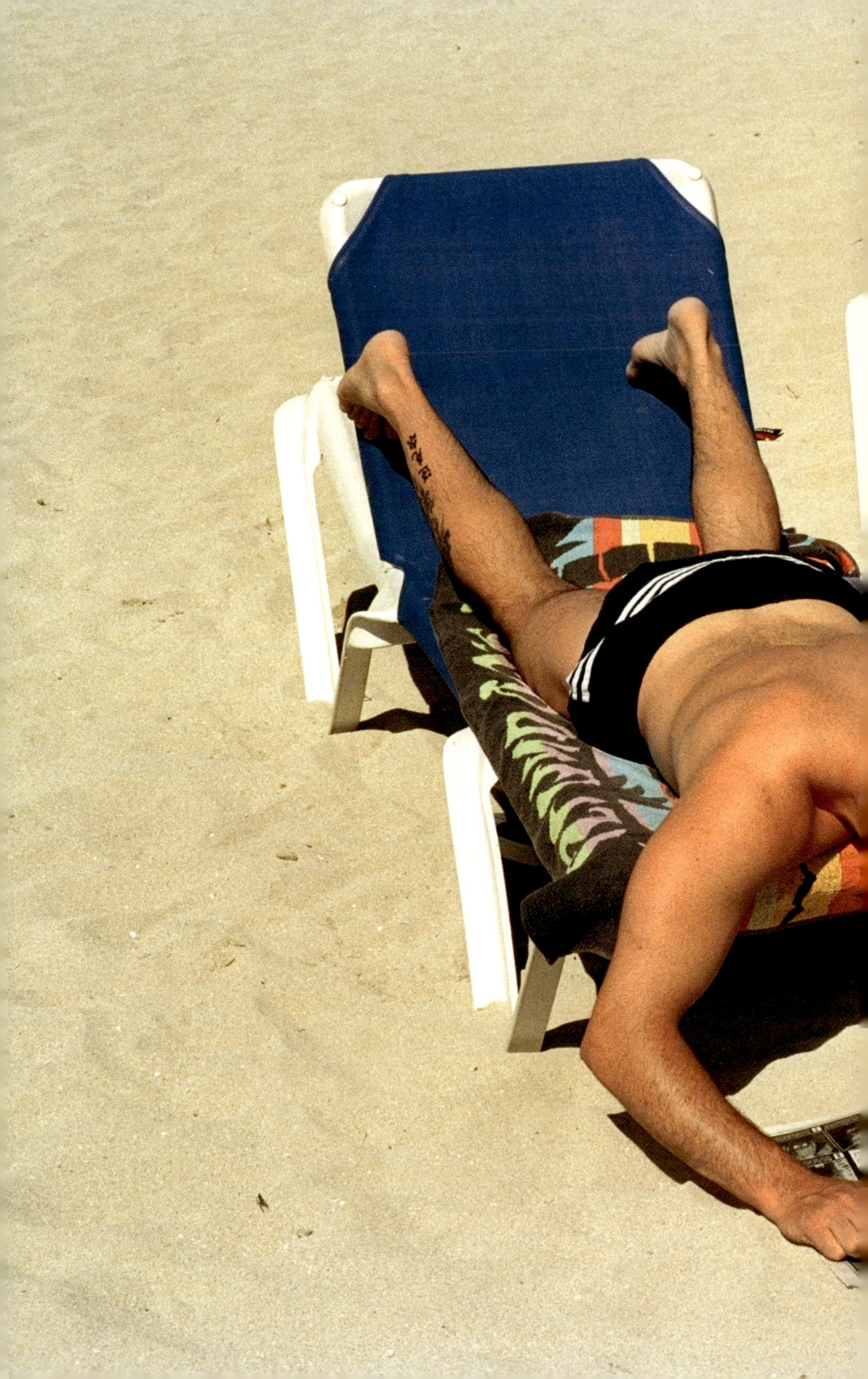

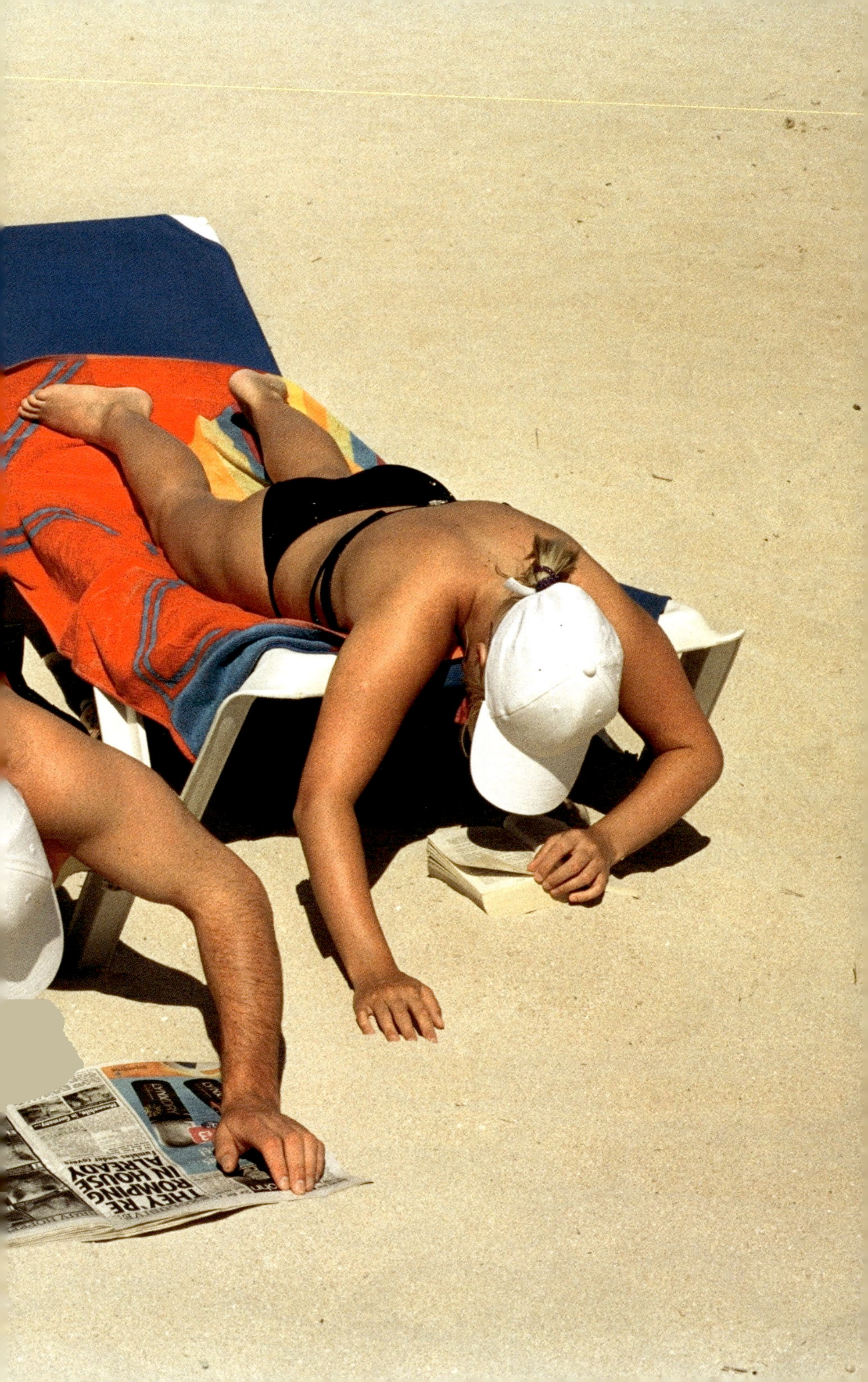
THEY'RE
ROMPING
IN HOUSE
ALREADY

has constantly modified her identity in her own way, first by means of disguise, then more recently by crudely manipulating her images. Romina Ressia (p. 139) and Hellen van Meene (pp. 164, 165) show that the body is an envelope that we are trying to tame from the time of adolescence. After that, we are mainly aware that the body can abandon us at any moment and that we therefore need to monitor it carefully. Even the elderly feel that they need to have a healthy and muscular body, as Erwin Olaf (p. 138) shows us. For on the one hand there are bodies that attract us ('a healthy mind in a healthy body') and on the other there are bodies that repel and that need to be transformed. We are living in the era of the body as ornament.

This raises a question: what is the exact relationship we want to maintain with our body? Is it an enemy or a friend? Do we hate it, enjoy it, or see it as a weapon for asserting our specific nature, as stated by the FEMEN activists photographed by Bettina Rheims (pp. 168, 169)? Fellow activist Zanele Muholi (pp. 170, 171), who is known mainly for her portrayals of the LGBTQIA+ community in South Africa, also poses this question and encourages us to question the manner in which we perceive race and gender roles today.

←(Previous) **Martin Parr,** *Magaluf, Majorca, Spain,* 2003

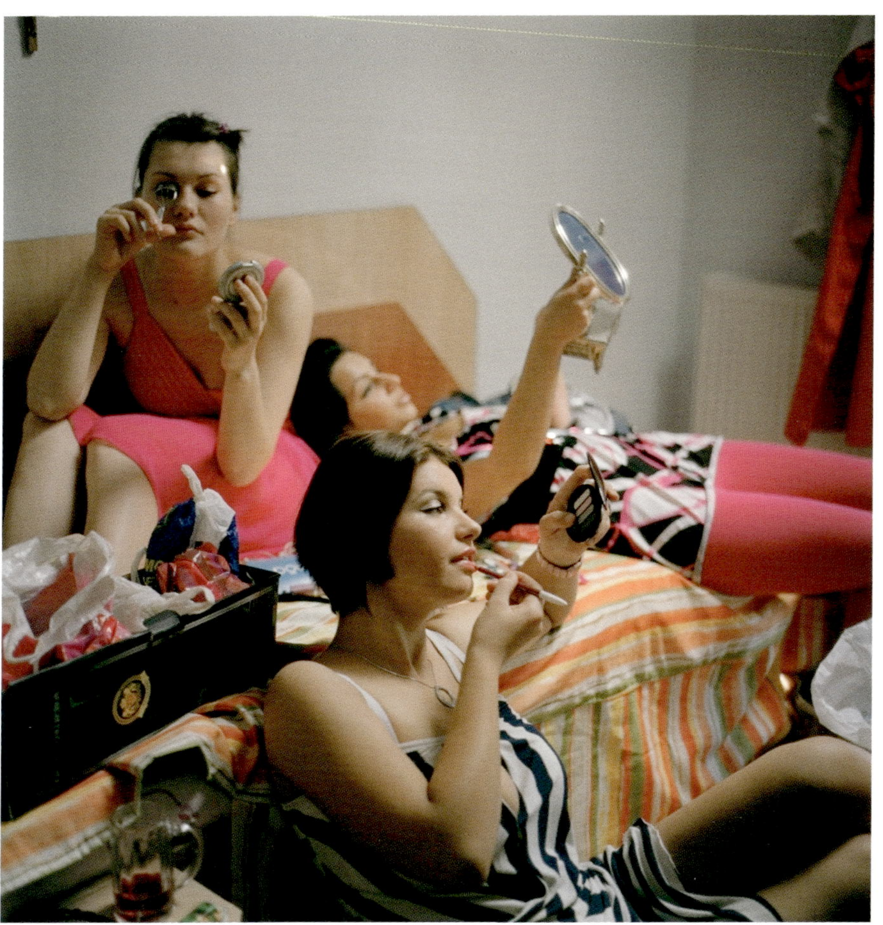

↑ **Dana Popa,** *'You must marry a German citizen and skip these queues,'*
says one mother to her young daughter while both had been waiting in
a long queue overnight in front of the German Embassy in Bucharest,
Romania, 2010

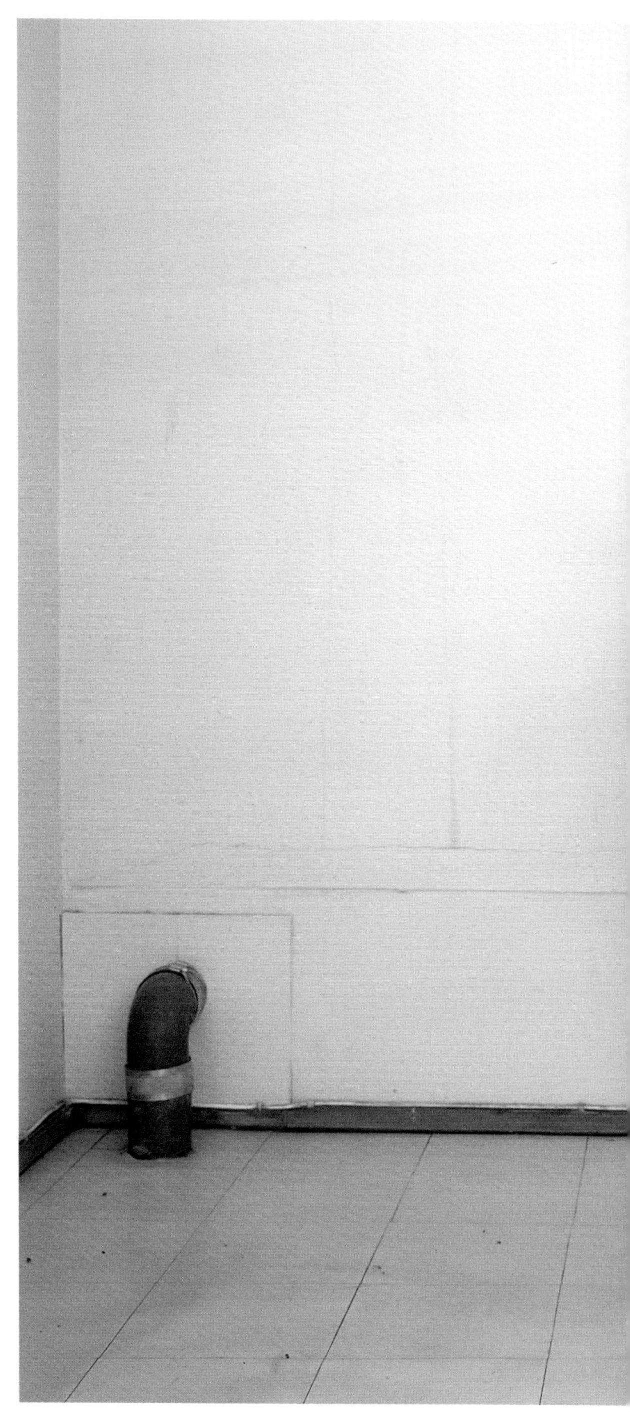

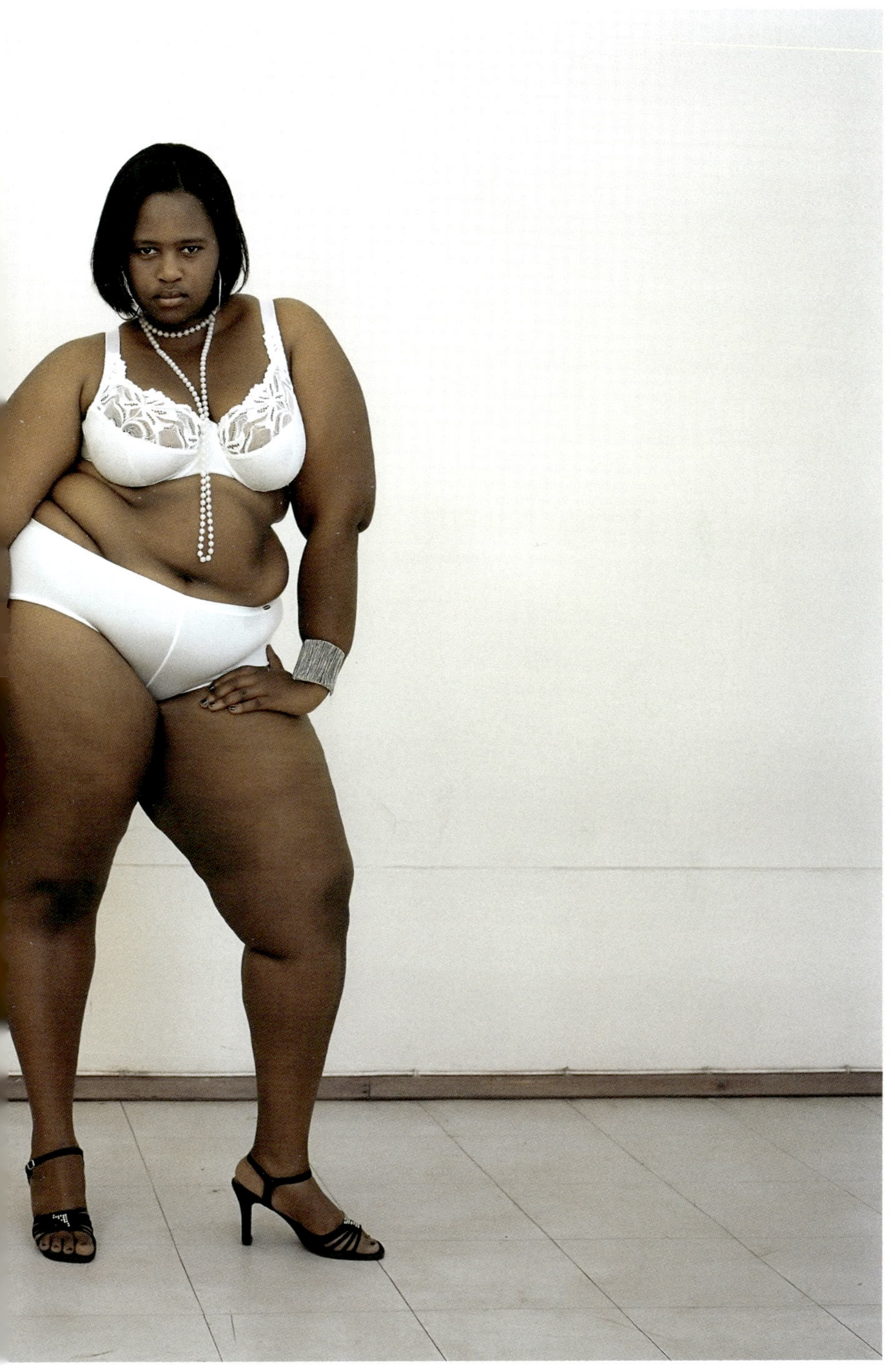

↑ **Jodi Bieber,** *Babalwa*, from the series 'Real Beauty', 2008

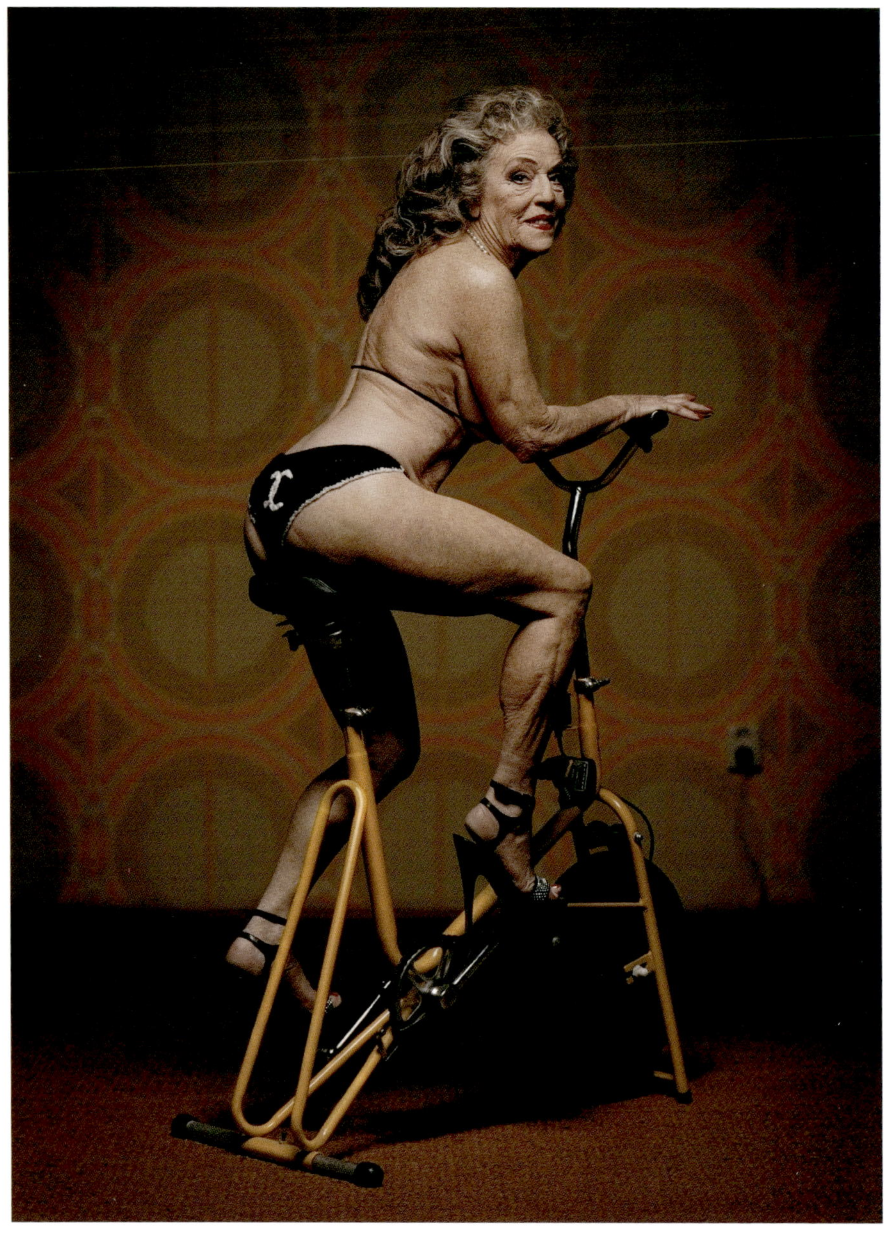

↑ **Erwin Olaf,** *Cindy C., 78,* **** from the series 'Mature', 1999

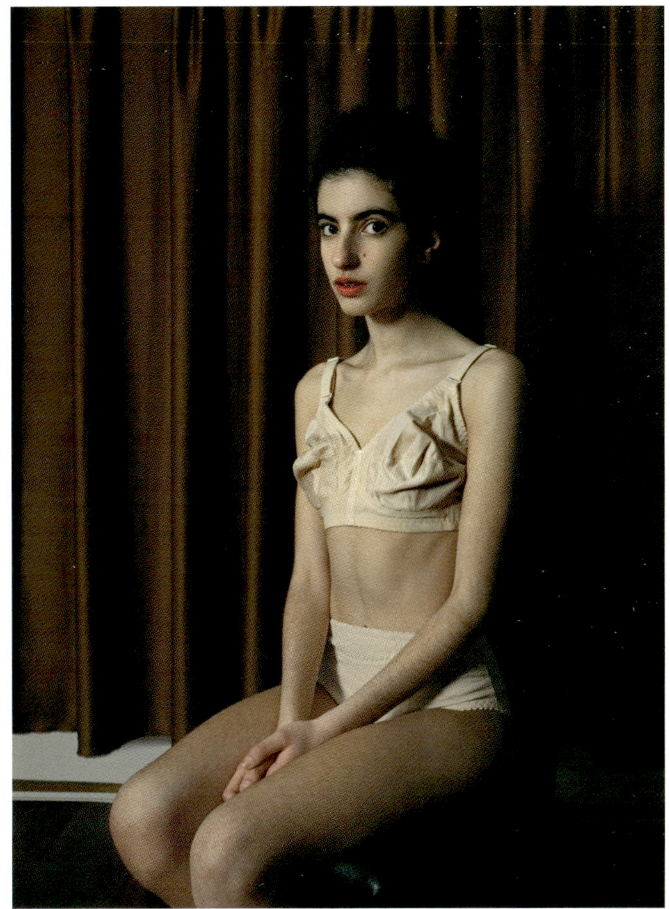

↑ Romina Ressia, *Mica*, 2016

→**Cara Phillips,** *Blue Liposuction Machine, Century City, CA, 2007*

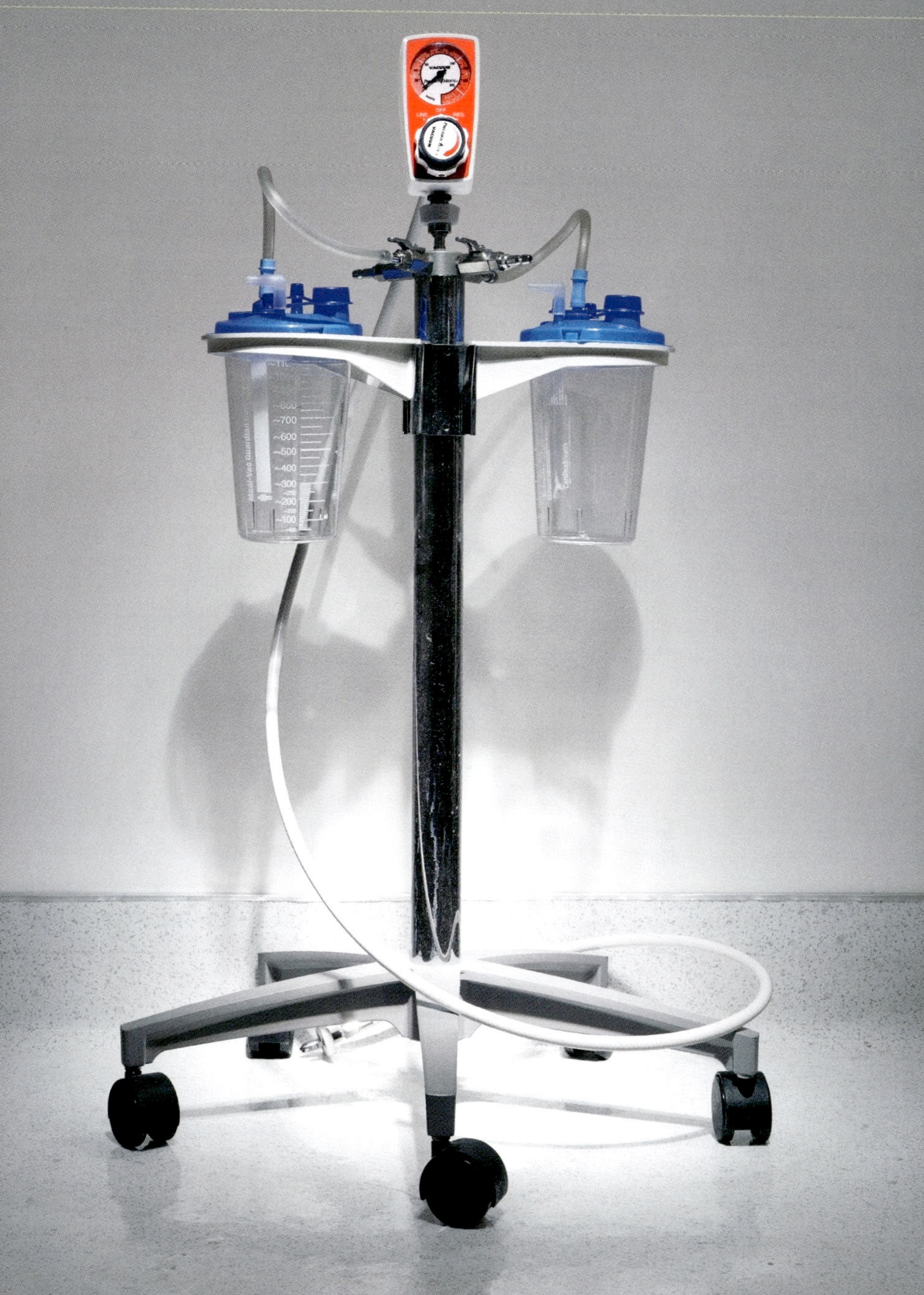

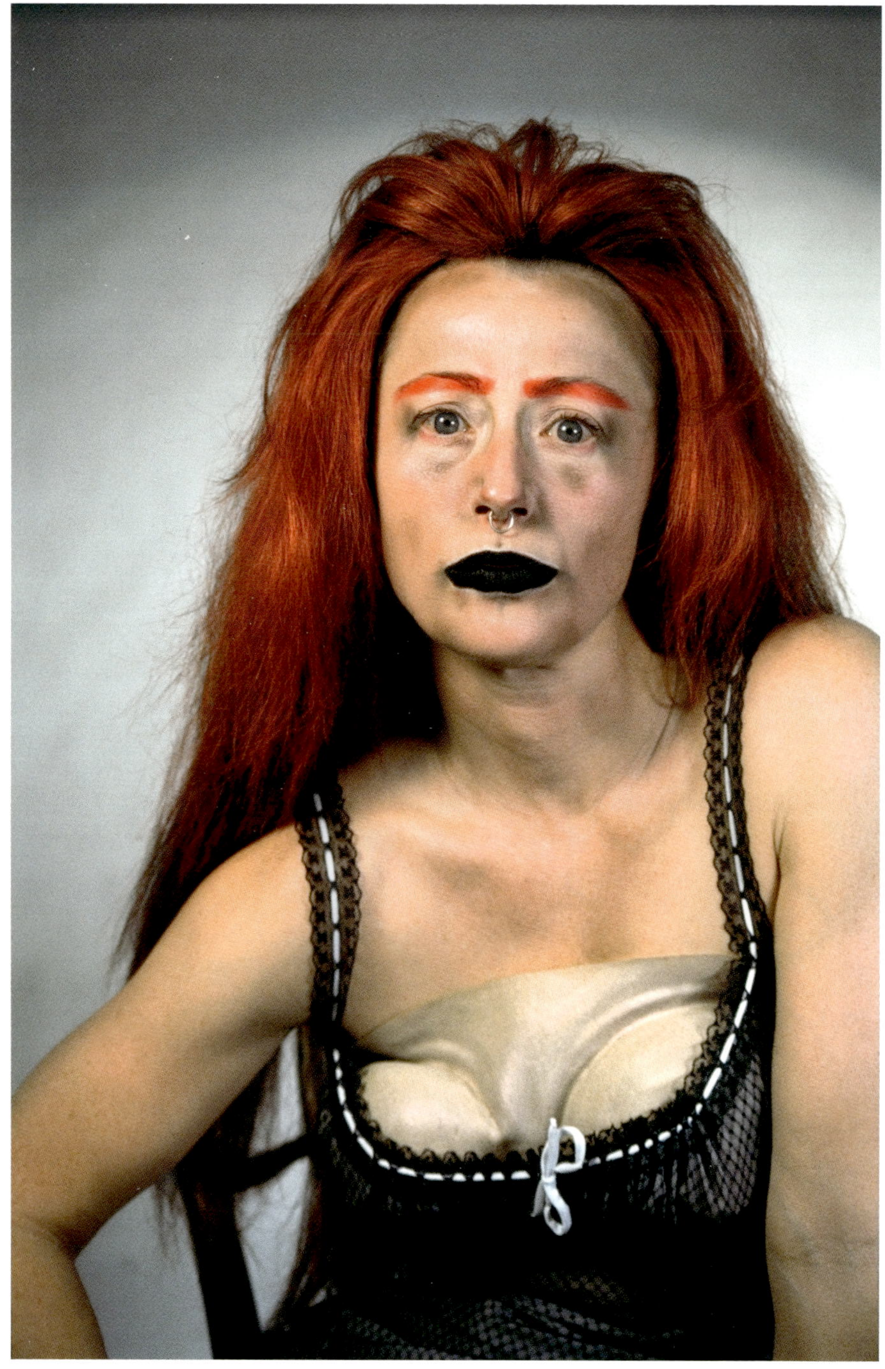

↑ **Cindy Sherman,** *Untitled #352,* 2000

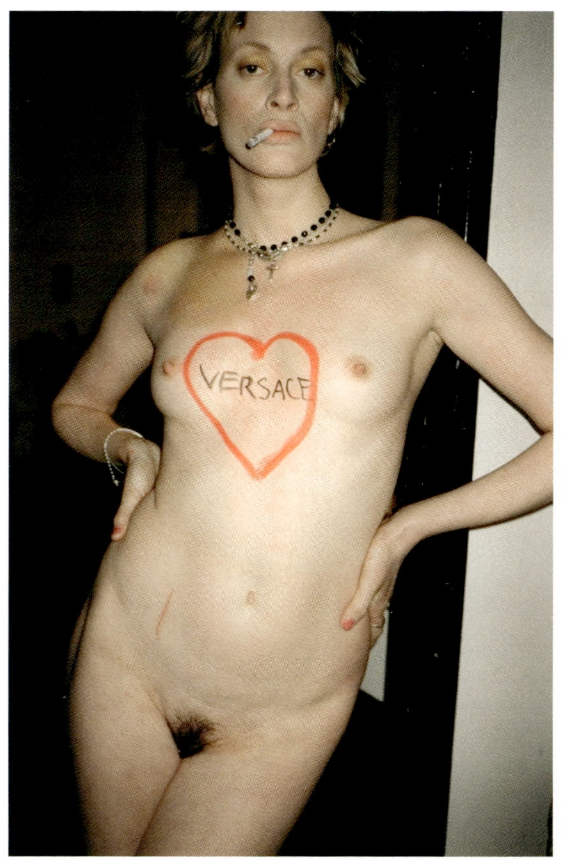

↑ **Juergen Teller,** *Kristen McMenamy No. 3, London,* 1996

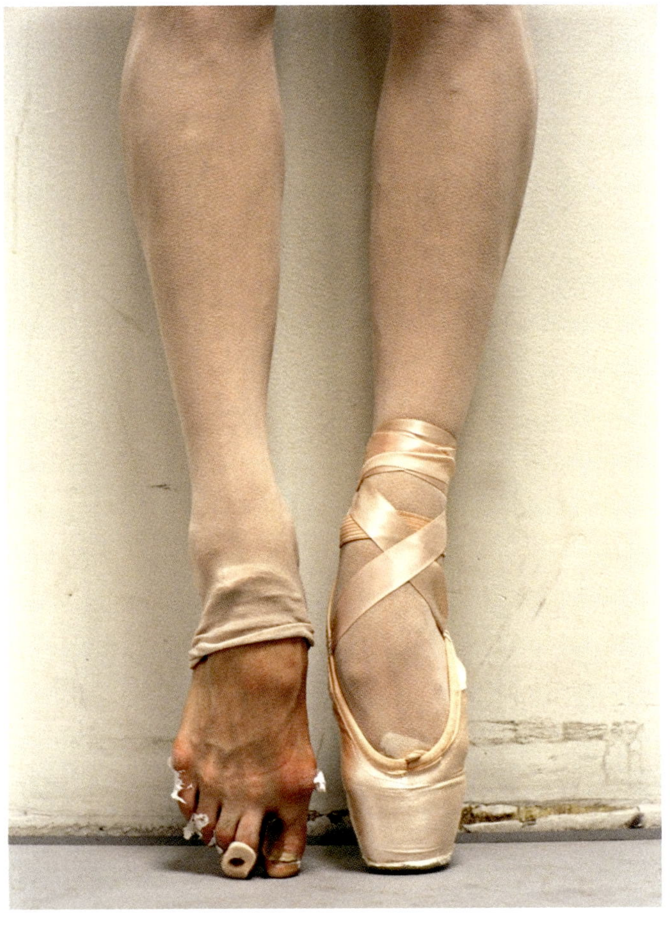

↑ **Henry Leutwyler,** *Megan LeCrone, soloist, New York City Ballet, 2011*

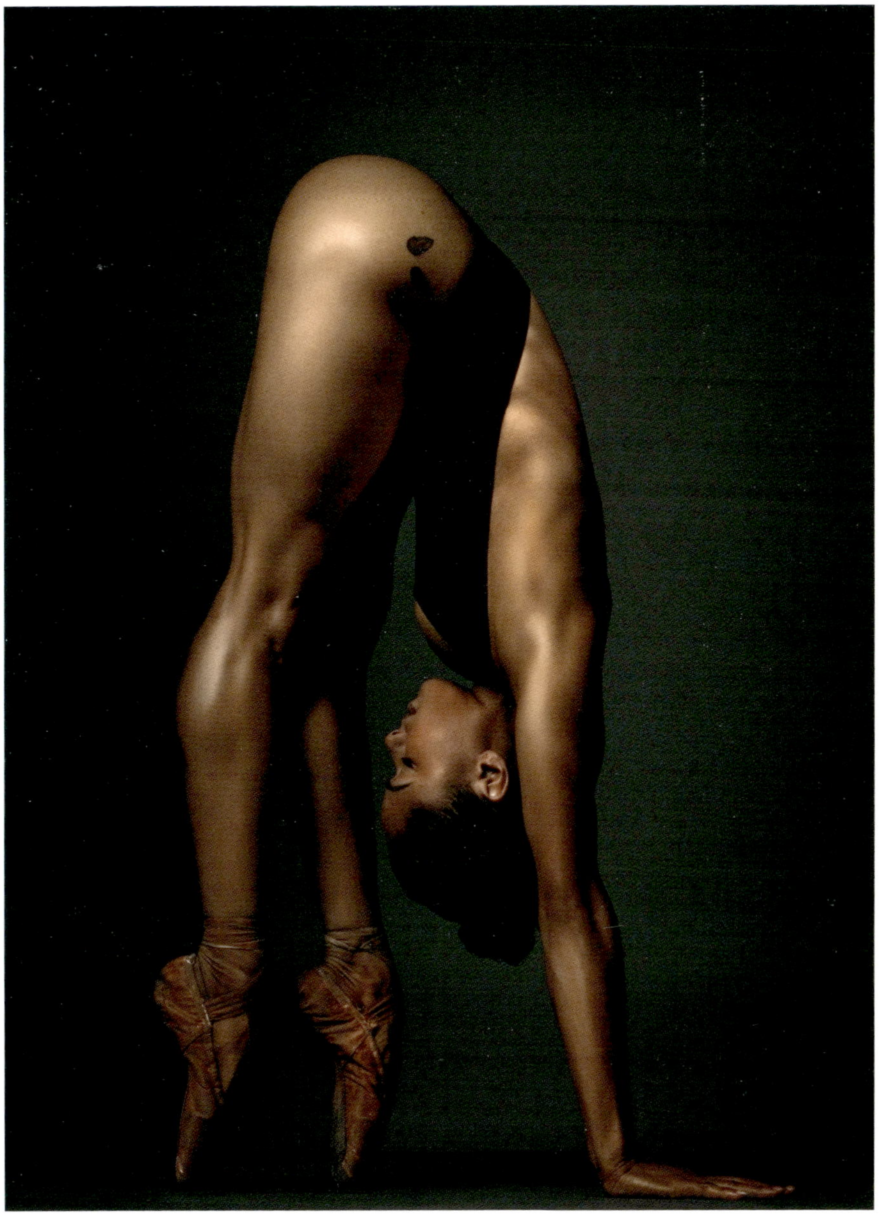

↑ **Henry Leutwyler,** *Misty Copeland, studies,* 2013

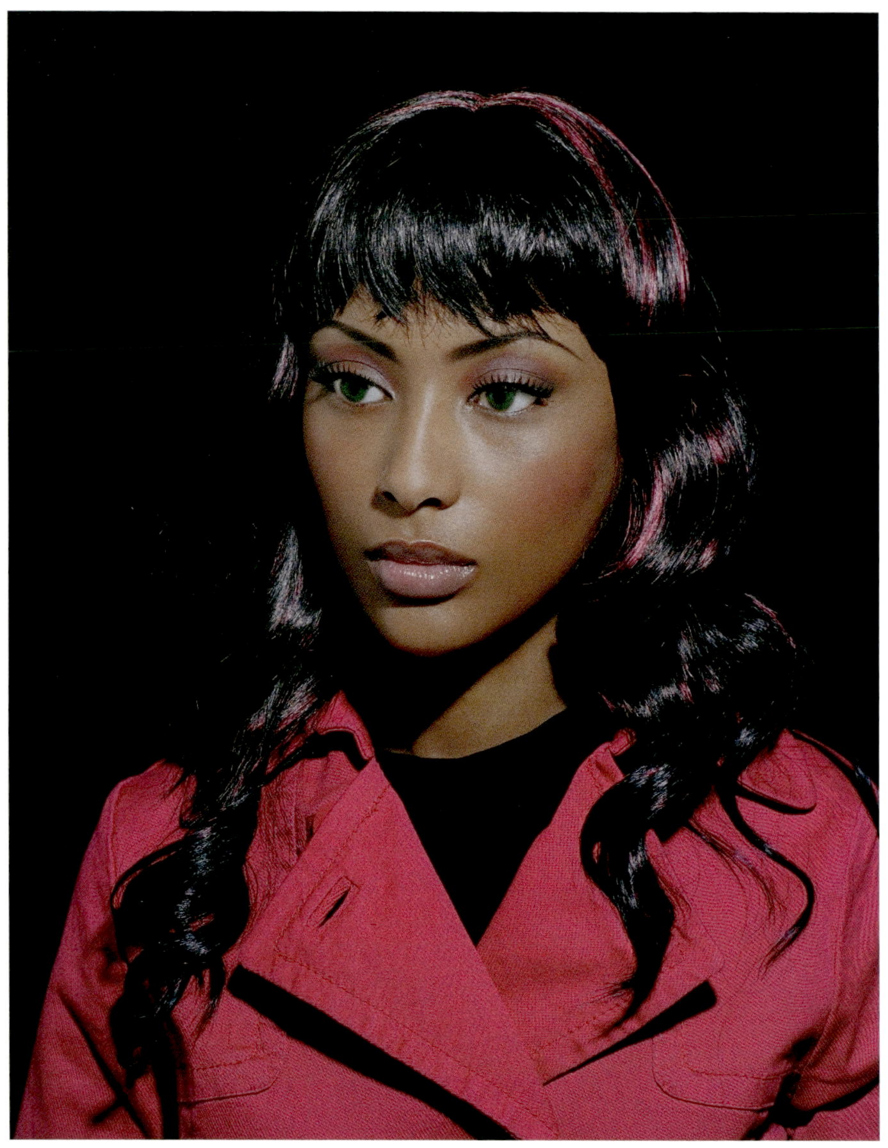

↑ **Valérie Belin,** *Untitled*, from the series 'Black Women II', 2006

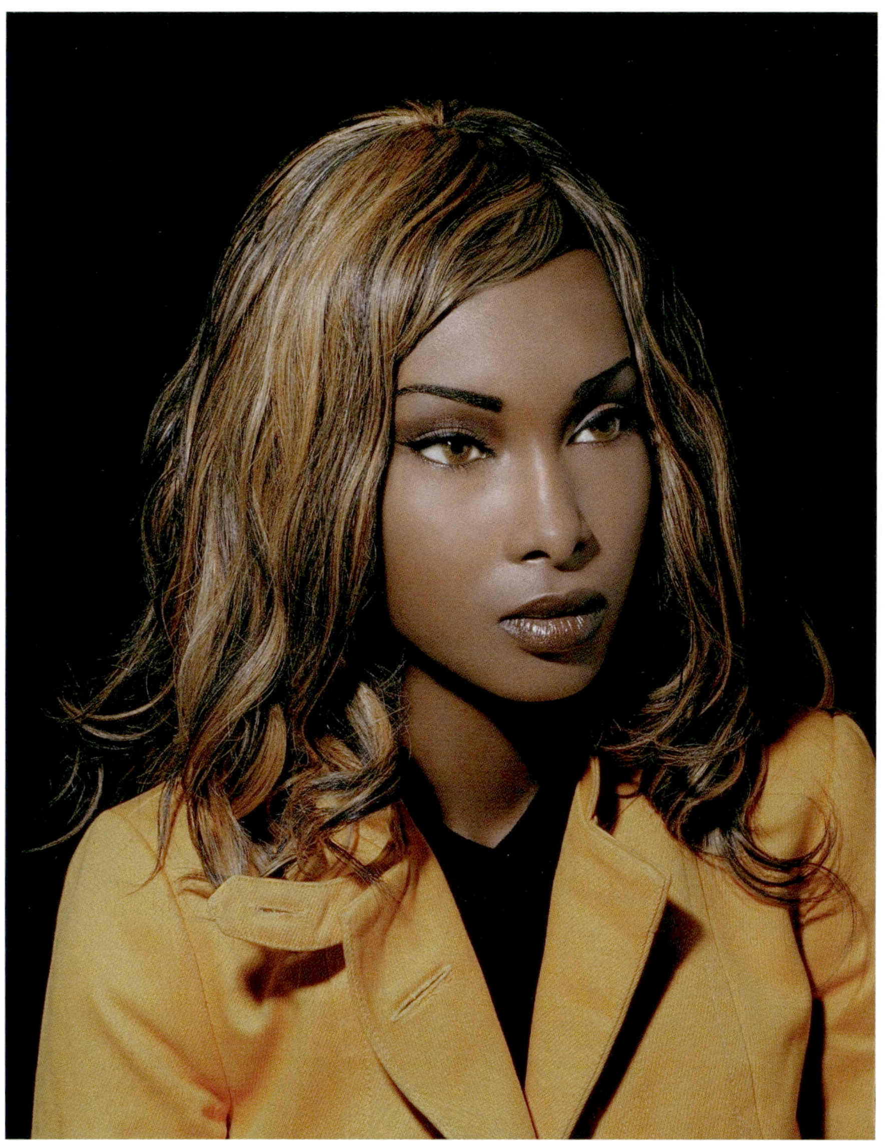

↑ **Valérie Belin,** *Untitled*, from the series 'Black Women II', 2006

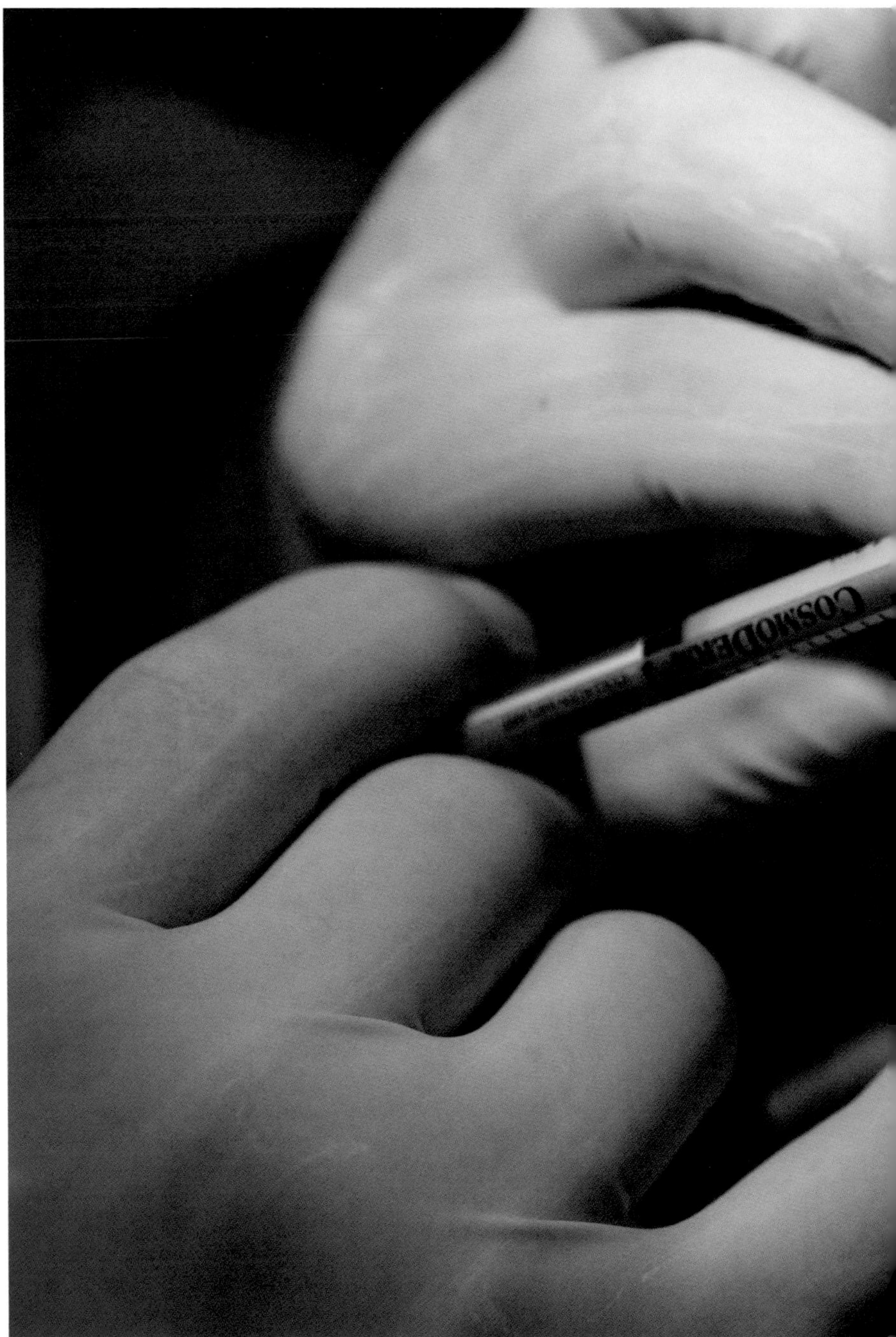

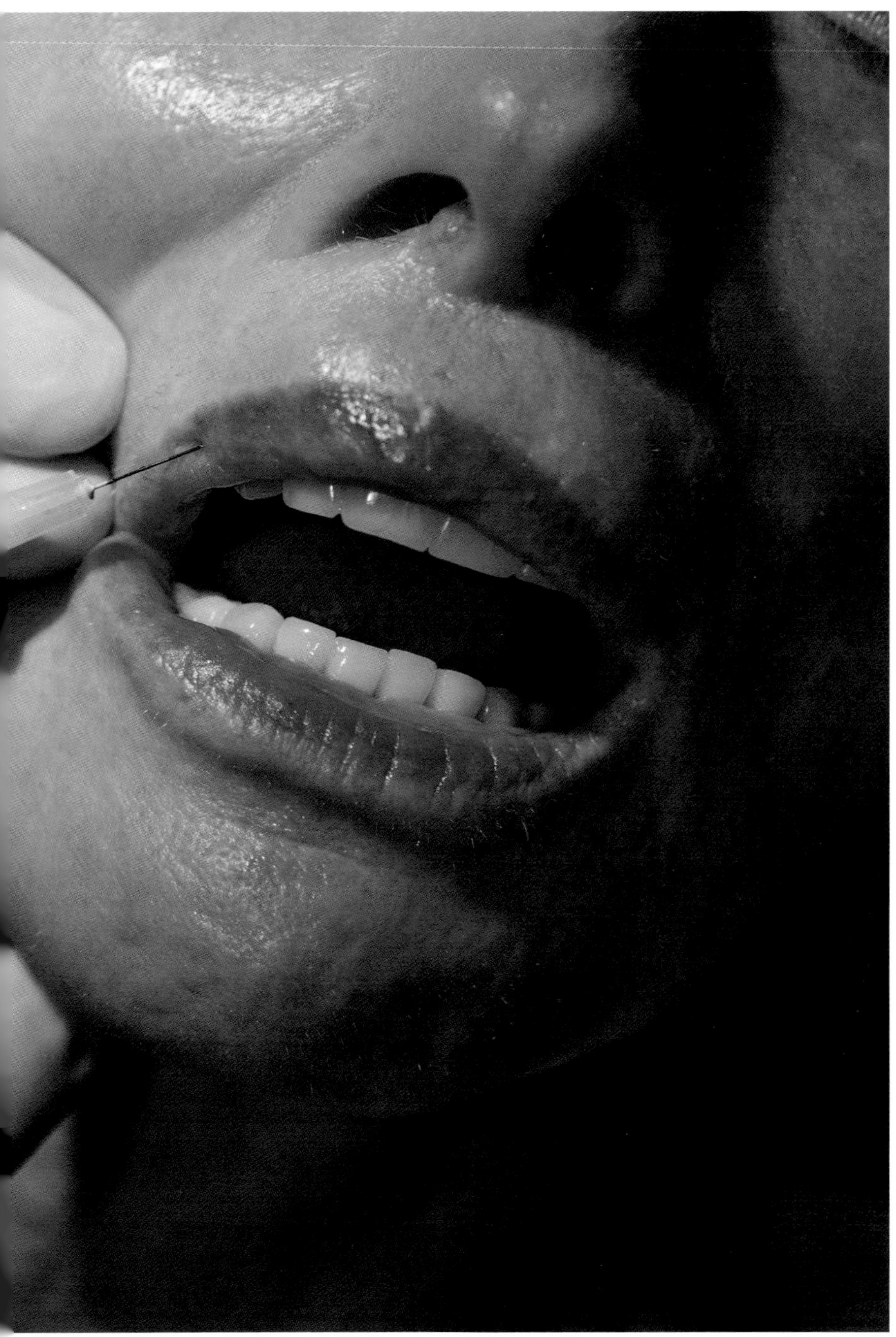

↑ **Lauren Greenfield,** *Dermatologist Dr Arnold Klein, 61, dubbed 'the King of Lips', injects 'the Pink Lady' Jackie Goldberg, 72, with collagen, Beverly Hills, 2005. 'I'm just hitting that great stage of Restylane, Botox,' she says. 'I love it. I'm hoping by the time I'm eighty-eight or ninety, there'll be something new for me to do.'*

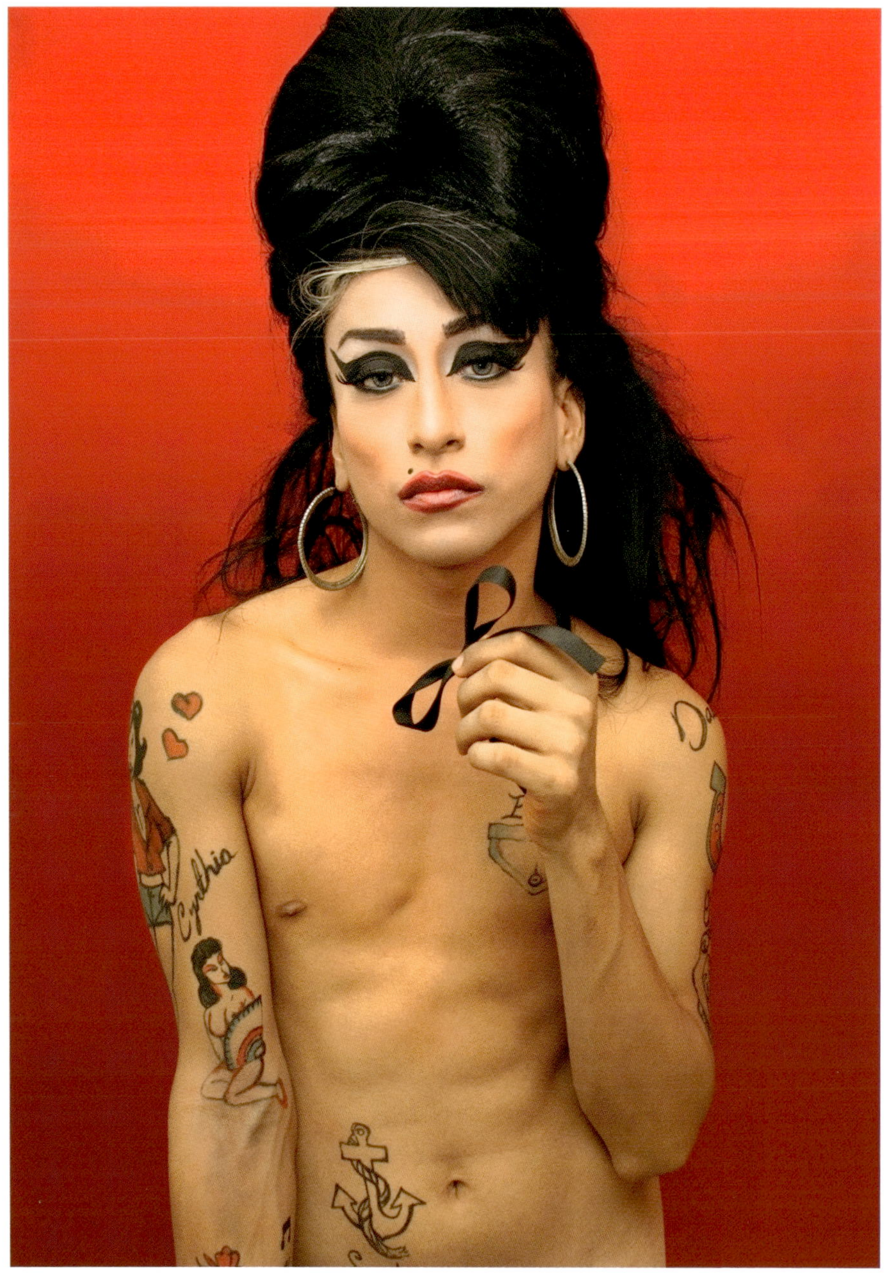

↑ **Luis Arturo Aguirre,** *Phoebe,* from the series 'Desvestidas', 2011

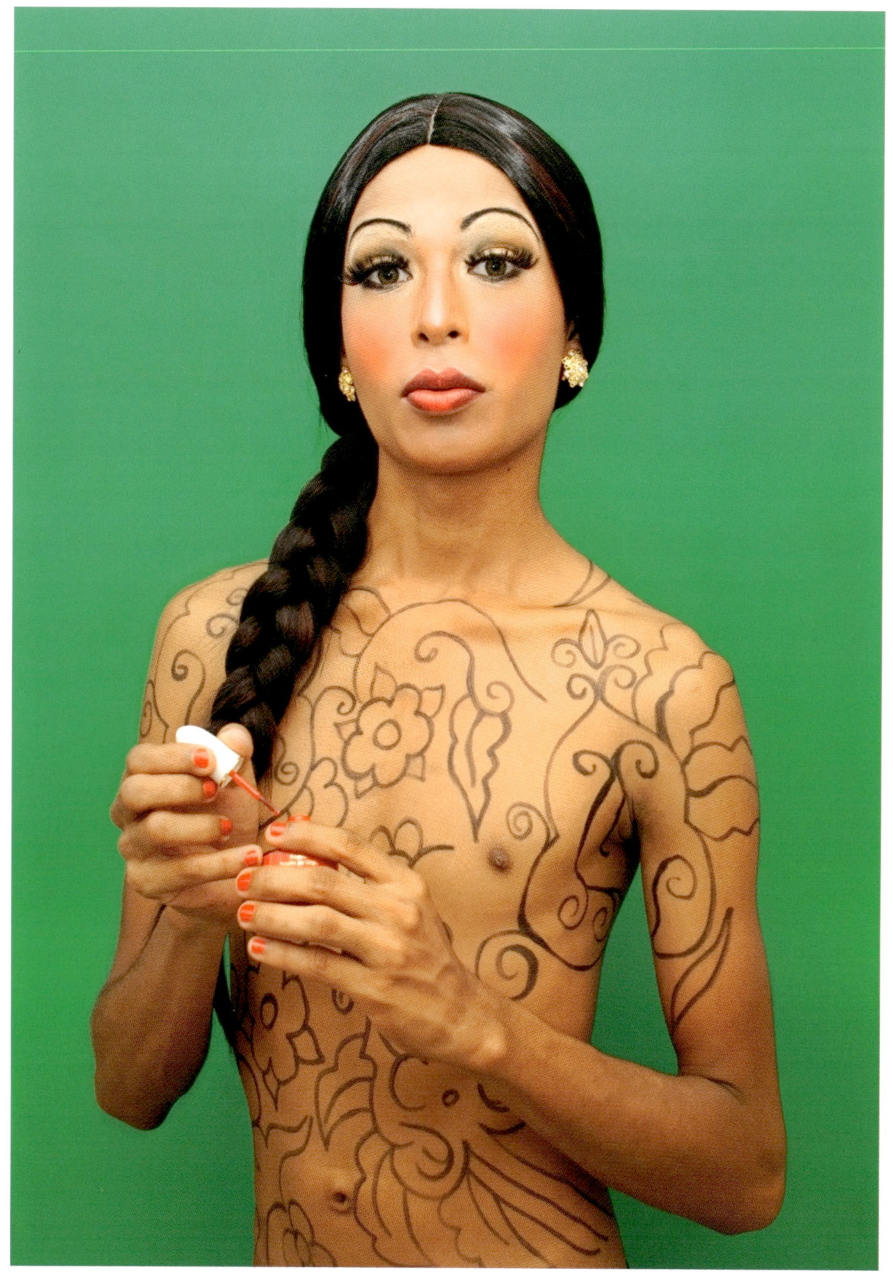

↑ **Luis Arturo Aguirre,** *Yajaira,* from the series 'Desvestidas', 2011

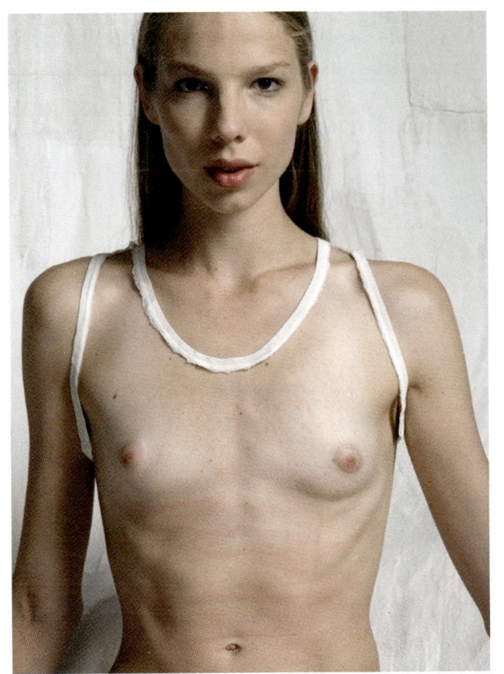

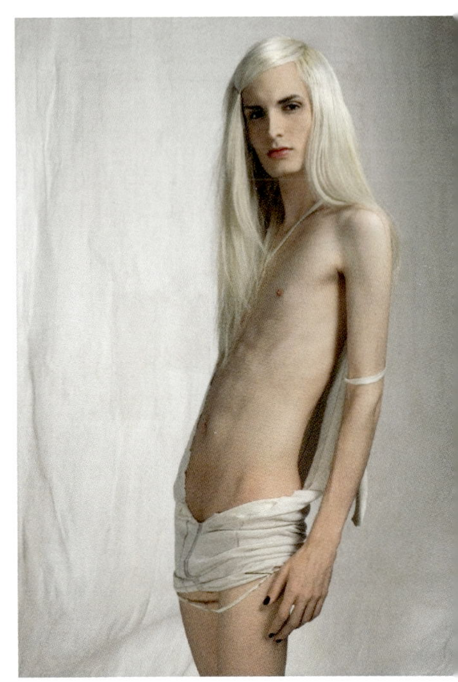

↑ (Left) **Bettina Rheims,** *Valentijn de H. II, June, Paris,*
from the series 'Gender Studies', 2011
↑ (Right) **Bettina Rheims,** *Miles D., June, Paris,*
from the series 'Gender Studies', 2011

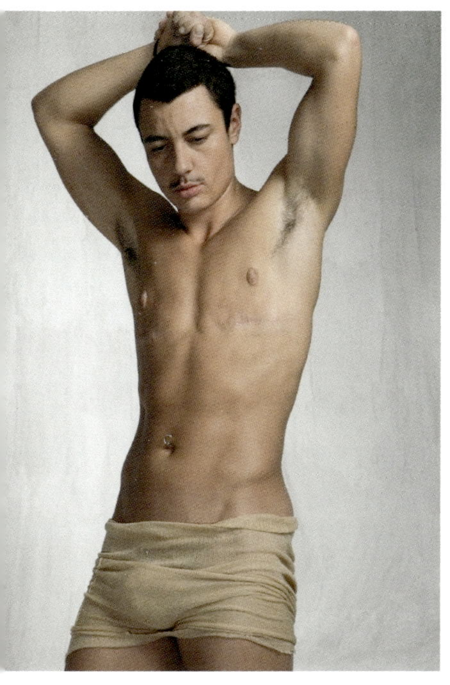

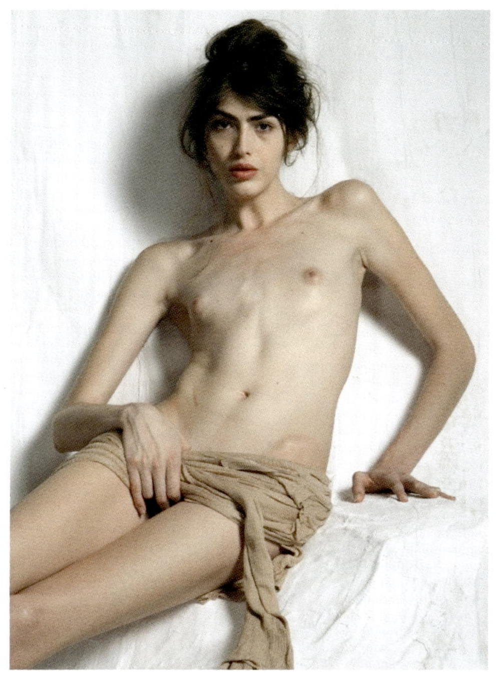

↑ (Left) **Bettina Rheims,** *Mattia S., June, Paris,* from the series 'Gender Studies', 2011
↑ (Right) **Bettina Rheims,** *Dafné C. II, June, Paris,* from the series 'Gender Studies', 2011

→**Annette Messager**, *Mes Voeux* [My Vows], 1989

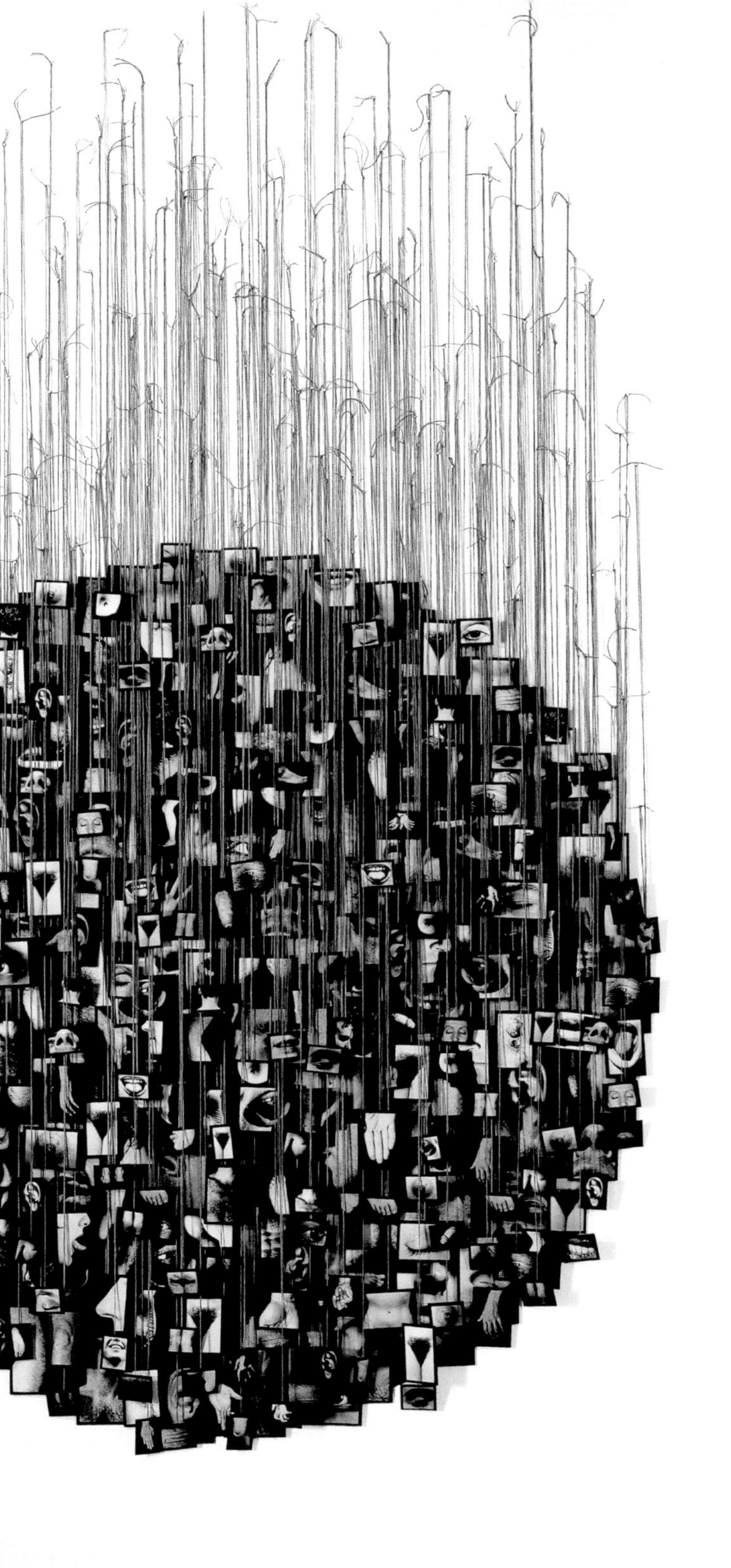

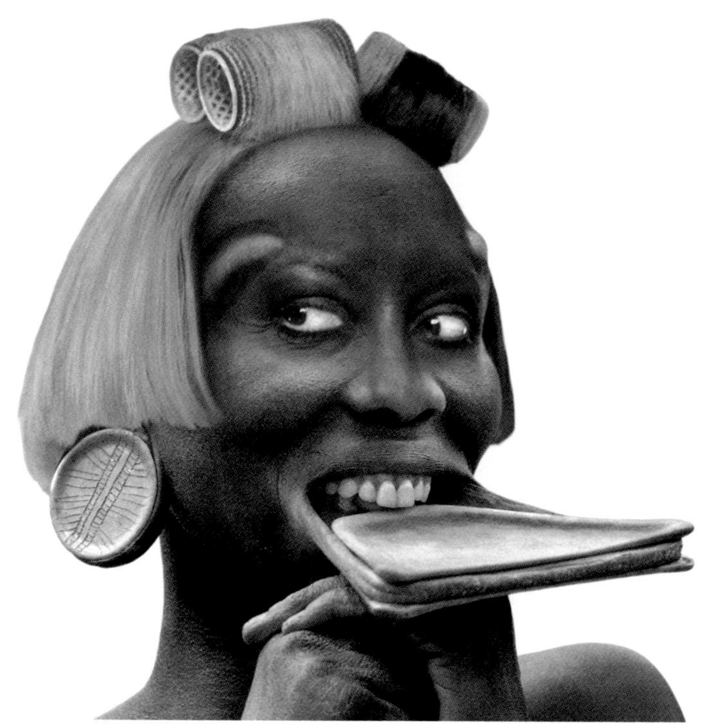

↑ **ORLAN,** *African Self-Hybridization. Surmas Woman with Lip Plug and Face of Euro-Stéphanoise Woman with Rollers, 2000.*

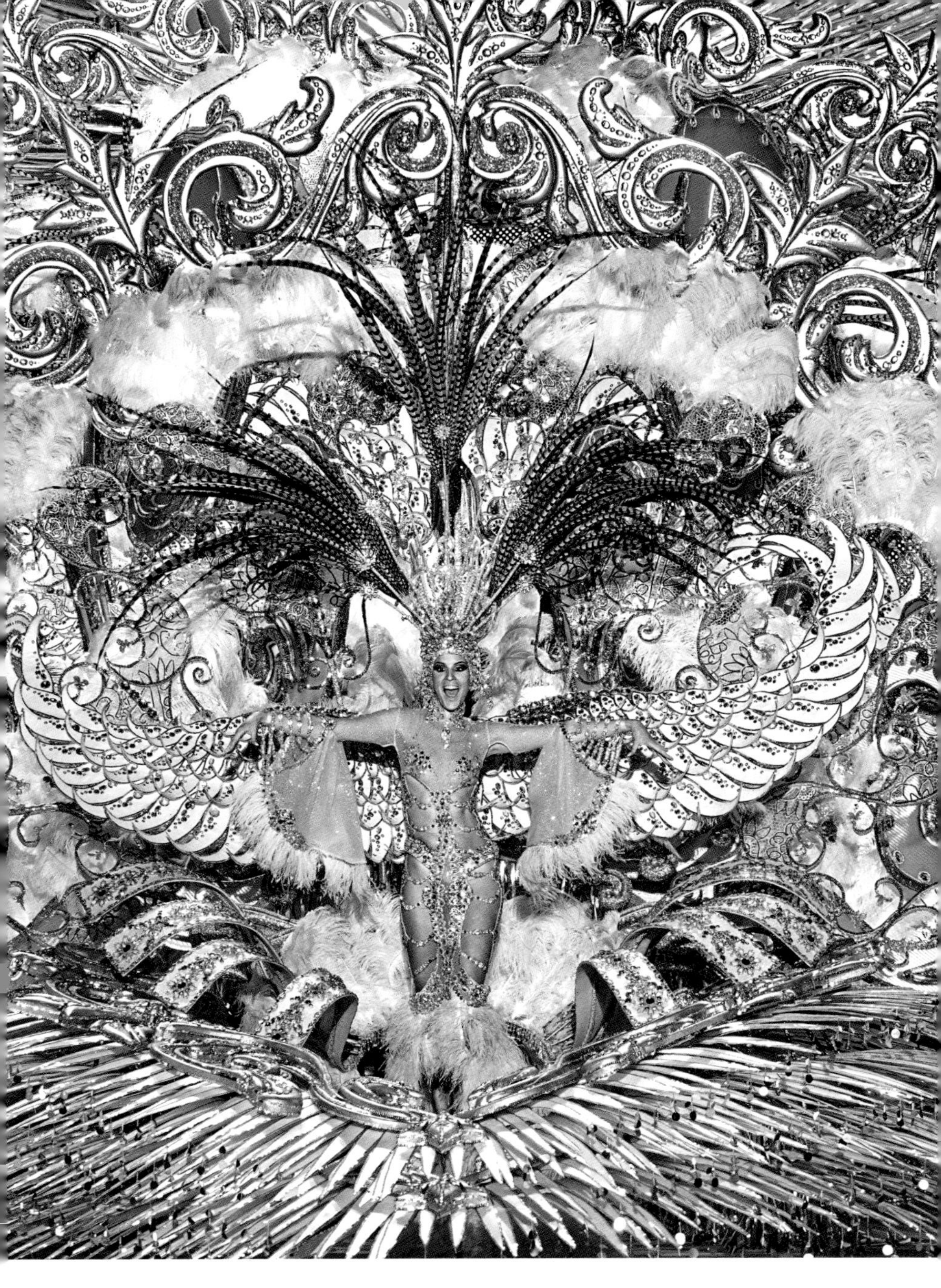

↑ **Cyril Porchet**, Untitled, from the series 'Reina', 2014

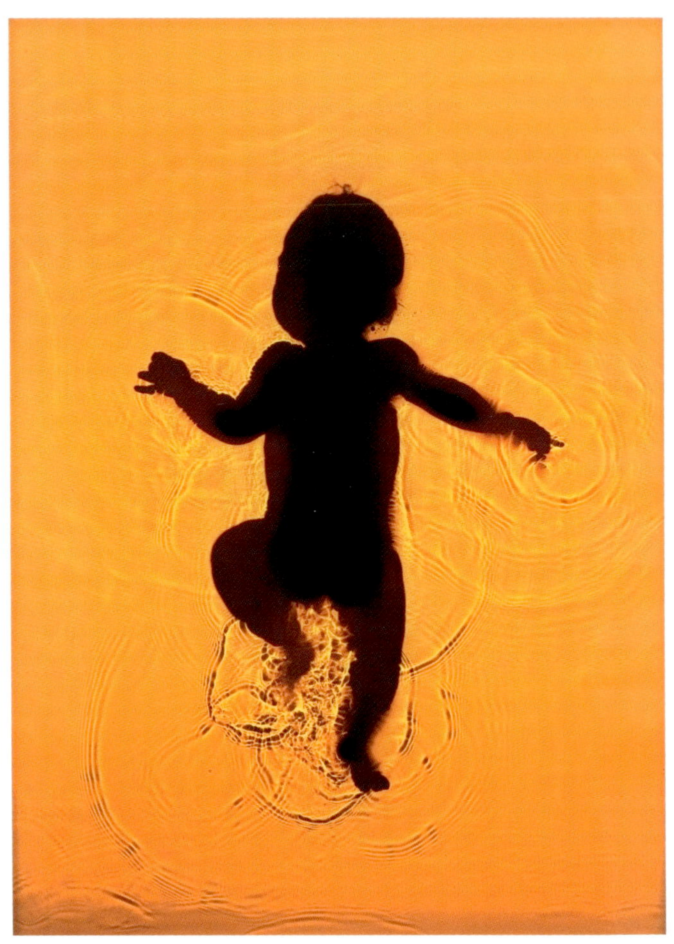

↑ **Adam Fuss,** *Untitled,* unique Cibachrome photogram, 2017
→**Catherine Opie,** *Self-Portrait / Cutting,* 1993

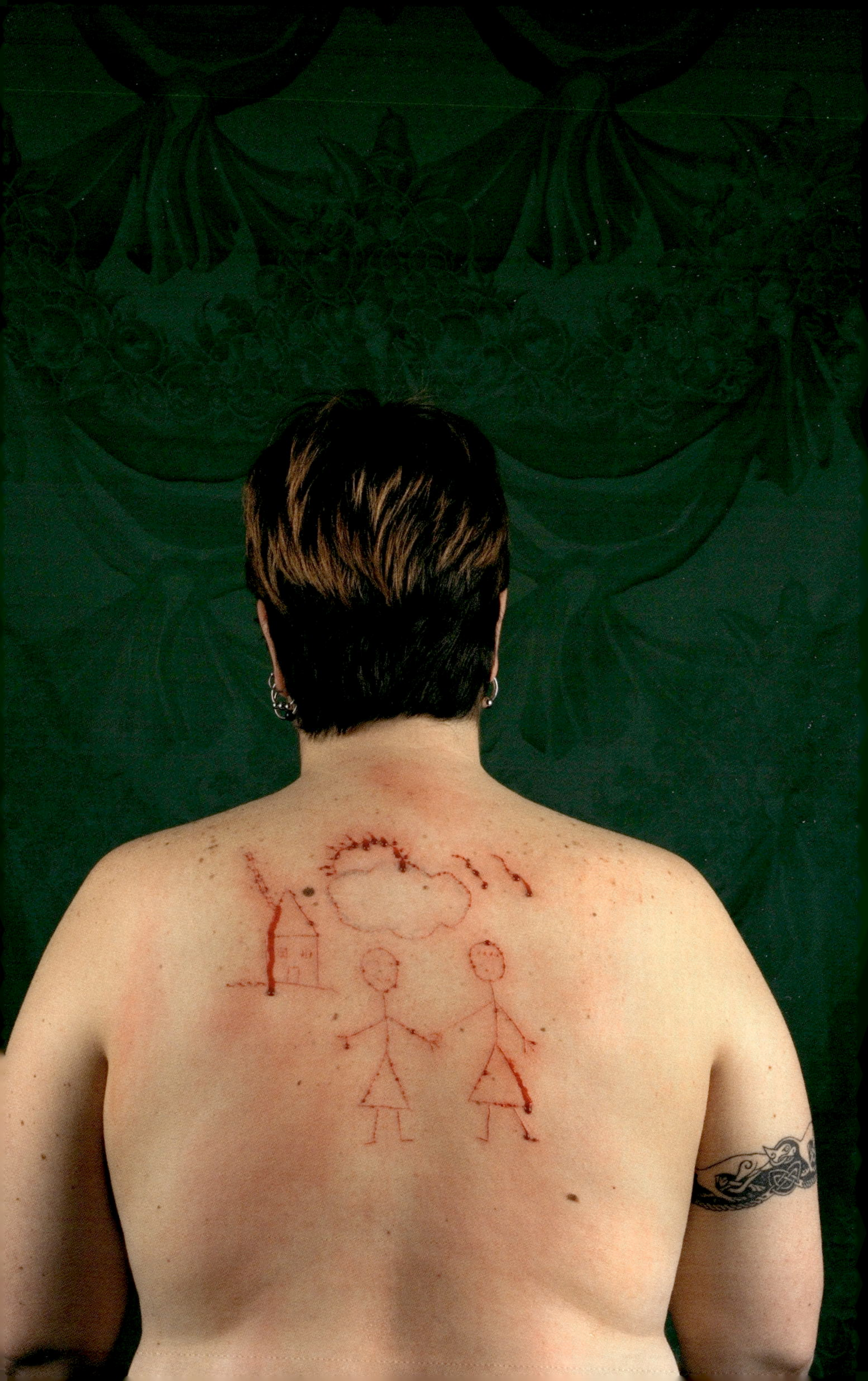

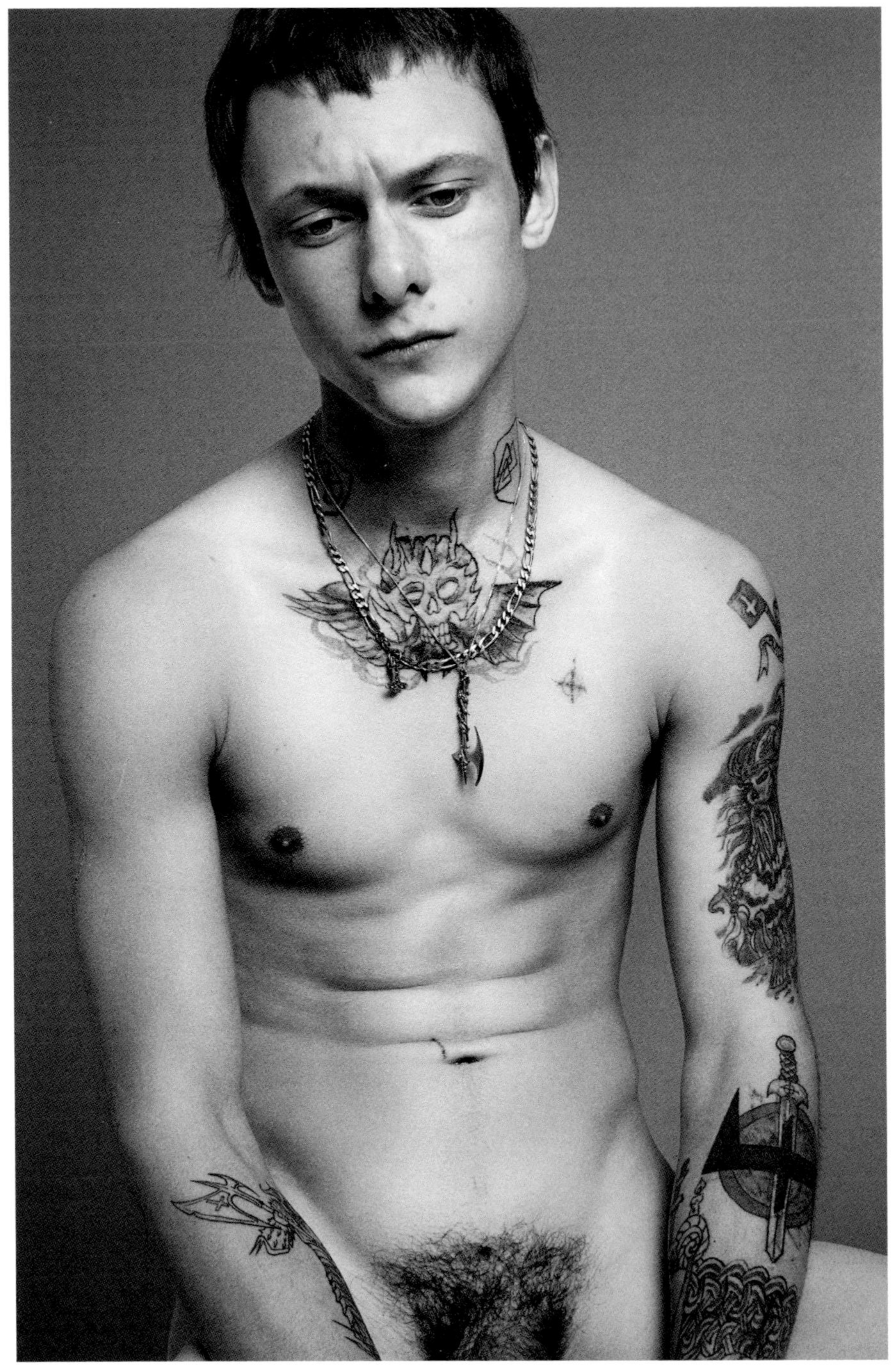

↑ Ryan McGinley, *Jasper*, 2010

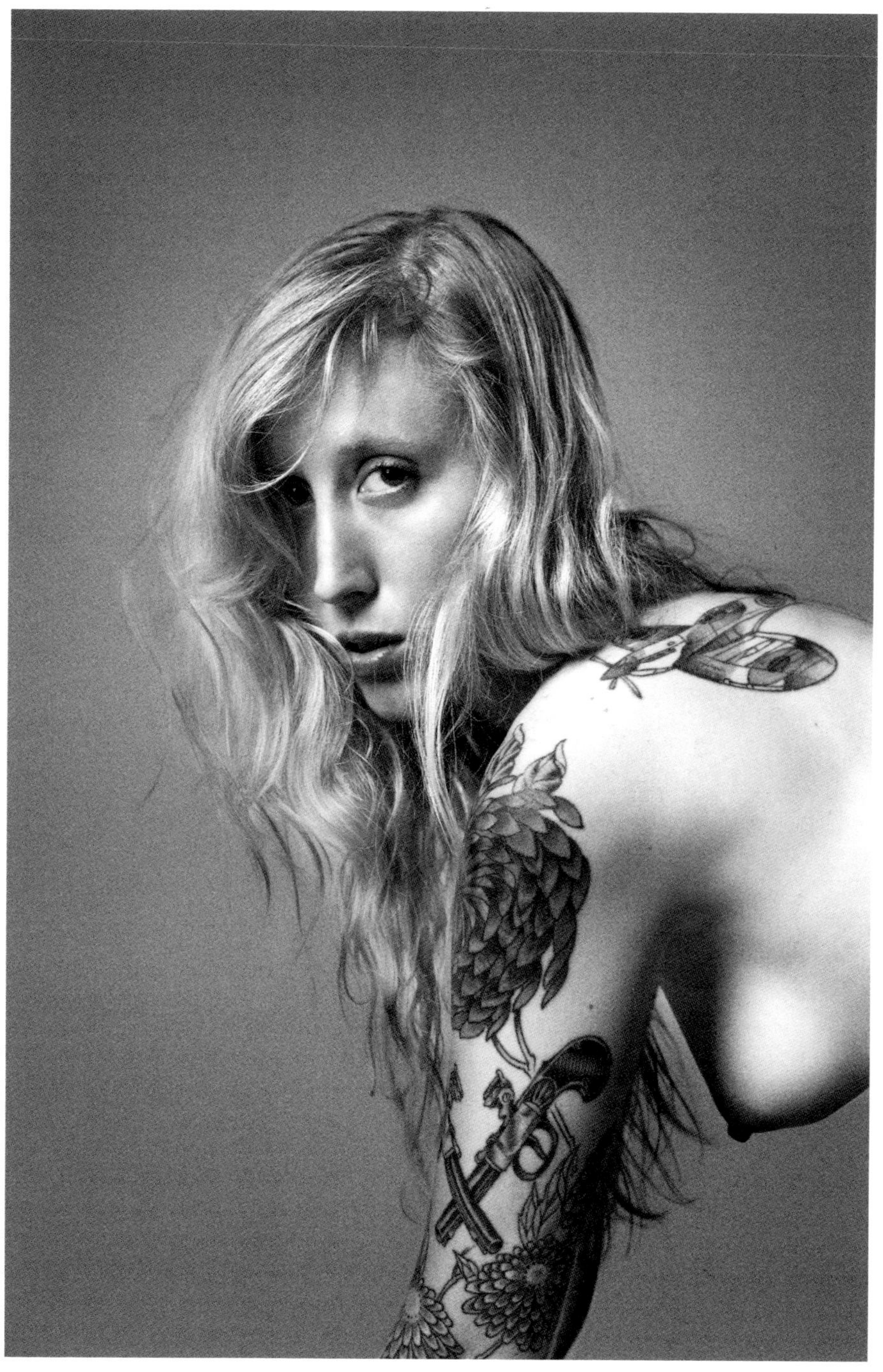

↑ Ryan McGinley, *Rachel*, 2011

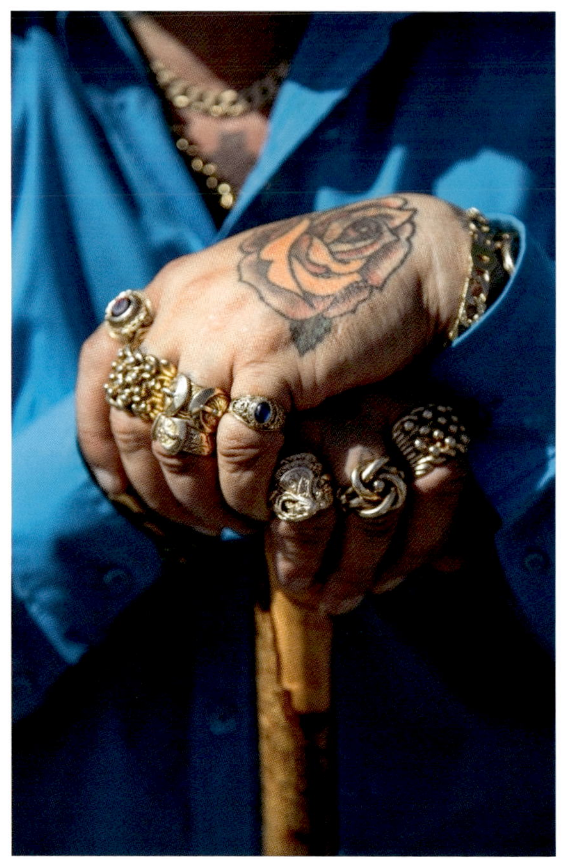

↑ **David Julian Leonard,** *William of Cork, Ireland,* 2014

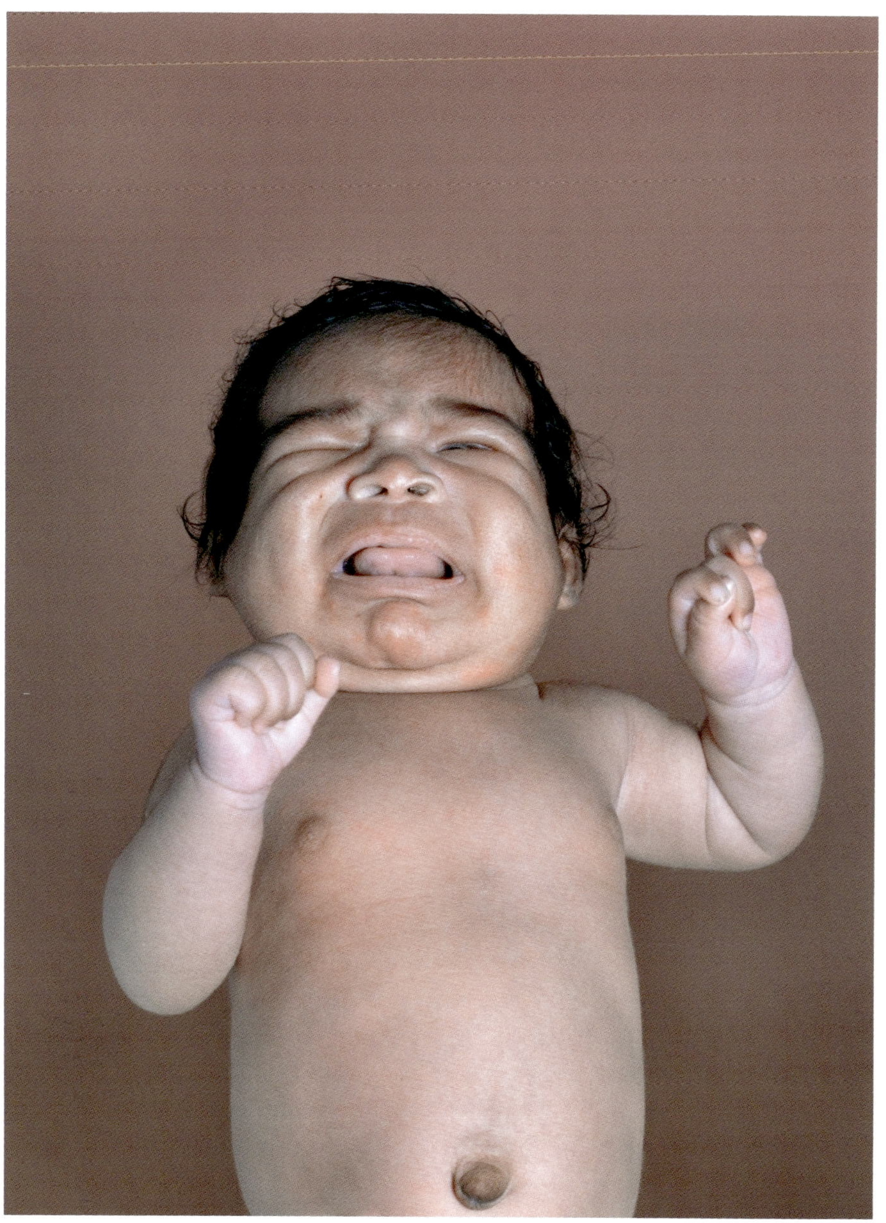

↑ **Romina Ressia,** *Shamira,* 2017

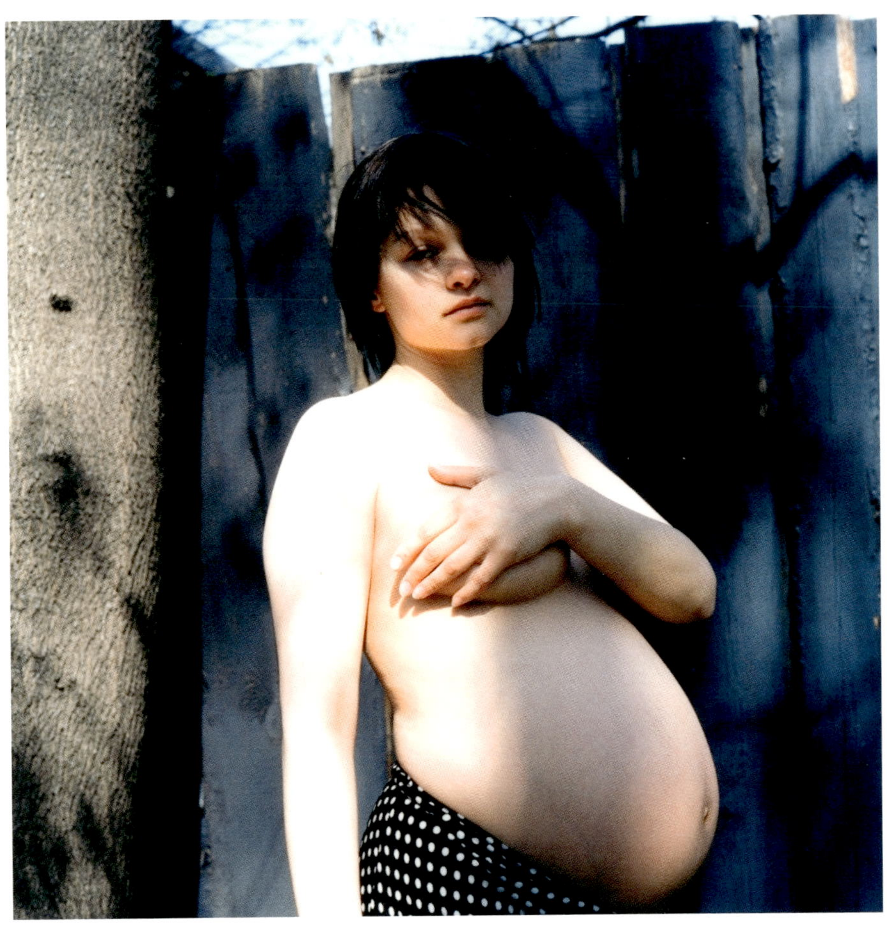

↑ **Hellen van Meene,** *Untitled, Riga, Latvia, 2004*

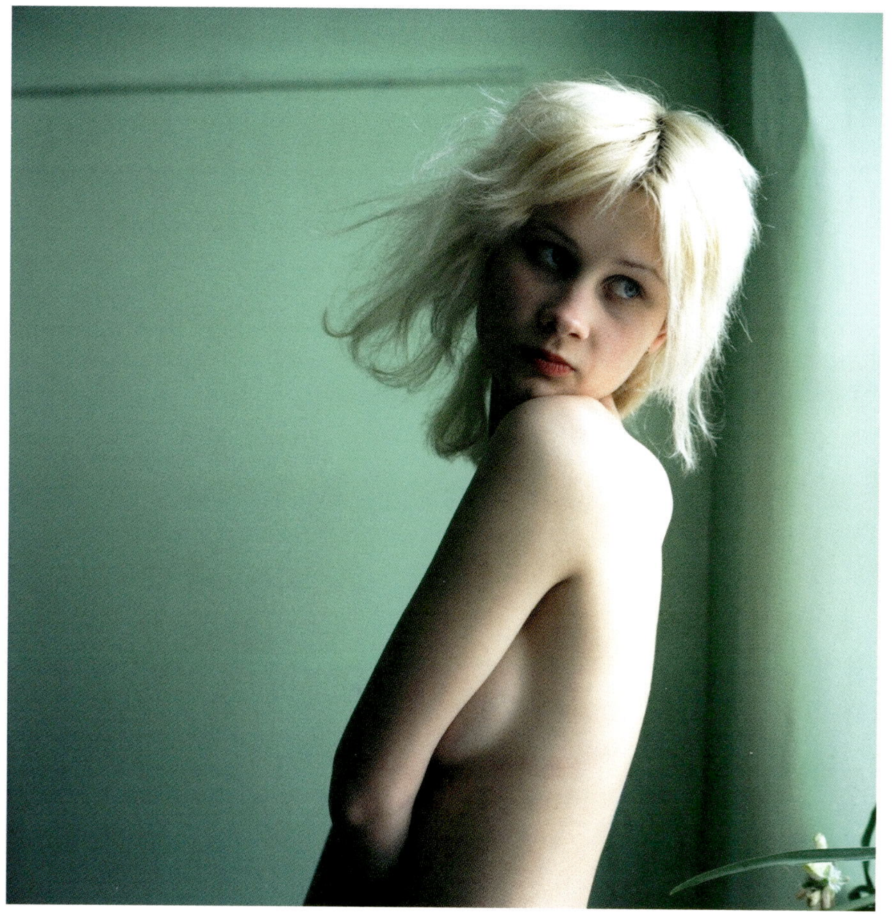

↑ **Hellen van Meene,** *Untitled, Riga, Latvia,* 2004

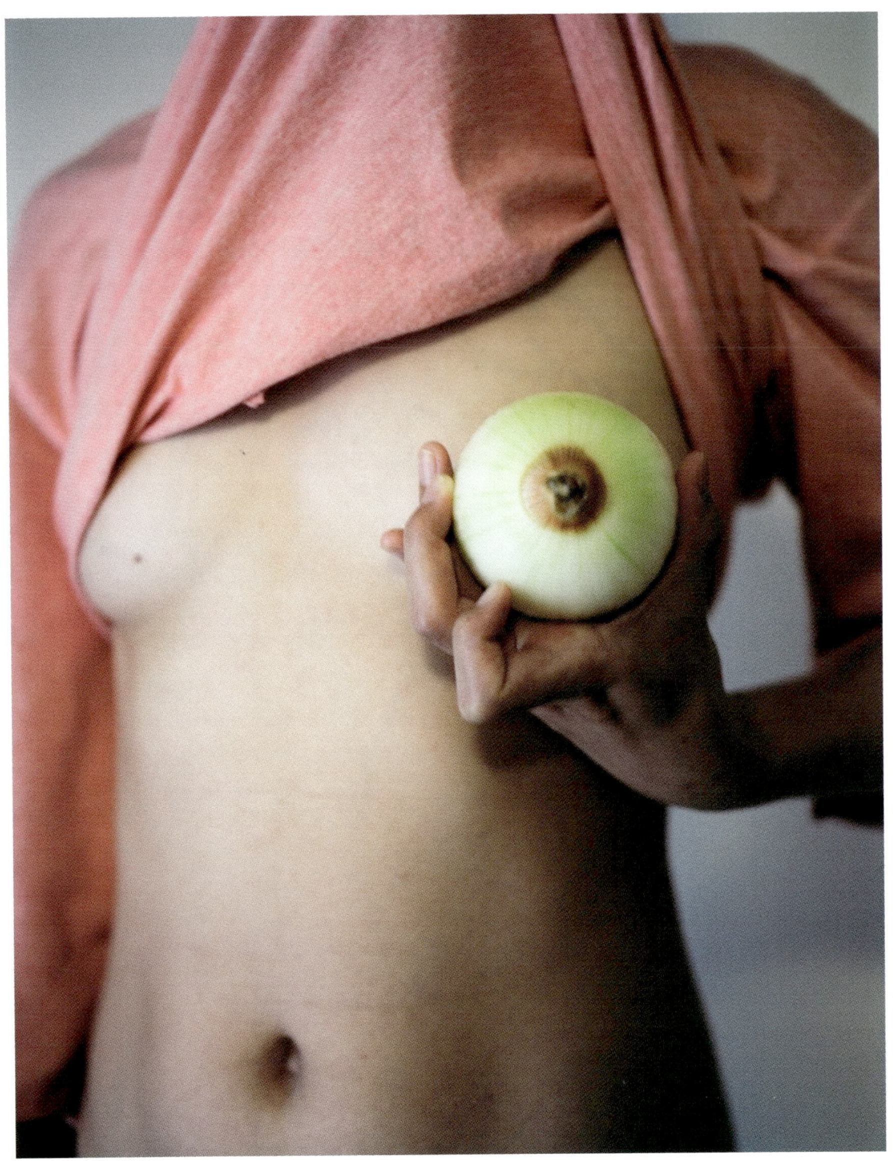

←**Yurie Nagashima,** *Self-Portrait,* 2001

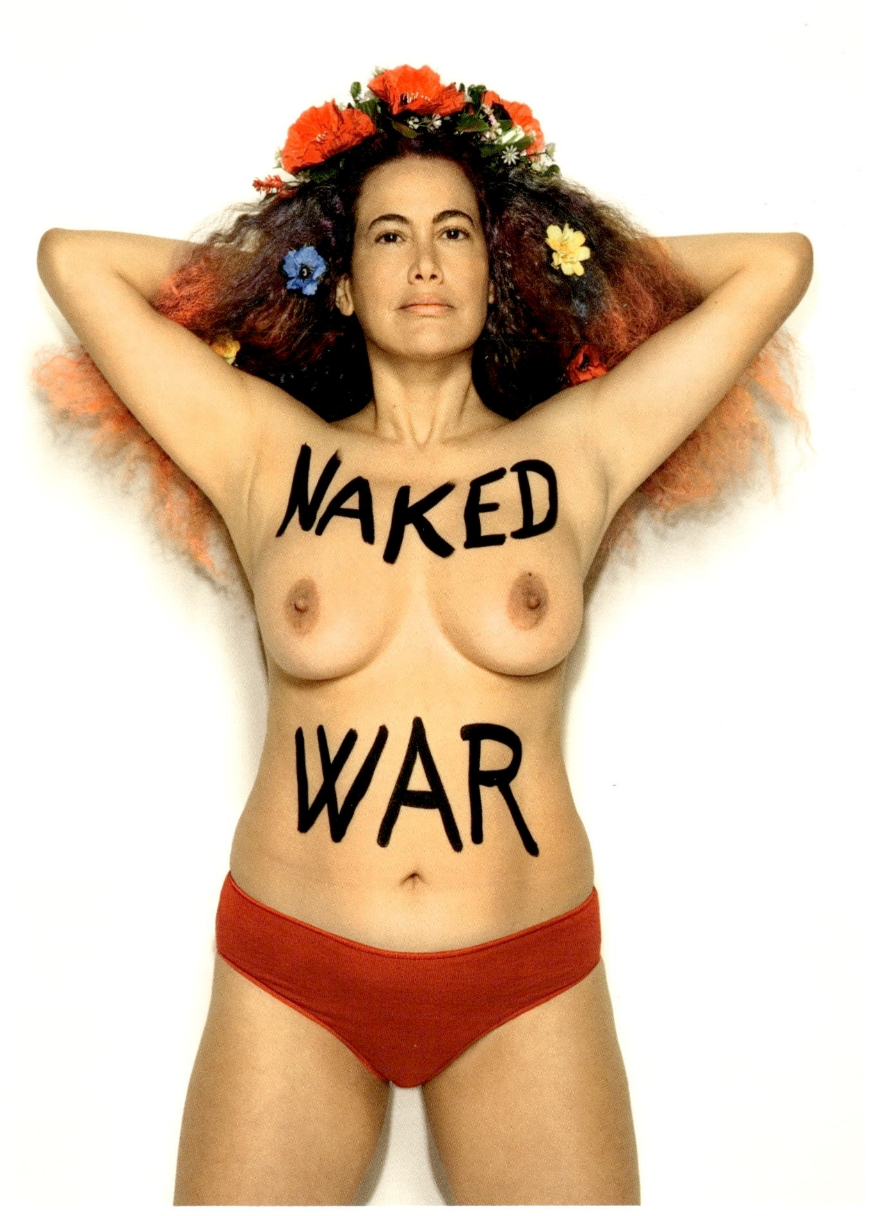

↑ **Bettina Rheims,** *Fleur d'Aboville, Naked War, May, Paris,*
from the series 'Naked War', 2017

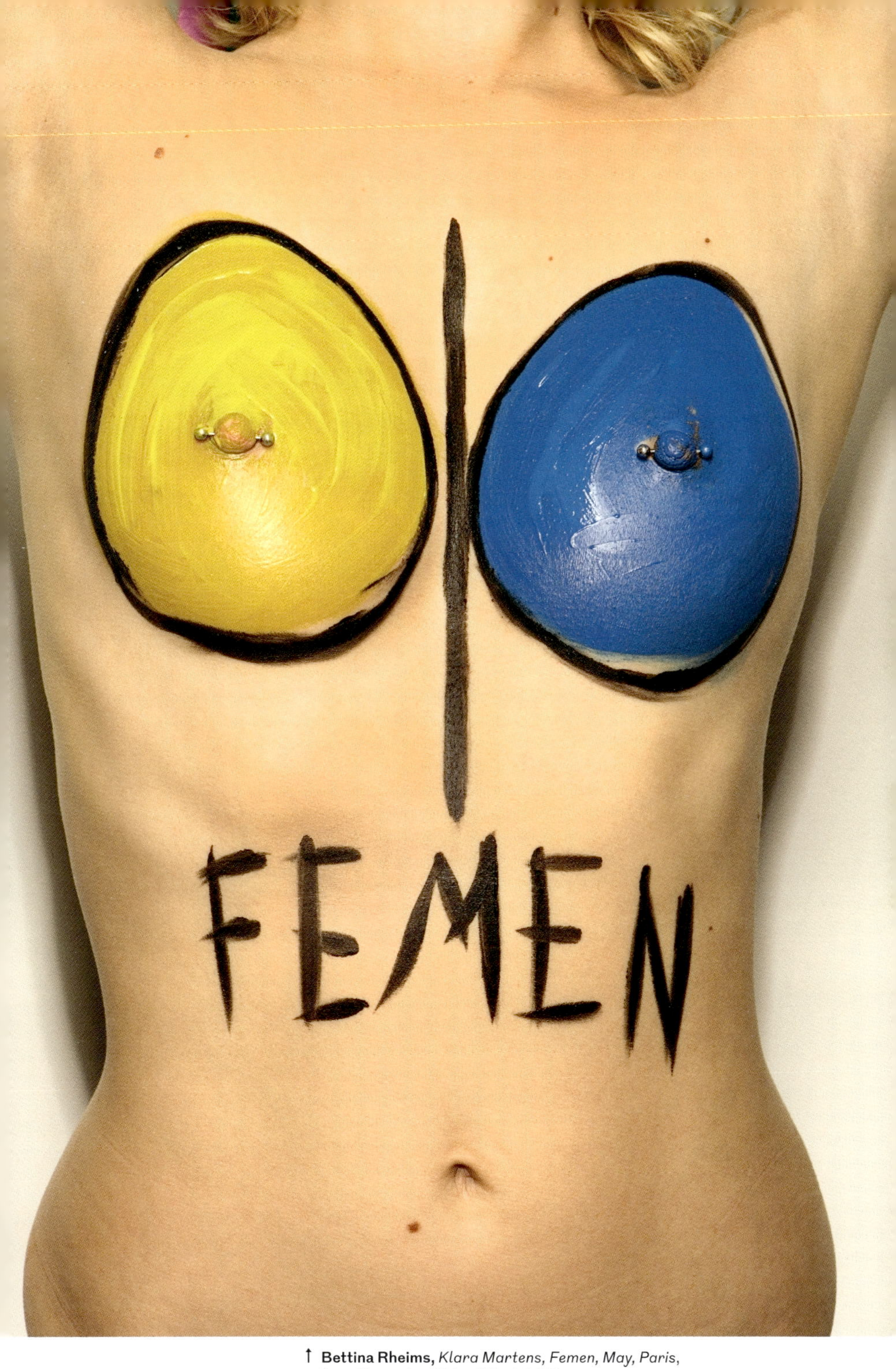

↑ **Bettina Rheims,** *Klara Martens, Femen, May, Paris,*
from the series 'Naked War', 2017

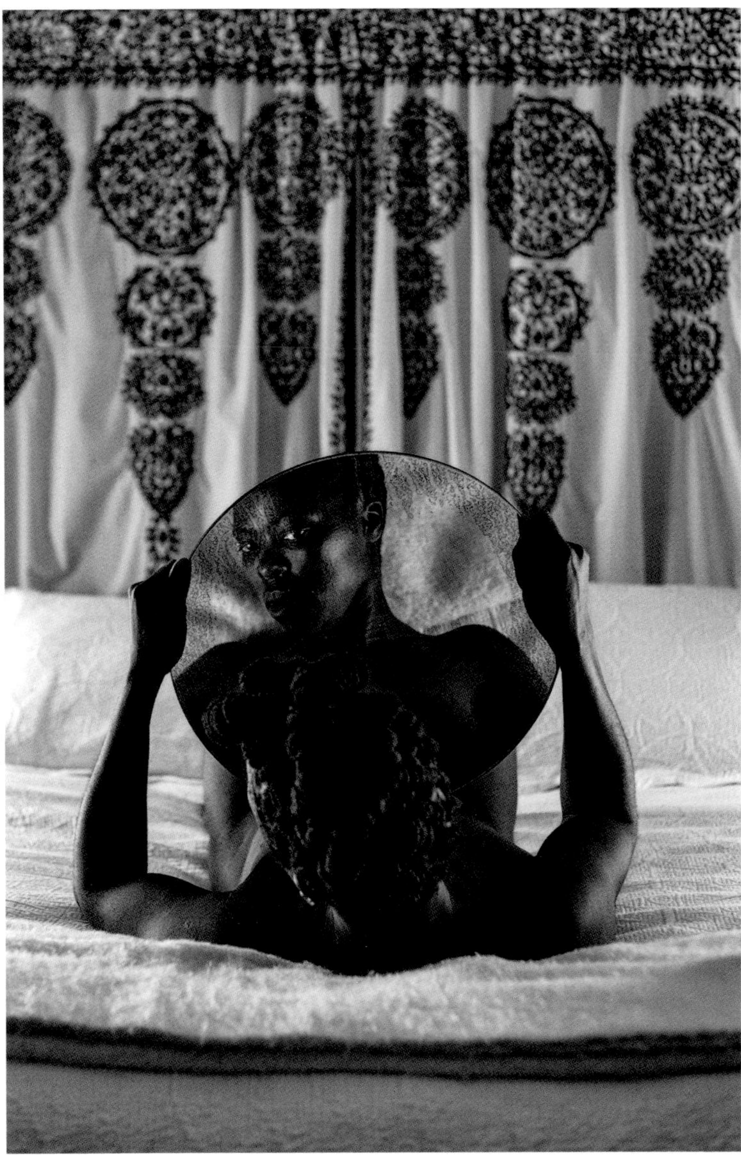

↑ **Zanele Muholi,** *Bona, Charlottesville,* 2015

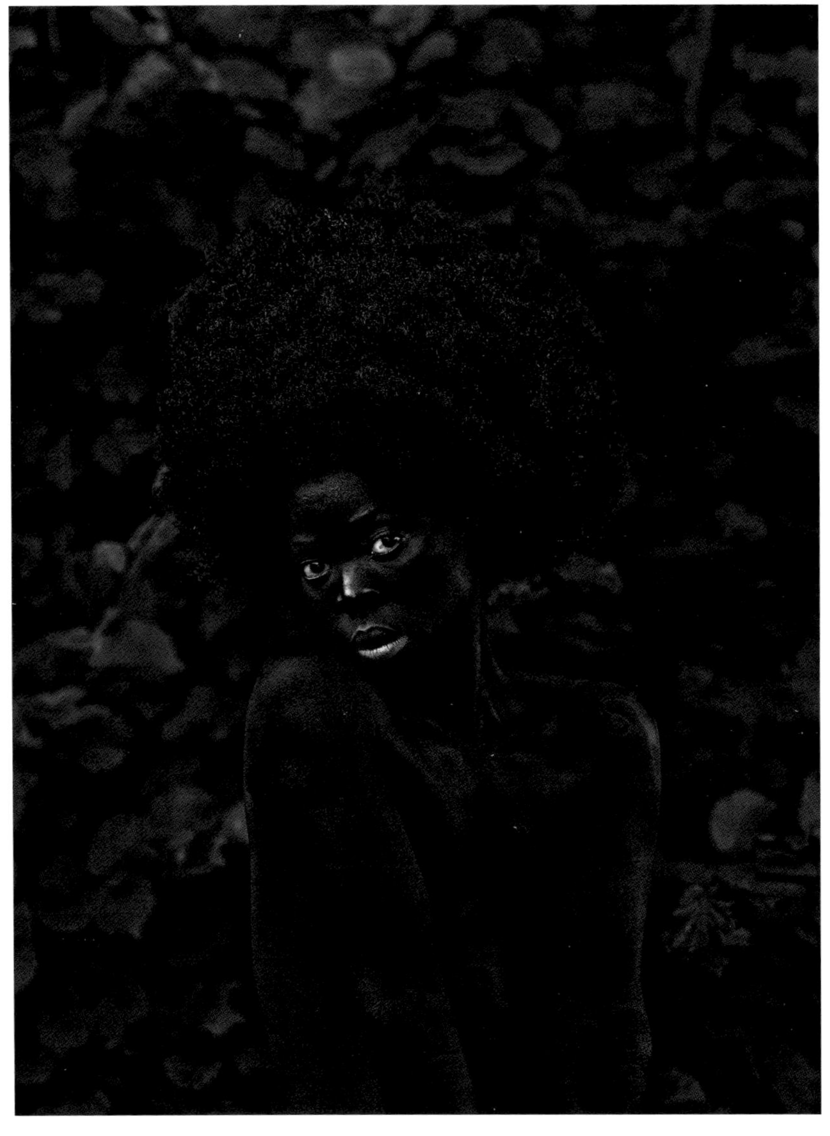

↑ Zanele Muholi, *HeVi, Oslo*, 2016

MUTATIONS

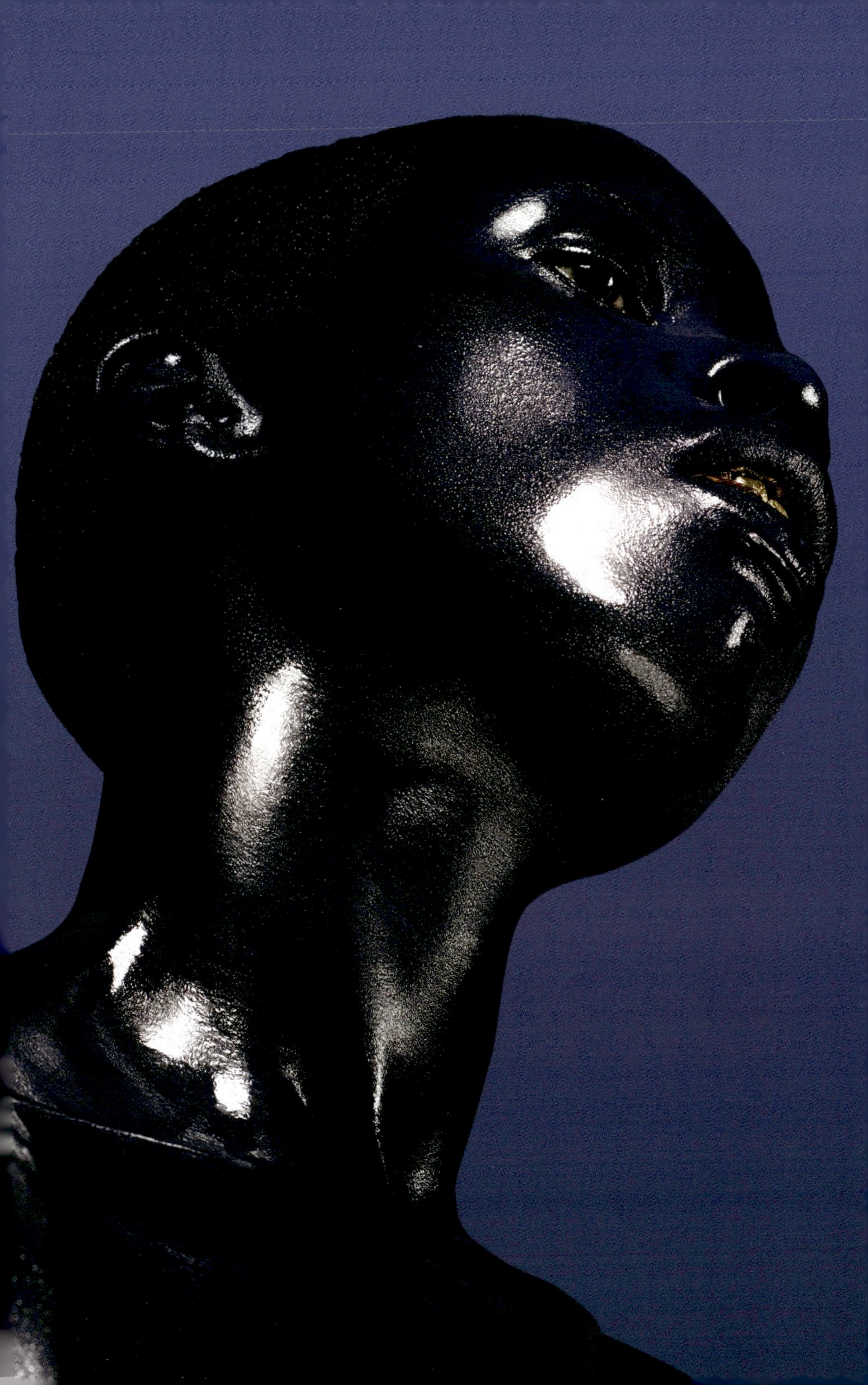

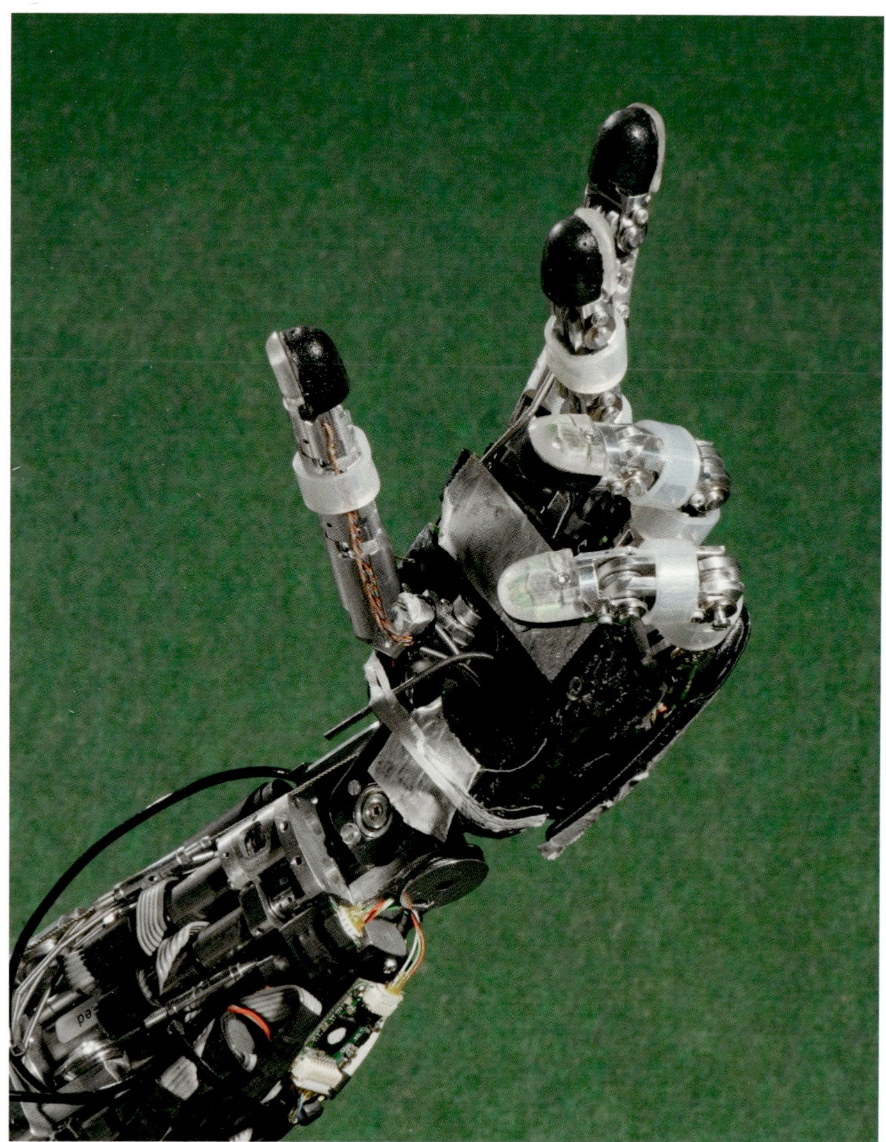

↑ **Maxime Guyon,** from the series 'Technological Exaptation', 2015
←(Previous) **Daniel Sannwald,** Camper campaign, Autumn/Winter 2015

The history of photography shows us what a vast subject the body is for photographers, because it can be subjected to an infinite number of photographic transformations and reconfigurations. Retouching and photocollage already existed in the 19th century, but it took until the first decades of the 20th century to discover the extent to which photographers can use their imaginations (and expertise) to create new compositions, fusions and abstractions of the body. We need only think back to the Surrealists, whose work was inspired by their obsessions and their dreams. They were seeking to distance themselves from the anatomy and to transcend the human being. The works of Arno Rafael Minkkinen (p. 228), who has been photographing himself nude in nature for forty years, and of Jenny Saville (p. 195), who observes her own body from different angles, follow in the same tradition. Viviane Sassen (pp. 188, 189) and Ren Hang (pp. 196, 197) transform the body by constantly playing with composition, while Daniel Gordon (p. 186) and Alix Marie (pp. 202–03) fragment and rebuild the body. In the case of Spencer Tunick (p. 205), who since 1994 has been gathering together thousands of people all across the world and getting them to pose in the nude, the performance becomes an installation that goes beyond the issue of nudity in public spaces to touch on political, environmental and social questions. The disappearance of the individual is also a theme of the photographs taken by Liu Bolin (pp. 182–83), who poses alone in front of his lens. Working on the basis of magazine images, Ina Jang (pp. 206–07) and Patrick Weidmann (pp. 208, 209) also raise questions about the disappearance of the individual — and of women as sexual objects, in particular.

Photography has always involved framing the subject (choice of scale, crop, tone, etc.) and it is clear that there can be many, and often surprising, interpretations. Yet it is not only the image that can be transformed; the contemporary body can also be reconstructed in a multiplicity of ways. Recent developments in cosmetic surgery and the variety of methods used to change the body (cloning, the use of drugs, organ transplants, prostheses and implants, surgical sex changes, fertility treatments, etc.) are paving the way towards the emergence of a mutant being. Artists are observing these interventions and venturing into new

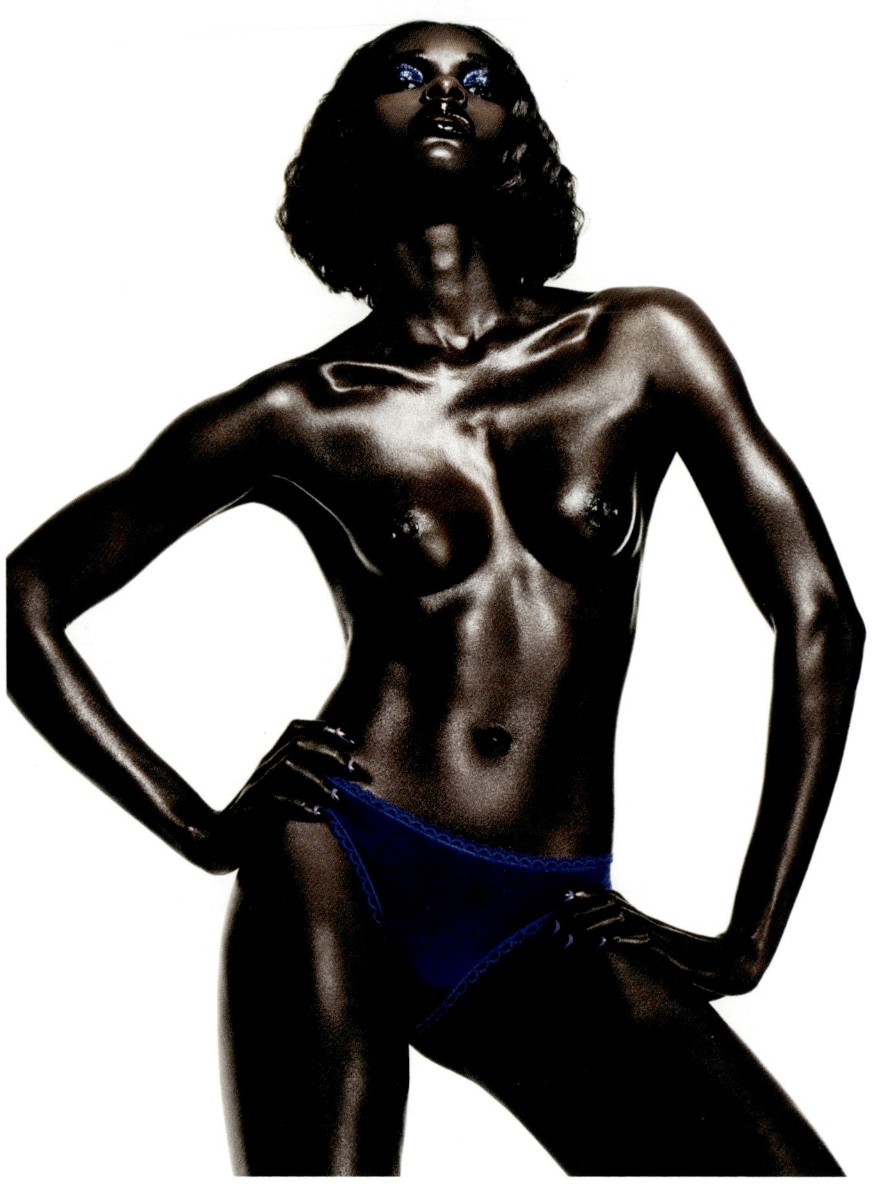

↑ **Daniel Sannwald,** *Pop* magazine, Fall/Winter 2012

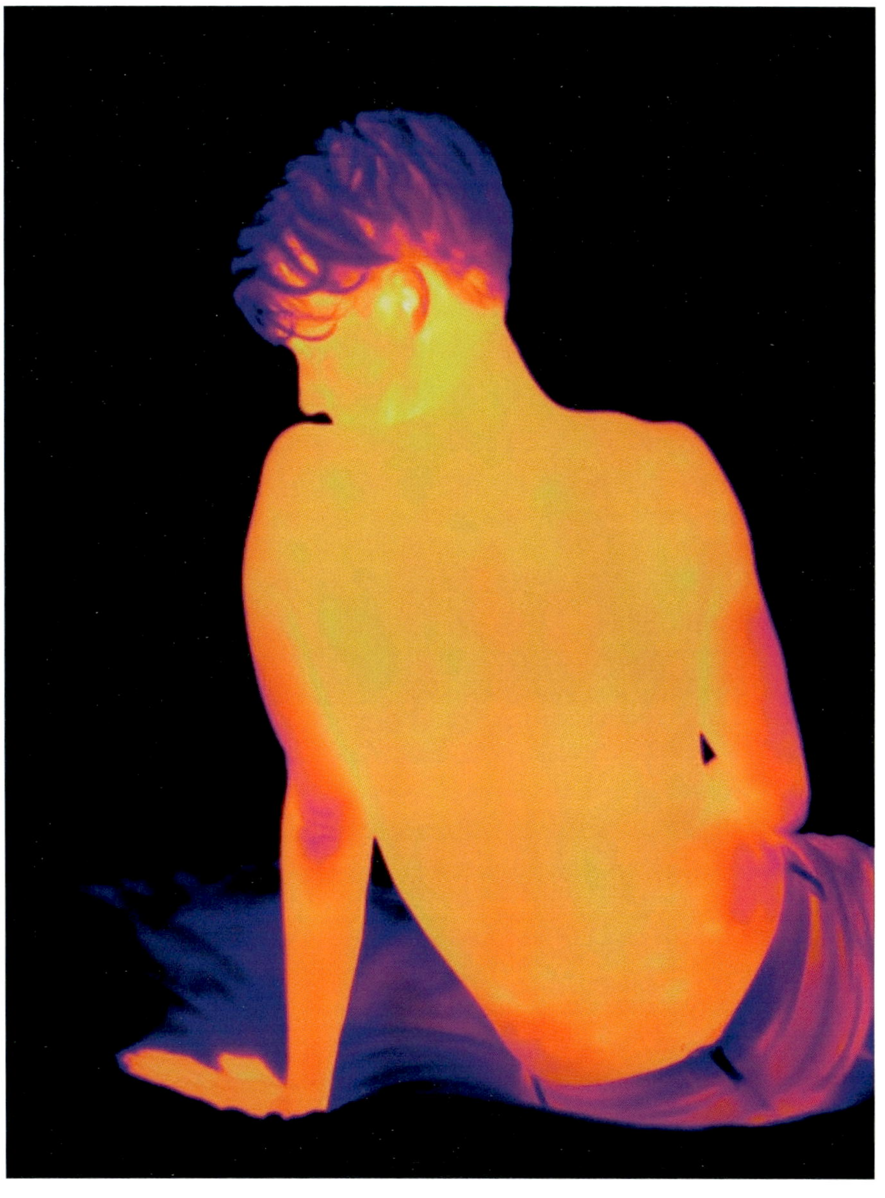

↑ **SMITH,** Untitled, from the series 'Spectrographies', 2015

territories. In their case it is a question of documenting the developments and questioning the scientific advances through which human beings become dehumanized or simply go beyond their humanity. Article 1 of the Transhumanist Declaration, dating from 1998, announced this new human being in the following terms: 'Humanity will be radically changed by technology in the future. We foresee the feasibility of redesigning the human condition, including such parameters as the inevitability of ageing, limitations on human and artificial intellects, unchosen psychology, suffering, and our confinement to the planet earth.' Back in the 1990s, the works of the artist Matthew Barney, the film-maker David Cronenberg and the performance artist ORLAN were the precursors of this new era. Today photographers document in depth the way transhumanism has already changed our bodies. Technological transformations are well underway.

The potential that artificial intelligence, genetic modification and robotics can offer our species no longer lies in the realm of utopian dreams. The bionic body has become a reality. Humans have always sought to amplify bodily functions, to achieve a superhuman strength, an infallible memory, to prolong life and hold back mortality. They have never been so close to achieving this as in the 21st century. A number of artists have looked at trans/posthumanism and questioned the future of this modified human being, generally referred to as the augmented (or enhanced) human. Matthieu Gafsou (pp. 214–17) has chosen to observe these mutations in documentary form. This is no longer science fiction but the real world. In 2000, Aziz + Cucher (pp. 220–21) offered us a dystopian vision of these new bodies by looking at the potential effects of a trans/posthumanism that dreams of discarding organs perceived as inadequate and erasing distinctions between the human and non-human in order to produce a purified organism. We cannot prevent ourselves from imagining future factories for making improved bodies when we look at the photographs that Xing Danwen (p. 204) took in a factory in China. Asger Carlsen (pp. 226, 227) goes even further and toys with the apocalyptic imagination by showing us distorted archaic bodies.

The utopian body that is exalted by transhumanism is certainly not as distant from us as it might seem. We already

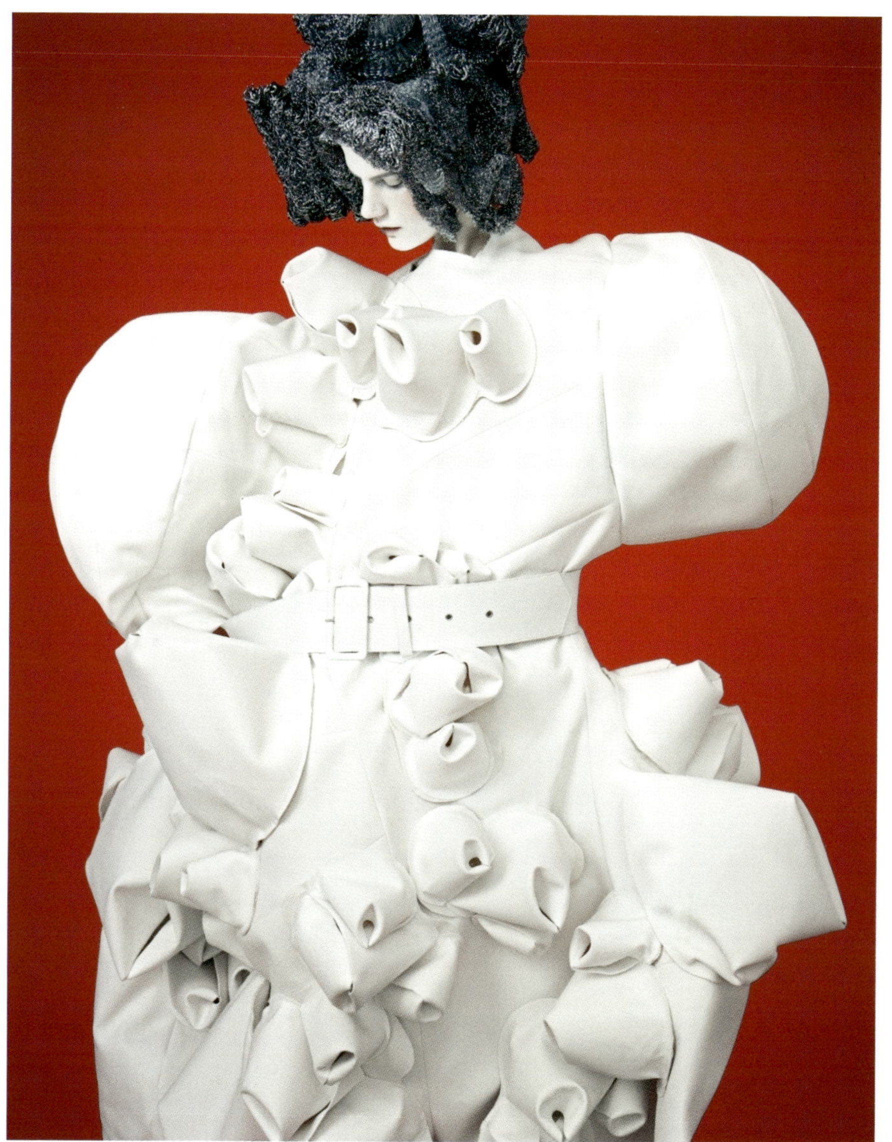

↑ **Erik Madigan Heck,** *Saskia in Comme des Garçons,* 2017

know how to subjugate and mould the body by mechanical, chemical, biological and pharmaceutical means, and this corresponds to our obsession with a high-performance and eternal body. With the help of the new technologies (nanotechnology, biotechnology, computer science, research in the cognitive sciences), which are advancing at a great pace, human life is being created, improved and prolonged. Perhaps we do not yet routinely have implants under our skin but we take pills during our lifetime that are supposed to make us more efficient or simply delay disease. Soon we will be wearing integrated underwear under our clothes that will stimulate and train the body, i.e. augment it. Engineers are testing artificial organs that can connect with the brain, developing sensors that can restore sensations, and working on stem cells that are designed to renew the cells, tissues and then the organs of the body. In our hyper-industrial society, the hybridization of the human being is already underway and is affecting us at different rates. We are seeing an increasing number of parallel worlds thanks to our new 'organs' (computers, mobile phones) and these are producing multiple, mixed humans. Indeed, we already have social media avatars that allow us to meet new people and experience emotions via on-screen interaction. These new humans, who transcend gender and sexual identity, already seem to be with us, as shown by Daniel Sannwald (see p. 173). The life sciences and engineering are confronting us all with societal and ideological challenges. Artists are encouraging us to keep a keen eye on the newly developing tools and technologies and to contribute to the public debate. The ethical challenges relating to the new human being concern each and every one of us.

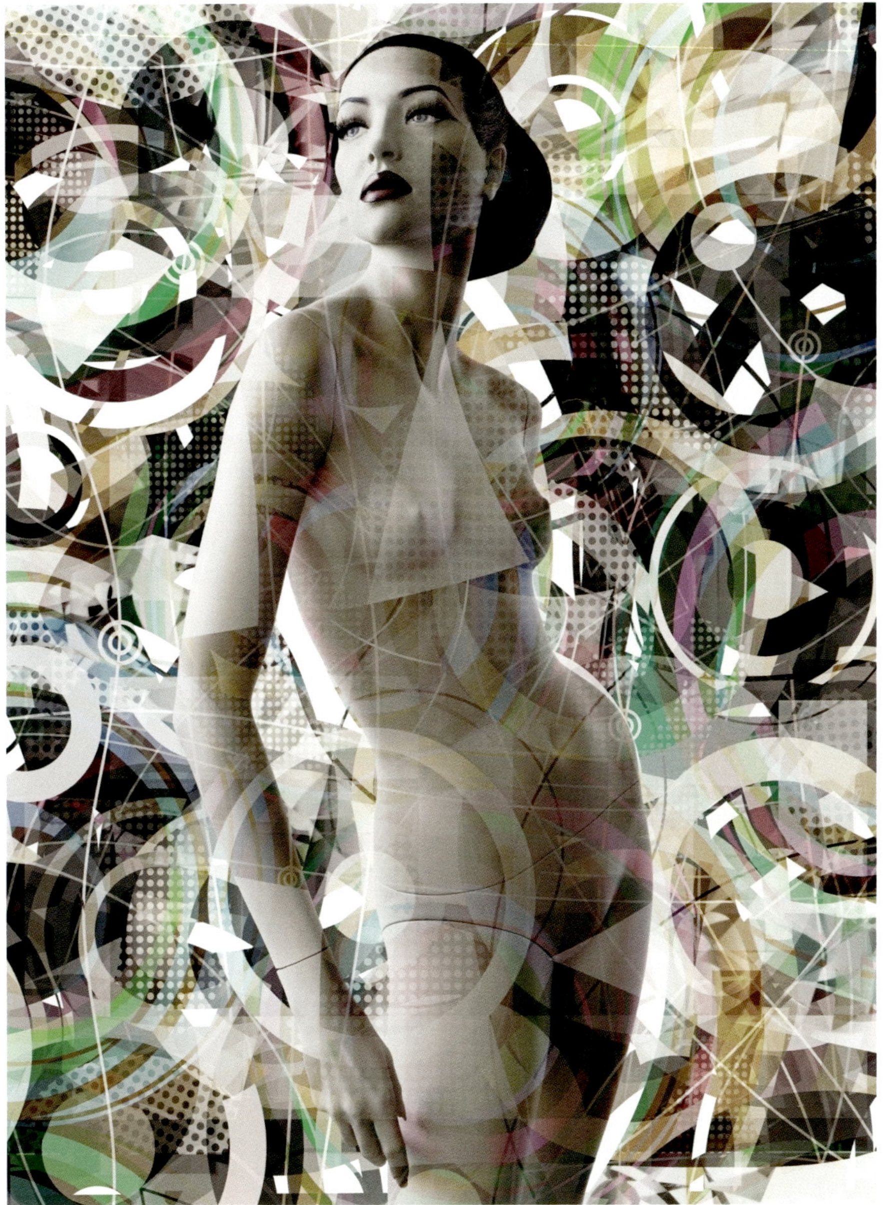

↑ **Valérie Belin,** *Electra*, from the series 'Super Models', 2015
→(Overleaf) **Liu Bolin,** *In the Woods*, 2010

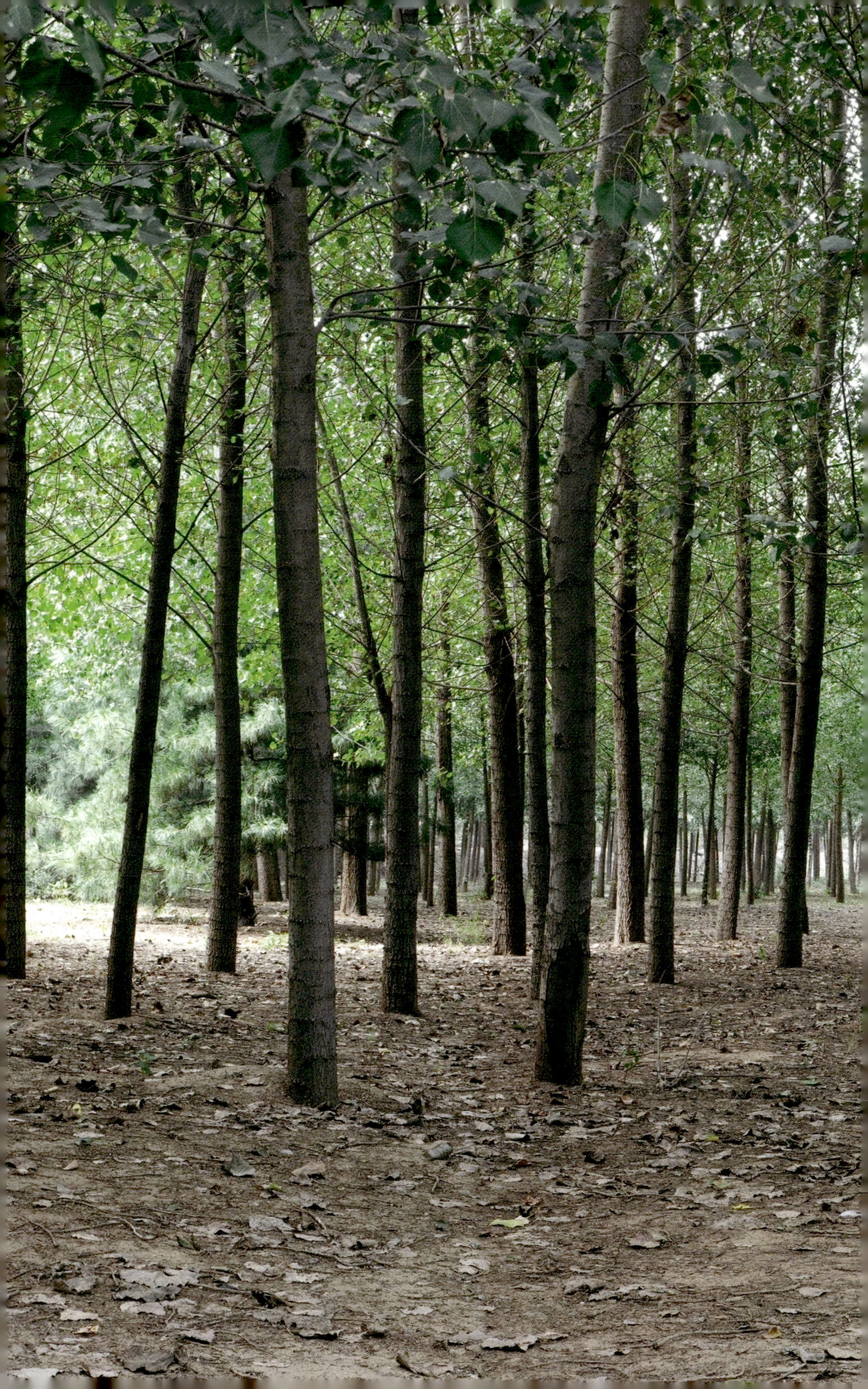

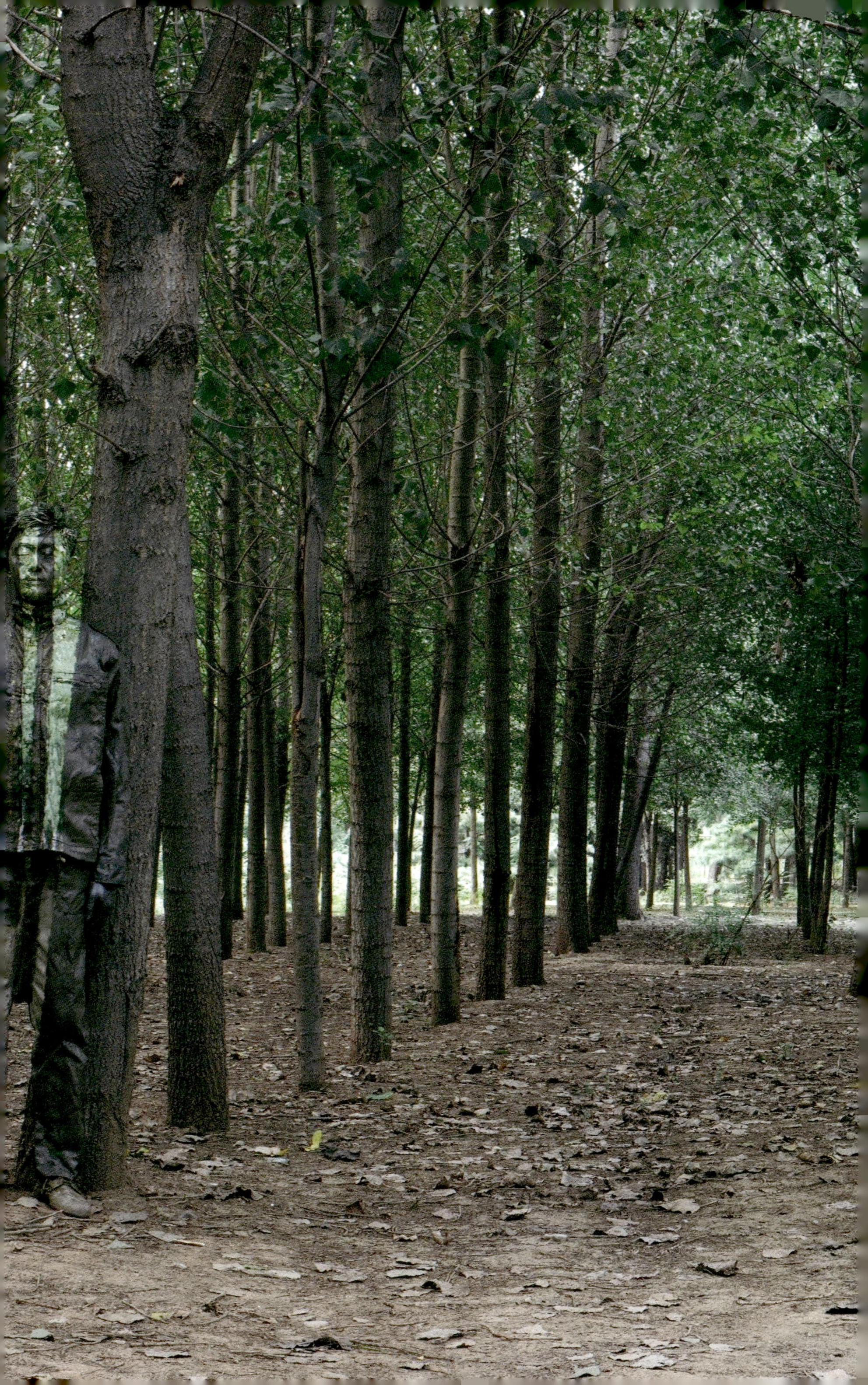

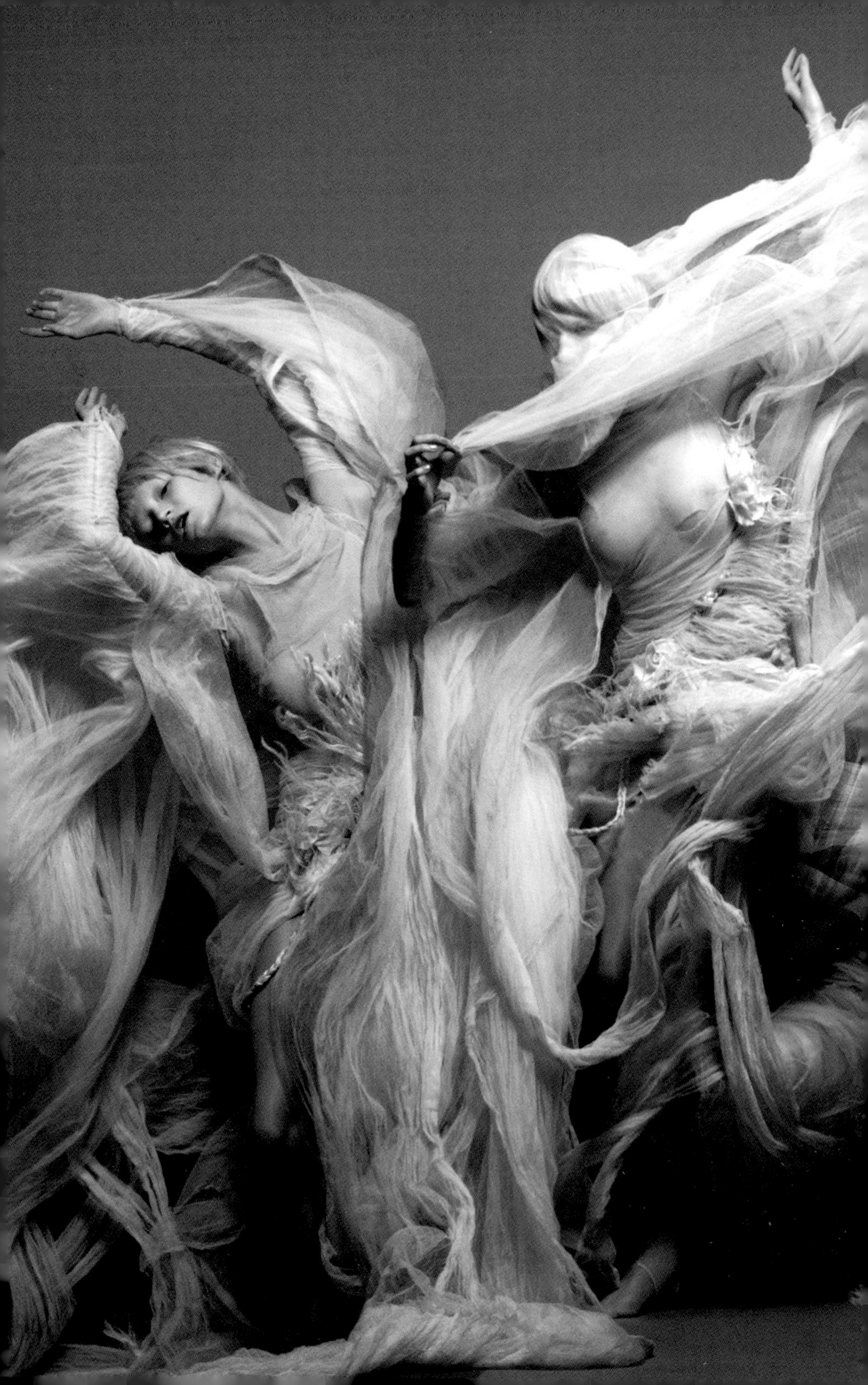

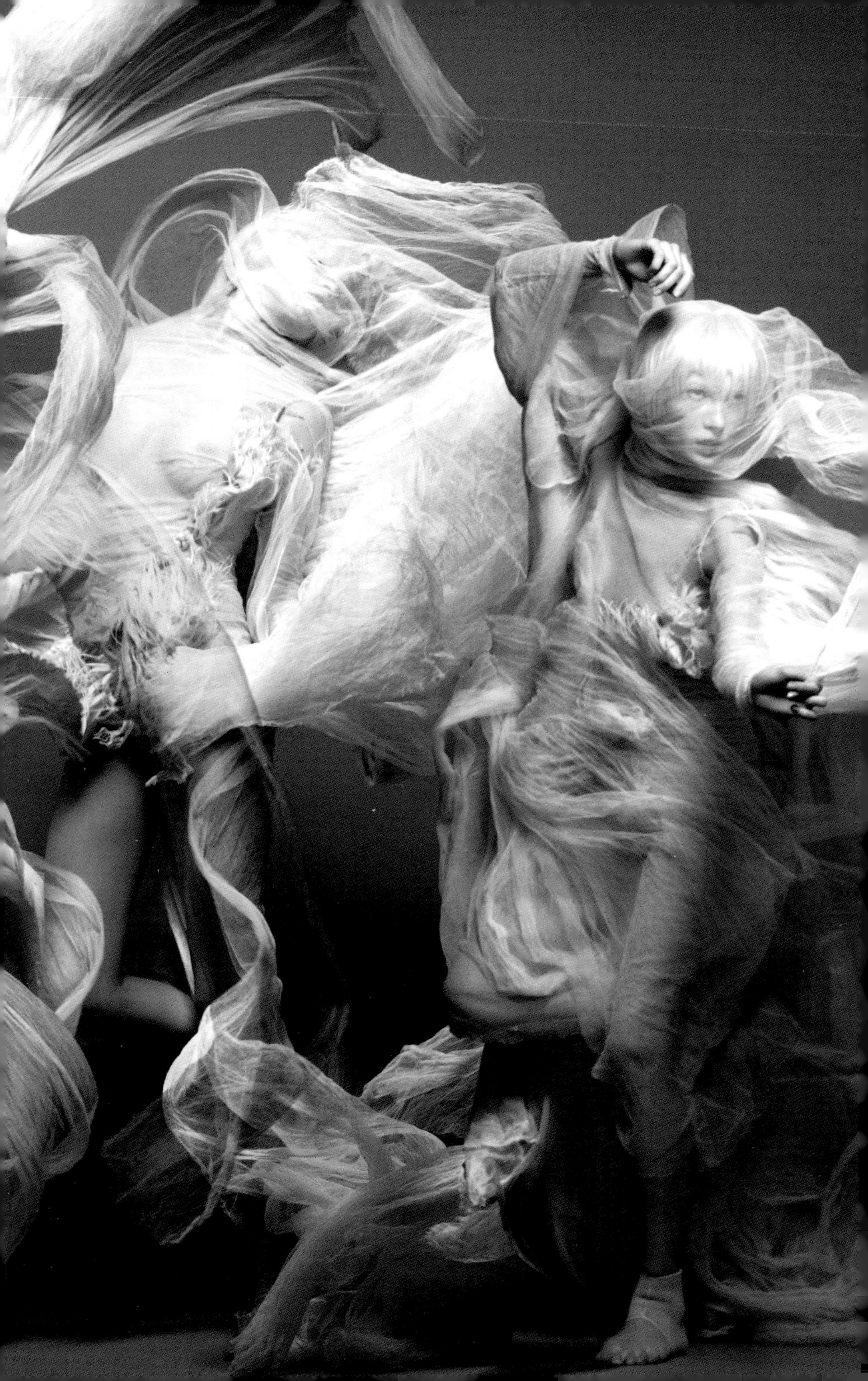

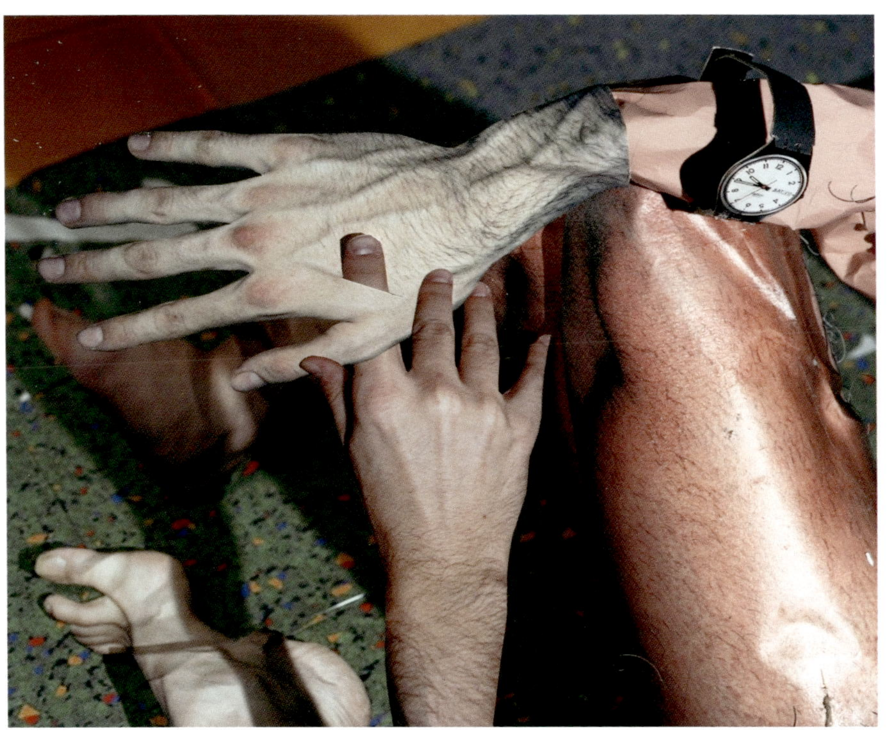

↑ **Daniel Gordon,** *July 1, 2009,* 2009
←(Previous) **Sølve Sundsbø,** *Elena in Gaultier,* 2007

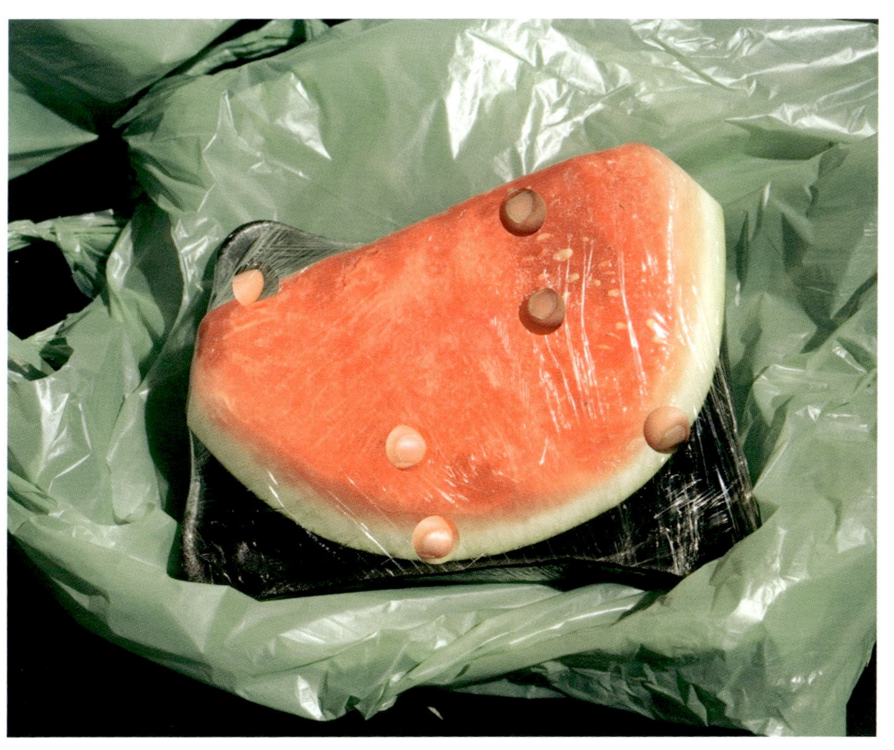

↑ **Lucas Blalock,** *A Physical Feeling,* 2014

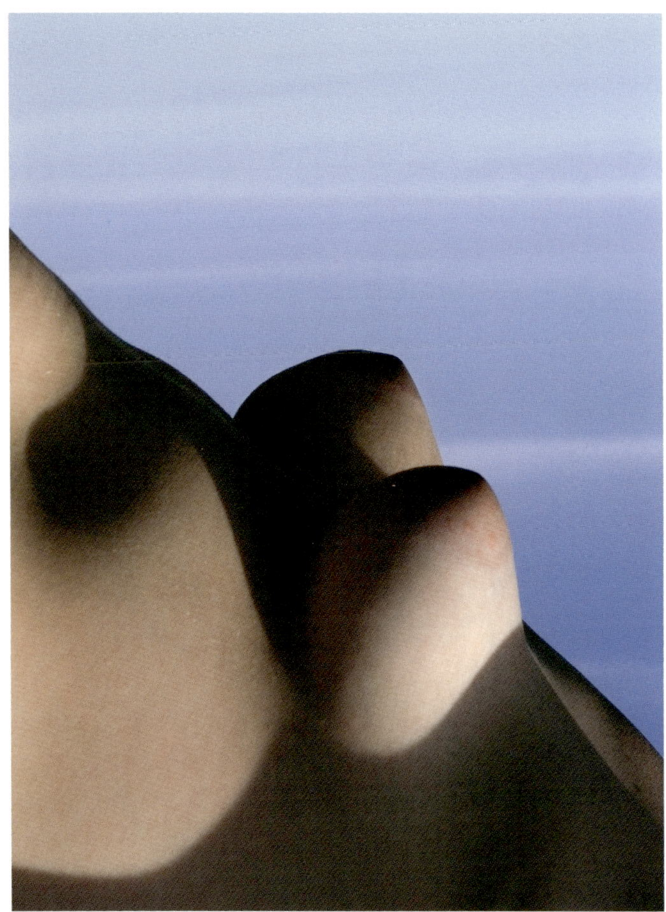

↑ Viviane Sassen, *Uppsala,* 2017
→Viviane Sassen, *Marte #02,* from the series 'UMBRA', 2014

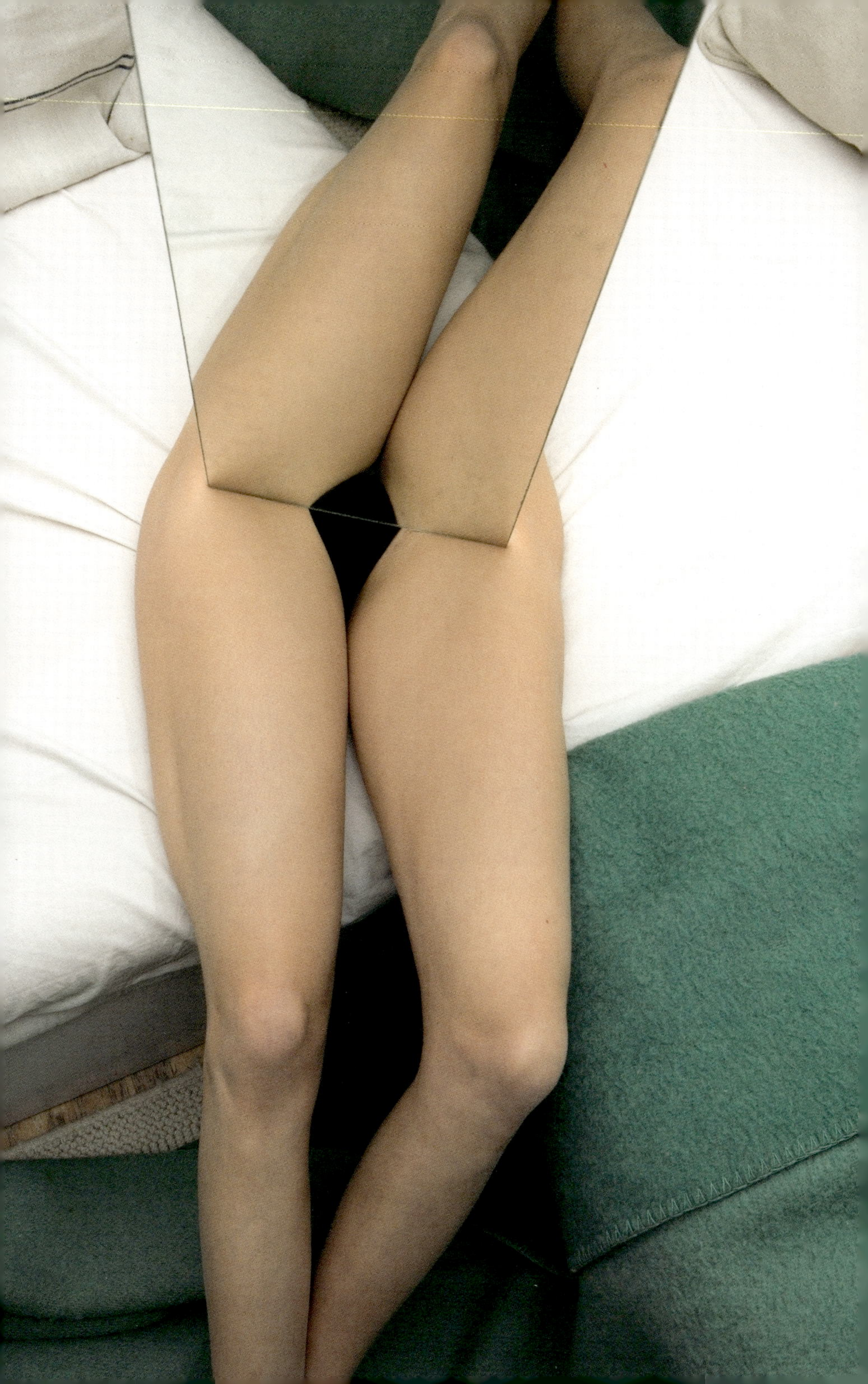

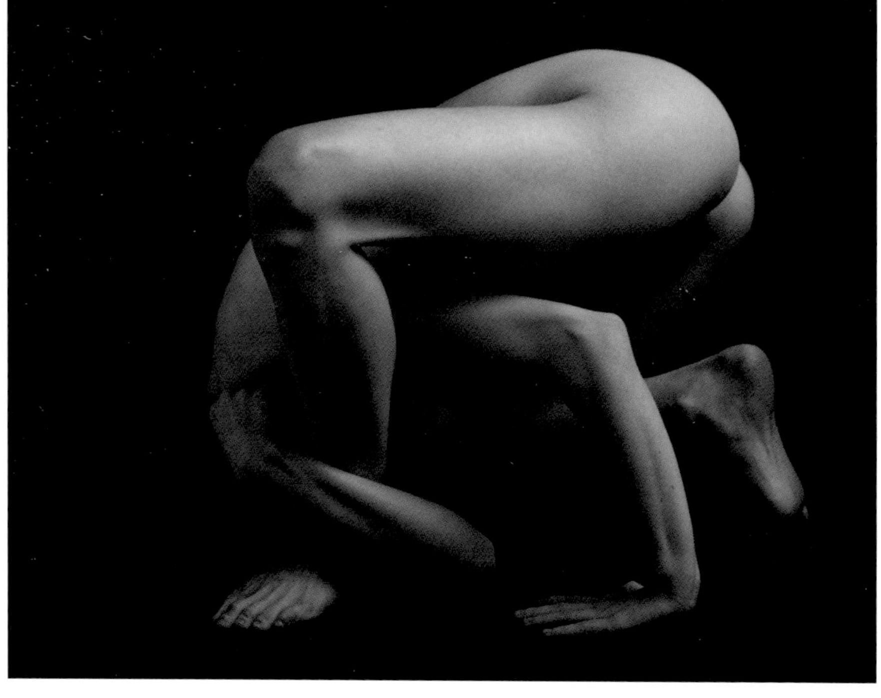

↑ **Juul Kraijer,** *Untitled (L.P. #2),* 2014–15

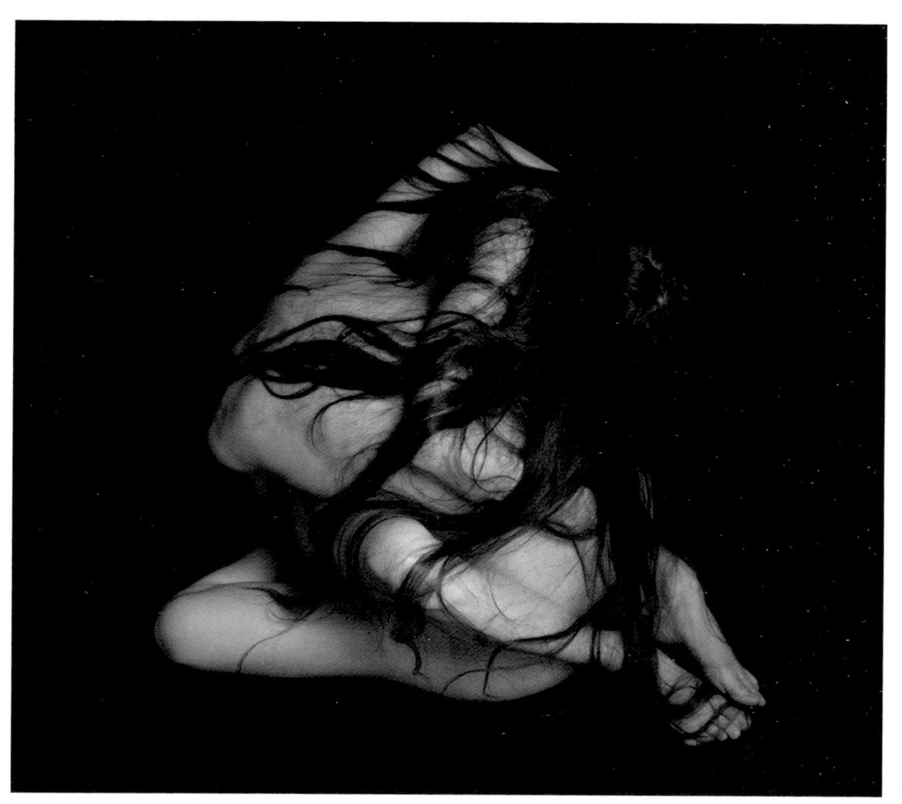

↑ **Juul Kraijer,** *Untitled (C.M.&L.P. #1),* 2016–17

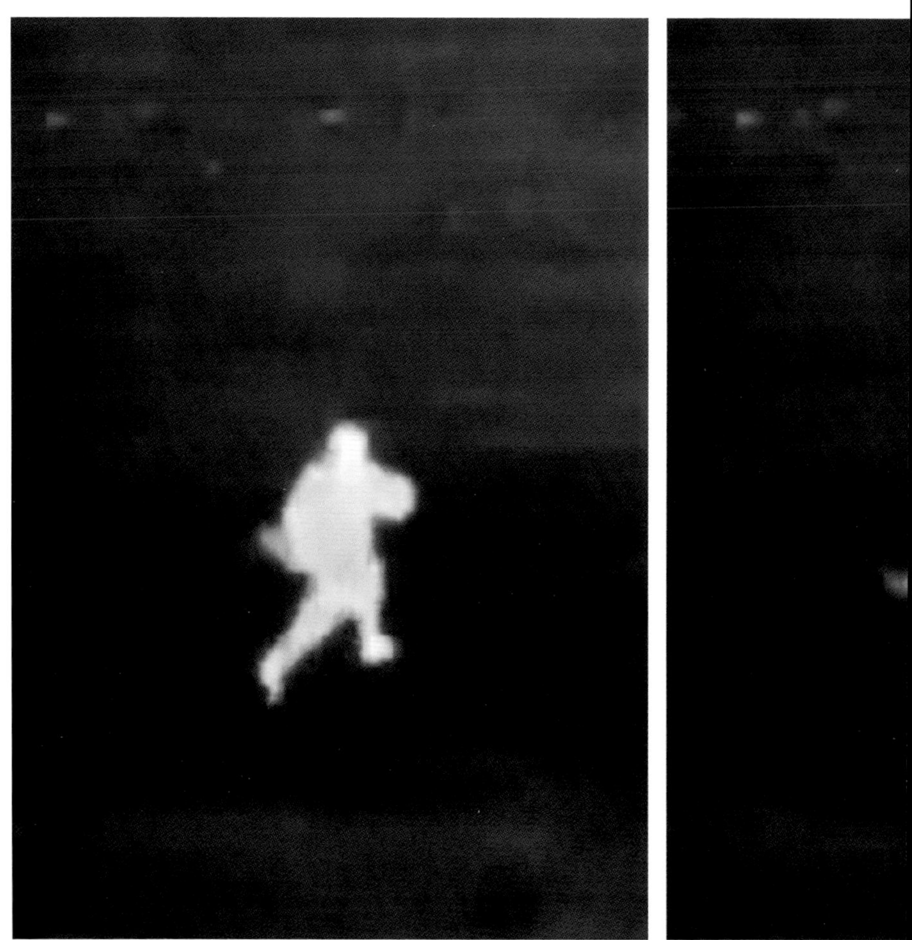

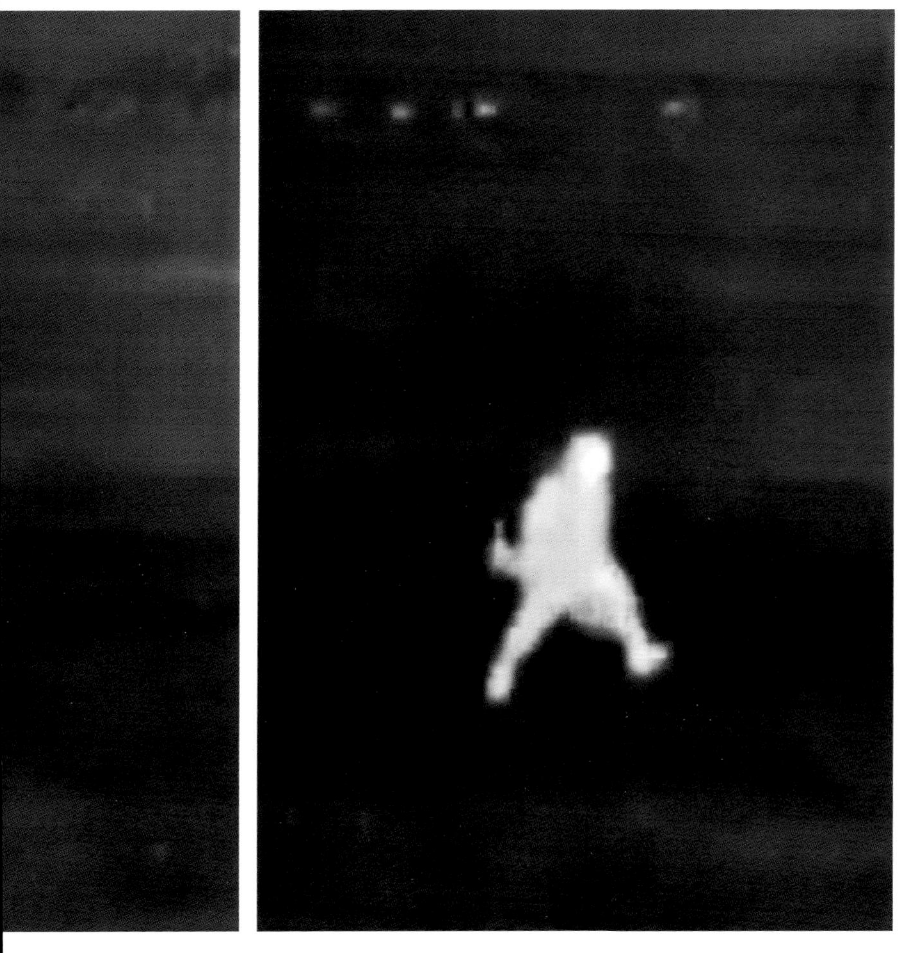 Clément Lambelet, Untitled, from the series
'Two Donkeys in a War Zone', 2016

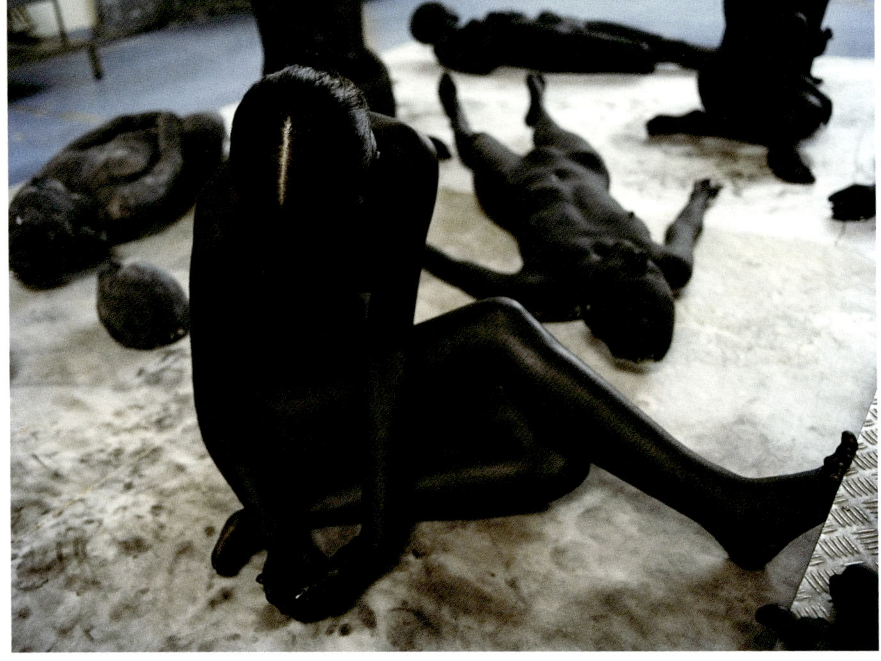

↑ **Vanessa Beecroft,** *VB66.141.VB*, 2010–11

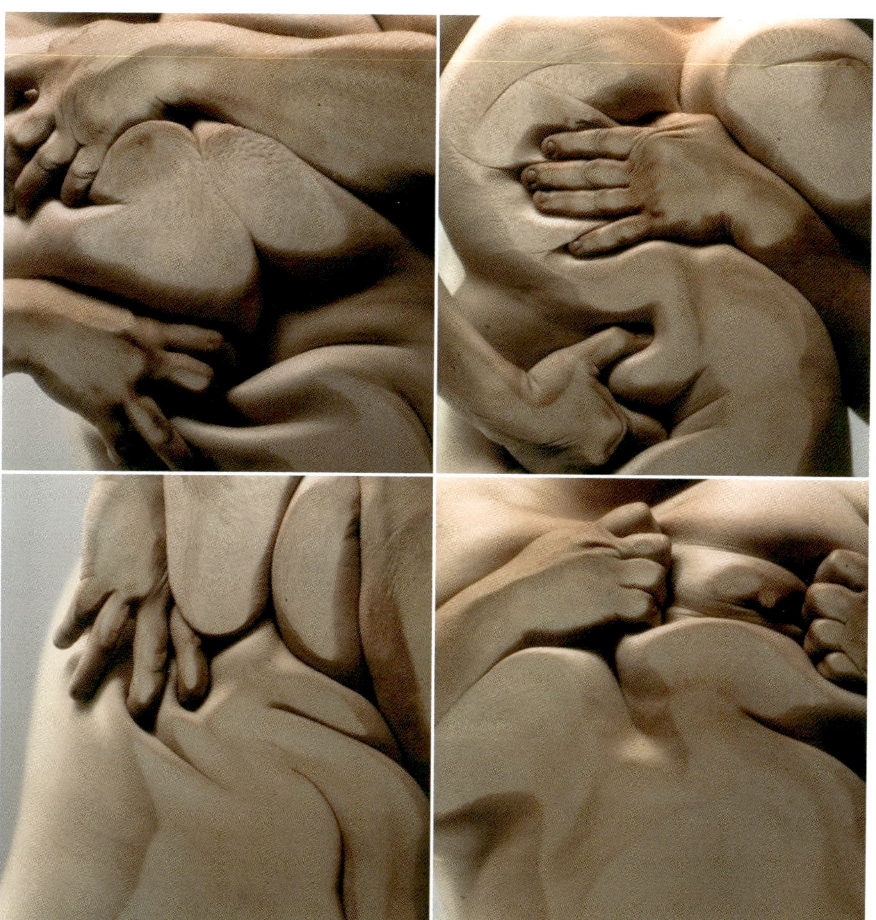

↑ (Clockwise from top left) **Jenny Saville & Glen Luchford,**
#2, #1, #4, #3, 1995—96

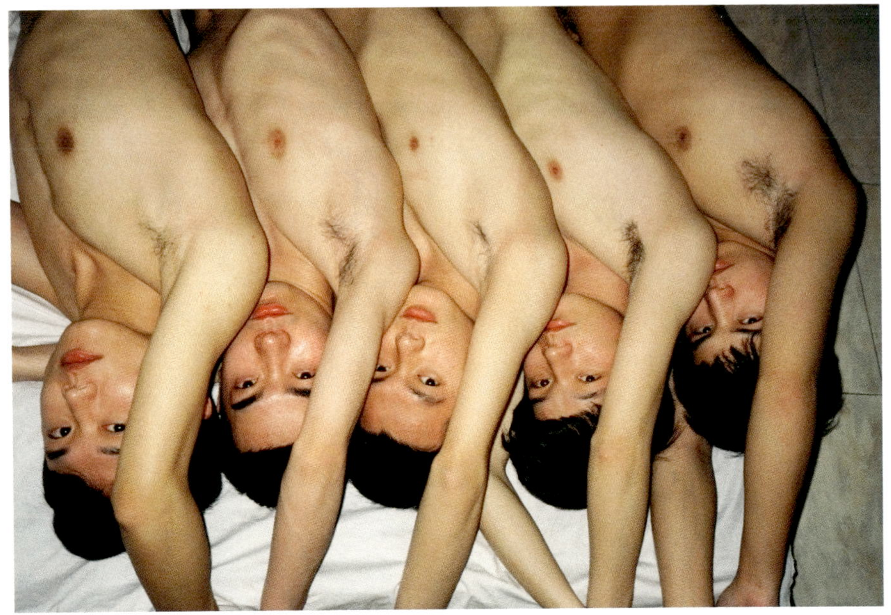

↑ Ren Hang, *Untitled 27,* 2012

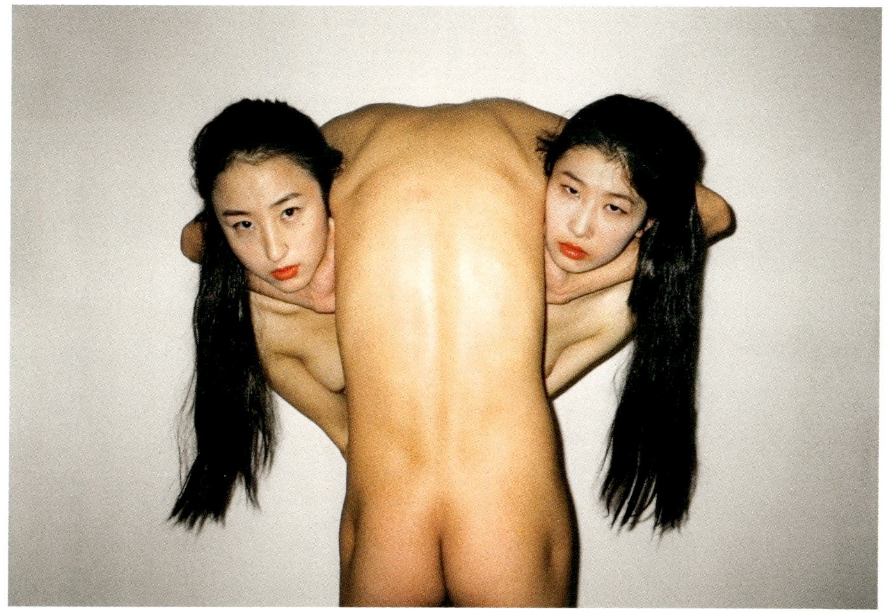

↑ **Ren Hang,** *Untitled 12,* 2011

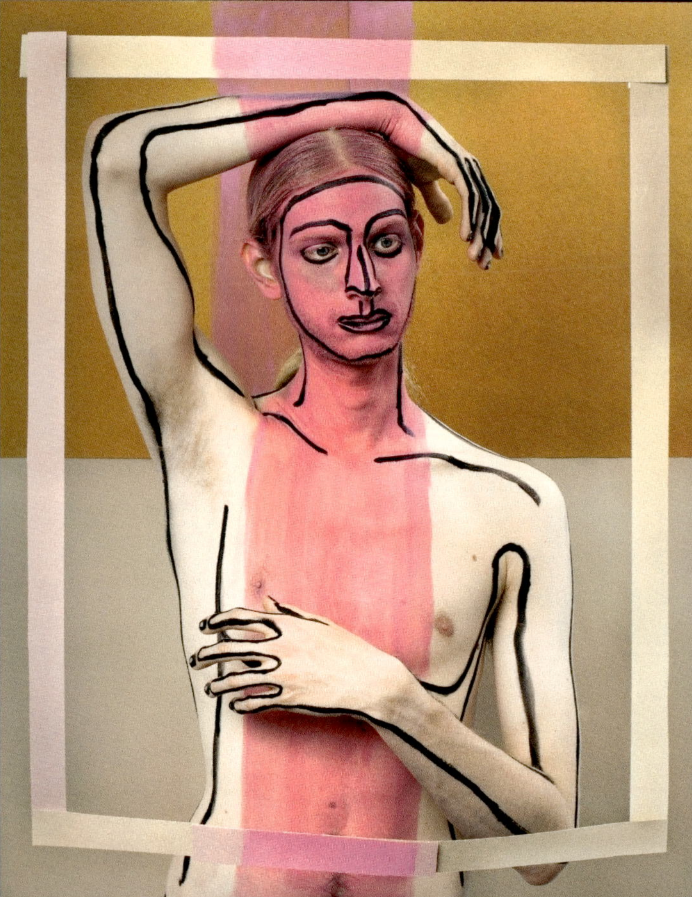

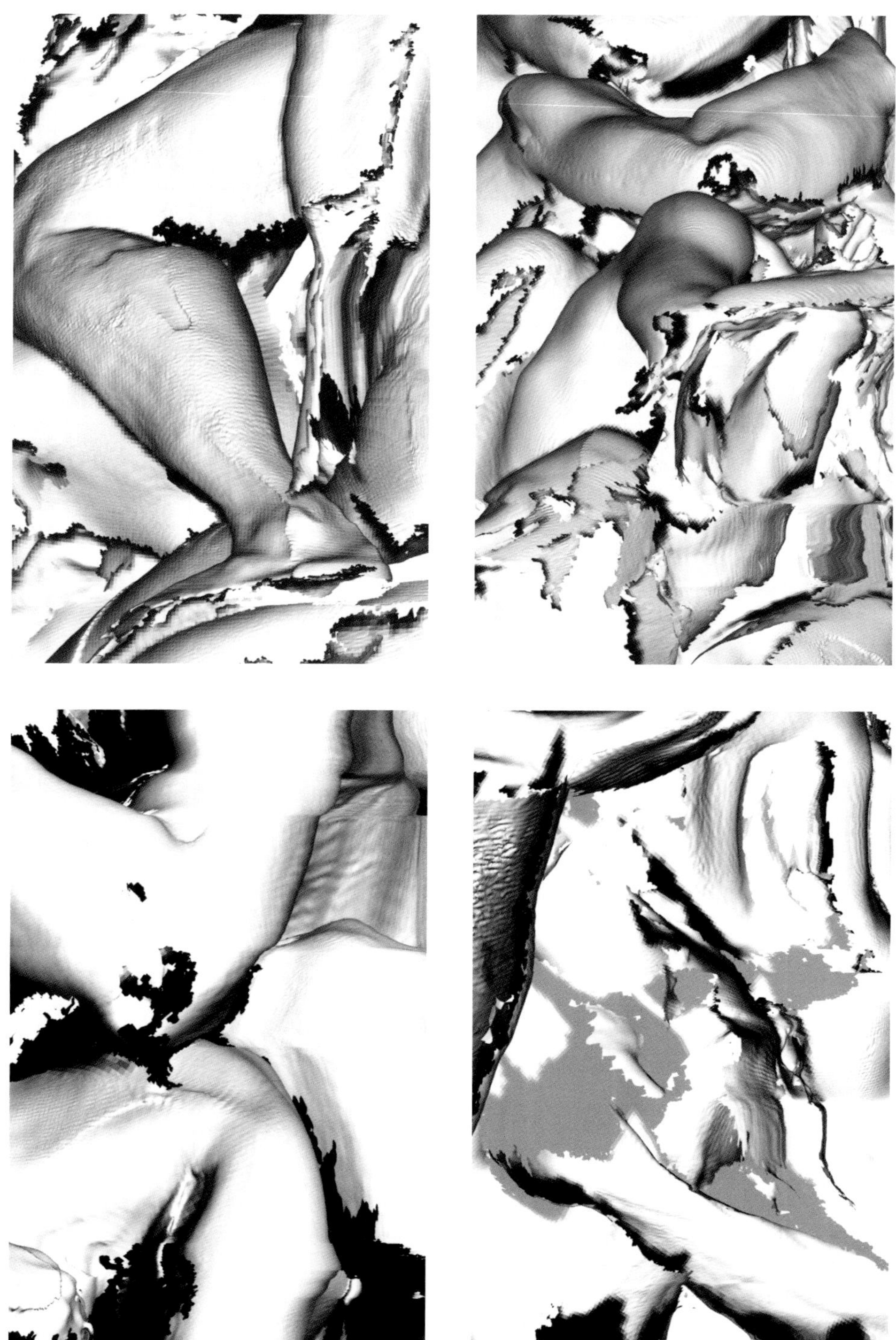

↑ (Clockwise from top left) **Taisuke Koyama,**
VESSEL - XYZXY #030, #039, #016, #012, 2016

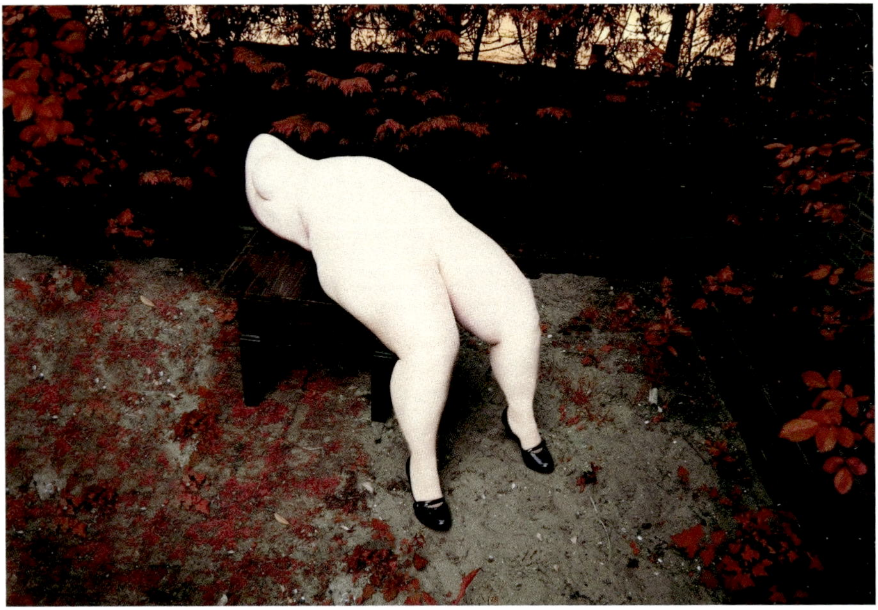

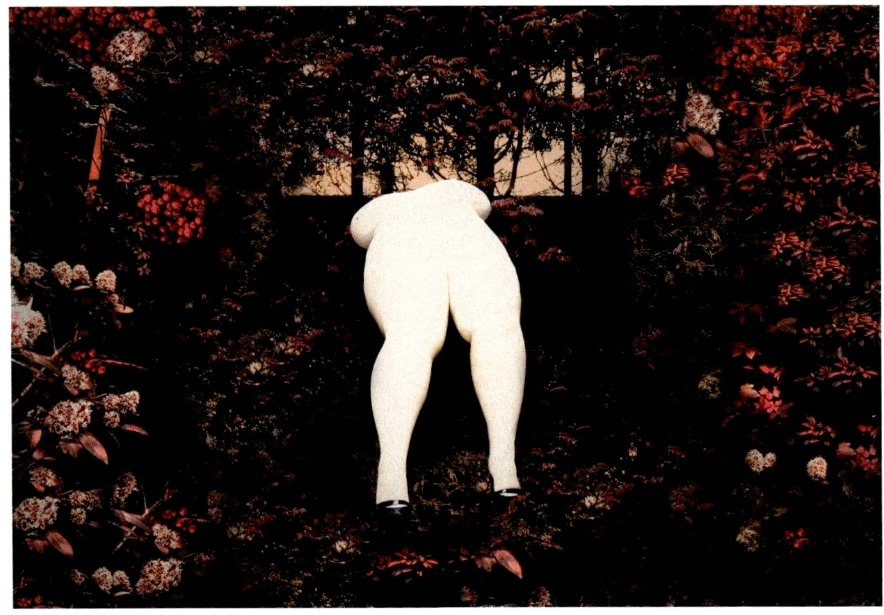

↑ (Top) **Paul Kooiker,** *Sunday 43,* 2011
↑ (Above) **Paul Kooiker,** *Sunday 52,* 2011

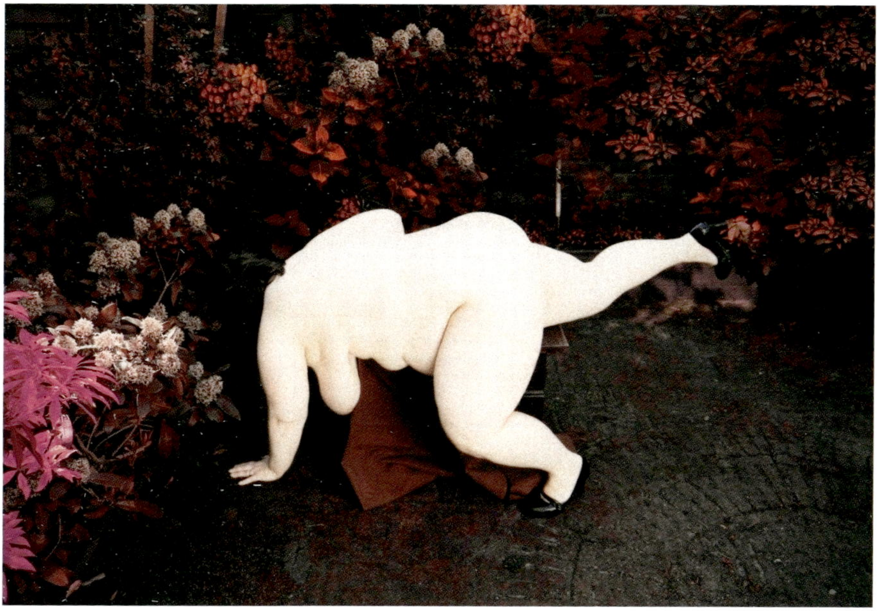

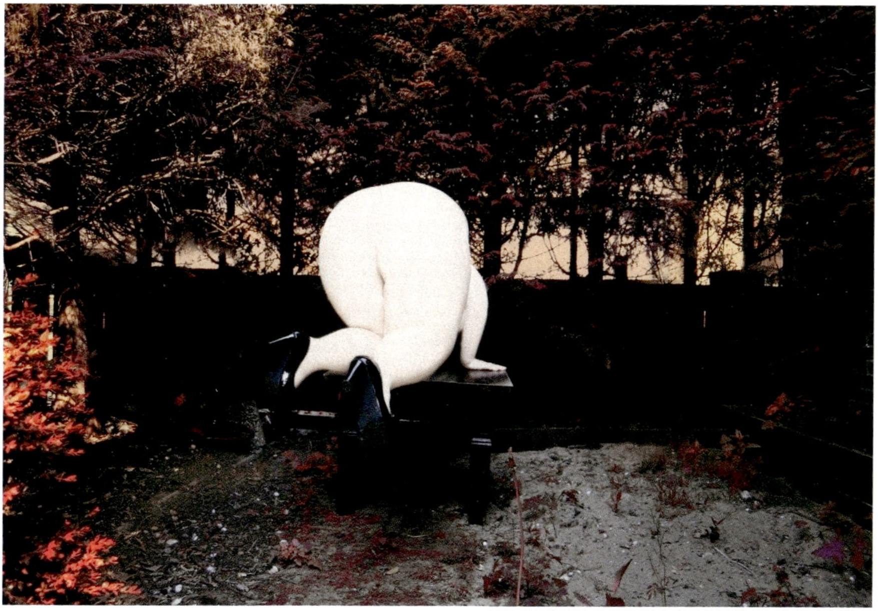

↑ (Top) **Paul Kooiker,** *Sunday 20,* 2011
↑ (Above) **Paul Kooiker,** *Sunday 24,* 2011

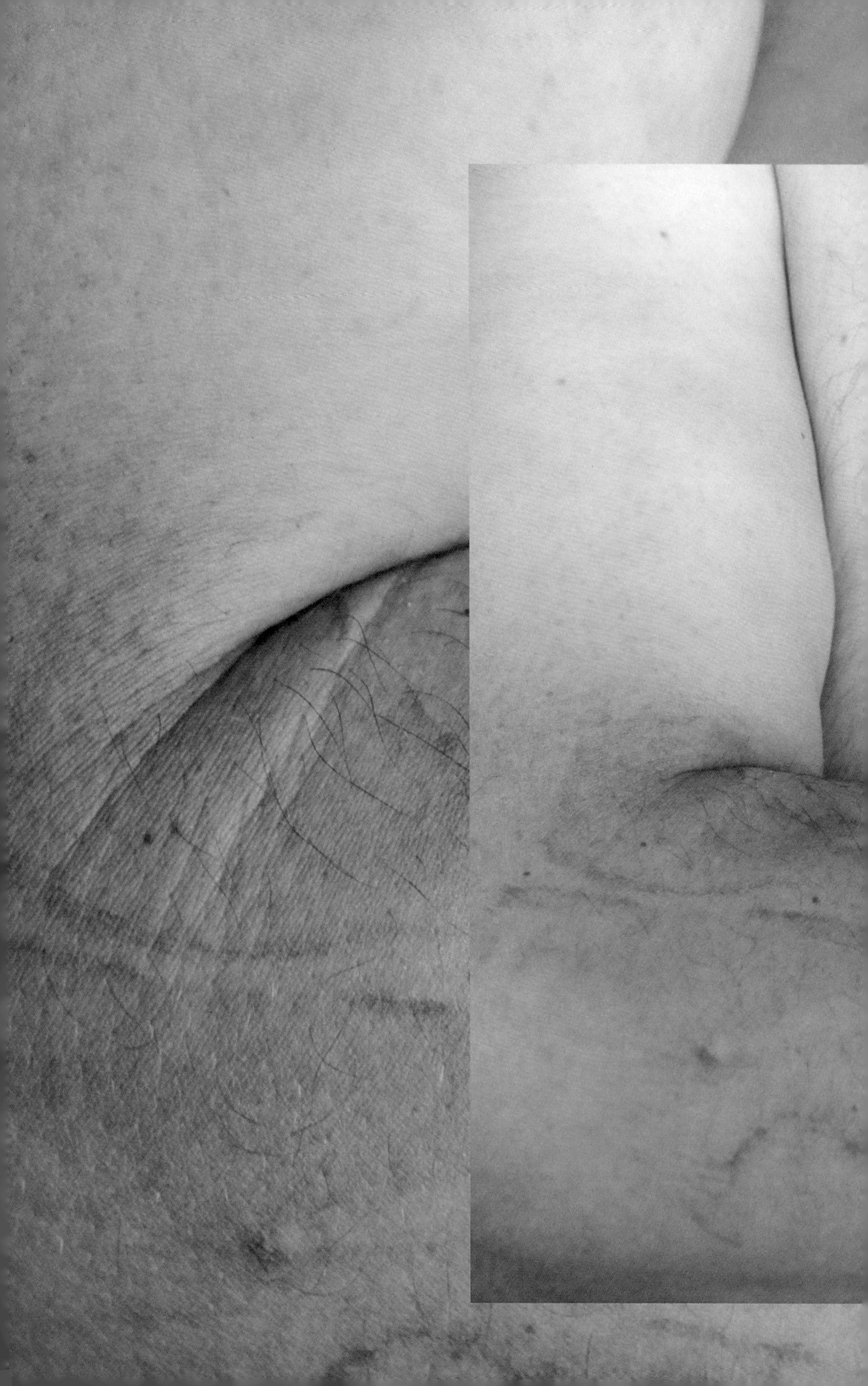

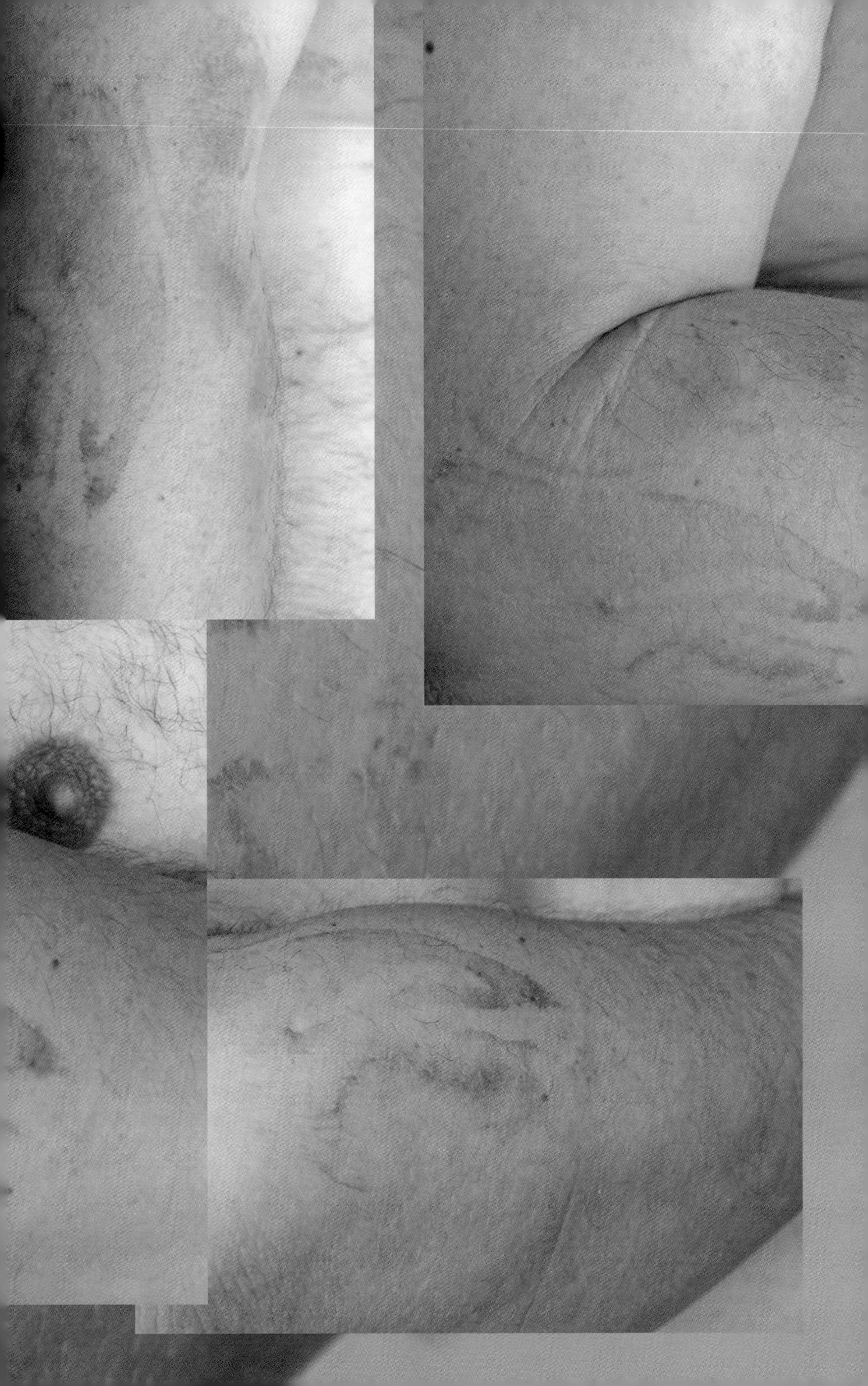

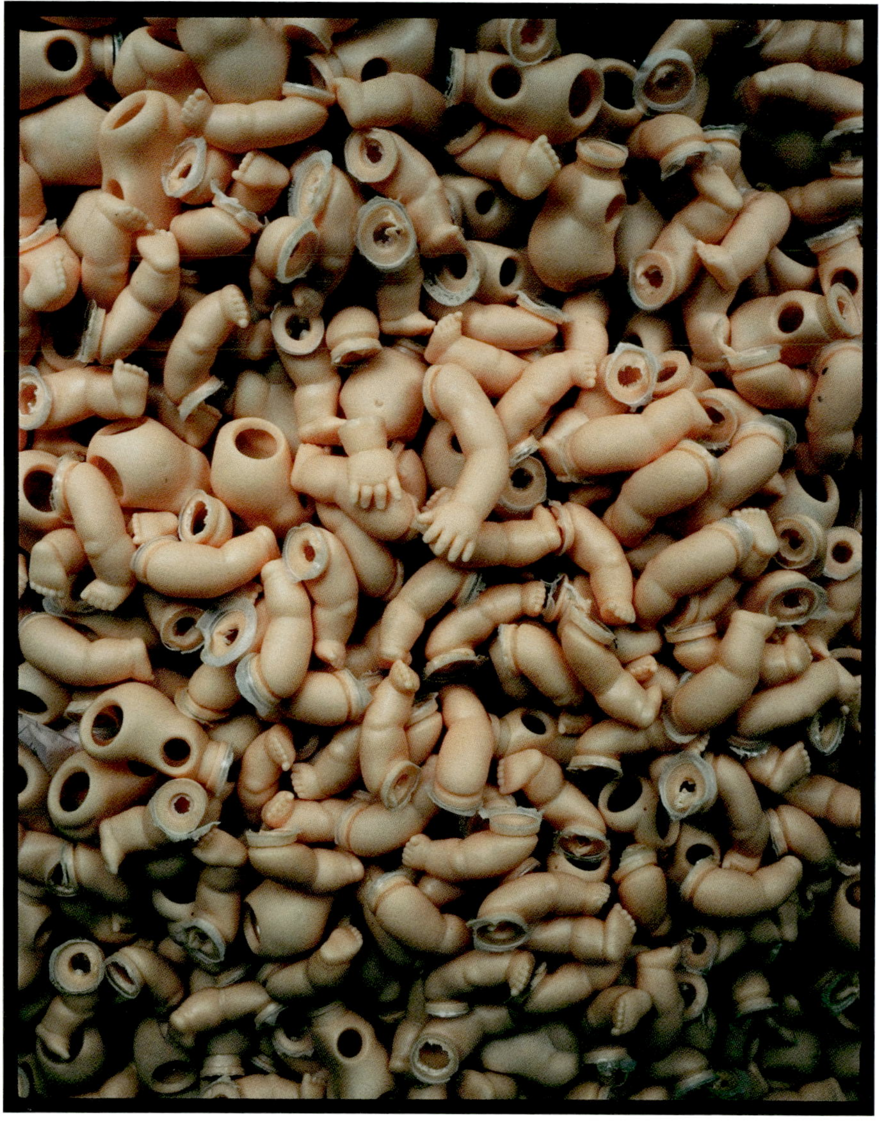

↑ **Xing Danwen,** *Image 3*, from the series 'Duplication', 2003
←(Previous) **Alix Marie,** *Ice Burn*, 2017

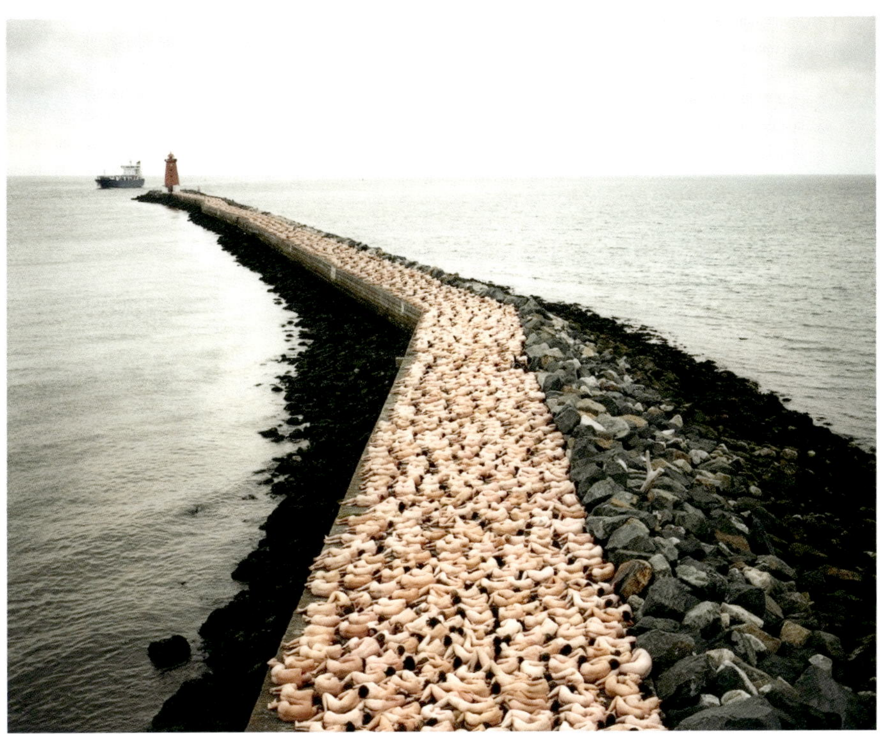

↑ **Spencer Tunick,** *Ireland 3 (Dublin),* 2008

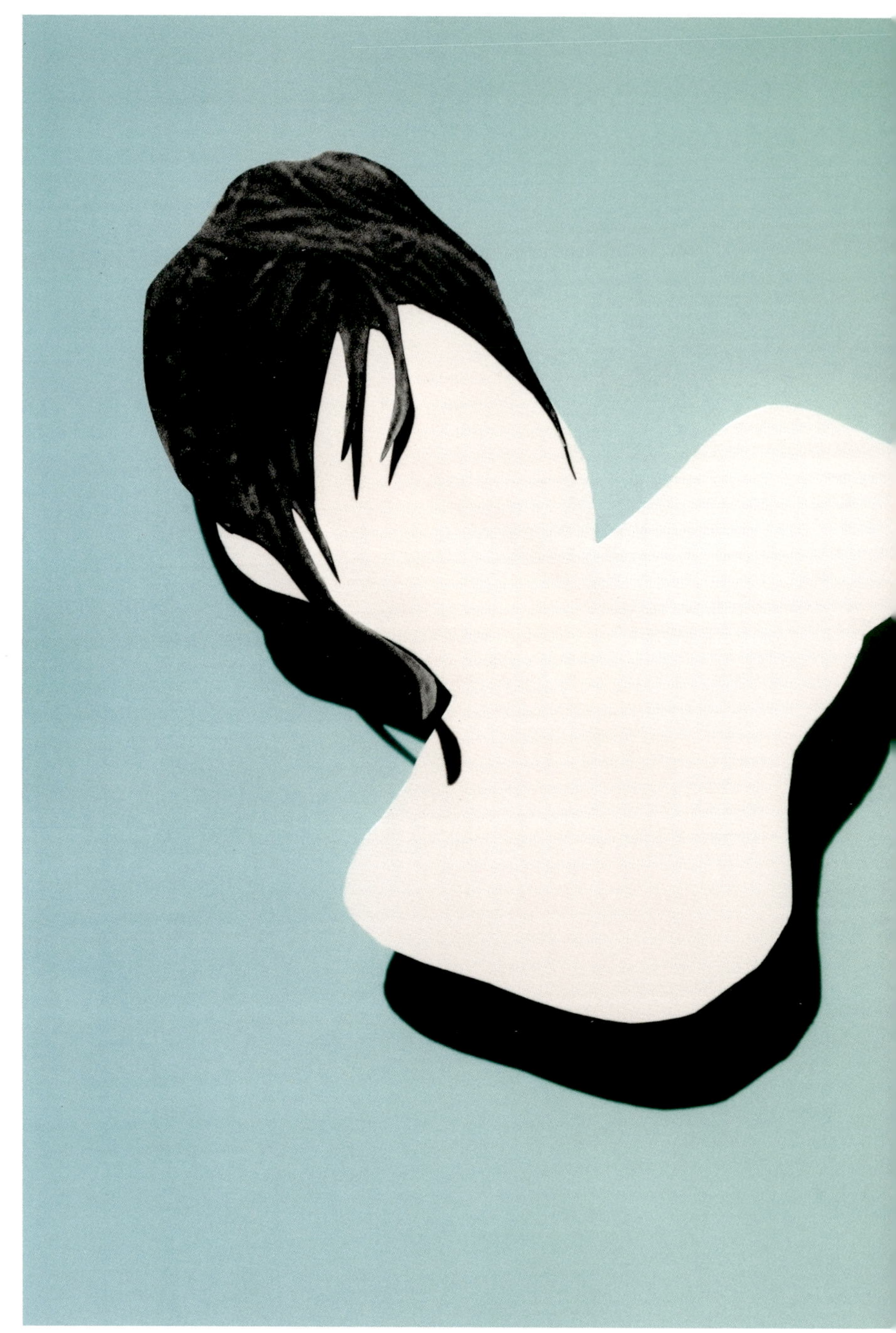

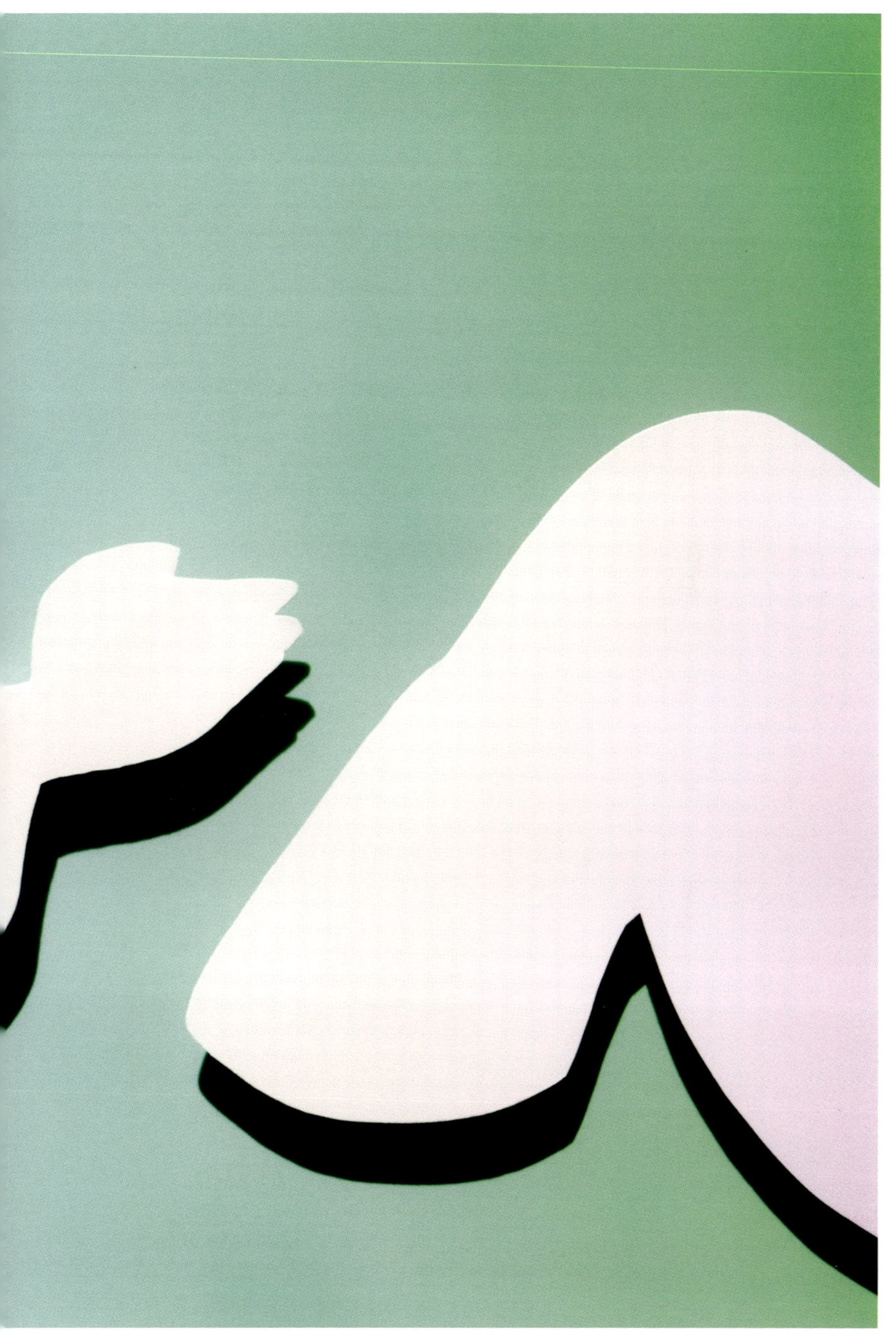

↑ **Ina Jang,** *Watermelon,* 2016

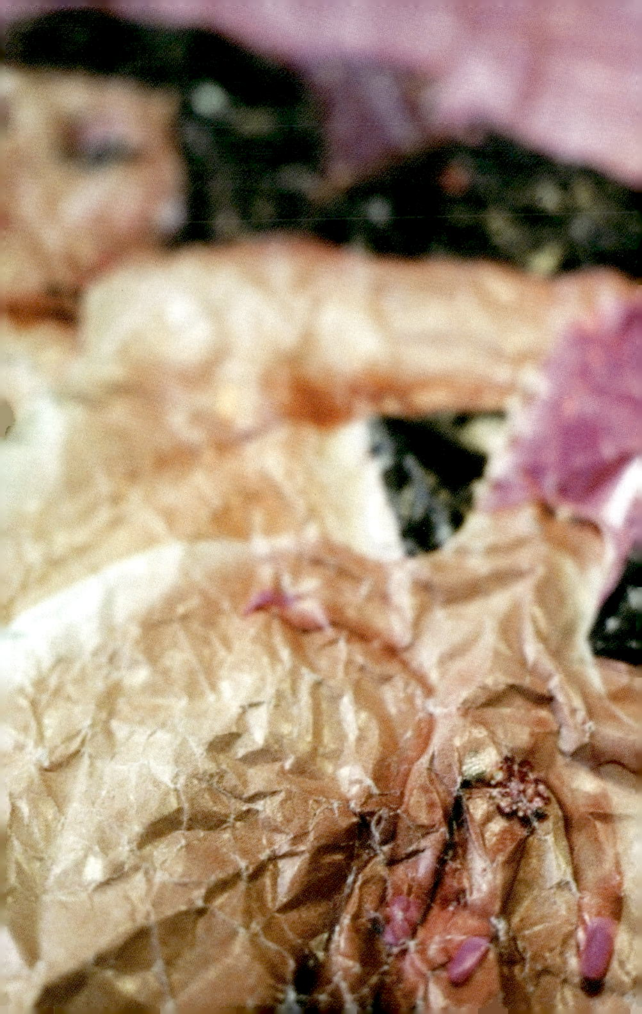

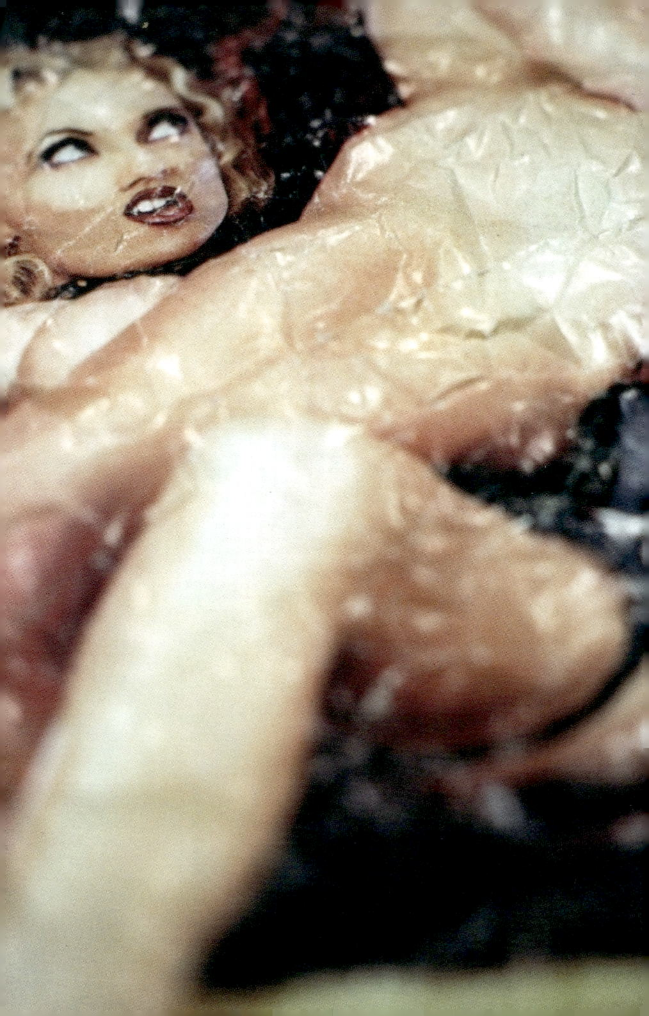

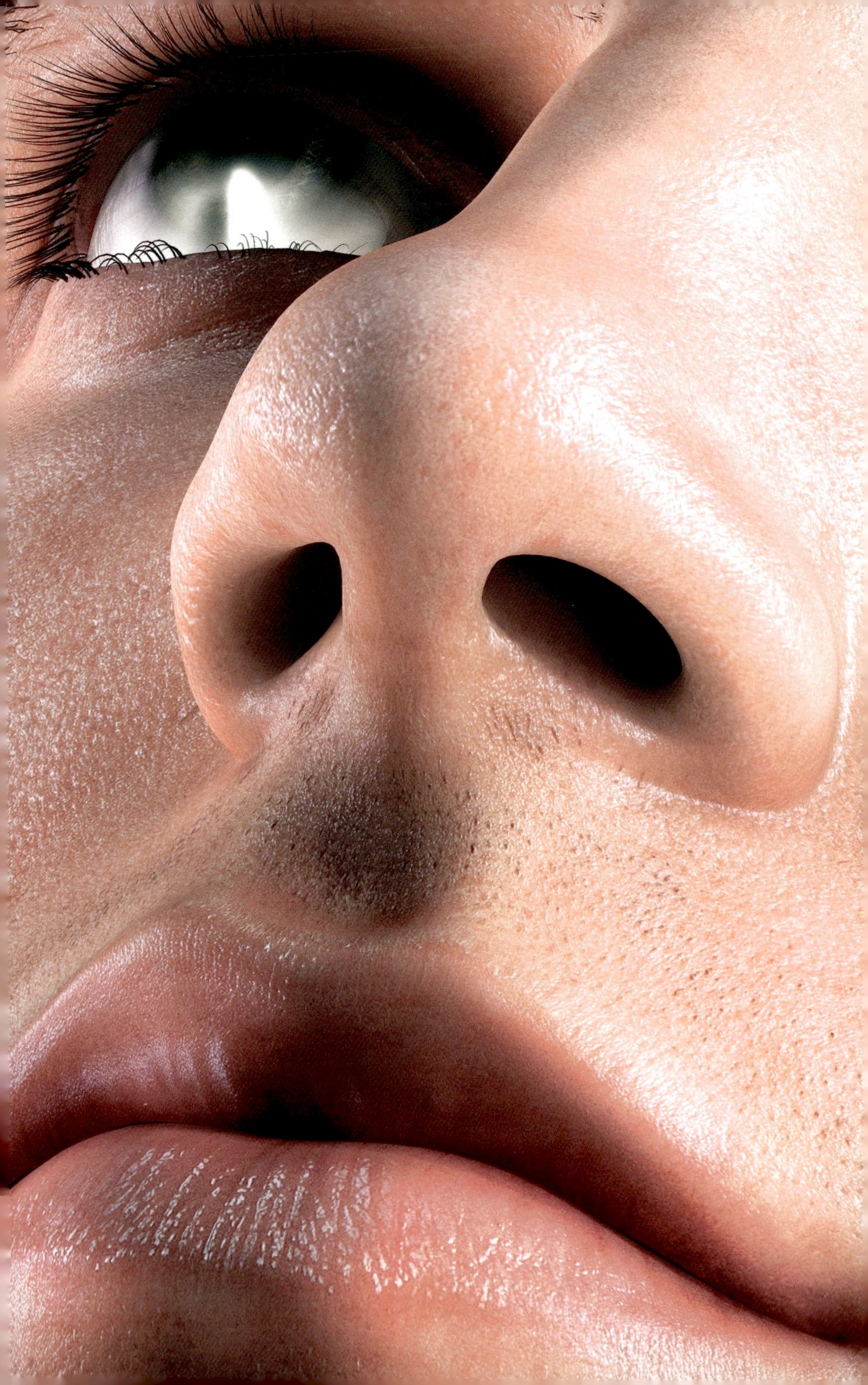

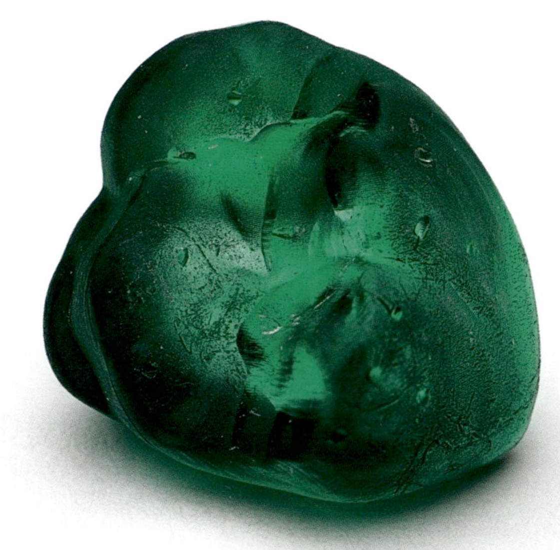

↑ **Catherine Leutenegger,** *New Artificiality / Failed 3D-Printed Dental Crown,* 2015
←**Nicolas Garner,** *Genesis 1:27,* 2017

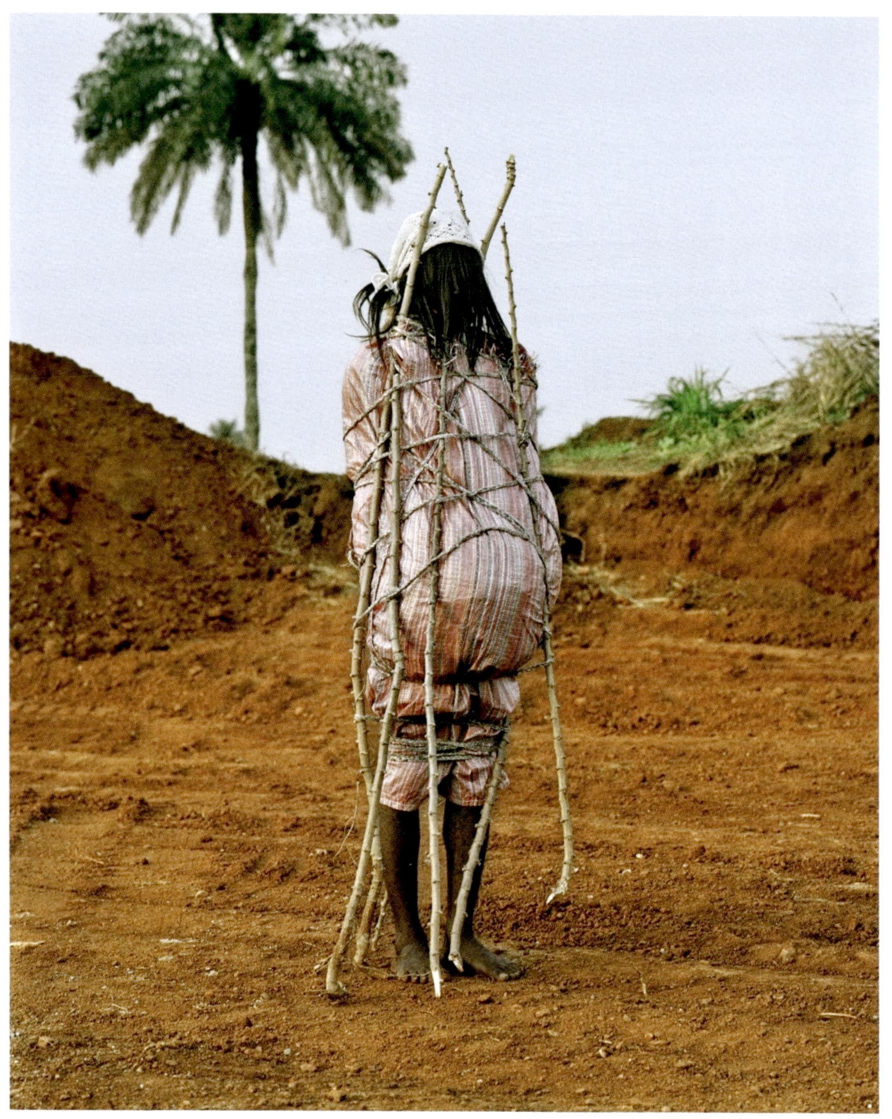

↑ **Namsa Leuba,** *Statuette Kafigeledio Prince Guinée,* 2011

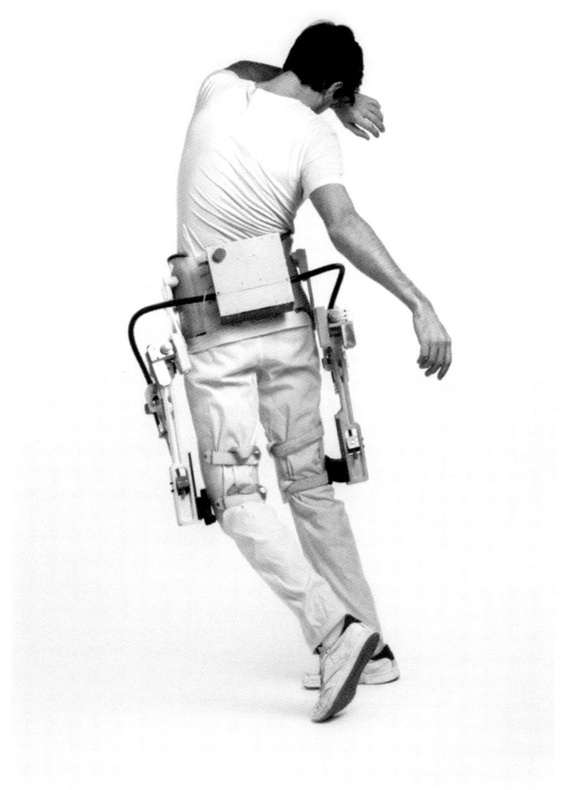

↑ **Yul Tomatala,** *Exo Metazoa,* 2016

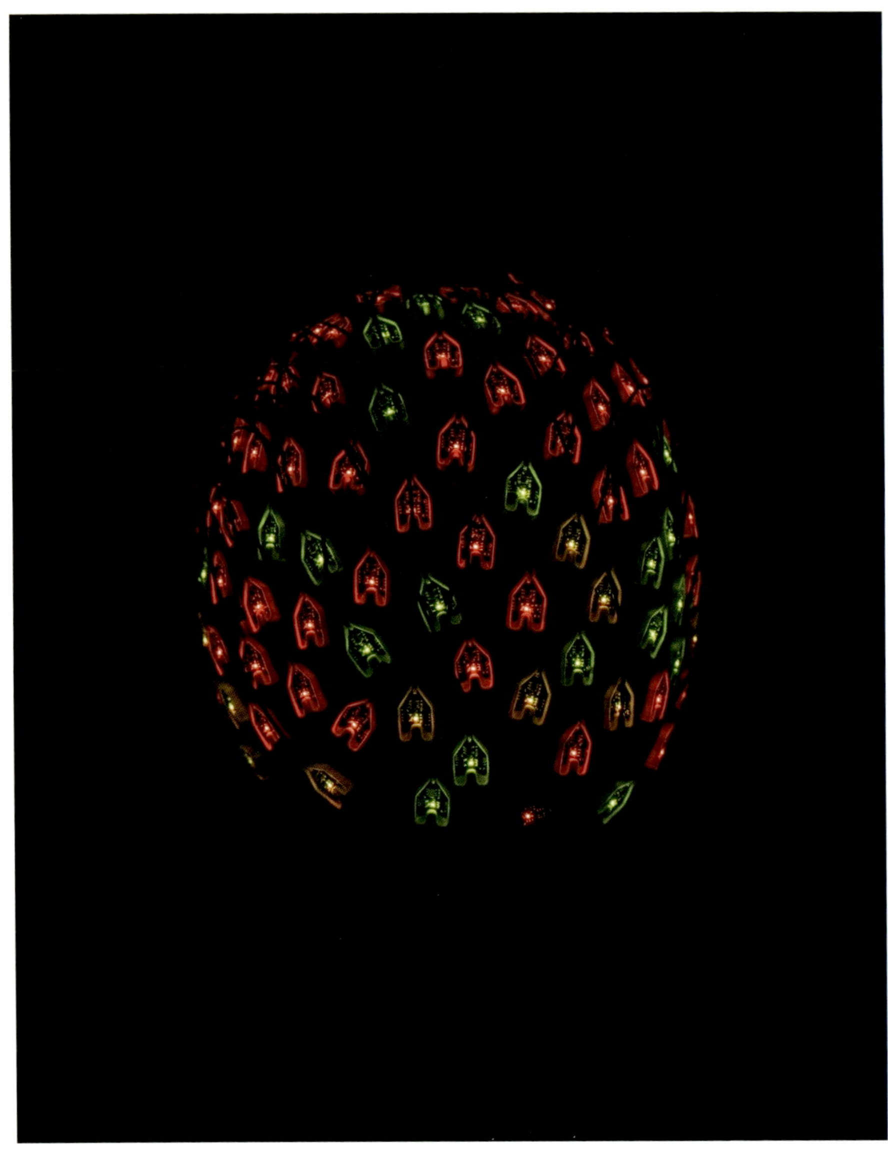

↑ **Matthieu Gafsou,** 2016. 'The electroencephalogram (EEG) measures the brain's electrical activity. It can establish direct communication between the brain and the machine; it does not require a mechanical movement (fingers on a keyboard, the hand on a mouse).'

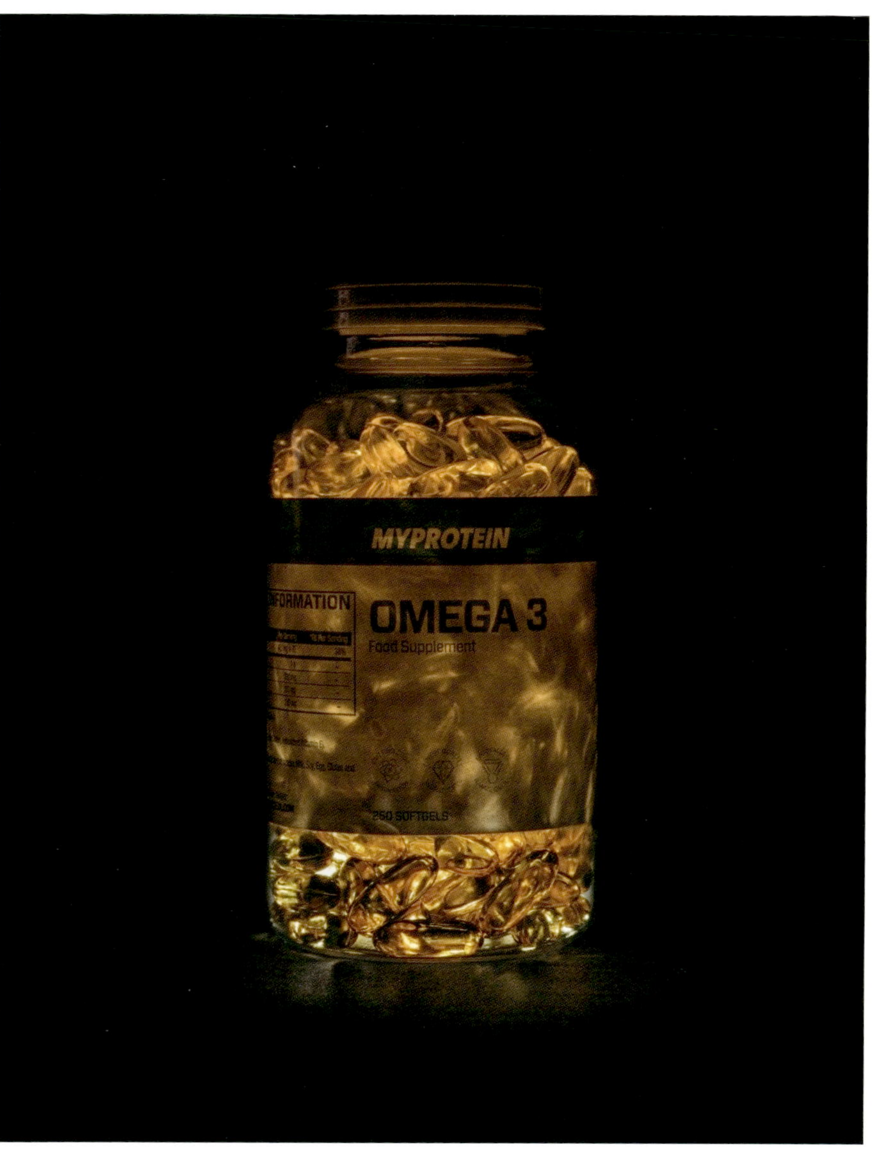

↑ **Matthieu Gafsou,** 2015. 'Dietary supplements can limit diseases and consequently increase life expectancy. Ideologically, this apparently harmless practice is paving the way for the cyborg, because it allies man with embodied technology.'

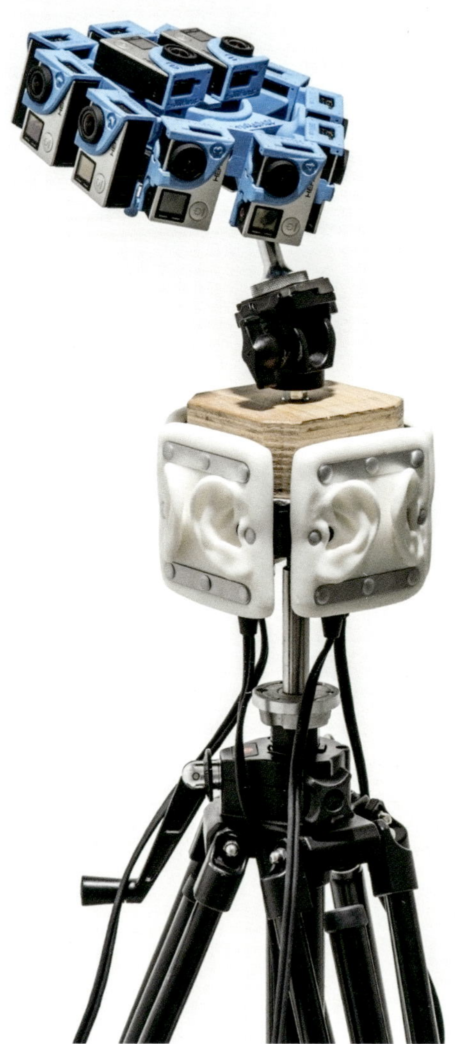

↑ **Matthieu Gafsou,** Device for the fabrication of virtual reality, 2016

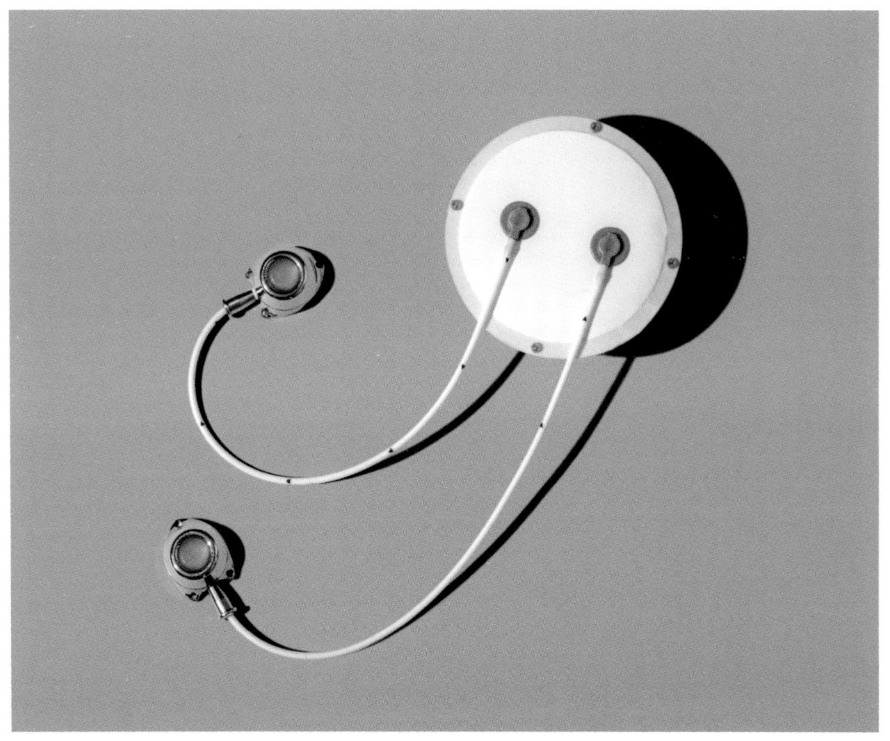

↑ **Matthieu Gafsou,** 2016. 'For years, Defymed has been working on this prototype of an artificial pancreas. Mailpan is an implant filled with stem cells that can secrete insulin.'

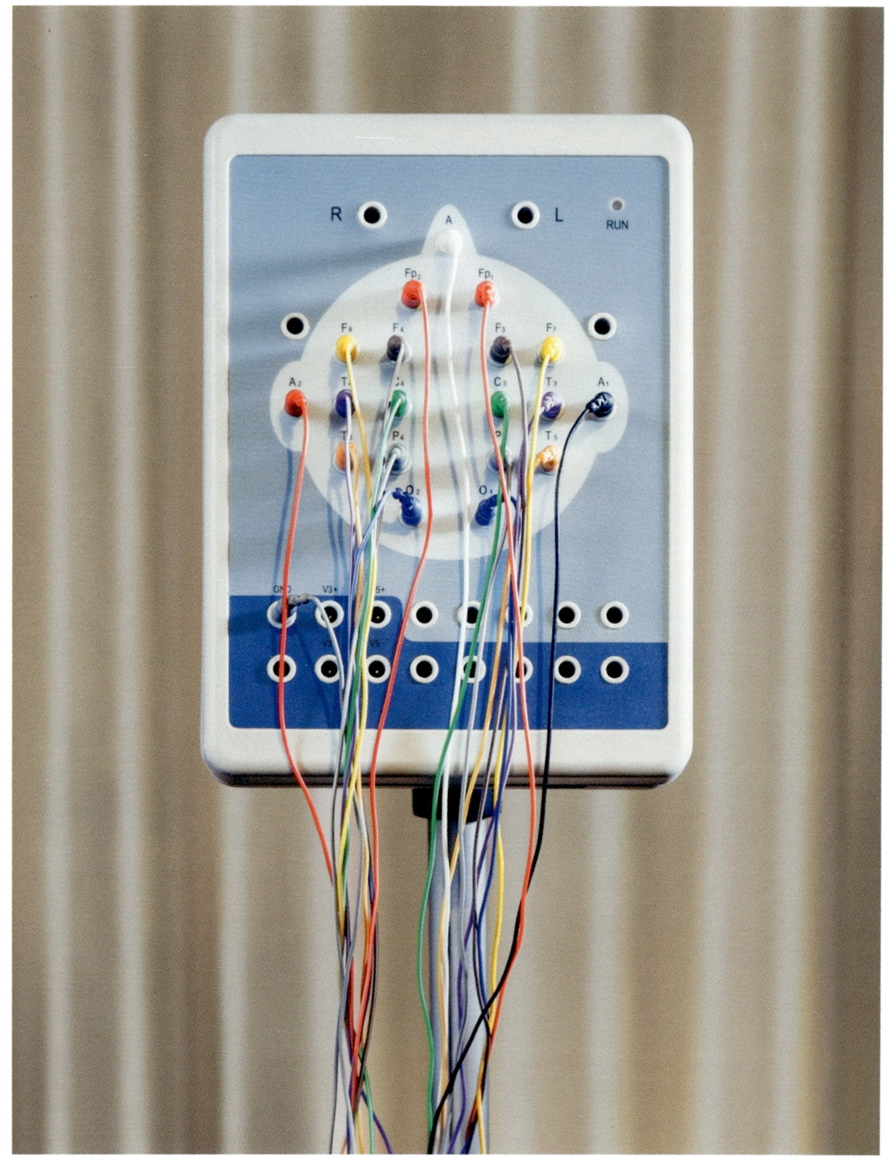

↑ **David Vintiner,** *EEG*, from the series 'Futurists', 2015

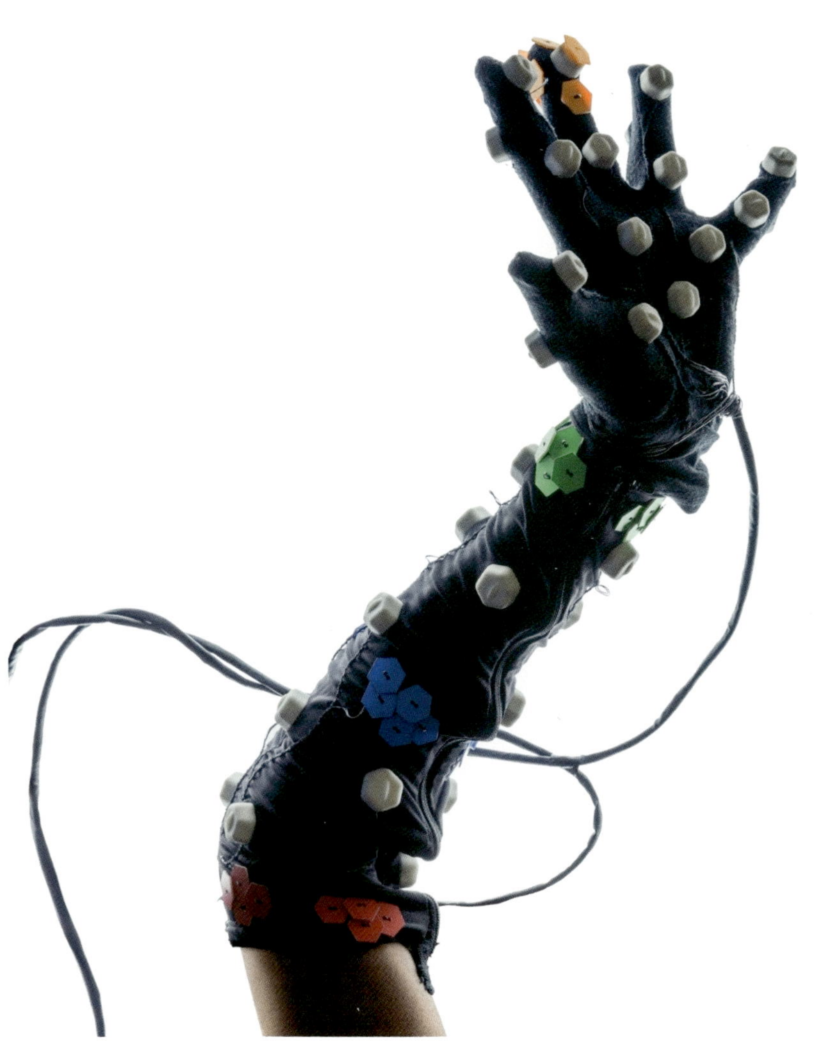

↑ **David Vintiner**, *Skinterface*, from the series 'Futurists', 2016

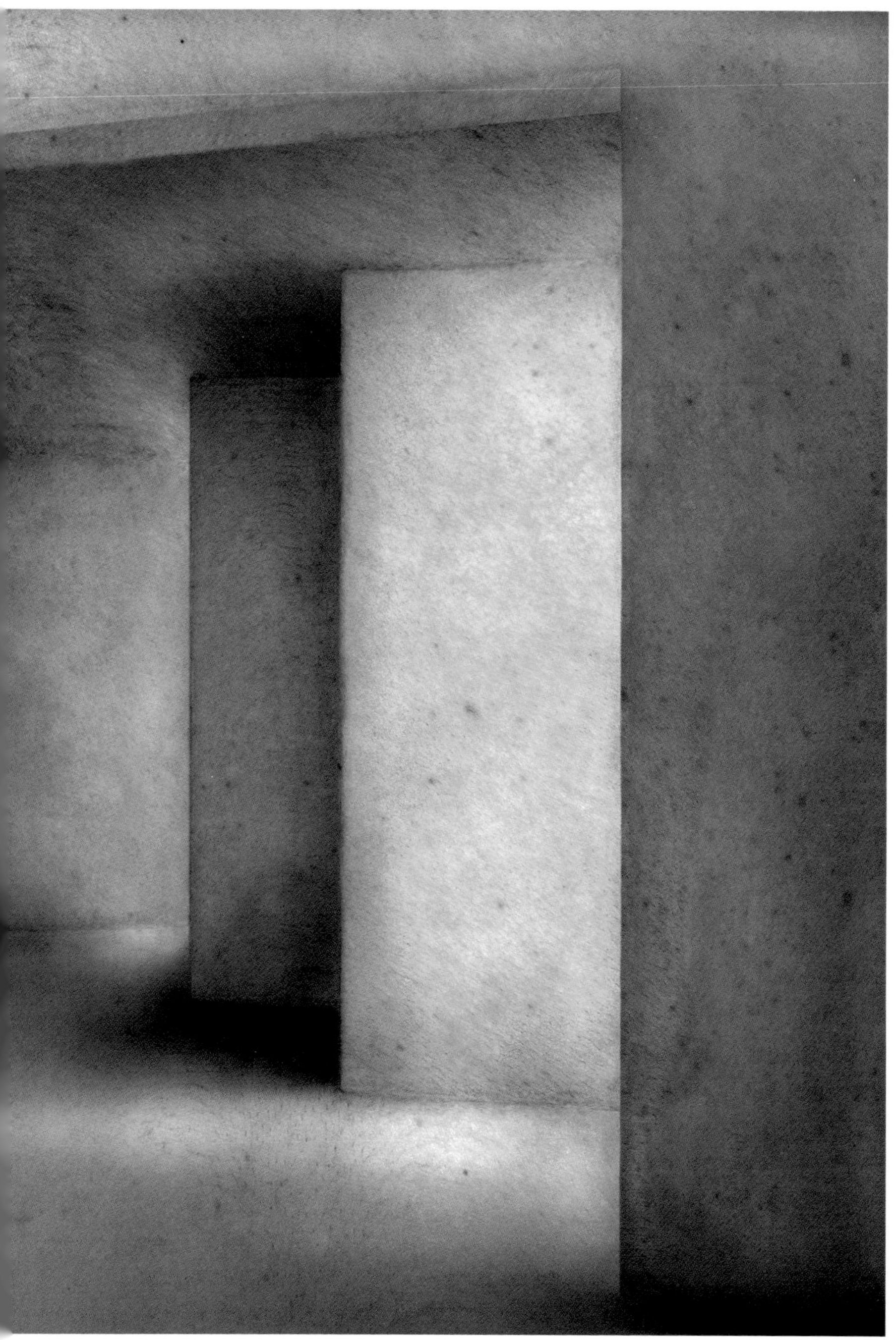

↑ **Aziz + Cucher,** *Interior #5,* 2000

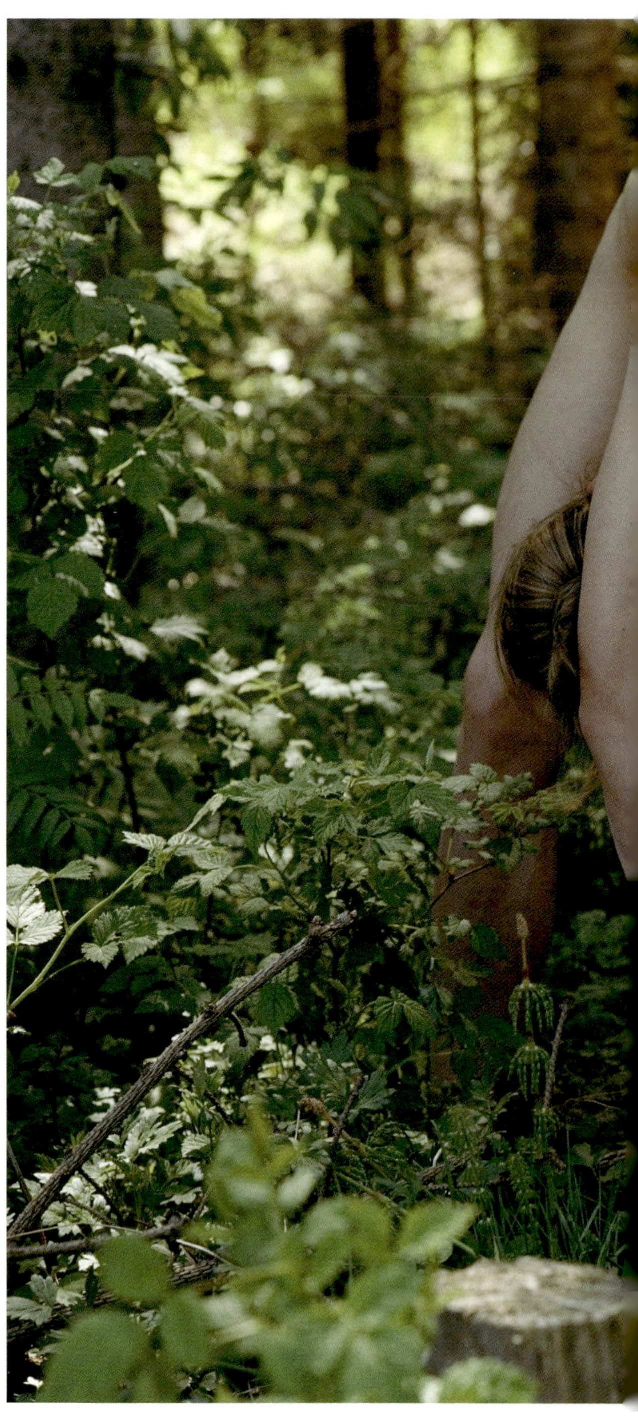

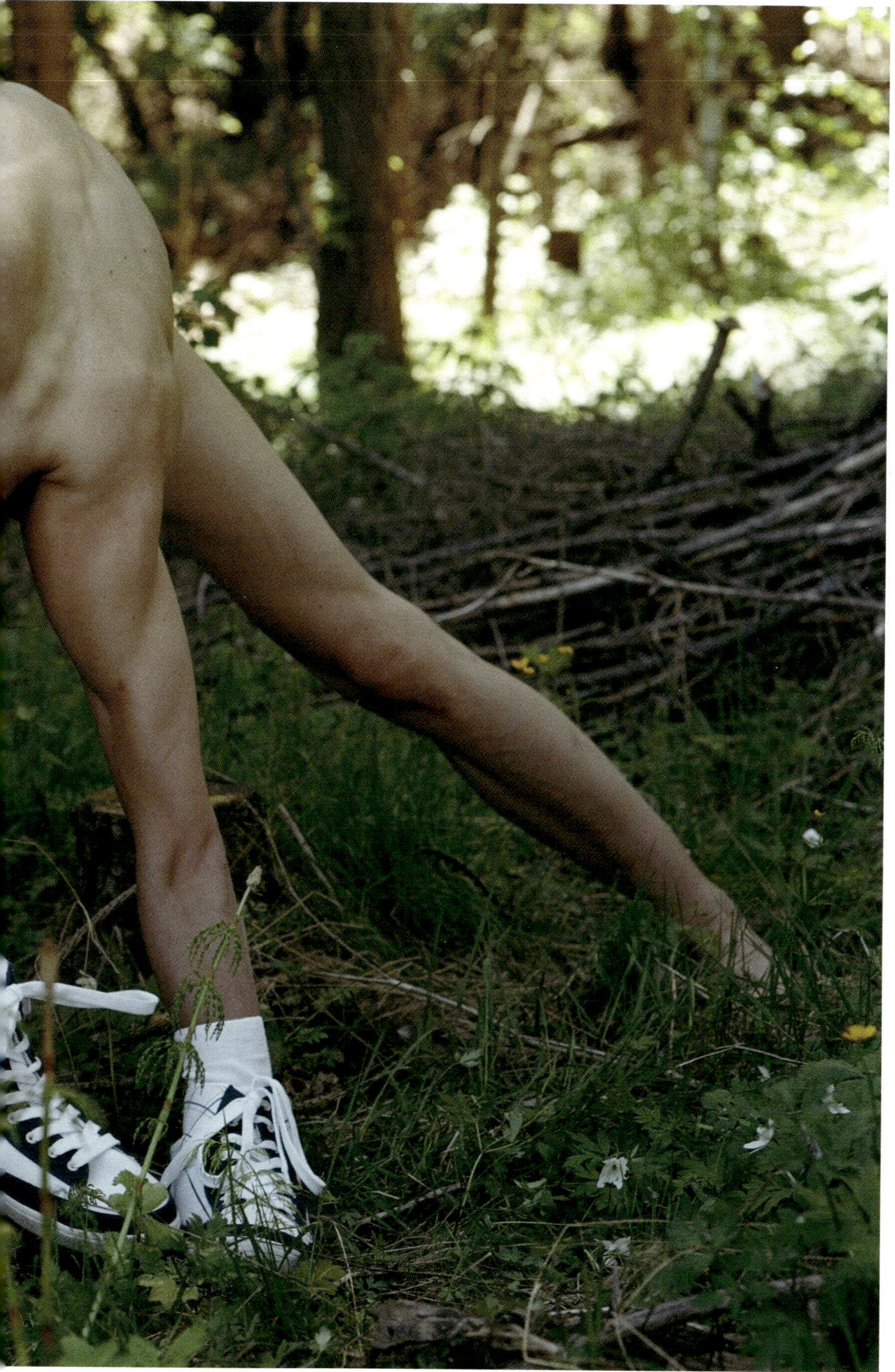

↑ **Torbjørn Rødland,** Untitled, 2009–15

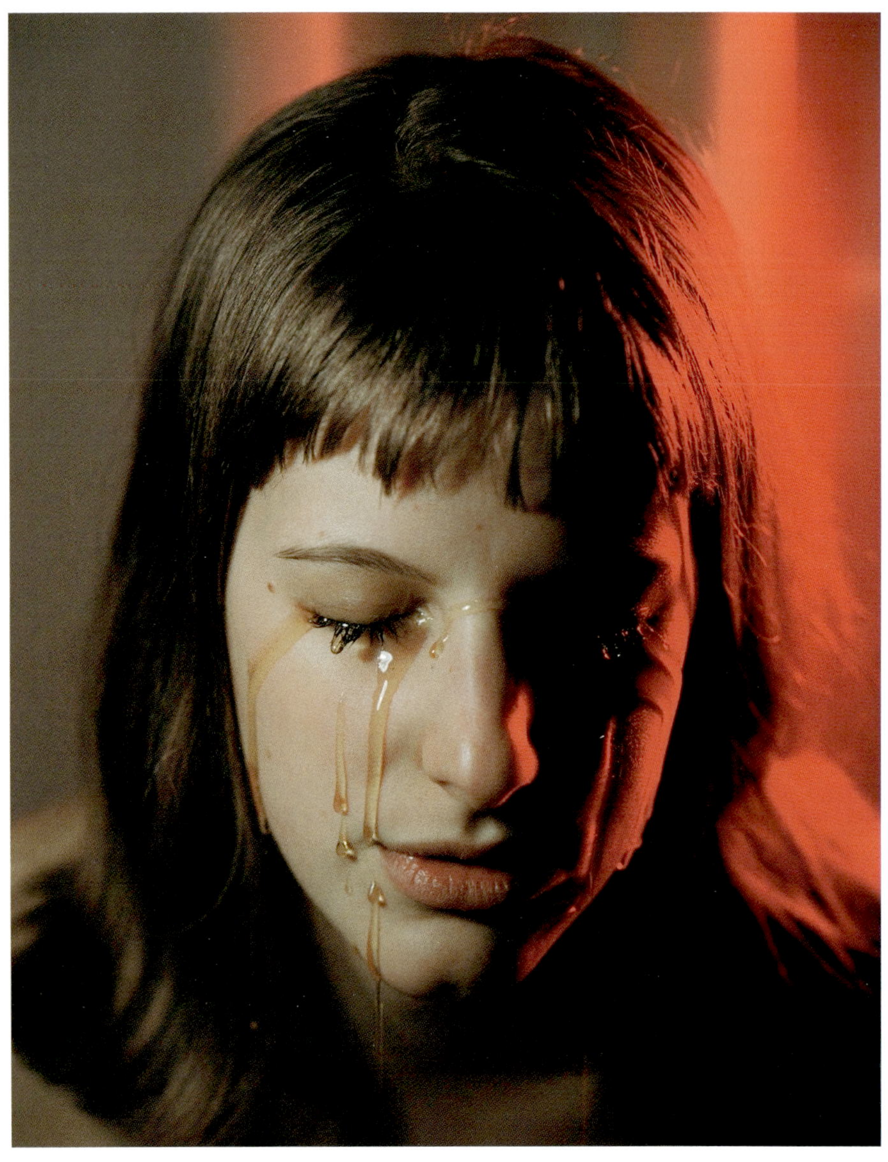

↑ **Torbjørn Rødland,** *Goldene Tränen* [Golden Tears], 2002

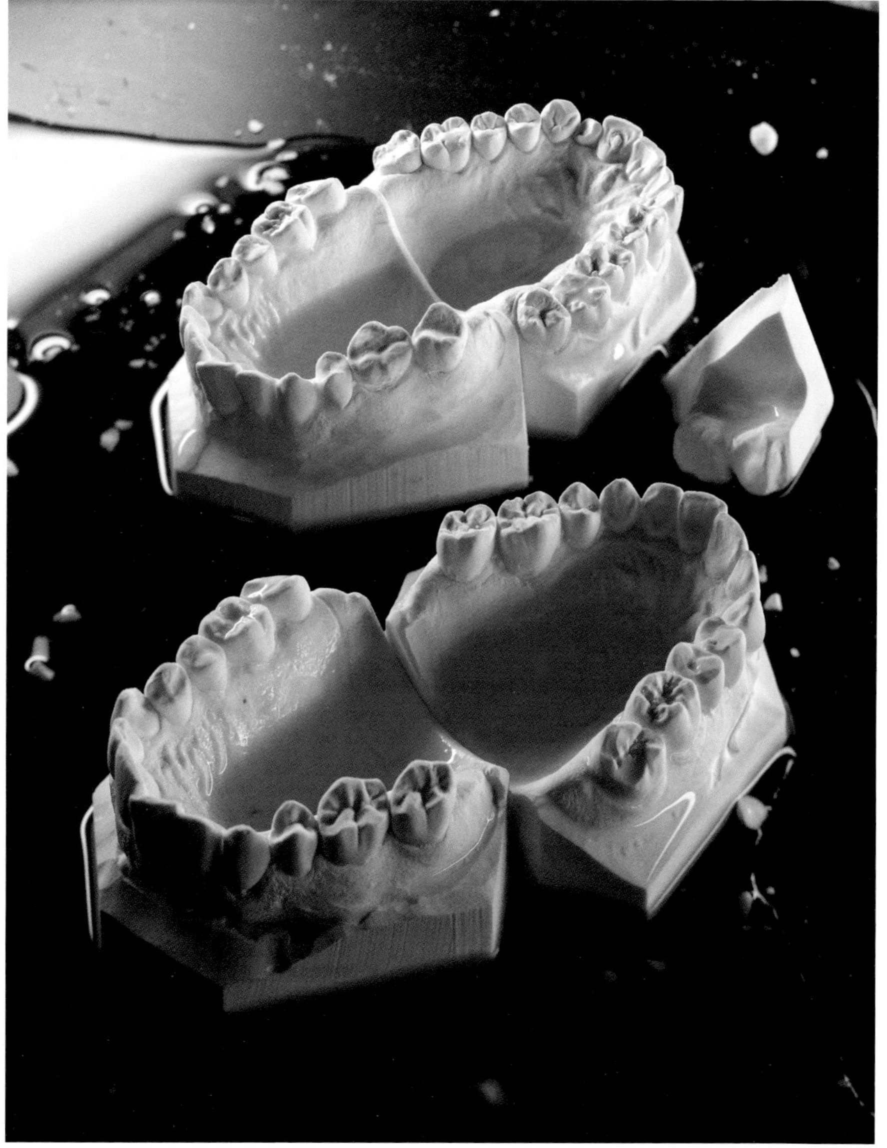

↑ **Torbjørn Rødland,** *Impressions,* 2015

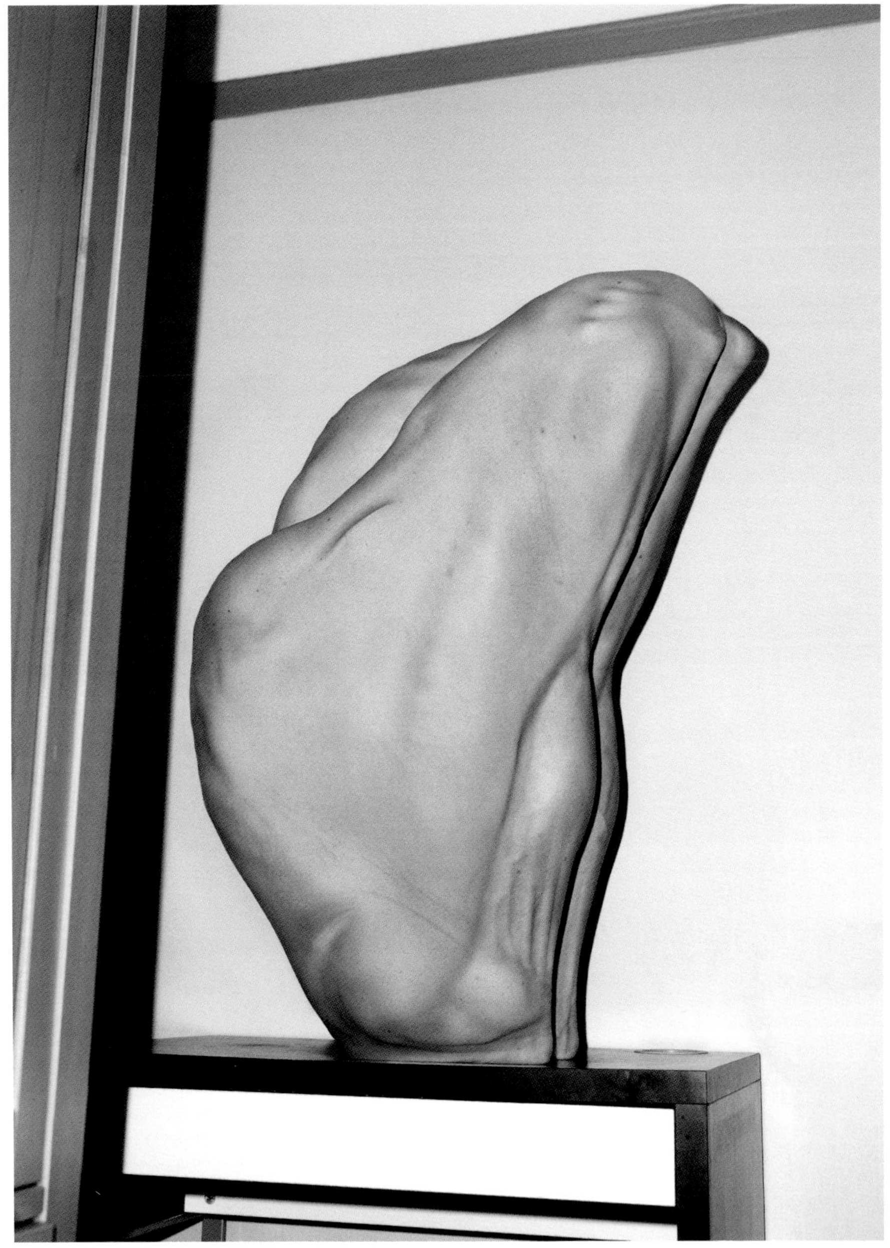

↑ **Asger Carlsen,** Untitled, from the series 'Hester', 2013

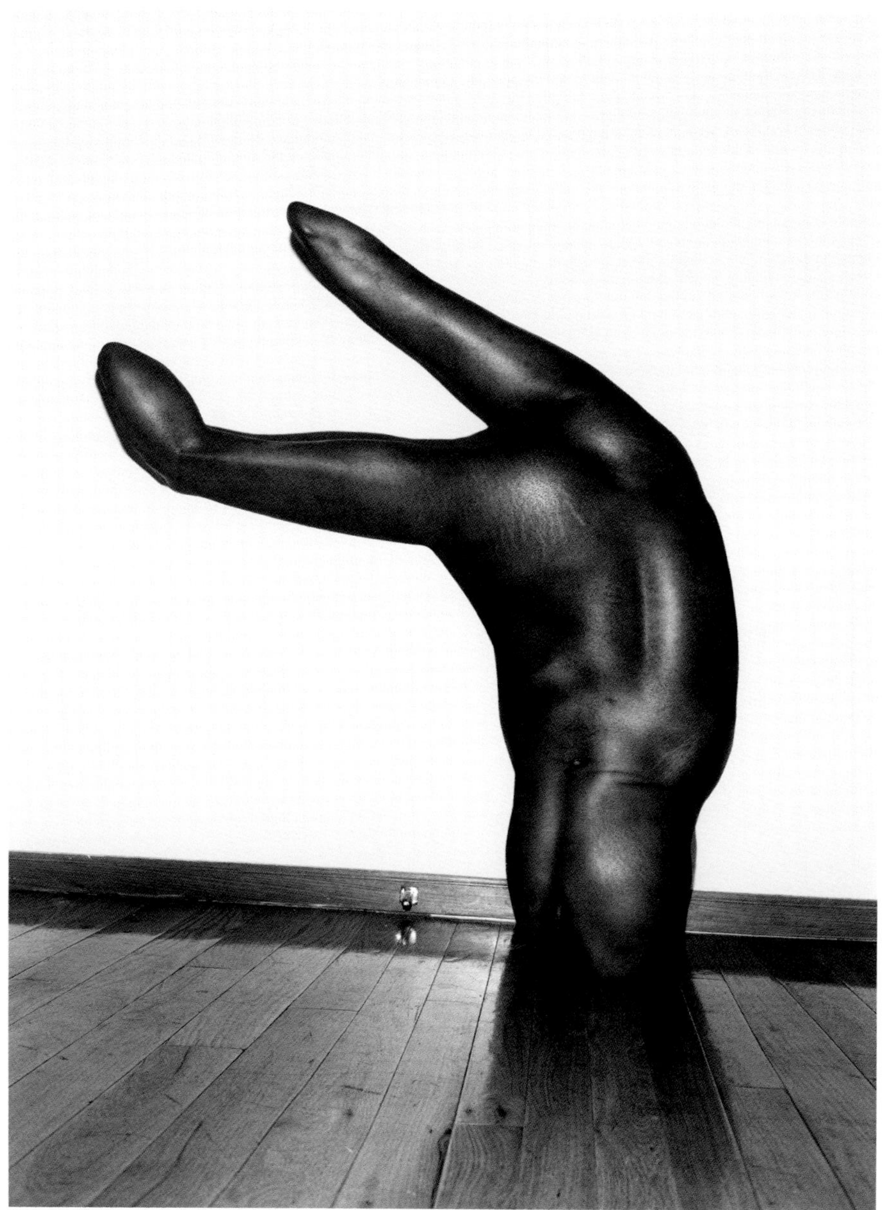

↑ **Asger Carlsen,** Untitled, from the series 'Hester', 2013

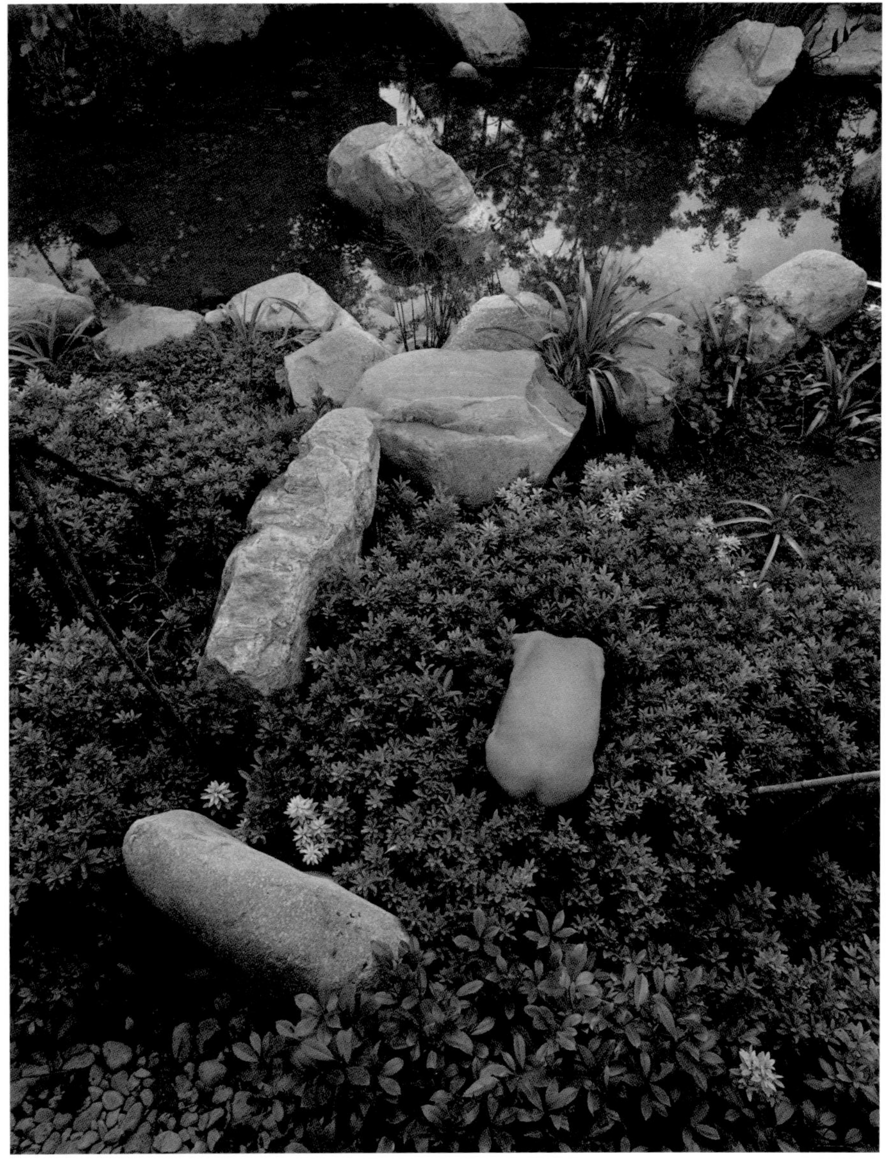

↑ **Arno Rafael Minkkinen**, *Eighteen Rocks, Dali City, China*, 2010

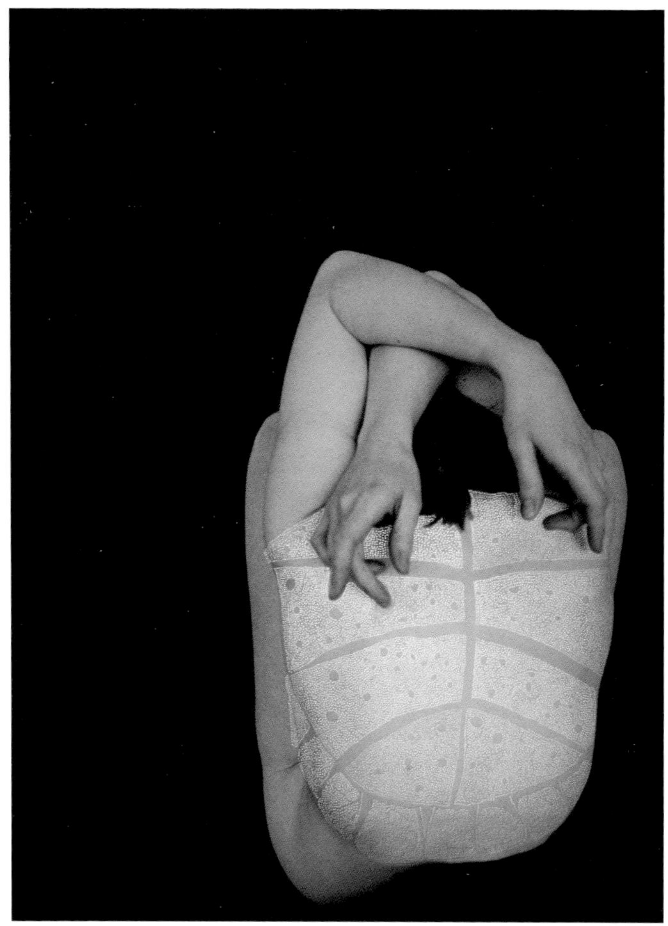

↑ **Jessa Fairbrother,** *Inscription I (armour study),* hand-embellished with perforations made by needle marks, 2015

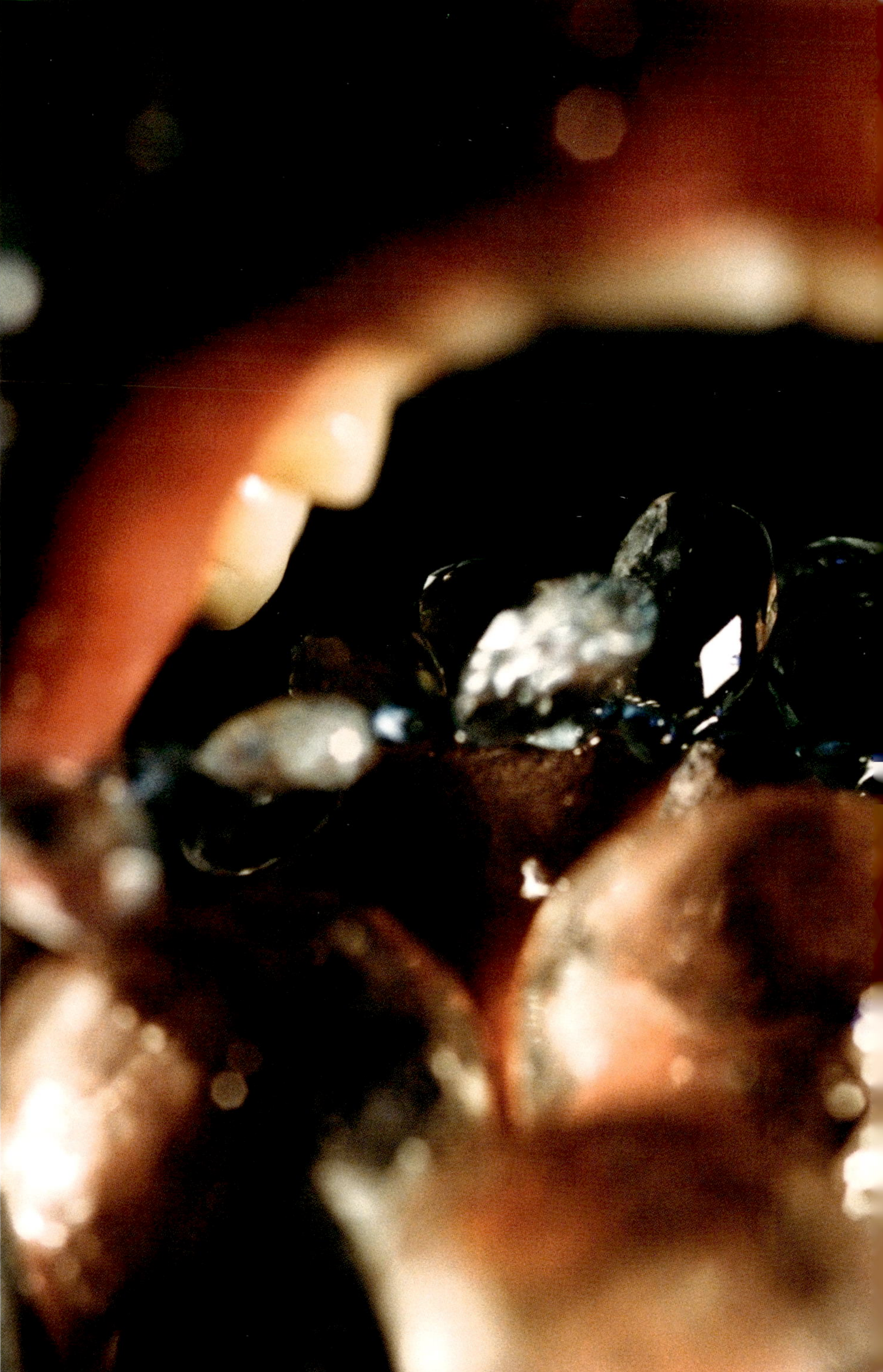

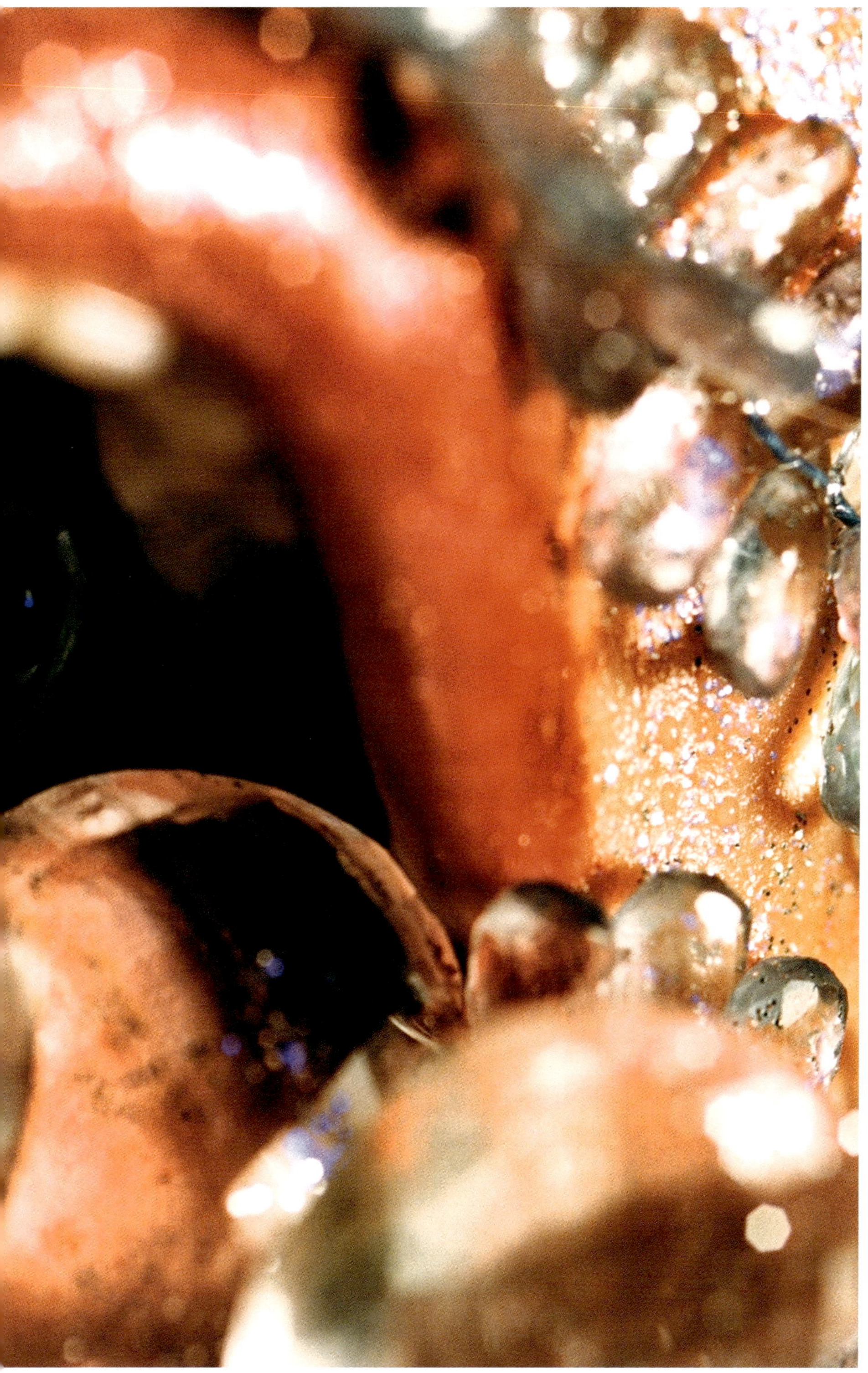

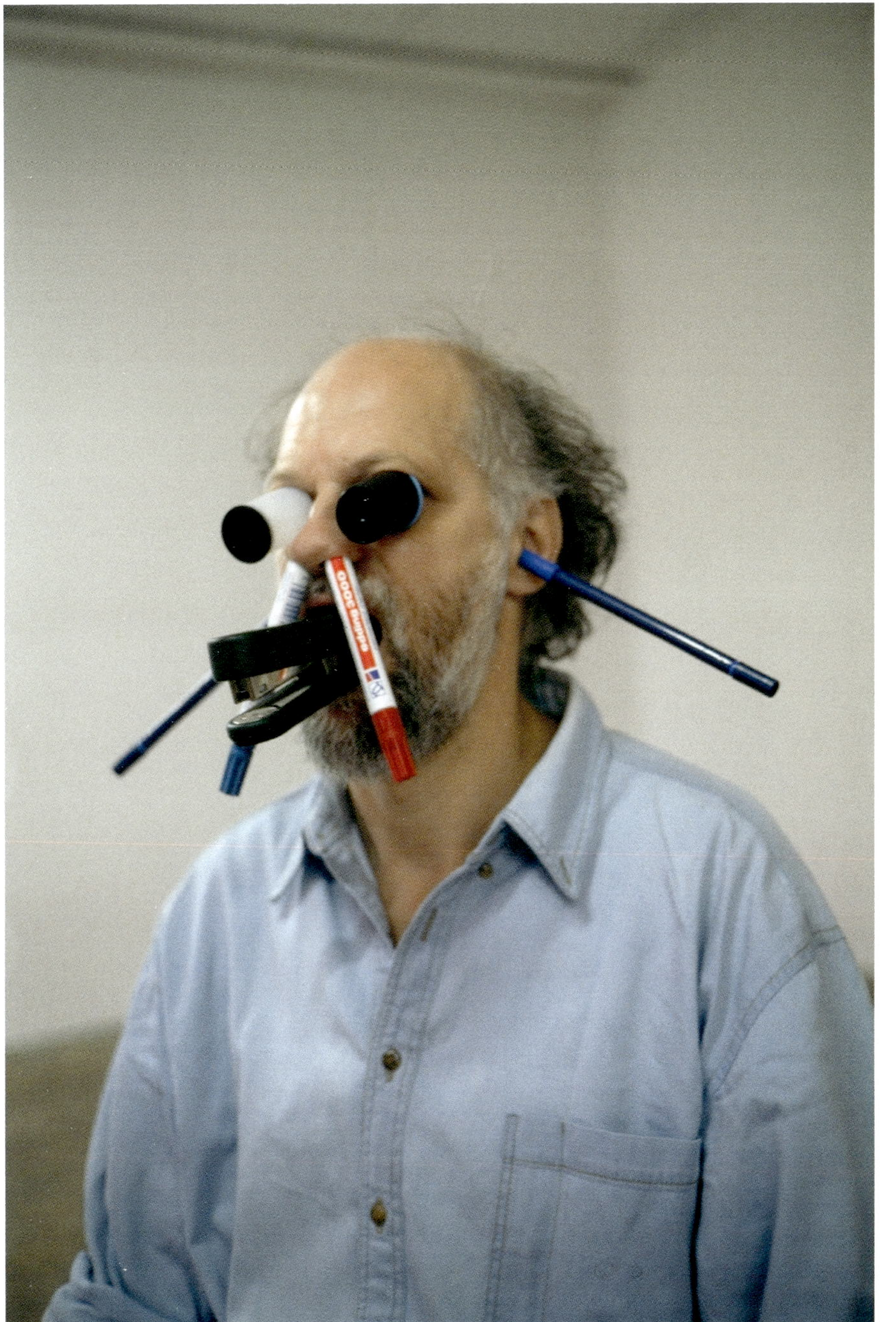

↑ **Erwin Wurm,** *One Minute Sculpture,* 1997

'Let us then conceive that the soul holds her principal seat in that little kernel in the midst of the brain, from whence she diffuses her beams into all the rest of the body by intercourse of the spirit, nerves, yea and the very blood … through the arteries into all the members.'

René Descartes
The Passions of the Soul, Article 34

MIND AND BODY

David Sander

Photography depicts the endlessly diverse and expressive physicality of the body. But what does it tell us of the mind? The relationships between the mind and the body have been extensively studied in disciplines interested in human nature, such as philosophy, psychology, neurosciences and artificial intelligence. But debates around the exact nature of this relationship continue, in particular when it comes to building models of how the mind works: does the mind need the material body (including the brain) to exist? If the mind needs matter, could it be simulated in non-biological material, such as a computer? Can we understand the mind by studying the material body? Though Cartesian dualism posits that the mind (what Descartes called 'the soul'; see p.235) and body were closely linked but essentially separate, current research into the interrelation of the mind and the brain tends to reject this approach, leading to disciplines such as 'neuropsychology', 'behavioural neurology' or 'cognitive neuroscience', which study how the mind works by investigating how the brain works. Adopting this 'materialistic' approach we can discuss how the mind is embodied, first by considering how the brain represents the state of various parts of the body, and then by assessing the role of bodily feelings in emotions.

THE EMBODIED MIND

Evidently the brain is a part of the body. But it is a unique part of the body, in that activity in the brain represents activity elsewhere in the body, such as the muscles and the viscera. Indeed, our central nervous system plays a key role not only in driving behaviour and in regulating bodily reactions and homeostasis (the maintenance of physiological equilibrium), but also in representing bodily states. Classical studies in neuroscience and neurology, in particular the landmark work of the neurosurgeon Wilder Penfield and his colleagues, have allowed the description of a so-called *cortical homunculus*, whereby motor and sensory systems are mapped to specific areas of the cerebral cortex — known as somatotopic arrangement — corresponding to distorted representations of anatomical features. Such work shows the extent to which various parts of the body are specifically represented in the cortex, with some parts being 'over-represented': e.g. anatomical regions such as the mouth or the hand use a proportionally larger number of neurons, and thus appear proportionally larger on cortical homunculi.

Since the work of Penfield and his colleagues, the somatotopic arrangement of motor and sensory systems has been extensively studied using modern neuroimaging techniques, including functional Magnetic Resonance Imaging (fMRI), greatly improving our understanding of how bodily reactions are elicited, perceived, represented and regulated by the human brain. In particular, with the work of scholars such as Bud Craig, Antonio Damasio and Hugo Critchley, both cortical and sub-cortical somatosensory maps have been identified, sub-serving various perceptions such as interoception, i.e. the perception of one's own physiological signals from internal bodily states (e.g. heart rate or respiration), and proprioception, i.e. the perception of the position and movement of one's own body (e.g. where one's hands are in the dark). According to several research traditions, integration of external information through exteroception (e.g. vision or olfaction) together with interoception and proprioception contribute fundamentally to self-consciousness and the sense of being a unified self.

The very fact that some aspects of the physical state of the body (e.g. position of limbs, heart rate, respiration and temperature) are represented in the brain has led some researchers to consider whether, given the distributed nature of mental representations in the neural networks, even psychological mechanisms that are not *a priori* bodily-related may be modulated by bodily-related mechanisms. In this tradition, the notion of an 'embodied mind' (or 'embodied cognition') refers to the idea that cognition is body-dependent, meaning that seemingly 'pure' psychological functions, such as decision-making, reasoning, language, learning, memory, creative thought or emotional response are constrained by the nature and activity of bodily systems (other than the brain). However, accepting that the body may play an important role in the elicitation of emotions raises further questions about the nature of 'an emotion'.

EMOTIONS AND BODILY FEELINGS

What is an emotion? When responding to this question, famously asked by the philosopher and psychologist William James in the title of his landmark 1884 article, different research traditions have found a variety of answers, typically focusing on differing aspects of an emotional response. In particular, a seminal debate is still alive in contemporary research concerning the role of the body during an emotional episode. Some scholars, such as William James, Jesse Prinz or Antonio Damasio, argue that one's own bodily reaction is what elicits the emotion. For instance, in his aforementioned provocative definition of emotion William James suggested that 'bodily changes follow directly the PERCEPTION of the exciting fact, and that our feeling of the same changes as they occur IS the emotion'. On the other hand, scholars such as Walter Cannon, Nico Frijda, Richard Lazarus or Klaus Scherer would counter-argue that, while important to consider if one is to properly understand a full-blown emotion, bodily reactions are secondary to the psychological mechanisms involved in the appraisal of emotion-eliciting situations.

Obviously, internal physiological signals perceived by the brain during motivational states such as hunger or thirst will drive our actions in order to fulfil our needs. However, the role of this perception of internal physiological signals (i.e. interoception) in the elicitation of an emotional response (e.g. surprise, anger, fear, disgust, joy, interest, admiration, pride, shame or guilt) remains fiercely debated. Though there is some consensus that during a typically experienced emotional episode our body is involved, its specific role remains unclear. Research indicates that changes in the body accompany an emotion, and can be measured in the autonomic nervous system (e.g. changes in heart rate, skin temperature, respiration, pupil dilation) and also in the somatic nervous system, with voluntary changes in motor activity (e.g. a smile or the position of the body). However, the causal nature of these manifestations in an emotional episode is debated: is the bodily reaction primary or secondary to the emotion itself? And if it is the bodily reaction that elicits the emotion, then what is it that elicits the bodily reaction in the first place?

One way to resolve this debate is to adopt a so-called componential approach to emotion, according to which an emotion is not a unitary phenomenon but rather corresponds to changes in five components: (1) the appraisal of (real or imagined) events will lead to (2) motor reactions (e.g. facial expressions and vocal expressions), (3) psychophysiological reactions (e.g. increase in heart rate and skin temperature), (4) action preparation (e.g. approach towards or avoidance of the eliciting stimulus) and (5) a feeling (a conscious experience). With such an approach to emotion, the bodily reaction corresponds to an aspect of the emotion that is integrated with other information when a conscious feeling emerges. Embodiment theories of emotion, such as the one proposed by Paula Niedenthal, help resolve this debate by considering that the body does not need to be actually aroused during each and every emotional episode: the mere cerebral representation of the bodily reactions in somatosensory maps may be sufficient. This notion of an 'as-if body loop', as proposed by Antonio Damasio, links the simulation of a body state (or the 'imagination' of a bodily state, constructed from memory, which is not actually taking place in the organism) to felt emotions.

Contemporary research on the interrelationship between the mind, the brain and the (rest of the) body tends not only to accept that studying the brain is a useful way to understand the mind, but also that studying the interactions between the body and the brain proves useful in better understanding the (embodied) mind. In addition to methodological developments in the ways we can measure bodily reactions, future research into the interrelationship of the mind and body will benefit from technological innovations that engage the full body of participants in experimental settings, using, for instance, virtual reality immersions. Such research will allow a better understanding of how the body, both when actually aroused and when arousal is simulated in the brain, might play a key role in the mind.

CELEBRATION

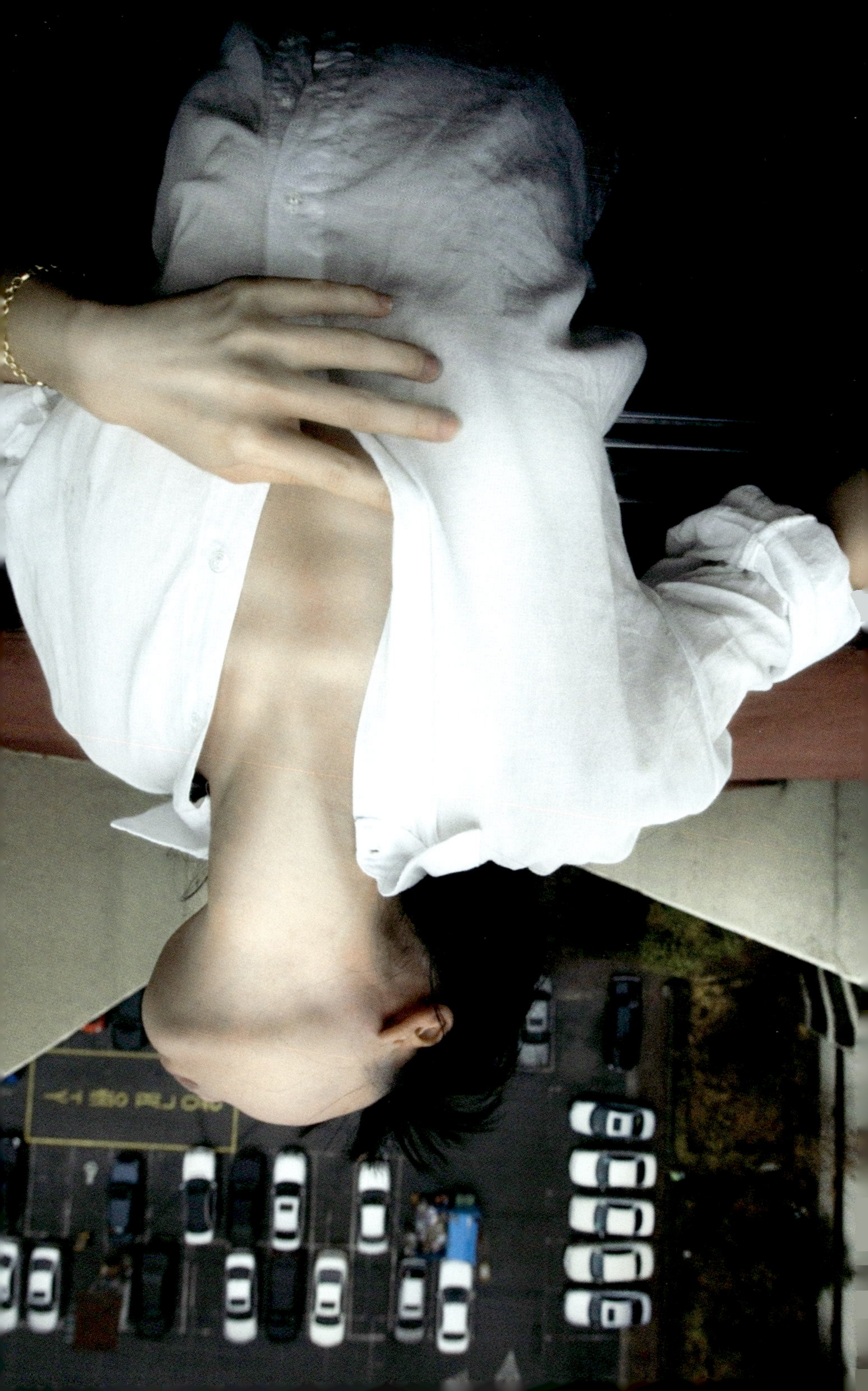

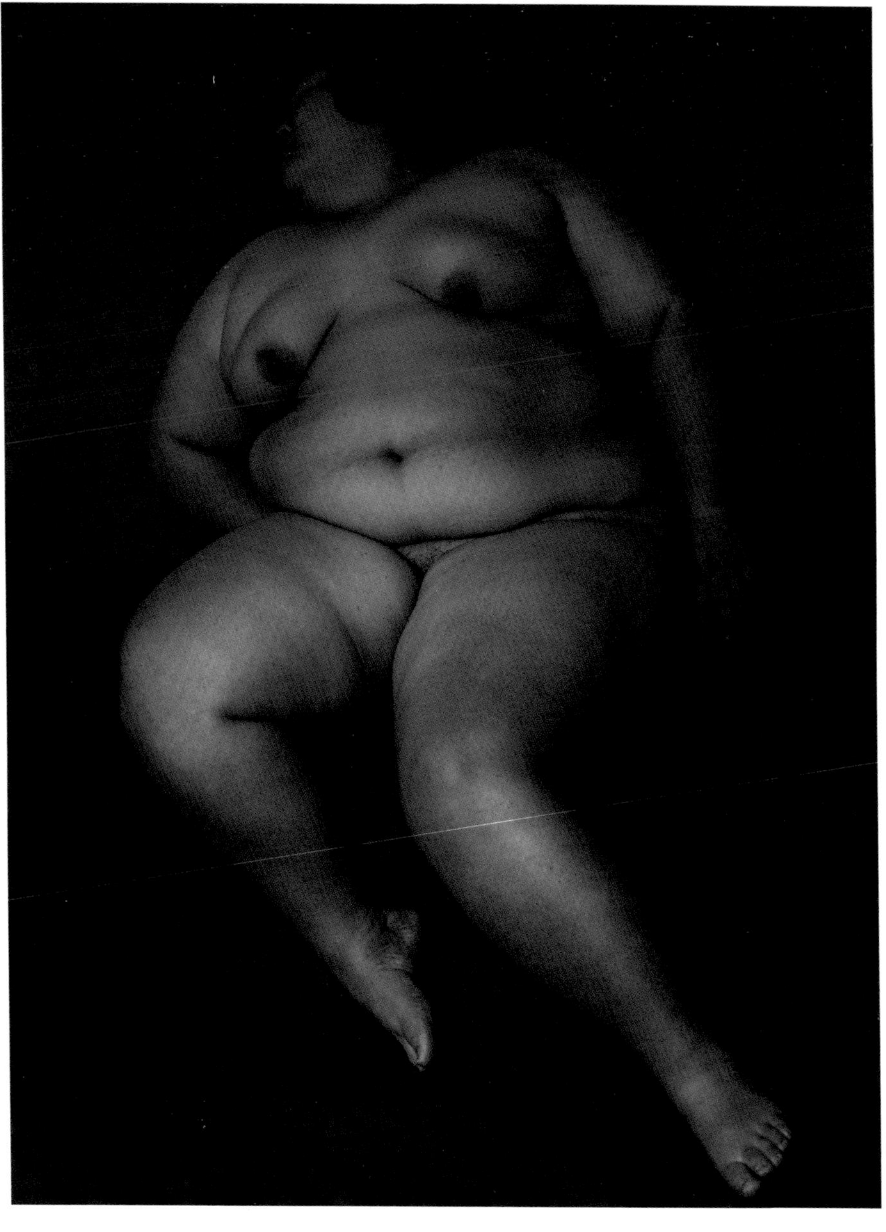

↑ **Kiki Xue,** *The Form of the Body,* 2015
←(Previous) **Jun Ahn,** *Self-Portrait,* 2008

Twentieth-century photography forged the image of a beautiful, slim, young, clean, luminous, strong, infinite, virtually incorporeal body, as the philosopher Michel Foucault noted in reference to the utopian body to which we are all presumed to aspire. The images of beauty and health filling our magazines and commercials celebrate a body — usually female — that exists to be looked at, admired, dreamed of. The nude has become a significant genre in the history of photography. The English language draws a clear distinction between the nude (sculptural, seductive and eternal, posing before the spectator, usually in a studio) and the naked (unclothed, often showing little confidence, and rendered fragile by the fact of being displayed so intimately). But this same exposed body can take on another, different sense when it is shown in nature, close to the elements. It becomes the symbol of individuals liberated from society. Over a number of years, the photographer Jock Sturges (pp. 262–63) has taken portraits of families who spend the summer on nudist beaches. His photographs go beyond the traditional representation of the naked body. His models express authenticity, purity and innocence. Similarly, Erik Madigan Heck (pp. 252, 253) marvels at his family and creates images in which nature, love and bodies merge.

The body and its appearance play a central role in our culture. Representations of ideal and fantasy bodies feed the industries of fashion, beauty and wellness. These are clearly imaginary bodies, retouched, always desirable; in fact, model bodies. For more than a century Western society has idolized what it perceives to be highly photogenic, sculptural beauty. Indeed, it is worth remembering that woman has been deified since antiquity. The Egyptians and Greeks represented her as a goddess, a queen or an image of fertility. Whether Venus, concubine or symbol of maternity, woman has served as a model of beauty throughout the history of sculpture and painting. Naturally, photography has continued that tradition, manufacturing new ideals of archetypes that include the femme fatale and the woman as object. The Hollywood dream was based on the femme fatale figure and has filled the pages of glossy magazines. Haunted by seduction and obsessed by beauty, humans like to project themselves onto these mythical figures. Fashion photographers have responded to this need dictated by the fashion industry and cinema. The top models, with their long and slender bodies that these photographers have created or enhanced, are with us forever. Herb Ritts's images (pp. 270, 271) celebrate modern-day standards of physical perfection while portraying bodies that are like the sculptures of classical gods. Representations of women, as indeed also of men, reflect the aesthetic, sociological and moral concepts of the time, even as ideals ebb and flow.

Curvaceous, naked, generally light-skinned women are certainly the vector of today's dreams but they tend to be submissive to men, who for their part are generally represented with a square-jawed face, darker skin and a more rugged look. On one side there is the 'perfectly formed' body of the flesh-and-blood male model (or *mannequin*); on the other, the effortfully formed body of the athlete. Dance photography, which dates back to the early 20th century, glorifies such muscular, tense, curved bodies. Lois Greenfield, in particular (pp. 272, 273), has devoted her career to this genre. This fantasy body, fashioned with hard graft by members of a society that celebrates the cult of the honed body, reflects a homogenized image of our icons and explains why our culture puts such a high value on bodily beauty. In her book *The Beauty Myth* (1990), Naomi Wolf explains how images celebrating female beauty are used against the emancipation of women. Instead of showing images of women who vary in size, age and ethnicity, our society has produced millions of images showing a very narrow ideal of physical perfection.

Such representations have recently changed thanks to the work of women photographers who have taken a different look at the body. Dana Lixenberg (p. 247) captures her subjects in everyday life and creates intense portraits, observing from a distance that is not invasive but is close enough to create a link and focus on details and body language. Viviane Sassen (pp. 188, 189, 281, 282–83, 400) has found new ways to represent bodies in both her personal work and her fashion photography. The young artist Senta Simond (p. 284) celebrates the female body in its intimate aspects, while Deanna Templeton (pp. 300, 301, 426) pays tribute to both the female and the male nude by observing the dancing curves of bodies photographed in a swimming pool.

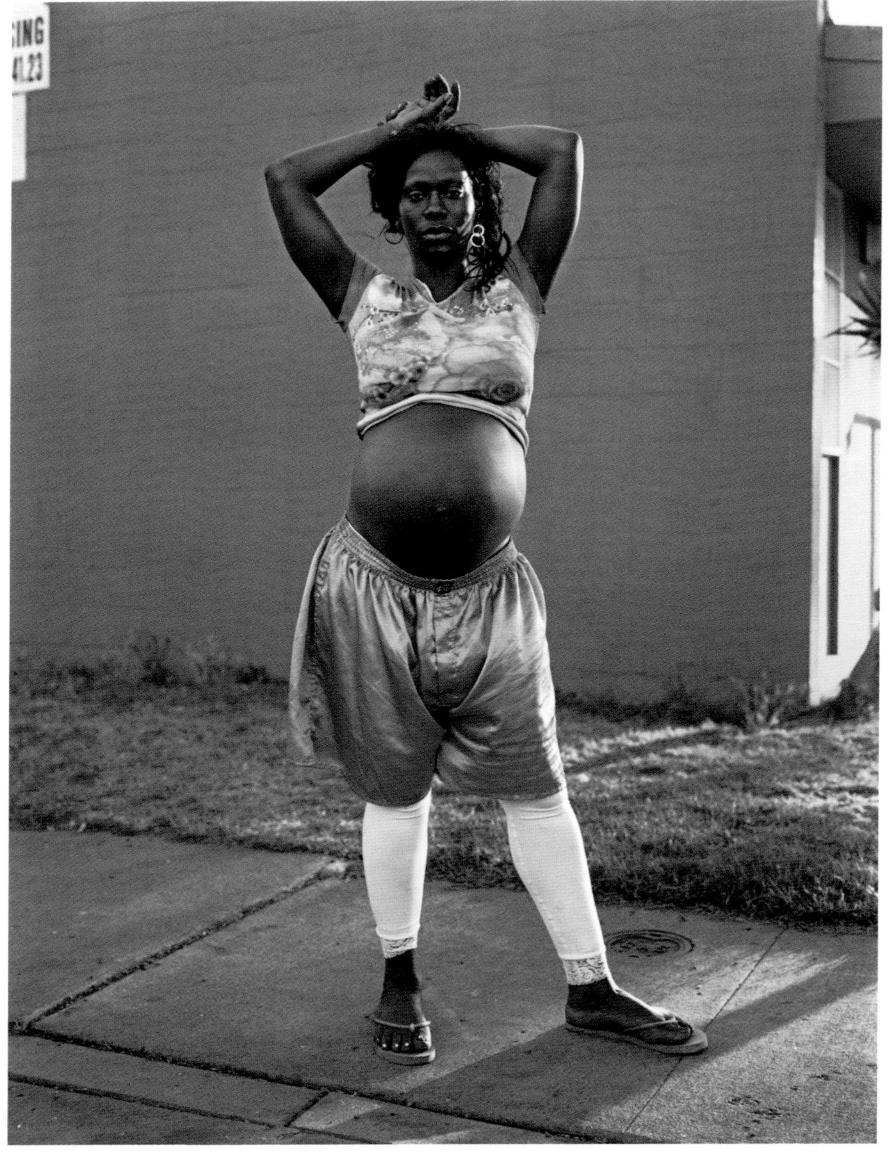

↑ **Dana Lixenberg,** *J 50, 2008,* from the series
'Imperial Courts 1993–2015', 2008

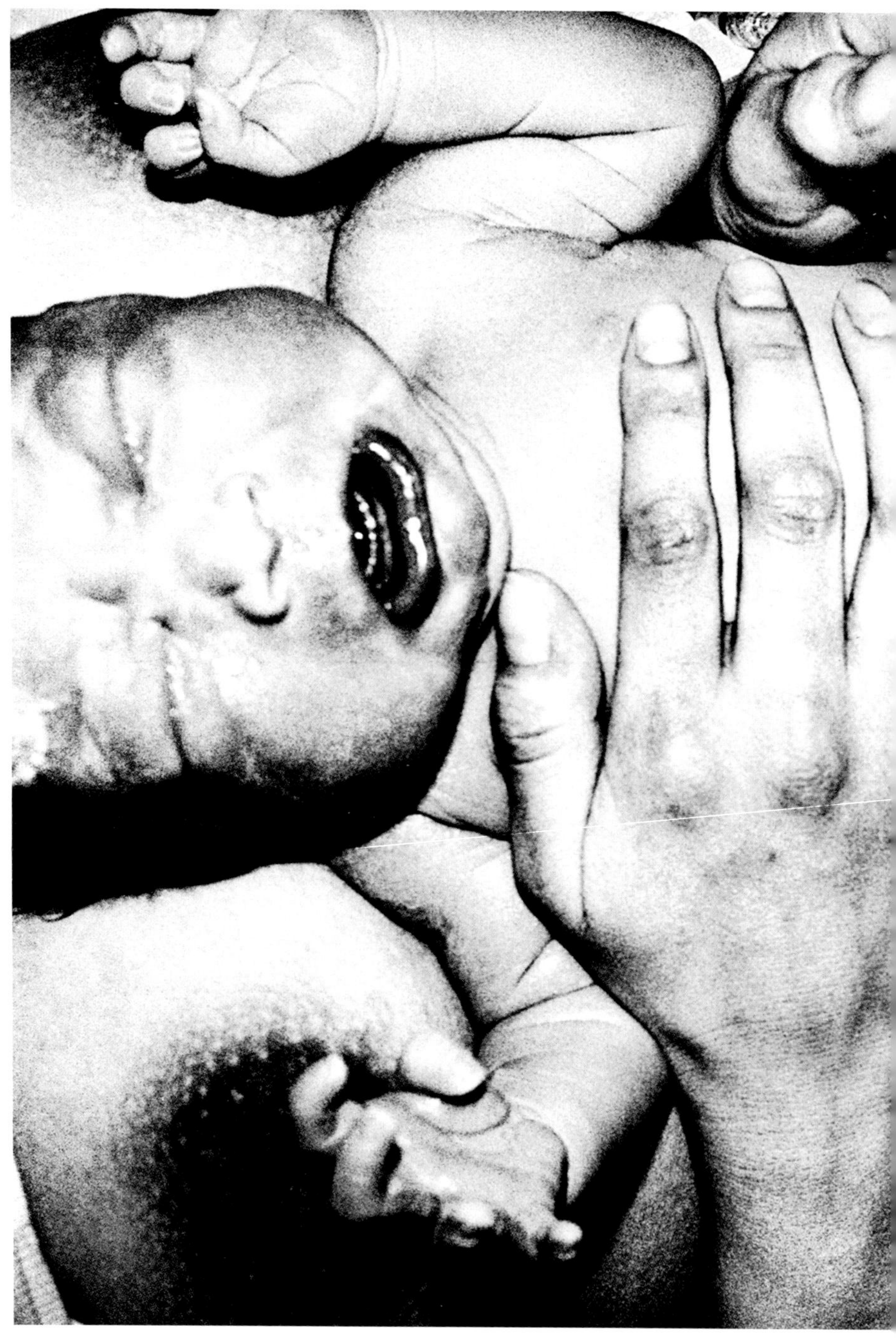

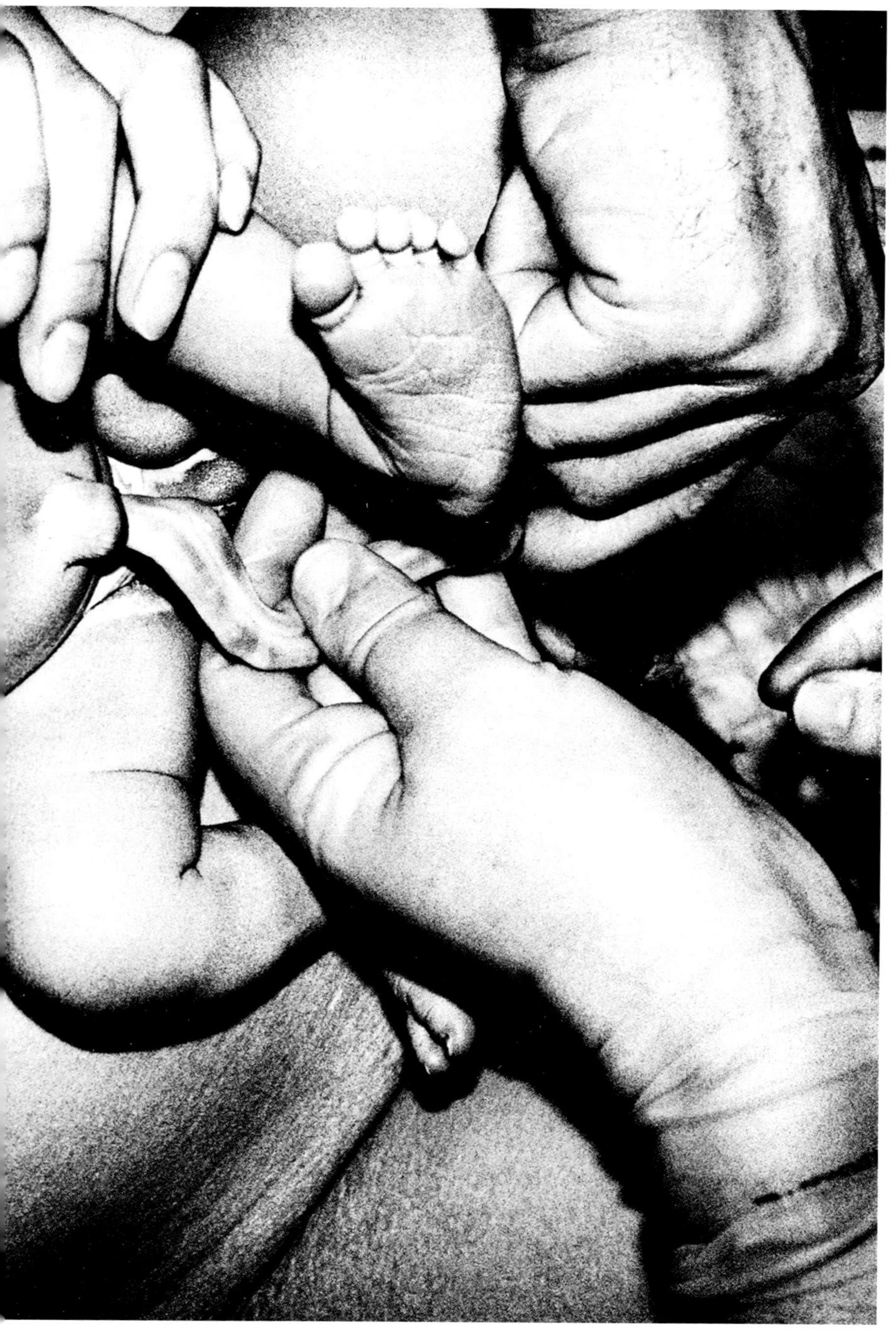

↑ **Jacob Aue Sobol**, *Tiniteqilaaq, Greenland*, 2000

For her part, Mona Kuhn (pp. 4, 122–23, 288, 289) constantly experiments with new compositions around bodies that are both nude and naked, opening up fresh perspectives for a genre that some believed a little dated.

As shown by the works of these women artists, male nudity, long considered as too sexual, is being shown more and more frequently outside homosexual circles. Wolfgang Tillmans's work (pp. 294, 295, 410, 411) is celebrated in the most prestigious museums. It opens our eyes to new representations of liberated bodies. Ryan McGinley (pp. 296, 297) has become an ardent proponent of images that celebrate the untrammelled bodies of men and women who embrace a hedonism practised in the heart of nature. In the world of fashion, too, men have gradually become sexualized, if not feminized. Photographers are distancing themselves from iconic and idolized bodies: today the body is celebrated in its diversity and shown as politicized, feminist.

The tyranny of appearance is beginning to lose some of its power now that images are circulated globally. The photographed body is no longer solely a reflection of the mainstream but also of the margins, and it no longer has to comply with the canons of beauty set by a Western society that has defined the contours of its citizens. Jocelyn Lee (pp. 308, 309, 314) aims her camera at women who are plump and of all ages, their silhouettes marked by life. Beauty is no longer found only in model bodies and standard representations but is seen primarily through the eye of the beholder; and the more the eye sees of images of different bodies that display their freedom, the freer the imagination becomes.

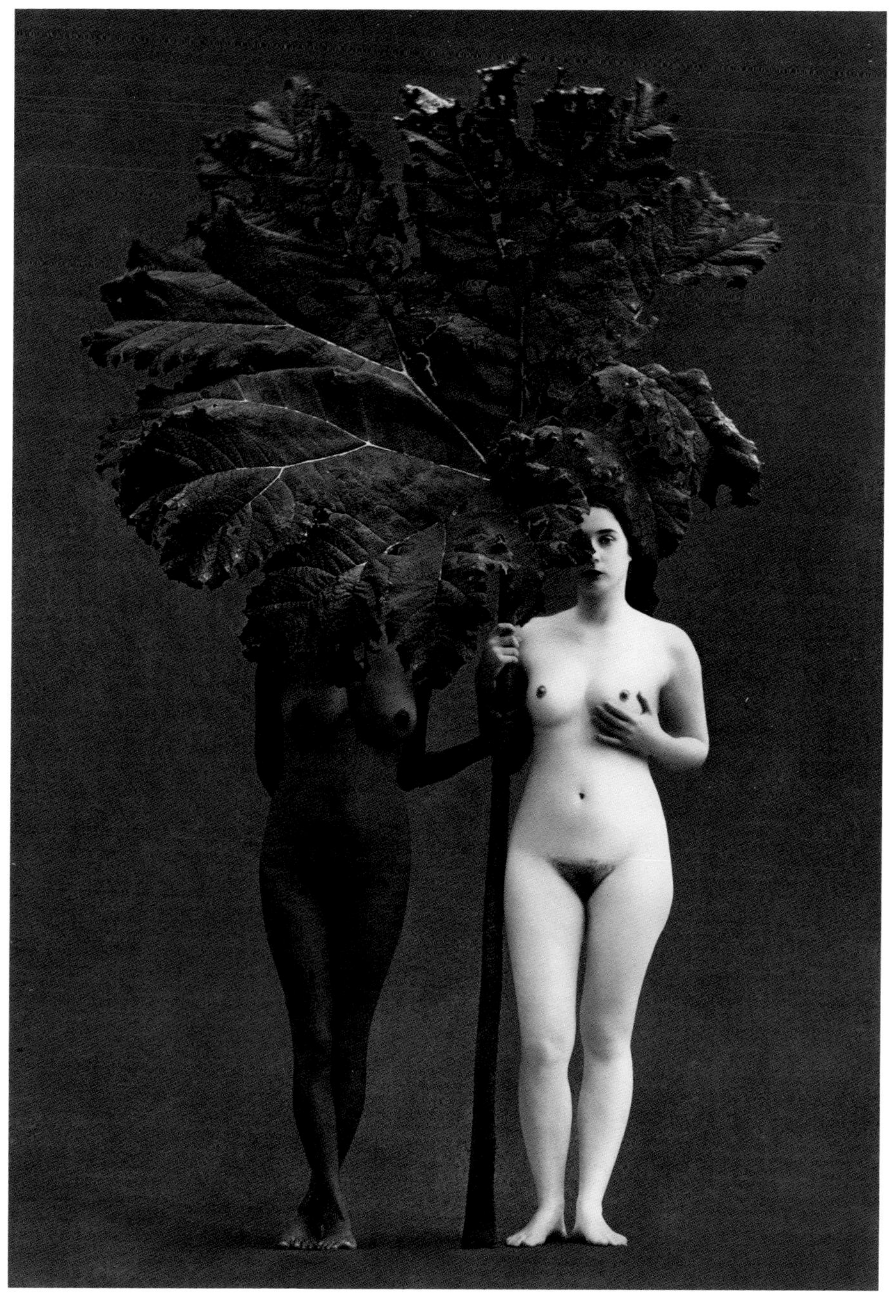

↑ **Flor Garduño,** *Eden, Switzerland,* 2001

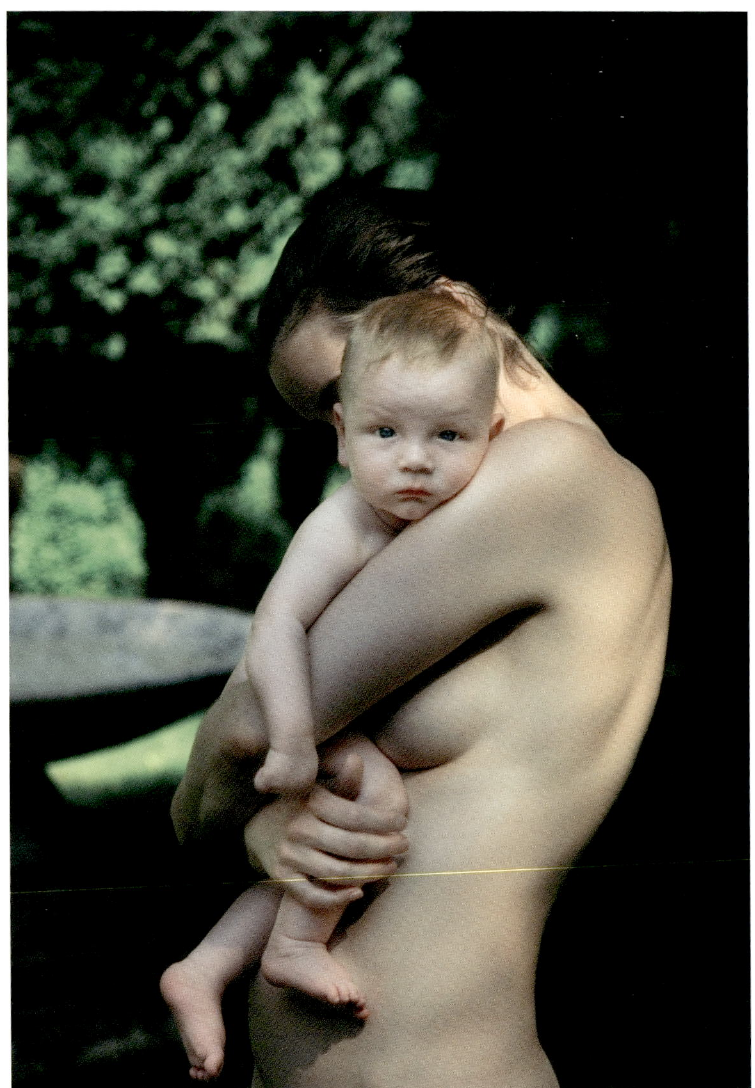

↑ **Erik Madigan Heck,** *Winston and Brianna in The Garden,* 2017

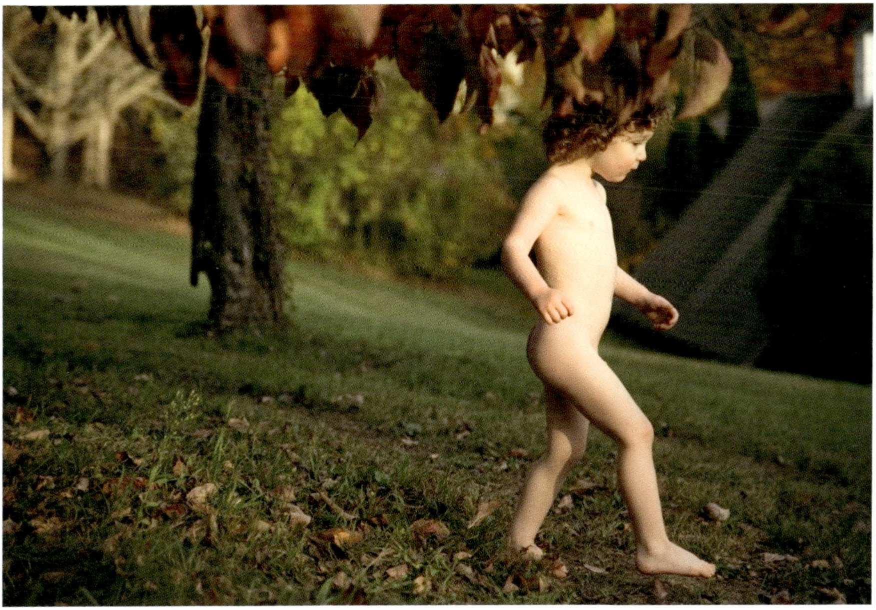

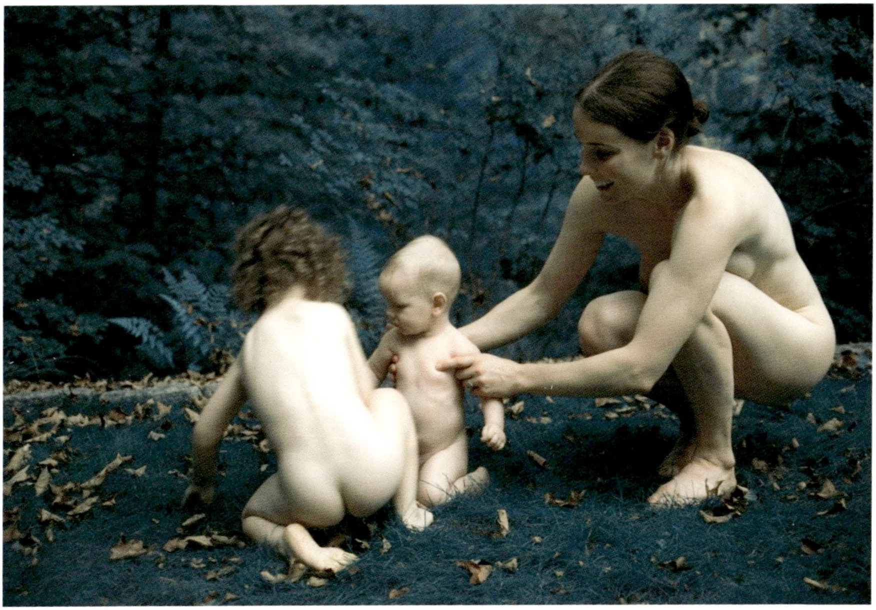

↑ (Top) **Erik Madigan Heck,** *Felix Running,* 2017
↑ (Above) **Erik Madigan Heck,** *Turquoise Family,* 2017

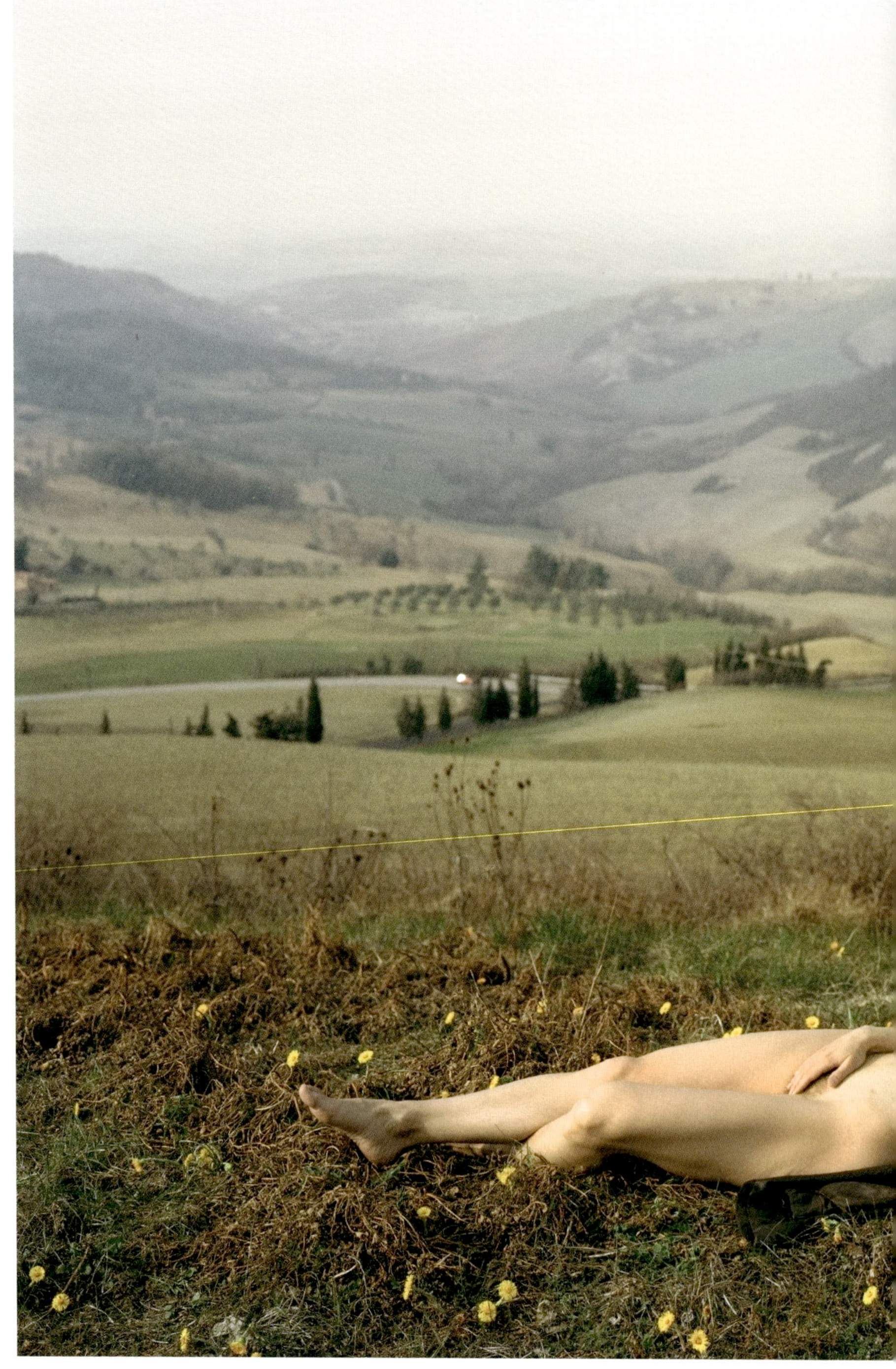

↑ **Elina Brotherus**, *Nu endormi* [Sleeping Nude], from the series 'The New Painting', 2003

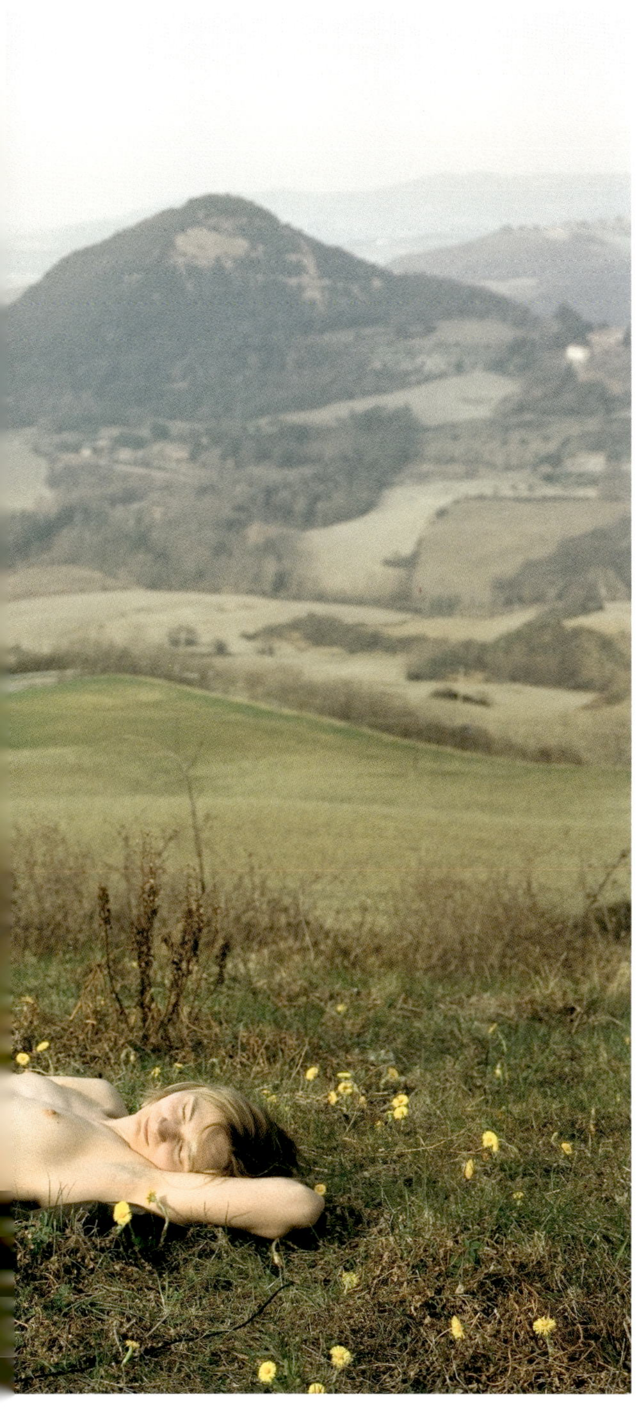

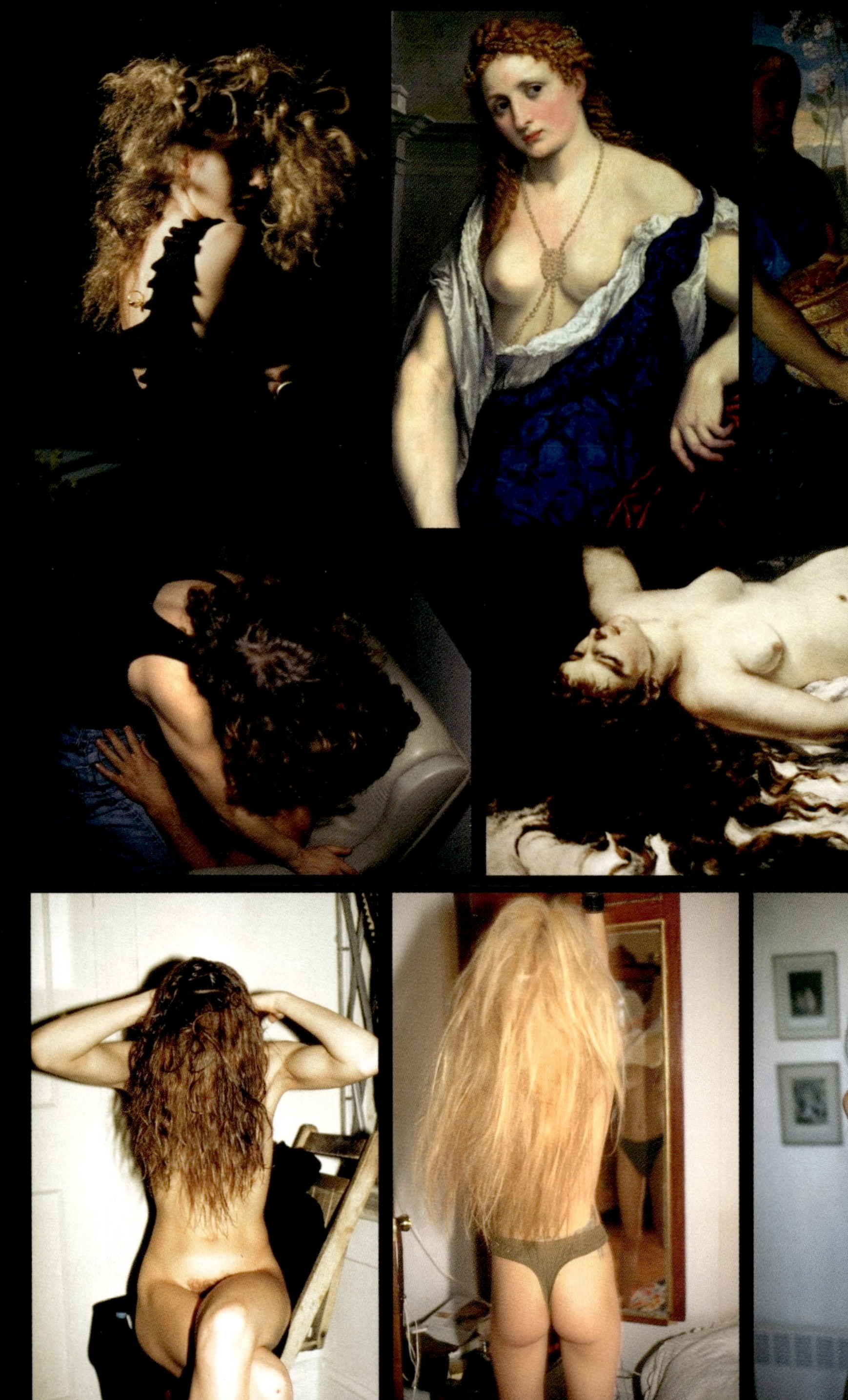

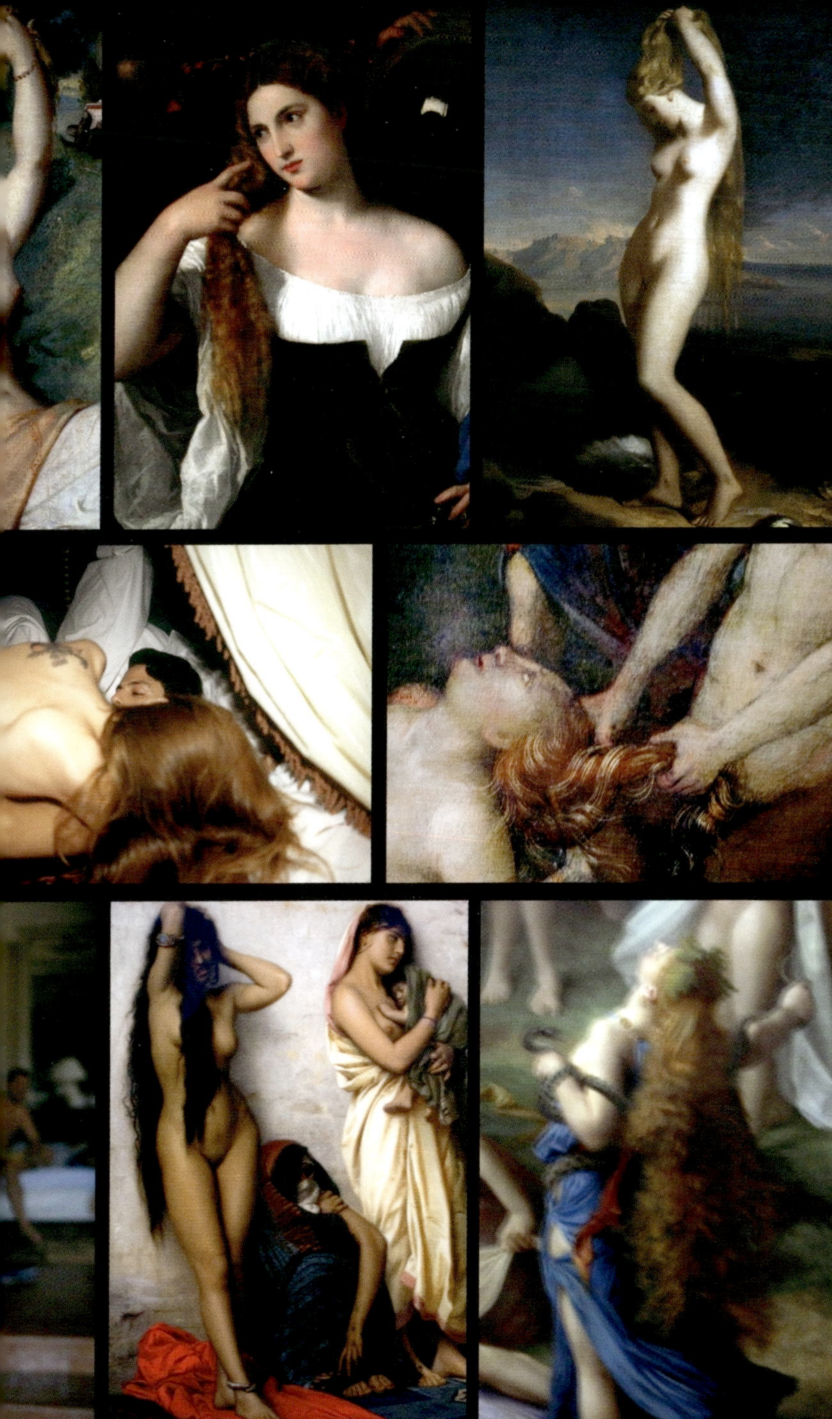

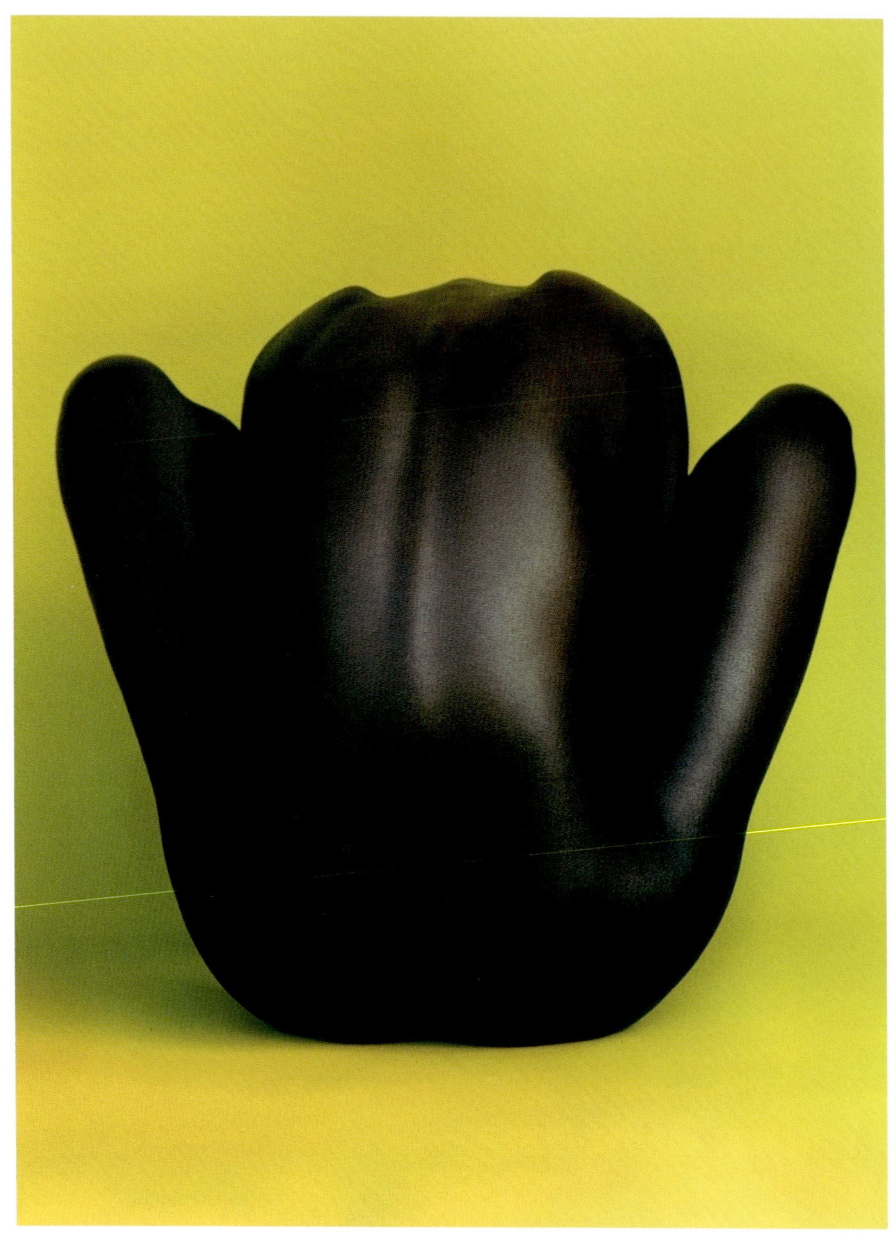

↑ **Koto Bolofo**, *Black Beauty*, 2008
←(Previous) **Nan Goldin**, *Hair*, 2011

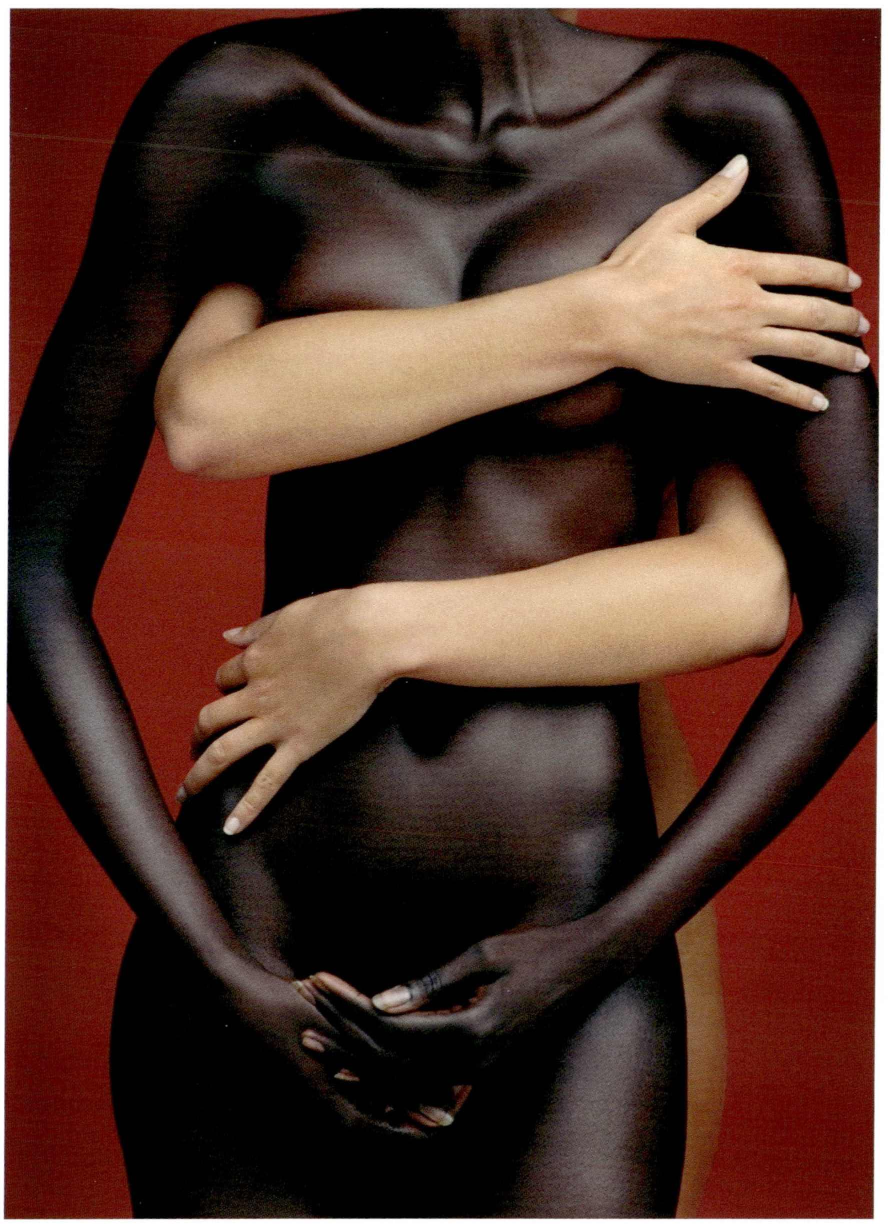

↑ **Koto Bolofo,** *Skin Deep*, 2008

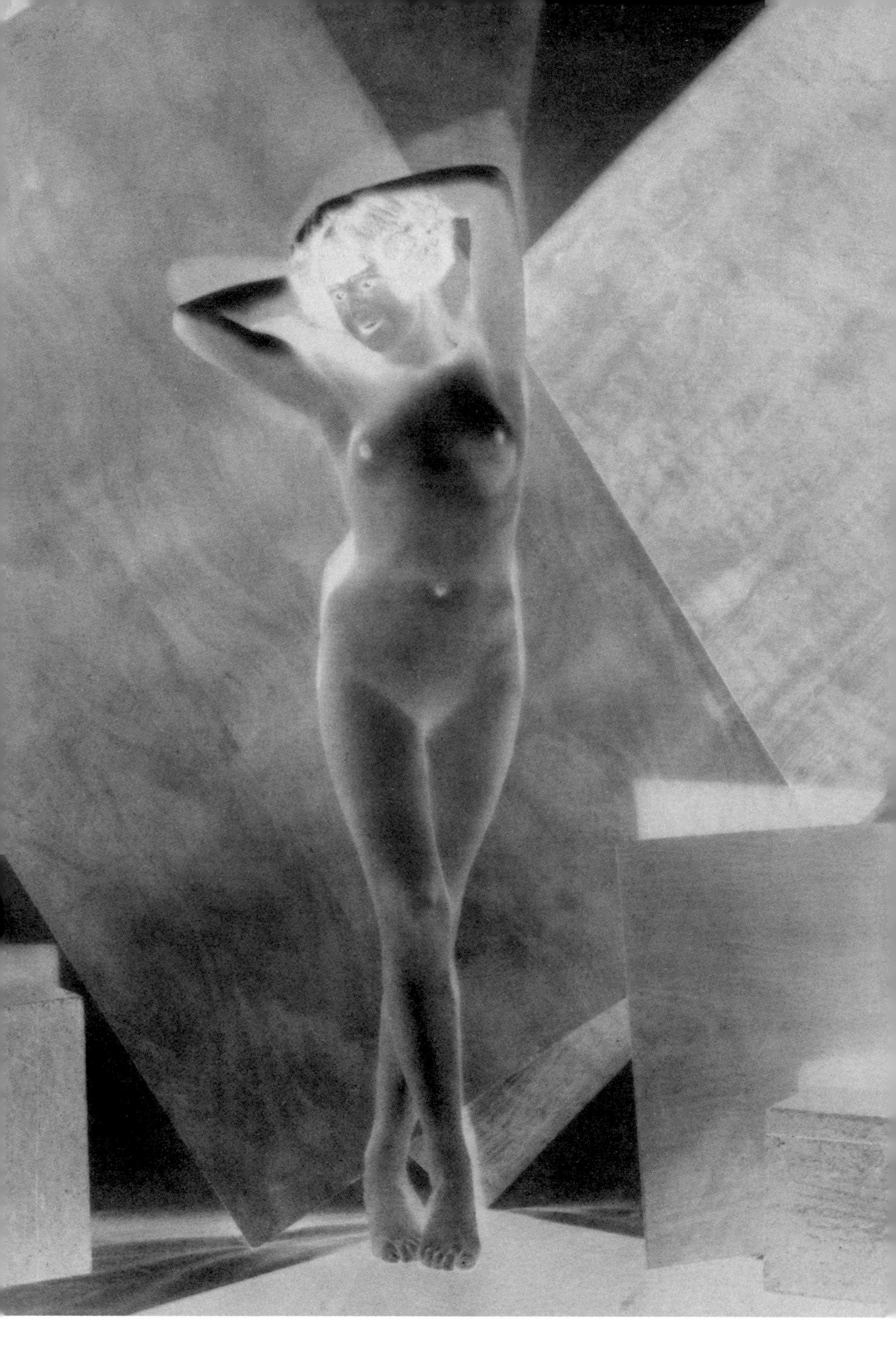

↑ Thomas Ruff, *neg◊nus_45*, 2014

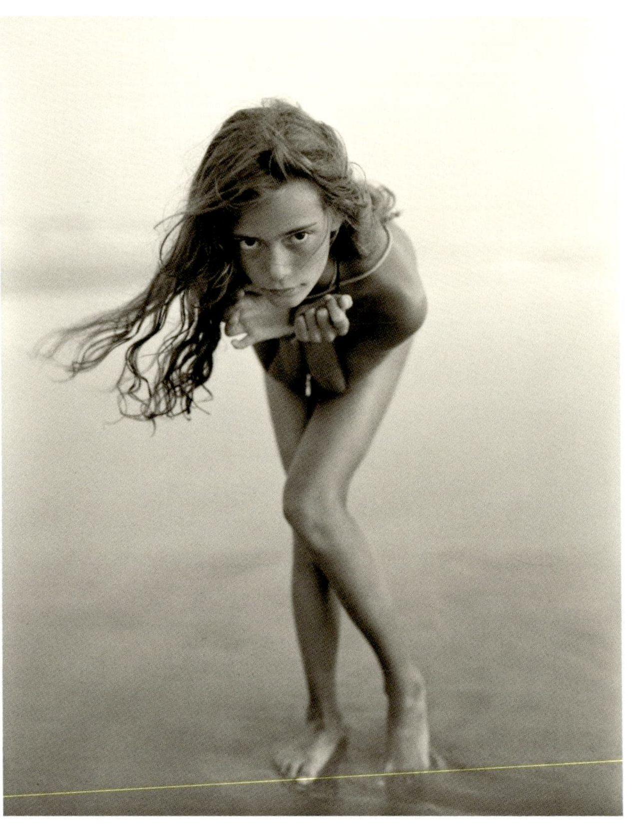

↑ (Left) **Jock Sturges,** *F; Montalivet, France,* 1995

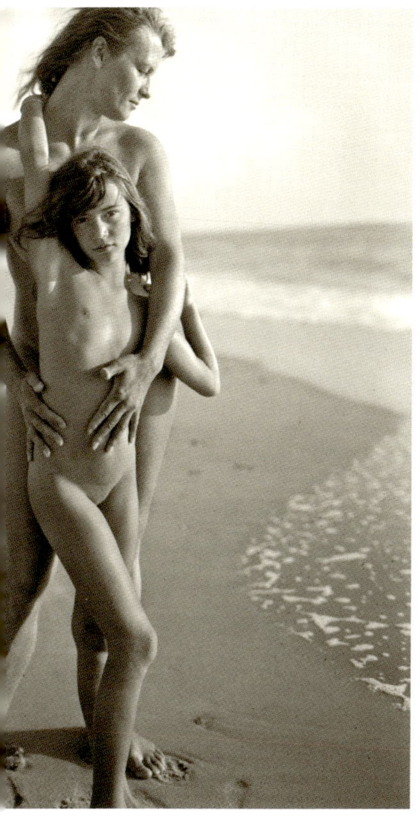

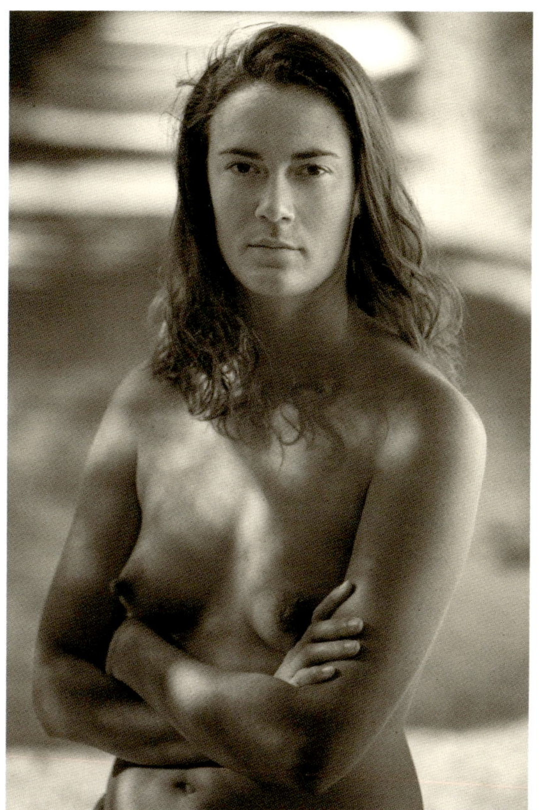

↑ (Centre) **Jock Sturges,** *F and C; Montalivet, France,* 1993
↑ (Right) **Jock Sturges,** *F; Montalivet, France,* 2016

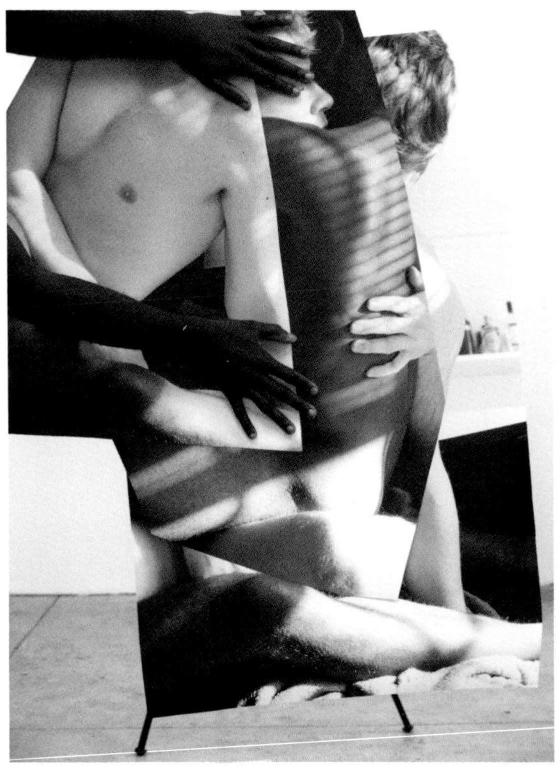

↑ **Paul Mpagi Sepuya,** *Mirror Study for Joe (_2010980),* 2017

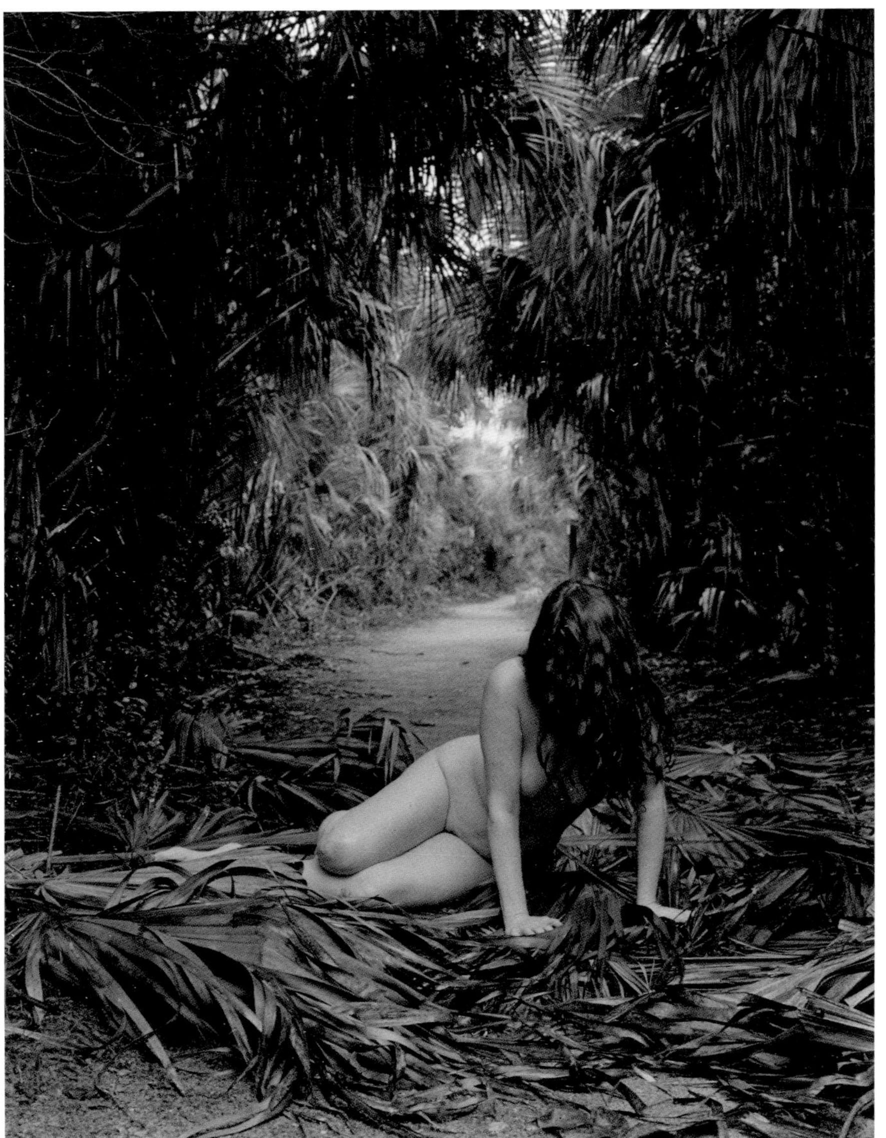

↑ **Esther Teichmann,** Untitled, from the series 'Heavy the Sea', 2018

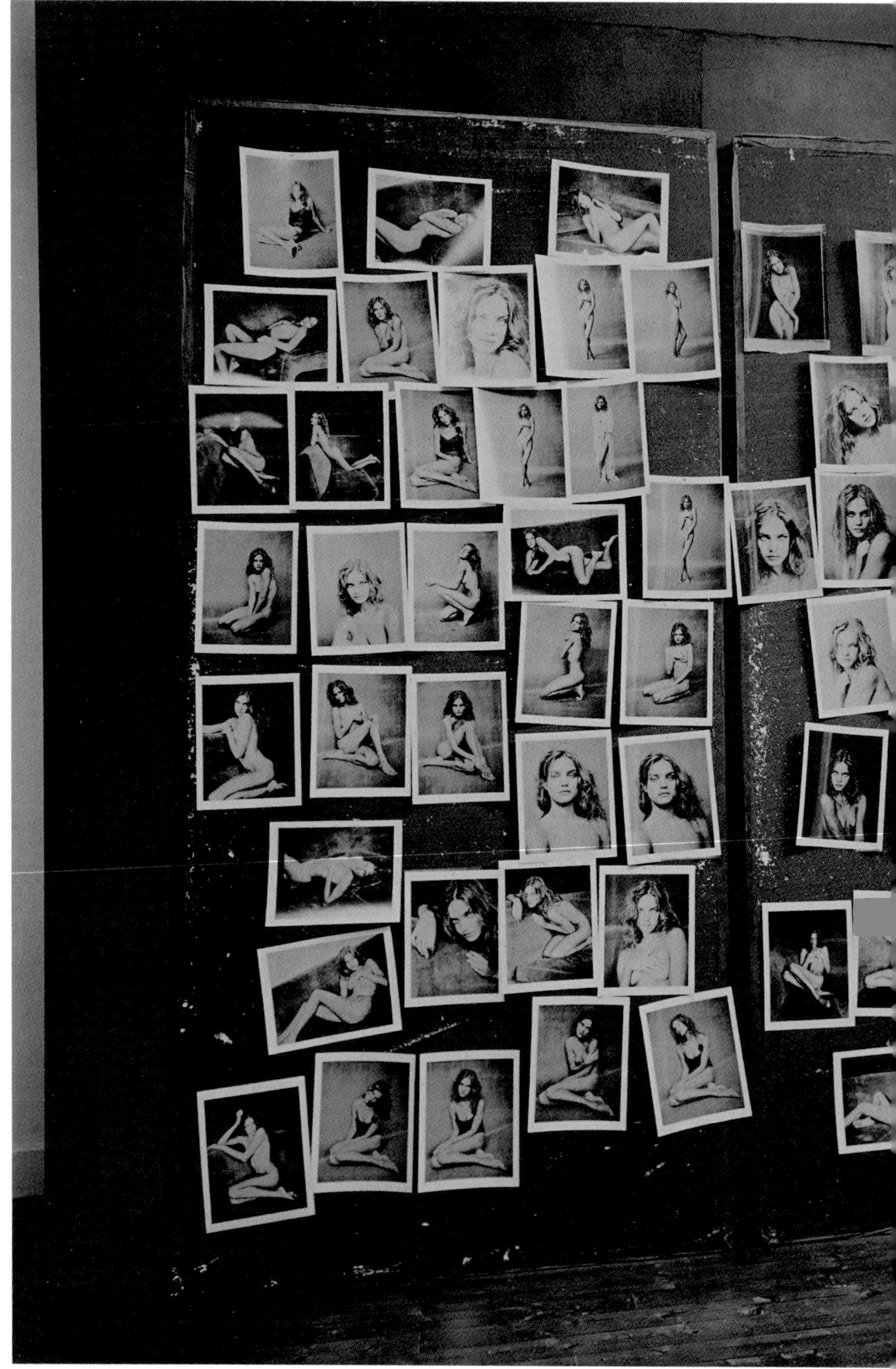

↑ **Paolo Roversi,** *Ravenna, Paris,* 2003

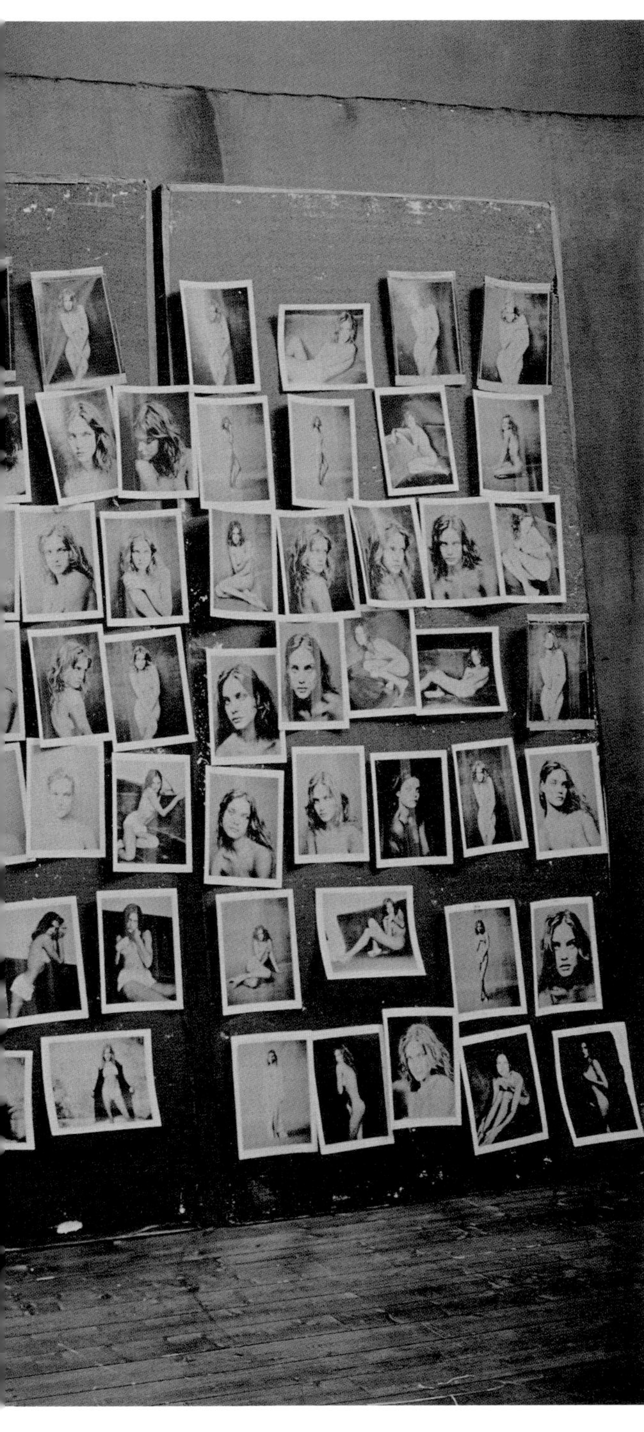

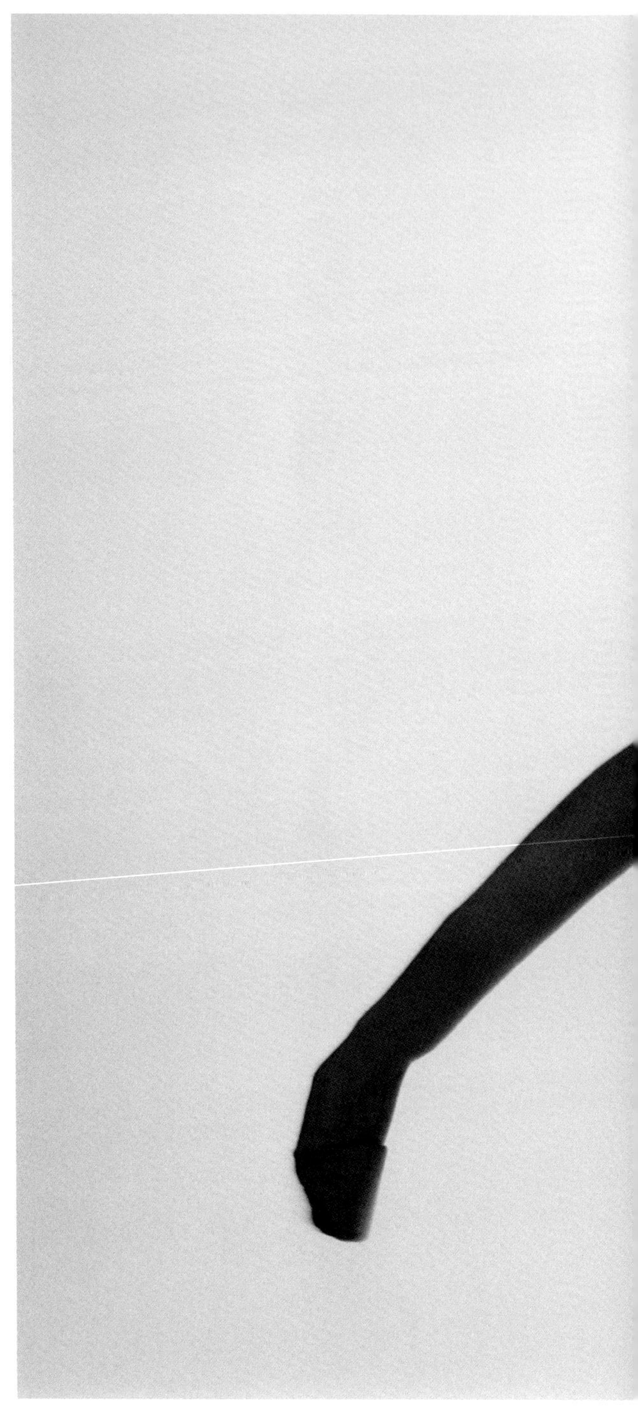

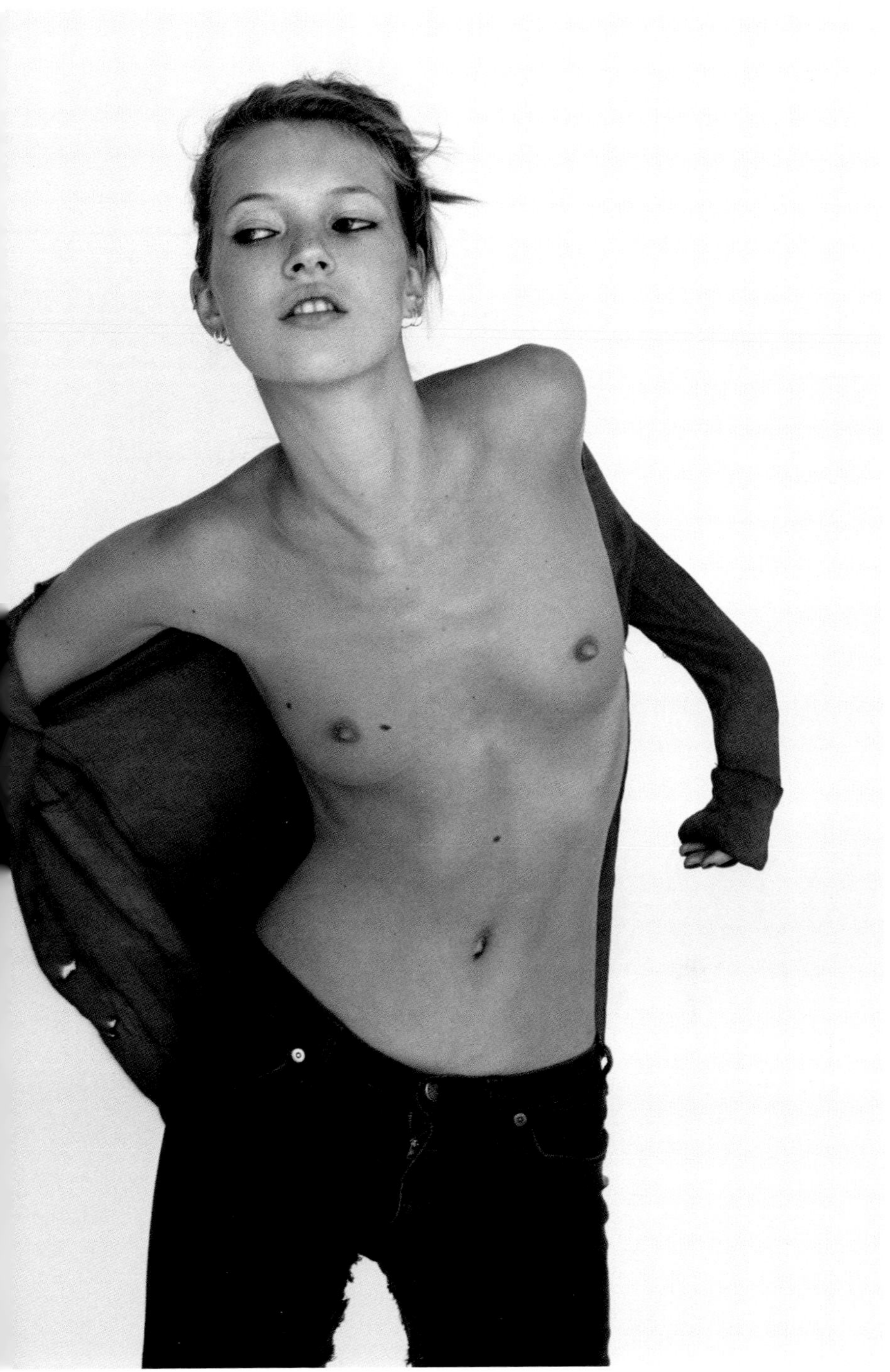

↑ **Corinne Day,** Kate Moss for *Vogue UK*, January 1993

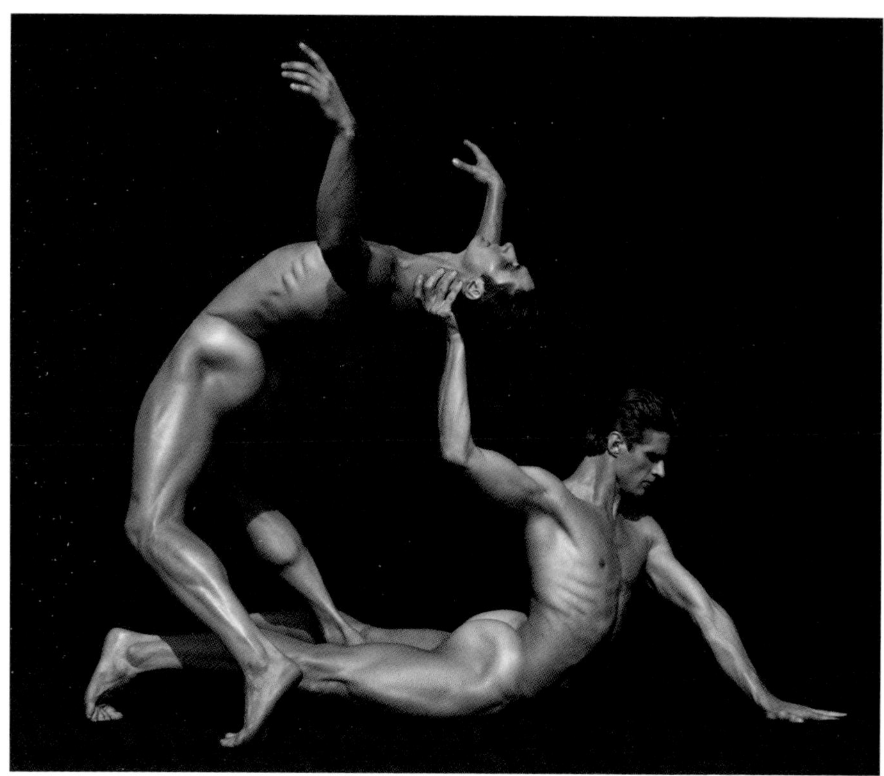

↑ **Herb Ritts,** *Vogue France*, January 2000

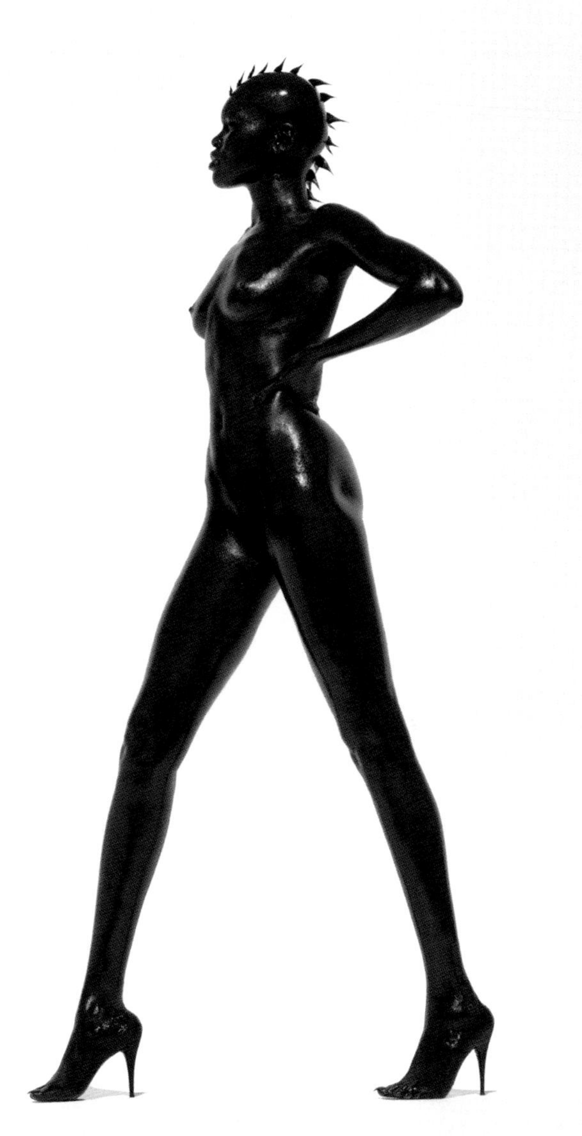

↑ **Herb Ritts,** Alek Wek, Pirelli Calendar, 1998

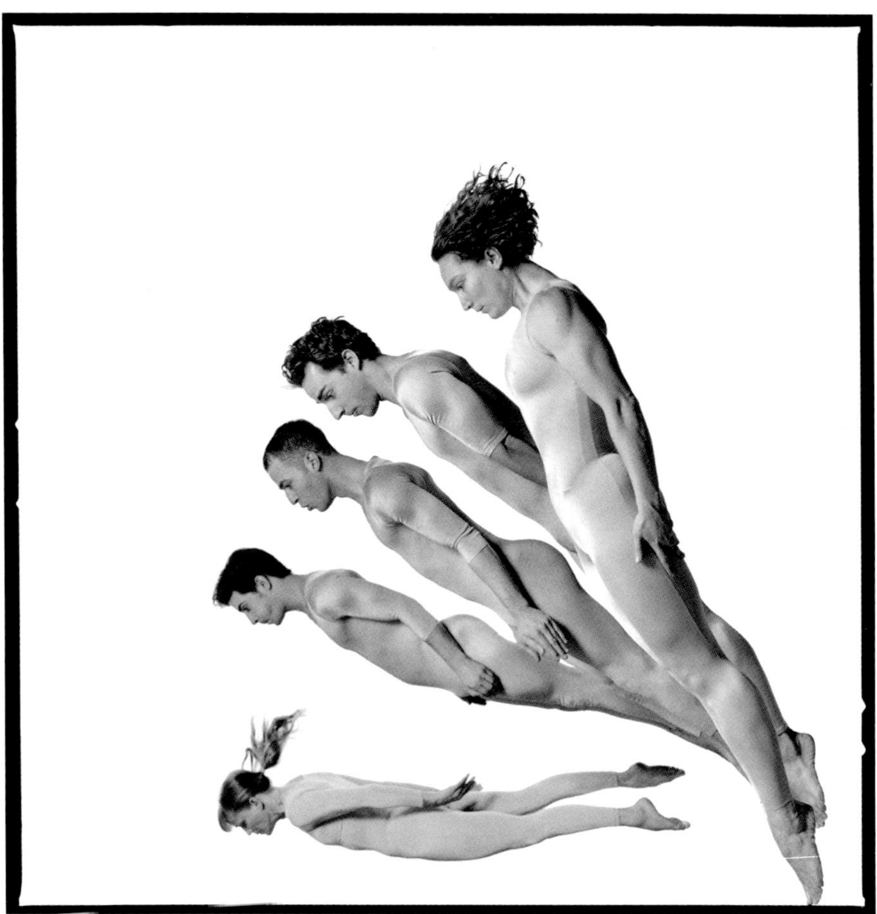

↑ **Lois Greenfield,** *Streb Extreme Action,* 1996

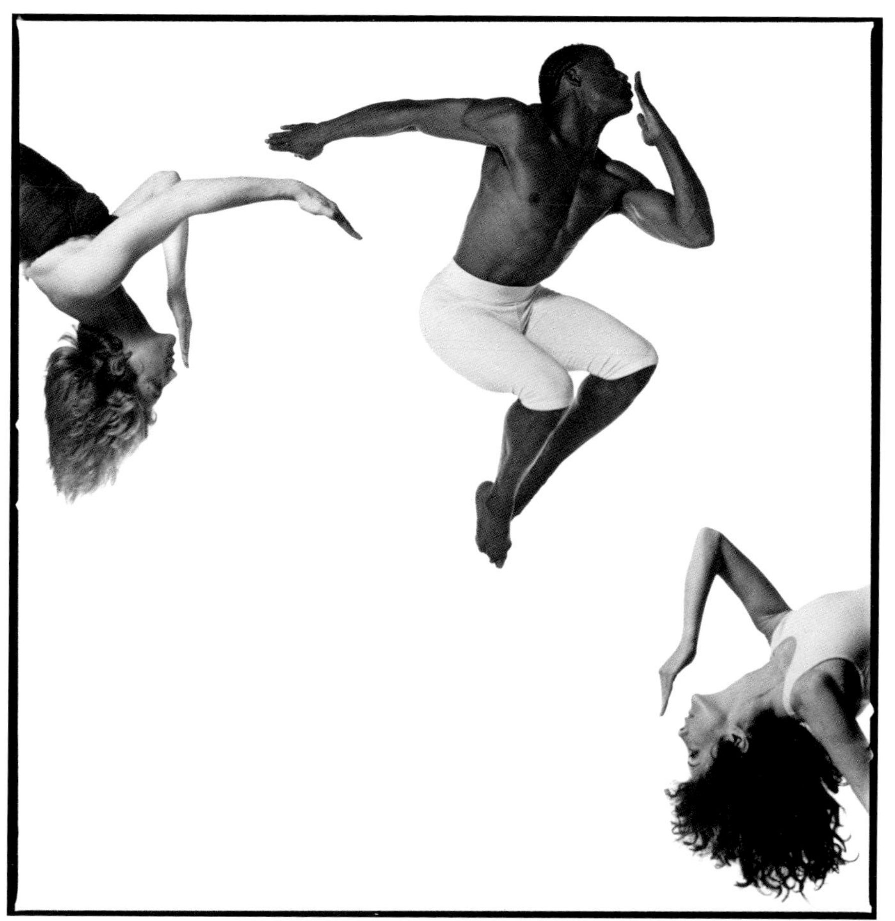

↑ **Lois Greenfield,** *'Chatter', Bill T. Jones/Arnie Zane Dance Company,* 1998

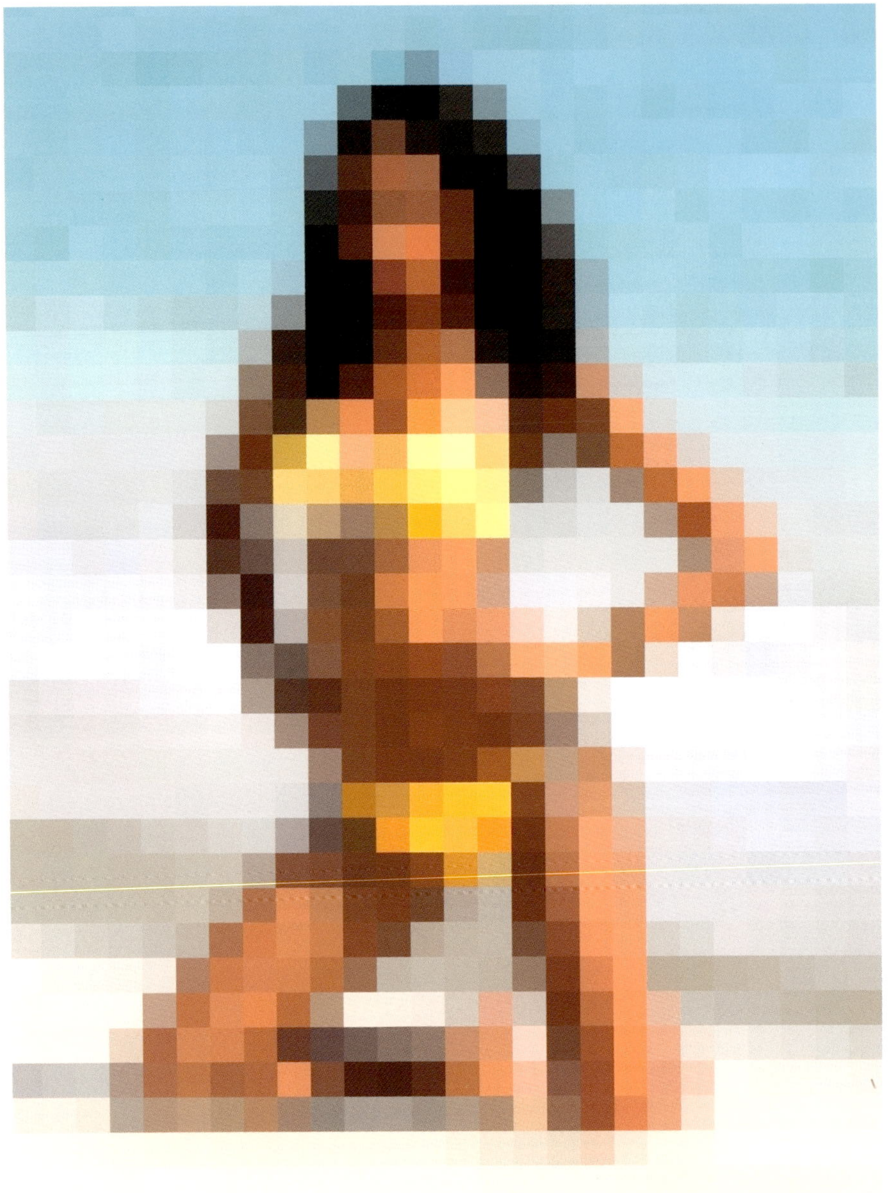

↑ **Gregory Eddi Jones,** *Untitled #4*, from the series 'Paradise Island', 2016

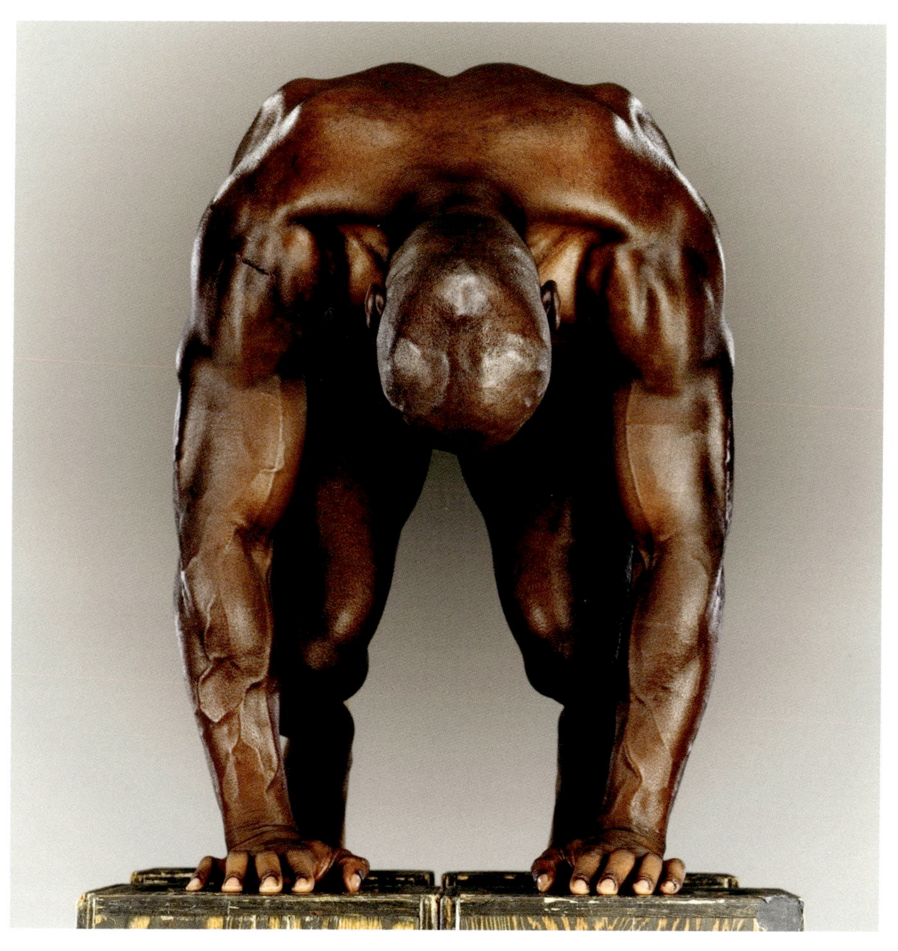

↑ **Howard Schatz,** *Human Body Study 1255 (Bryan Scott),* 2011

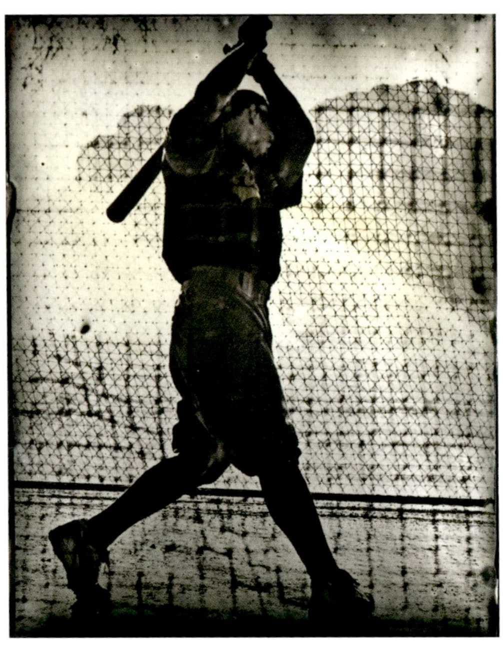

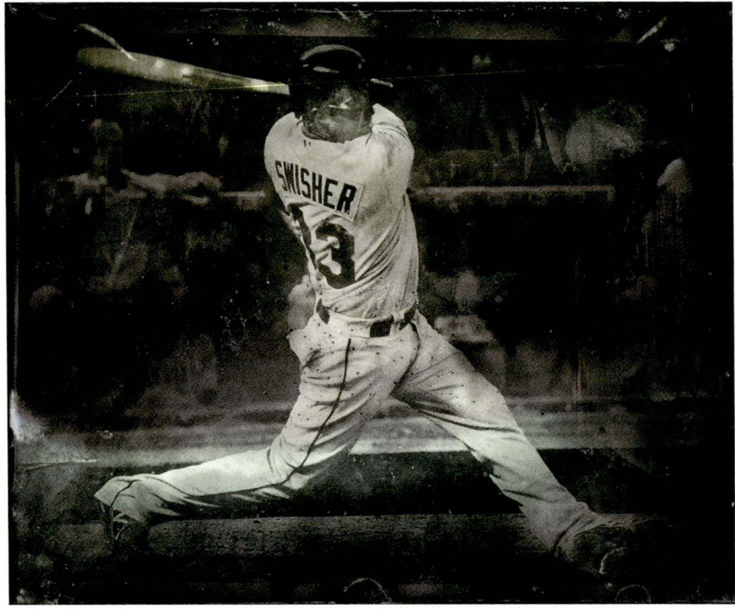
SWISHER
13

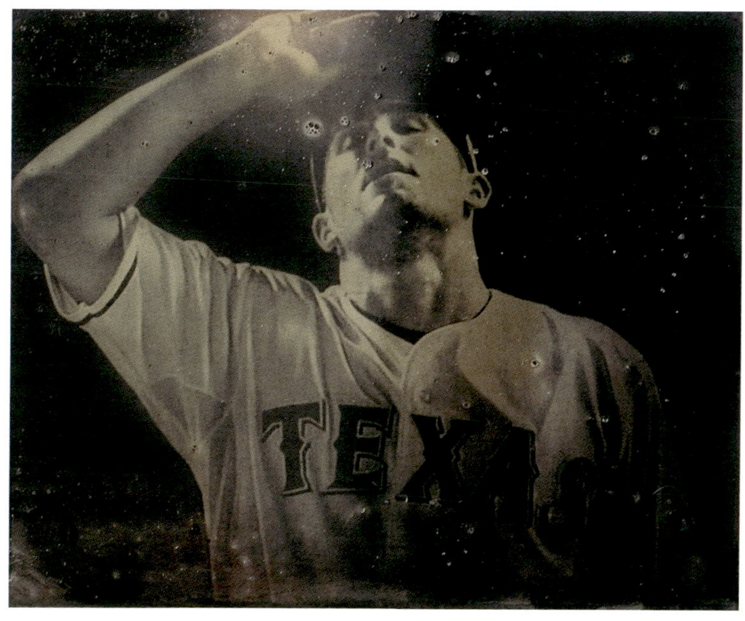

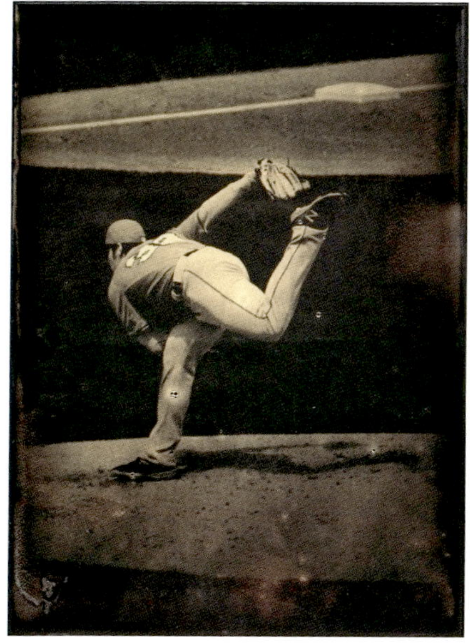

← (Clockwise from top left) **Tabitha Soren,** *Steve Stanley, Oakland A's outfielder, Scottsdale, AZ, 2004; Cliff Lee, Texas Rangers pitcher, Fort Worth, TX, 2010; Pitcher C. J. Wilson, Los Angeles Angels of Anaheim, 2014; Nick Swisher, Cleveland Indians first baseman, Minneapolis, MN, 2013, all from the series 'Fantasy Life: Baseball and the American Dream'*

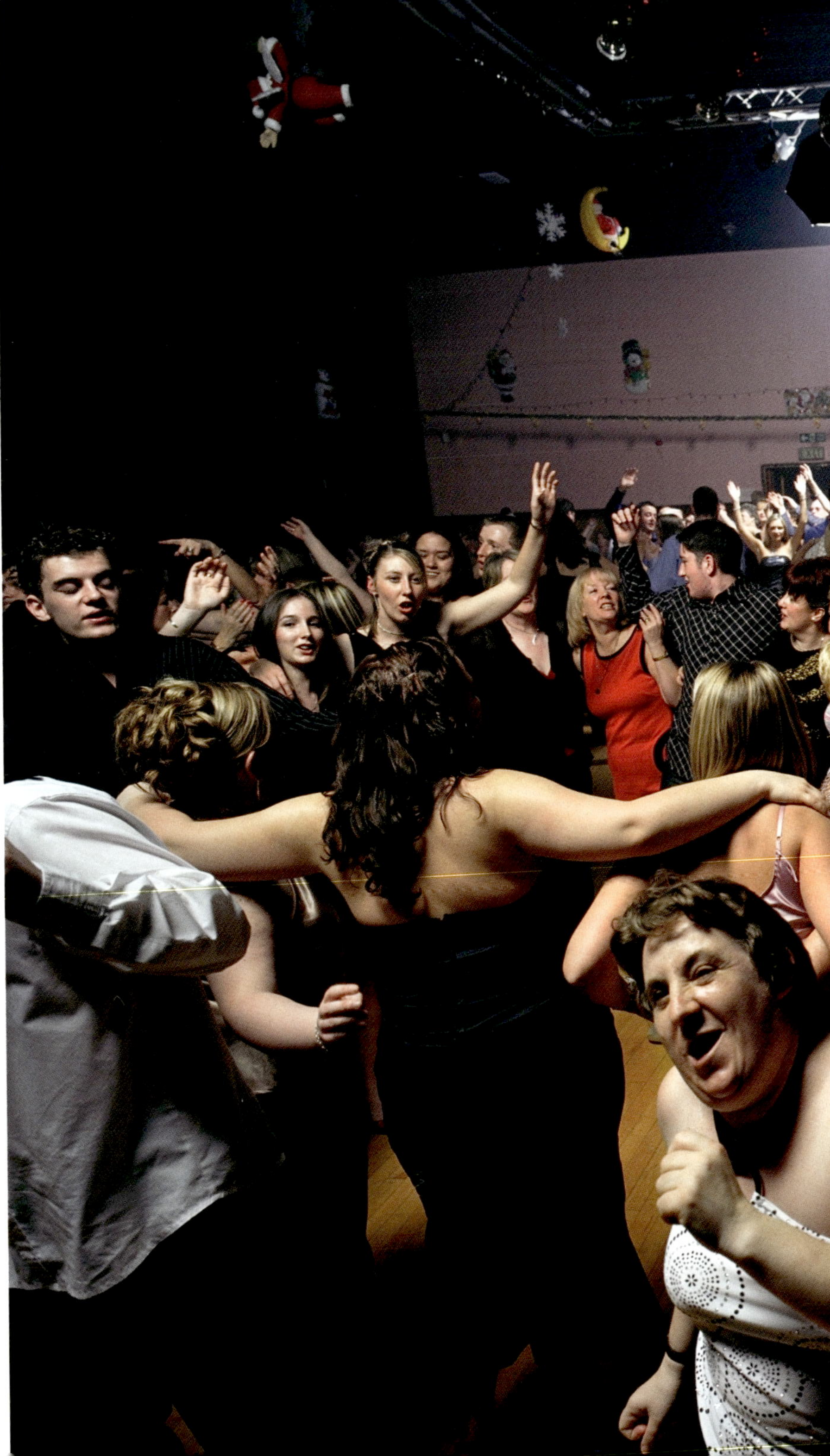

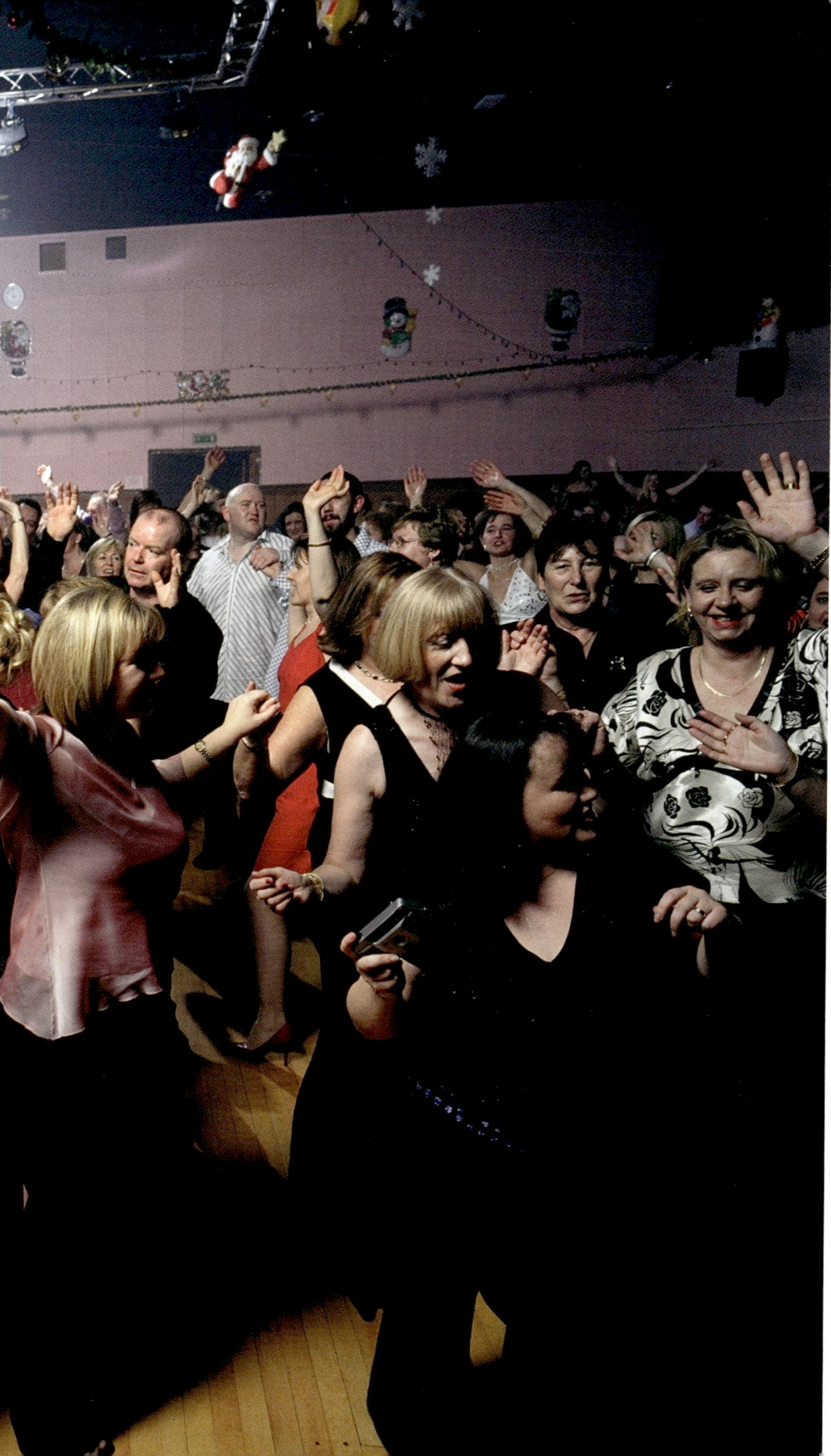

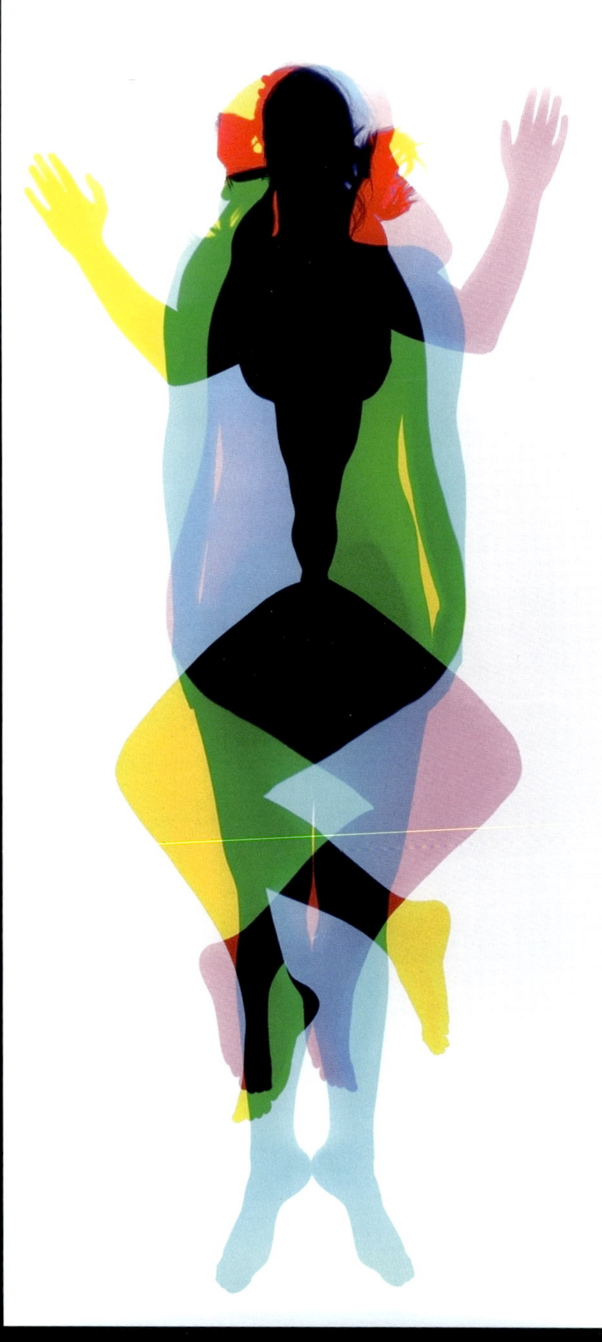

Floris Neusüss, *Untitled H 2,* 2007
(Previous) **Mark Neville,** *Betty at Port Glasgow Town Hall Xmas Party,* 2004

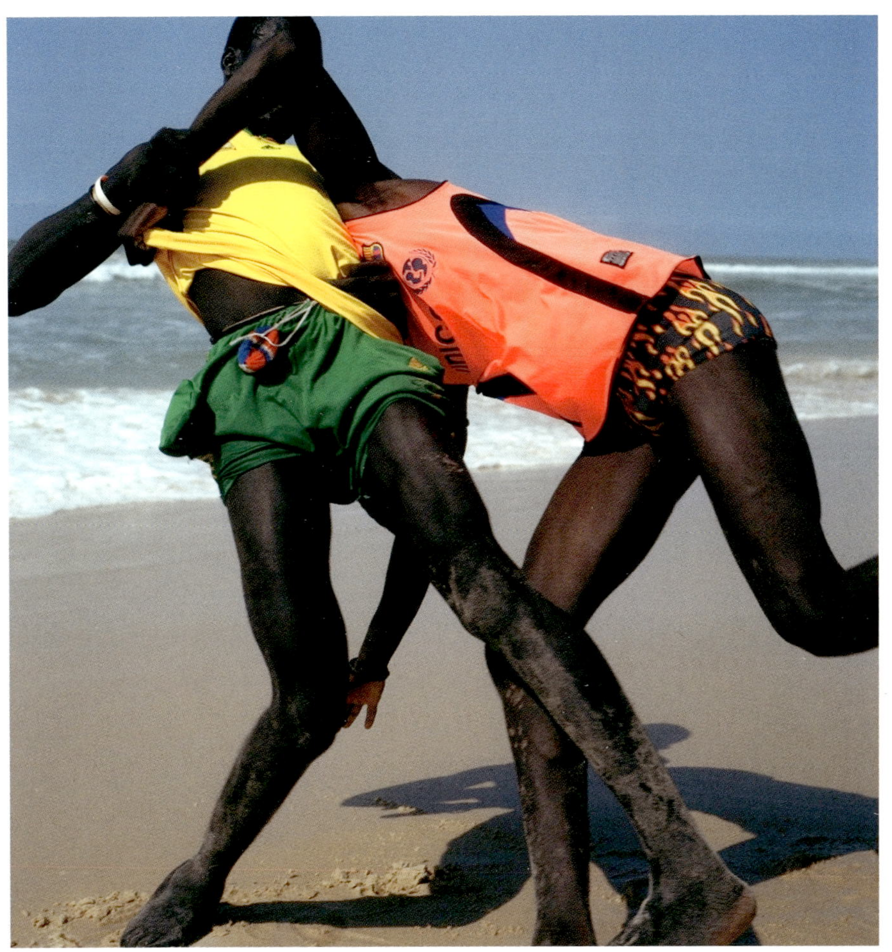

↑ **Viviane Sassen**, *La Lutte* #2 [The Fight #2],
from the series 'Parasomnia', 2011
→ (Overleaf) **Viviane Sassen**, *Hoover*,
from the series 'In and out of Fashion', 2011

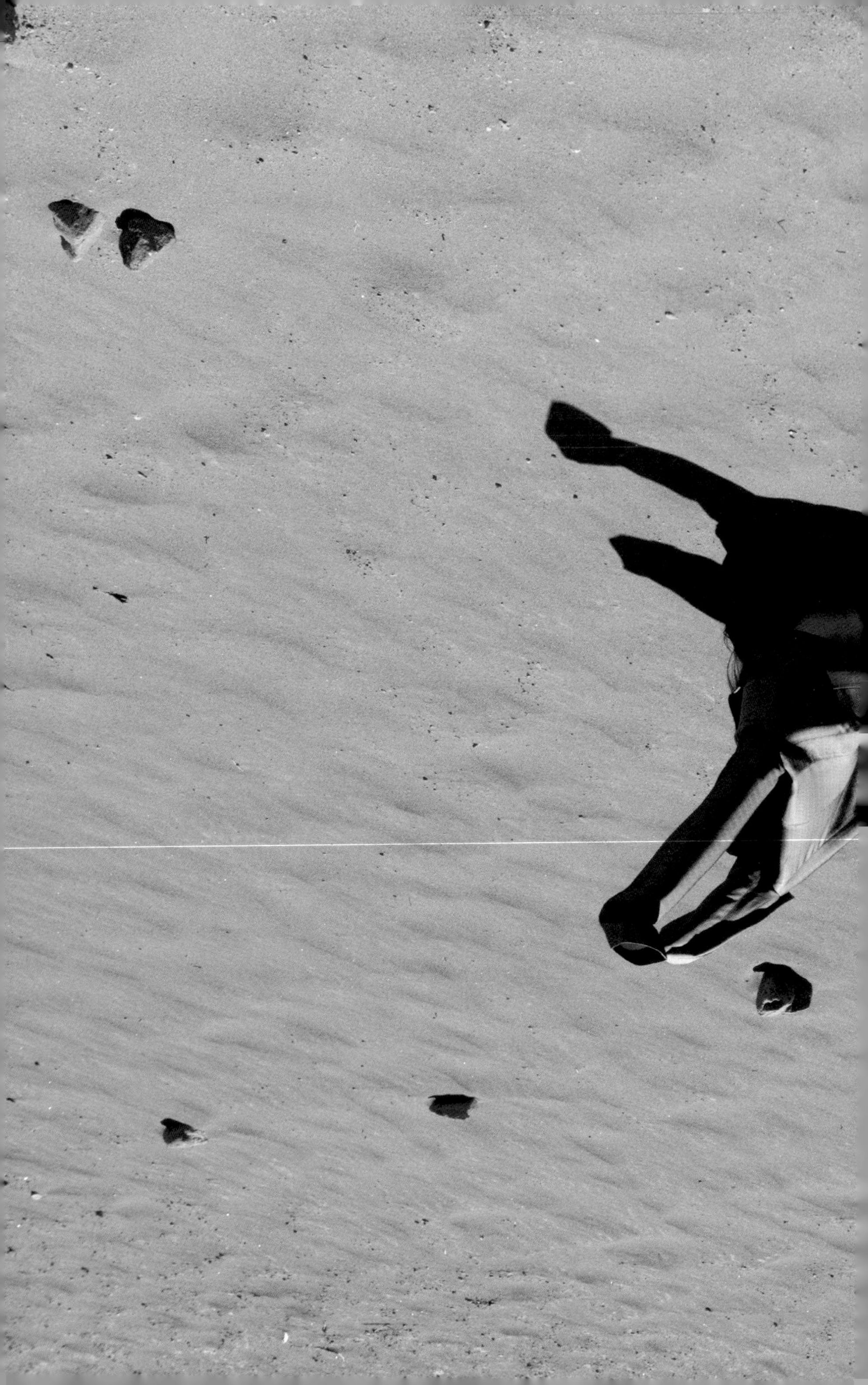

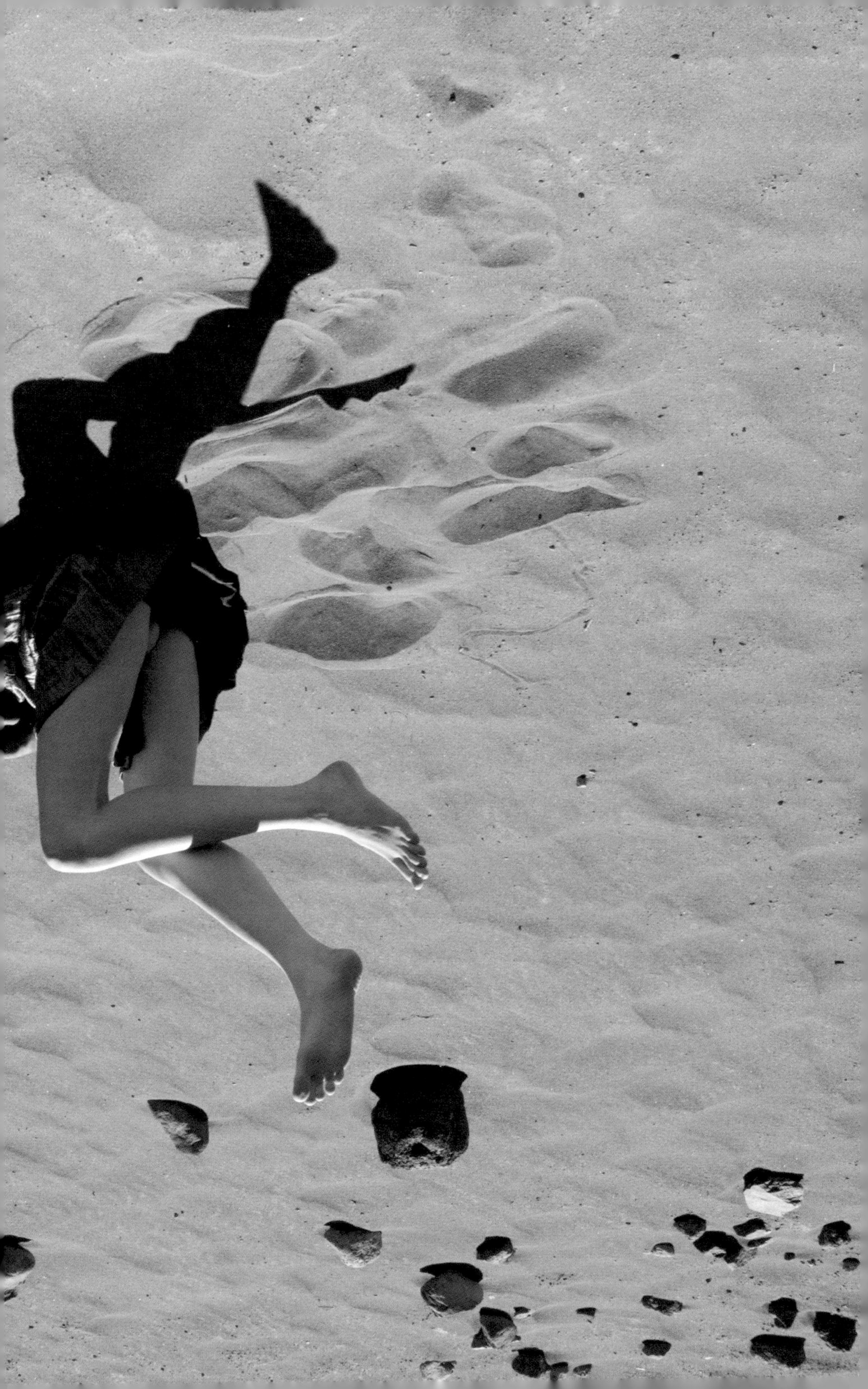

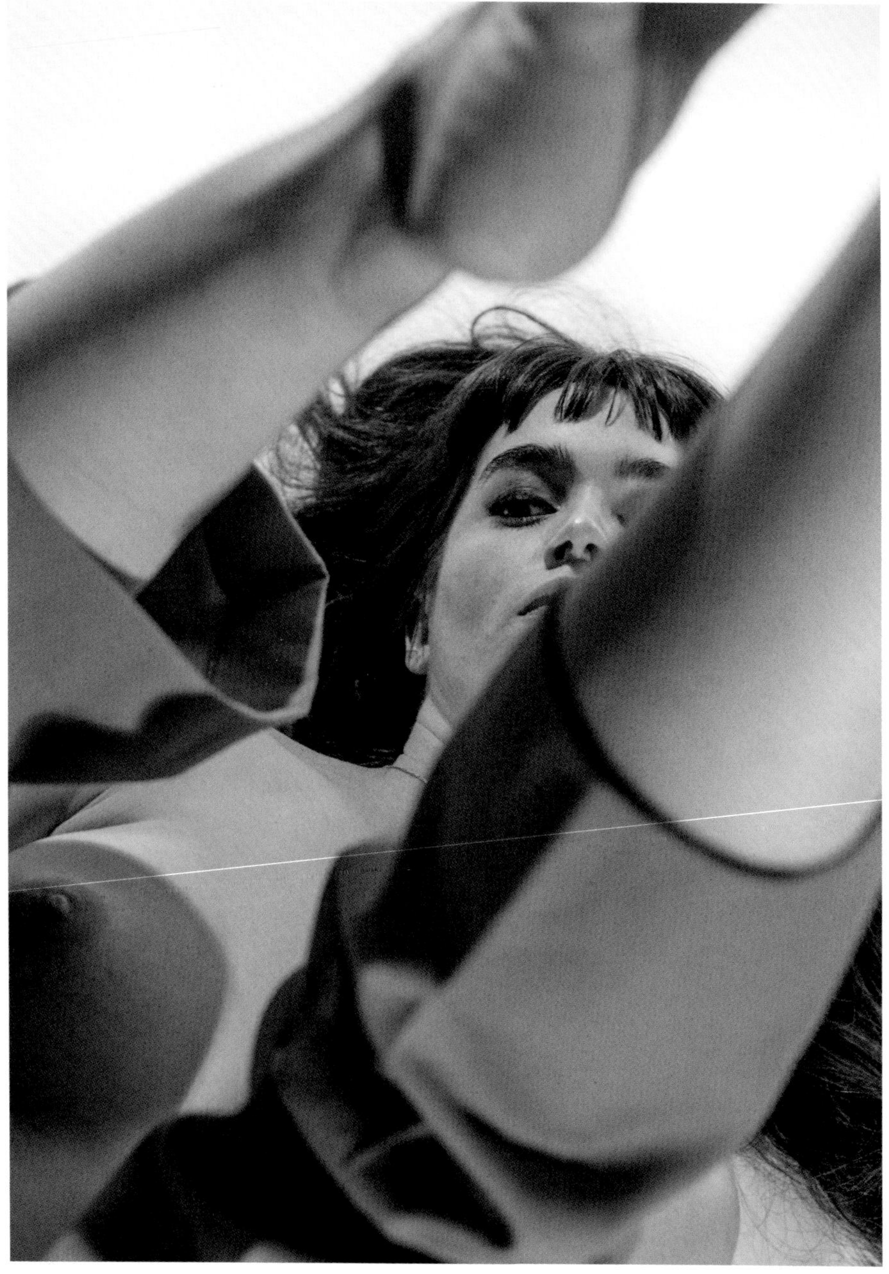

↑ **Senta Simond,** *Laurence #1, 2016*

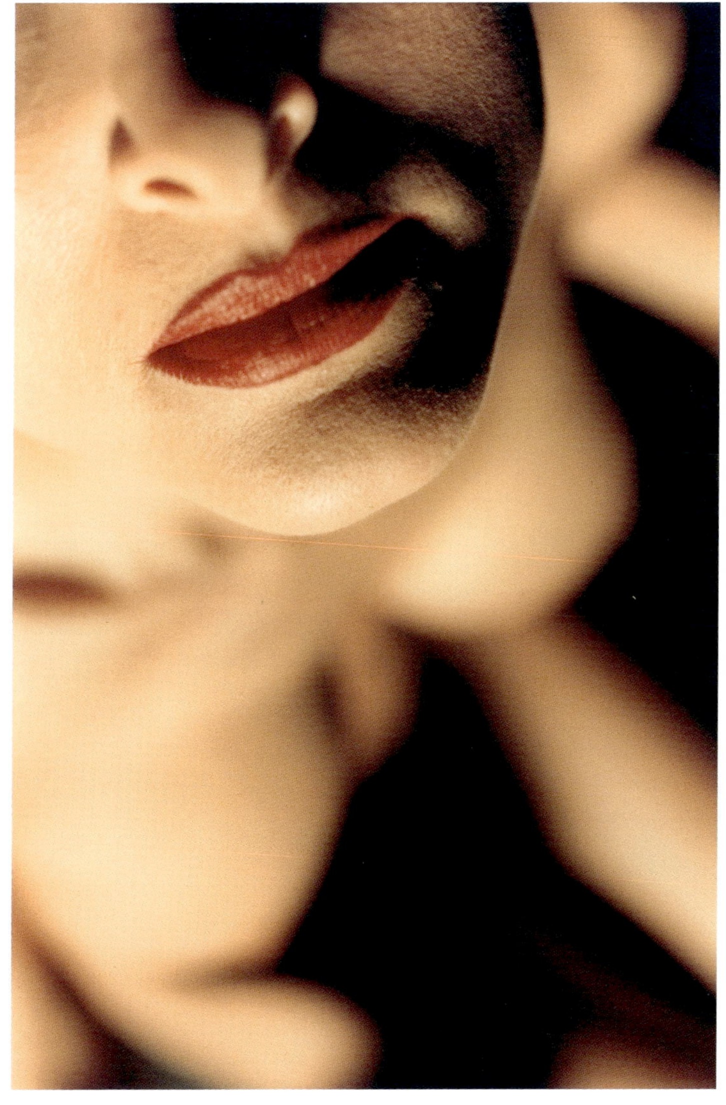

↑ **David Lynch,** Untitled, from 'Nudes' series, 1992

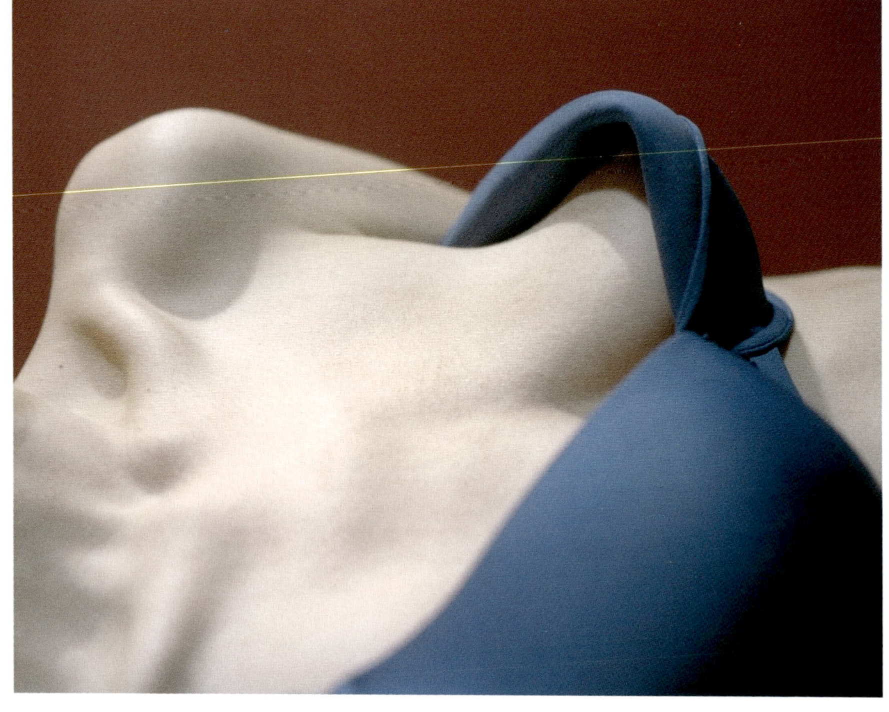

↑ **Marton Perlaki,** *Female Torso,* 2014

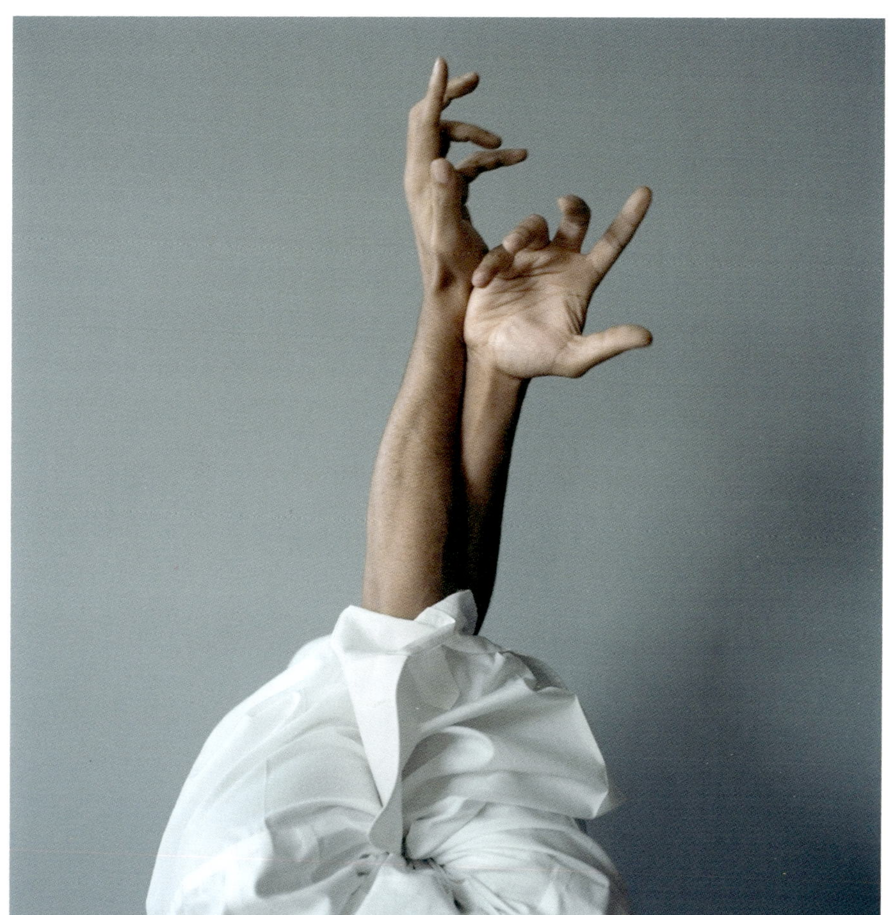

↑ **Marton Perlaki,** *Bonebreaking,* 2017

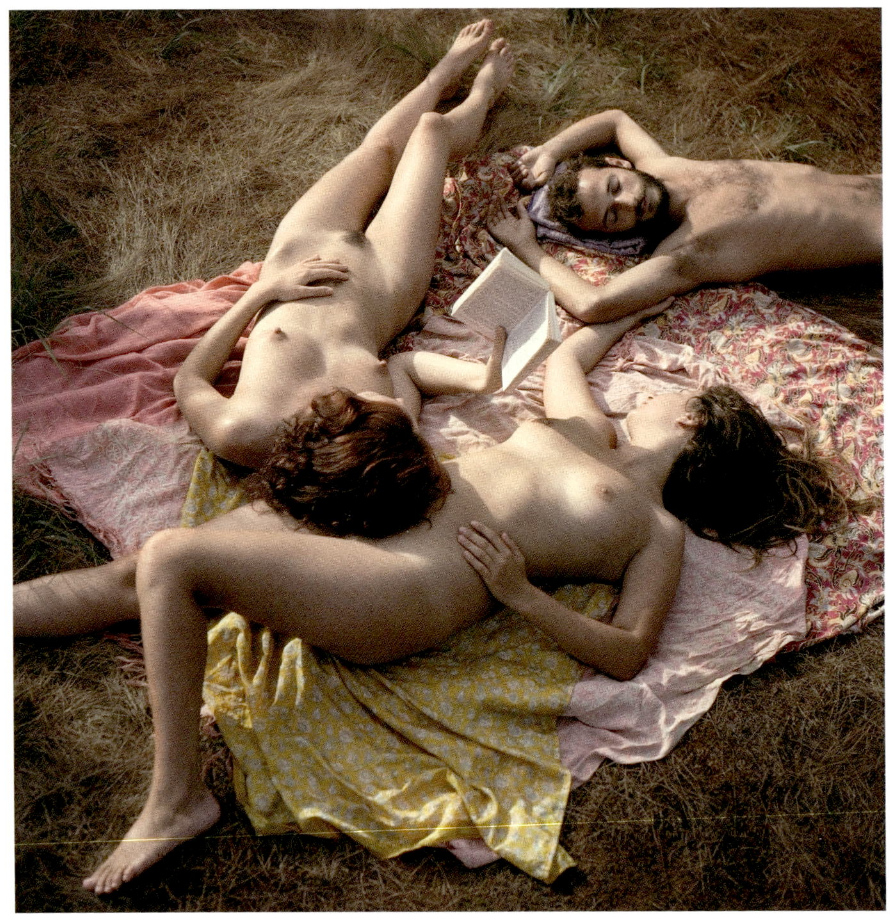

↑ **Mona Kuhn,** *Poem 3*, 2016

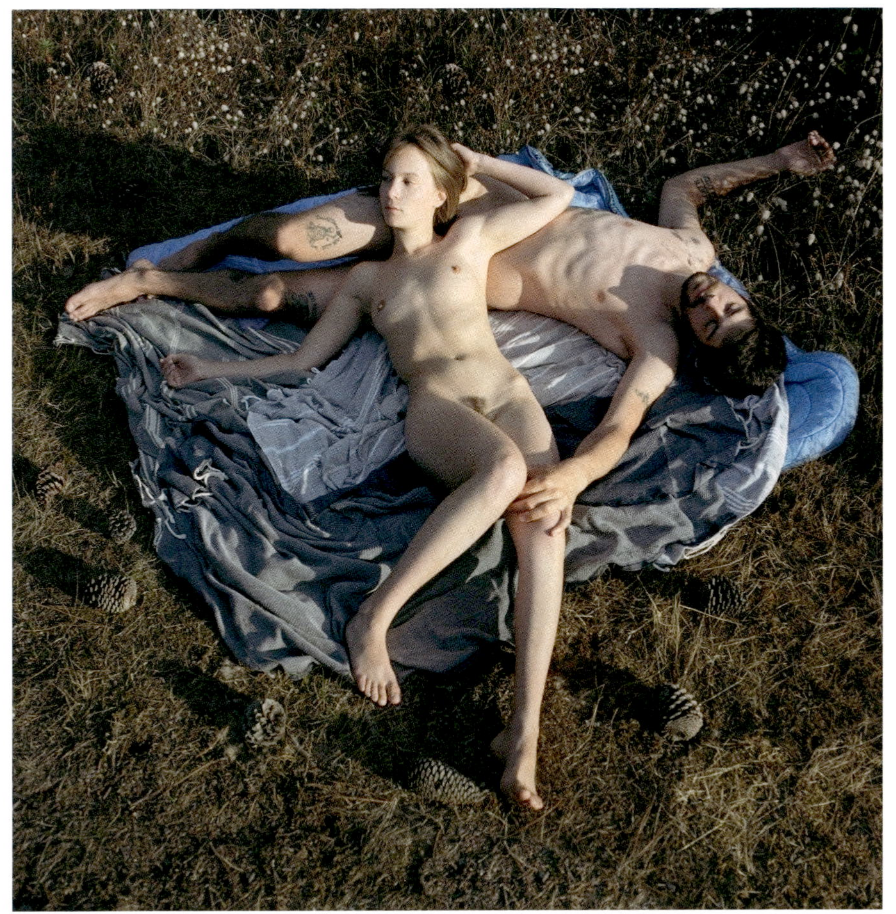

↑ **Mona Kuhn**, *Poem 2*, 2016

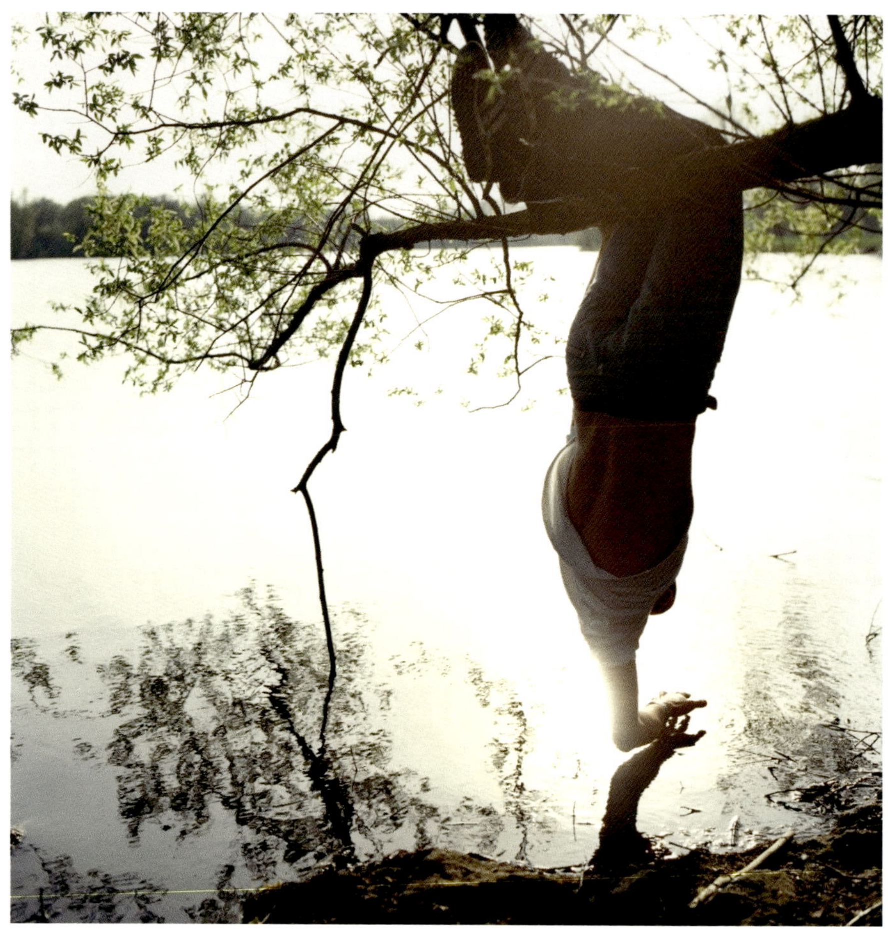

↑ Sascha Weidner, *Touché II*, 2005

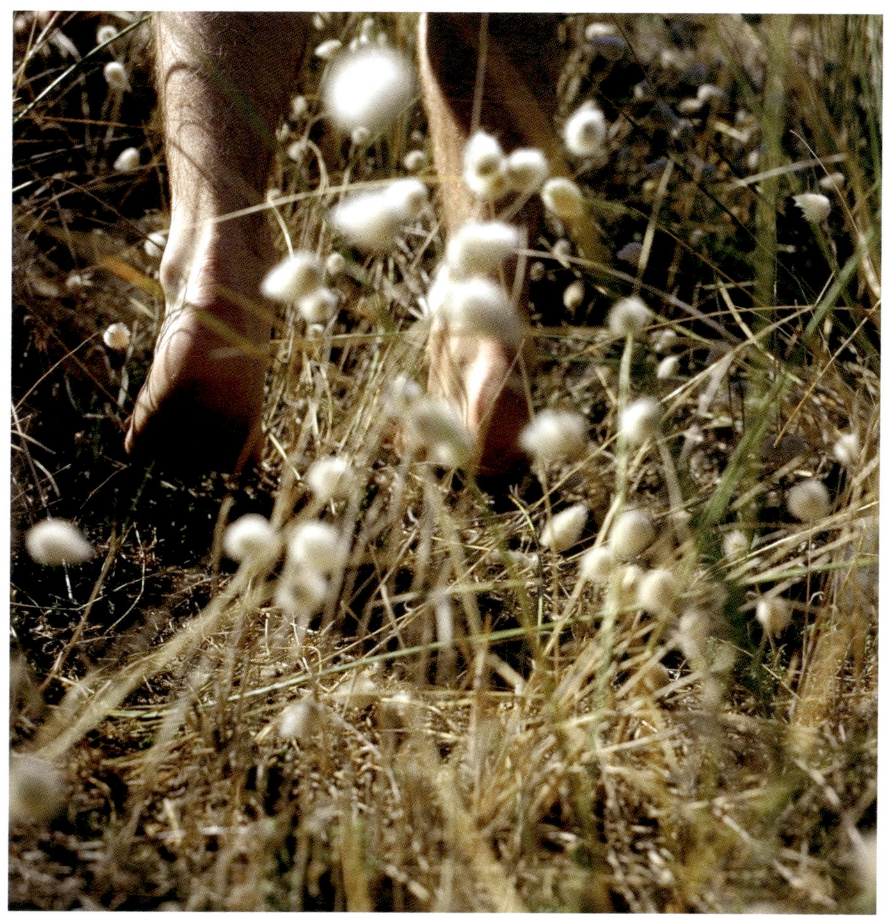

↑ Sascha Weidner, *Weidekätzchen II*, 2011

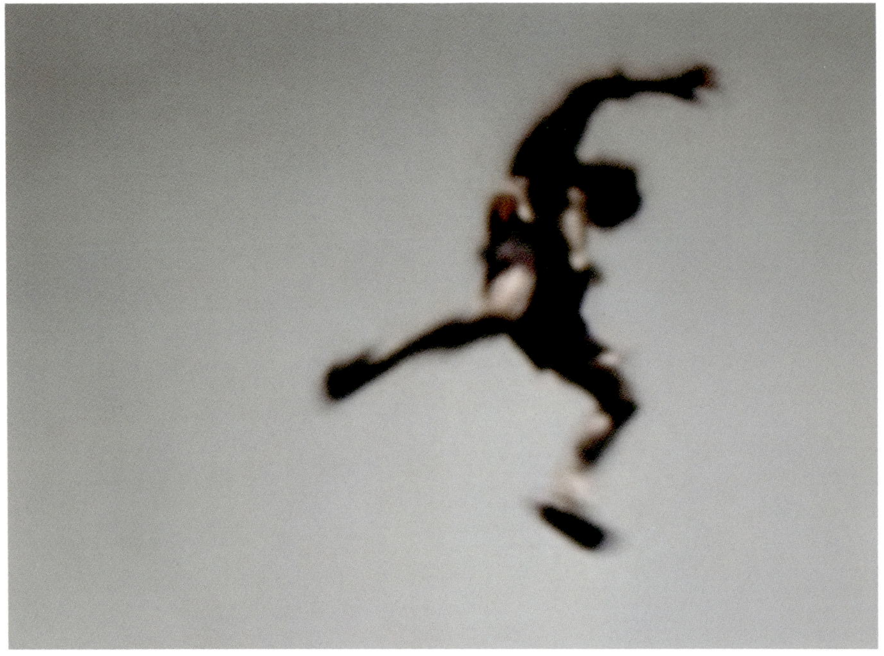

↑ Sascha Weidner, *Jumper II*, 2011

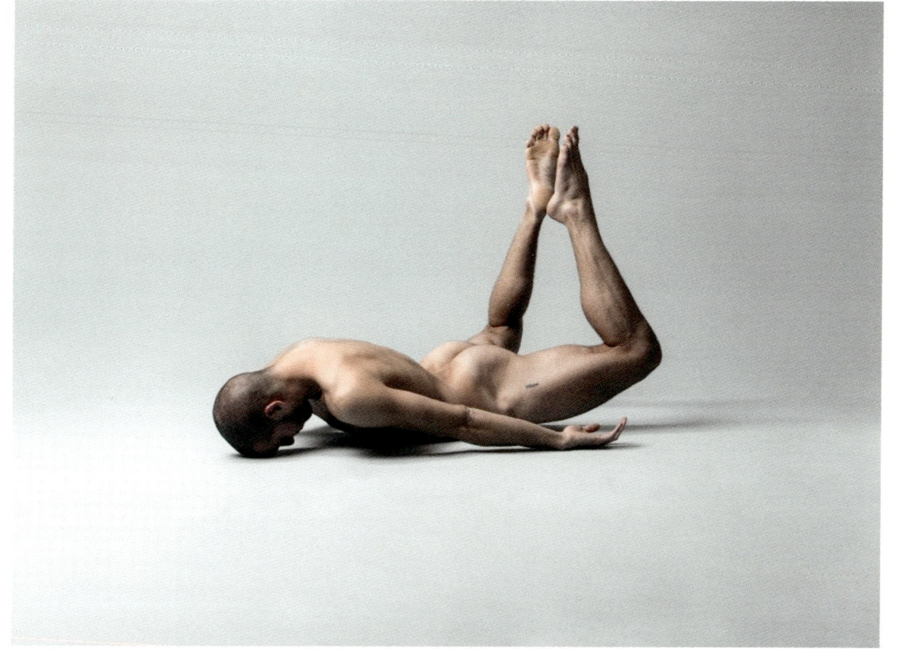

↑ **Gerardo Vizmanos**, *Thibaut*, 2016

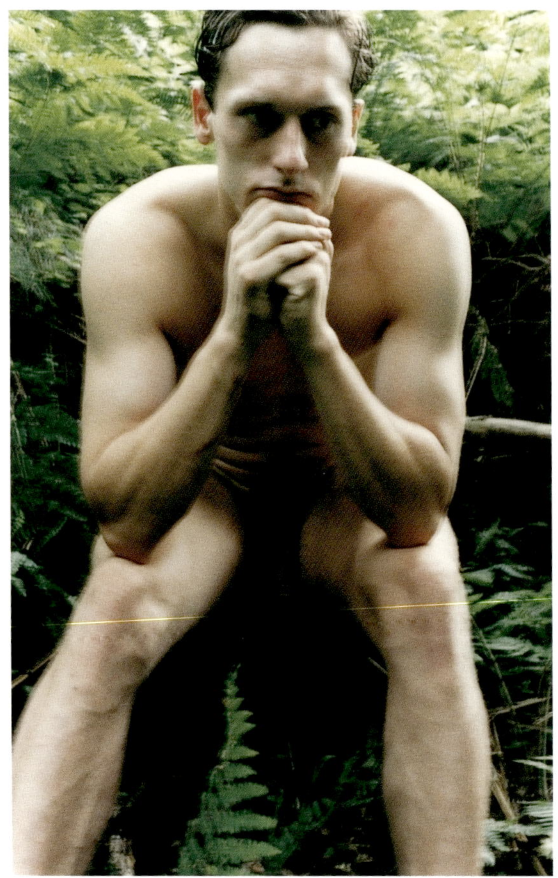

↑ **Wolfgang Tillmans,** *Arnd, nude, sitting,* 1991

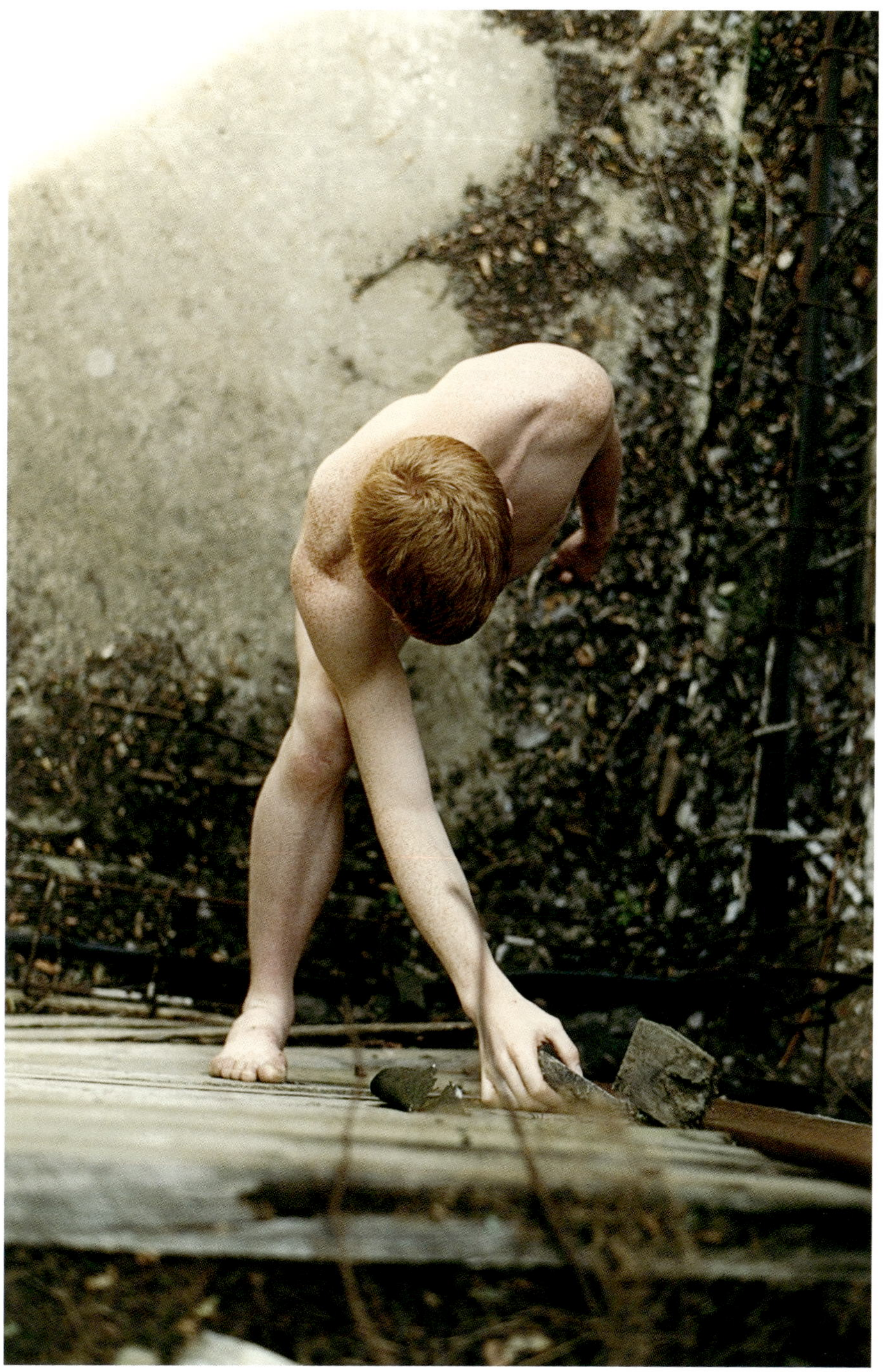

↑ Wolfgang Tillmans, *Dan*, 2008

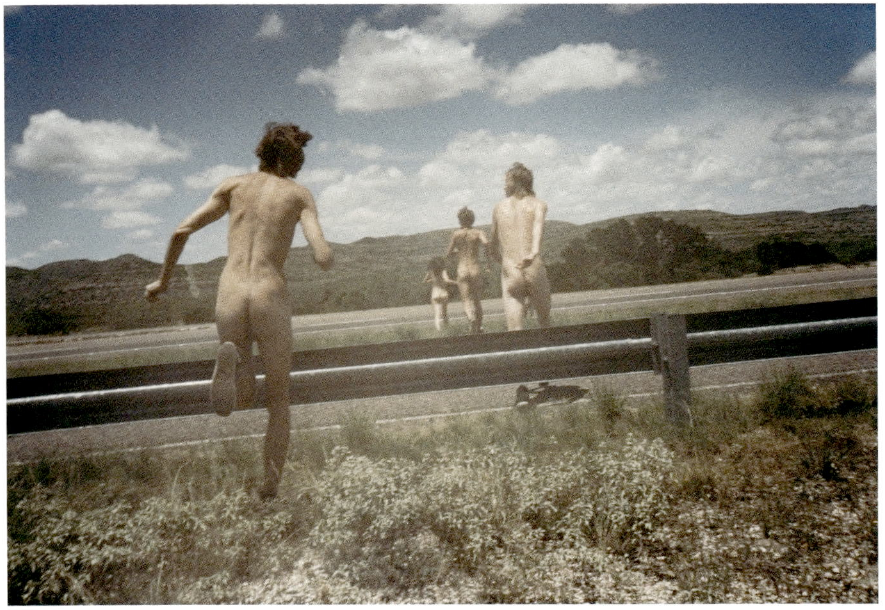

↑ Ryan McGinley, *Highway*, 2007

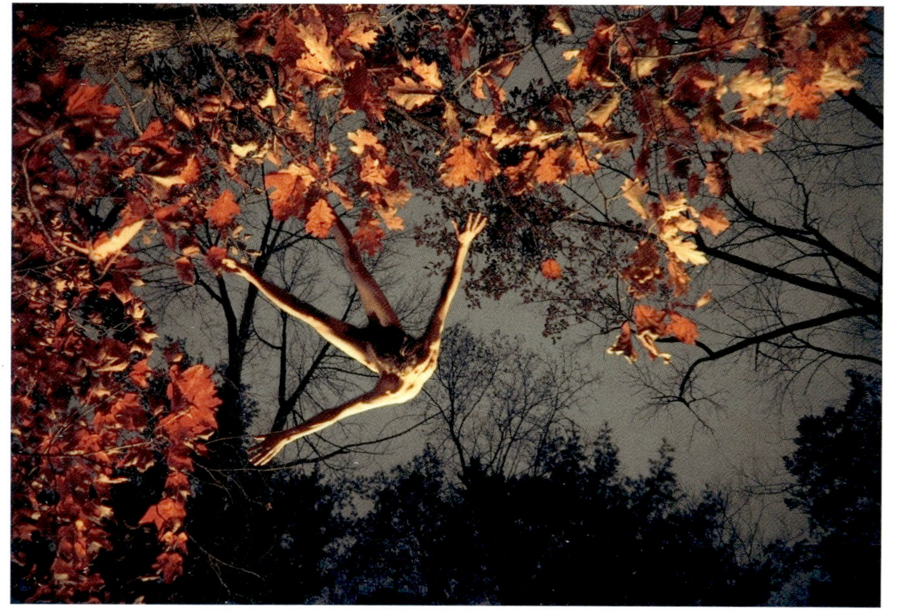

↑ **Ryan McGinley,** *Jake (Fall Foliage),* 2011

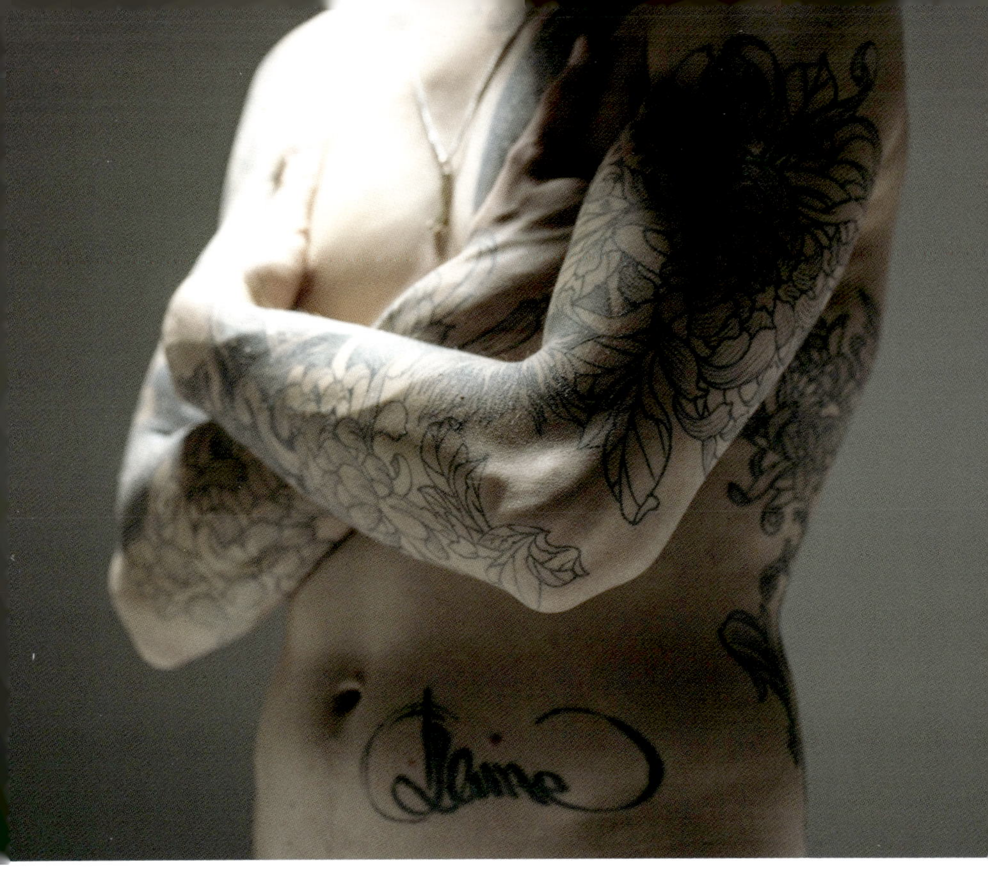

↑ **Angélique Stehli,** *Antoine,* from the series 'InDogWeTrust', 2015

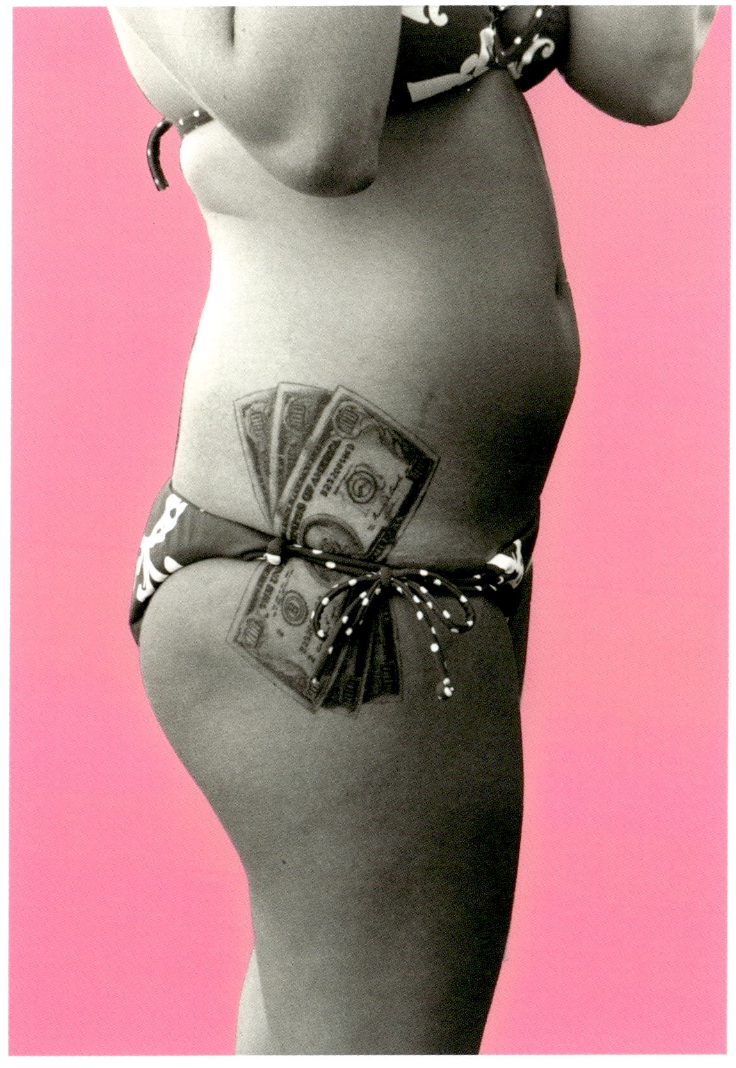

↑ **Ed Templeton,** *'Money Tattoo', Huntington Beach,* 2011

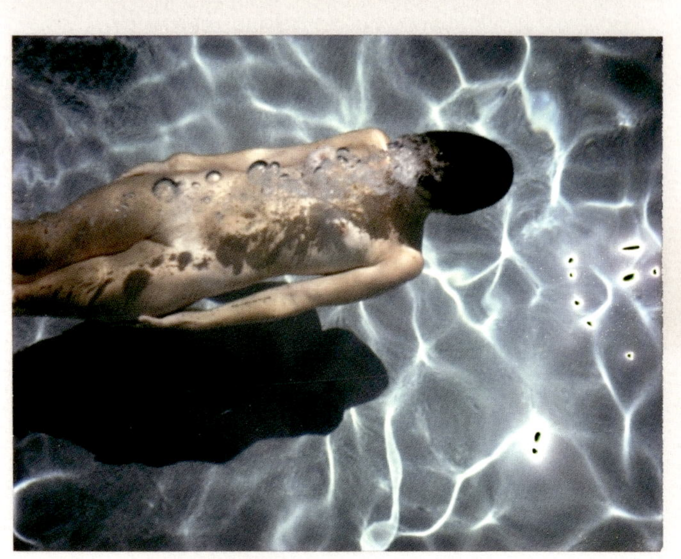

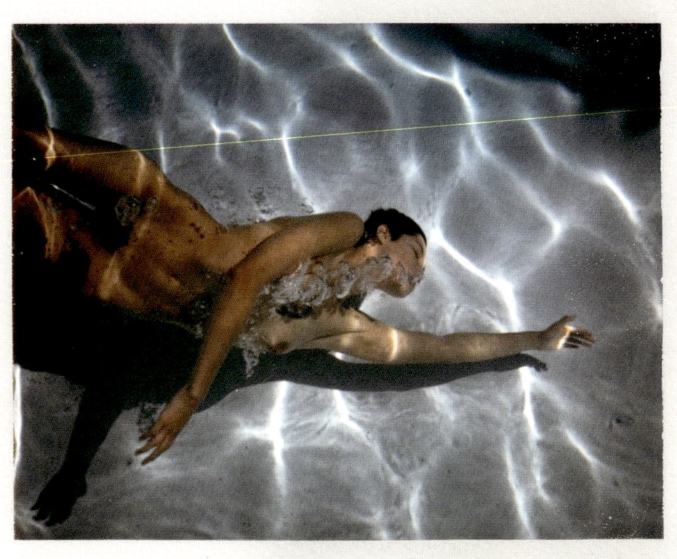

↑ (Top) **Deanna Templeton,** *Andi*, from the series 'The Swimming Pool', 2015
↑ (Above) **Deanna Templeton,** *Dani*, from the series 'The Swimming Pool', 2009

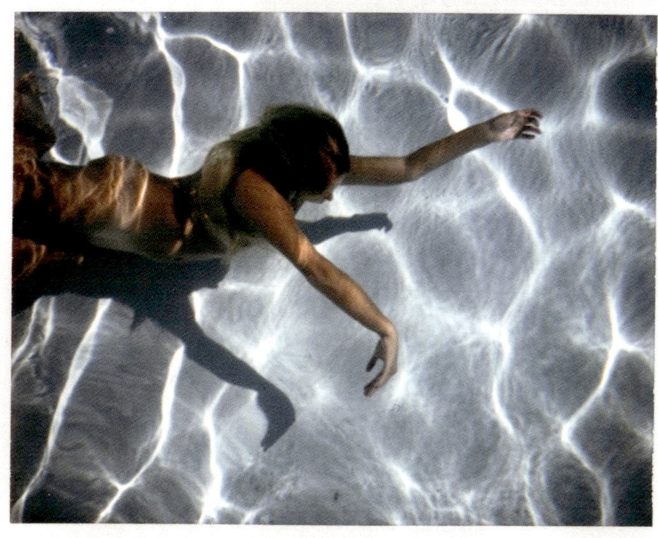

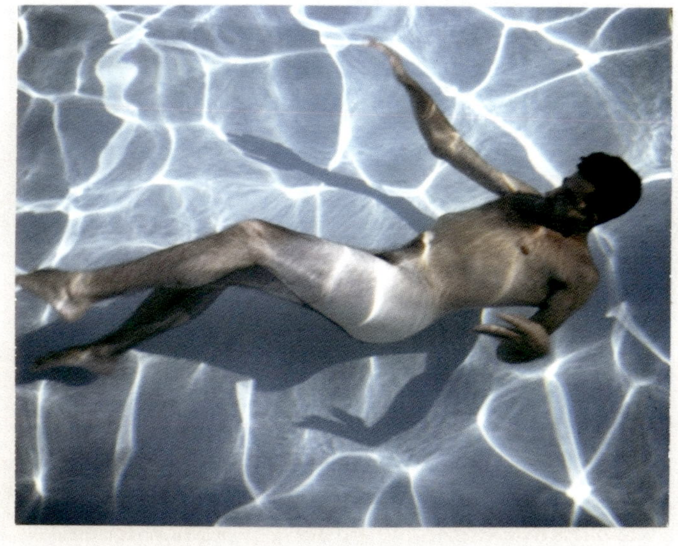

↑ (Top) **Deanna Templeton,** *Brooke,* from the series 'The Swimming Pool', 2009
↑ (Above) **Deanna Templeton,** *Kevin,* from the series 'The Swimming Pool', 2008

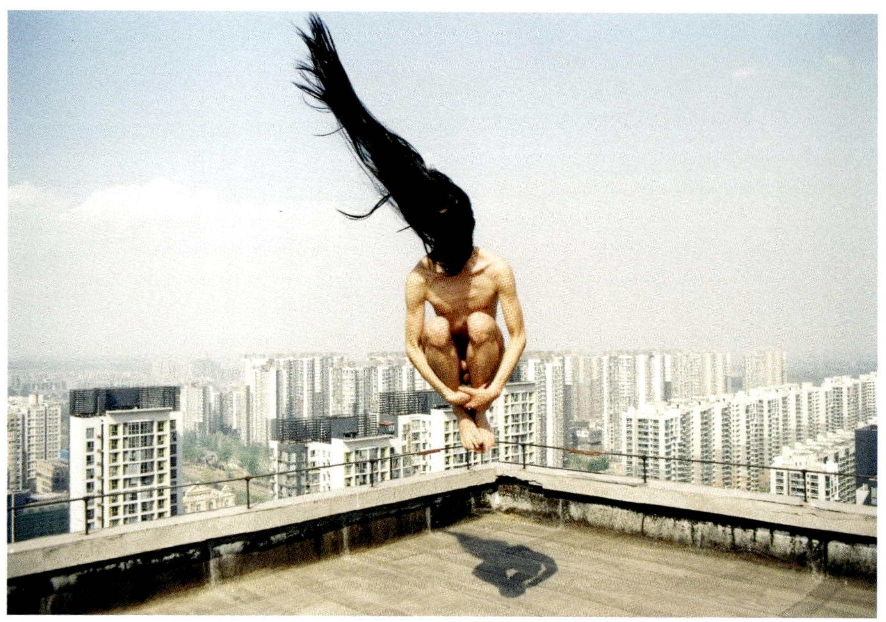

↑ **Ren Hang,** *Untitled 22,* 2012

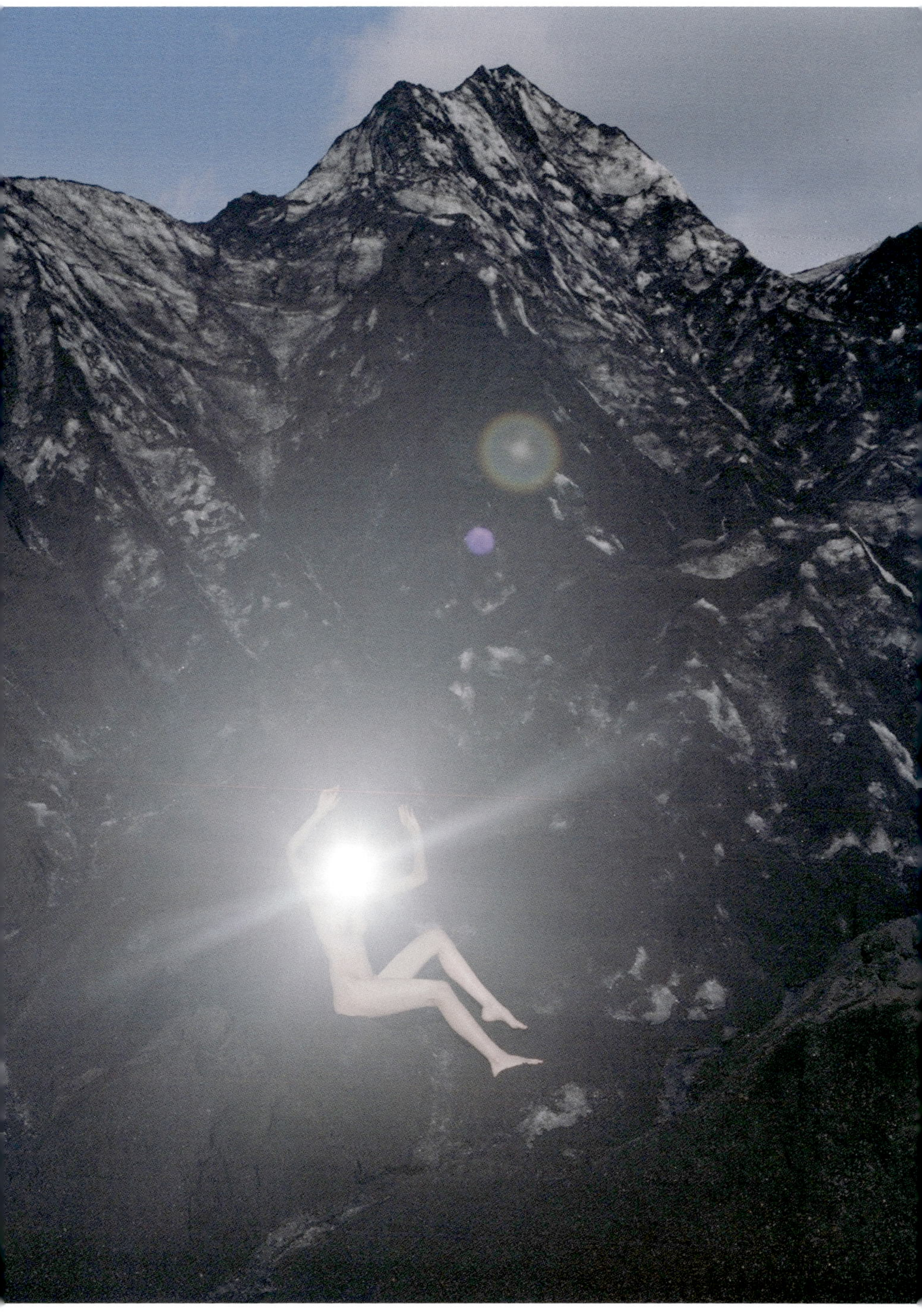

↑ **Synchrodogs,** Untitled, from the series 'Reverie sleep', 2013

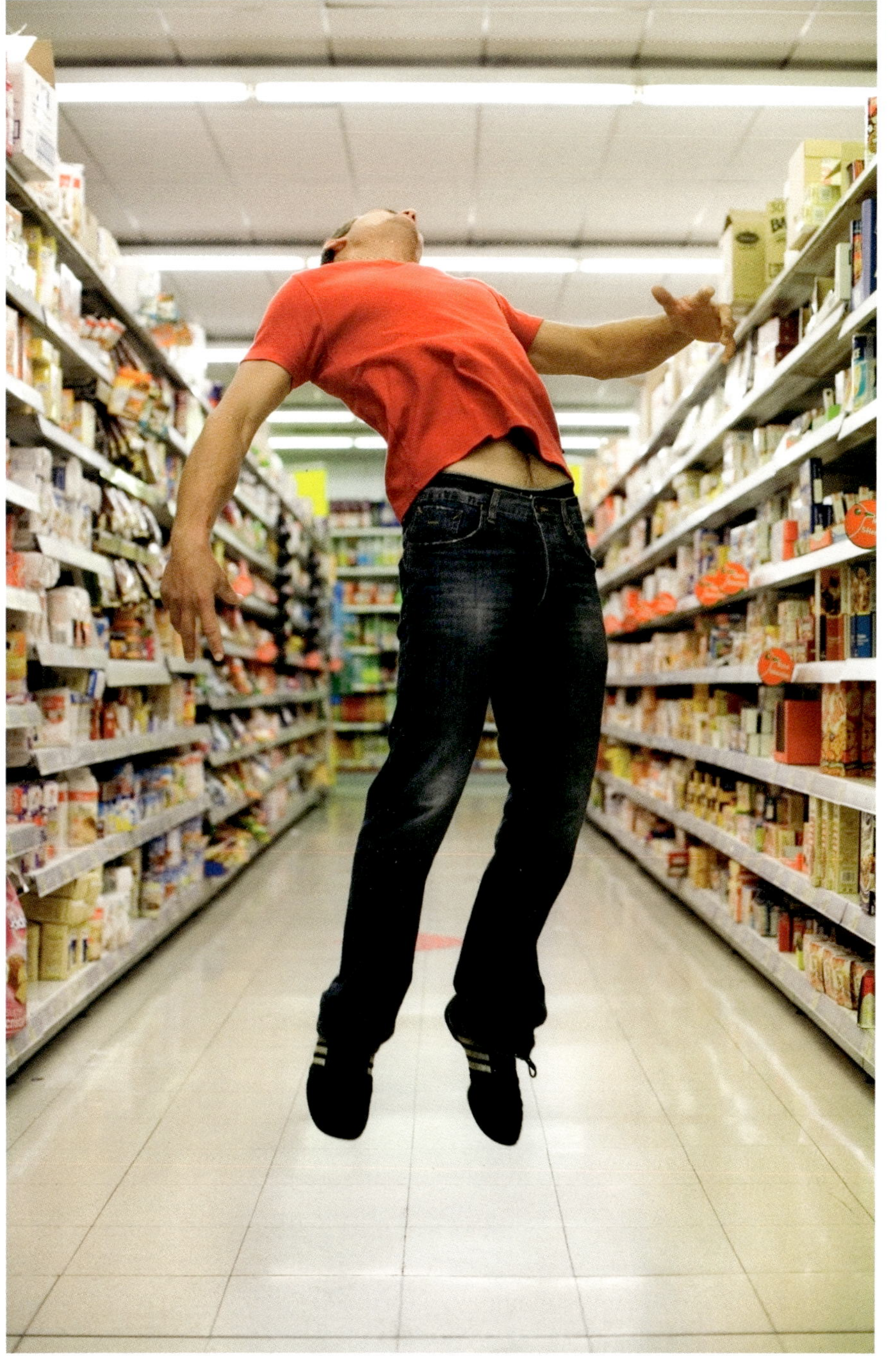

↑ **Denis Darzacq,** *Hyper n°20,* 2007
→(Overleaf) **Bill Henson,** *Untitled,* 2009–10

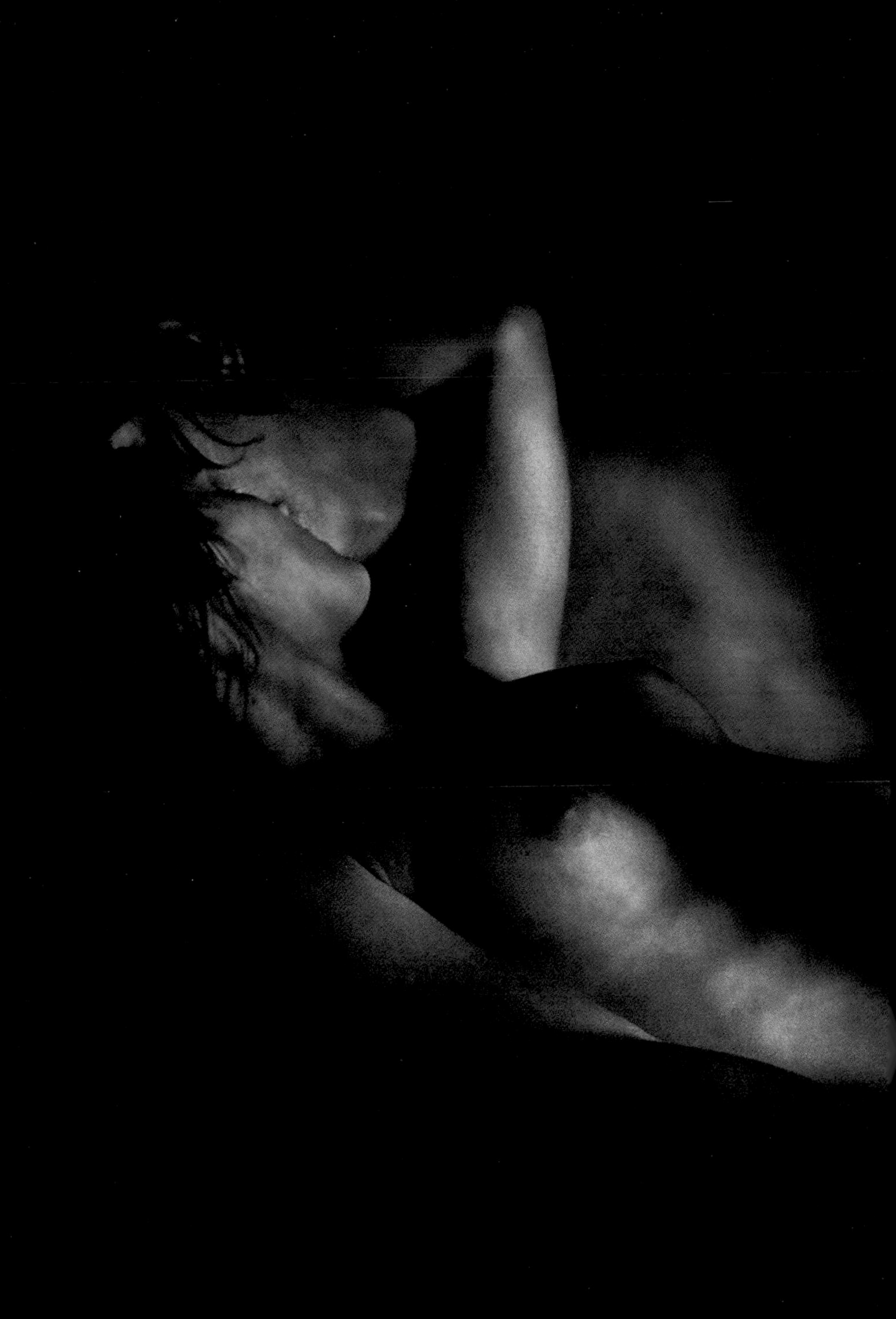

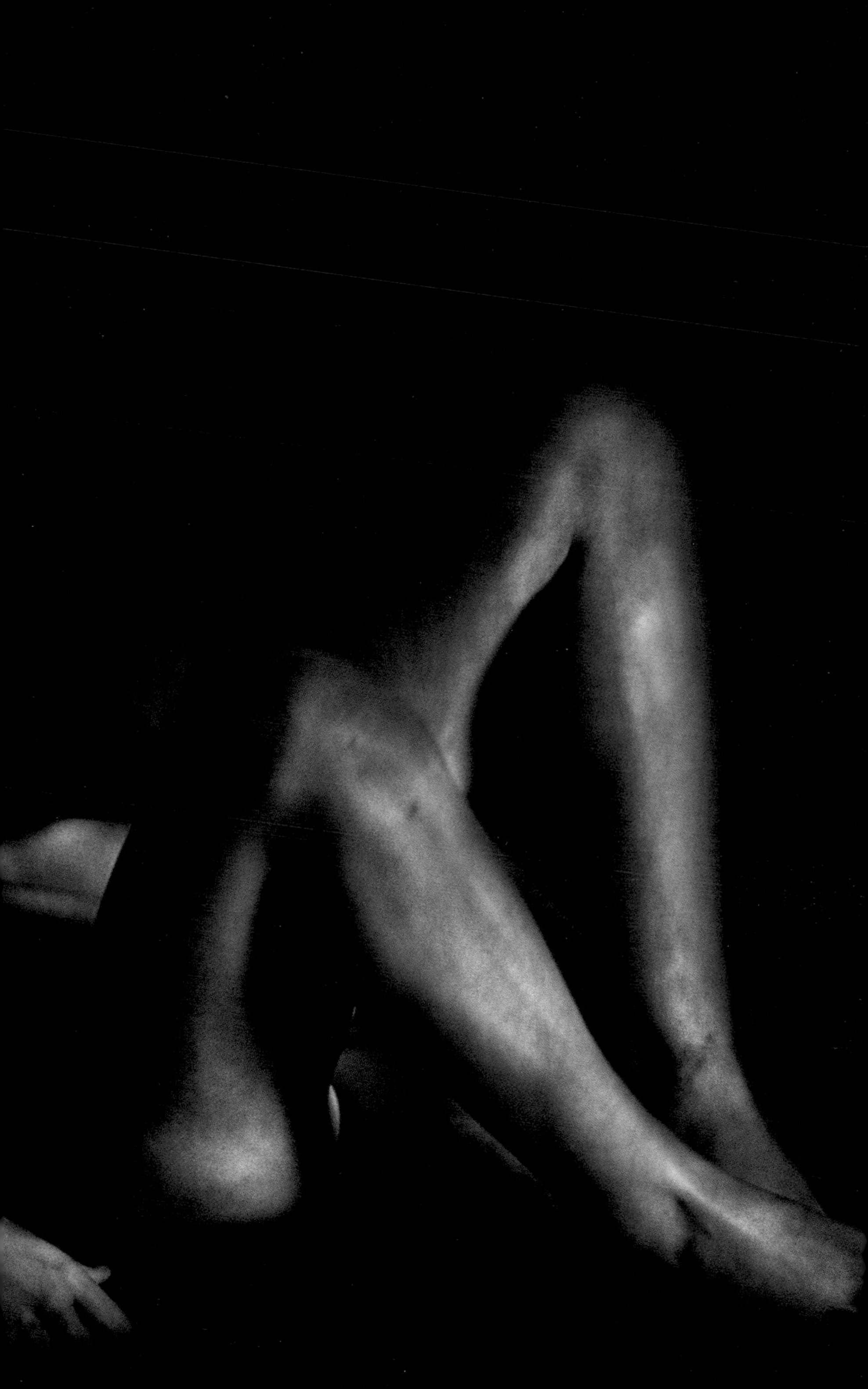

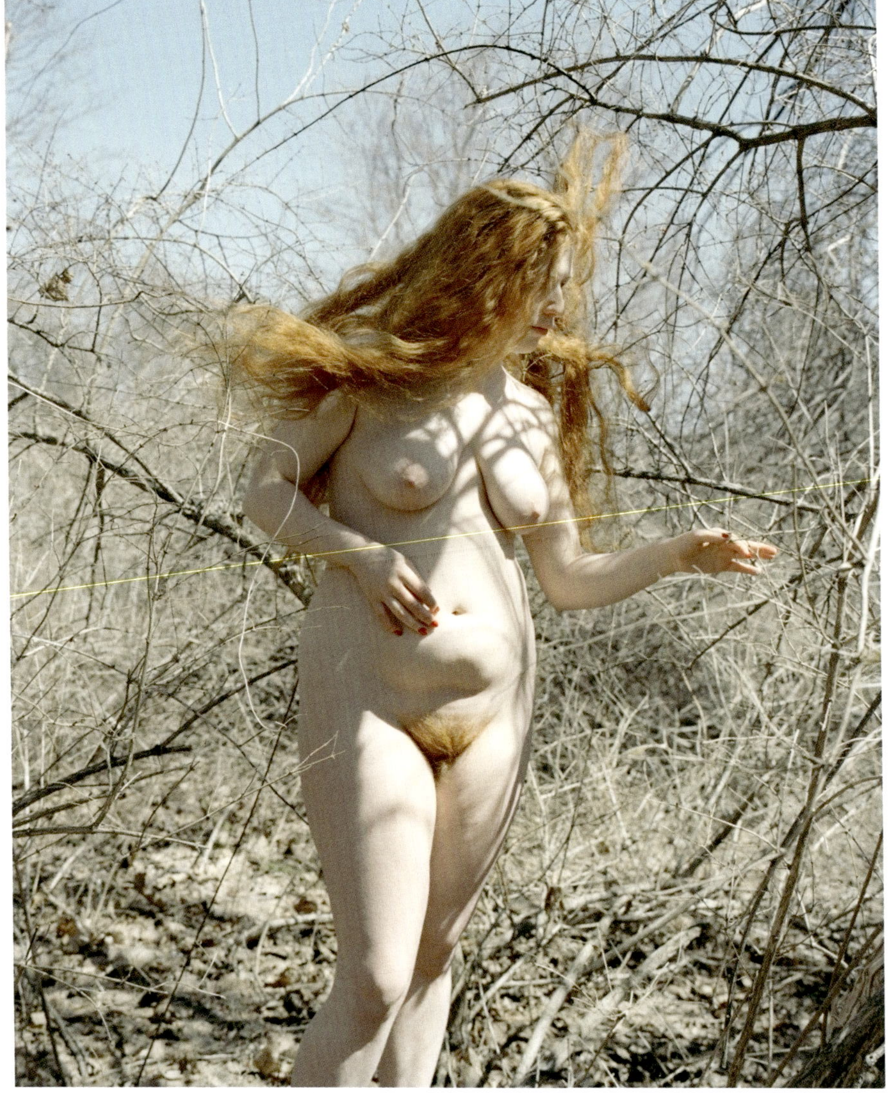

↑ **Jocelyn Lee,** *Winter Venus*, from the series 'The Appearance of Things', 2016

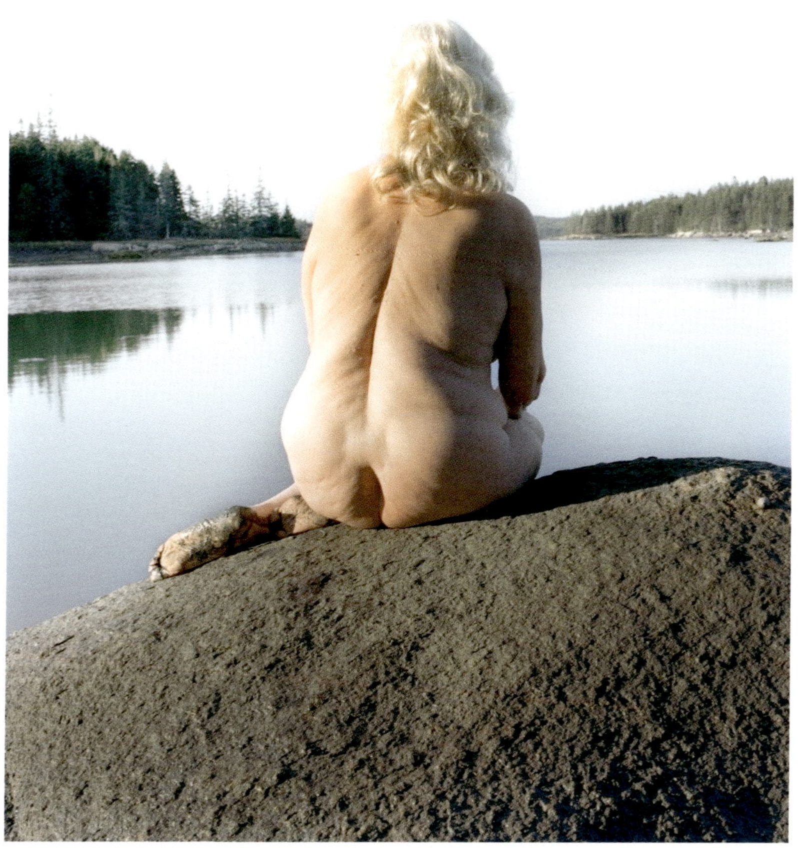

↑ **Jocelyn Lee,** *Late September #1,* from the series
'The Appearance of Things', 2017

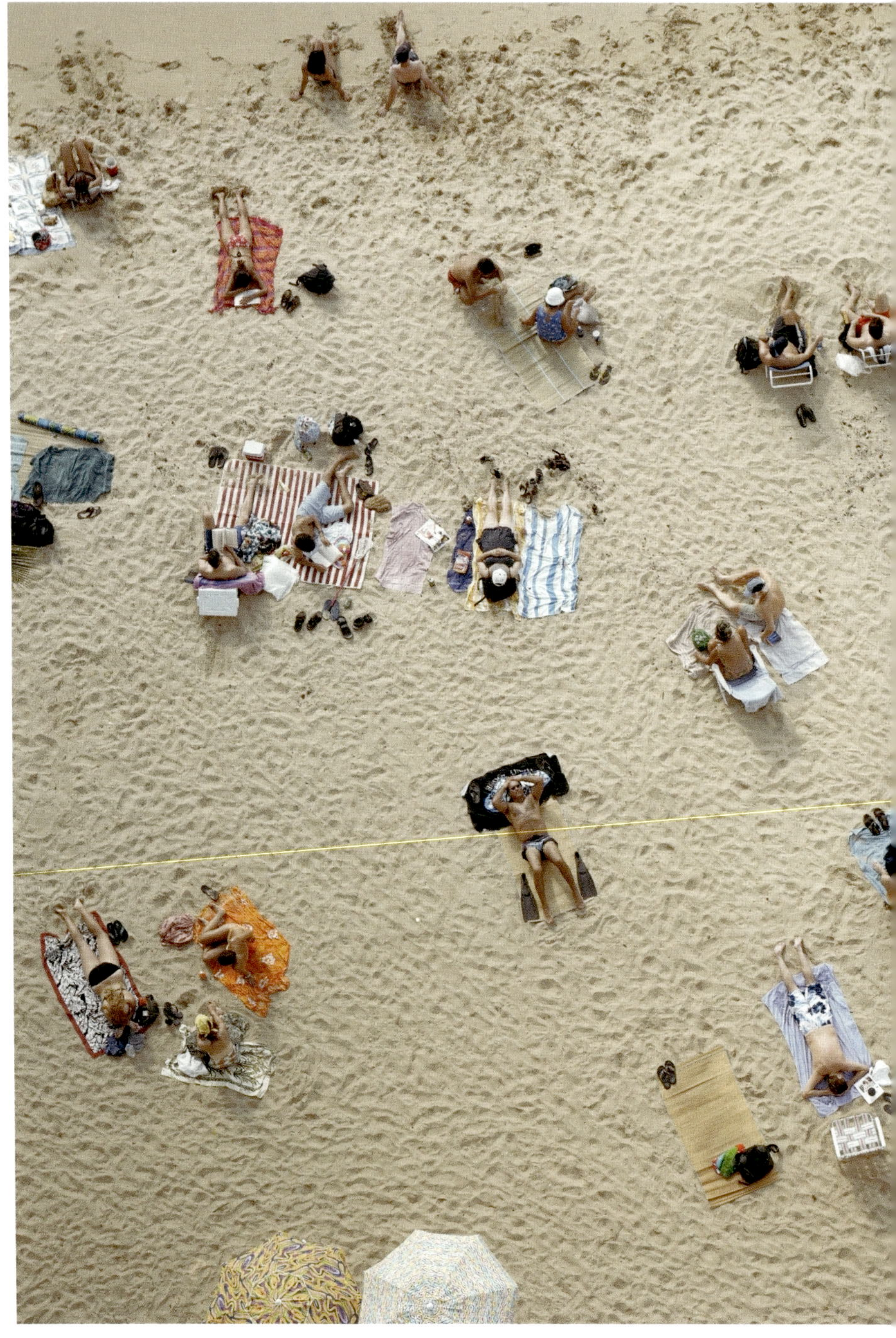

↑ **Richard Misrach,** *Untitled,* 2004

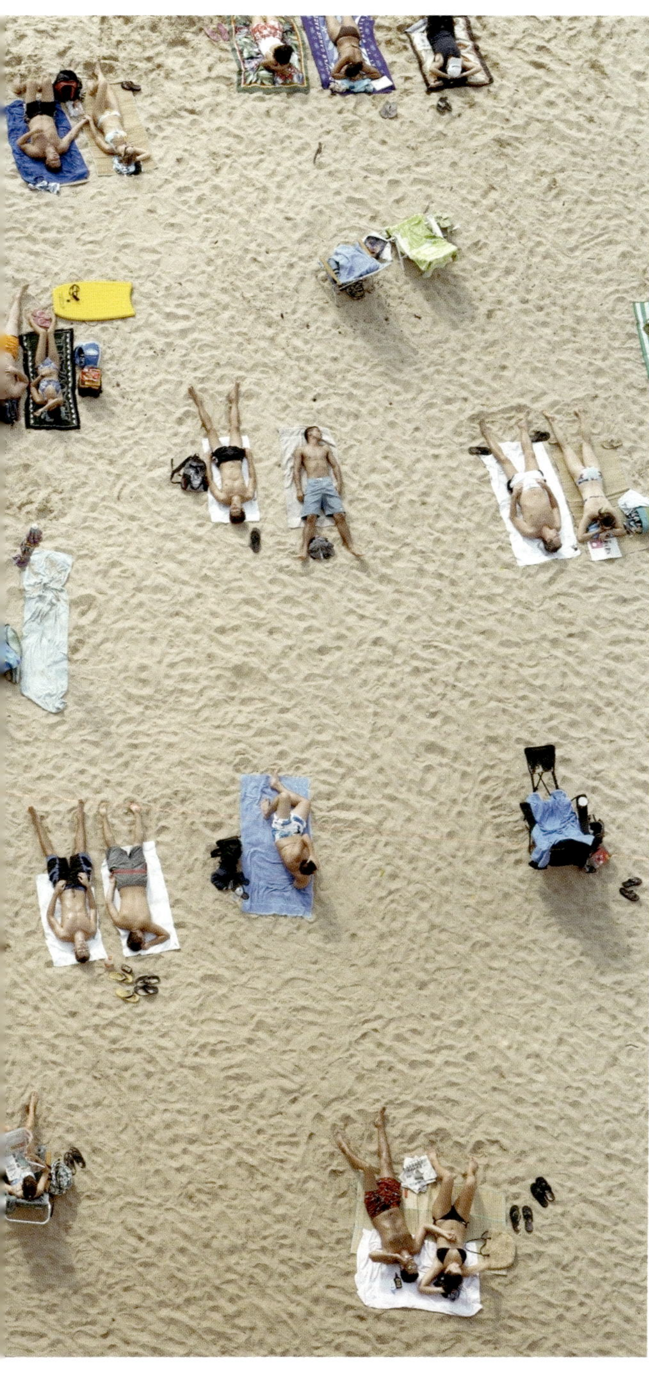

FLESH

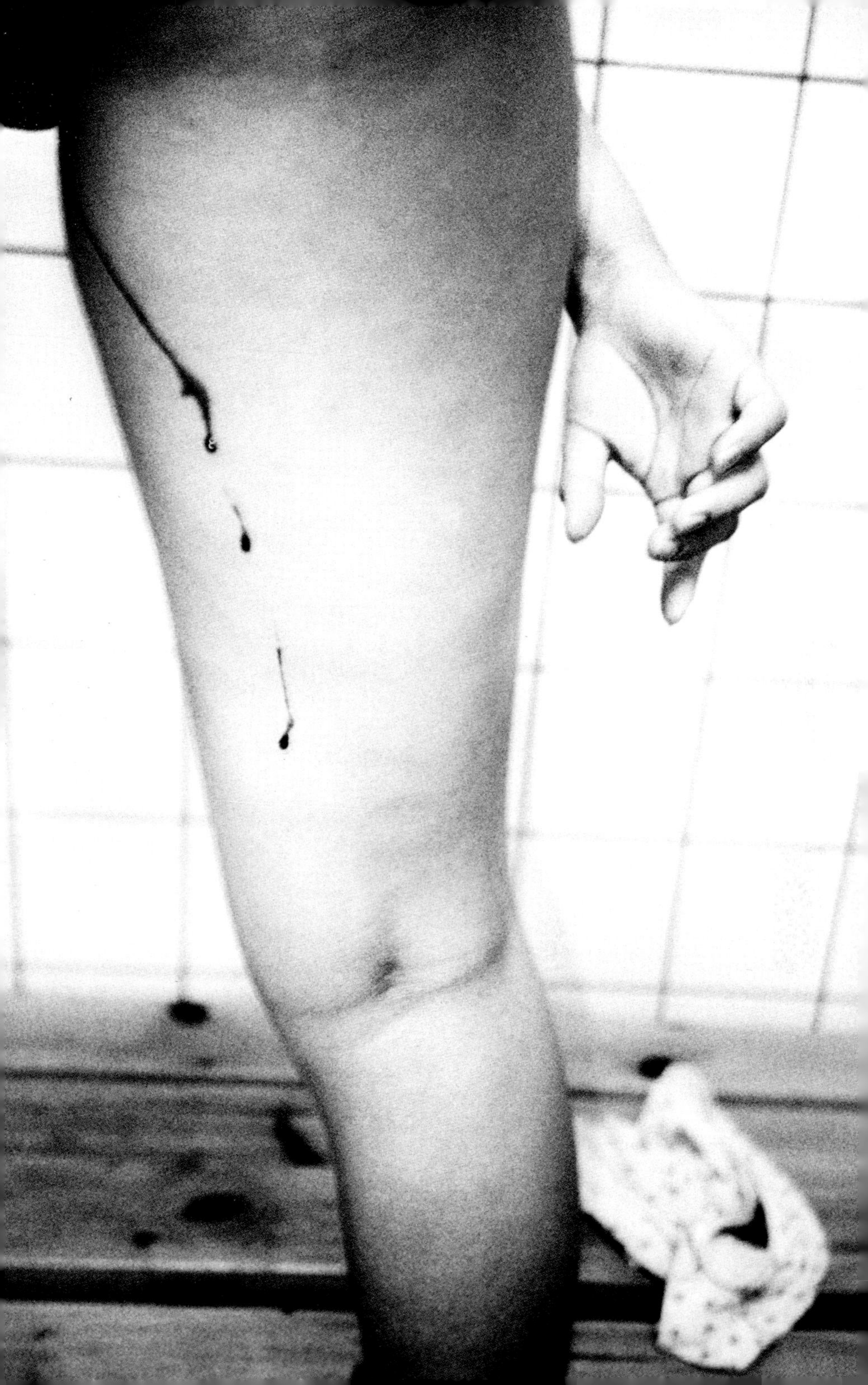

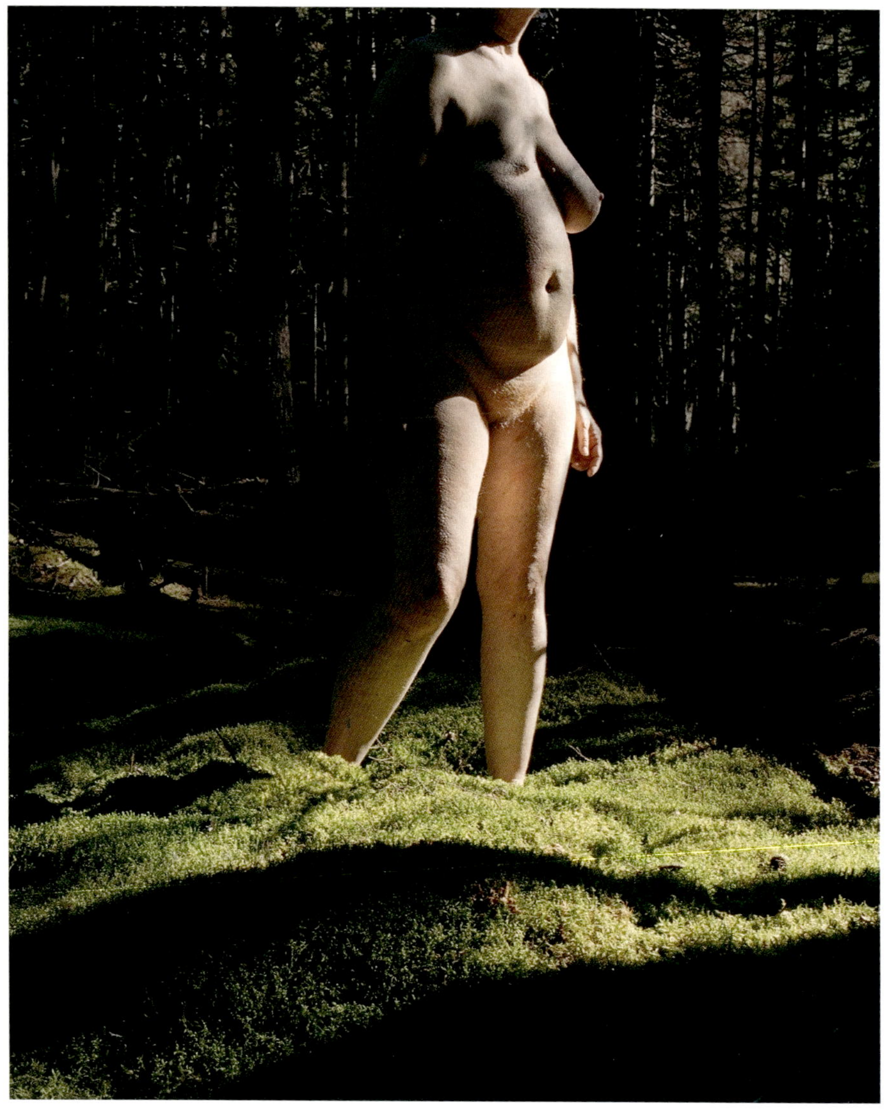

↑ **Jocelyn Lee,** *The Perfect Breast*, 2017
←(Previous) **Jacob Aue Sobol,** *Greenlandic Sabine Maqe, Tiniteqilaaq, Greenland*, 2001

We have an ambivalent relationship with our bodies: we wish them well and take care of them, but we battle against them throughout our lives. We often find the idea of a weak, sick, suffering and dying body unbearable. So we fight it in order to meet the targets set by our society (health, vitality, well-being, etc.). Yet our bodies nonetheless bear the traces of our personal history, in the little marks here and there, the wrinkles, the extra pounds, the tattoos, scars and other traces of injury and illness. We are tenaciously fighting this ordinary human body – a body that causes us anxiety – because we know that it may suffer and break down at any moment. It is sometimes difficult to accept the idea that we will die one day. It is true that medicine is helping us in this constant battle. With average life expectancy now at around 71 years, humans have never lived so long. As it ages, however, the body is more and more likely to fall ill despite all the preventive, protective or precautionary measures that we take. We are very much confronted with this fact when it comes to caring for the elderly. We find it reassuring to put them into the care of old people's homes, followed by hospitals and hospices, kept apart from our world, because we are so disturbed by the sight of the sick.

Photography is able to erase spots, lumps, wrinkles, hairs and other bodily protuberances – this was already accomplished in the 19th century since, even then, photographers were expected to make the human being look more impressive – yet there are times when we cannot avoid facing our flesh, for example beginning the day in front of our mirror which shows us an image that has not been retouched. Accepting the reality of the flesh and its 'defects' conflicts with the mass-produced images of young and smooth skins created by our society. Richard Learoyd (pp. 318, 319) is renewing the genre of the nude by posing flesh-and-blood humans who do not necessarily match up to the aesthetic canons to which photography has accustomed us. His work expresses a fragility, which his camera obscura technique makes particularly evident. Erica Deeman (pp. 344–45), meanwhile, poses men in front of a background chosen on the basis of her own skin tone as a means of highlighting individual variations in skin colour and idiosyncratic facial features, thus questioning simplistic ways of stereotyping.

Images of people suffering, wounded or deformed by disability were for a long time restricted to the medical profession. But we have not been spared images of war. We need only remember haunting photographs of war veterans of 1918, or the survivors of the holocaust in 1945, or more recently the scars of torture survivors, as in an image by Jim Goldberg (p. 317) showing the back of a man tortured by the Taliban. Andreas Rentsch (pp. 324, 325), whose work is the result of drawing with light, takes a singular approach to the suffering body, depicting the appalling treatments that were meted out in Abu Ghraib prison in Iraq in 2003. Then there are the unbearable images of people suffering or shown dead that we see in the papers. Even if we look with indifference at many of these press images, sometimes we are still shocked by images of the dead and look away. In his 'Morgue' series, Andres Serrano (pp. 348–49) prevents us from closing our eyes and turns us into voyeurs.

It took until the late 20th century for photographers to become interested in ageing flesh, a flesh that becomes an increasing burden with the passage of time. This is very much the case with Susan Copen Oken (p. 351). The unease we feel in the face of images of a body that is quite simply withering shows that we have great difficulty in identifying physically with it. It seems impossible to feel in harmony with something that we fear and that makes us so anxious. We may remember the series the Swiss artist Ferdinand Hodler painted in 1914–15 of his mistress, Valentine Godé-Darel, on her deathbed. One hundred years later, the viewer remains as shocked as ever. Sally Mann (p. 353) reverses the role when in her series 'Proud Flesh' she observes the body of the man who has been her husband for thirty-nine years. These photographs go beyond the classical idea of the nude.

We in the 21st century still find it hard to confront the body that bears the marks of its suffering, even at a time when we are being exposed to more and more images. In his series 'Fragile', Raphaël Dallaporta (pp. 358, 359) concentrates on organs examined by forensic surgeons looking for causes of death, as well as medical instruments used by the physicians. Aida Silvestri (pp. 360, 361) depicts women who have been

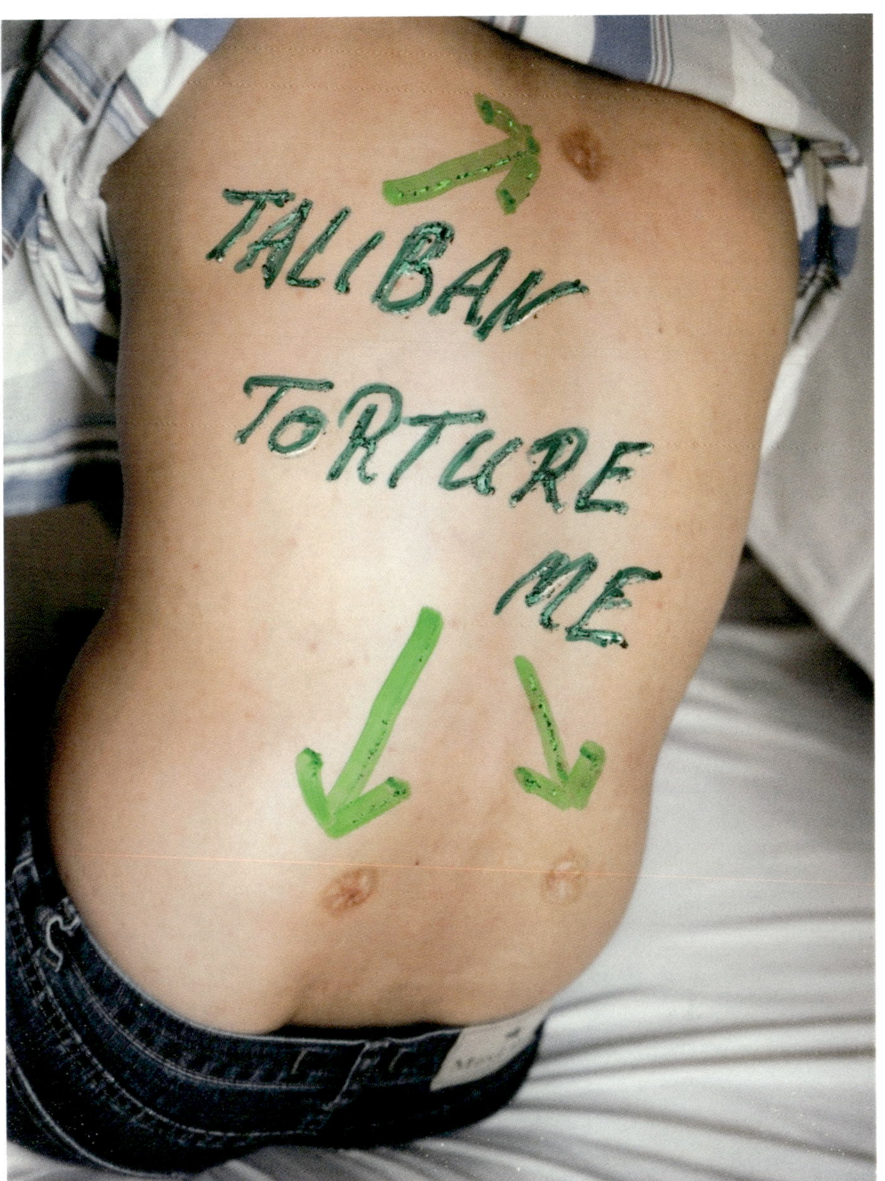

↑ **Jim Goldberg,** *Detained Afghani refugee shows scars received from Taliban torture. Lavrio Detention Centre, Greece, 2005*

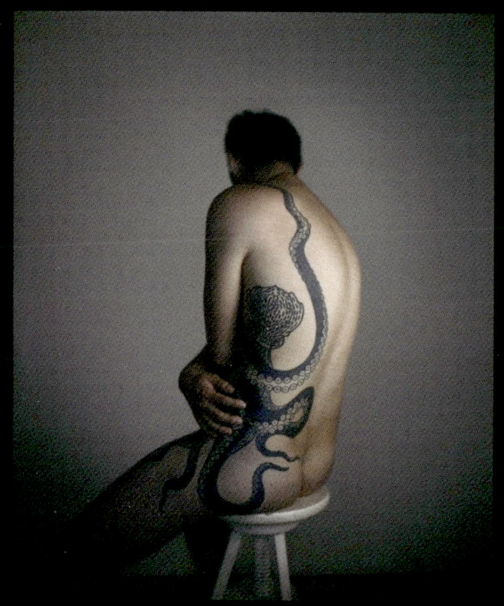

↑ **Richard Learoyd,** *Man with Octopus Tattoo II*, 2011

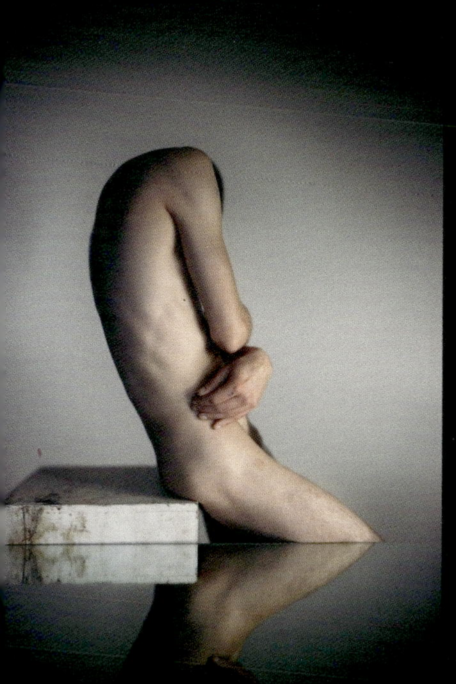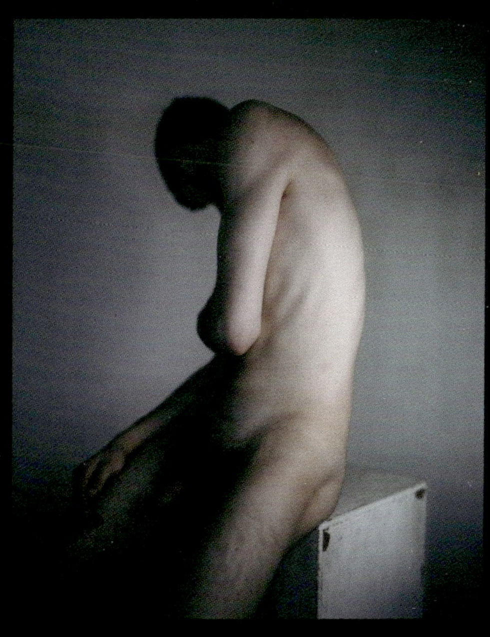

↑ (Left) **Richard Learoyd,** *Headless Man with Mirror,* 2016
↑ (Right) **Richard Learoyd,** *A New Man,* 2015

subjected to genital mutilation. In order to protect them she does not show their faces but only their silhouettes. Yet their suffering is clearly expressed by the screaming leather vaginas sewn on in place of their mouths.

In St Petersburg, Pyotr Pavlensky photographs himself supporting jailed members of the female punk band Pussy Riot (pp. 332–33): he has literally sewn up his mouth. Oliviero Toscani (pp. 362–63) confronts us directly with the emaciated body caused by anorexia. Such suffering bodies push us away; they are at odds with the 'beautiful' and healthy bodies we are told we must have. We have always been disturbed by this alternative reality. Fifty years ago, Diane Arbus gave us examples of it. After directing her lens at the extra-ordinary (dwarfs, giants, twins, tattooed people at fairgrounds), she turned her attention to the so-called ordinary people she met in the street. While the giants and dwarfs began to look human, normal people suddenly began to reveal themselves as strange. Denis Darzacq (p. 321) arouses the same feeling with his photographs of people suffering from physical disabilities, showing them as though they were contemporary dancers making unusual movements.

We live in a world where 'the other' is often hidden from us and compelled to live in horrendous conditions. Richard Mosse (pp. 366–69) uses a thermal camera to take a look at the way we dehumanize illegal migrants, while Seba Kurtis (pp. 370, 371) mimics the systems set up at borders to detect the heartbeats of people in hiding by using an unusually long exposure to create apparently blank film, which he then processes to reveal the information that is 'hidden' in the image. Our society has developed a strong sense of dissociation from the human body, whether others' or our own. This body cannot, however, avoid fatigue, hunger, disease or death. To this day, we remain flesh.

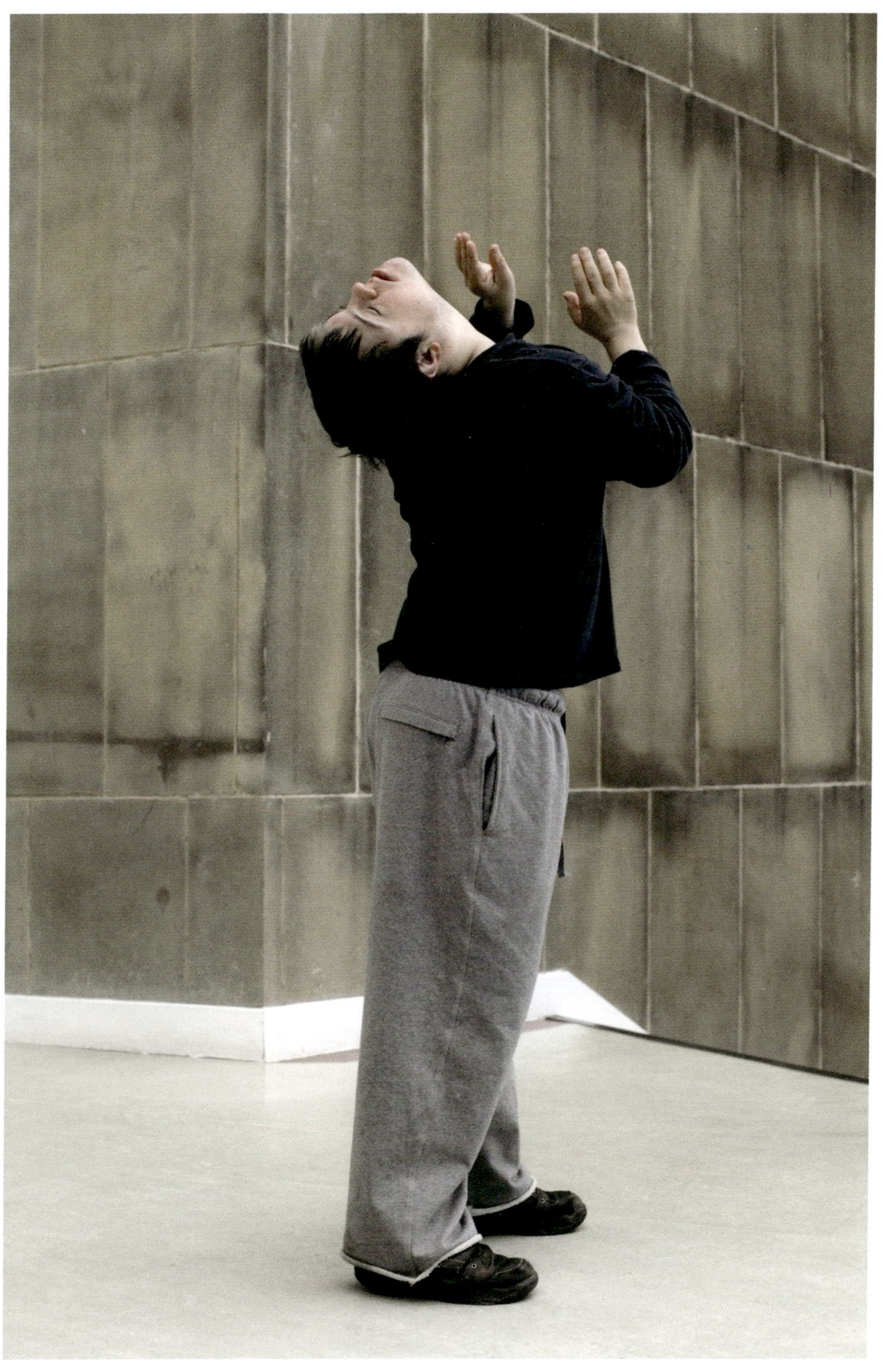

↑ **Denis Darzacq,** *ACT n°21, Jack Riley,* 2010
→(Overleaf) **Nadav Kander,** *Elizabeth with elbows hiding face,* 2012

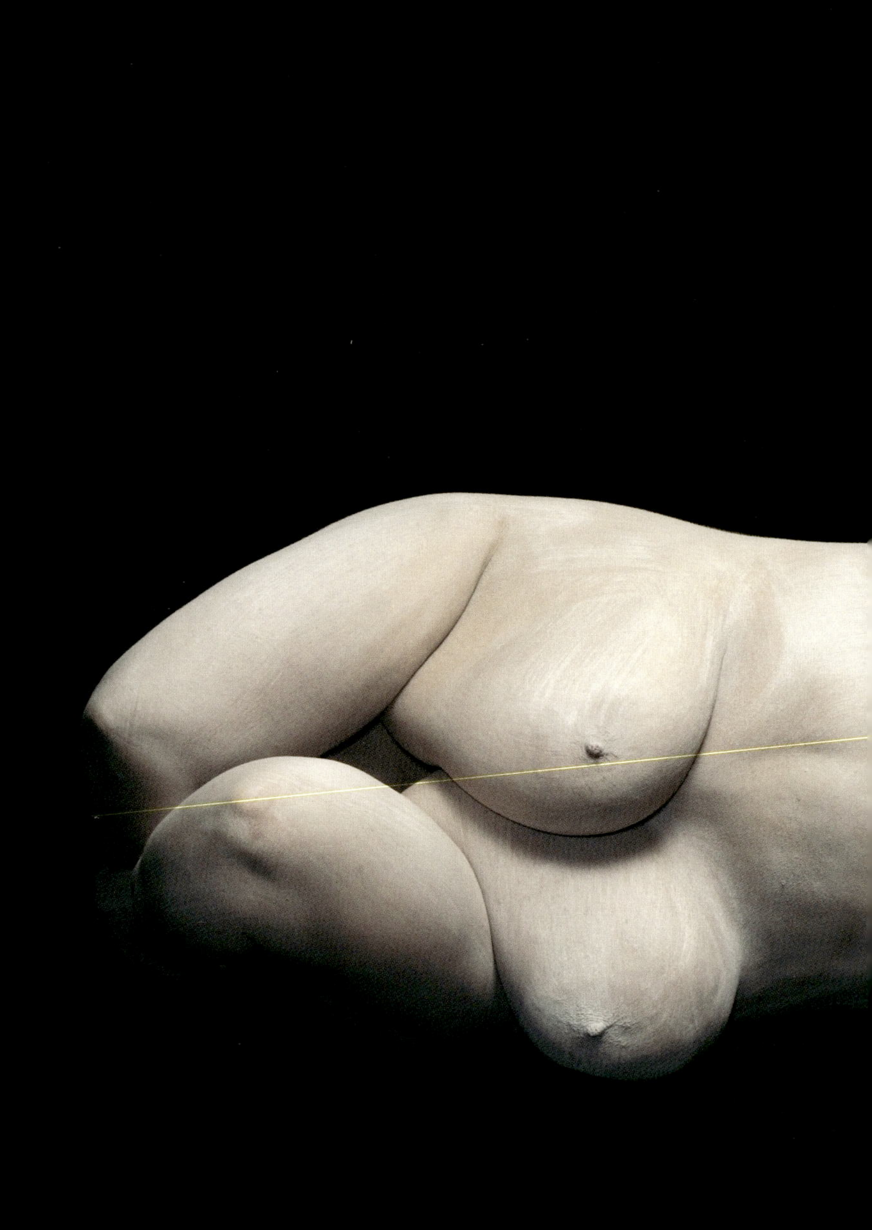

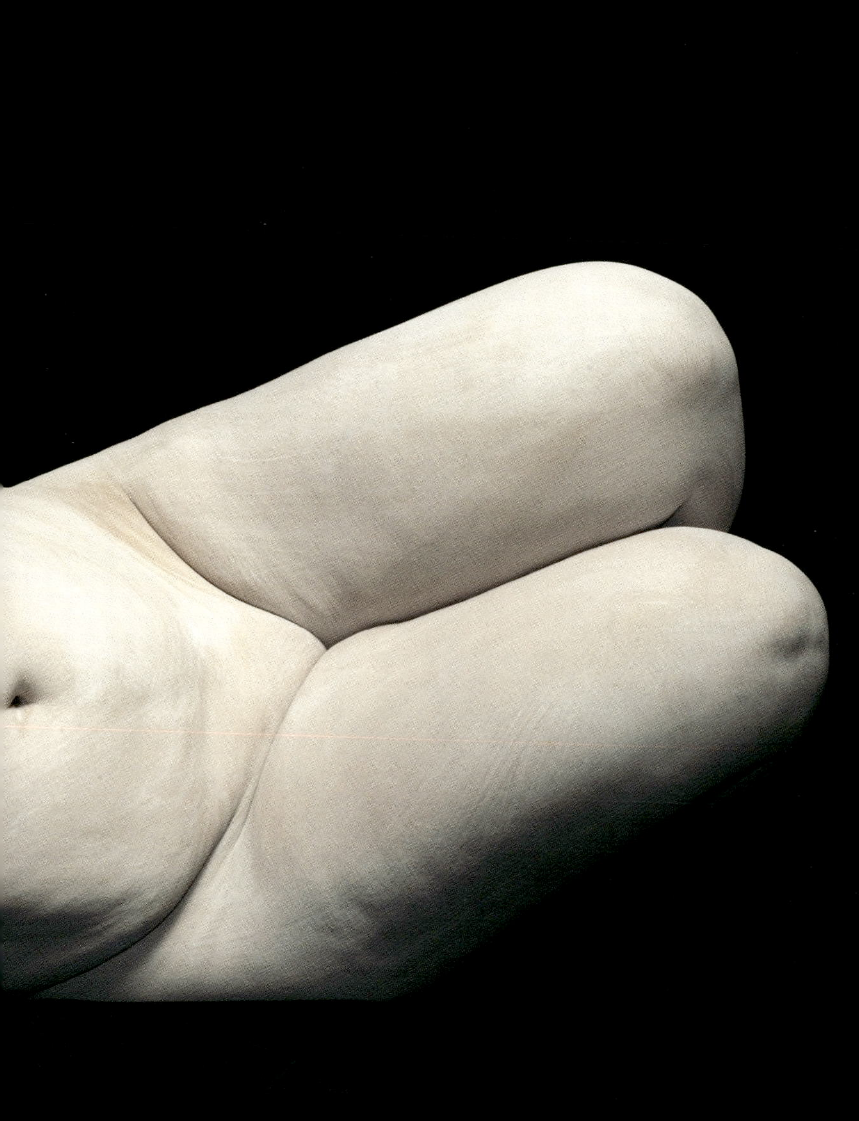

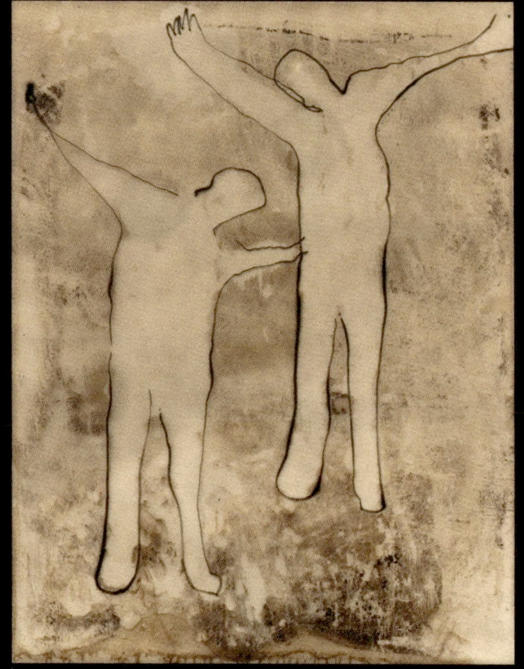

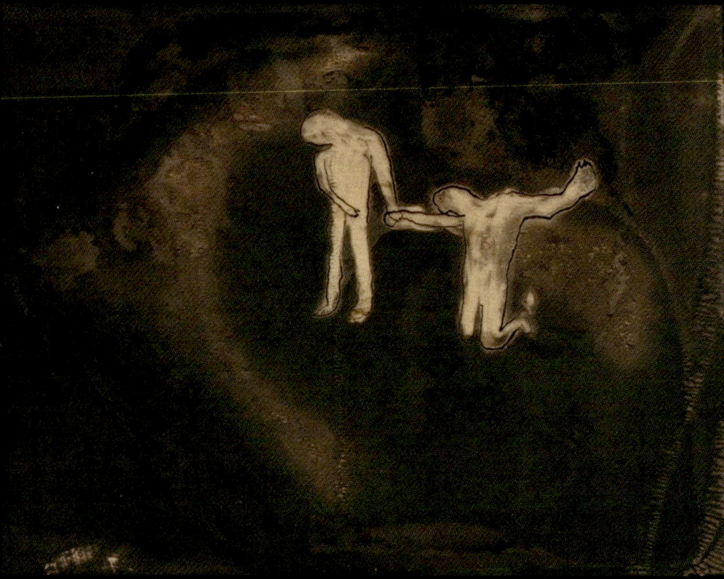

(Top and above) **Andreas Rentsch,** *Untitled,*
from the series 'Entangled with Justice', 2008

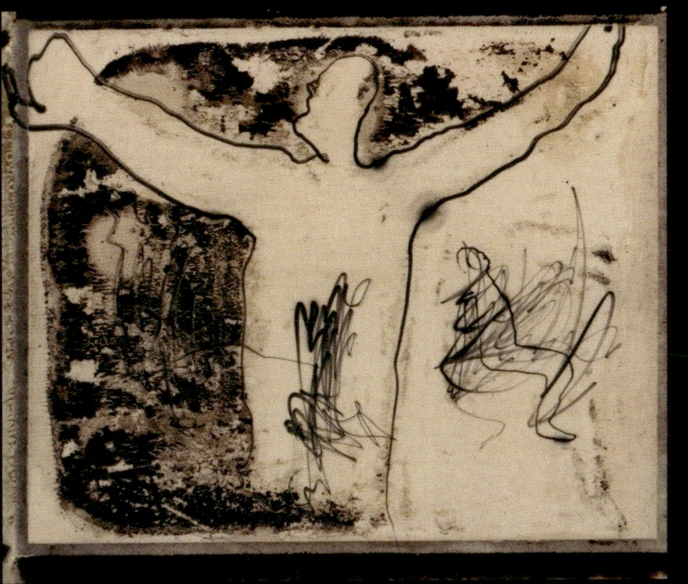

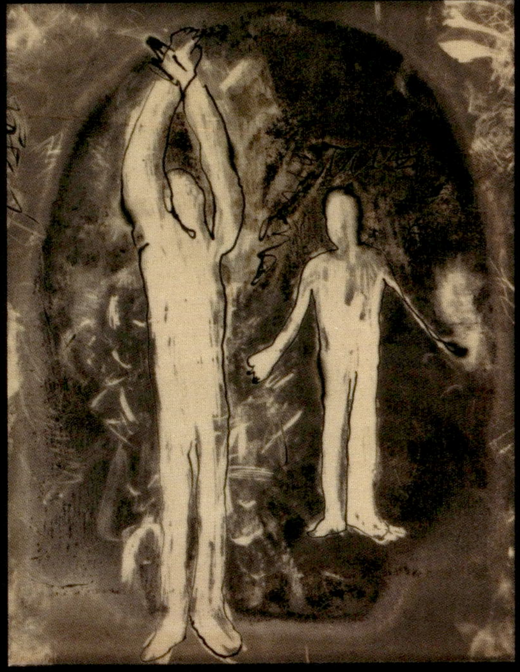

↑ (Top and above) **Andreas Rentsch**, *Untitled*,
from the series 'Entangled with Justice', 2008

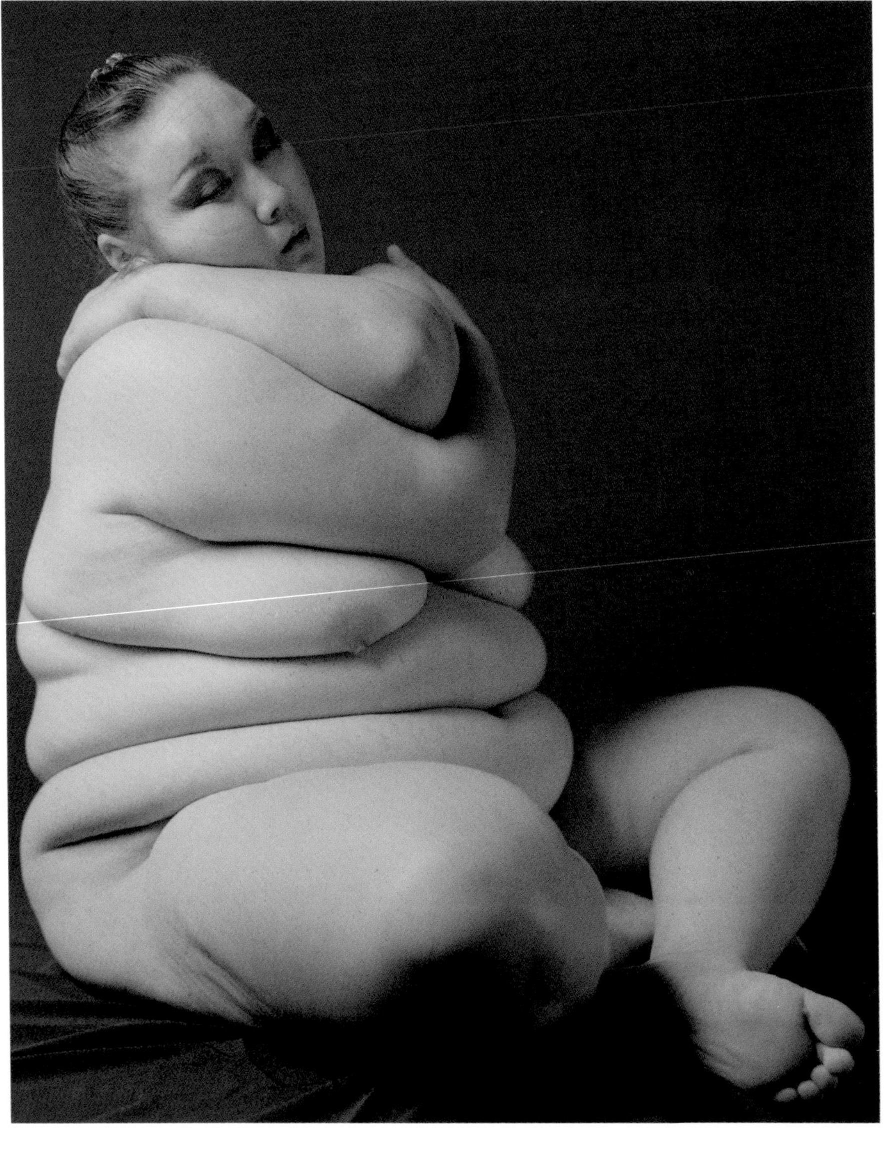

↑ **Liu Zheng,** *A Fat Woman,* 2008

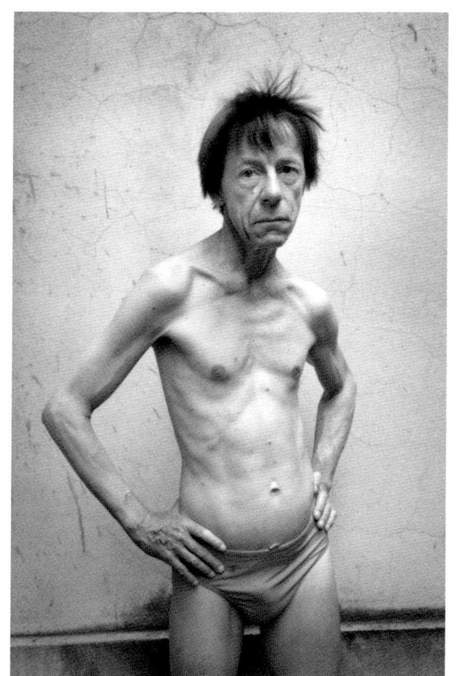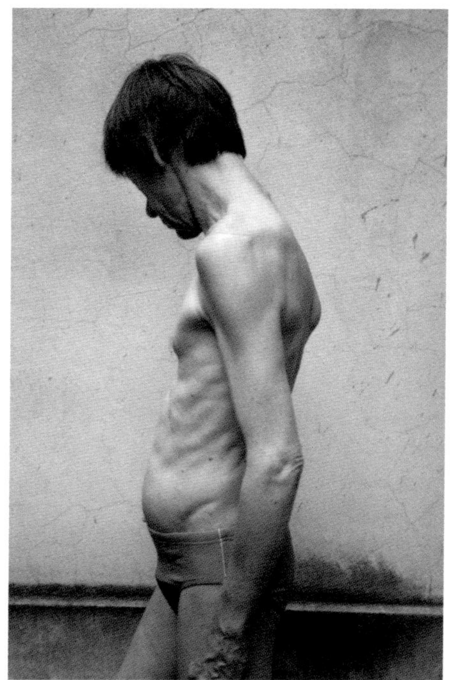

↑ (Left and right) **Alexandra Catiere,** *Michel,* from the series 'After Walser', 2015

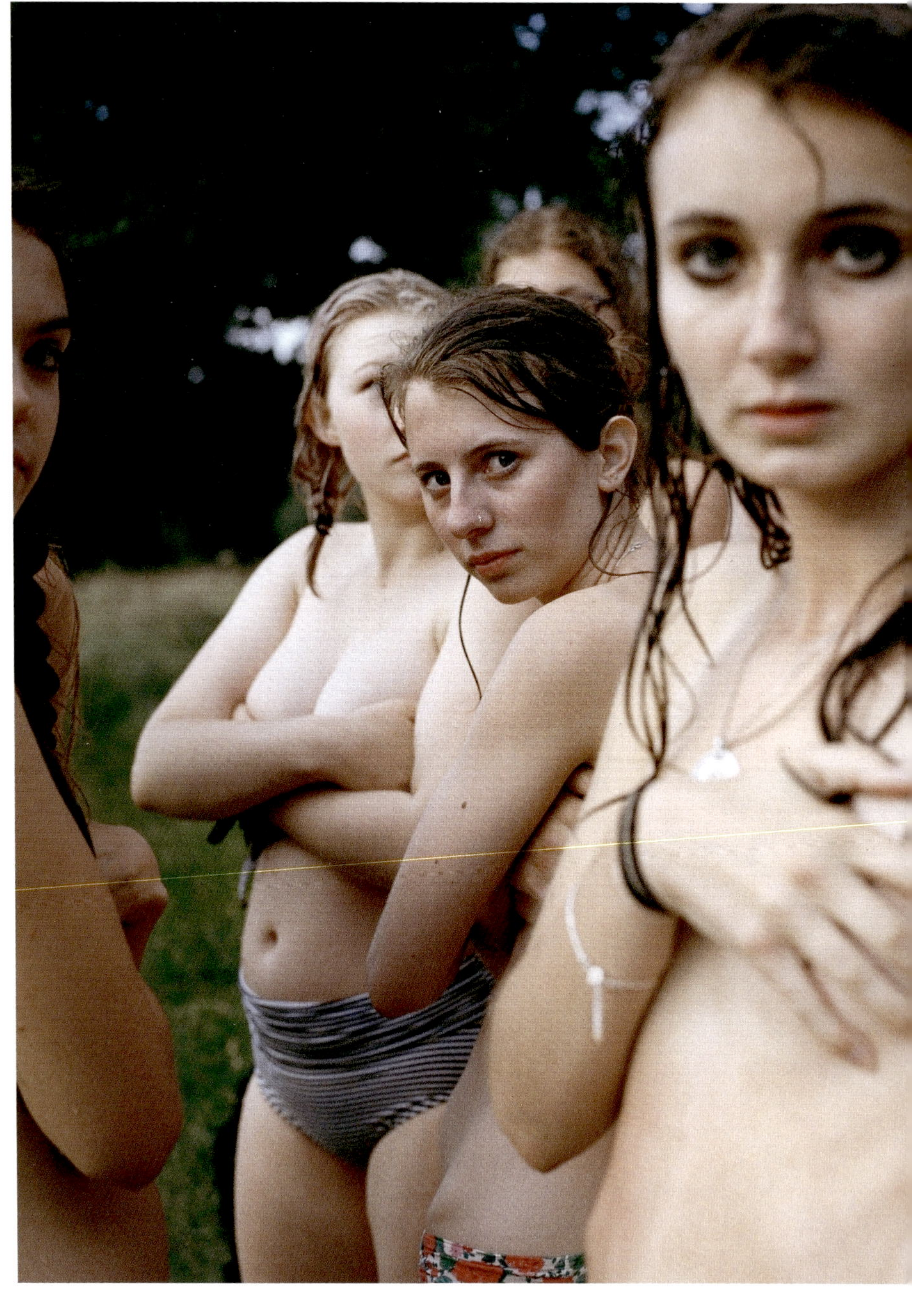

↑ **Siân Davey**, *After the Swim (iii), May, 2016*

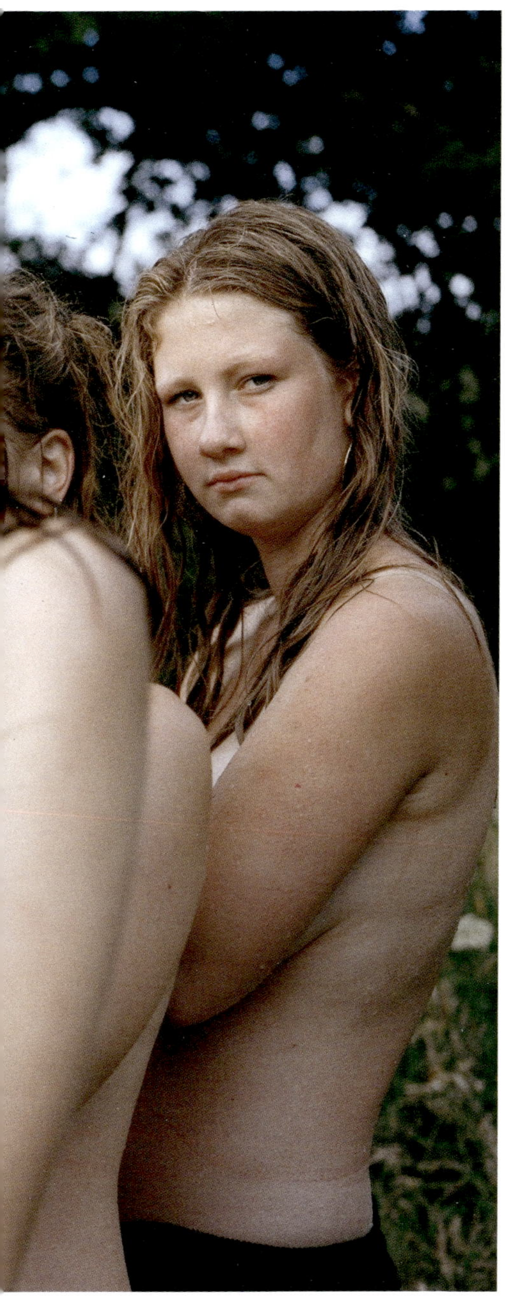

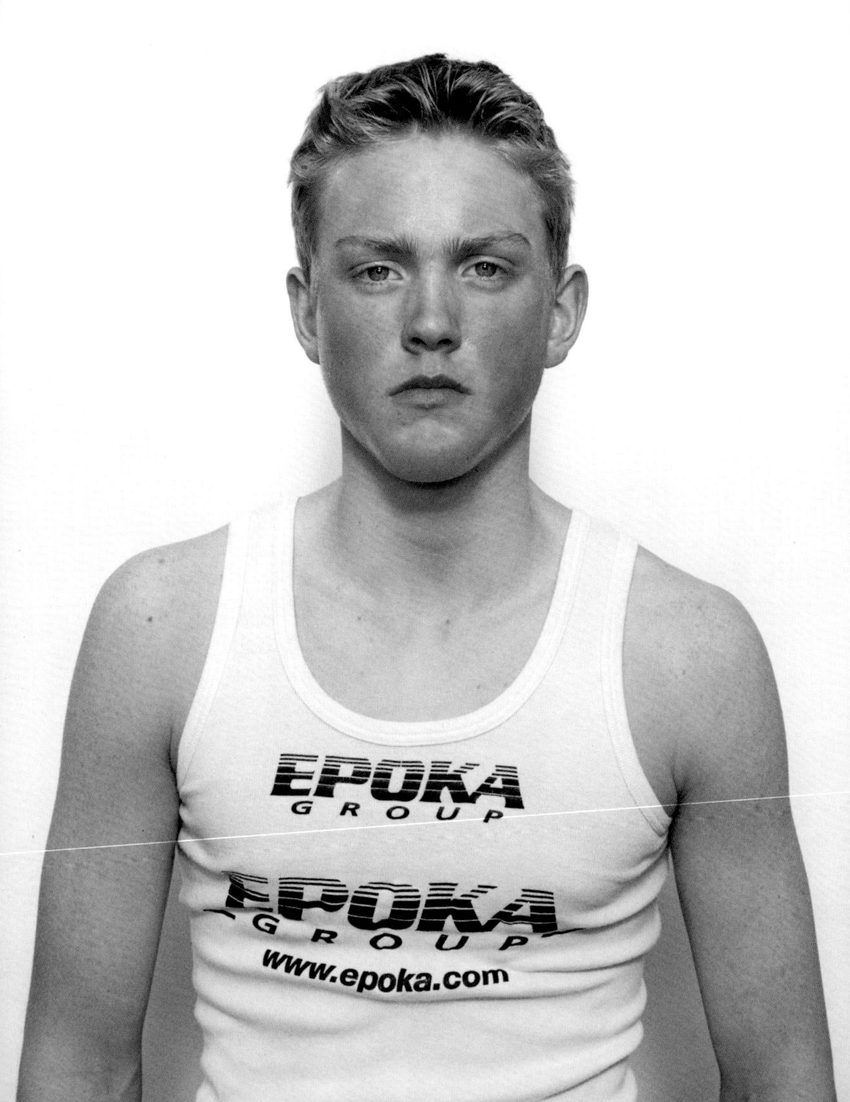

EPOKA
GROUP
EPOKA
GROUP
www.epoka.com

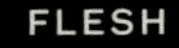

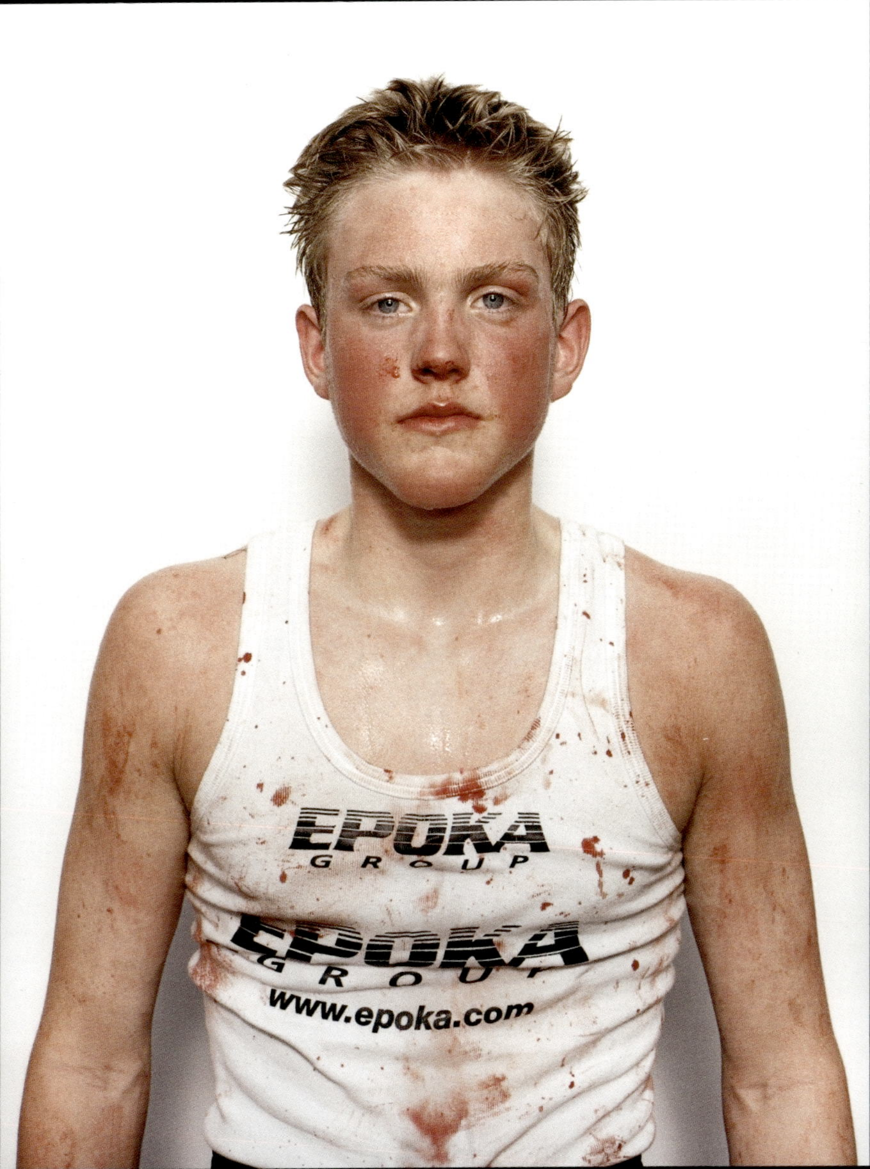

EPOKA
GROUP
EPOKA
GROUP
www.epoka.com

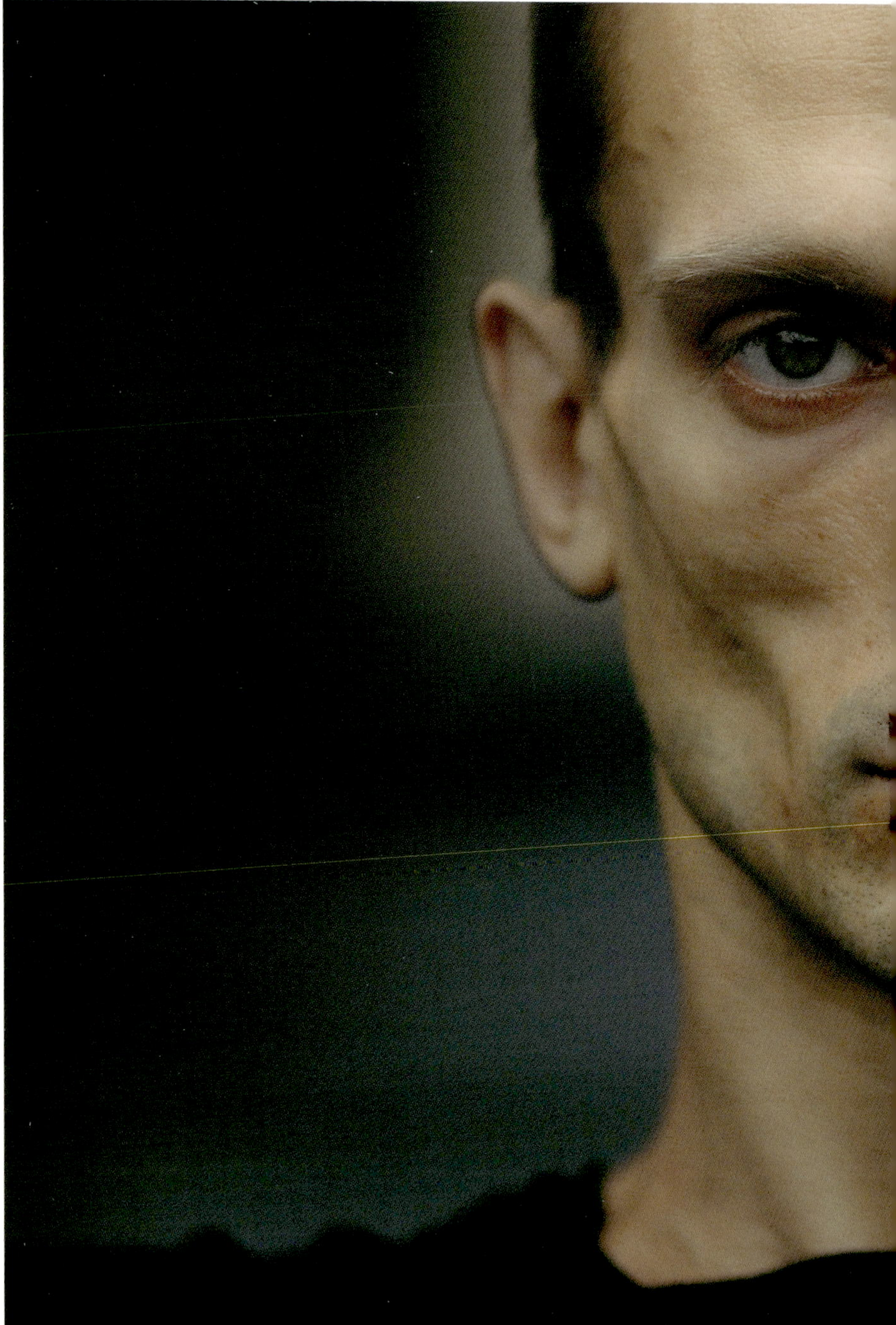

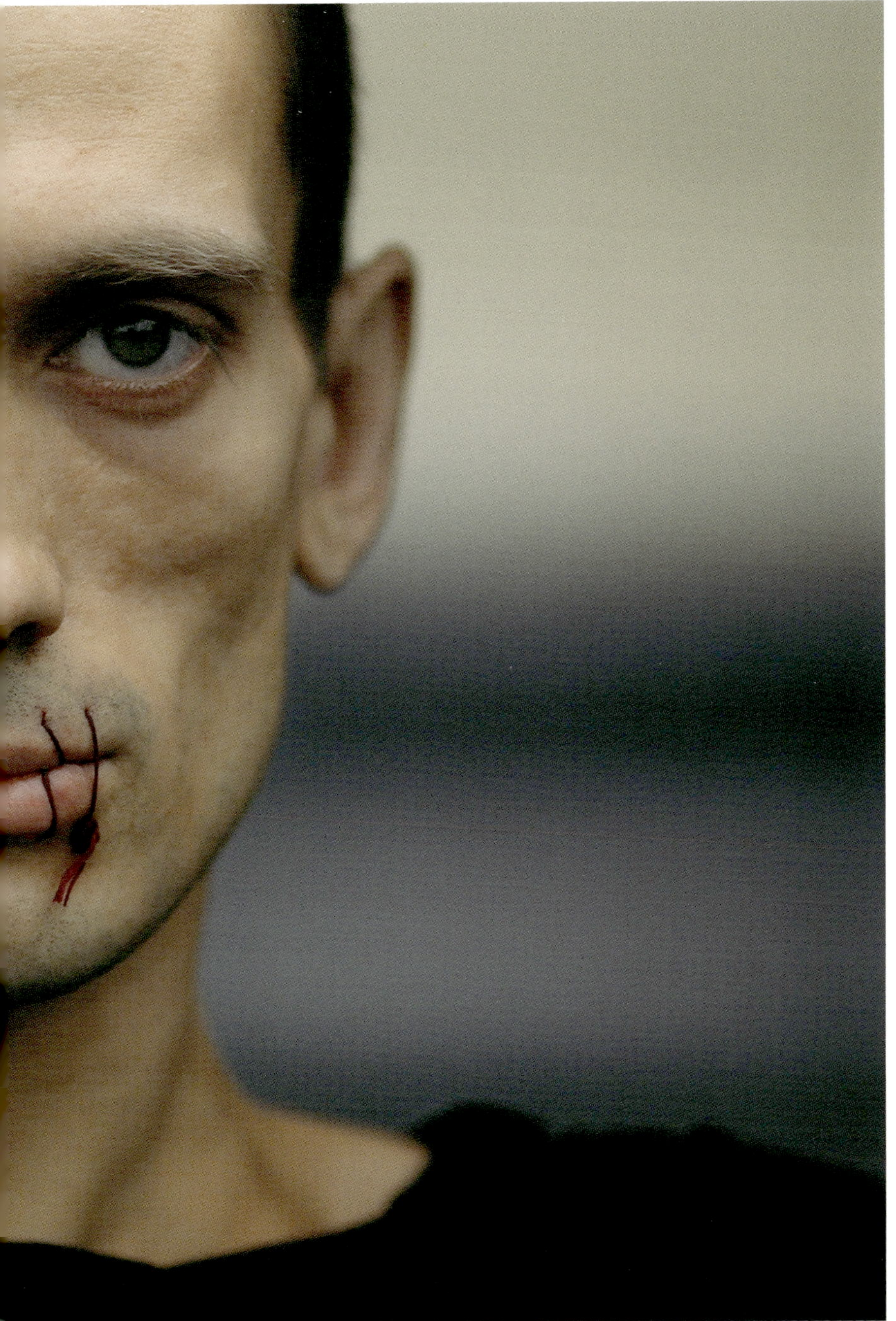

↑ **Pyotr Pavlensky,** *Seam,* 2012

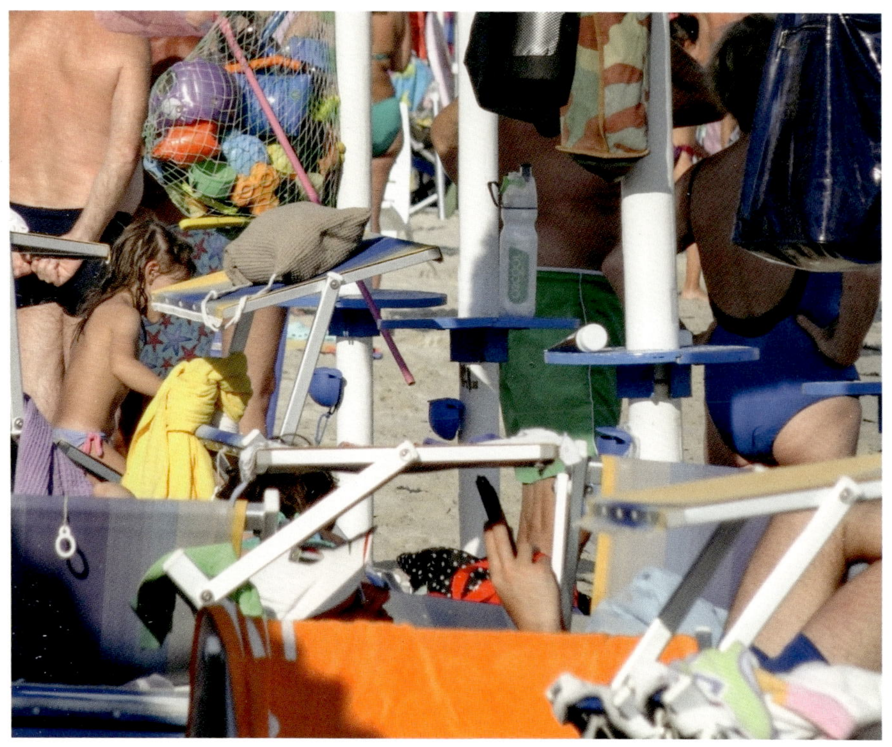

↑ **Olivier Christinat,** *Untitled*, from the series
'Une place au soleil', 2015

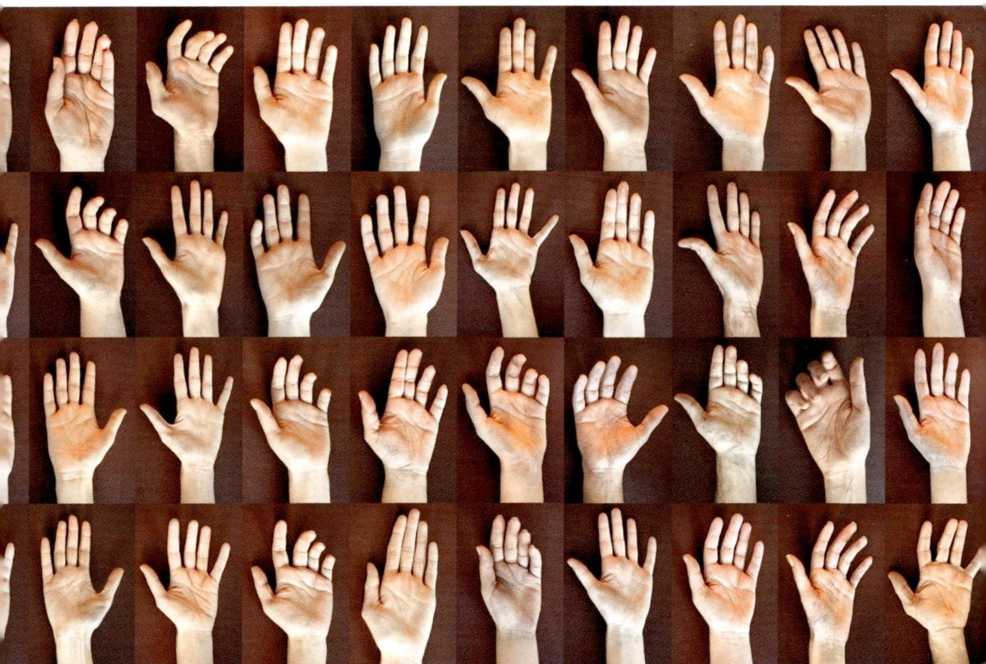

↑ **Francesca Catastini,** *Study of Hands,* from the series
'The Modern Spirit is Vivisective', 2013

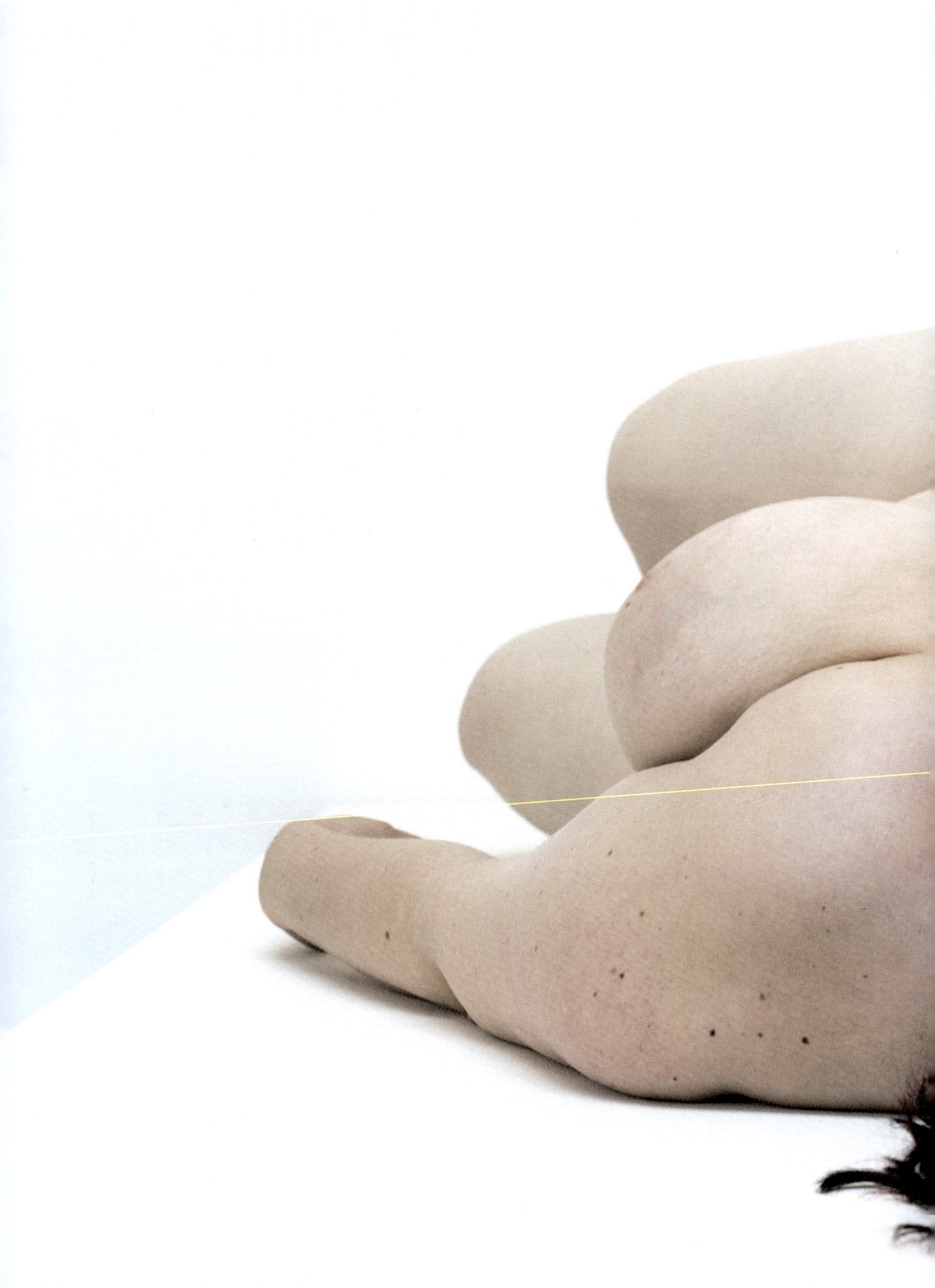

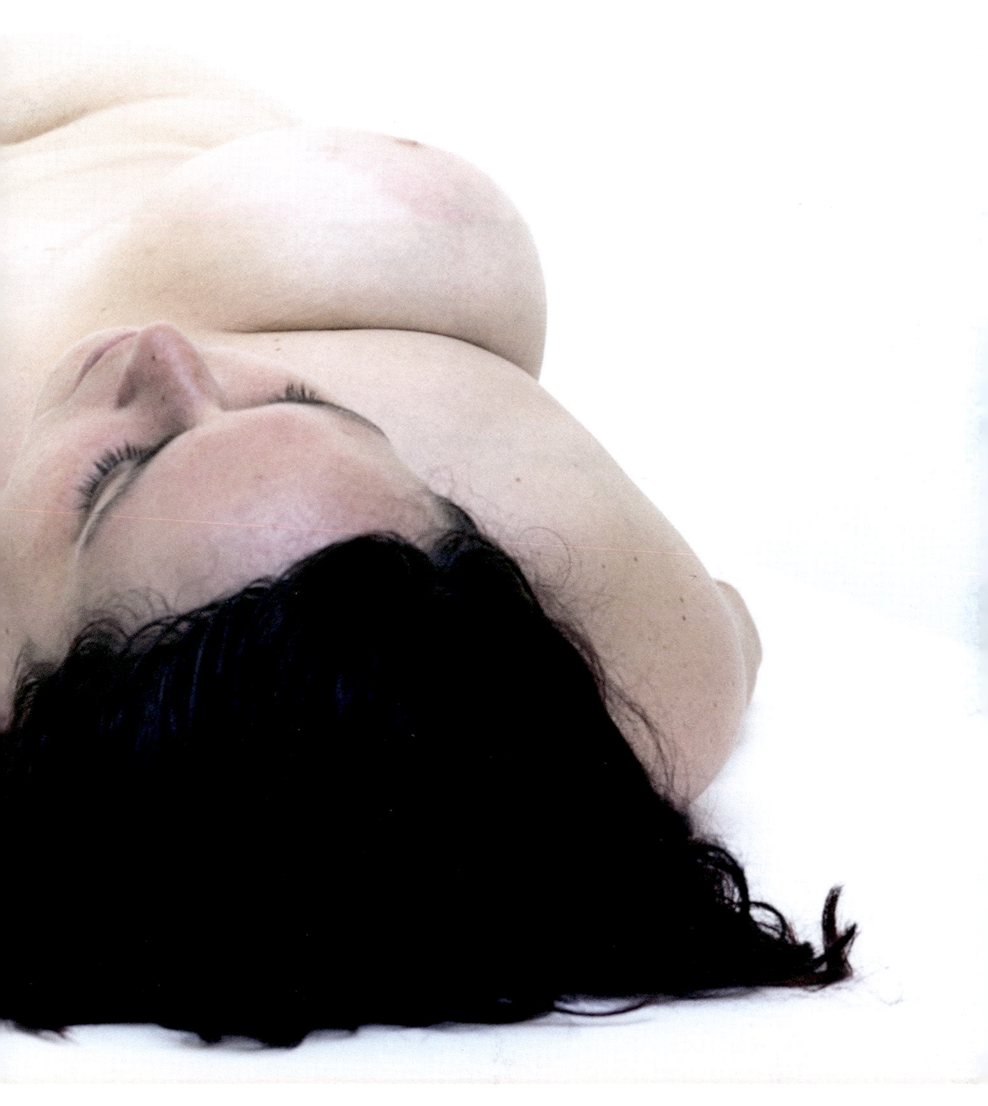

↑ **Eric Poitevin,** *Untitled*, 2010

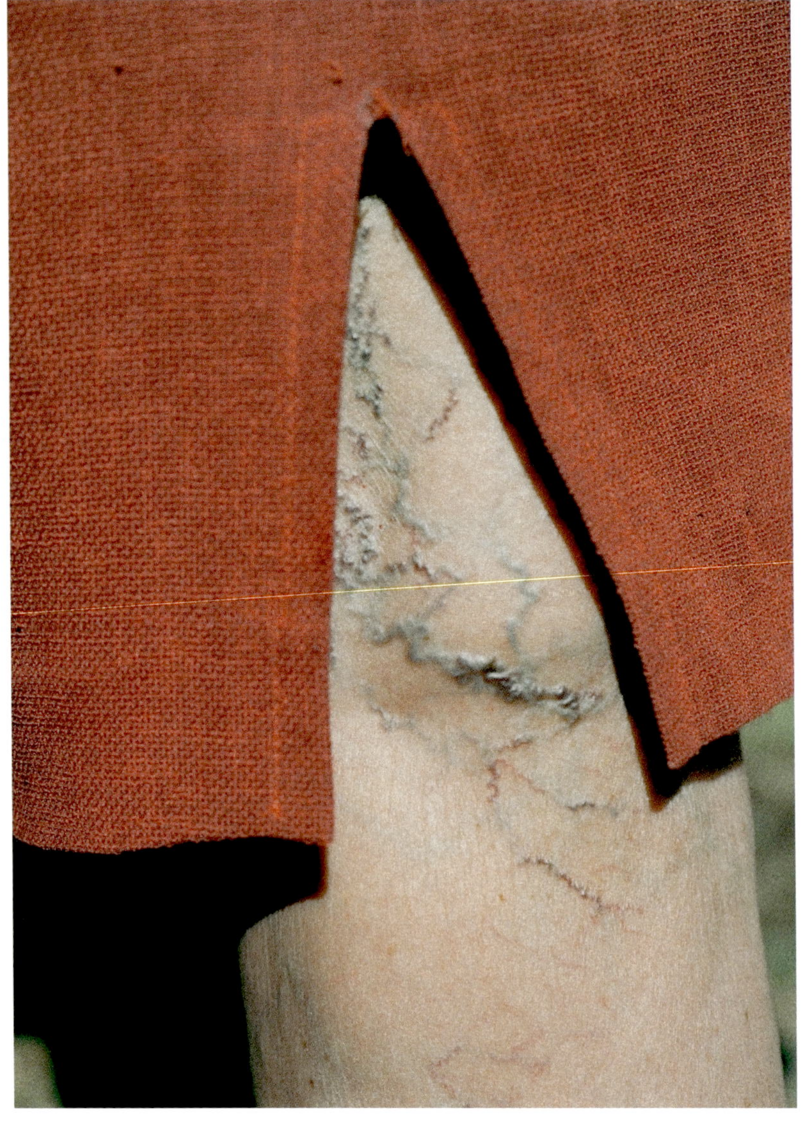

↑ **Lucile Boiron,** *Untitled*, from the series 'Bodies', 2017

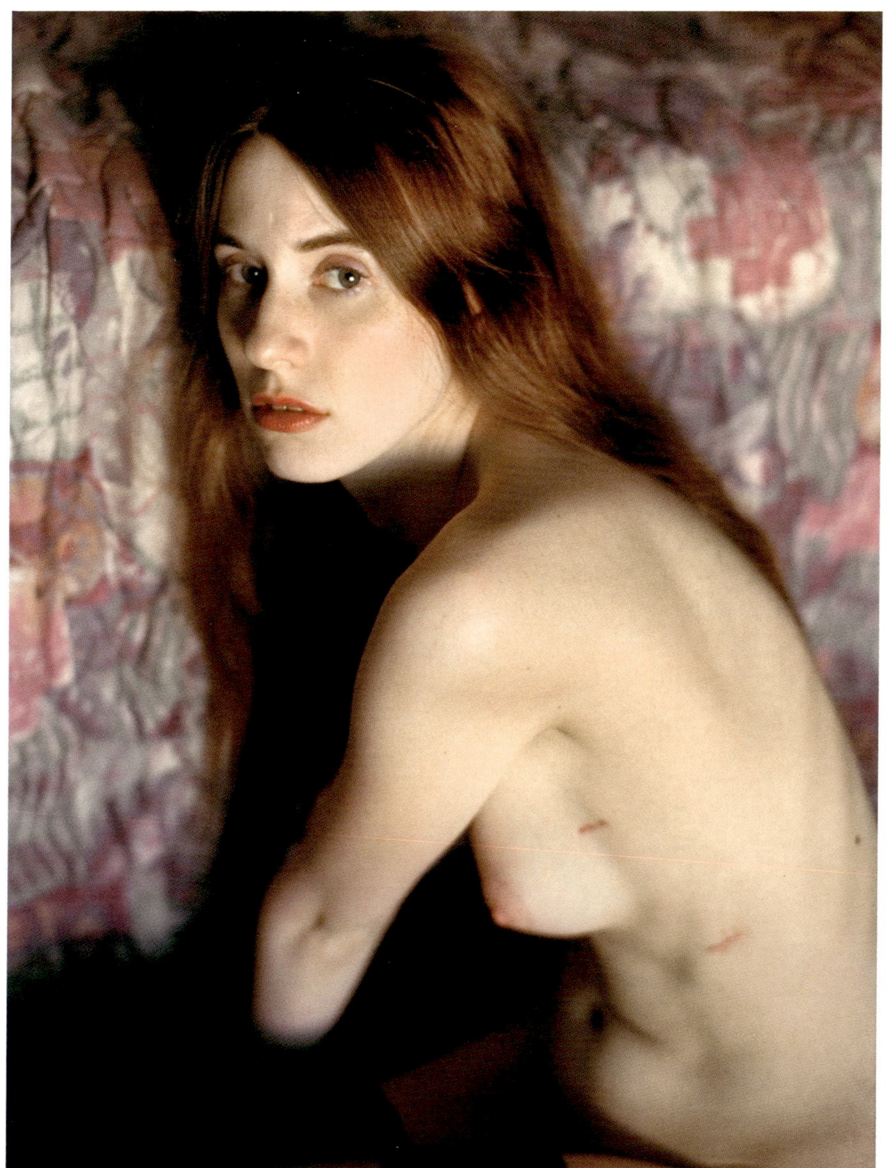

↑ **Todd Hido,** *Untitled, #10622-8,* 2011

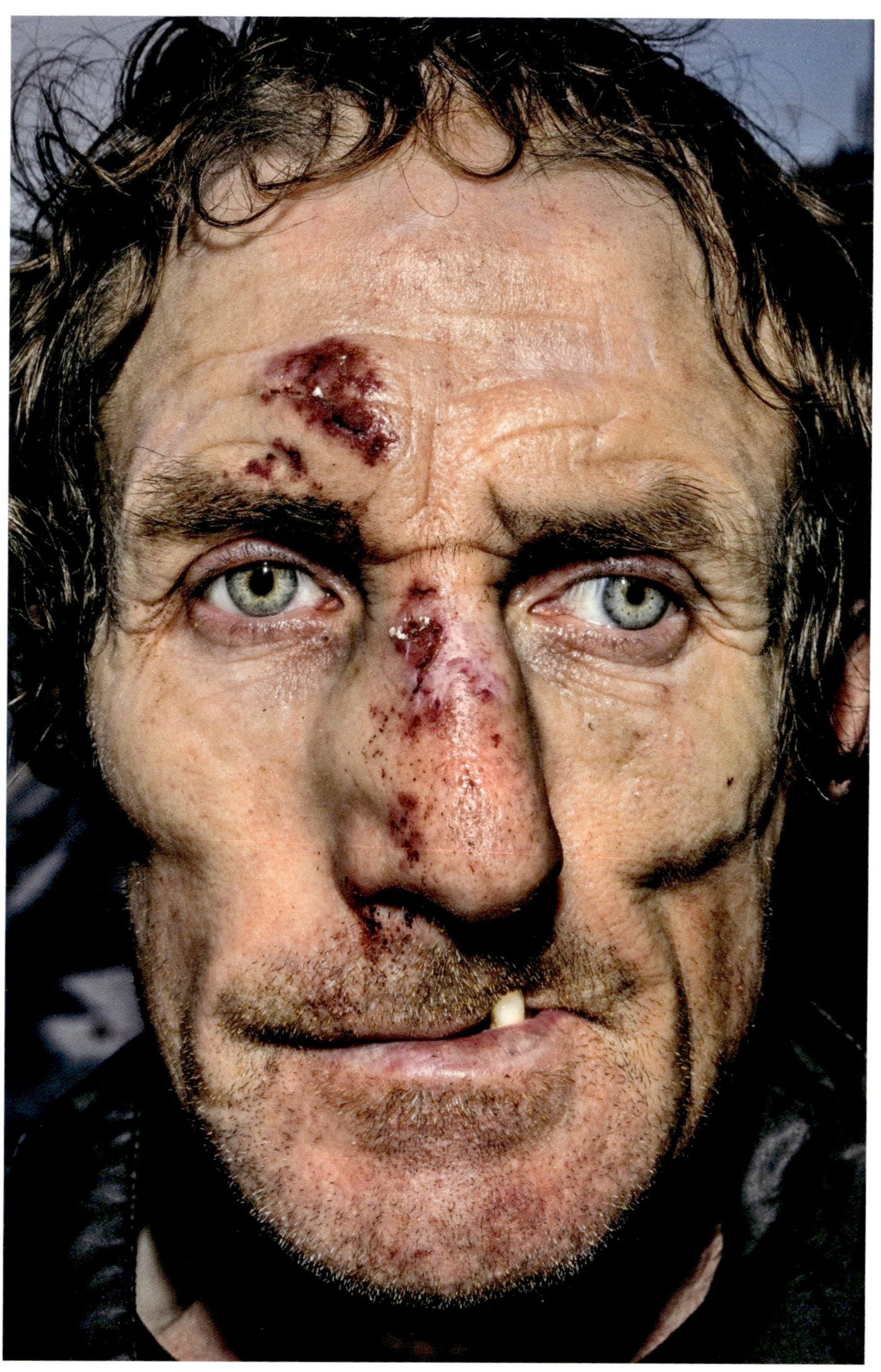

↑ **Bruce Gilden**, *James, Beat-up Man, Wolverhampton, Great Britain*, 2013
→ (Overleaf) **Jeff Mermelstein**, *New York City*, 2016

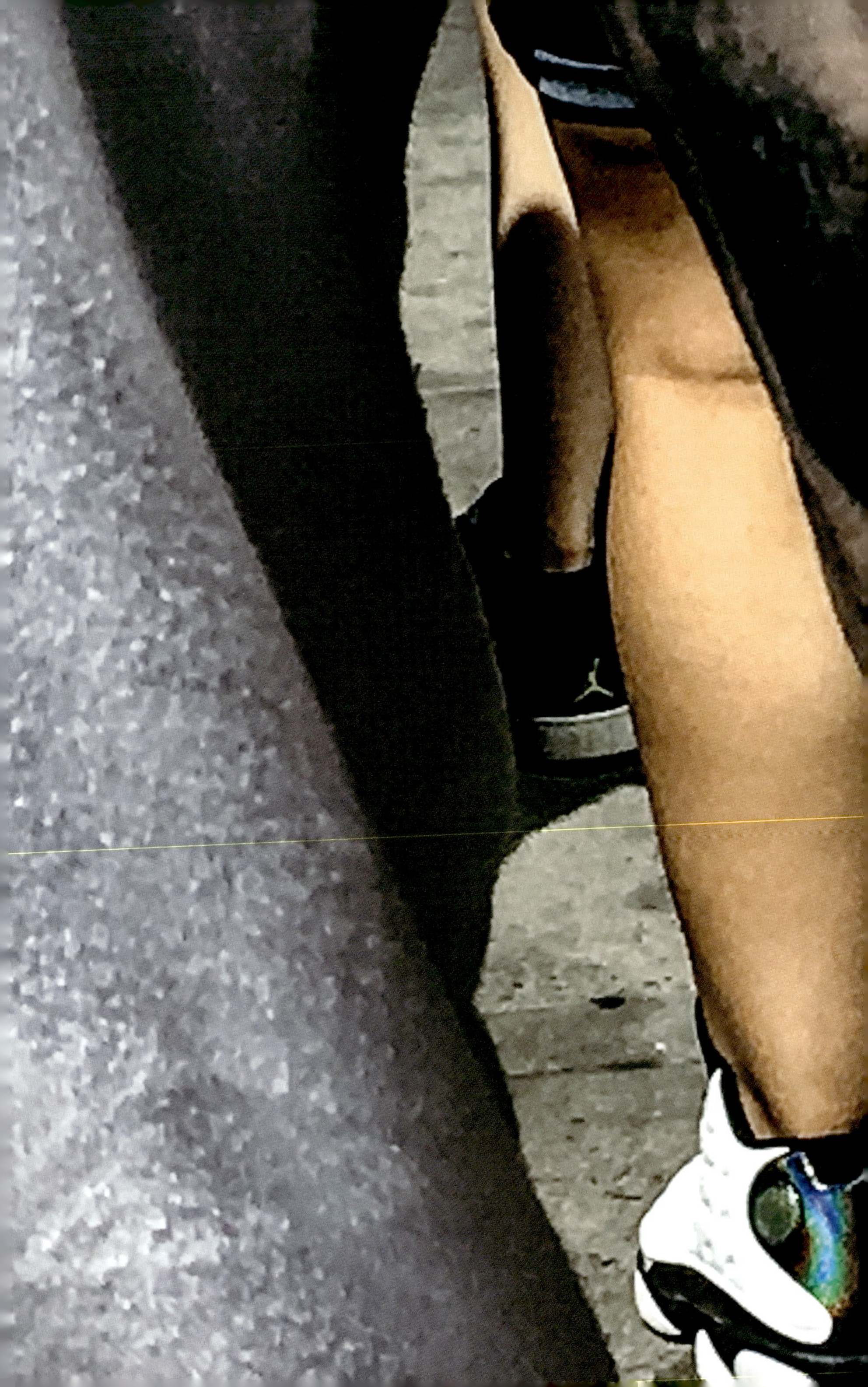

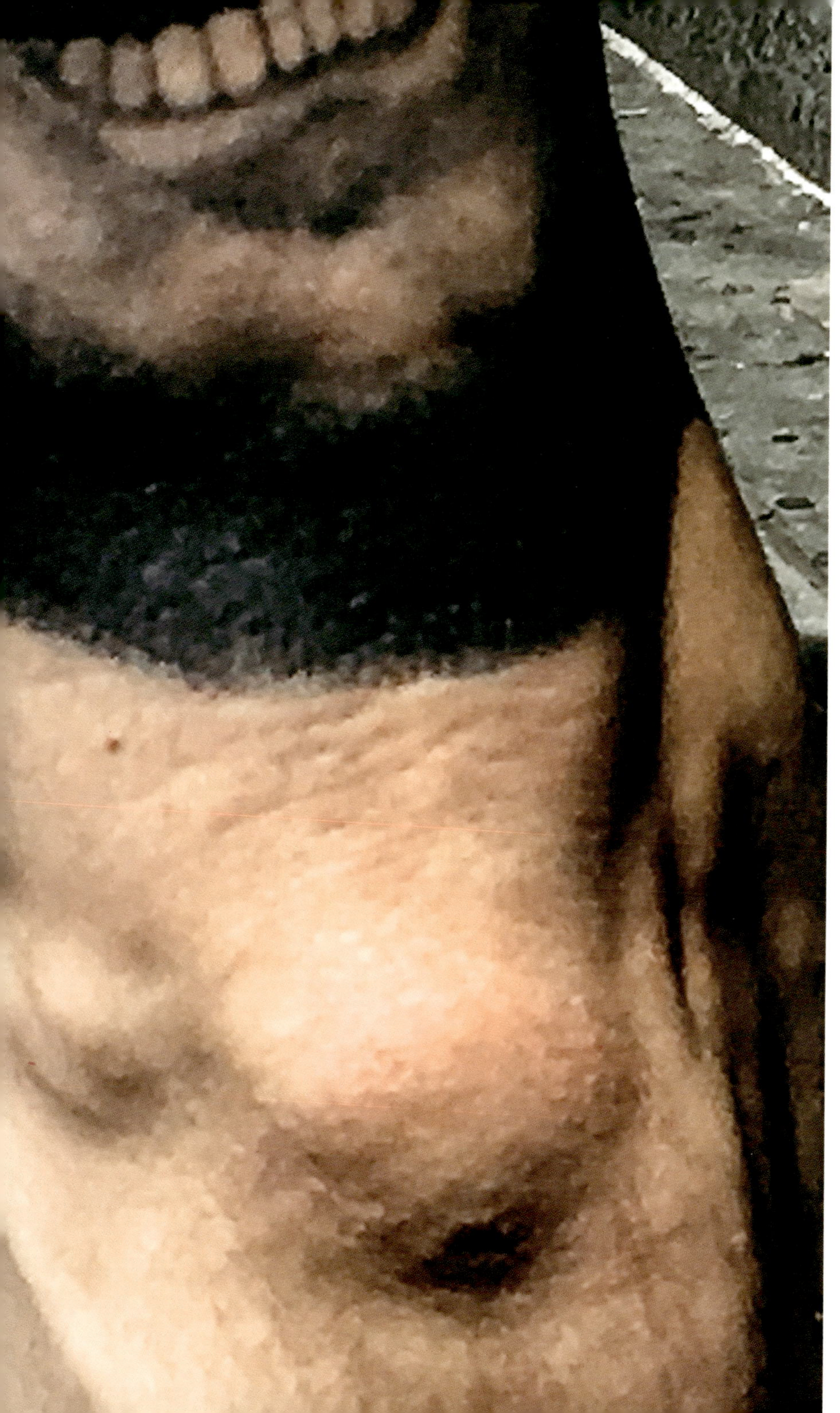

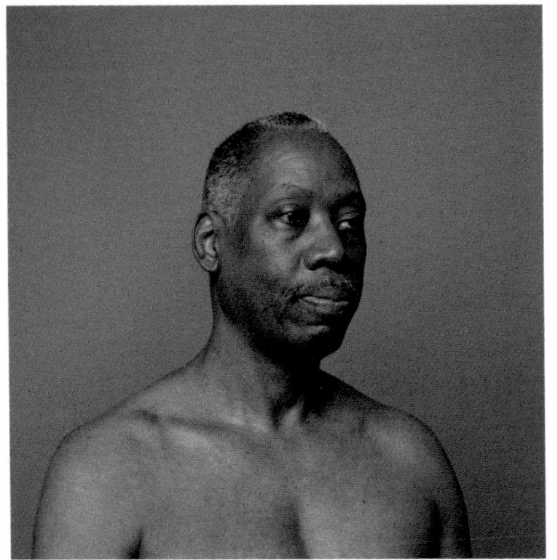

Chris, 2016

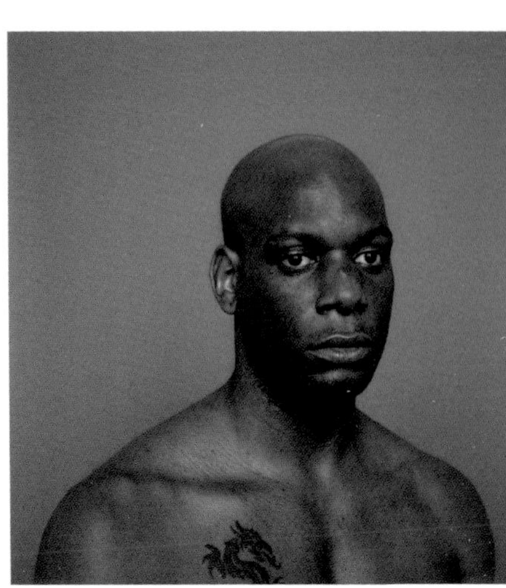

Derek, 2016

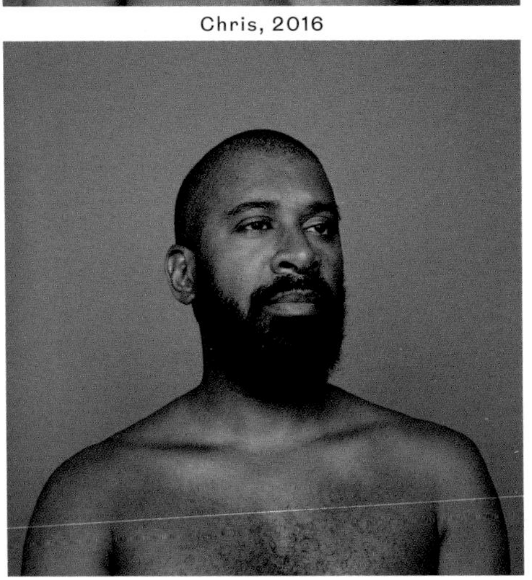

George, 2016

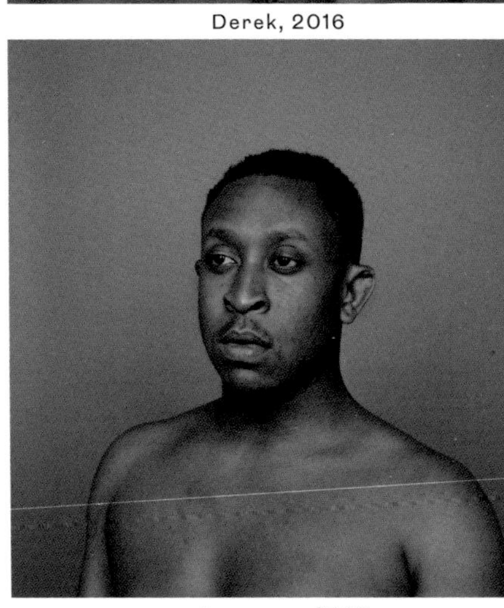

Jocquese, 2016

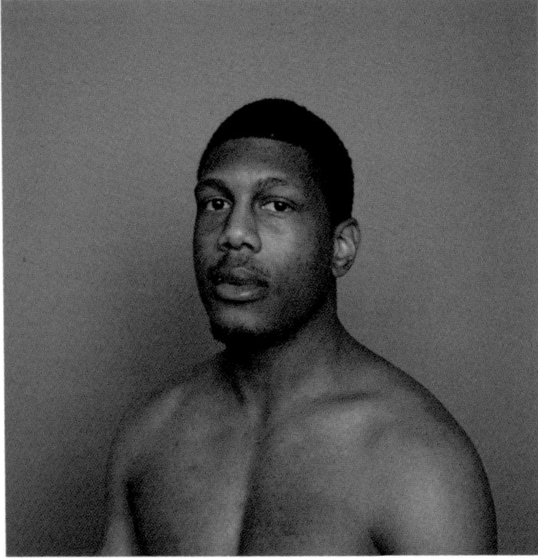

Nathan, 2015

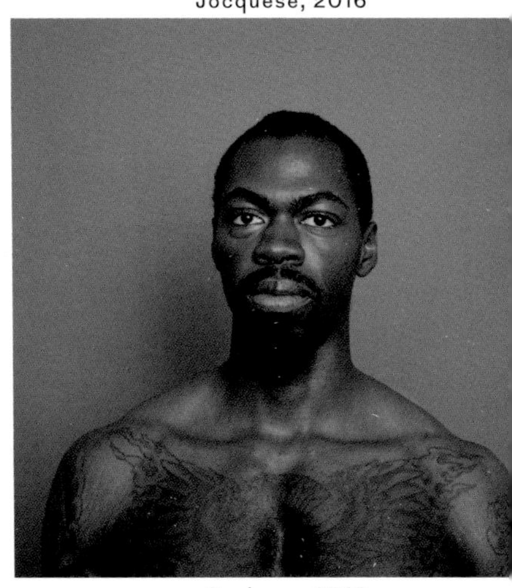

Orobosa, 2015

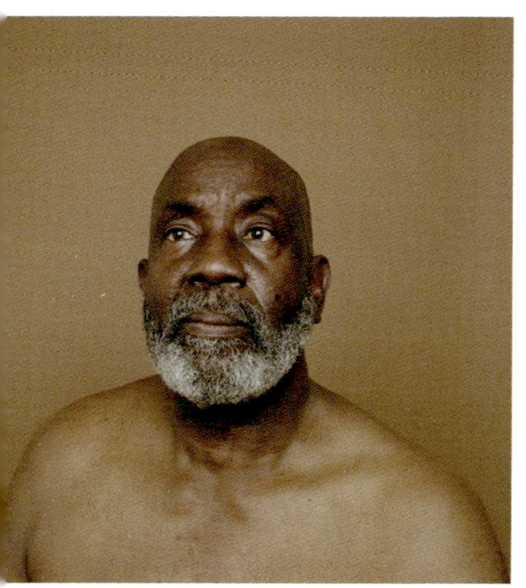

Eli, 2016

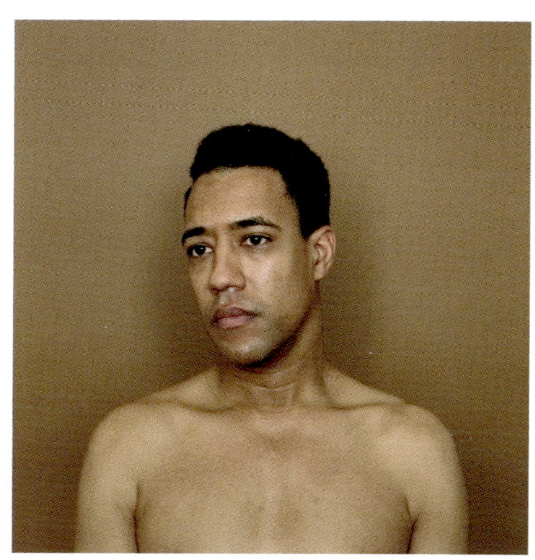

Eric, 2016

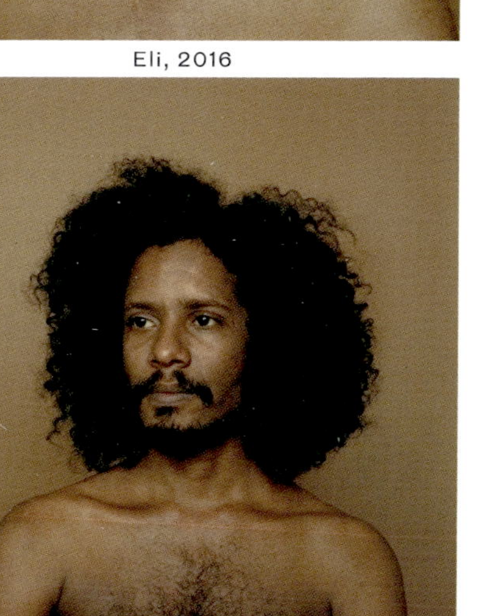

Llane, 2016

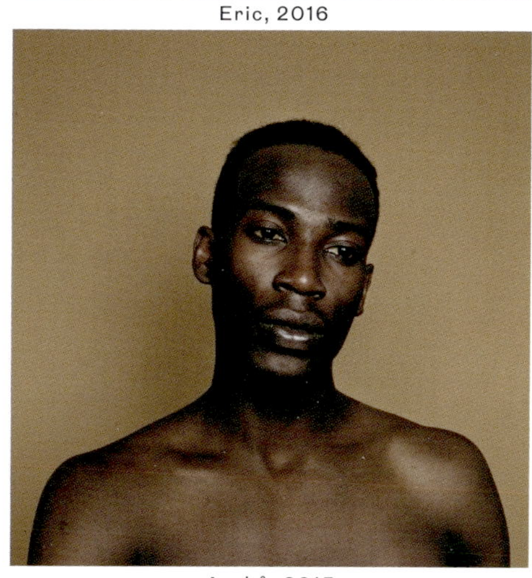

Asabå, 2015

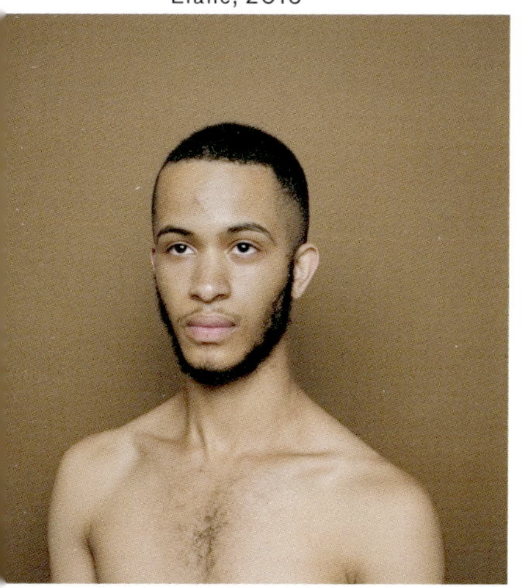

Reed, 2016

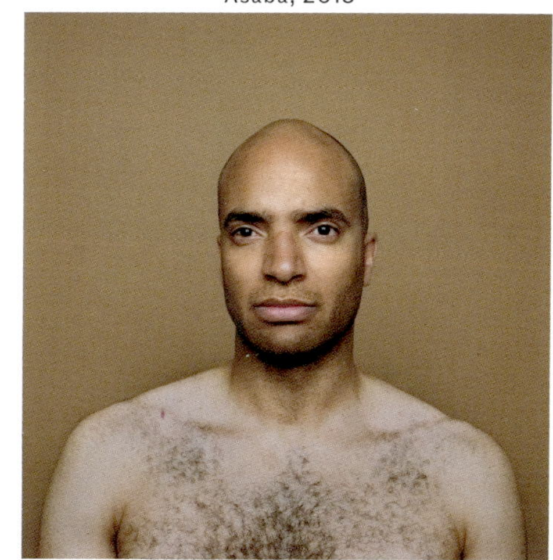

Stefano, 2016

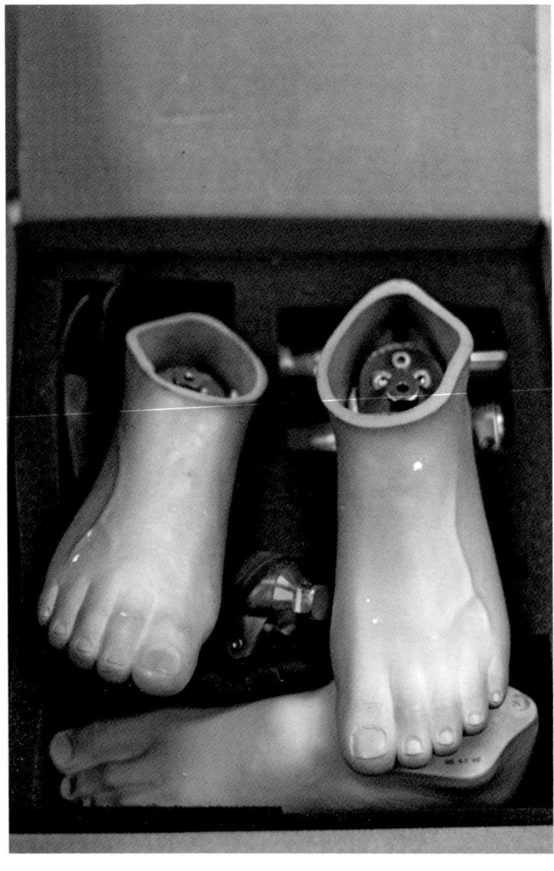

↑ **Louie Palu,** *Prosthetic Feet in a Workshop, Walter Reed Army Medical Center, Washington, DC,* 2009
← (Previous) **Erica Deeman,** from the 'Brown' series, 2016

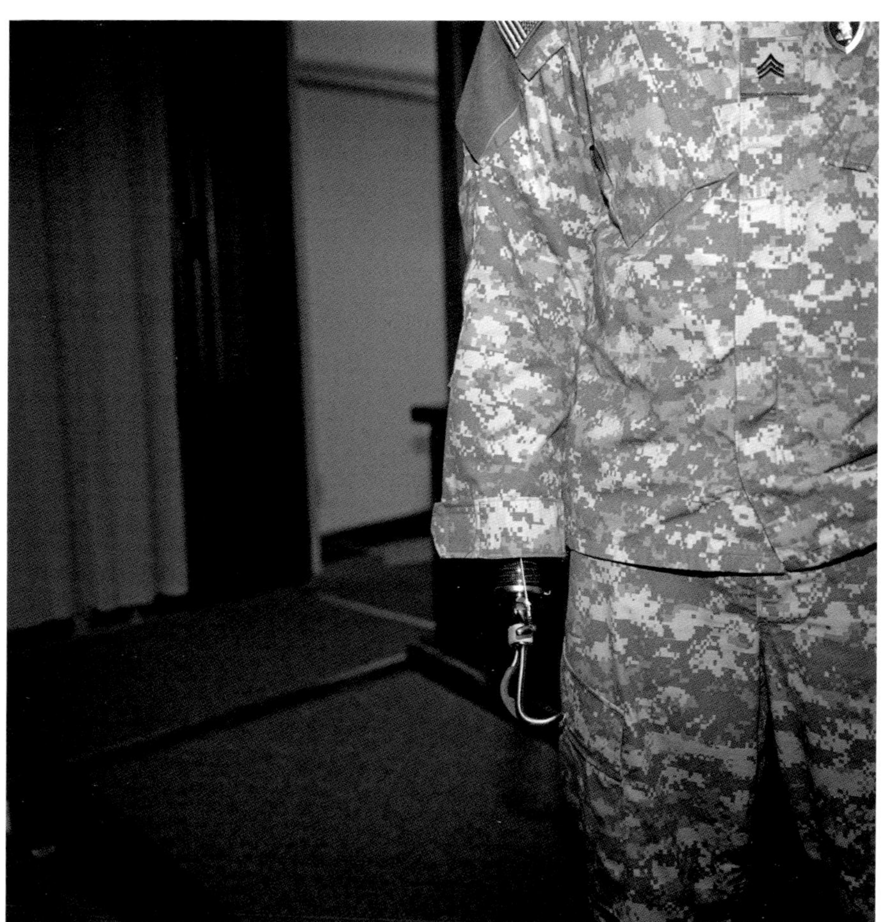

↑ **Louie Palu,** *Iraq War Veteran, Walter Reed Army Medical Center, Washington, DC,* 2008

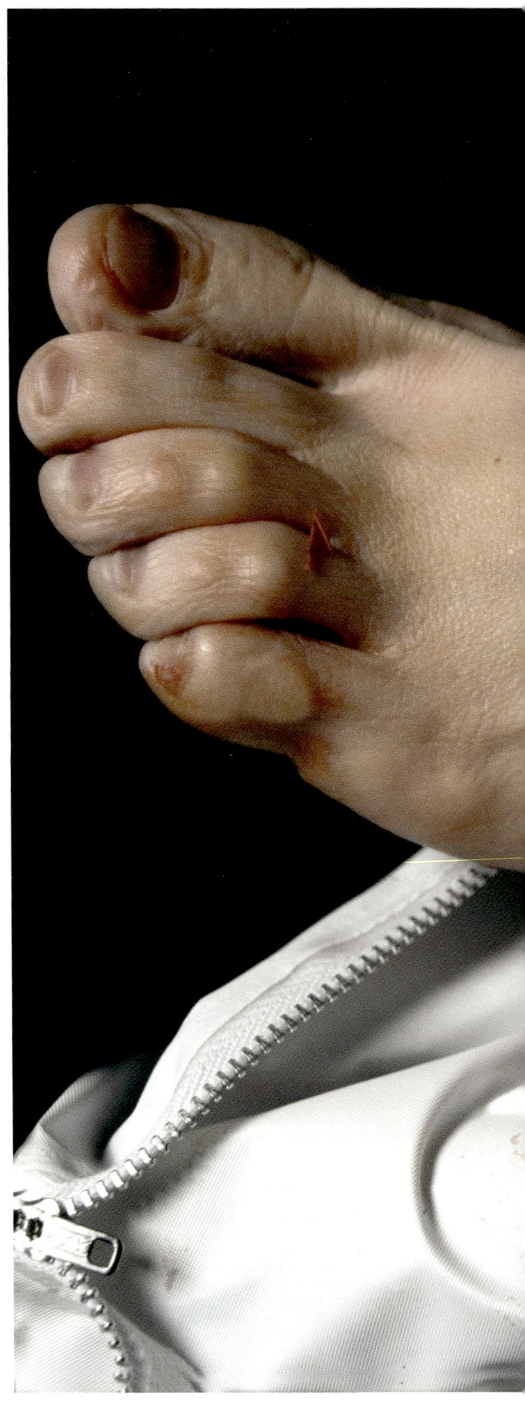

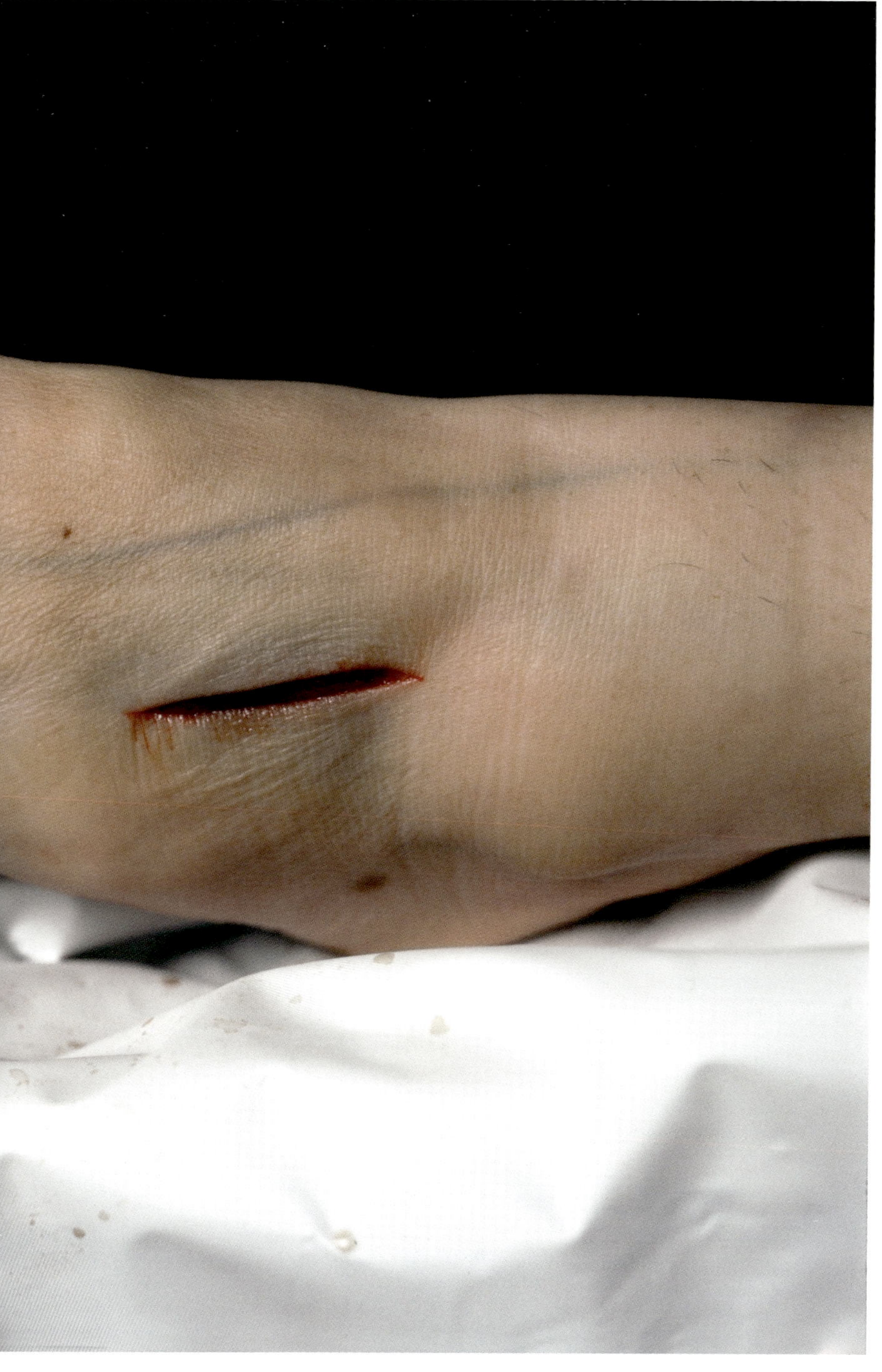

↑ **Andres Serrano,** *Rat Poison Suicide II (The Morgue),* 1992

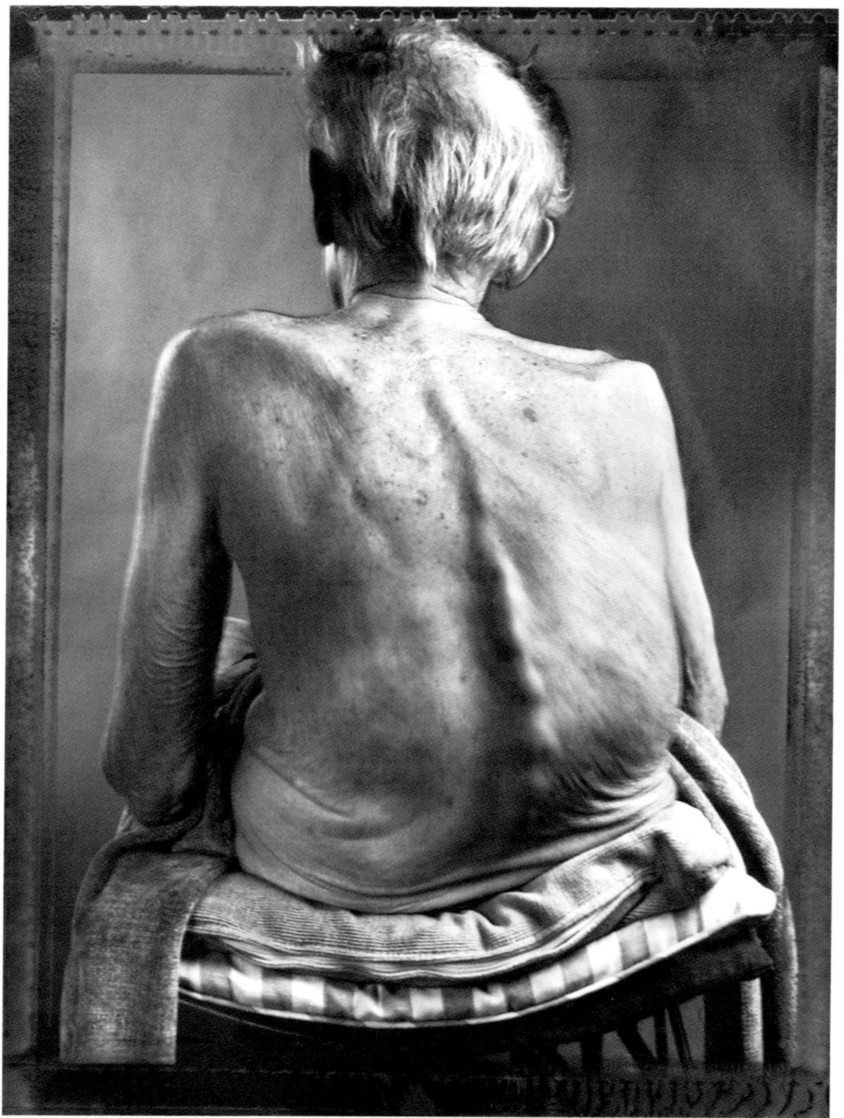

↑ **Susan Copen Oken,** *The Last Decade,* 2004

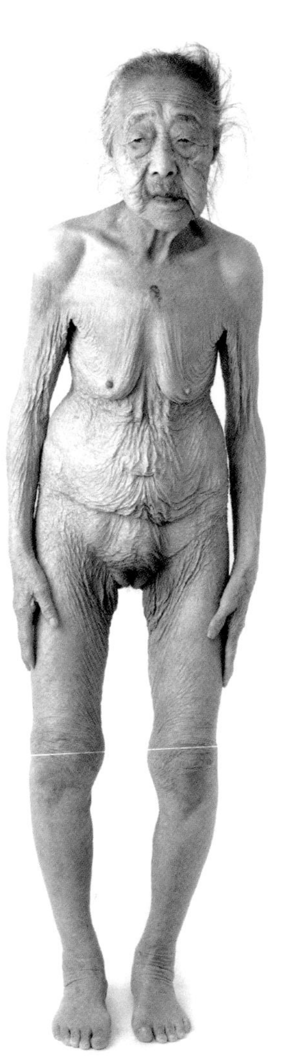

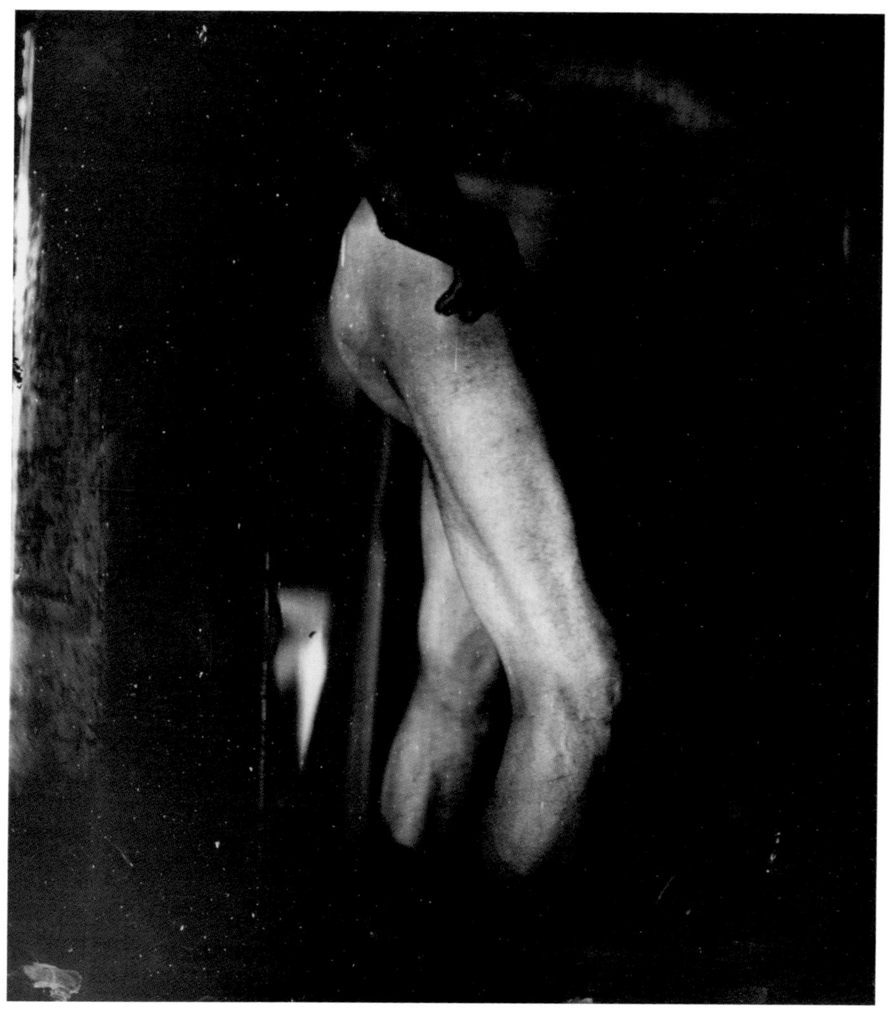

↑ **Sally Mann,** *David*, from the series 'Proud Flesh', 2008

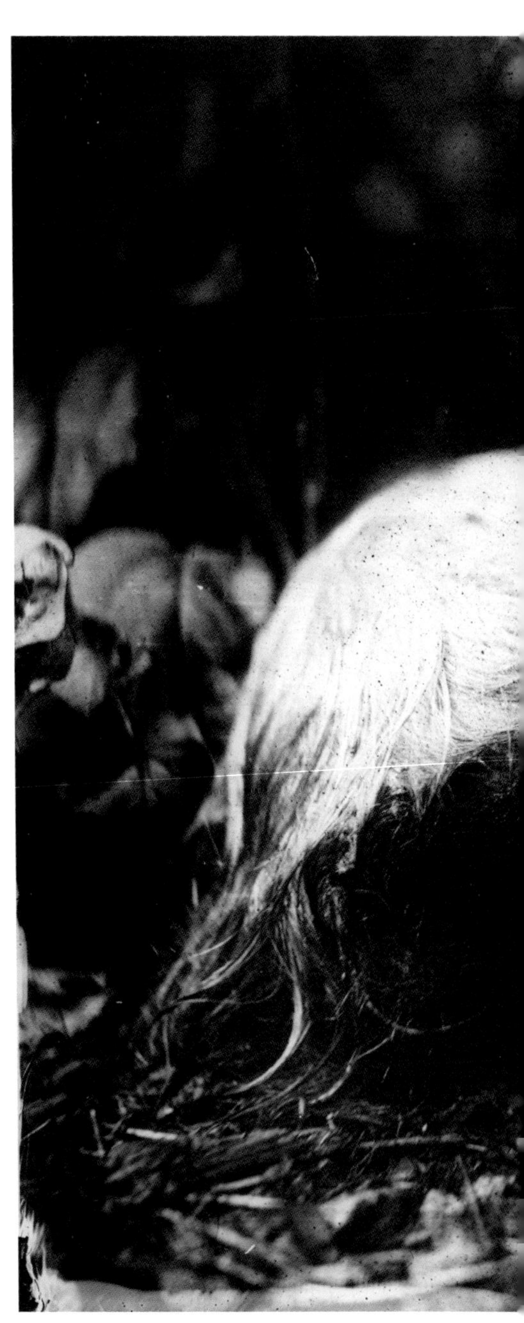

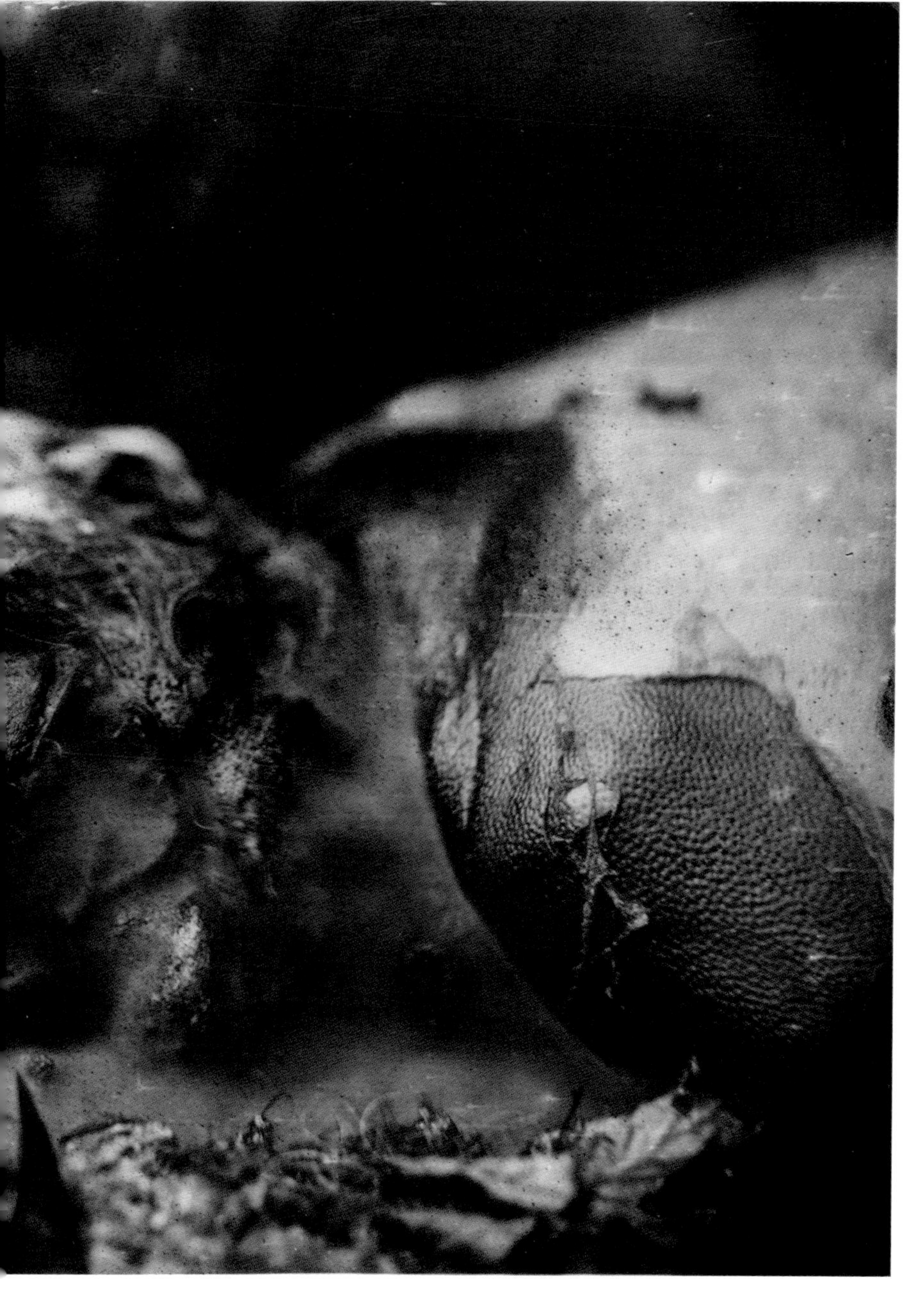

↑ **Sally Mann,** *Untitled*, from the series 'What Remains', 2000

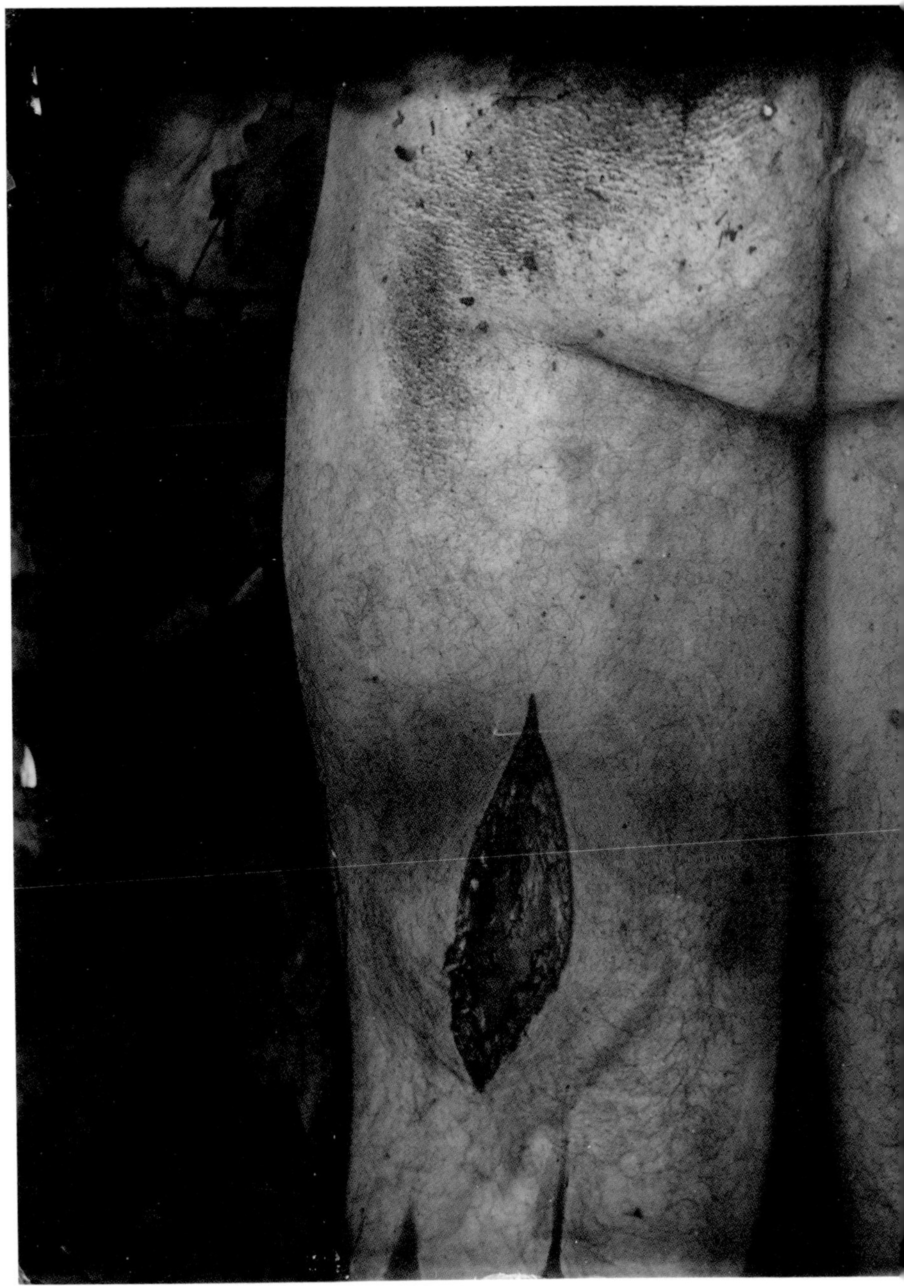

↑ **Sally Mann,** *Untitled*, from the series 'What Remains', 2000

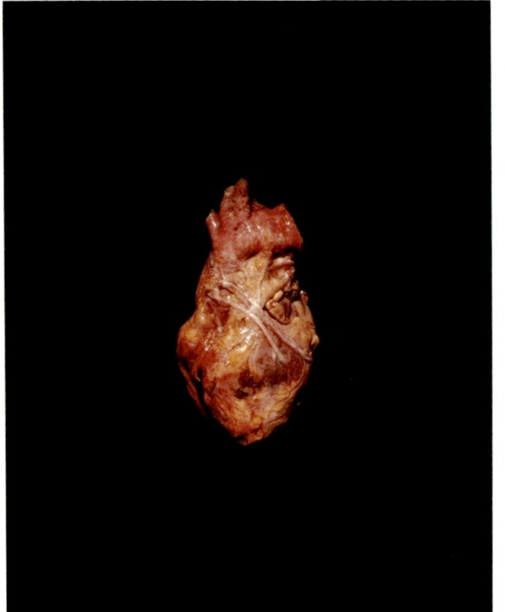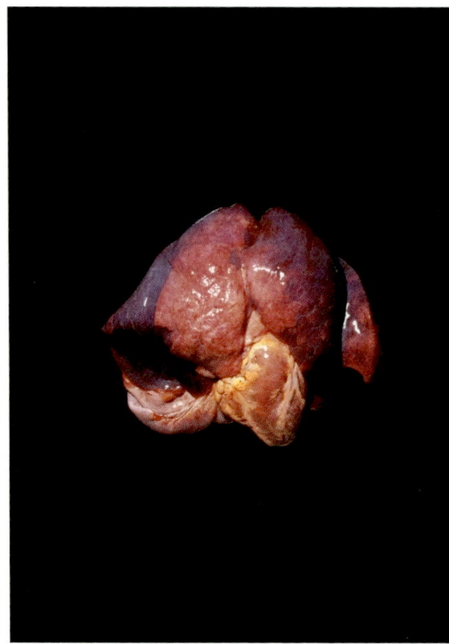

↑ (Left and right) **Raphaël Dallaporta,** from the series 'Fragile', 2010

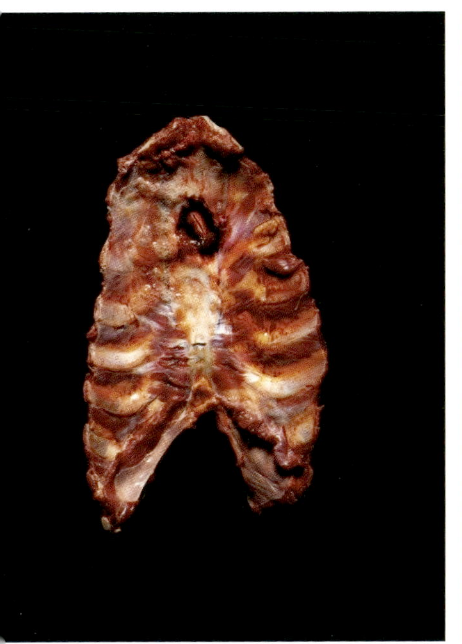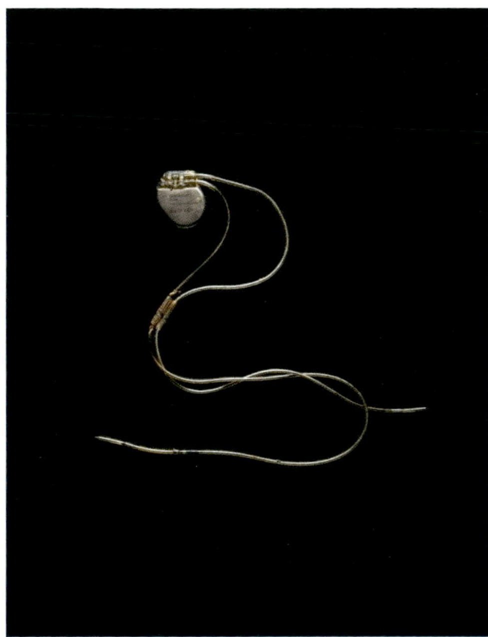

↑ (Left and right) **Raphaël Dallaporta,** from the series 'Fragile', 2010

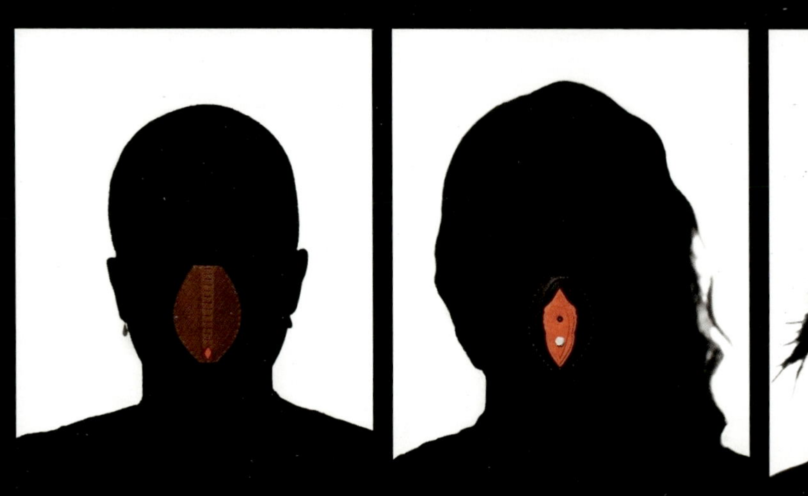

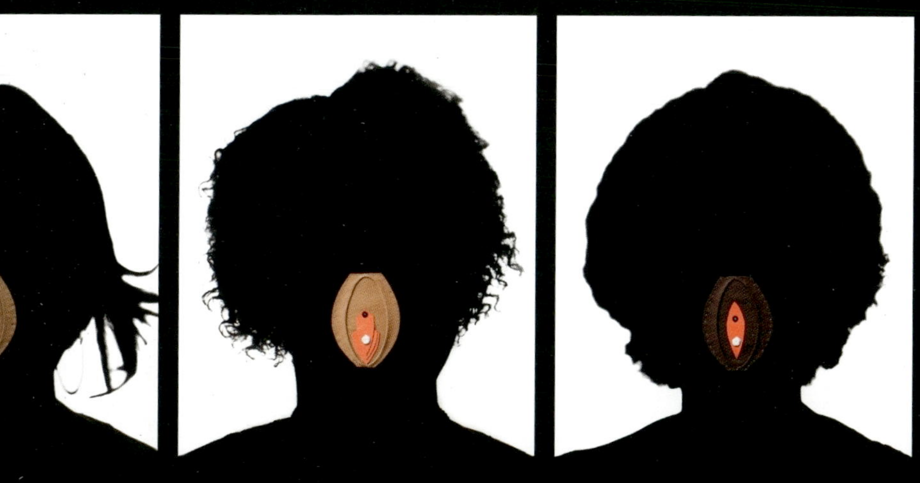

↑ (From left) **Aida Silvestri**, *Type III C; Type I C; Type II C; Type II E; Type II H*,
all from the series 'Unsterile Clinic', 2015

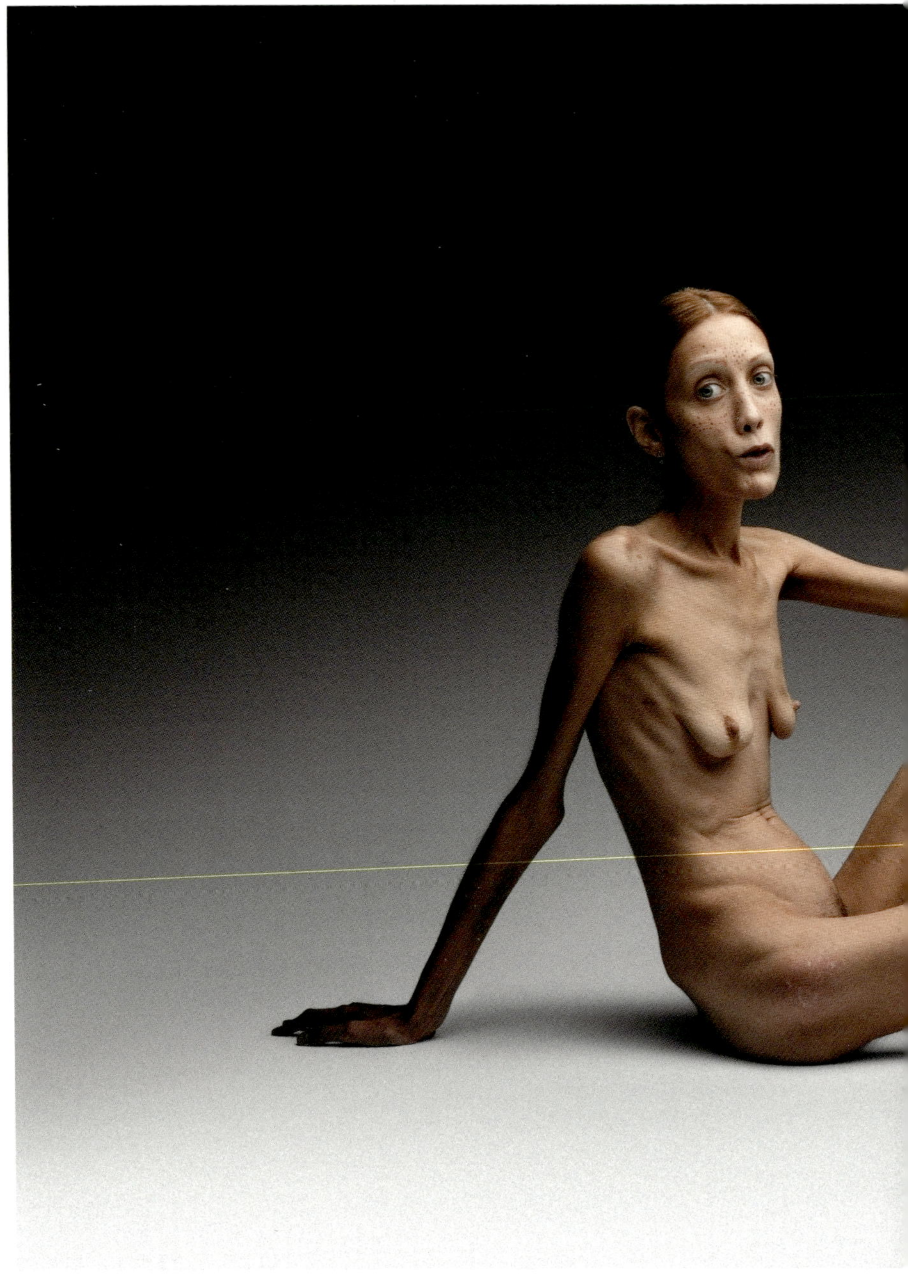

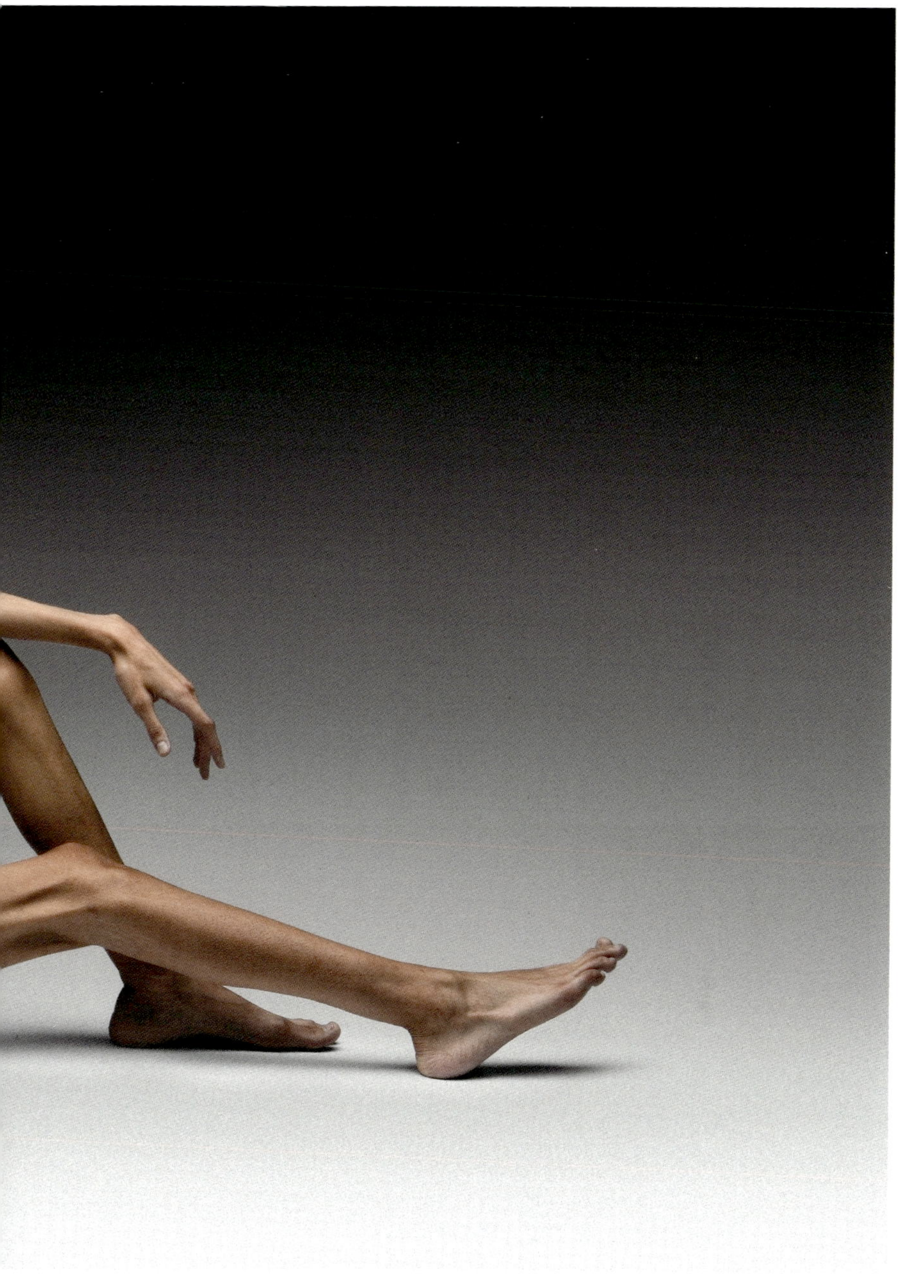

↑ **Oliviero Toscani,** *No anorexia (ad campaign)*, 2007

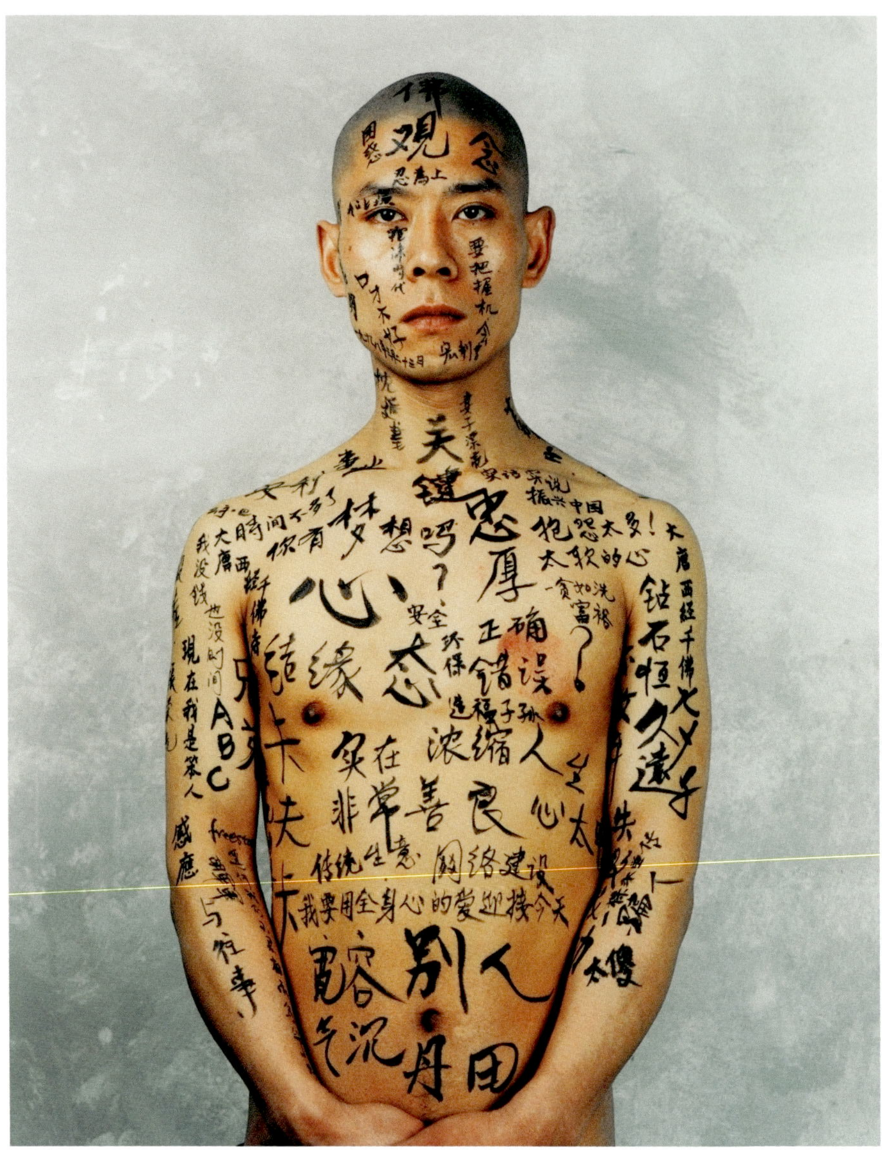

↑ Zhang Huan, *1/2*, 1998

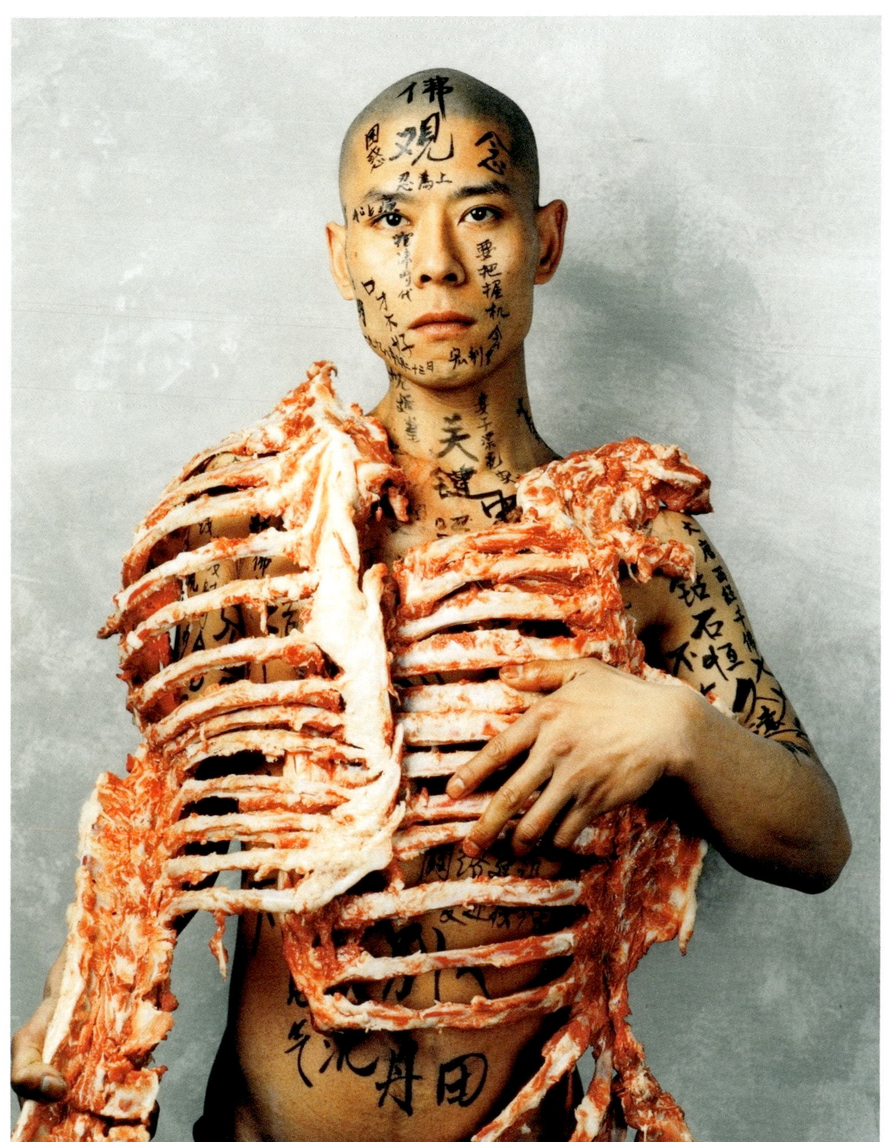

↑ Zhang Huan, *1/2*, 1998

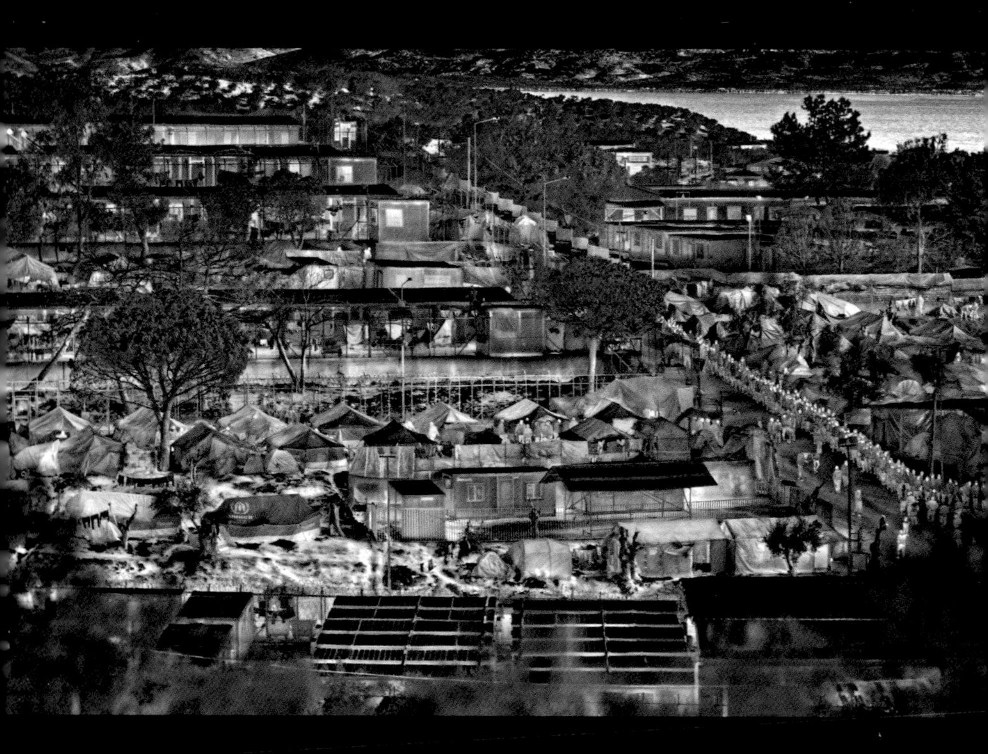

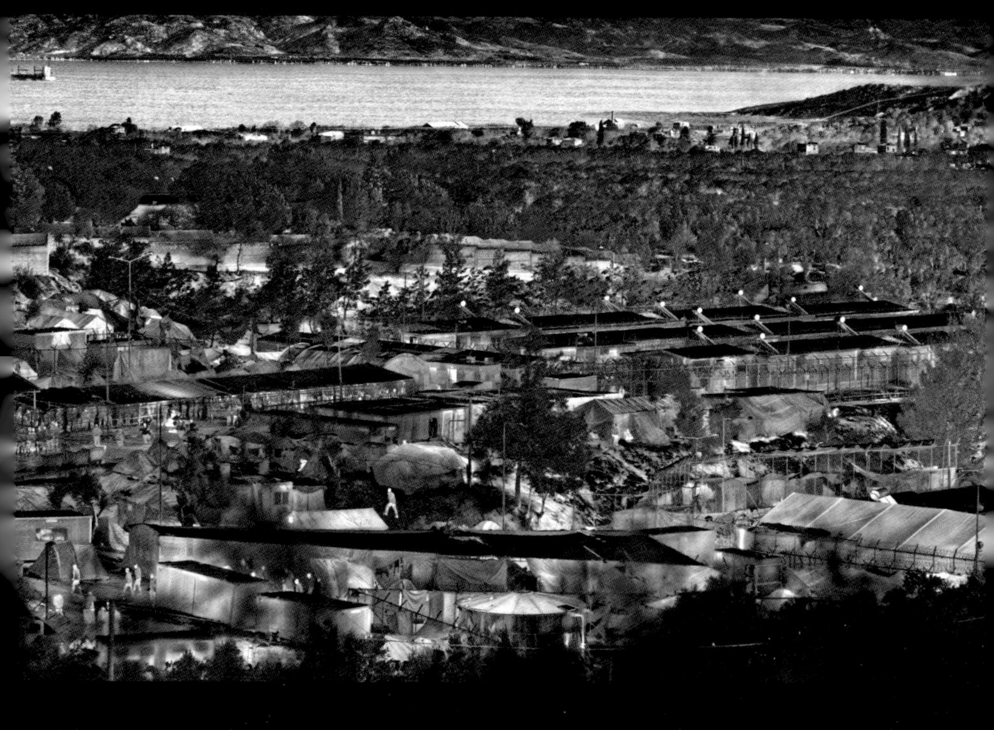

↑ **Richard Mosse,** *Moria in Snow,* 2017

↑ **Richard Mosse,** still from *Incoming* (three-screen video installation), 2017

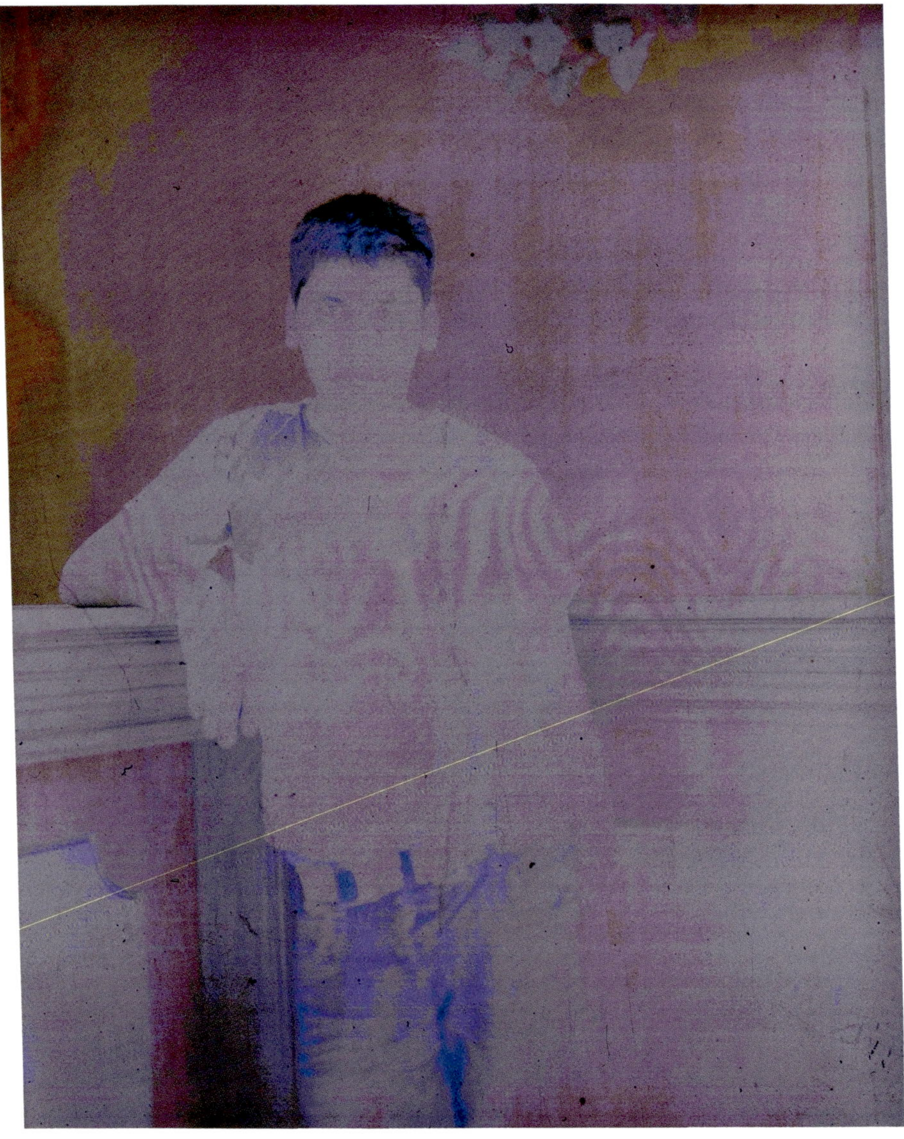

↑ **Seba Kurtis,** *HeartBeat (Study-10)*, 2012

↑ **Seba Kurtis,** *HeartBeat (Study-8)*, 2012

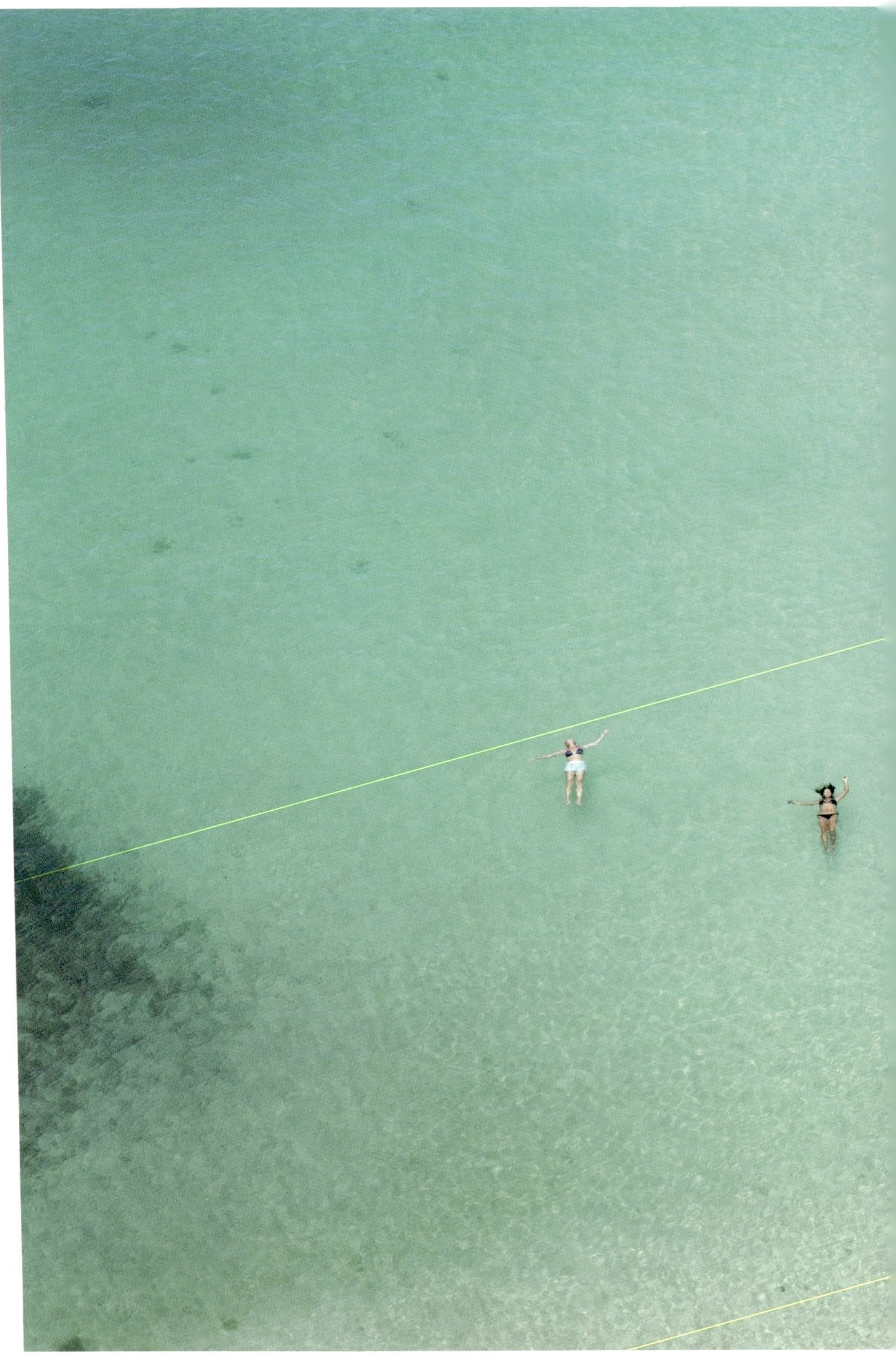

↑ **Richard Misrach**, *Untitled #394-03*, 2013

LOVE

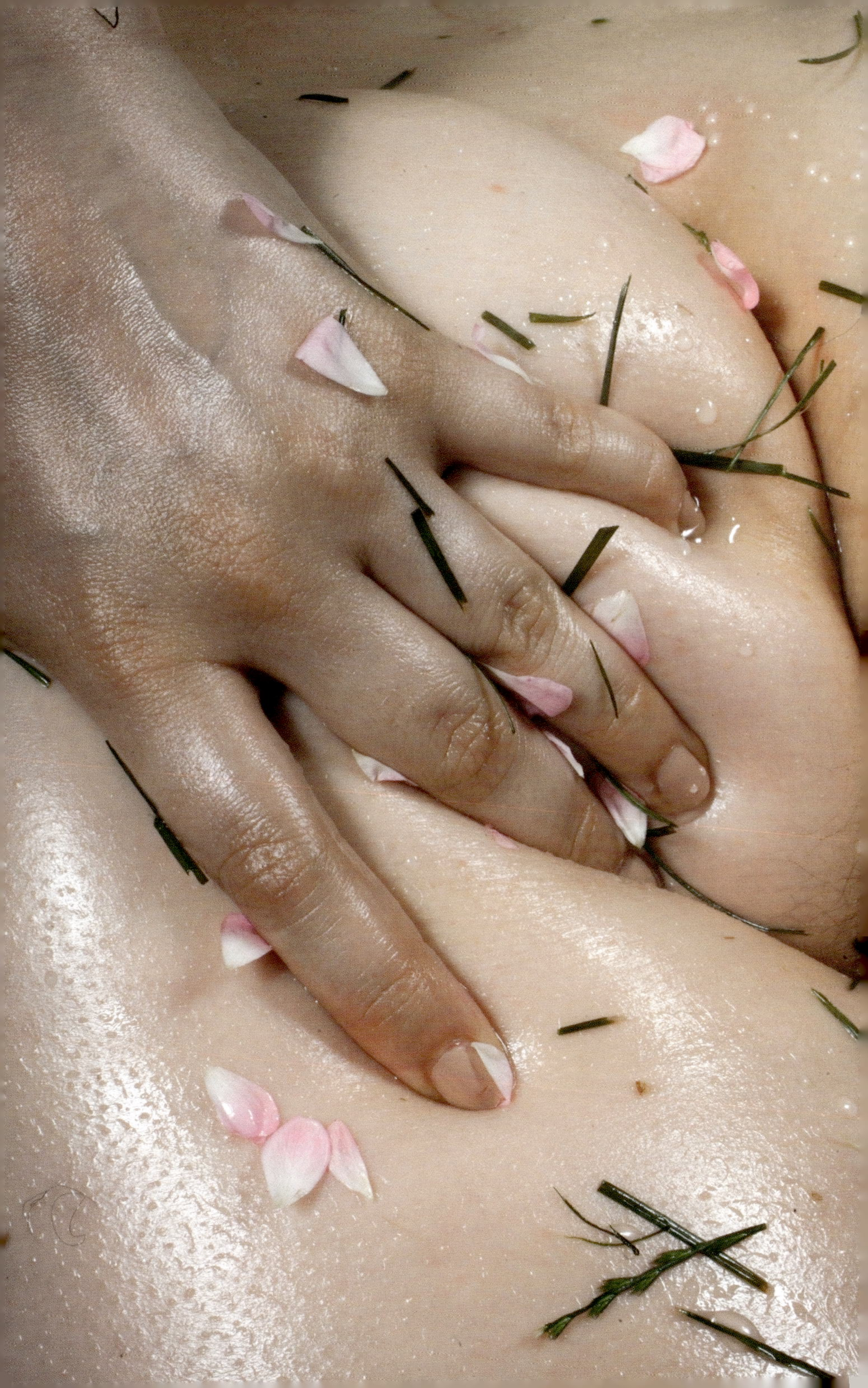

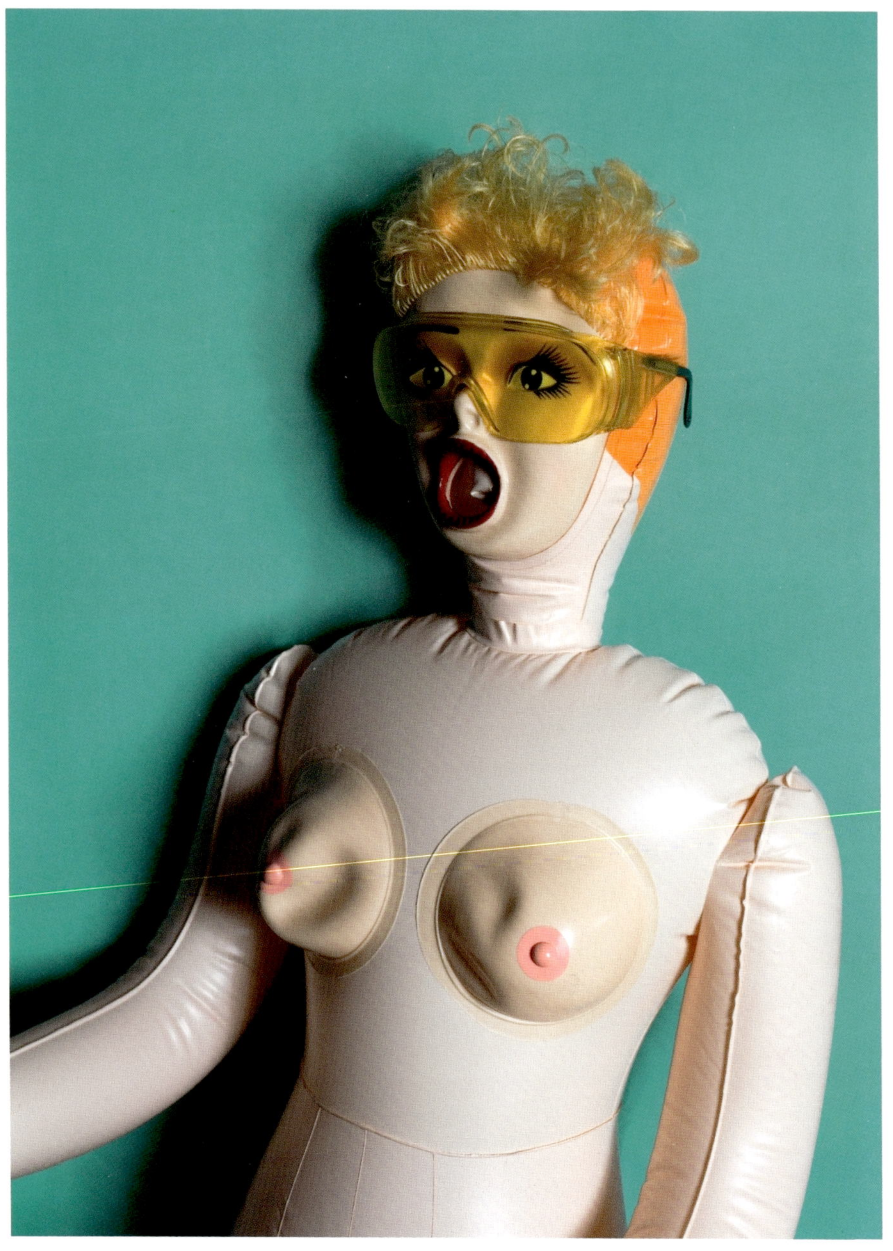

↑ **Romina Ressia,** *Doll,* 2017
←(Previous) **Maisie Cousins,** *Grass Bum,* 2015

Testimony to our relationship with the world and with others, the body quivers and trembles and the heart beats more quickly when faced with the beloved. The skin is something that the other can touch, caress, kiss. It is a surface but it is in no way superficial. That is why we speak of being 'happy in our skin'. Pleasure is felt via the physical body, the site of the sensations and emotions, especially in the case of love. Throughout the ages, artists have represented the body as a means of expressing emotions, above all desire and pleasure. Feelings manifest themselves physically and are reflected in the face, in gestures and postures, and in the sensuality of the body. Love has been a prime subject for sculptors and painters since antiquity, and photographers have naturally continued this tradition. Their success was immediate, since the photographic image can likewise reveal every detail of the contours of the bodies exposed to a viewer.

It has often been hard, however, to draw a line between sensual images and images of a pornographic nature. It is difficult to know how to react to Gustave Courbet's *The Origin of the World*, or to Hokusai's *shunga* prints. Are these scenes erotic, or are they obscene? Such questions about images of a sexual nature are particularly applicable to photography, which is capable of showing the flesh in minute detail, wrinkles and all. The viewer ultimately has to make up their own mind. But we can also seek the answer from the photographers themselves. What was their original intention? Artists often chose to show erotic representations of the sex act long before the invention of photography. The female nude has been associated with concepts of sexual availability, seduction and submission for centuries. The production and proliferation of images of this kind have clearly merely grown with the advent of photography. In the 19th century, 'obscene' pictures were sold under the counter. From the mid-20th century on, they made the fortunes of 'adult' magazines such as *Playboy*, *Penthouse* and *Lui*. The craze for pin-up photography trivialized the sight of the naked female body. We need only remember the success of the Pirelli calendars that have been published since 1964 and contain pictures by some of the world's greatest fashion photographers, from Richard Avedon to Bruce Weber and including Herb Ritts, Helmut Newton and Peter Lindbergh.

The advertising world has also embraced sensual imagery and, since the late 1990s, has even ventured into what has come to be known as 'porno chic', an expression that was first used in relation to various 1970s films and that reappeared twenty years later in connection with the pages of Paris *Vogue* under editor Carine Roitfeld, and ads for Gucci and Tom Ford. The two mingling tongues photographed by Sølve Sundsbø for a fashion magazine (p. 379) show how widely images of a sexual nature have come to be displayed. Male heterosexual culture has been forged by images of this kind, initially distributed by men's magazines and then via the internet. Daido Moriyama (p. 383) distorts the sexual body and it takes a moment or two to understand that the undulating and fluid forms of his photographs actually represent the legs of women wearing fishnet tights.

Today, in the West, very few would be shocked by direct photographs of the sex act. Yet we must remember that — in France, at least — it took until the time of the May 1968 revolution for sexual practices and discourses on sexuality to be combined publicly. Images of physical love showing mingling bodies that desire and enjoy one another have certainly sold well for a long time, but they are no longer regarded as taboo or to be hidden, as proved by the enormous success of the exhibitions and books of Nobuyoshi Araki (pp. 390–93), whose work is characterized by an abundance of sexual scenes. Edouard Levé (p. 395), with his astonishing pornography-inspired scenarios, and Thomas Ruff (pp. 396, 397), who is interested in the proliferation of X-rated films on the internet, show the degree to which sex is displayed and omnipresent in contemporary society. For her part, Lina Scheynius (pp. 402, 403, 404) has chosen to provoke the viewer's attention, rather than to shock, with her images of female sexuality and pleasure, images that would until recently have been taboo.

Scenes of homosexuality have appeared in art for 2,000 years but have also become more visible thanks to the new horizons opened up by photographers such as Robert Mapplethorpe and Peter Hujar in the 1970s to 1980s. Wolfgang Tillmans (pp. 294, 295, 410, 411) and Sascha Weidner (pp. 290, 291, 292, 401) show the sensuality of the male body. Laurence Rasti

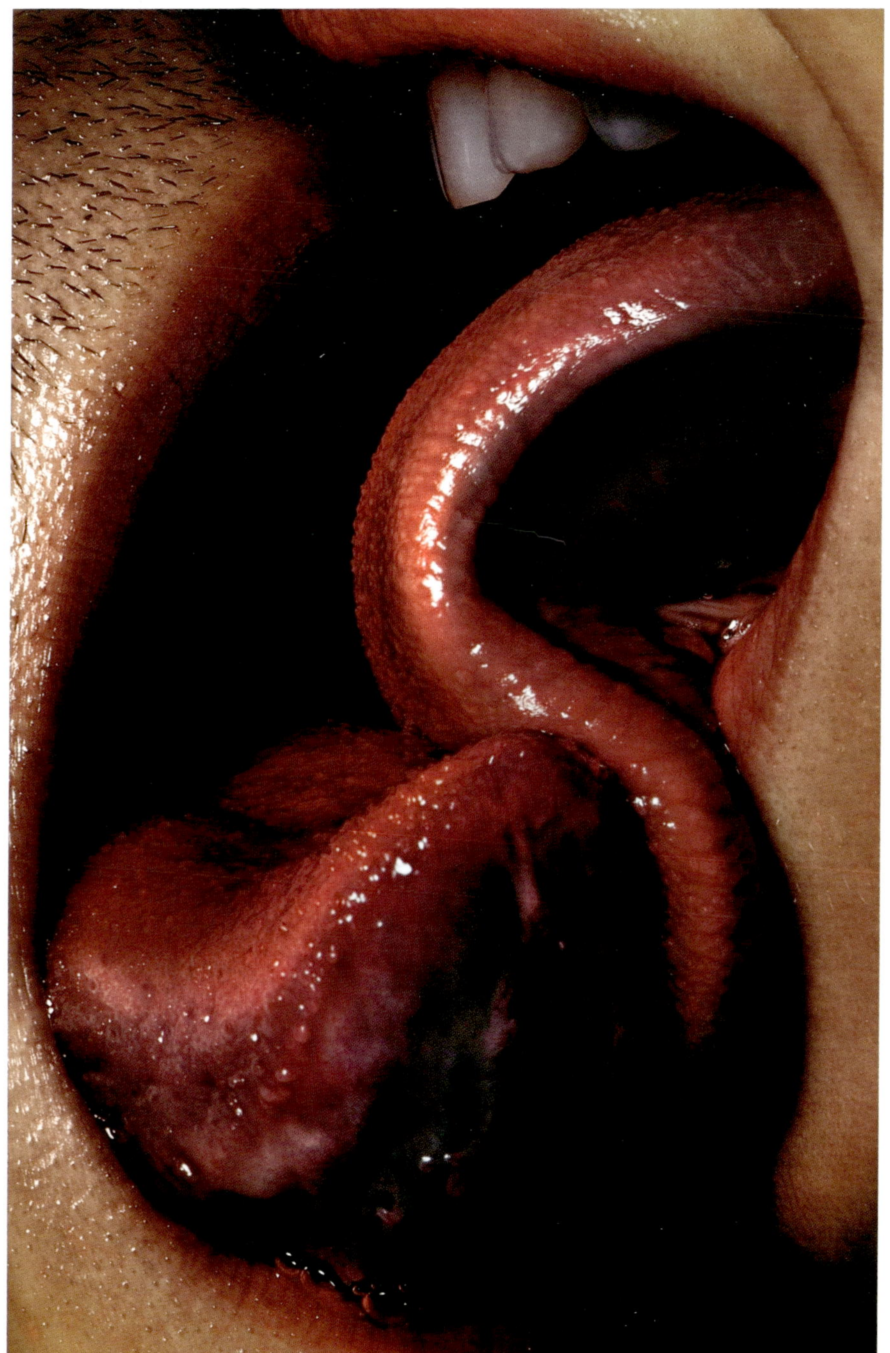

↑ **Sølve Sundsbø**, *Kiss*, 2010

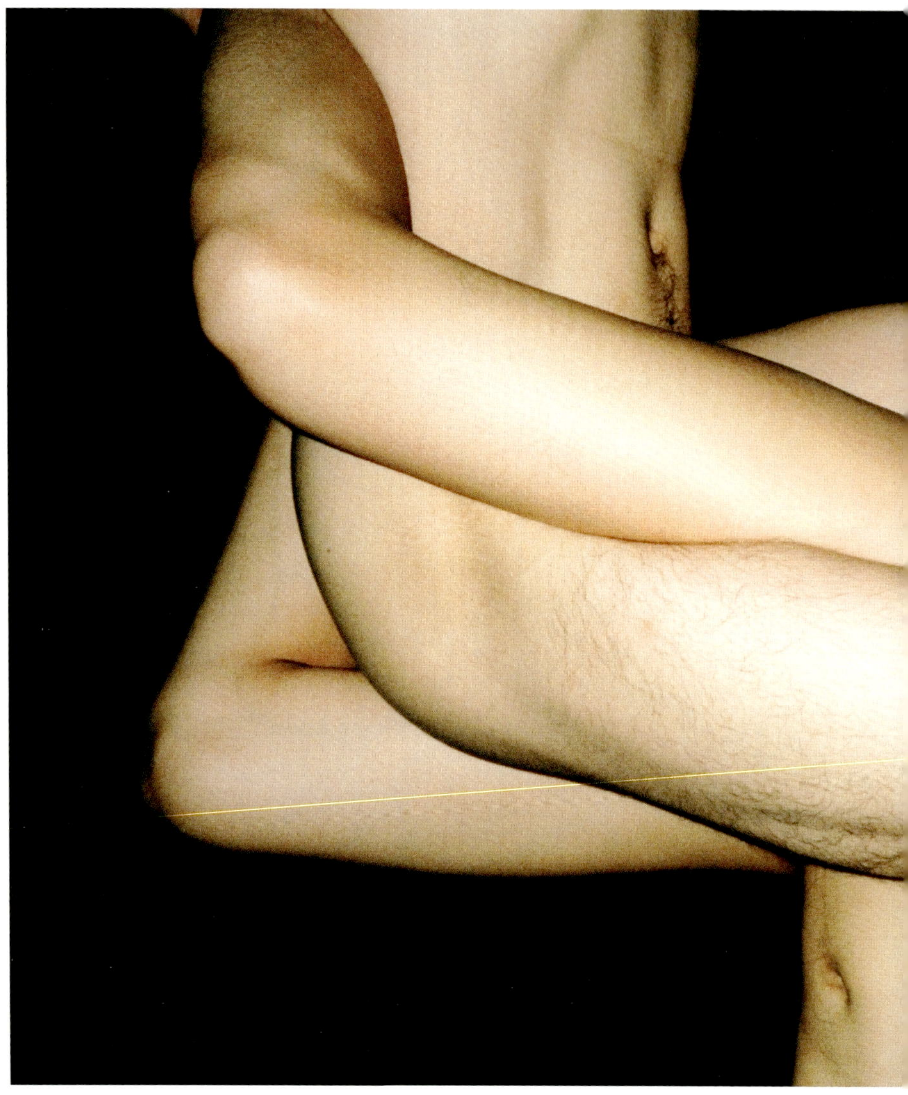

↑ Ren Hang, *Untitled 11*, 2011

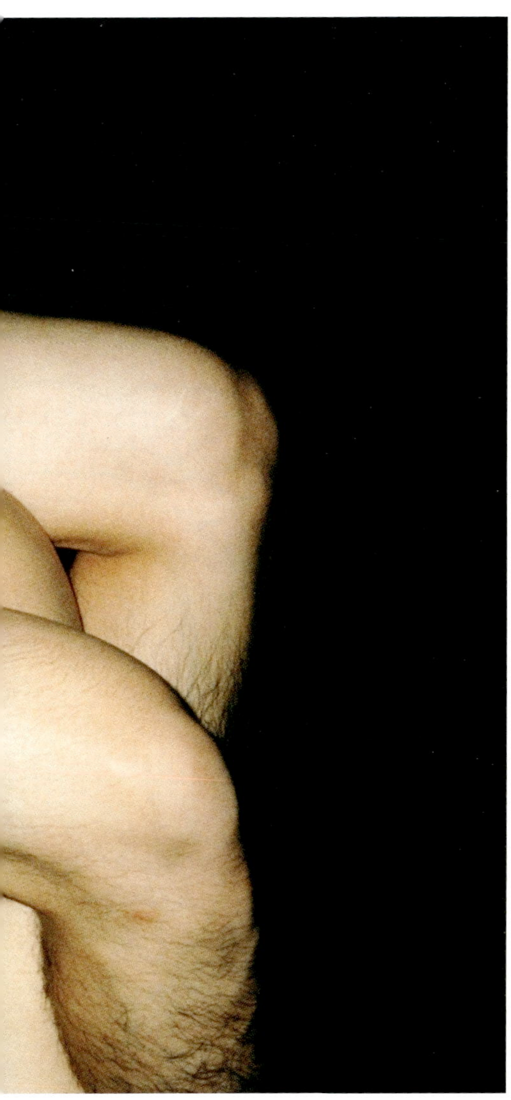

(p. 409) reminds us that homosexual love still remains forbidden in many countries in the 21st century. The couples she has photographed live in hiding and have fled their country of origin, Iran, because they are considered subversive and in breach of the social order.

In some regards, love seems to be an almost taboo experience in our times. It seems easier today to refer to sexuality than to love. In the photographs of SMITH (see pp. 414–15), the individual grows through his or her relationship with another, for surely it is indeed through our bodies that we are linked to others. Along the same lines, Jacob Aue Sobol (pp. 416, 417) captures the intensity of moments of physical closeness. Obviously, love and the coming together of bodies are not just a question of sex. There is a powerful sense of tenderness in Nicholas Nixon's photographs of himself with his wife (pp. 418, 419). The same is true of Elinor Carucci (p. 421), who has centred her work on self-portraits for many years, and here shows herself expressing the force of maternal love. Meanwhile, Alessandra Sanguinetti (p. 423) looks at the link between two cousins in her series 'The Adventures of Guille and Belinda', which she began in Argentina in 1999 and which has become a lifelong project. Working in China — a country where nudity is heavily censored — Ren Hang (pp. 196, 197, 380) has been able to capture intimate portraits of his generation, where bodies are mingled in a playful and sensual way. These images once again show that love is an emotion anchored in the fleshly physical world.

→ **Daido Moriyama,** *Tights, 1987–2011*

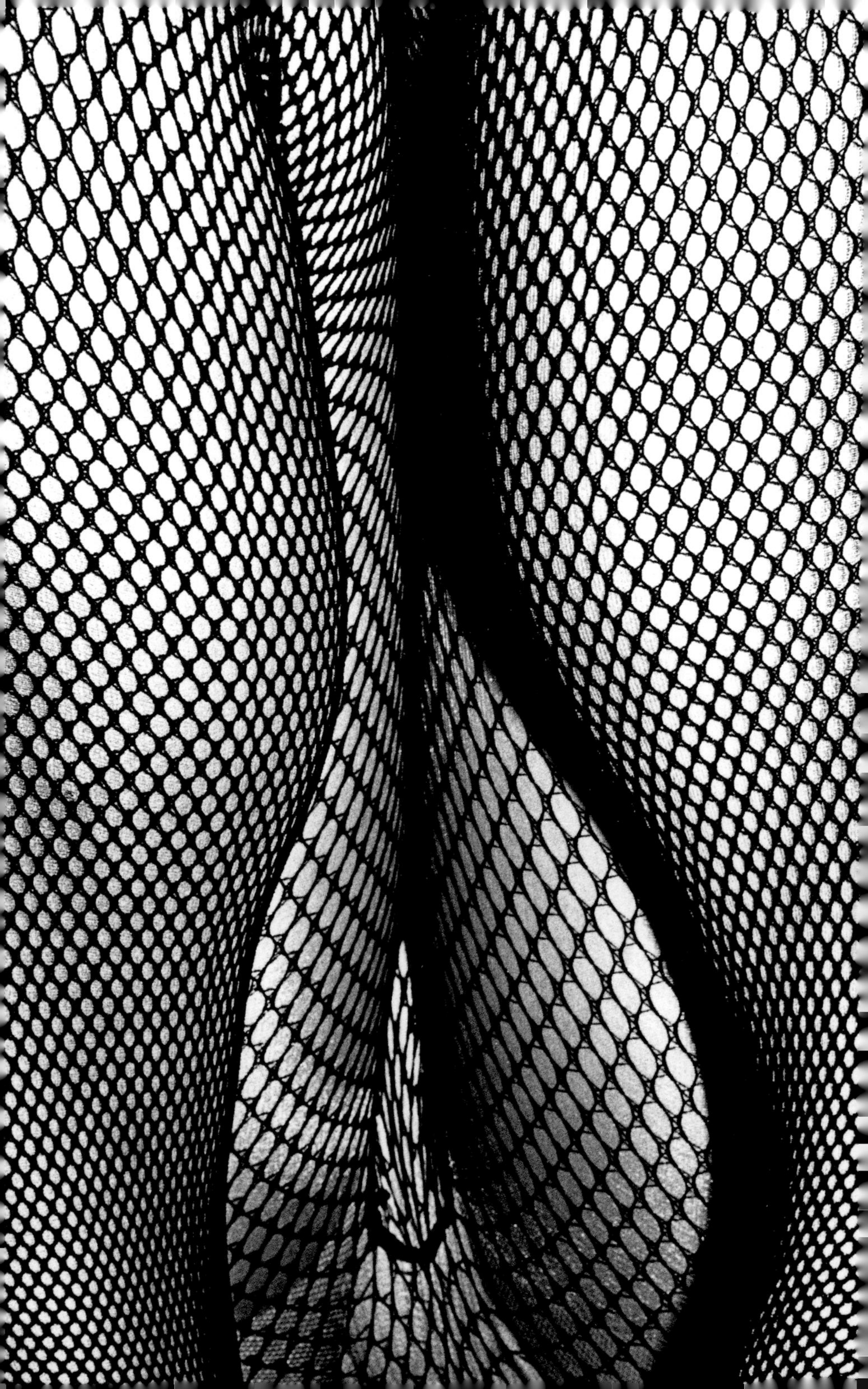

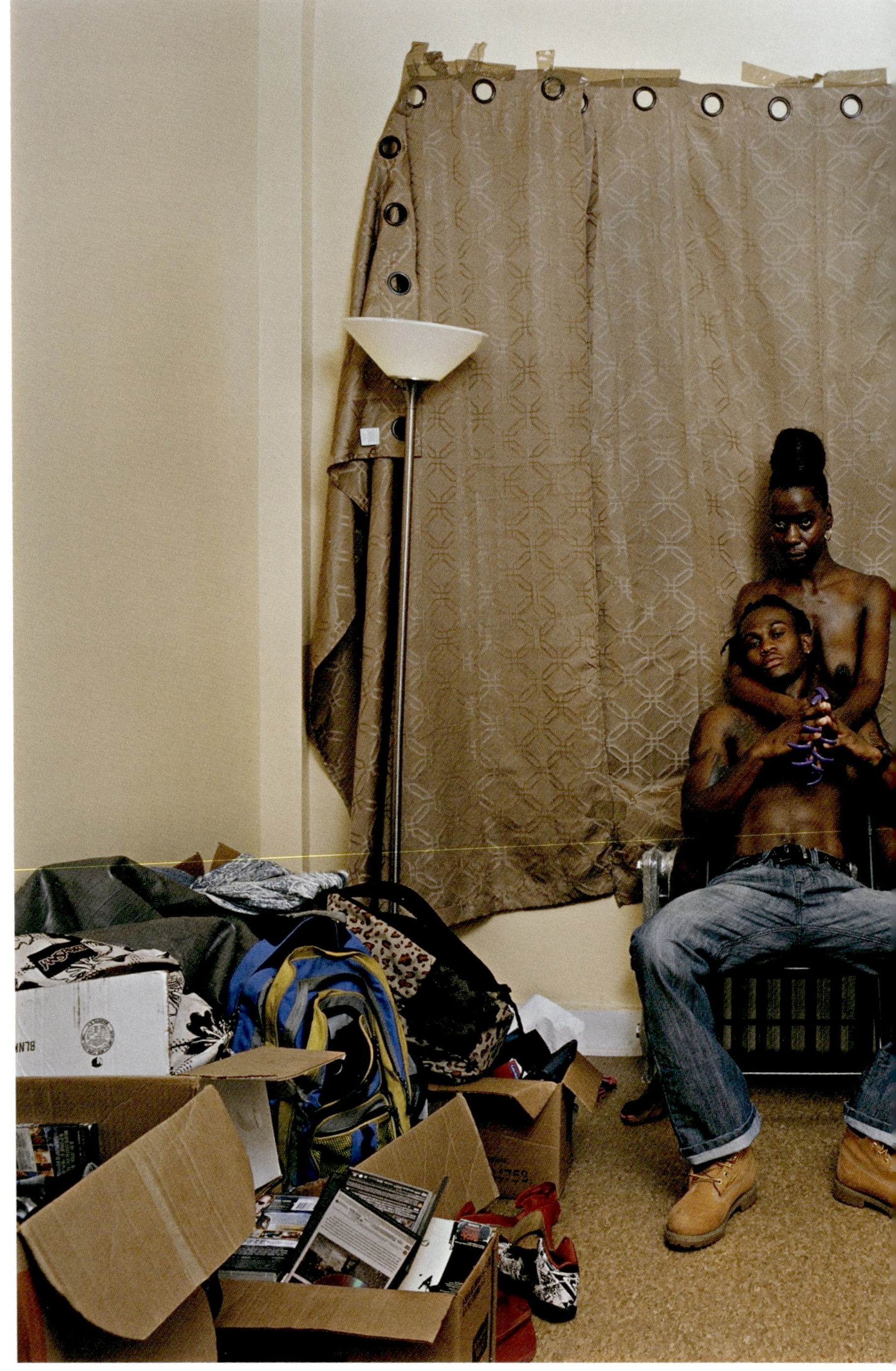

↑ **Deana Lawson,** *Living Room, Brownsville, Brooklyn,* 2015

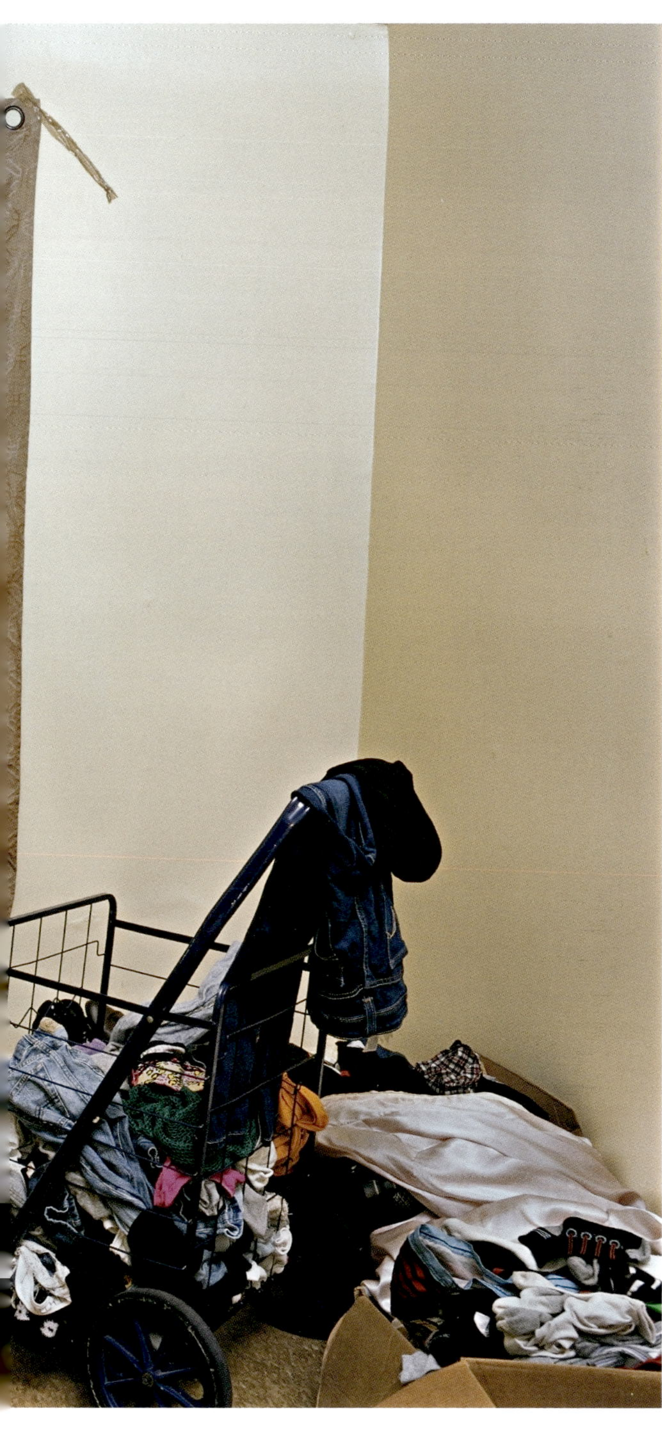

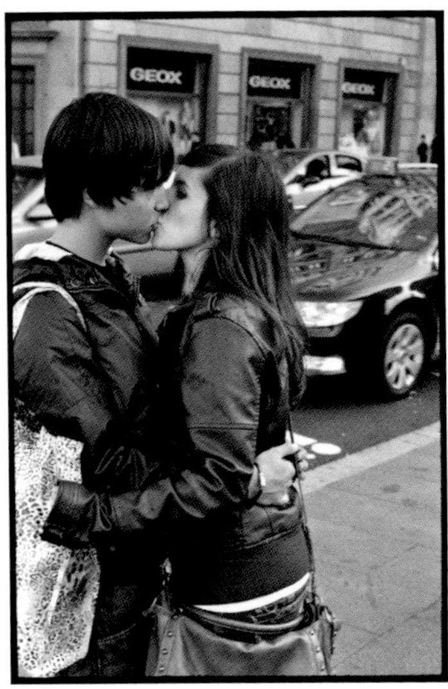
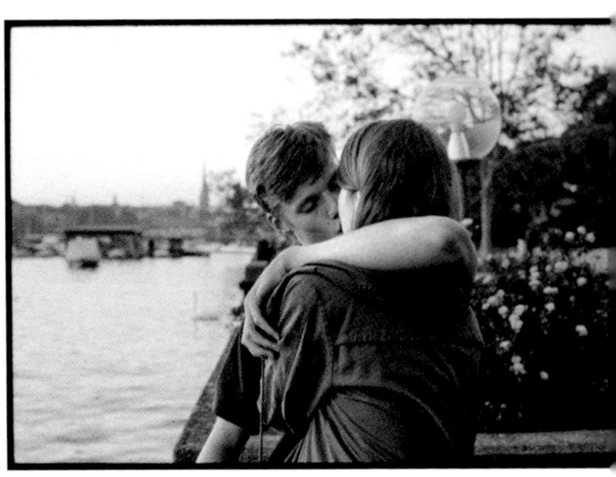
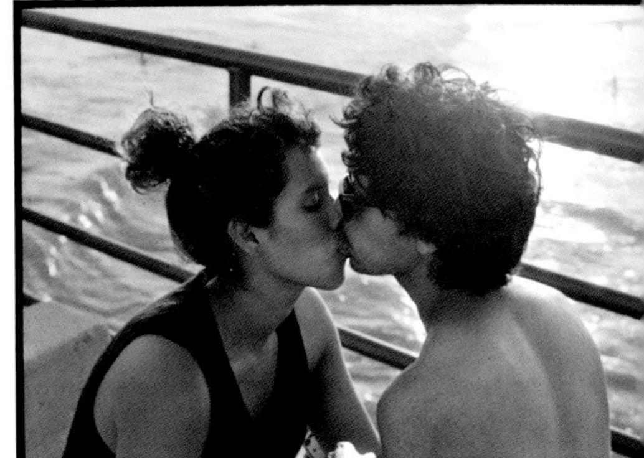
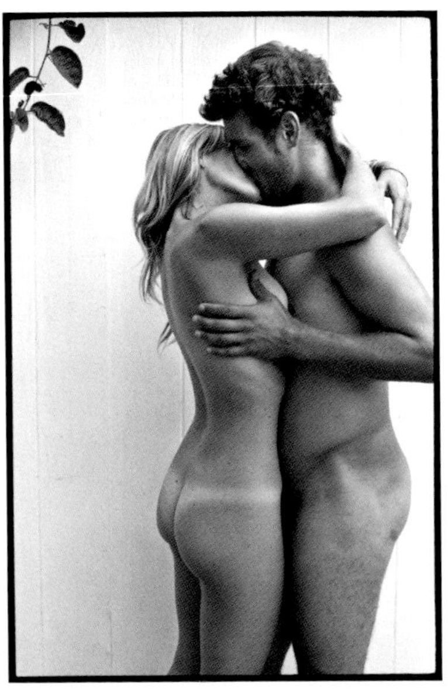
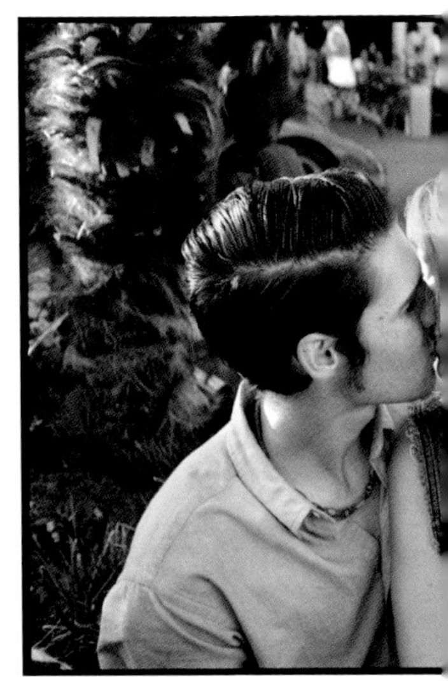

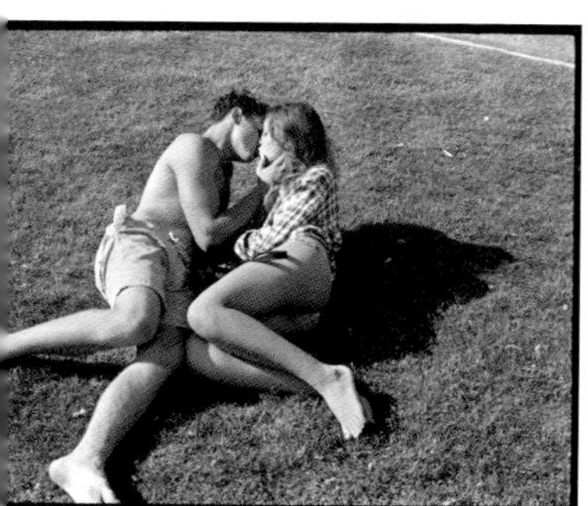

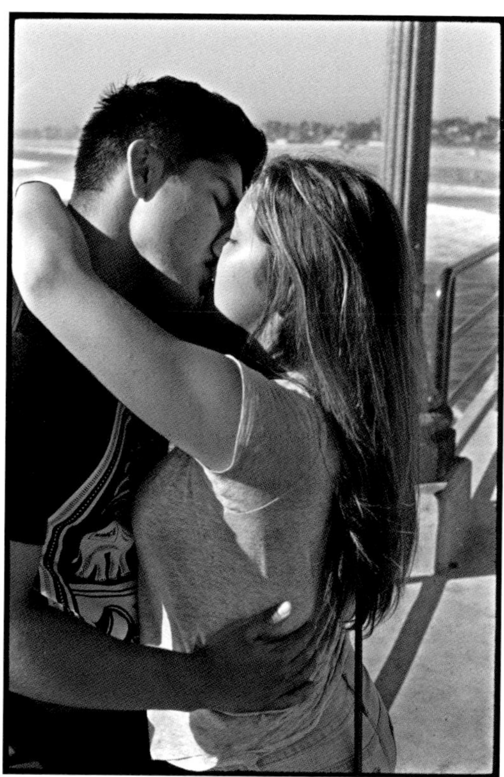

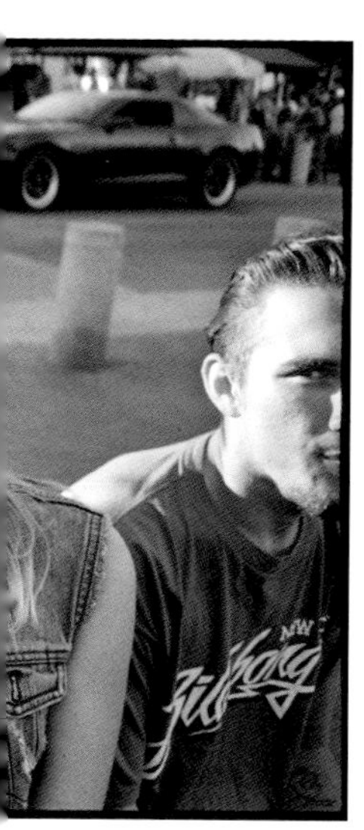

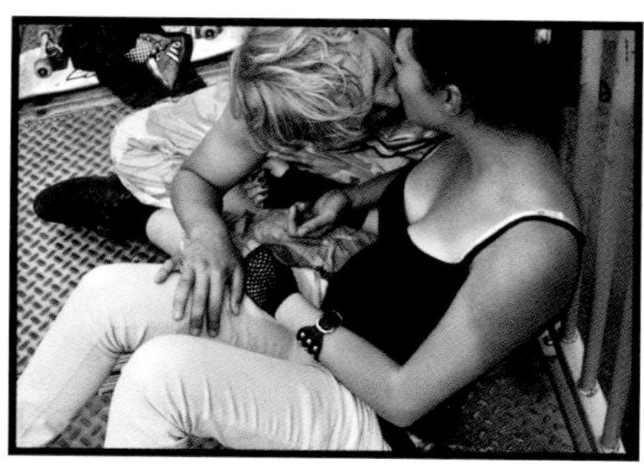

← (Clockwise from top left) **Ed Templeton,** *Teenage Kissers, Barcelona,* 2012; *Teenage Kissers, Zurich,* 2013; *Teenage Kissers, Huntington Beach,* 2013; *Teenage Kissers, Huntington Beach,* 2015; *Teenage Kissers, Birmingham,* 2007; *Teenage Kissers, Huntington Beach,* 2012; *Arto and Mimi, Los Angeles,* 2009; (centre, p. 386) *Teenage Kissers, Huntington Beach,* 2013

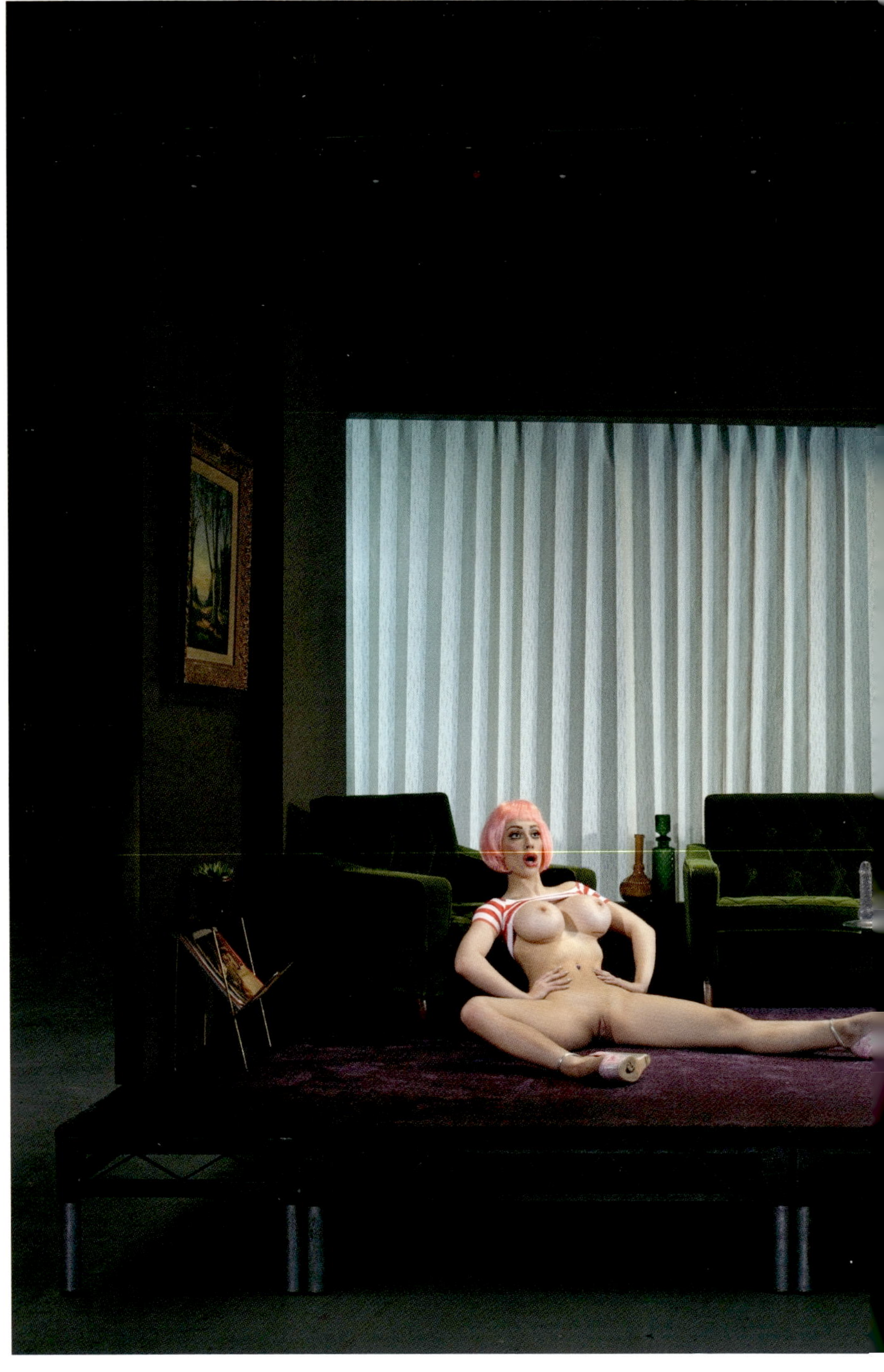

↑ **Julia Fullerton-Batten,** *Chessie Kay, Pornstar,* from 'The Act' series, 2016

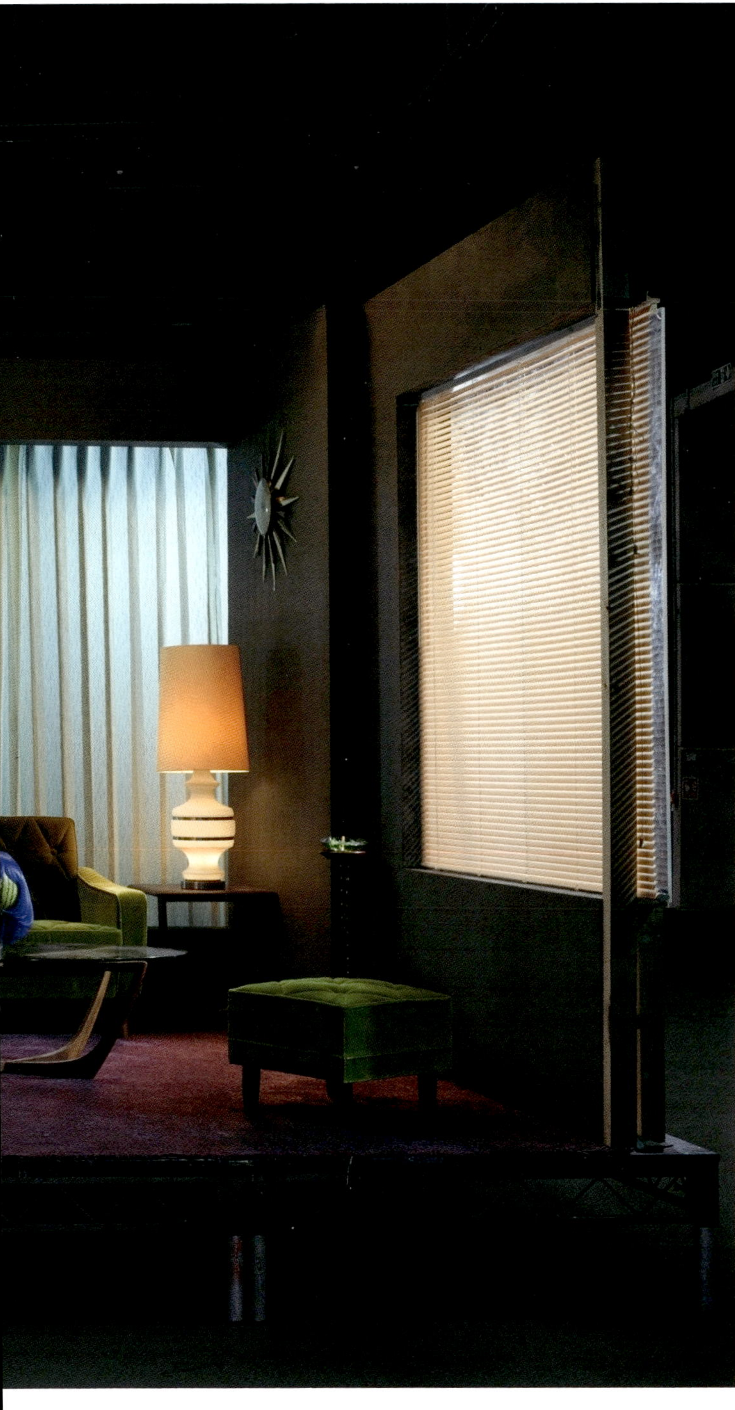

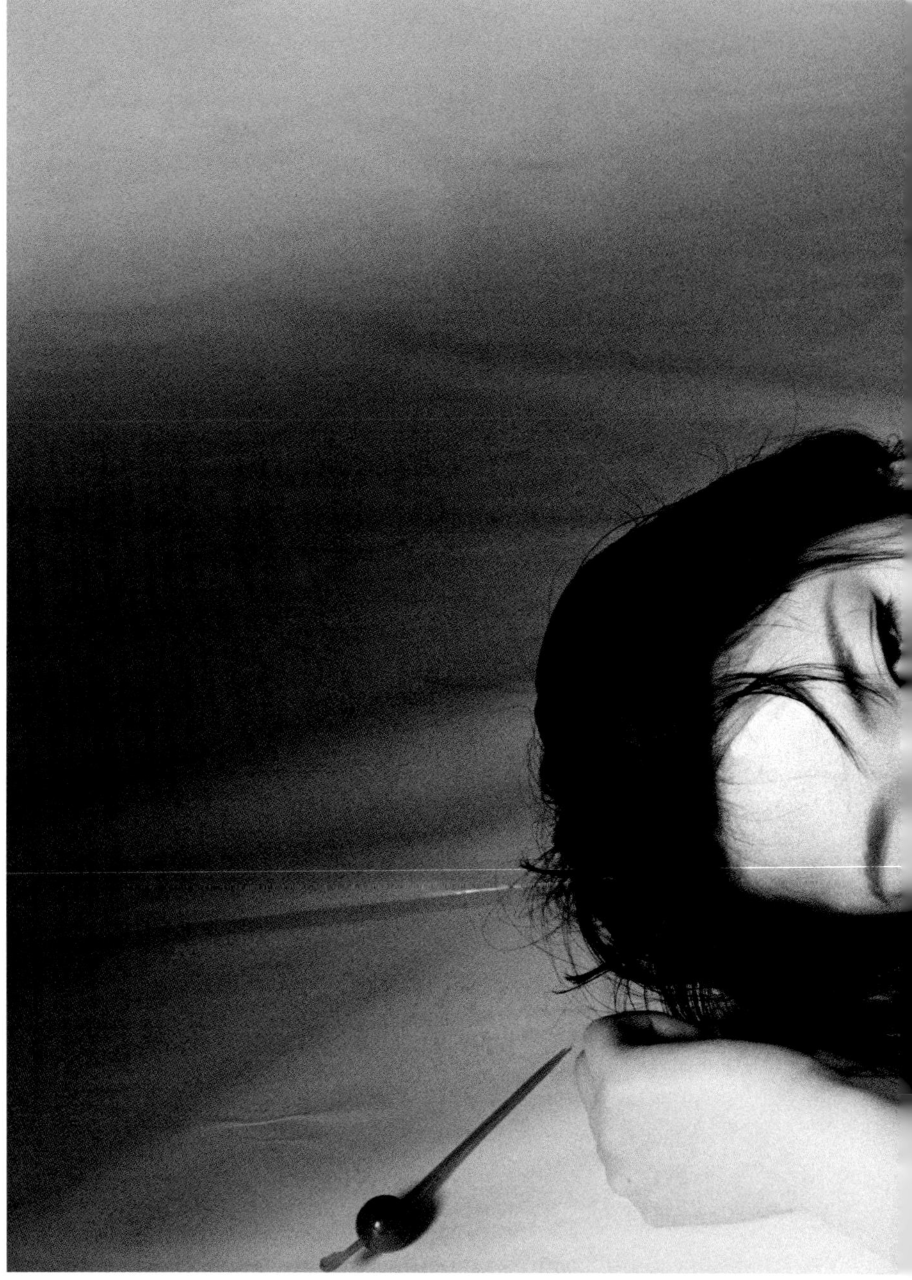

↑ **Nobuyoshi Araki,** *LOVE by Leica*, 1997

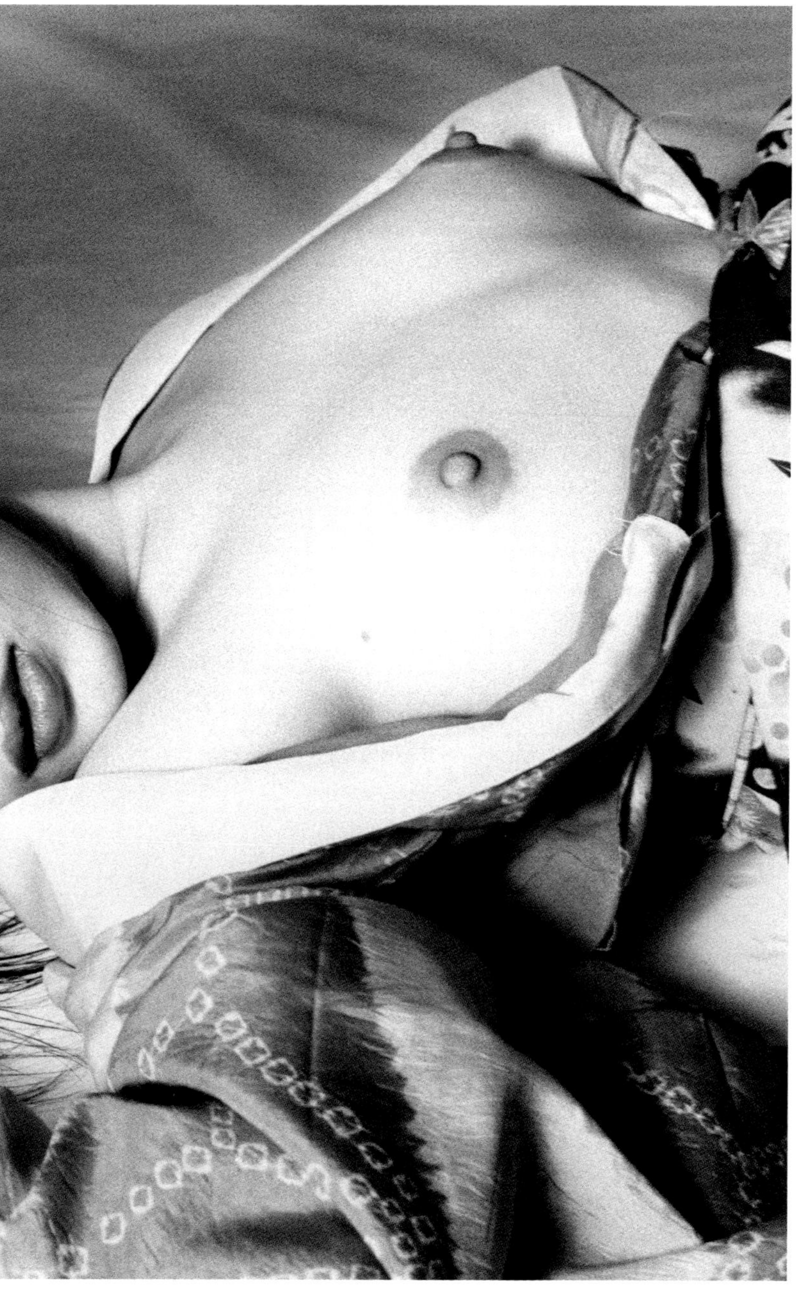

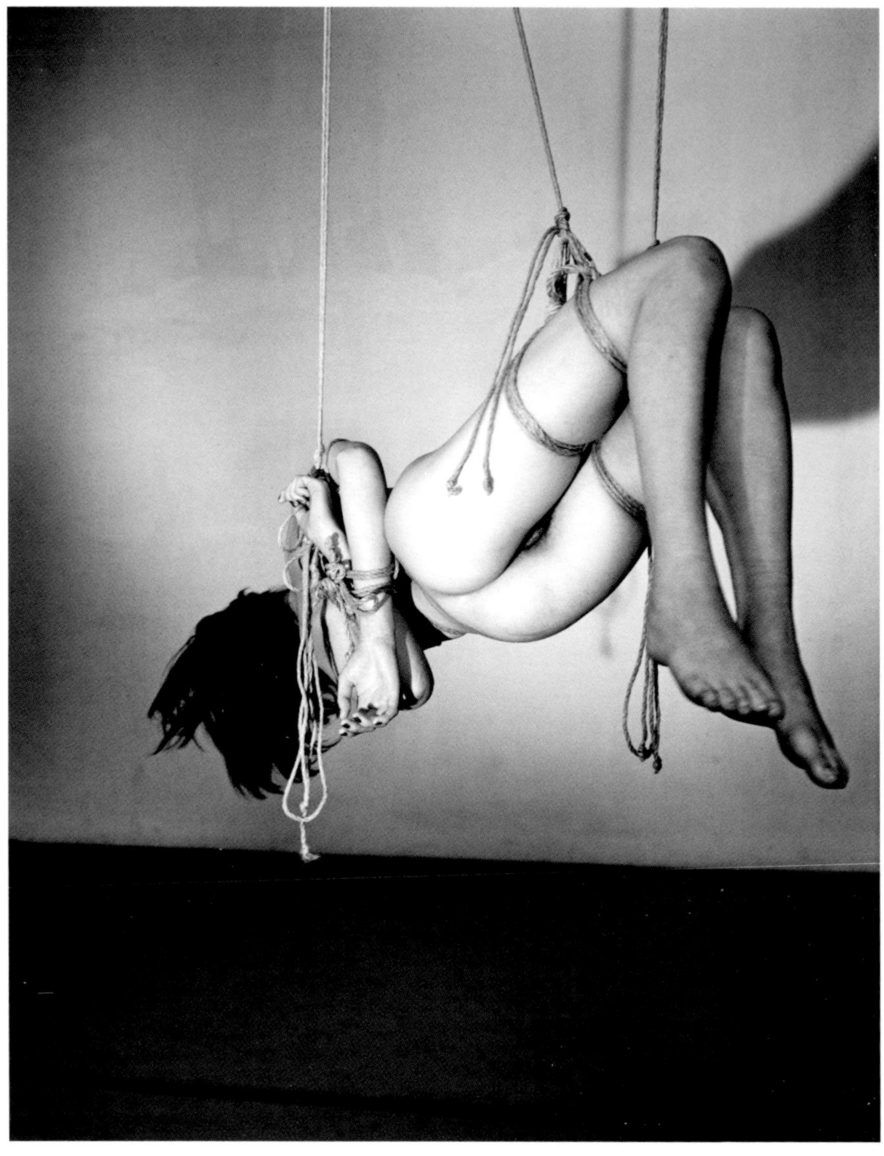

↑ **Nobuyoshi Araki,** *Kinbaku (Bondage)*, 1979

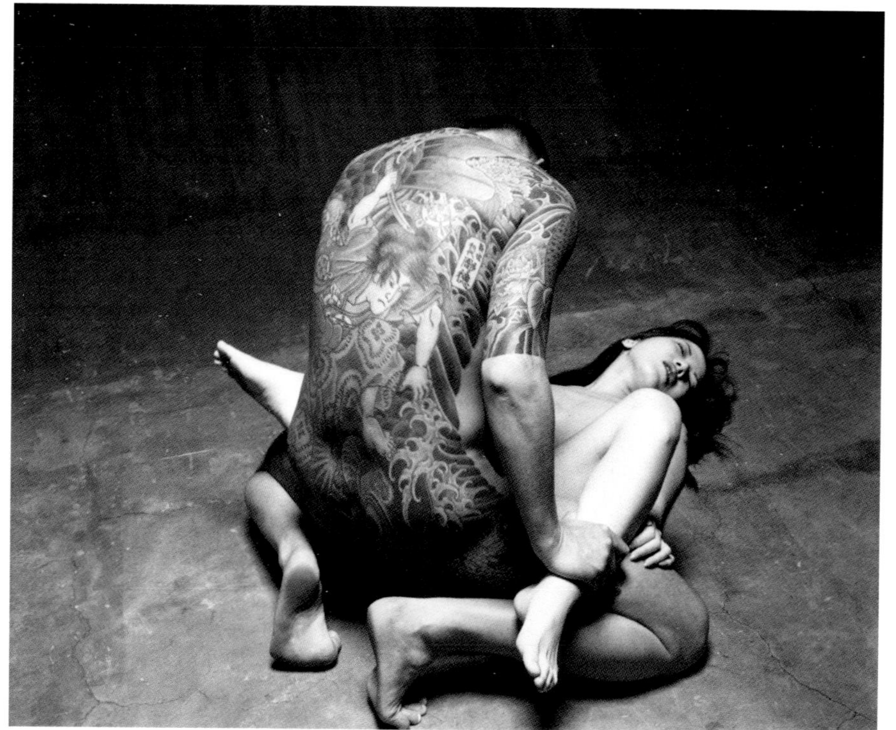

↑ **Nobuyoshi Araki,** *Tokyo Comedy,* 1997

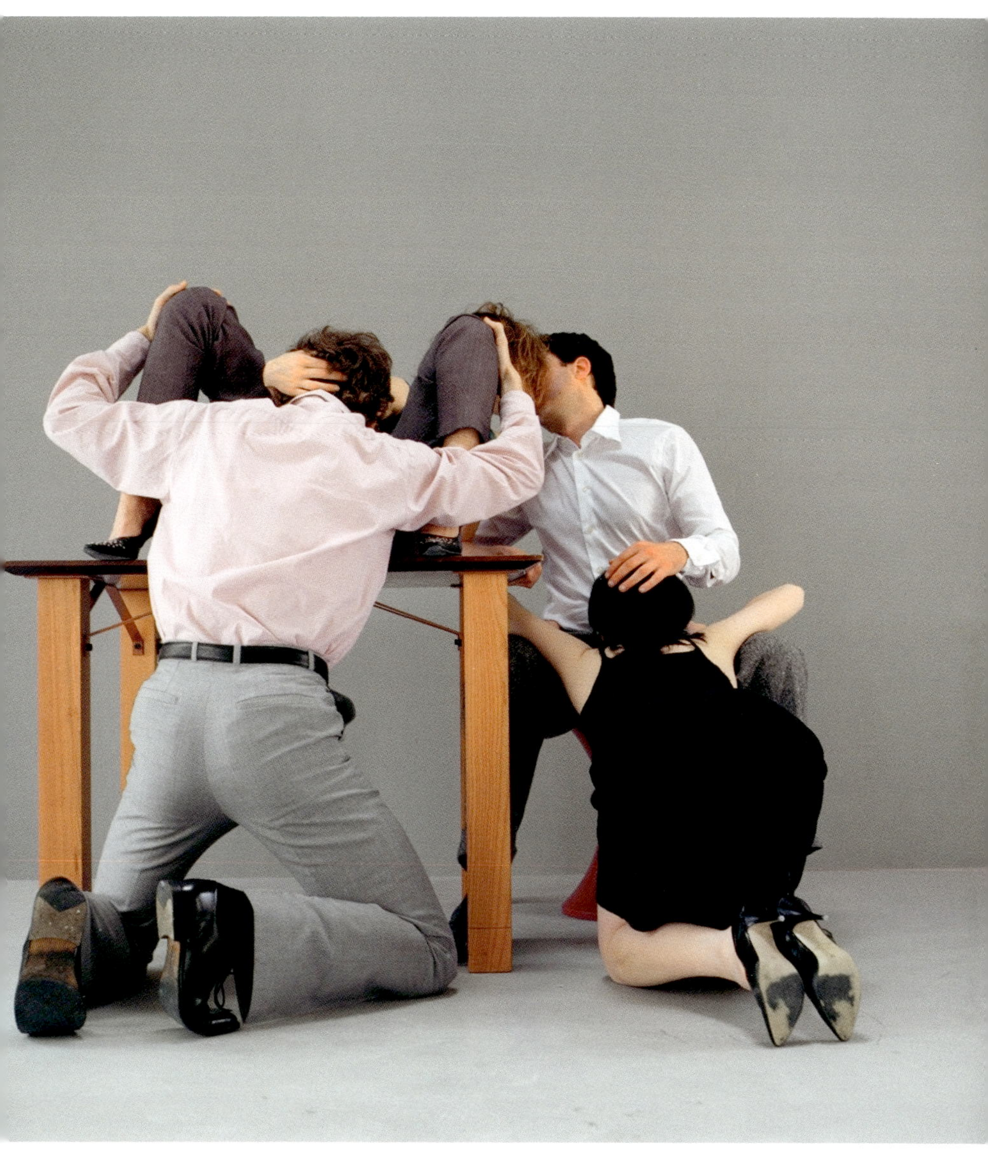

↑ **Edouard Levé,** *Untitled,* from the series 'Reconstitutions, Pornographie', 2002

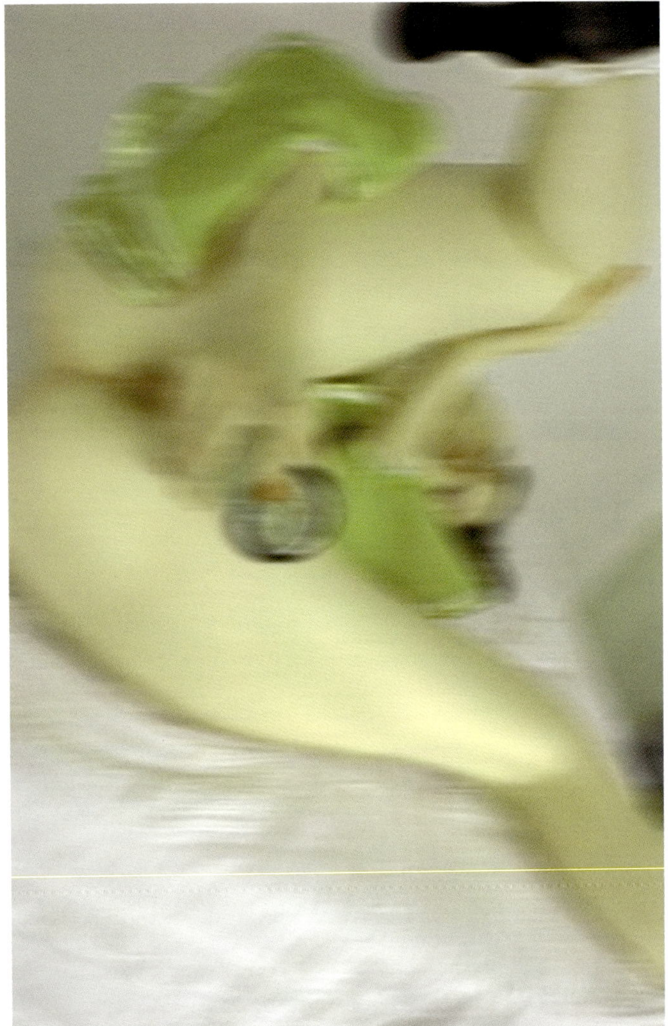

↑ **Thomas Ruff,** *Nudes bs15*, 2001

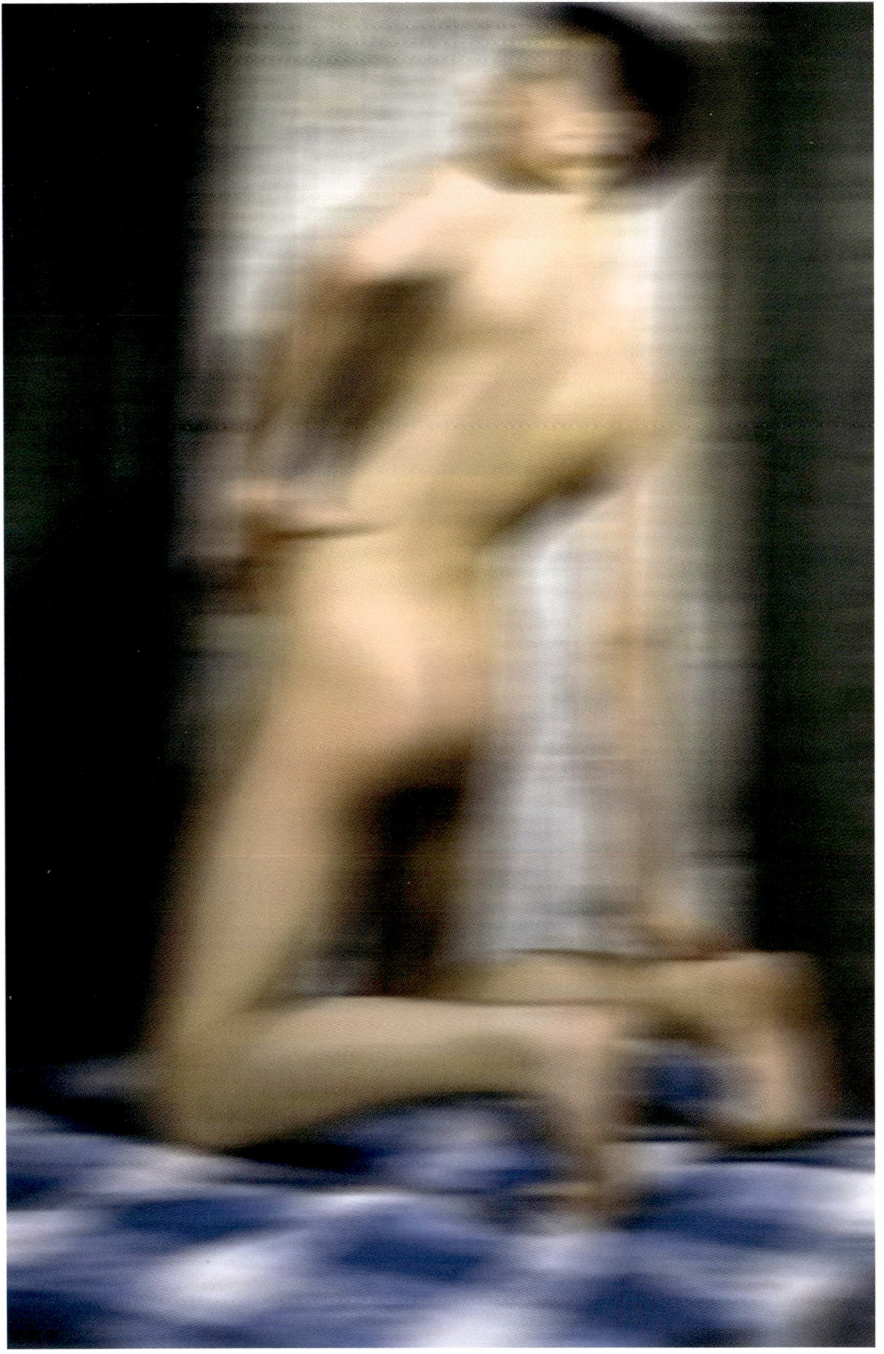

↑ **Thomas Ruff,** *Nudes lk18,* 2000

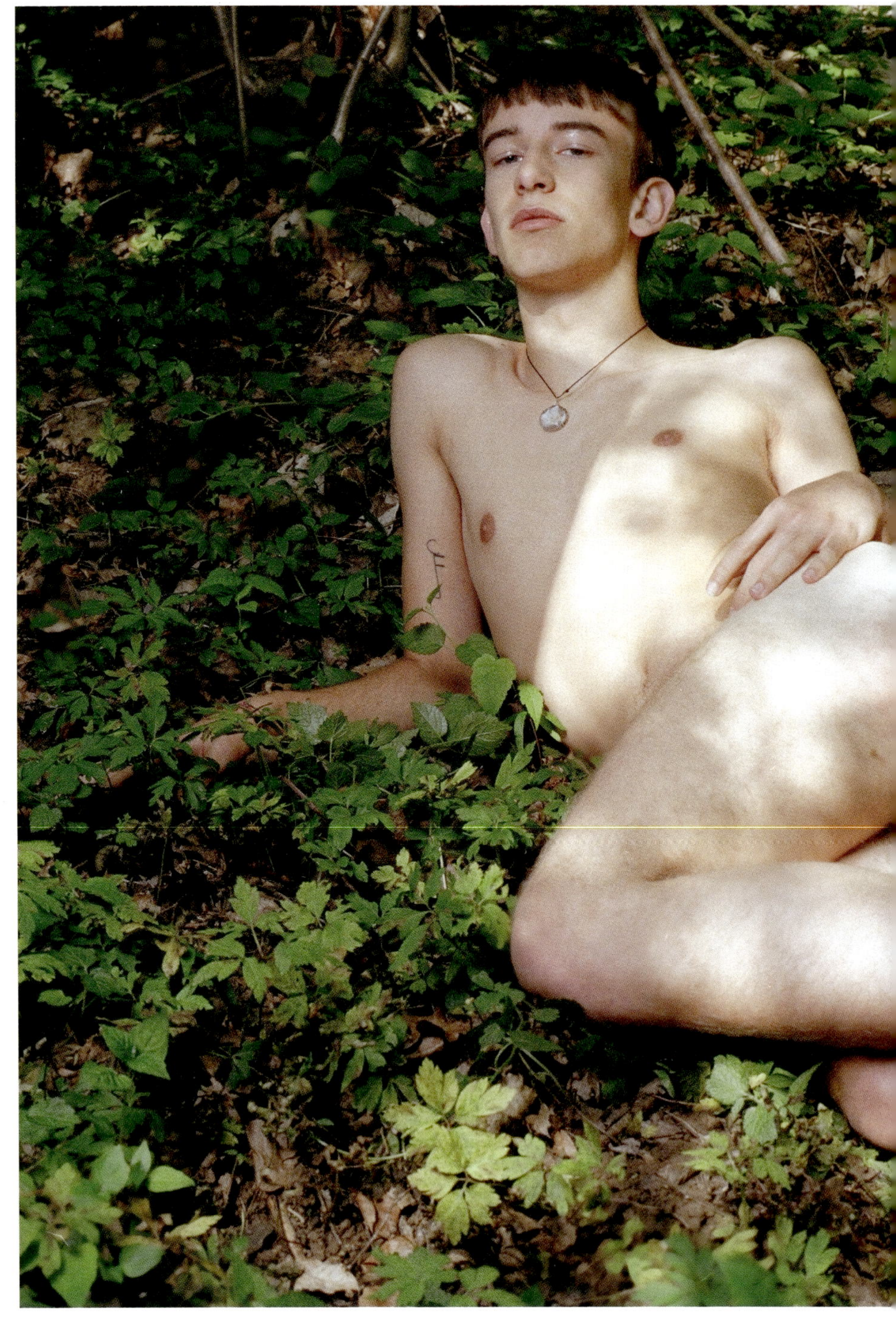

↑ **Margaux Piette & Emma Panchot,** *Danny on the Grass,* 2017

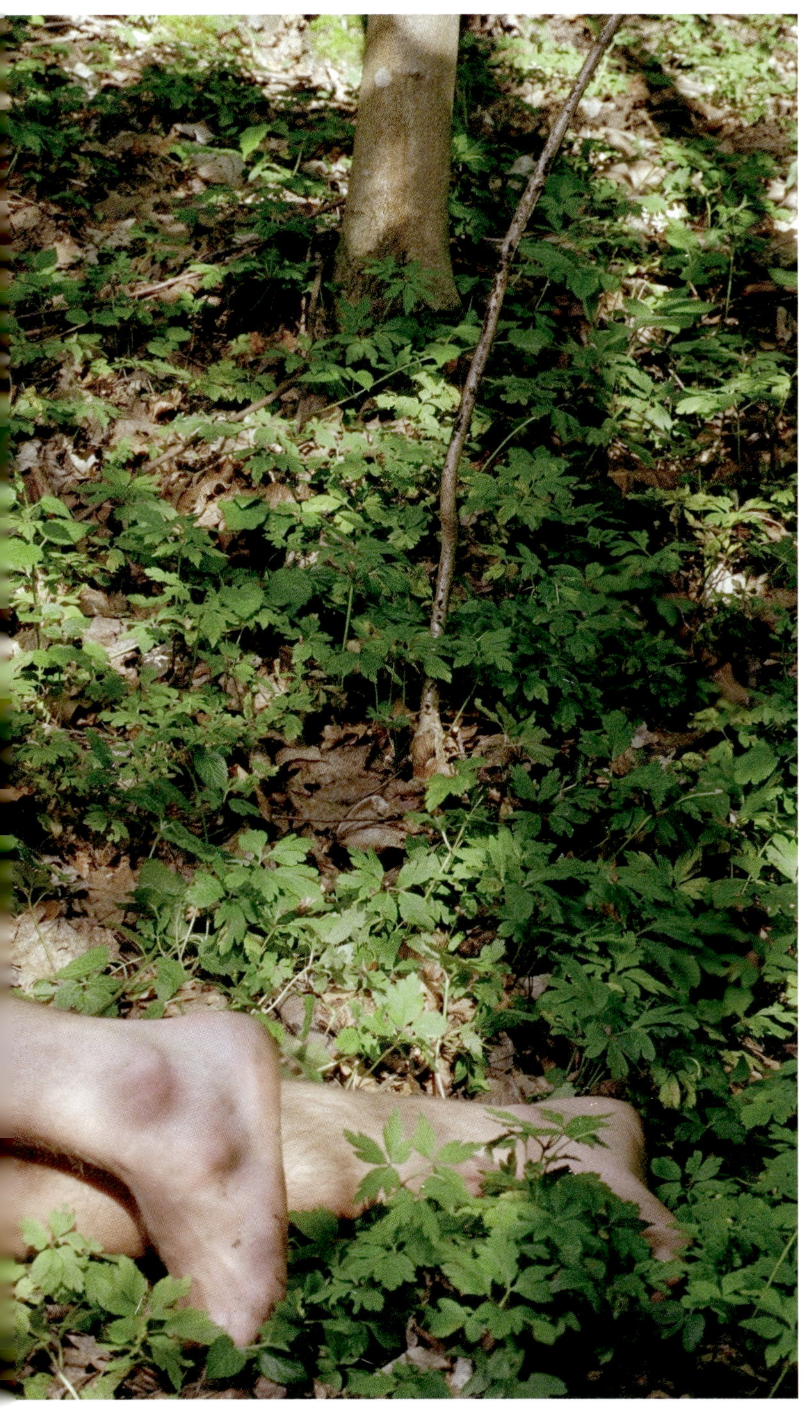

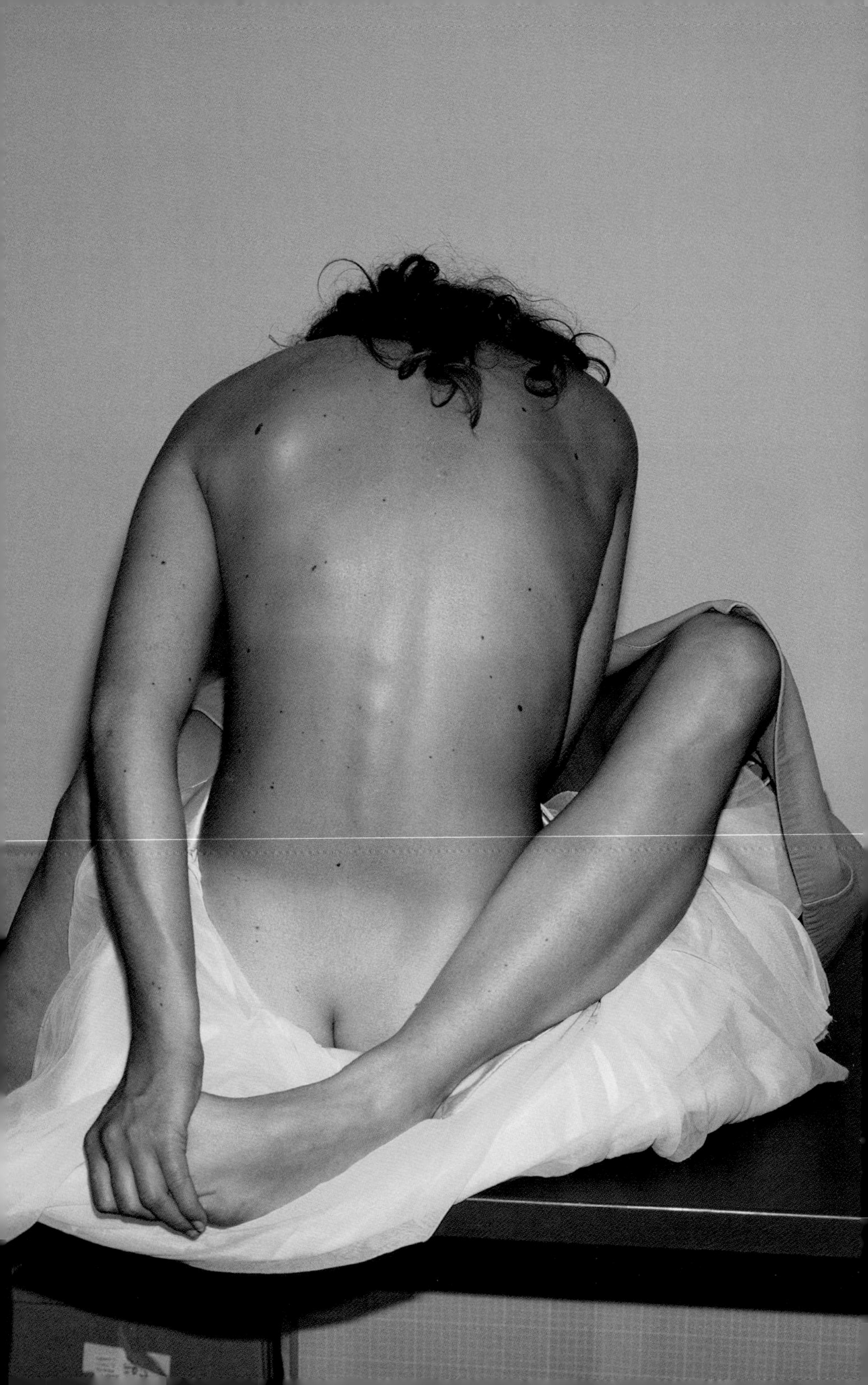

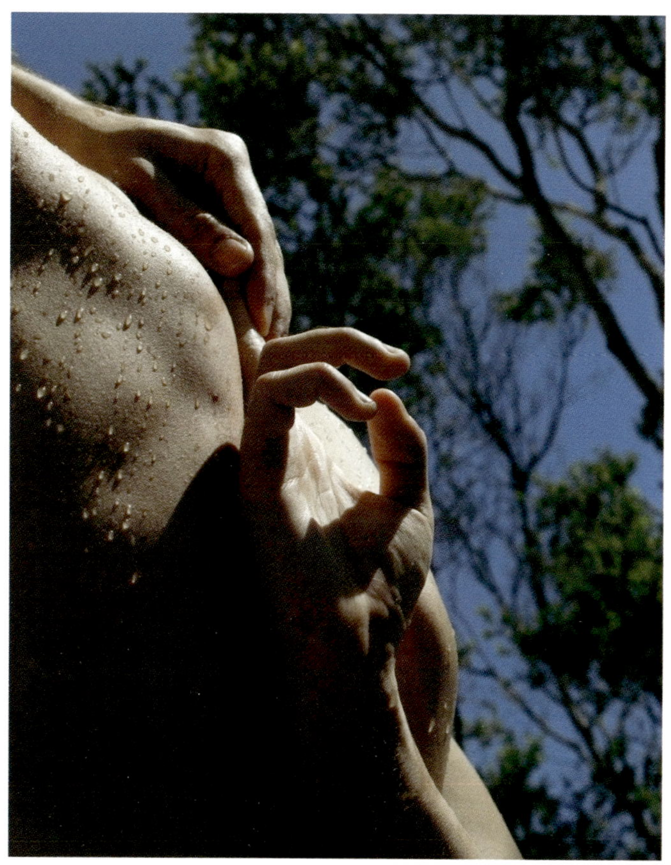

↑ Sascha Weidner, *Circle II*, 2012
←Viviane Sassen, *#3*, from the series 'Kutt', 2003

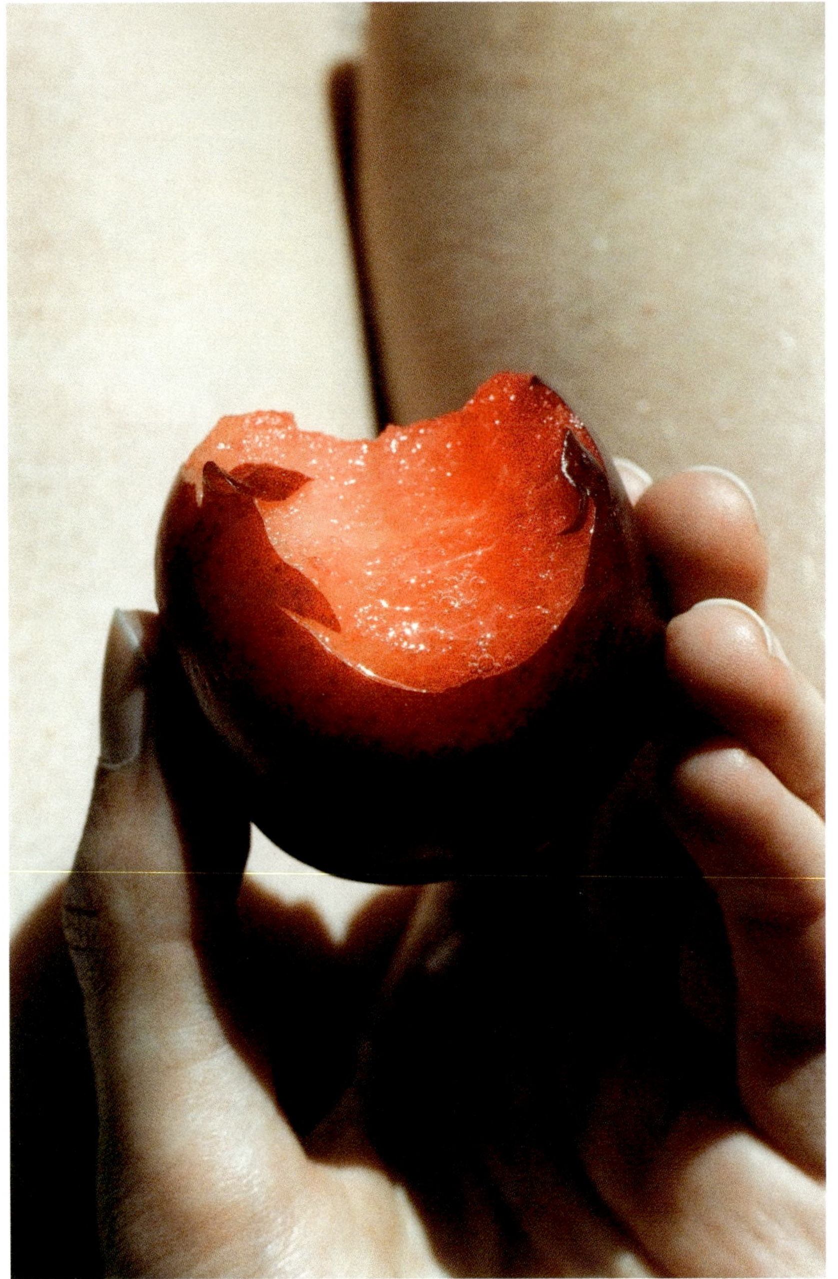

↑ **Lina Scheynius,** *Me in London, Summer, 2015*

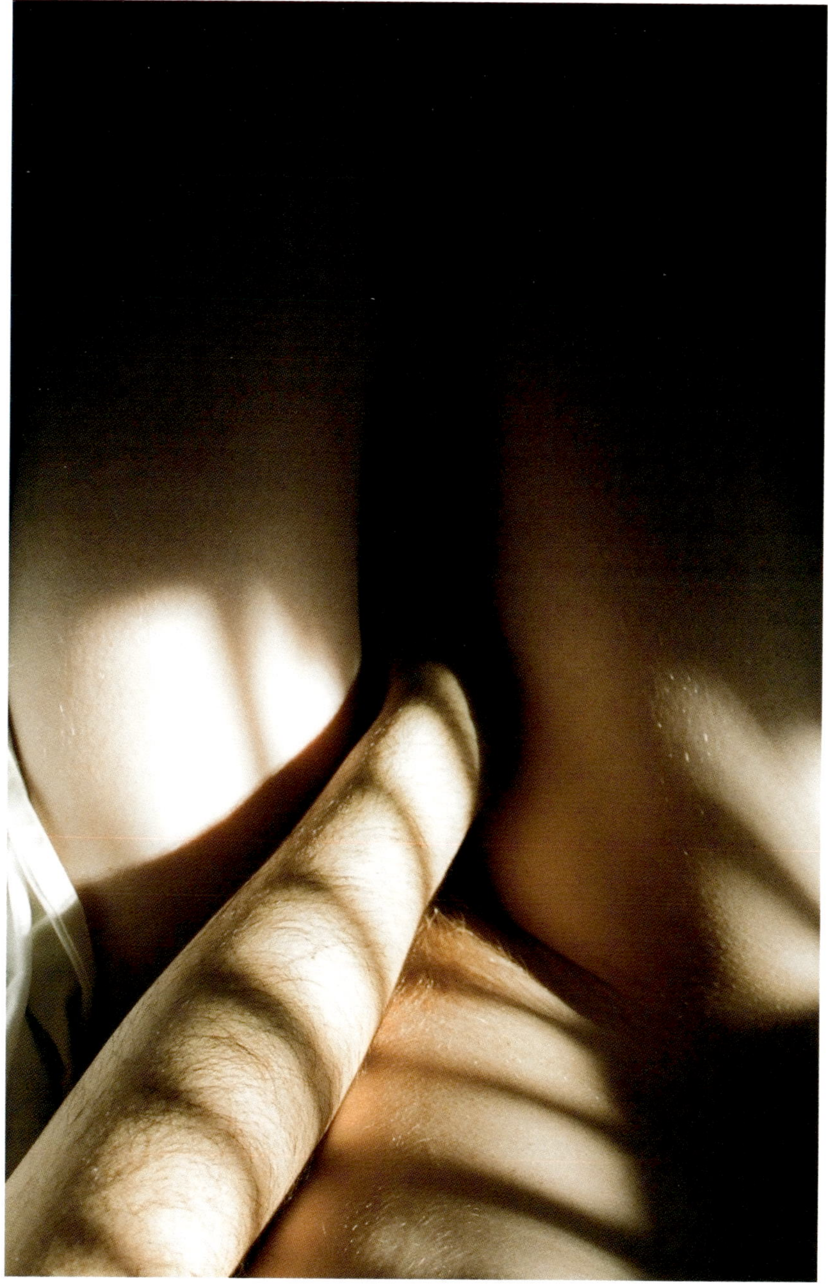

↑ **Lina Scheynius,** *David and I in New York, 2015*

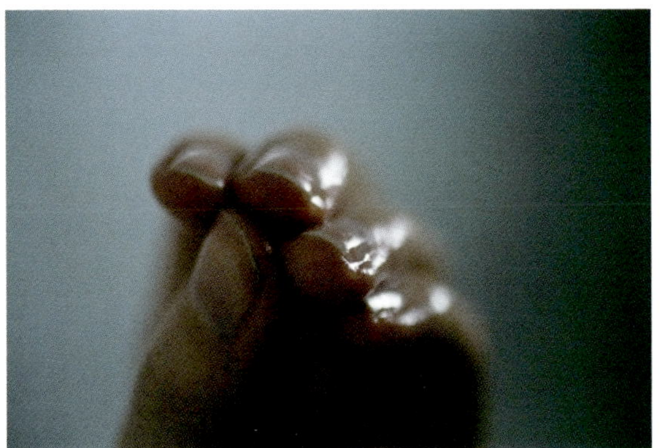

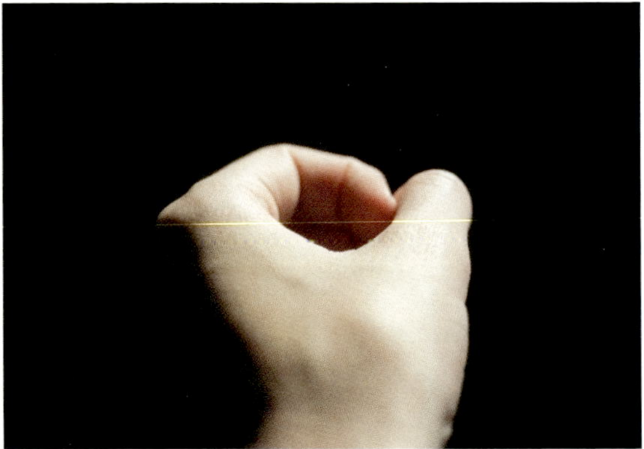

↑ (Top) **Lina Scheynius,** *Me in London, Spring, 2015*
↑ (Above) **Lina Scheynius,** *Untitled (Diary), 2013*

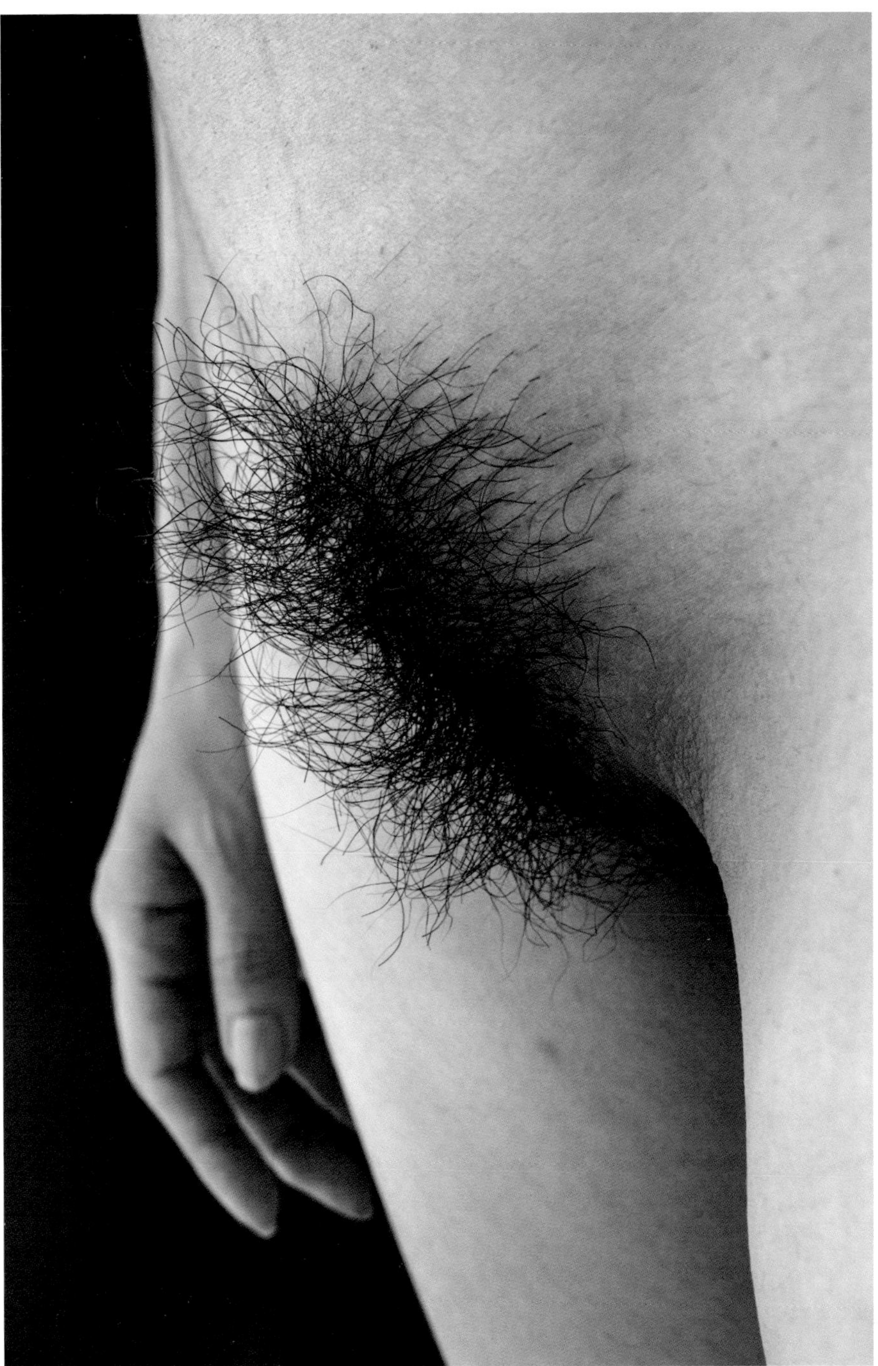

↑ **Augustin Rebetez,** *Untitled,* 2017

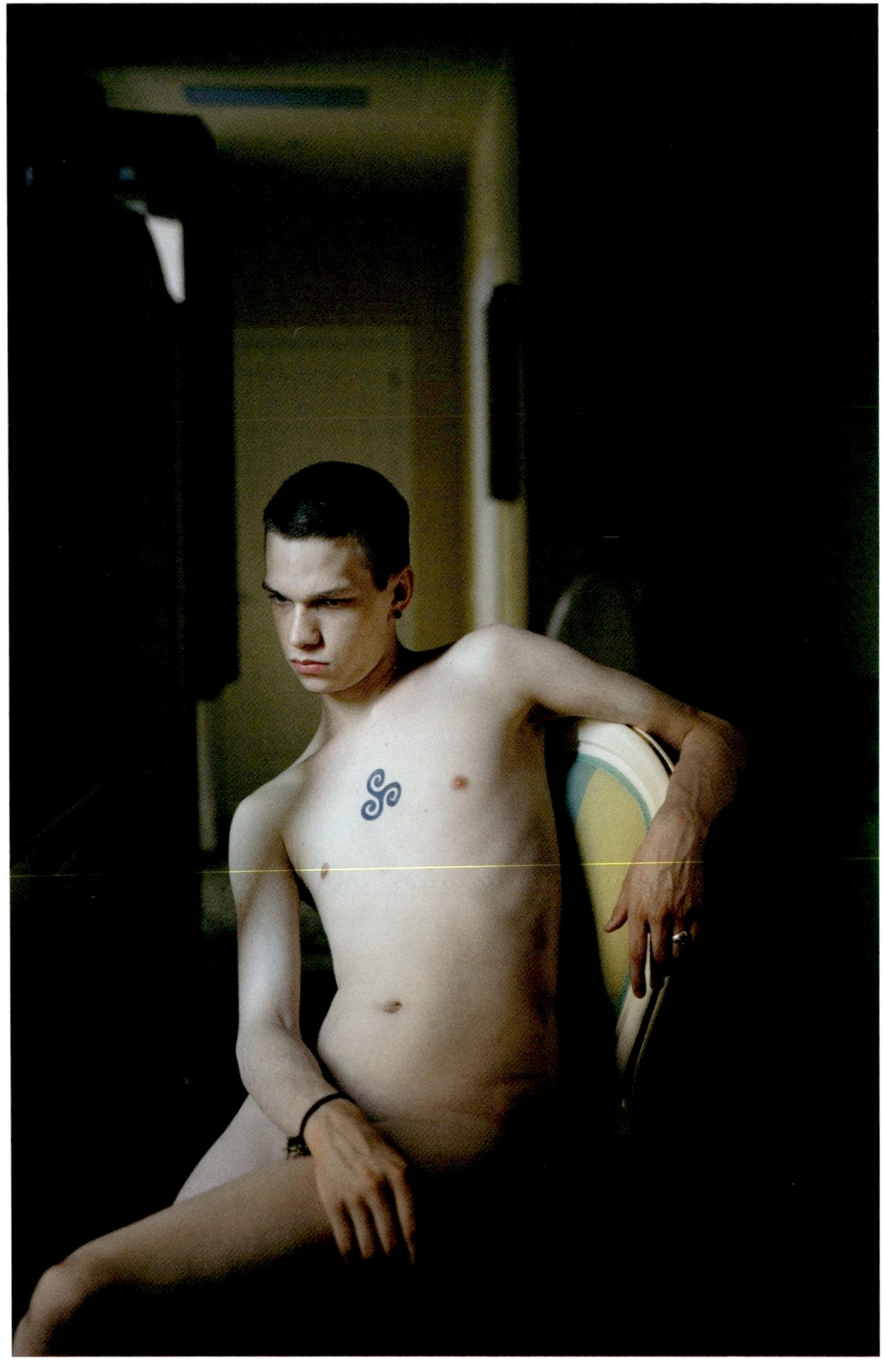

↑ **Margo Ovcharenko,** *Untitled (Maxim),* from the series 'Hermitage', 2010

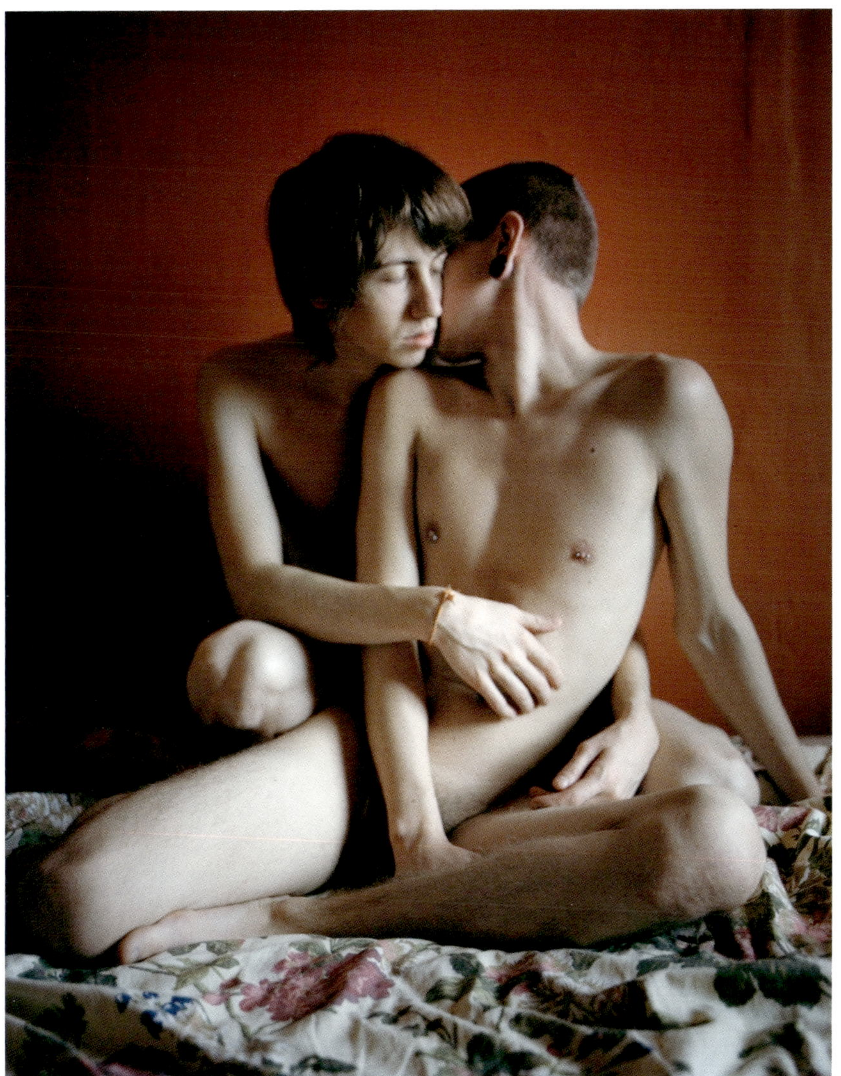

↑ **Margo Ovcharenko,** *Untitled*, from the series 'Hermitage', 2010

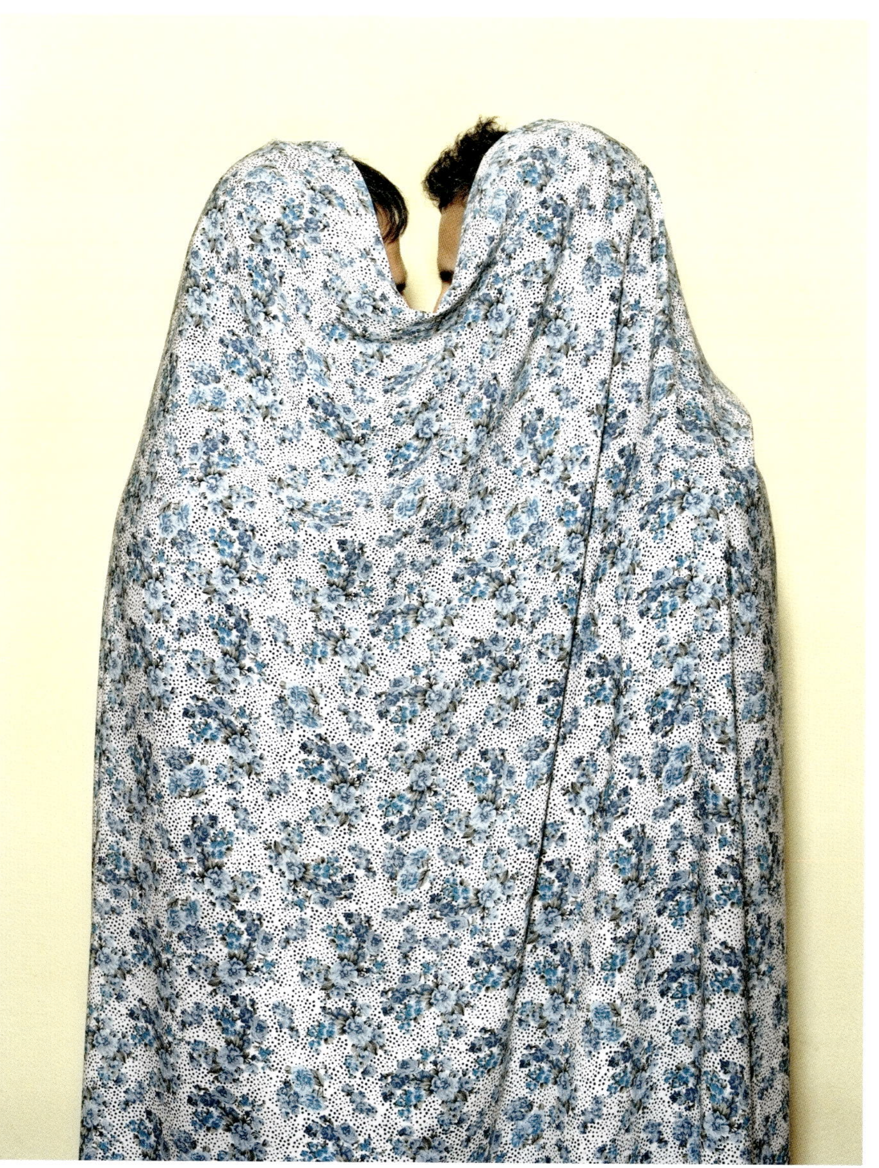

↑ **Laurence Rasti,** *Untitled*, from the series
'There Are No Homosexuals in Iran', 2014

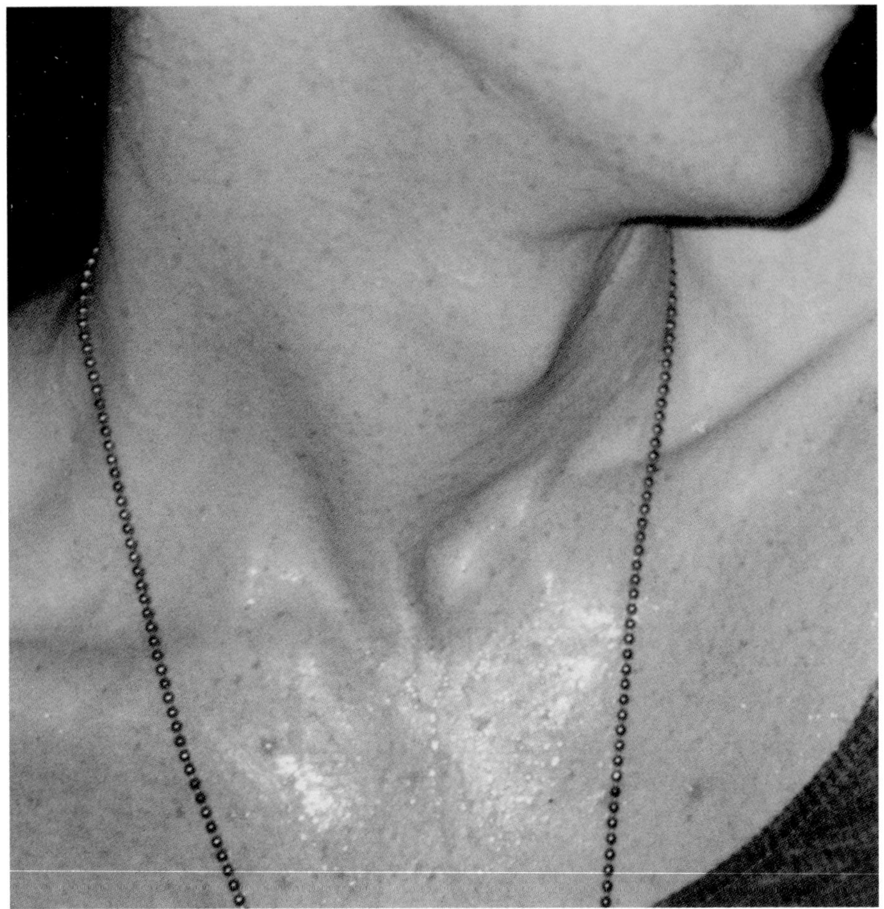

↑ **Wolfgang Tillmans,** *Chemistry square, neck & chest,* 1992

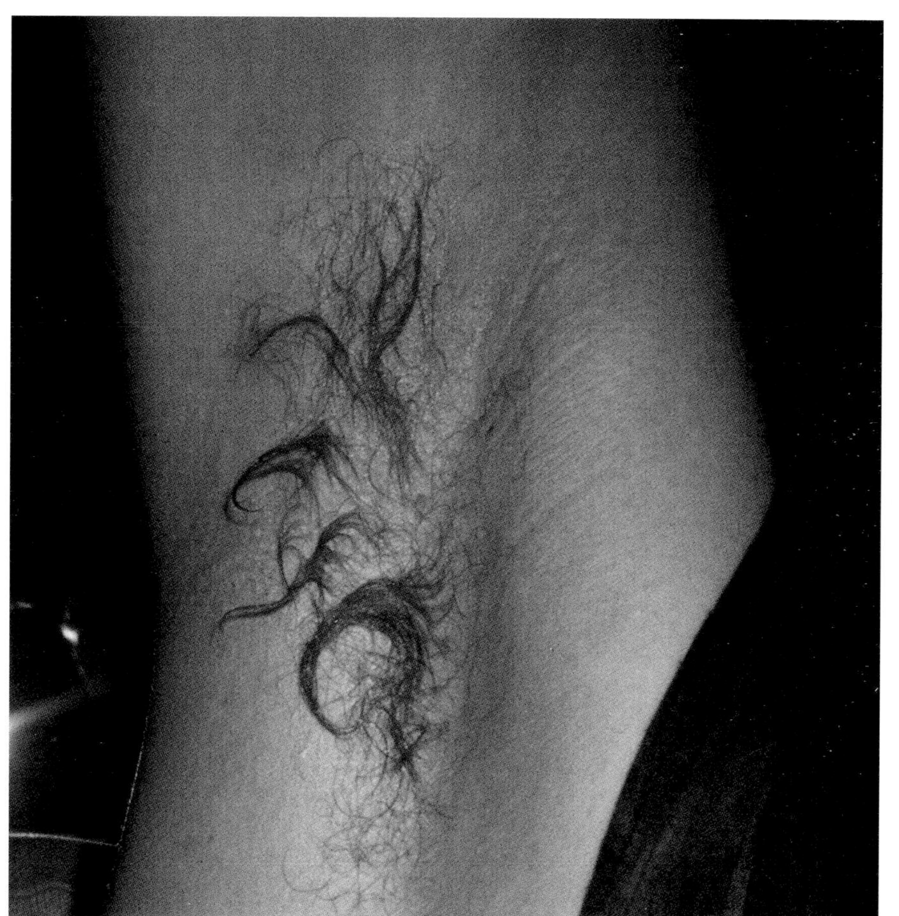

↑ Wolfgang Tillmans, *Armpit*, 1992

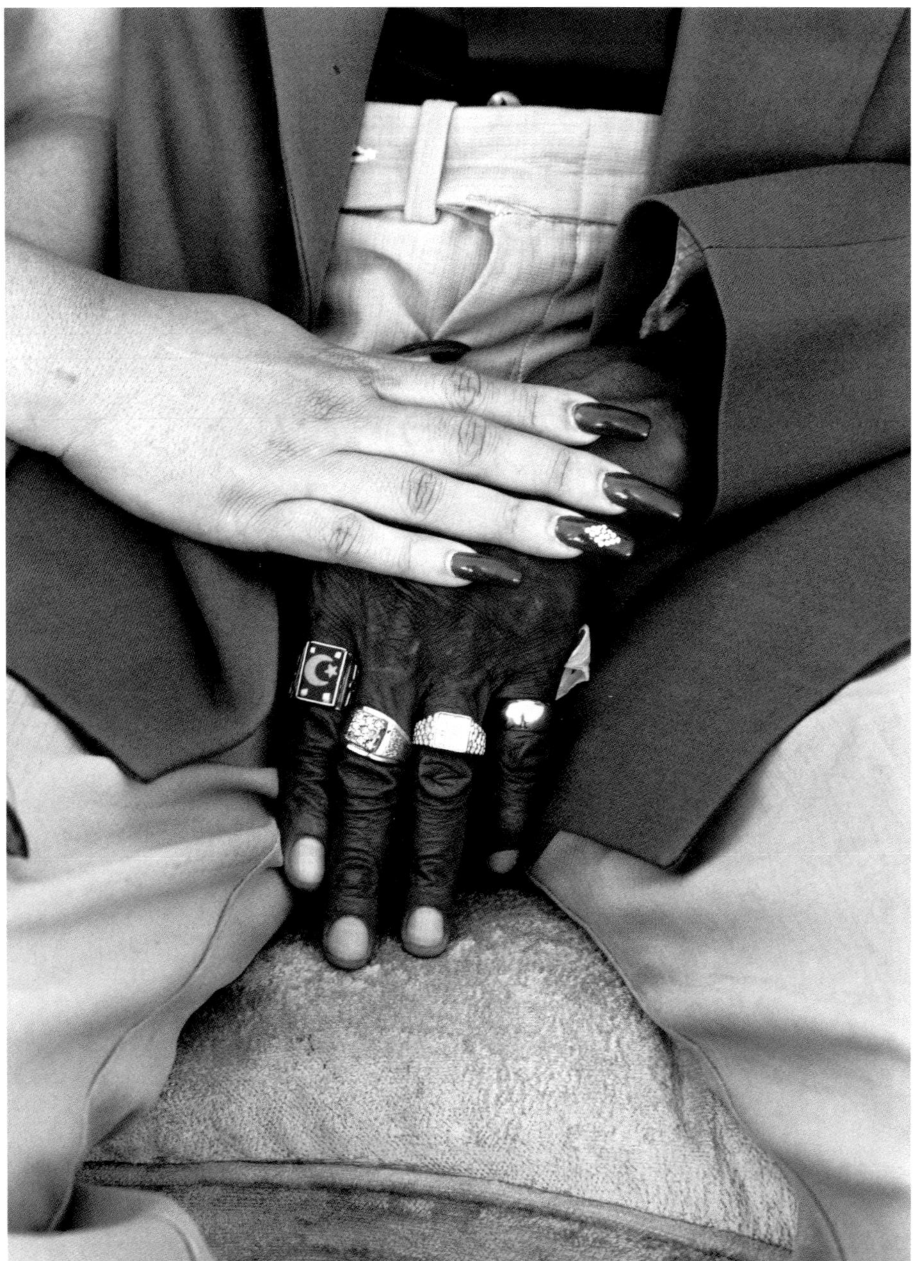

↑ **LaToya Ruby Frazier,** *Mom and Mr. Yerby's Hands*, 2005

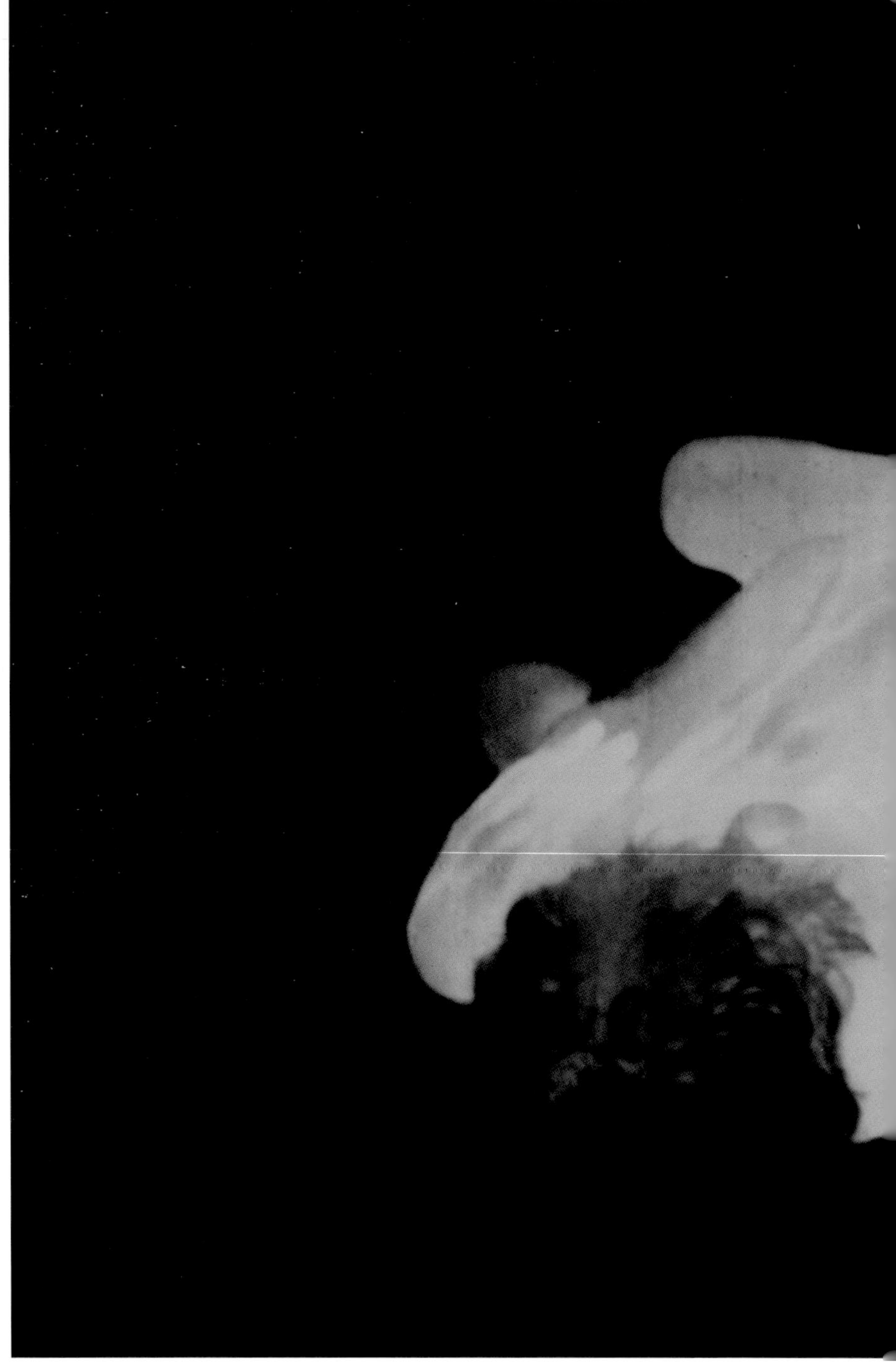

↑ **SMITH,** Untitled, from the series 'Spectrographies', 2015

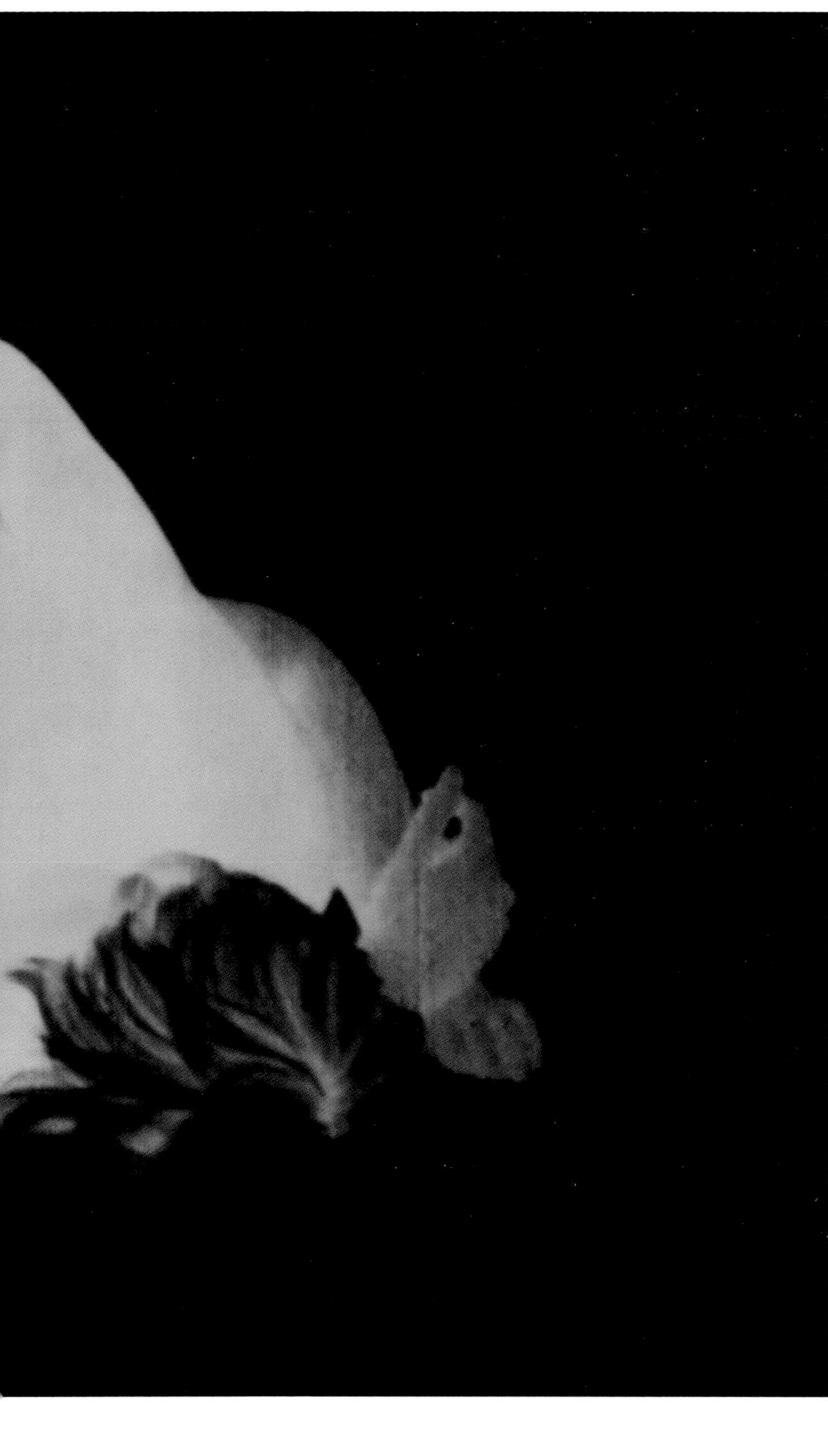

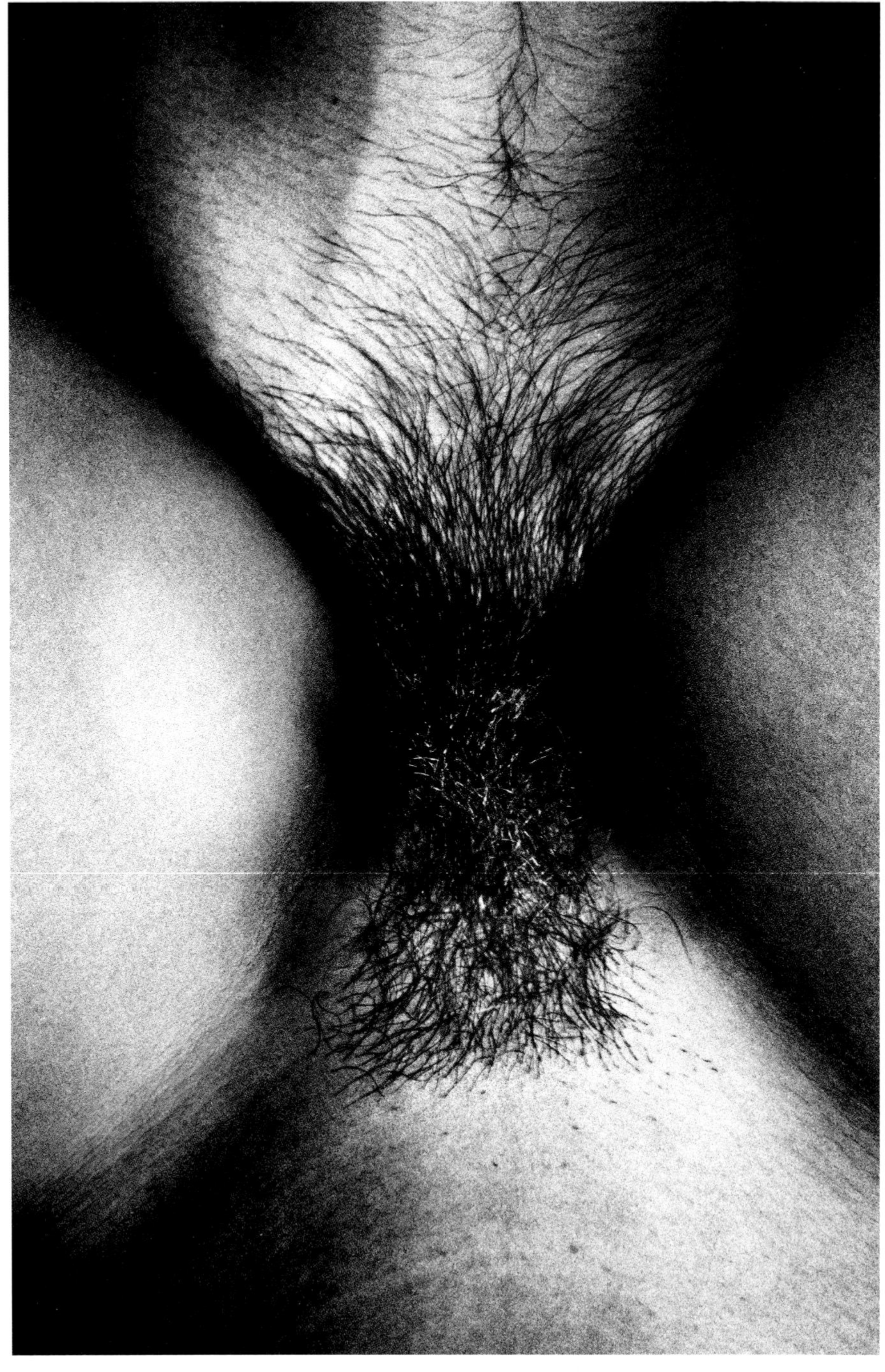

↑ **Jacob Aue Sobol,** *Tokyo, Japan,* 2007

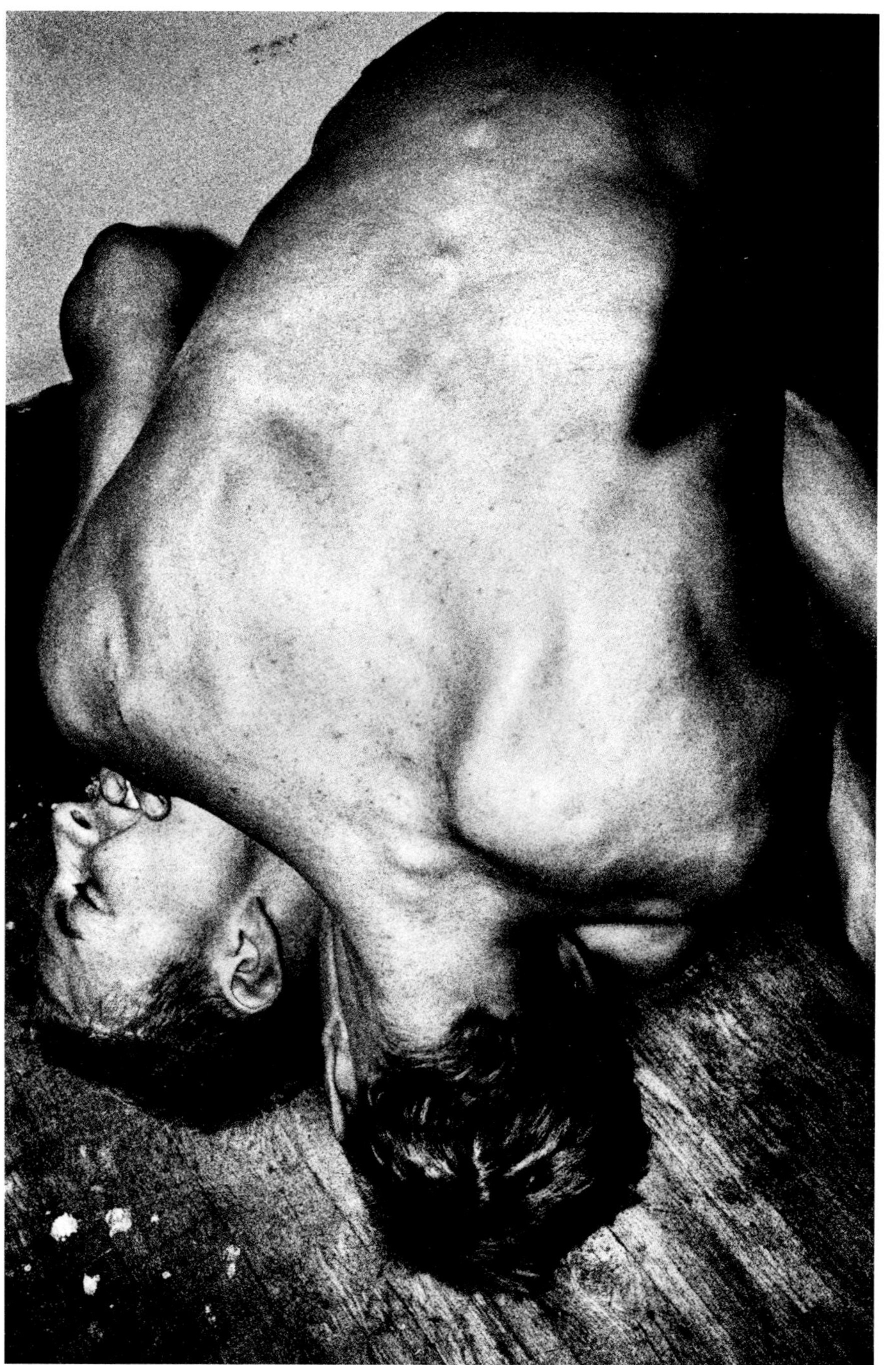

↑ **Jacob Aue Sobol,** *Copenhagen, Denmark,* 2010

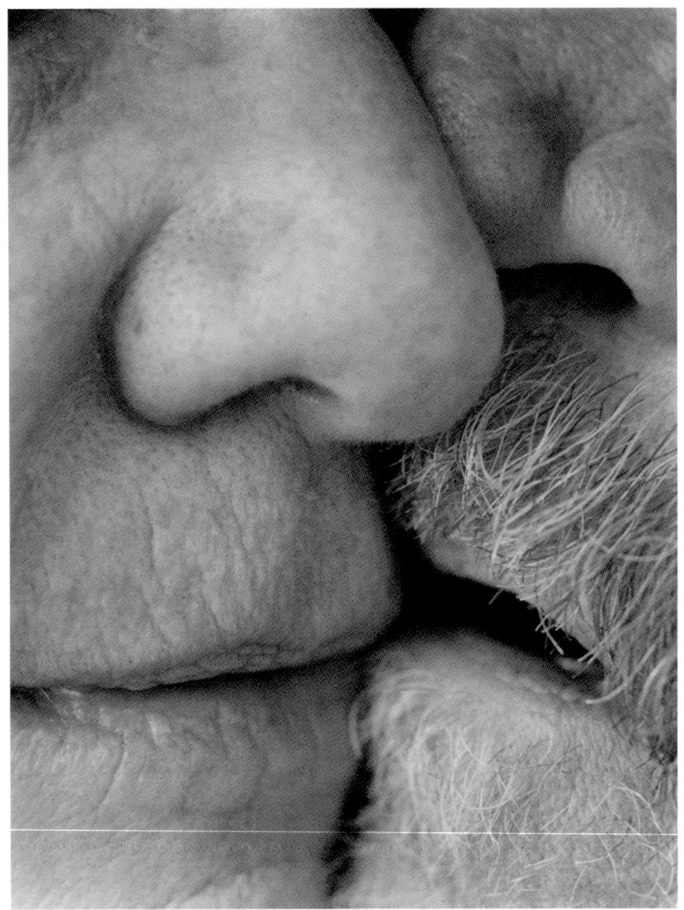

↑ **Nicholas Nixon,** *Bebe and I, Brookline,* 2011

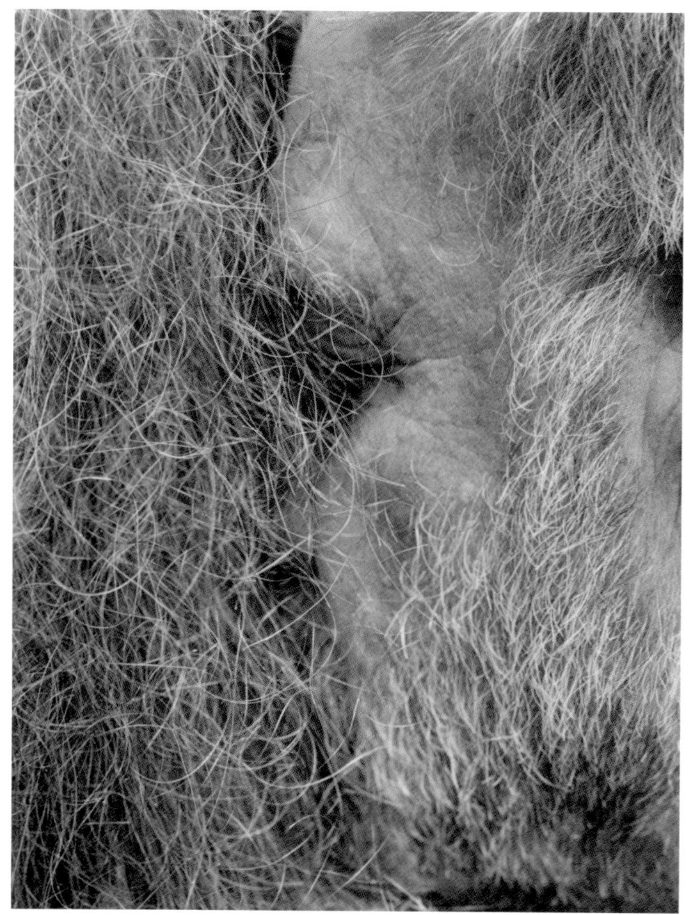

↑ **Nicholas Nixon,** *Bebe and I, Brookline,* 2012

→**Elinor Carucci,** *Holding Emmanuelle*, 2008

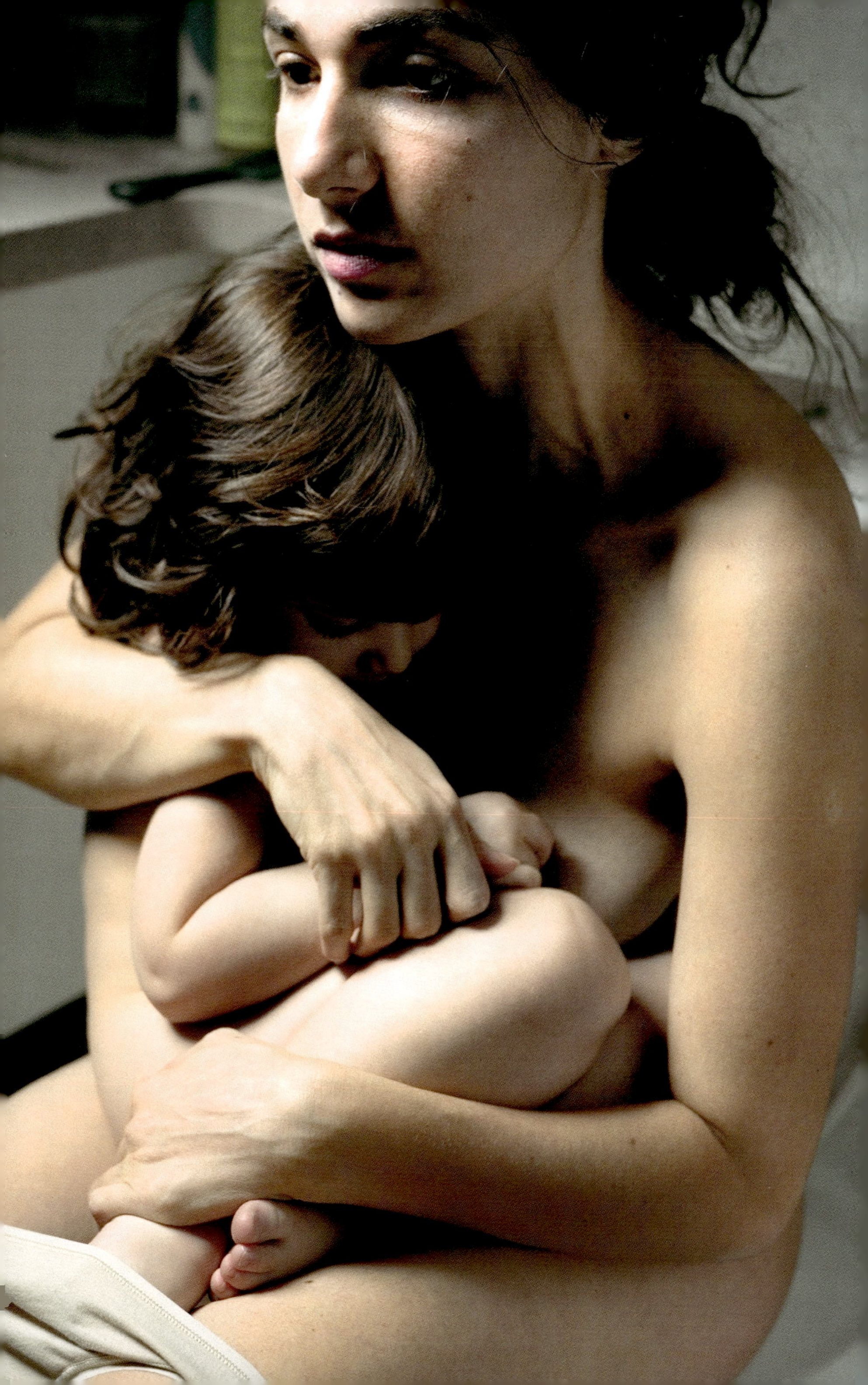

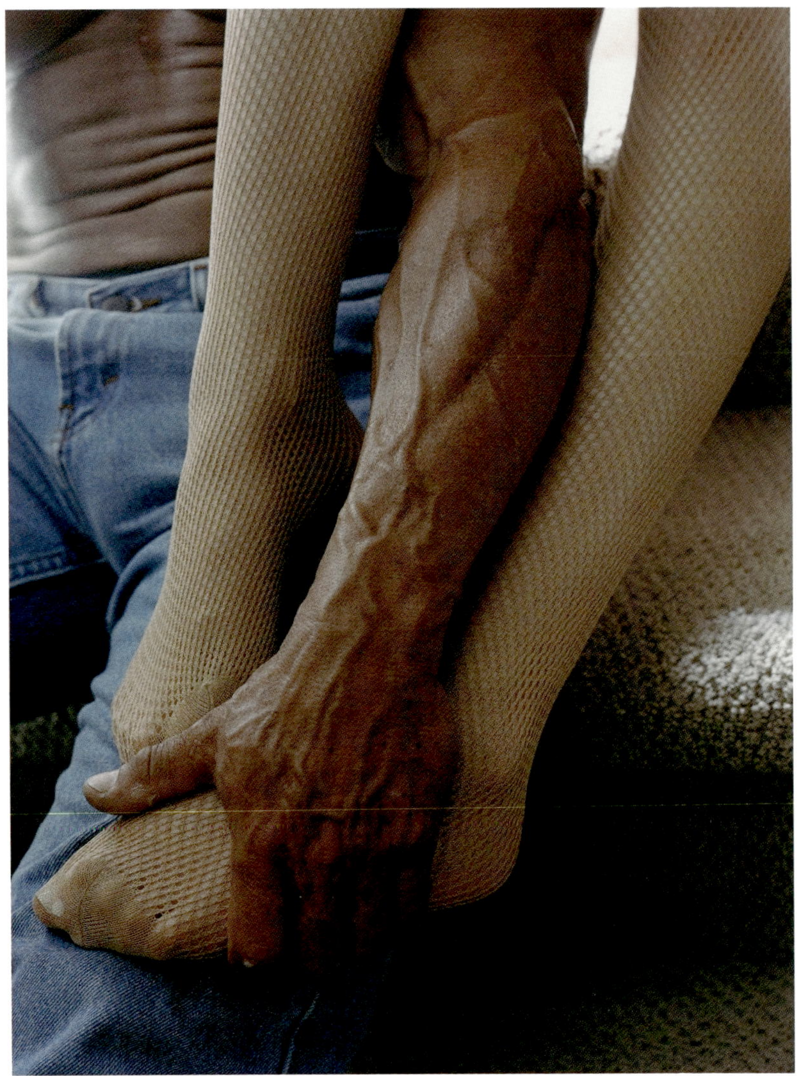

↑ **Torbjørn Rødland,** *Stockings, Jeans and Carpeted Stairs,* 2013–17

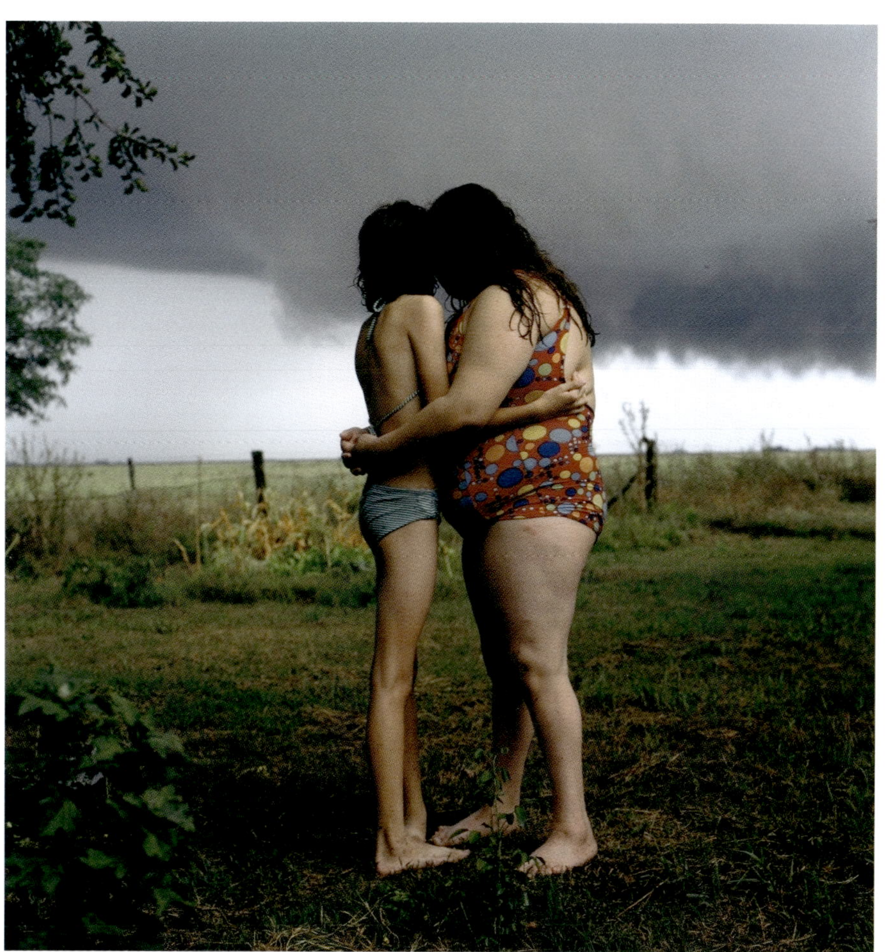

↑ **Alessandra Sanguinetti,** *The Black Cloud, Buenos Aires, Argentina,* from the series 'The Adventures of Guille and Belinda', 2000

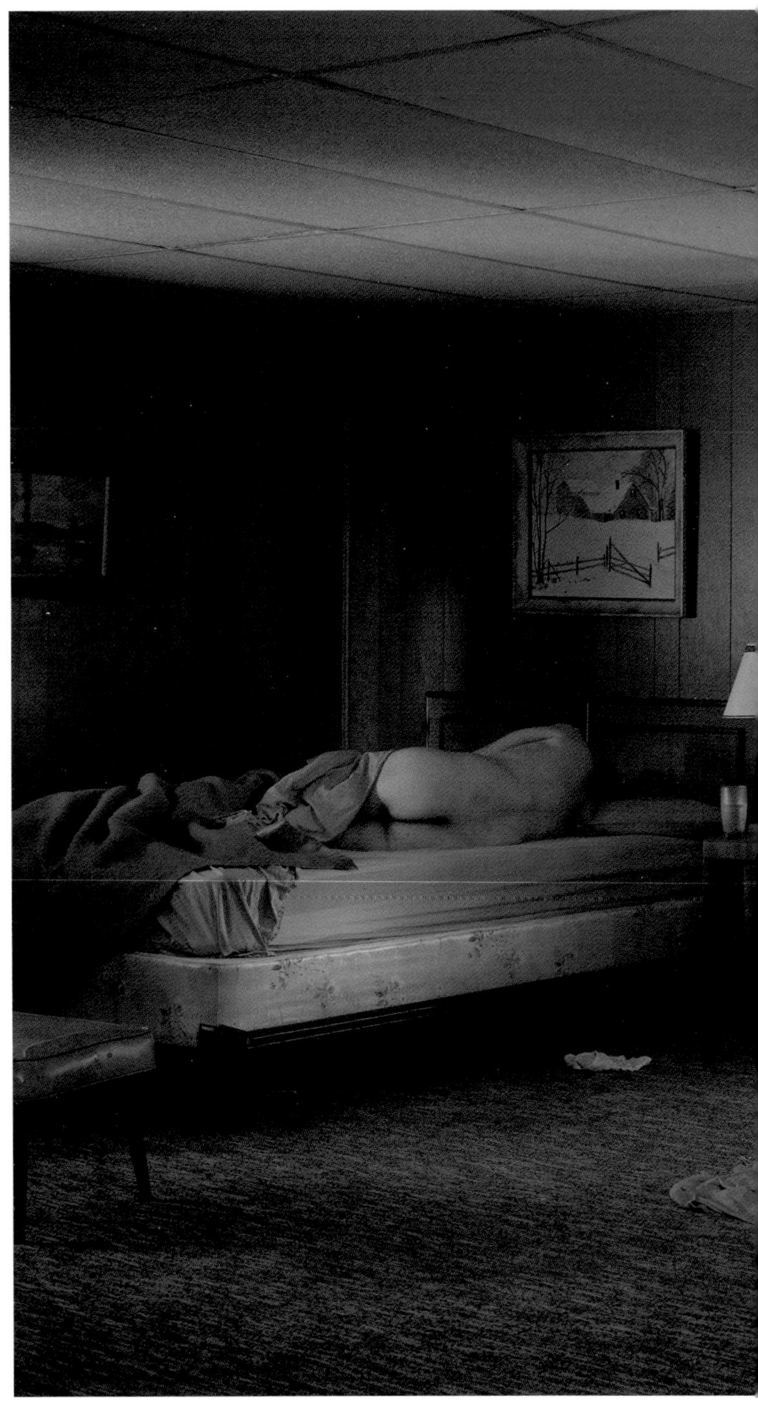

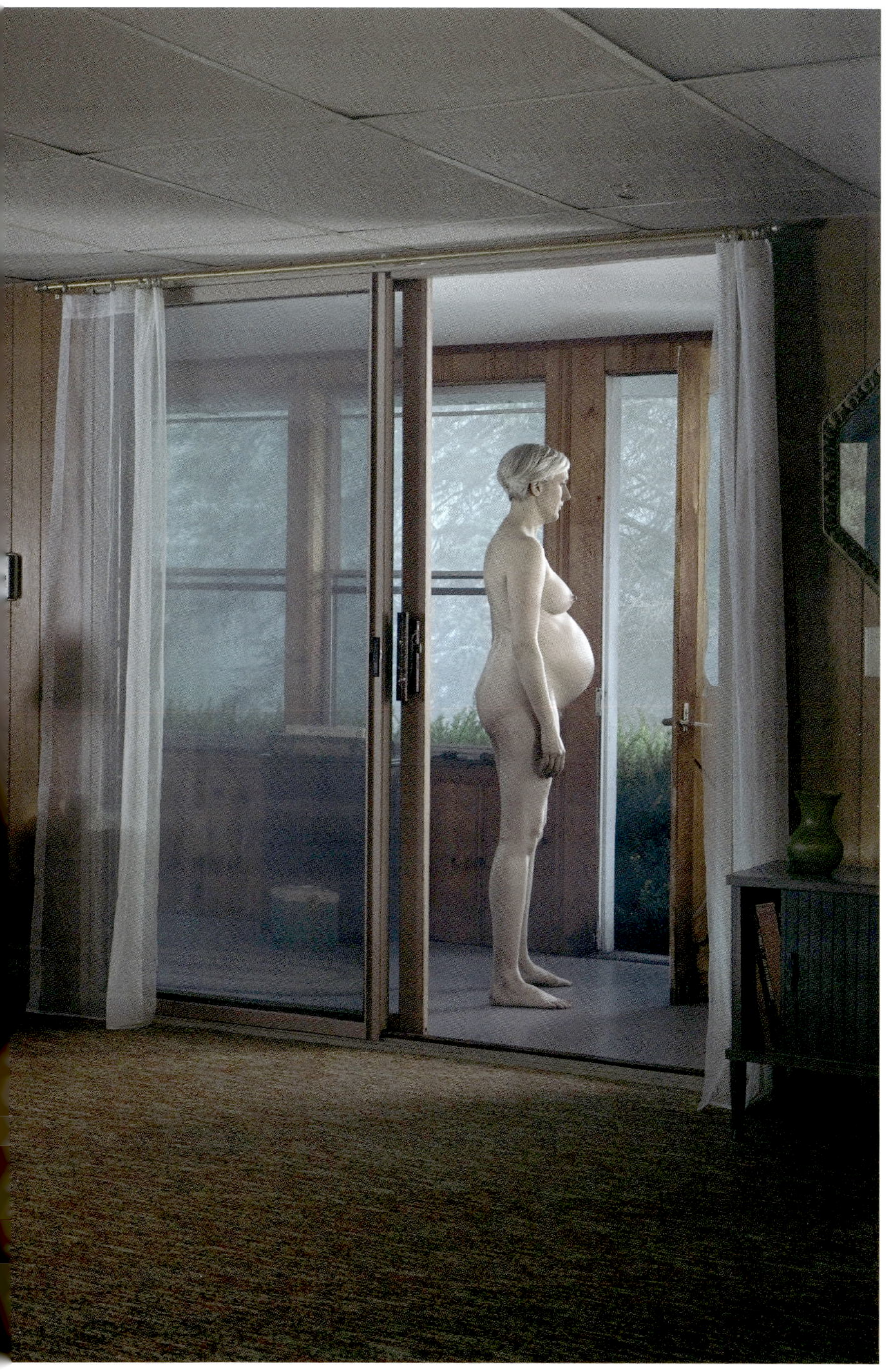

↑ Gregory Crewdson, *Pregnant Woman on Porch*, 2013

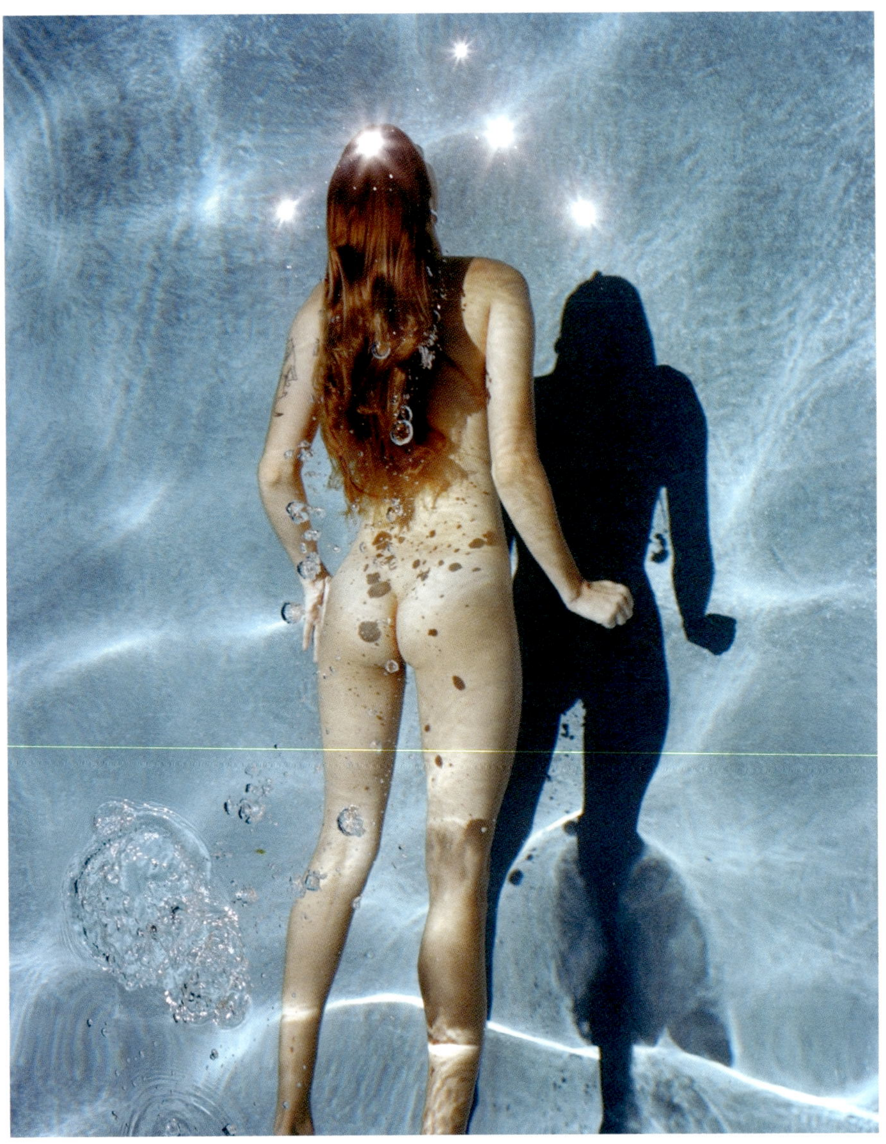

↑ **Deanna Templeton,** *Erin*, from the series 'The Swimming Pool', 2015

'If anything is sacred,
the human body is sacred.'

Walt Whitman
'I Sing the Body Electric', *Leaves of Grass*

a = above, b = below, l = left, r = right

pp. 2–3 © Gerber Loesch

pp. 4, 122, 122–23, 123, 288, 289 © Mona Kuhn

pp. 8, 31 © Institut de la Vision/Fondation Voir et Entendre

p. 15 © Barbara Kruger. Courtesy Sprüth Magers

p. 17 © Angélica Dass

pp. 18, 21 © Nolwenn Brod. Courtesy Galerie VU'

pp. 22–23 © Sean Lee

pp. 25, 342–43 © Jeff Mermelstein

pp. 26–27, 38–39 © Thomas Struth

pp. 28–29, 84 © DR

pp. 30, 34 ar © Science Photo Library

p. 33 © Daniel Berger, Narayanan Kasthuri, Jeff Lichtman/Harvard

pp. 34 al, 37 ar © Steve Gschmeissner/Science Photo Library

p. 34 bl © K. H. Fung/Science Photo Library

p. 35 ar © Susumu Nishinaga/Science Photo Library

p. 35 bl © Thierry Berrod, Mona Lisa Production/ Science Photo Library

p. 35 br © Science History Images / Alamy Stock Photo

p. 36 a © Science Photo Library / Alamy Stock Photo

p. 36 b © Blue Brain Project/EPFL 2005–2018. All rights reserved

p. 37 al © Dr Yorgos Nikas/Science Photo Library

p. 37 bl © Prof. P. Motta/Dept. of Anatomy/University La Sapienza, Rome/Science Photo Library

p. 37 br © Steven Daniel

p. 40 © Maija Tammi

p. 41 Courtesy of Dr Bernard Benoit, Princess Grace Hospital, Monaco

pp. 42, 43 © Eamonn Doyle

pp. 44–45, 148–49 © Lauren Greenfield. Courtesy INSTITUTE

pp. 46–47 © Howard Schatz and Beverly Ornstein

pp. 48, 49, 190, 191 © Juul Kraijer

pp. 50, 51 © Pieter Hugo. Courtesy Stevenson, Cape Town/Johannesburg

pp. 52, 53, 54–55, 421 © Elinor Carucci. Courtesy Edwynn Houk Gallery, New York

pp. 56–57, 348–49 © Andres Serrano. Courtesy Andres Serrano and Galerie Nathalie Obadia Paris/ Brussels

pp. 58–59 © Jamie Hawkesworth

pp. 60, 61, 418, 419 © Nicholas Nixon. Courtesy Fraenkel Gallery, San Francisco

pp. 62, 63, 322–23 © Nadav Kander

p. 64 © Anne Golaz. Courtesy of Galerie C, Neuchâtel

pp. 65, 66, 67 © Rinko Kawauchi. Courtesy Christophe Guye Galerie, Zurich

pp. 68–69 © Mike Brodie. Courtesy Yossi Milo Gallery, New York

pp. 70, 71, 230–31 © Marilyn Minter. Courtesy of the artist and Salon 94, New York

pp. 72–73, 114–15, 116–17, 166 © Yurie Nagashima

pp. 75, 76 © Laia Abril

p. 77 © Neige Sanchez

pp. 78–79, 305, 321 © Denis Darzacq. Courtesy Agence VU'/Galerie RX

pp. 80, 81 © ECAL/Yuliya Khan

pp. 83, 88, 89, 131 © Ole John Aandal

p. 84 All rights reserved

p. 87 © Aneta Bartos

pp. 91, 93, 94, 95 © Collier Schorr. Courtesy 303 Gallery, New York

p. 92 © ECAL/Jeanne Tullen

pp. 96, 97 © Kim Kardashian West

pp. 99, 339 © Todd Hido

pp. 100–01 © Pierre et Gilles

pp. 102, 103, 384–85 © Deana Lawson. Courtesy of Sikkema Jenkins & Co., New York

pp. 104–05, 106, 107 © Aneta Grzeszykowska. Courtesy of Raster Gallery

pp. 108, 109, 127, 146, 147, 181 © Valérie Belin. Courtesy of Galerie Nathalie Obadia, Paris/Brussels and Edwynn Houk Gallery, New York/Zurich

pp. 110, 111 © Roger Ballen

pp. 113, 276, 277 a © Tabitha Soren

pp. 119, 159 © Catherine Opie. Courtesy Regen Projects, Los Angeles

pp. 120, 121 © Alec Soth/Magnum Photos

pp. 124–25, 364, 365 Courtesy Zhang Huan Studio

p. 128 © Sarah Maple

pp. 132–33 © Martin Parr/Magnum Photos

p. 135 © Dana Popa

pp. 136–37 © Jodi Bieber

p. 138 © Erwin Olaf. Courtesy Galerie Wagner + Partner, Berlin

pp. 139, 163, 376 © Romina Ressia

p. 141 © Cara Phillips. Courtesy of Robert Morat Galerie and the artist

p. 142 © Cindy Sherman. Courtesy of the artist and Metro Pictures, New York

p. 143 © 1996 Juergen Teller. All rights reserved

pp. 144, 145 © Henry Leutwyler

pp. 150, 151 © Luis Arturo Aguirre

pp. 152, 153, 168, 169 © Bettina Rheims. Courtesy Galerie Xippas

pp. 154–55 © Annette Messager. Courtesy of the artist and Marian Goodman Gallery/Collection Centre Georges Pompidou

p. 156 Collection Michèle Barrière. Courtesy ORLAN and Galerie Ceysson & Bénétière

p. 157 © Cyril Porchet. Courtesy Galerie C, Neuchâtel

p. 158 © Adam Fuss. Courtesy Cheim & Reid, New York

pp. 160, 161, 296, 297 Courtesy of Ryan McGinley and Team (Gallery, inc.), New York

p. 162 © David Julian Leonard

pp. 164, 165 © Hellen van Meene

pp. 170, 171 © Zanele Muholi. Courtesy Stevenson, Cape Town/Johannesburg

pp. 173, 176 © Daniel Sannwald

p. 174 © ECAL/Maxime Guyon

pp. 177, 414–15 © Dorothée Smith. Courtesy Galerie les Filles du Calvaire, Paris

pp. 179, 252, 253 © Erik Madigan Heck

pp. 182–83 © Liu Bolin

pp. 184–85, 379 © Sølve Sundsbø/Art + Commerce

p. 186 © Daniel Gordon

p. 187 © Lucas Blalock

pp. 188, 189, 281, 282–83, 400 © Viviane Sassen. Courtesy Stevenson, Cape Town/Johannesburg

pp. 192, 192–93, 193 © ECAL/Clément Lambelet

p. 194 © Vanessa Beecroft. Courtesy Lia Rumma Gallery Milan/Naples

p. 195 © Jenny Saville and Glen Luchford. Courtesy Gagosian

pp. 196, 197, 302, 380–81 © Ren Hang. Courtesy Gao Guilan and Blindspot Gallery

p. 198 © Manon Wertenbroek

p. 199 © Taisuke Koyama in collaboration with Kohei Nawa| Damien Jalet

pp. 200, 201 © Paul Kooiker

pp. 202–03 © Alix Marie
p. 204 © Xing Danwen
p. 205 © Spencer Tunick
pp. 206–07 © Ina Jang. Courtesy Christophe Guye
    Galerie, Zurich
pp. 208, 209 © Patrick Weidmann
p. 210 © ECAL/Nicolas Garner
p. 211 © Catherine Leutenegger
p. 212 © Namsa Leuba
p. 213 © ECAL/Yul Tomatala
pp. 214, 215, 216, 217 © Matthieu Gafsou. Courtesy
    Galerie C, Neuchâtel / MAPS
pp. 218, 219 © David Vintiner. Art Director Gem
    Fletcher
pp. 220–21 © Aziz + Cucher
pp. 222–23 © Torbjørn Rødland. Courtesy of David
    Kordansky Gallery and STANDARD (OSLO)
p. 224 © Torbjørn Rødland. Courtesy of the artist and
    Nils Stærk
p. 225 © Torbjørn Rødland. Courtesy of the artist and
    Galerie Eva Presenhuber
pp. 226, 227 © Asger Carlsen
p. 228 © Arno Rafael Minkkinen. Courtesy Edwynn
    Houk Gallery, New York
p. 229 © Jessa Fairbrother
p. 233 Erwin Wurm © DACS 2019
p. 243 © Jun Ahn
p. 244 © Kiki Xue
p. 247 © Dana Lixenberg
pp. 248–49, 313, 416, 417 © Jacob Aue Sobol/
    Magnum Photos
p. 251 © Flor Garduño
pp. 254–55 © Elina Brotherus. Courtesy of the artist
    and gb agency, Paris
pp. 256–57 © Nan Goldin
pp. 258, 259 © Koto Bolofo. Courtesy Kahmann
    Gallery, Amsterdam
pp. 261, 396, 397 Thomas Ruff © DACS 2019.
    Courtesy Sprüth Magers
pp. 262, 262–63, 263 © Jock Sturges
p. 264 © Paul Mpagi Sepuya. Courtesy the artist,
    DOCUMENT gallery, Team Gallery, and Yancey
    Richardson Gallery
p. 265 © Esther Teichmann
pp. 266–67 © Paolo Roversi
pp. 268–69 © Condé Nast UK/Corinne Day/Trunk
    Archive
pp. 270, 271 © Herb Ritts/Trunk Archive
pp. 272, 273 © Lois Greenfield
p. 274 © Gregory Eddi Jones
p. 275 Bryan Scott © Howard Schatz and Beverly
    Ornstein
p. 277 b © Tabitha Soren. Courtesy Los Angeles
    County Museum of Art, Los Angeles
pp. 278–79 © Mark Neville
p. 280 © Floris Neusüss. Courtesy of the artist and Von
    Lintel Gallery
p. 284 © Senta Simond
p. 285 © David Lynch. Courtesy the artist and Kayne
    Griffin Corcoran, Los Angeles
pp. 286, 287 © Marton Perlaki
pp. 290, 291, 292, 401 © The Estate of Artist Sascha
    Weidner
p. 293 © Gerardo Vizmanos
pp. 294, 295, 410, 411 © Wolfgang Tillmans
p. 298 © ECAL/Angélique Stehli
pp. 299, 386–87 © Ed Templeton. Courtesy Roberts
    Projects, Los Angeles
pp. 300, 301, 426 © Deanna Templeton
p. 303 © Synchrodogs
pp. 306–07 © Bill Henson
pp. 308, 309, 314 © Jocelyn Lee. Courtesy Pace/
    MacGill Gallery, New York
pp. 310–11, 372–73 © Richard Misrach. Courtesy
    Fraenkel Gallery, San Francisco / Pace/MacGill
    Gallery, New York / Marc Selwyn Fine Art, Los
    Angeles
p. 317 © Jim Goldberg/Magnum Photos
pp. 318, 319 © Richard Learoyd. Courtesy Fraenkel
    Gallery, San Francisco
pp. 324, 325 © Andreas Rentsch
p. 326 © Liu Zheng. Courtesy of the artist and
    Blindspot Gallery
p. 327 © Alexandra Caticrc
pp. 328–29 © Siân Davey
pp. 330, 331 © Nicolai Howalt. Courtesy Martin Asbæk
    Gallery & Bruce Silverstein Gallery
pp. 332–33 © Pyotr Pavlensky
p. 334 © Olivier Christinat
p. 335 © Francesca Catastini
pp. 336–37 © Eric Poitevin. Courtesy Galerie Albert
    Baronian
p. 338 © Lucile Boiron
p. 341 © Bruce Gilden/Magnum Photos
pp. 344–45 © Erica Deeman
pp. 346, 347 © Louie Palu
p. 351 © Susan Copen Oken
p. 352 © Manabu Yamanaka
pp. 353, 354–55, 356–57 © Sally Mann. Courtesy
    Gagosian
pp. 358, 359 © Raphaël Dallaporta
pp. 360, 361 © Aida Silvestri. Courtesy of the Artist
    and Autograph ABP, London
pp. 362–63 © Studio Toscani
pp. 366–67, 368–69 Courtesy of Richard Mosse and
    Jack Shainman Gallery
pp. 370, 371 © Seba Kurtis. Courtesy Christophe Guye
    Galerie, Zurich
p. 375 © Maisie Cousins
p. 383 © Daido Moriyama Photo Foundation. Courtesy
    Christophe Guye Galerie, Zurich, and Taka Ishii
    Gallery, Tokyo
pp. 388–89 © Julia Fullerton-Batten
pp. 390–91, 392, 393 © Nobuyoshi Araki. Courtesy
    of Taka Ishii Gallery, Tokyo, and Michael Hoppen
    Gallery, London
p. 395 Courtesy Succession Edouard Levé et Galerie
    Loevenbruck, Paris
pp. 398–99 © ECAL/Margaux Piette & Emma
    Panchot
pp. 402, 403, 404 © Lina Scheynius. Courtesy
    Christophe Guye Galerie, Zurich
p. 405 © Augustin Rebetez
pp. 406, 407 © Margo Ovcharenko
p. 409 © Laurence Rasti
p. 413 Courtesy Latoya Ruby Frazier and Gavin Brown's
    enterprise, New York/Rome
p. 422 © Torbjørn Rødland. Courtesy of the artist and
    Air de Paris
p. 423 © Alessandra Sanguinetti/Magnum Photos
pp. 424–25 © Gregory Crewdson. Courtesy Gagosian

Page numbers in *italic* refer to illustrations

To Salomé and Flore

ACKNOWLEDGMENTS

I would like to thank William A. Ewing, author of the seminal 1994 book *The Body: Photoworks of the Human Form*, who gave his blessings to this project and whose book has been a source of inspiration throughout my broader research into the history of photography. I am grateful to the staff at Thames & Hudson, in particular Andrew Sanigar, Sam Palfreyman and Jenny Wilson. My heartfelt thanks go to Ramon Pez for his elegant design, and to Morgane Paillard for her assistance on this project. Finally, I would like to thank the many photographers, along with their studios and their representatives, whose work has been reproduced in this book.

Nathalie Herschdorfer
is a curator and art historian specializing in the history of photography. She is the Director of the Museum of Fine Arts, Le Locle, Switzerland. Among her other books are *Afterwards*, *The Thames & Hudson Dictionary of Photography* and *Coming into Fashion*, all published by Thames & Hudson.

David Sander
is a Professor of Psychology, Director of the Swiss Centre for Affective Sciences and Director of the Laboratory for the study of Emotion Elicitation and Expression at the University of Geneva, Switzerland. He was awarded the 2013 National Latsis Prize for his research and publications.

Cover **Koto Bolofo**, *Black Beauty*, 2008. © Koto Bolofo. Courtesy Kahmann Gallery, Amsterdam

pp. 2–3 **Gerber Loesch**, *Exoskeleton*, 2016

p. 4 **Mona Kuhn**, *Three Figures*, 2006

First published in the United Kingdom in 2019 in hardback by Thames & Hudson Ltd, 181A High Holborn, London WC1V 7QX

First published in the United States of America in 2019 in hardcover by Thames & Hudson Inc., 500 Fifth Avenue, New York, New York 10110

This compact paperback edition published in 2022

Body © 2019 Thames & Hudson Ltd, London
Mind and Body © 2019 David Sander

All other texts © 2019 Nathalie Herschdorfer
Translation of original French texts by Francisca Garvie
All images © 2019 the copyright holders: see pages 428–29 for details

Design by Ramon Pez

British Library Cataloguing-in-Publication Data
A catalogue record for this book is available from the British Library

Library of Congress Control Number 2018956117

ISBN 978-0-500-29656-1

Printed and bound in Slovenia by DZS-Grafik d.o.o.

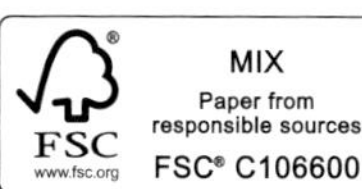

Be the first to know about our new releases, exclusive content and author events by visiting
thamesandhudson.com
thamesandhudsonusa.com
thamesandhudson.com.au